T0365646

and The WORLD

The india
and The WORLD
Wonder of Shame and Uncertainty!

KRISHNA KUMAR SINGH

PARTRIDGE
A Penguin Random House Company

To order additional copies of this book, contact
Partridge India
000 800 10062 62
www.partridgepublishing.com/india
orders.india@partridgepublishing.com

CONTENTS

Krishna Kumar Singh

A Strong believer in destiny as well as pray to Almighty for the welfare of people!

K.K. Singh

In memory of my mother Sudama Devi and father Satyanarayan Singh, who fought for the political emancipation of my country—India—from British imperialism during national movement of the Independence and now they are no more!

PROLOGUE

But I, being poor, have only my dreams;
I have spread my dreams under your feet;
Tread softly, because you tread on my dreams.
                                                W B Yeats.

To walk safely through the maize of human life,
one needs the light of wisdom and the guidance of virtue—
                                                Gautam Buddha.

At the fag end of my life, I had a dream to publish a book to highlight the misdeeds, spread in the society socially, and miseries as well as poverty among huge population in the globe and economically and other vices spreading like poison not only in India but throughout the Globe. Almighty helped me and I could succeed a little in this great venture! I started writing essays, articles, analysis, etc. on various subjects, especially on social issues like poverty, atrocity on women, children and poor, lack of health facilities, illiteracy etc, prevalent throughout the world, particularly in India, known as the largest democracy of the world but pervaded by all the ills and problems, especially among poor, downtrodden, women and children. The entire world is today threatened with arms race, particularly in nuclear armaments and other lethal weapons, which could ruin the man-kind once a button is pressed! Corruption and crimes, particularly against weaker sections of society, children and women throughout the world are eating the vitals of the society. Sadly, majority of people of the world are afflicted with hunger, malnutrition and various other ills in the society.

My book is mainly compilations of essays and articles, written time to time in the last two and half years. I have tried my best to explain the above mentioned facts by quoting extensively authenticated newspaper reports, various books as well as data and figures in various governments of the world and also from other authenticated sources.

This has been never my intention to blame or malign some one for all these ills in the society of the world, which is now called 'global village' I have tried to explain that after all who should and could be blamed for such malpractices and ills in the society of the world nations. A few of my essays have highlighted about global warming because of environment changes, more caused by men than the nature. About economy of the world, less said is better. In the name of liberalizing our economy, we, world people, are creating more imbalances in the society of the nations. Terrorism and militancy, which have become very common throughout the globe, appear to be the results of suppressing the people from respective society to raise their voices for just causes! It is not surprising that huge number of people in the world are still alienated from their national mainstreams. Still, we super power, developing and developed nations, boast of their respective supremacy. World nations are more concerned about their supremacy than to look the poor plight of majority of people on the Earth.

There are much and much and more and more in the book! Now I leave entire things to readers to judge. There may be many things, lacking in the book—I welcome suggestions from the readers! Last but not the least, I am grateful to the Almighty for giving me strength in writing this book at this fag end of my life. I am also grateful to those hidden and open forces, who encouraged and discouraged me in bringing out my this maiden venture in print line in the form of a book. Just I want to conclude by Introduction of the book with one quotable quote of Nirad C Chaudhari—"Nobody could be more conscious than I am of the pitfalls which lie the path of a man who wants to discover the truth about . . . ."

K K Singh.
Place: A/154, in front of A/74, Housing colony,
Lohianagar, Kankarbagh, Patna-800020,
BIHAR, INDIA
20 November 2013

INDIAN BUREAUCRACY, LEGACY OF BRITISH EMPIRE, ARE MOST CORRUPT IN LEAGUE WITH POLITICAL CLASSES!

Tuesday, 29 October 2013

Indian bureaucracy—Indian Administrative Service (IAS), Indian Foreign Secrvice (IFS), Indian Police Service (IPS), and other central services and states services—have become much-maligned today in the wake of the degeneration of India with creeping corruption, inefficiency and of all lack of vision because of the encouragement of corrupt and thug political classes, ruling the India successively since independence! Among the many things our bureaucrats are worse legacies of the British Empire! The Indian civil servants have become massively corrupt. Even Pundit Jawahar Lal Nehru, the first Prime Minister of India had little respect for the bureaucrats in India. As Pundit Nehru put in his autobiography, written in 1935, 'few things are more striking today in India than the progressive deterioration, moral and intellectual, of the higher services, more specially, the Indian Civil Services (ICS). This is most in evidence in the superior officials, but it runs like a thread throughout the services'. Nehru had called officials as 'imperialists stooges'. The time changed. And after independence, Nehru entrusted the officials of the ICS to conduct the gigantic tasks of 1952 general elections, the first elections in independence India hesitatingly because there were no alternatives. Moreover,'great credit is due to those who are in charge of this stupendous first experiment in Indian history. Bureaucracy has certainly proved its worth by honestly discharging the duties imposed on it by an honest prime minister', Lucknow based sociologist D P Mukherji commented. The author of the book—India after Gandhi-Ramachandra Guha has written," in this respect, the 1952 elections was a script jointly authored by historical forces for so long opposed to one another: British colonialism and Indian Nationalism.

Between them these forces had given this new nation what could be fairly described jump-start to democracy."

In fact the bureaucracy, as it exists today, is essentially, a creation of British Raj. At that time, it gave slaved India, and administration that was impartial but insensitivity. Eminent bureaucrat of independent India T N Seshan, in his book—The Degeneration of India—with his co-author journalist Sanjoy Hazarika has written, "The close association of the administration with the ruling colonial regime bred a natural suspicion of them among political activists. After all, the politicians were involved in the independence movement. The job of the administration was to suppress that campaign—any movement that constituted a challenge to colonial authority—and toss people in jail. The suspicion and hostility of the politicians towards civil servant and vice-versa has continued even after independence. Each saw the other as a threat to his or her position and a competing centre of power. The main civil service as it operates across the country's districts, which is where its impact is most pronounced, has two arms: the Collector (also known as the district magistrate or deputy commissioner) and the Superintendent of police. Several collectors are grouped under a senior administrator, known as commissioner to form a division. The senior police officials, who ranks at the same level as the commissioner, is a deputy inspector general of police, some time an inspector general . . . At the second tier, the state level, the top officials is the chief secretary director general of [police is similar the top layer in the whole country comprises, the cabinet secretary, who is supposed to do on a national level what the chief secretary of a state does." In nut sell this is the structures of bureaucracy in India.

There were a few officials like Lalan Prasad Singh, ICS, and former union home secretary. P C Alexander, secretary to Indira Gandhi ands Rajiv Gandhi, K Pradhan, former union home secretary, T N Seshan, former Chief Election Commissioner of India, former rural development secretary N C Saxena etc, who proved their metal and did not buckle under political pressures and remained officials of proven integrity. Although political interferences in administrative work started just after independence, Pundit Nehru, Sardar Patel, the chief ministers, B C Roy (West Bengal, B G Kher (Bombay), S K Sinha (Bihar), G V Pant (Uttar Pradesh), R S Shukla (central province), Kamaraj (Tamil Nadu) were the political personalities, who never tolerated any interferences in the domains of bureaucrats by ruling or opposition political elites and rather, they protected the officials from any wrong-doings of ruling political classes in the respective states and at the centre.

But the deterioration in civil service began in 1960s. The successive brand of politicians in league with officials started indulging in corruption to mint money. Not only in corruption, they indulged but both officials and political classes bended rules, acts, and some cases even the Constitution for 'wrong doings.' Both the groups ganged up together in defeating India's first post-independence experiment with devolution of power to the villagers or the panchayati raj system. Both the groups ganged up in such way while implementing the system, the experiment ended up in joke in early 1950s to 1970s. It was corrected only the prime minister ship of Rajiv Gandhi when an Act for Panchayati Raj was enacted. Another casualty in the confrontation between the civil service and politicians was the police, especially the lower constabulary and the general administration. Officials began siding with the ruling politicians because they were more vulnerable. Police connived with the ruling politicians for creating jungle raj instead of rule of law. In the merciless attack on bureaucracy, the American humorist P J O'Rourke says that since the 'actual work of government is too unglamourous for the people who govern us', they create' bureaucratic departments to perform the humdrum tasks of national supervision. Government proposes; bureaucracy disposes. And the bureaucracy must dispose of government proposals by dumping them on us' (O'Rourke, 1992)

These days civil service is confused it is in search of an identity, but its role is determined by the perception of its political masters, not by the people. In this manner, the Indian bureaucracy, like other arms of governance in India is on 'slippery downward slope' Rewards are sought and given not for merit and efforts but for those who can cut deals, broker arrangements. Seshan says in his book, "India's political structure and philosophy now says that everything is acceptable unless you are caught or being blackmailed. Civil servants have taken a leaf from politicians in this regard: if you find some thing illegal, like accepting or demanding dowry, then there are two options before you. Neither option is honest one. It is a choice, these days, between resorting to influence peddling to get out of a fix and just brazening it out. In addition, civil servants are battered to death, openly assaulted in their offices, intimidated in other ways including transfers and threat of foisted corruption charges".

The Indian civil service is still on the same pattern of frame built by the British Raj. In India, IAS and other allied services men are considered 'highest elite classes' in the society even today. These IAS officials get training in British pattern since they join as probationers in Mussoorie. IAS probationers have been allotted to stay at the grandest, the Charleville, that stood on a ridge in Happy Valley and boasted a stay by the Prince of Wales (later George fifth) and Princess Mary of Teck, who in 1906 could never have envisaged that 50 years later everything devised for their comforts—the kitchens, the stables, the dinning rooms, the linen cupboards—would be in the hands of the people banned from the mall. Ian Jack has written in the Guardian, "everything has changed, nothing has changed. The era that produced hill stations also laid down the foundations of the Indian Administrative Service, the IAS, which together with the Indian Foreign Service used to attract (and arguably still does) the brightest from each generation. The IAS owes its structures to the British India Civil service, the ICS, which administered the country as a colonial possession from 1858 until 1947 through district officer system, in which a young Briton, public school and Ox bridge educated, passed a highly competitive examination and after some tuition in Indian languages and customs was given charge of an Indian district as populous as an English country, where under various titles (collector, district magistrate, deputy commissioners) he took charge of law and order and land revenues and any other piece of government policy that needed enforcing . . . ."

". . . . Lloyd George called it "the steel frame on which the whole structure of our government and of our administration in India rests" and the IAS has kept the steel frame pretty much intact. Its officers exercise enormous authority over a district population of between one and two million, some time barely familiar with the local language, apt to be lonely, forever facing the temptation of bribery. And they start so young, so terribly young. The new recruits in Mussoorie, the lucky thousands who have been chosen from 500,000 candidates by excelling in exams and interviews, are young enough to address visitors as Sir or Madam, but in a year or two they will sit as rulers of their small kingdoms, having been examined in Hindi, the Constitution and the Laws. A young ICS man, setting out from Tilbury to India in 1910, would have felt no less blessed or anxious."

In a country that over the past 20 years has been transformed— some would say disfigured—by private money, the IAS has survived as a still-impressive public institution. As the College's deputy director Ranjana Chopra, said, speaking to the IAS's ability to handle natural disasters better than George Bush's Washington. "Everything may not work well in India, but here is something that does."

But the facts are otherwise about IAS, IFS, IPS and central and state services, these cadre men have now become most corrupt, barring a few. One politicians quipped, "it is the officers who teach us the first lesson of wrong doings by bending rules, laws and ultimately the Constitution, for minting money in present day India". Entire edifice of these cadres have crumbled under the pressure of corruption to mint money and also to give favours to persons of influence and in this game poor people of India are worse sufferers!

Before I sum up the essay, I think it proper to quote T N Seshan, who has said, "I spend sleepless nights worrying about the degeneration of the country and wandering what my contribution to the regenerative process . . . ." and also the dream of Mahatma Gandhi for just and equatable society! In both the sections, these elite bureaucrats have failed miserably by succumbing to the pressure of successive brands of politicians!

ACCUMULATION OF BLACK MONEY IN INDIA HOLDING DEVELOPMENT AND WELFARE MEASURES FOR POOR!

Saturday, 26 October 2013

INDIA has notoriety in gaining top positions in many ills in the society, being a largest democracy in the globe, among the world's nations! Black money, discrimination against poor and dalits, atrocity on women, malnutrition, illiteracy etc are the few examples, which have put INDIA on 'shame list' in among the global countries. Today, I will put a few facts on accumulation of black money and deposited by Indian illegally in the foreign countries and cases of corruption, posing a serious threat on the development agenda of India.

Sadly and curiously, INDIA ranks eighth and among the top ten in developing countries with illicit fund outflow at $ 1.6 billion. India particularly saw black money outflow of $ 123 billion from 2001-2010; according to the Global Financial Integrity (GFI) in December 2012. Apart from these black money of Indian stashed abroad, in the country itself over Rs 10 lakh crore are hidden by Indian capitalists, political classes, professionals, industrialists, corporates and multinationals etc, without being accounted. This is what is happening in India where development projects and welfare measures for over 70 percent of persons, below poverty line, are suffering due to lack of fund!

The report of the GFI has said that the total outflow of black money from India since independence until 2010 was $232 billion. The aggregate value of illicit assets held by Indians from 1947 to 2010 is estimated at $ 487 billion. The report, titled ILLICIT FINANCIAL FLOWS, has found that only 27.8 percent of India's illicit assets are held domestically and 73 percent make their way overseas. But independent surveys have put the figures just vice-versa. Crores of black money inside the country is in the shape of benami illicit money and other assets, owned through black money. This black money is kept in fake bank accounts besides stashed in bags in the respective houses, especially by professionals and industrialists, capitalists etc.

THE GFI has said, in 2012 alone, India was ranked 94 out of 176 countries in the Transparency Internationals Corruption Perceptions Index. India was tied with Benin, Columbia, Djibouti, Greece, Moldova, Mongolia and Senegal. Apart from that, The Transparency International, which has put India as one of the most corrupt countries in the world, has said, in its report in 2008 that 40 percent of Indians have paid bribes to get a job done in public offices. This figure was 62 percent in a study conducted by the same firm in in 2005.

The Indian government report itself has admitted that as of December 2012, the government has conducted 2603 surveys and has detected Rs 8255 crore in undisclosed income in the country. This figure was Rs 6572.75 crore in the year 2011-12 when 3706 surveys were conducted. In a White paper on black money, tabled in the Indian Parliament in 2012, the Indian government conceded that real estate sector is one of the largest holders of illicit income and unaccounted funds. A large number of transactions are not reported and a vast number are under-reported. As the realty sector contributes 11 percent to GDP, this huge amount of under reporting is a huge dent to the treasury.

Independent surveys have, however, while confirming the government's facts on realty sectors, also pointed out that professionals like doctors, lawyers, contractors, neo-rich business men etc have huge black money and undisclosed income. BUT successive union and state governments have failed in its endeavour to unearth illicit and black money because of the connivance of political classes in black money holders in last many years. Not only Swiss banks, there are many countries' banks, especially Nepal banks, where Indians have deposited or accumulated huge amount of black and illicit money. In the name of religion, many religious places like temples, matths, mosques, religious trusts are under the control of huge property and cash, totalling over Rs two five lakh crores without any account to the government.

According to Yahoo news Website report; Swiss National Bank's report also states as of end 2012, out of the total 2.18 billion Swiss franc, deposits by Indian individuals and entities—1.34 billion Swiss francs were held directly by Indian individuals and entities and the rest 77 million Swiss franks was via 'fiduciaries' or wealth managers. The Swiss

Bank report has said that Indians hold Rs 9,000 crore or 2.18 billion Swiss franks in Swiss banks at the end of 2012, according to data released by Swiss National Bank. The overall amount held in Swiss banks by entities from across the world is estimated at around Rs 90 lakh crore.

India will now be able to track down the illicit money of Indians deposited in Swiss banks with an international agreement among 58 countries worldwide with Swiss government. The agreement is called, "Multilateral Convention on Mutual Administration Assistance in Tax Matters. Switzerland has finally agreed to share information on funds held in its banks to fight tax evasion and concealment of illicit funds. Switzerland was under tremendous pressure for co-operating with countries across the globe and divulges data on funds parked in Swiss Banks. It may be recalled that Swiss Banks have had strict client confidentiality clause and hence are a popular haven for illicit income. Now with the agreement Swiss Banks will have to bring down the wall of secrecy around its account holders and divulge information regarding overseas money held in the banks.

REFERENCES:—THE WEBSITES OF INDIA AND SWISS GOVERNMENTS, THE SWISS NATIONAL BANK, THE GLOBAL FINANCIAL INTEGRITY, THE TRANSPARENCY INTERNATIONAL, THE INDIAN PARLIAMENT, the YAHOO NEWS

MANMOHAN GOVT BENT TO WEAKEN RTI ACT!

Tuesday, 22 October 2013

I have no knowledge of Arabic Text as written in The Koran. Just I am mentioning the English translation of HUD, "In the name of God, the compassionate, the Mercuful" translation of Arabic text in English by the writer J N Dawood, born in Bagdad in his book in the chapter on JONAH***"The Koran—with parallel Arabic text" The writer translates the HUD in English—"—they cover up their breasts to conceal their thoughts from Him. But when they put on their garments, does He not know what they hide and what they reveal? He knows their inmost thoughts***"

Exactly this verse of the Koran reveals the surreptious move of the Manmohan Singh Govternment to exempt the Central Bureau of Investigation (CBI) from the perview of the Right to nformation Act despite vehement opposition by different sections of the society and government's other departments' views. Strangely bringing such move the union government has also ignored the Parliament and even National Advisiory Committee led by Sonia Gandhi. This is what is happening in democratic secular country—India. A very good thing enacted by UPA-1 as weapon to provide the citizens to secure aceess to information under the control of public authorities in order to promote transparency and accountablity in the working of every public authority. But the Act is being silently and surreptiously being tramplated by the Manmohan Singh Government! What has gone wrong withis great economist Manmohan singh, prime minister of India? Manmohan will ultimately answerable to all these misdeeds not only for future generation but also the people of the country living presently!

Sadly, the Law Ministry had mooted the partial proposal to exempt CBI from RTI Act—the Department of Personnel initially opposedthe move. And final curtain was down with the Attorney-General of India

G E Vanamati pushing for total exemption of the CBI from the perview of RTI Act.

Suspicion of people arose right from the very beginning over the proposal to keep the CBI from the perview of the Act. Because the CBI handles important corruption cases, involving big politicians, top officials etc. Successive union governments always put the CBI under the thumb to help the big culprits from the net. Now it has been justified hundred percent that union government wants to keep CBI under thumb to suit its political intesrest. Right to Information Act weapons of people were always putting the CBI and the union government under tenterhook by knowing what is happening and progress in the investigations of much-maligned cases, involving big politicians and officials as well as cronies of the ruling elites.

Originally RTI Act has exempted 18 public authorities under central government from disclosure of information under Section 24 of The Act, which included intelligence and security organisations in the interest of the country. For further exemption, the union govternment could broaden the areas in the name "security of the nation" without seeking any permission from the Parliament for its sanction but it is mandatory to place every such exemption and subsequent notification before each houses of the Parliament. Now the Indian people will must watch how the representatives of different hues in the both houses react over this exemption to the CBI! Moreover the Union cabinet okayed the exemption to the public authorities like CBI, National Investigation Agency, (NIA) And National Intelligence Grid in its meeting in the first week of June 2011 and exemption notices were issued by the Joint Secretary in the Ministry of Personnel, Public Grievances and Pension on June 9, 2011. Instead of bringing more and arenas for under RTI Act for more and more transparency—this is what union government has been doing gradually to weaken the RTI Act. Vanamati has put very funny logic of the CBI that as the agency that cases are referred to it for lodging cases from the courts as well as the economic cases and economic security of the country at risk etc. Vanamati has placed hollow logic to exempt the CBI—CBI is not an intelligence gathering organisation and Section 24(1) of the Act clearly states that information pertaining the allegation of corruption andf human right violations shall not be execuled under this sub-section and that such information should be provided after the approval of the central Information Commission. Strangely, many government agencies were violating such provisions and not responding to the petitions, referred by CIC, Subhash agrawal, a noted RTI Act activist said, while deploring the exemption to the CBI.

Even the member of the A NAC Aruna Roy and Wajahat Habubullah former CIC have opposed the exemption and hacve pointed out that there were conpiracies from the very beginning to weaken this bright and people firiendly Act to expose the governments both at union level and state levels. CBI is not a intelligence gathering organisation but it is investigating serious corruption cases like loot of public funds manily by politicians and officials, they remarked. Vehement opposition are goning on to protest the exemption but the union government is in its deep slumber and opposition leaders do not have time to take up such important issues. Here we must remember the weakening of left parties in the country, which would have initiated protests strongly to condemn such morve of the union government and restore earlier position!

Sadly what has gone wrong with newsapers, news magazines, and electronic channels? Why they are silent over such serious development? Except Hindu and Front line fortnightly, none of of the media has paid attention over such serious issues! Are they realy under "undeclared censorship" imposed by the governments of Union and states and also the proprietors of media houses for their englightened self interest? This is freedom of expression and press, enshrined in the Constitution. And we the people have also become worse than Murda (dead bodies) or this country has become "murdon ka desh (country of dead bodies) and we are tolerating atrocities by the government in our decadent society.

At this moment I exactly remeber a verse of Upanishad, "uttishth jagrat prapy barniin bodhat! (Uttho jago aur bare se gyan prapt karo duniyan to jitene ke liye—awoke from deep slumber and finally become consicious.

INDIA RANKED FIRST IN PREVALENCE OF SLAVERY AND FORCED LABOUR IN THE WORLD; SURVEY!

Tuesday, 22 October 2013

One can never change his or her mind-set in the feudal-minded society in India! Discrimination of dalits and poor in India is order of the day. Untouchablity Act is rarely implemented hardly in the country. Untouchablity prevails everywhere in India. Cases of untouchablity are again order of the day in Tamil Nadu by Orthodox Tamilians, especially Brahimins. (Essays on discrimination in India on my link—www. kksingh1.blogspot.com) Notwithstanding, the India has abolished three decades back the bonded labour system under the Bonded Labour System (Abolition) Act, 1976, the system "continues to be prevalent" in the country. This year also, amendments were, enacted to the Penal Code, in the wake of Delhi gang rape uproar in the Indian Parliament, which Act now criminalises most forms of human trafficking and forced labour!

India has the largest number of people in the world, who are living in conditions of slavery caused by poverty, handed-down social customs and weak enforcement of anti-slavery laws. Of the 30 million people world-wide, living in slavery-like conditions, 14 million are Indians. The West African nation of Mauritania ranked highest in the index in terms of percentage of population living in slavery-like conditions (with about 150,000 out of a population of 3.8 million). But in absolute numbers, India ranked the highest; While India leads in forced labour, the Communist China has some 2.9 million and Pakistan just above two million. Bonded persons, Nigeria, Ethiopia, Russia, Thailand, the Democratic Republic of Congo, Burma and Bangladesh round out the top ten, measured in absolute numbers. With about 4,000 slaves each, the UK, Ireland and Iceland claim the bottom spot. There are many faces of modern slavery; according to a global survey report, published recently by the Australia-based rights group—Walk Free Foundation at Chatham House.

The global survey index, compiled by the Walk Free Foundation, is the first global survey cataloguing forced labour on a country-to-country basis. "Modern slavery is a hidden crime," notes Walk Free Foundation CEO Nick Grono. "It is forced labour, bounded labour. And everyone is tainted by it. The clothes we wear might be made from cotton picked by forced labour in Uzbekistan. The electronic games we play with might contain minerals extracted by forced labour in the Congo," Says Grono. Uzbekistan cotton pickers are not like U S's cotton-picking slaves of past generations; no body owns them. But they are in servitude nonetheless, children and adults forced by the government to work in cotton fields. The co-founder of the organisation' Free the Slaves' and the index's author Prof. Kevin Bales says, "Slavery takes place at the bottom of the ladder with small mom-and-pop criminal enterprises. But some of these concerns grow. For example, fish and shrimp processing in Bangladesh and India can get very big and these companies are supplying the European and North American frozen seafood market."

The report says, "Today some people are still being born into hereditary slavery, a staggering but harsh reality, particularly in parts of West Africa and South Asia. Other victims are captured or kidnapped before being sold or kept for exploitation, whether through marriage, unpaid labour on fishing boats or as domestic workers." The index ranked 162 countries based on human trafficking, forced labour, slavery or slavery-like practices including debt bondage, forced or servile marriage, sale or exploitation of children including in armed conflict/ (INDIA HAS BOOMING SEX TRADE—my essay on www.kksingh1. blogspot.com) The index says, "India, China, Pakistan, Nigeria, Ethiopia, Russia, Thailand, Democratic Republic of Congo, Myanmar and Bangladesh together constitute 75 percent of the total estimate of 29.8 million people in modern slavery. That estimates is higher than the INTERNATIONAL LABOUR ORGANISATION (ILO)'s estimate of 21 million victims of forced labour."

As the story goes if you visit a Haitian home and see a child making coffee or washing dishes, do not assume it is one of the family's children going about their weekly chores. It is more likely that the child is a restavek, forced domestic labour. A Port-au-Prince-based social entrepreneur and presidential adviser Hans Tippeenhauer has explained, "There is supposed to be a social contract whereby the employees take care of their restaveks and send them to school. But most often that is not the case. These children are abused". Though Mauritania is worse than

Haiti, restaveks make up the lion's share of the Caribbean nation's forced labour. Some 25,000 to 3000,000 children cook and clean for families in large cities. They have no choice because their own parents are unable to look after them. A Haitian construction executive Greg Figaro, has explained, "It is not even seen as abuse. It is also a bit of status symbol. If you have a restavek, it means you are better off than the child's parents

With regards to India, the report (index) points out the failure of the Indian government to make use of its "power and resources" to eradicate slavery. "Until recently, the response to human trafficking focused almost exclusively on the sexual exploitation of women and children and other forms of human trafficking including those affecting men were barely recognised", the report says and adds," national leaders tend not to recognise the violent criminality of bonded labour and instead see it as a vestige of poverty".

But the hidden crime by definition is hard to tackle. Andrew Forrest, the Australian mining magnate and founder of the Walk Free Foundation, was not even aware of forced until his daughter unwittingly worked alongside African slaves labourers during gap year. And corporations often turn a blind eye. Nintendo, for example is accused of remaining avalier about the possibility of slave labour in its supply chain. The anti-slavery group Walk Free has launched a petition to make the electronics company take further steps to ensure slave-minded minerals are not used in their gaming consoles. As the grassroots campaign against blood diamonds has shown, consumers can be a formidable power.: Slaves labour is becoming an increasing reputational problem" says Grono. "Even if companies do not want to end forced labour because it's unethical, they will be forced to do so because being tainted by slave labour is bad for business."

The Guardian Professional essay, written by Elisabeth Braw has disclosed that bowing to customer pressure, H&M and Machael Kors recently banned supplies that use Uzbek cotton. Now activists are pressing Nike to take similar action. While Nike has pledged not to buy Uzbek cotton, it still sources synthetics from Daewoo International, the largest processor of cotton in Uzbekistan. According to a recent report by the Enough Project, while Nintendo has made little efforts to eliminate conflict materials from its devices, manufacturers like Intel and HP have taken decisive action. But the consumer activism will not help the slaves whose toil never touches the global supply chain. In Haiti, no politician would dare tackle the restavek issue, reports Tippenhauer. "We need a law regulating how domestic work should be remunerated. The restaveks get food, board and nothing else. But parties do not win votes by having restaveks on their agendas and the parliamentarians have domestic workers themselves. Those domestic workers, in turn, often employ restaveks in their own homes. In Order to pay restaveks popular wages, you would have to pay your own employees better. So nothing happens."

REFERENCES:—Websites of The INTERNATIONAL LABOUR ORGANISATION; The WALK FREE FOUNDATION; THE TIMES WEEKLY; THE GUARDIAN; THE INDIA GOVERNMENT; THE GLOBAL SURVEY INDEX; THE UZBEKISTAN GOVERNMENT; AUSTRALIAN GOVERNMENT;THE H&M; THE MICHAEL KORS; THE DAEWOO INTERNATIONAL; etc

"INDIA'S SEX TRADE IS BOOMING": NEW YORK TIMES

Sunday, 20 October 2013

".... India's own sex trade is booming. The New York Times recently reported on widespread human trafficking of young girls in the state of Jharkhand and on the trafficking of impoverished girls into India from neighbouring Nepal. Girls are also exported from India and other South Asian countries to the GULF and south-east Asia . . . ." Says an EDITORIAL BOARD OPINION of the NEW YORK TIMES recently.

I have mentioned in my number of essays on my link—www. kksingh1.blogspot.com—about shames after shames in India, thanks to the lack-lustre approaches and attitudes of India's successive union and state governments in the last over 65 years, even being called one of the largest democracy in the world! Practically women are being treated in this present social structure of India as "toys". And the women are being discriminated without any rhymes and reasons even with the heralding of 20th century. No doubt, in the wake of brutal gang rape in last December, in Delhi, which grabbed national and international headlines and also caused public outrage, lamentably huge sex-trafficking in India have not attracted the same public attention or provocation in the last several years. India has been identified as a major hub in the international sex trade, a global phenomenon that may involve upwards of 27 million people, by the United States State Department, the United Nations and the India's Human Right Commission.

Corruption among officials, police and political classes is widespread in India. Trafficking in sex has become a thriving business in India! Particularly the political classes, except a few, in India give long ropes to the criminals and vested interests to thrive in the nefarious business in trafficking in sex of for money. The political classes get huge share and protection money for encouraging, protecting and shielding the persons, engaged in the business. Now it is generally said in India that these decadent political classes can go to any extent to stay in power and to earn money for their hegemony on the political scenes in the country. People by and large consider in India that politicians, except a few are roots of all the evils in the system! All hues of politicians are strangely united in running the inhuman and dishonest businesses for the sake of money and power secretly but daggers drawn in public. Business in the Parliament is installed invariably on flimsy issues, obviously to show the public that are raising the issues of public interest! Police and civil officials, for the sake of money and good posting involved themselves in corrupt businesses in league with politicians throughout the country. Entire system in India has been corrupted and degenerated. Trafficking is profitable and corruption is widespread in India! It is all too easy to buy off police and other law-enforcing agencies by traffickers.

Persistent poverty is a major factor. Many vulnerable women and girls are lured by promises of employment and some parents are desperate enough to sell their daughters to traffickers, Rapid urbanisation and migration of large numbers of men into India's growing cities creates a market of commercial sex, as does a gender imbalance resulting from sex-selective abortion practices that has created a generation of young men, who have little hope of finding female partners. India's a affluence is also a factor, luring European women into India's sex trade. The caste system compounds the problem. Victims of trafficking disproportionately come from disadvantaged segments of Indian society. Trafficking is profitable and corruption is widespread. It is invariably seen that traffickers, alluring the women and girls, sold them to Gulf. Many of them are forced to marry and girl lured from rural India are got married to Shiekhs in the Gulf and also sexually exploited. In many cases, women and girls of India are sold to European, American, Australian, African countries and they are either sexually-assaulted or forced to do menial and other domestic work. Women and girls, mainly lured from rural India are brought in cities and towns and they are sexually exploited in "big bazaars of prostitutes" and also sold to big people for sexual pleasures in the name of domestic work! Women and girls from Bihar, Jharkhand, eastern Uttar Pradesh, Assam, West Bengal and other eastern states are trafficked by sex-traffickers and after sexual assaults, they are forced to marry with people of old age in Haryana, Delhi, eastern Uttar Pradesh, Rajasthan for giving birth to their children and later they are formalised as wives and husbands after much hue and cry! Even in rural areas in India, girls and women of lower caste are made show-cases for "nautch and gaan". Nothing substantial is being done to improve the lots of women in India!

In March, in the wake of Delhi rape, India's Parliament passed a bill amending laws concerning sexual violence and making sex-trafficking a criminal offence. But the gap between enactment and enforcement remains unacceptable wide. Parliament acted in response to the recommendations of judicial committee led by the late Justice Jagdish Sharan Verma. In addition to urging tougher laws protecting women and children from abuse, the Verma report recommended stiffer penalties for sex related crimes as well as swifter justice for the perpetrators. Amending law is good step but law is only as good as its enforcement. Police are mainly very easily saleable, thanks to protection by political classes mainly in trafficking cases, Measures must be initiated so that police must face strong disciplinary consequences for turning a blind eye, and those who commit sex crimes must know that they risk speedy prosecution and stiff sentences.

Apart from that Indian government should address historic patterns of discrimination and focus increased resources on educating disadvantaged girls. Until attitudes in India towards women change and poor children gain the skills they need to control of their futures, sex-trafficking and the damage it inflicts will continue!

BOOK REVIFW:—BOOK ON BIHAR REKINDLES NEW HOPE AND ASPIRATION IN BIHAR MINUS NOT 'NITISHNOMICS' BUT 'NITISHOHYPOCRACY'!

Thursday, 17 October 2013

Before I start to come to the points about the book—THE NEW BIHAR: REKINLING GOVERNANCE AND DEVELOPMENT—, authored by N K Singh, retired IAS official and Rajya Sabha Member from Bihar, and his co-author Lord Nicholas Stern, an IG Patel Professor of Economics and Government at the London School of Economics, I want to put some of my old reminiscences of 1980s about Bihar when everybody in India has ruled out the state because of its growing backwardness and no sign of development. Some of them used to comment, "Bihar has withered away." I was in Delhi in late 1980s. Just out of curiosity, I went to meet an acquainted senior IAS official of Bihar cadre that time posted on senior slot in the Union Home Ministry (UHM). In course of talks of over half-an-hour, I usually asked him when he is returning to Bihar to his parent cadre. Just after that senior official first gazed the ceiling of his well-decorated office chamber in the magnificent North Block, which houses UHM and thereafter he started looking towards adjacent India Gate from across the room through big window. After after half a minute, he told me," who bothers for your Bihar . . . ., which have been ruled out because of misgoverning and no-sign of development . . . ." I was not amazed but simply I smiled! The senior IAS official was no other but N K Singh. Now after the long gap of over 24 years, the same IAS official, now retired, after holding important position in union government, is Janata Dal (U) MP from Bihar, has penned the book, arising new hopes and aspirations to the people of Bihar with regards to all round development of Bihar, which was in moribund stage over nine years back!

Apart from the NOTES THE PREFACE AND, THE INTRODUCTIONS by authors and co-author, the book is by and large compilations of essays on Bihar's economy and its tempo in all round development in recent years written by eminent economists, writers, analysts, commentators etc Mr N K Singh and Nicholas Stern have introduced the subject about Bihar's development in very lucid style. Other essayists including Nobel Prize winner in Economics Amartya Sen have also traced the facts very aptly about Bihar, its culture, glory, economy, education, society, health etc since ancient and medieval period. The Authors and essayists have simply argued the hopes of desired development of Bihar—"like as straw man lies dead, what is ignored is the development in the room . . ." Author and his co-author as well as essayists have failed to mention about lack of land reforms measures, the bane of poverty in the state. However here and there there are just passing references. Although the essayists and author and his co-author have heaped praise on the Chief Minister of Bihar, Nitish Kumar for bringing the backward state on the development path, there are many discernible factors about backwardness and recent tempo of developments in Bihar, which have rarely found place in the book—that is, in my opinion, percolating of the fruits of development at grass-root level for major sections of society in social indicator during the so called sharp rise in GDP of Bihar in comparision to other developed states of India. Many 'metaphors' like free market paradigm that economic growth in Bihar during Nitish regime has brought wide-ranging development. Whether Bihar developed at desired level or not but essayists have tried to rewrite the history of Bihar, which continues to languish on almost all parameters of development and social indicators. No doubt, both the authors and essayists of the book have been gifted with sense of history but lack in experimenting the economy of Bihar, which is primarily agriculture based.

After reading the book, exactly I remember the announcements of Nitish Kumar after assuming chief minister ship of the state about eight years back that his topmost priority will be improving of education and health sectors besides land reforms. But in all the cases, probably Nitish Kumar has failed to achieve desired result. Education and health are most important parameters of development—of course a number of measures have been taken by Bihar government but results are hardly 20 to 25 percent on the surface. All these failures of Bihar government and hammering of the subjects by the essayists for their success, remind me Rabindranath Tagore, who had once said, "In my view the imposing tower of misery which today rests on the heart of India has its sole foundation in the absence of education."

At least in one aspect, the author and his co-author have admitted that Bihar has long history of backwardness. Even as historically, Bihar has glorious past. They have also made honest appraisal of facts in the book that Bihar has lowest electrification rates in the country with only 16 percent of the households having access to electricity much lower than the national average of 67 percent. Forty percent of electricity is consumed only in the one city—Patna, the state capital, which also does not have constant power supply; the authors point out and add, "That it is surely extraordinary that having reached the nadir Bihar rejuvenated itself in less than a decade to become fastest growing state even as India's own growth gathered momentum. Many have attributed this rapid turn-around to Nitishnomics, meaning improved governance and a more inclusive growth strategy. There are many facetes of Nitishonomics. But the picture appears some thing different. There are many glaring mention of facts in the book, one can imagine how the Bihar is developing? There are many instances that it is not Nitishonomics but the so called turn around in Bihar "Nitishohypocracy"! Deprived majority are still languishing because of faulty implementation of welfare measures and large scale corruption, which have become greatest menace during Nitish regime in Bihar. The book does give a clean scenario of what are happenings in Bihar under democratic fabrics of India. Elites and neo-rich class, closure to corridor of power, are cornering all benefits, meant for poor in Bihar.

When I look such painful pathetic picture of human condition in rural areas in Bihar, it reminds the well-known Mahamta Gandhi's Talisman of 1948 when Gandhi had said, "I will give you a talisman. Whenever you are in doubt or when your self becomes too much with you, apply the following test, Recall the face of the poorest and weakest man and woman, whom you may have seen and ask yourself, if the step you contemplate is going to be of any use to him (her). Will he (she) gain anything by it? Will it restore him (her) to a control over his/her own life and destiny? In other words, will it lead to swaraj (freedom0 for the hungry and spiritually starving millions? Then you will find your doubts and your self melt away." If these things do not reflect the minds of ruling elite in Bihar, then we must call them thieves and looteras of public funds Nitish Kumar does behave like a feudal ruler of Bihar, which hardly finds place in the book. Nitish Kumar held Janata Darwars at his official residence once in a week after attending the so called darwar for registering their complaints, people returned disappointed and call the janta darwar a feudal darwar like of British Raj and landlords during pre-independence days! A recent essay on the website of Carnegie Endowment for International Peace (http://carnegieendowment, org) has compared Nitish Kumar no less autocrat than Narendra Modi. Both have autocratic tendencies Nitish has developed a worrying reputation for leveraging his state government'd hefty advertisement budget to punish media outlets who dare publish negative stories about his administration. Not only that Nitish Kumar has given free hands to officials and other government staffs to carry his programmes and policies without caring even the ruling class politicians, resulting into wide-spread corruption in government machinery. Virtually there is no democracy in Bihar but bureaucracy is prevailing—even ministers are not allowed to speak about officials, thanks to the autocratic style of Nitish Kumar! These are some hard facts which should have found mention in the books either by essayists or authors themselves. Is the book one-side about Nitish's dream Bihar? At one place in the book, one essayist Pawan Kumar Verma has virtually, while praising Nitish Kumar like a sycophant number one has heaped abuses—like words on Biharis and its culture, prior to what were happenings in Bihar. Were Bihar and Biharis before Nitish Kumar rule have had gone uncultured and forgotten the unique culture of Bihar? Shame to Pawan Kumar Verma for such remarks in N K Singh's book!

No doubt Bihar is developing during Nitish regime in the wake of allround economic turn around in India, it does not mean that it is because of Nitishnomics but to some extent streamlining of governance in Bihar, which had lacked during Laloo-Rabri regime as well as new economic policy being implemented in India as a whole and massive funds of centrally-sponsored programmes, Backwardness of Bihar is also contribution successive Congress governments in Bihar. But during Laloo Prasad regime, the poor, the dalits, the adivasis and downtrodden got their voices and Laloo was instrumental for that—but during Nitish regime dalits are being tortured by upper caste people. There are many instances of such atrocities in Bihar during Nitish regime. Both economically and politically, dalits are being deprived of their rights by land-owing classes and neo-rich classes, cropped during Nitish regime One essayist Meghnad Desai, an eminent economist and professor of Economics at the London School of Economics has rightly commented in his writings, "The collapse of the Congress hegemony at the national level in 1989 and the emergence of the Mandal reforms brought about the first profound change in Bihar . . . . This was assertion of power by the other backward class (OBC) . . . . The Janata Dal, which later became Rashtriya Janata Dal (RJD) during its 15 years tenure (1990-2005) concentrated on what one may call the 'respect' agenda. This was to give dignity and respect to the previously downtrodden social groups and challenge the upper caste hegemony with the help of state power. It was acknowledged by the leaders of the RJD that development was not his priority but the righting of the old oppression was it is correct to say that in the respect agenda the RJD was successful. As Jeffrey Witsoe says in his article in the Lall and Gupta volume: While Lalu systematically destabilised the institution of governance and state directed development, i suggest that this was catalysed a meaningful although partial empowerment of lower caste' A [popular RJD slogan was "vikas nahi samman chahiye" . . . ." But what happened to empowerment of dalits and backwards during Nitish regime, the agenda was not cared and today atrocity on them is continuing as reflected ion the National Crime Record Bureau (NCRB).

The importance of the N K Singh's book would have comparatively lesser impact about the development of Bihar with the recent blasting of Bihar government and its chief minister Nitish Kumar by the well known development economist Jean Dreze, a co-author of the book, written by Amartya Sen—AN UNCERTAIN GLORY: INDIA AND ITS CONTRADICTIONS while delivering a lecture on the food security at Patna. Dreze has said, "Bihar is capital of corruption and exploitation in the world. The living condition of the people in some of Bihar villages is more grim and horrifying than at most places in the world. In fact in terms of scheme implementation, corruption is at its zenith. Bihar is sitting on the hotbeds of poverty, hunger and malnutrition and could be potentially the biggest beneficiary of the National Food Security Act, 2013. Eighty-five percent of rural population and 62 percent of urban residents in Bihar have calorie deficiency during 2009-10 as per reports of the National Sample Survey office. In Fact Bihar ranked 74th in global hunger index of 88 countries, according to Survey of India State Hunger Index—2008. In the same survey Jharkhand ranked 76th, Odisha 67th and UP 61st all in the alarming zone.

However N K Singh and Lord Nicholas Stern's book has rekindled the hopes and aspiration among Biharis and if the measures to develop the state are taken in right direction till next 15 years, Bihar will regain its lost glory of development once again. For the first time in many years, a book on Bihar has pictured the ways and means for the real development of the State. The book is definitely a good reading in lucidity, style and detailed facts!

EU AND INDIA'S LOK SABHA SPEAKER CONCERNED OVER CASTE BASED DISCRIMINATION: DISCRIMINATION HAS CONSOLIDATED DALITS TO PLAY CASTE-BASED VOTING AND EMPOWERED THEM!

Sunday, 13 October 2013

The prevalence of consolidation of low caste men, on caste lines to protest against the caste based discrimination in different parts of the world, particularly in South Asia has raised hopes and aspirations for low caste Hindus in India, known as 'dalits'. And low caste men in India have started asserting and moving for bigger rights in India. Many important personalities including Mahatma Gandhi, Dr B R Ambedkar and a number of Indian right organisations had launched campaign to support dalits for being discriminated and living in India in apartheid conditions since pre-independence days. Dalits are not only beginning discriminated but taken in low stock by feudal mindset landlords, Upper caste men, and rich people!Two important factors of the recent past—the speech of the Speaker of the Lok Sabha, Meera Kumar, also a former Indian Foreign Service (IFS) official and daughter of veteran dalit leader and former Deputy Prime Minister, Babu Jagjivan Ram, in the Cambridge University on "elections and the factors that influence voting" and a powerful resolution of the Parliament of the European Union (EU) against caste based discrimination in South Asian countries like India, Nepal and Sri Lanka—have amply substantiated that caste-based politics is the need of hour to fight against discrimination and also get lever of power in the governance.

Notwithstanding many measures, like reservation of seats in Parliament and state legislatures and in services as well as reservation in job to backward classes to them, enunciated in the Indian Constitution, since independence, have been initiated for equal rights to all Indian without any discrimination, discrimination of dalits continued in India. Since their assertions in caste-based politics and vote their caste men, in elections in India have started giving dividends to them in asserting their rights. In her speech in the Cambridge University Lecture recently, Meera Kumar has pointed out that dalits' "preferences on the ballot, there was positive belief that consolidation on caste-lines was leading to empowerment of dalits as it gave them opportunity to assert themselves." Besides caste, she slammed the importance "that religion plays in elections" Reiterating that caste "decides a voter's preference in India, she, however, said, in her speech, that now "it is high time the caste system was destroyed completely" Kumar further has said in her speech, "generally the deciding factor is the case, which is discussed in hushed tones behind closed door caste system has caused and is continuing to cause unimaginable harm to the society. It needs to be destroyed completely and not encouraged to tighten its grip in our electoral system."

In a related major development, The EU's Parliament, which has recently discussed caste-based discrimination, has passed a resolution endorsing the views of the campaigners from South Asia about discrimination and decided to push the agenda in the ensuing at the trade talks between the EU and countries like India, Nepal and Sri Lanka, where discrimination are very rampant. (India's lowest caste, such as dalits, are often forced into dangerous work, despite a number of affirmative action initiatives) Speakers in the debate were critical of current EU commitments for tackling caste discrimination. The EU commissioner Cecilia Malmstorm told Parliament that the issue is "being tackled, MEPs disagreed". Alf Svensson, of the European People's Party group said, "I do not really agree that this is put on the agenda quite often." Michael Cashman, of the Progressive Alliance of Socialists and Democrats, said "if we have all these EU instruments and 260 million people still suffer caste discrimination, we are failing."

Jean Lambert, an MEP for the Green Party in the U K, who has been involved with campaigning on behalf of dalits for several years, says, "It will not be easy to move from a resolution to practical action. It is going to be tough to get anything into trade agreements . . . . It is always a battle to get human rights in, especially some thing as specific as this, but certainty in some programmes in the affected countries we will already be looking at the impact on the most deprived, and that would include dalits." To move towards action, she says, "Parliamentarians have to better understand caste issues so they can keep them in mind when they travel on business, trade and development trips. You would have to make sure that the people, who are going from the European Parliament, are really briefed to ask about this. They need to know what to ask and who to ask, so awareness—raising is important; seeing it as a human right issue. We are all required to raise issues of human rights."

ILO SURVEY:—In the meantime, the International Labour Organisation (ILO) estimates that overwhelming majority of bonded labour victims in South Asia are from lower castes, with forced and bonded labour particularly widespread in the agriculture, mining and garment production sectors. Surprisingly, some of these companies involved in these sectors supply [products to multinationals. Many countries of South Asia have launched awareness campaign against discrimination and atrocity against lower caste men. Caste system are very much common in south-east Asia, Campaigners estimate 260 million people around the world are affected. Caste divides people into social groupings; those in the lowest caste are regarded as unclean and are forced into unpleasant and dangerous work. They are put to live in slavery with landlords and feudal, Manjula Pradeedp of India Right Organisation—Navsarjan-point out, "you are born as a sub-caste within dalits, given the caste identity and an occupation linked to that caste. If I belong to this caste, the first work that is forced upon me is cleaning human excrement with my hands and to carry it my heads. People are not able to get out of this slavery. India is seen as a large democracy, but it would not address these people should do this work; it is mind-set."

Campaigners from India have welcomed the EU initiatives, particularly discrimination against low-caste Hindus, known as dalits at such high-level forum. Pradeep says, "When we started the process of lobbying the European Parliament in 2007 we had to explain what (caste discrimination) was. Now, we do not have to say what it means to be dalit, so it is reward, but we stll have to do a lot of work." Confirming India's affirmative action programmes to support dalits, Pradeep says, "some inbuilt prejudices are coming in the way of long-term methodology to tackle the situation. When we were listening to the statements of European Parliament, I thought about my own members of Parliament and I wonder if they are ready to speak on this issue. Very few are ready . . . . they do not want to address it at a larger level, most often these issues related to caste have never been addressed at a national level in our country"

Pradeep Says, "The EU result is in the positive direction and the result is beginning of recognition that caste-based discrimination can be tackled internationally as well as at domestic level. Non-recognition of dalits and their rights is a challenge to all of us. The Indian government has failed to protect the rights of people who have been living in a situation that is like apartheid. That process has happen in our country; ultimately, it has to happen on the ground. But when you do not get support from your own government, you need to address it internationally. It is not a local issue, it is global issue."

REFERENCES:—WEBSITES OF THE EU, THE GUARDIAN, THE TIMES OF INDIA, THE ILO, THE GOVT OF INDIA, THE PARLIAMENT, THE CAMBRIDGE UNIVERSITY

WOMEN OF THE WORLD, ESPECIALLY INDIA, MUST UNITE AND TAKE UP ARMS TO FIGHT INJUSTICES!

Friday, 11 October 2013

One of the saddest aspects in the globe today is that nearly half of the population—female—are by and large have become subjects of rape, atrocity, torture, manhandling, cruelty, domestic violence, discrimination etc in almost all countries of the World The countries of Asian continent, which are the most populous continent with 4.2 billion around 60 percent of world population, have surpassed in this nefarious activities beyond imagination! Today the women are most in secured in the world. Out of total population on the earth—7.117 billion—, the proportion of sex ratio is approximately 1.01 male to 1 female as per global sex ratio count in 2012, drawn by the United States Census Bureau (USCB). Almost all countries on the earth, are male dominated with little window of opportunity to the opposite sex. And the women are tolerating, almost silently, all the injustices, meted out to them! Almost all print and electronic media through out the world are, today, flooded with incidents of rapes and other atrocities on women of the world. My two essays— Women of the Globe becoming Most vulnerable . . . . written on July 20, 2012 and Women are Not Safe in India . . . . , written on July 28, 2012 on my link—www.kksingh1.blogspot.com clearly reflect such ills in the society. Now the appropriate time has come for women of the world to unite and take up arms to fight against injustices on them throughout the GLOBE!

WOMEN IN INDIA:—Such inhuman practices are very much common in other cities, towns and villages in India, which is the second largest populous country in the world. Less said is better about developed countries in Europe, America etc. Various surveys and reports by United Nations and other agencies, published in The Guardian and other newspapers and magazines have confirmed the incidents of atrocity

44

on women in the globe. When incidents of such heinous crimes on women happen, much hype is created but nothing tangible is done to stop such things. Persons, involved in inflicting such crimes on women, usually get away without any sever punishments! Apart from that women in the world, particularly in India are isolated from the respective mainstreams by successive brands of political classes in the globe. At least in India, efforts of empowering women are not working despite clear cut provisions in our Constitution. Women are almost half of the population in India. Women of India are neglected lots in India since ancient days. They are not allowed to come out from the houses. All political classes are supporting 50 percent reservation to women in the "lever of power" for Parliament and state legislatures. Matter is hanging fire since many years, thanks to the lack of determination and guts power among political classes of all hues! Instead, women are target of atrocities in India openly if one considers reports of abuses on women by dominant and powerful males In India!

"There is undoubtedly a cultural dimension to violence against women and at the very least the U N Study demonstrates that the legal frame work for dealing with sexual violence in many Asian states is barely fit for the purpose. But we do not solve that problems by exaggerating it to the point of absurdity or pretending that we can treat diverse populations with essentially nothing in common as upholding some kind of ubiquitous misogyny." Instead of giving equal or lever of power under much-publicised social justice, the male bastion of the world believe in looking women as sex symbols. In such inhuman games males including politicians, sadhu, sants, officials are involved in many cases of sexual abuses in the name of blind faiths and belief. They are involved in criminal cases for raping and perpetuating other forms of atrocity on women at least in India today. Almost on daily basis, the crime of rapes are being committed in every parts of the country. Notwithstanding the rape and murder of a young woman in Delhi last year, and the subsequent death handed out to the four perpetuators, has prompted all manner of soul searching in India, women's rights have-finally-come the forefront in a country where the concept remains curiously alien to many of its inhabitants.

25pc ADMITS RAPES:—Recent verdict in rape case in Delhi in India coincided with the release of U N-led study on sexual violence in Asia and Pacific. Although survey did not include India in its sample-survey, it did not fail to dissuade commentators from drawing a parallel between the findings and the Delhi case. The U N survey has shockingly revealed that 25 percent of the men surveyed admit to raping a partner or a stranger. Such report amply authenticates the unequivocal confirmation that the Asian women are the victims of a deep-rooted-cultural problem. The study, published in The Guardian, covered a small, but diverse number of Asian countries—Bangladesh, Cambodia, China, Indonesia, Sri Lanka and Pappua New Guinea. In each country, men were asked about their experiences both within and outside of relationship. In most cases, the samples were not nationality representative. In case of Papua New Guinea for instance, all of the respondents were based on the island of Bougainvillea. as the samples were not nationally representatives, "it is impossible to use the figures to make any generalisations about the populations in these countries (for less the continent of Asia).—More importantly, out of all of the locations surveyed, the only territories in which positive responses to the questioned on rape were 25 percent or higher were Bougainvillea and the Indonesian province of Papua. In both instances the number "yes" responses from men were staggering: 43.8 percent for Papua and 59.1 percent in Bougainnville. Both the areas have a recent history of conflict, which might explain the appalling prevalence of sexual violence indicated by the study. Indeed if the two samples had not been included, the overall figure of men admitting to rape could have dropped to 18 percent. The Guardian essay says "In itself that is still a deeply worrying statistics, but the extent to which two isolated cases cam swing our perception of an entire continent should be enough to prompt a little caution"

Perhaps most troubling of all, though, is the nature of questions used which varied across different countries. In Bangala Desh, the first country included in the study, the questions related strictly to "forced sex". In all of the other countries, an additional question was asked which attempted to measure the prevalence of "coerced sex". The wording of these questions made no explicit mention of coercion, however, and simply asked: "have you had sexual intercourse with your partner when you knew she did not want to, but believed she should agree because she was your wife/partner?" But there are many defence of study—say China has a population of around 1.35 billion while Bougainville sits less that two lakh. It may well be the case that a quarter of the survey's respondents indicated they had raped someone during the course of their life but that is an entirely different thing from saying a quarter of the people in the surveyed countries has committed rape.

Whatever may be report of UN Study, the Indian women are standing up to "abuse". A recent BBC report says India has cases of atrocity on women in many ways. Women are beaten and tortured in India in case of not delivering male child apart from rampant rise in cases of rapes. Situation is terrible for Indian Women. But one discernible facts have come surface that tortured women have mustered courage to approach police station in case of tortures, rapes etc unlike previously when they used to keep silence despite tortures after tortures. But cases of rapes are increasing in Delhi, the capital of India. Police have registered 1036 cases of rapes up to August 15, 2013. But the fate of such rape incidents in other cities and rural areas, which are flooded with such complaints of rape, are not assailable to the public. If one compares the incident of rapes and subsequent convictions to the culprits in other countries, such rates are far below in India. The National Crime Records Bureau (NRBC) has said that conviction rates in rape cases are only 21.4 percent in s current year in comparison to much higher figures in the last year, says BBC report and adds during October 2013—BBC has organised "100 WOMEN SEASON", which will seek shine on life for women in their respective countries—theme "is risk, challenges and opportunity, the women face everyday in every country".

Examples of crime and rapes on women are enormous in India! According to India's NCRB, crimes against women have been on the rise in Indian cities in recent years. In 2012, Delhi accounted for ten percent of all crimes against women, in the 53 cities with more than a million people. Mumbai followed with 6.4 percent, Bengaluru was third at 6.2 percent and Kolkata had 5.4 percent.

URBAN PLANNING FAULTY IN INDIA:—According to New york Times report on sexual violence in India; urban planners and designers argue that apart from better policing, gender-sensitive city planning and design can help make India's cities safer for women. Pattern of crimes in a city, according to experts, vary according to its urban design. One of the most striking components of urban infrastructures in New Delhi is the Ring Road, a massive circular road that circles the city. It passes through several desolate areas of the city and has vast stretches without any traffic lights for miles. An Urban designer K T Ravindaran, who retired as the head of School of Planning and Architecture in New Delhi, has said, "One of the most common places of rape in Delhi is a moving vehicle. They can just go on until the fuel runs out." The best-known instance of such a crime was the gang rape and subsequent death of a 23-year-old paramedical student in a moving bus in Delhi in December last year. Vehicular speeds in Indian cities have increased in the past decades with the construction of multiple over passes and several major road ways that eliminated the need of traffic lights. These changes saw a parallel increase in motor-borne crimes from snatching, road rage and assault on women in moving vehicles. Ravindran said, "The speed of the city is critical. You can have fast-track lanes for public transport and cars because the city has to move. But it should have safe havens for pedestrians. That is primary condition for a city to become safe.

Usually crimes and rapes on women in India are committed in "dark shadow" or in desolate areas in Indian cities and rural areas. In most of the Indian cities, street lights are positioned to light roads, foot-paths or side-walks of the roads remain in darkness. The emergence of gated neighbourhoods in India has also added to creation of empty, potentially dangerous spaces outside their confines., vulnerable to crimes. Gsutam Bhan, a senior consultant at the Indian Institute of Human Settlements, has said, "When cities become fortified, they create non-space or residual space outside the walls of their gated colonies. Those spaces then belong to no one and create empty landscapes that violence then fills." Yet urbanisation experts are aware that sensitive planning is not enough to prevent crime in a city. Amitabh Kundu, an Economics Progfessor in Jawahar Lal Nehru University in New Delhi, who specialises in urbanisation has said, "Creating exclusionary urban spaces tends to develop an atmosphere of deprivation and violence among the excluded." The perpetrators in Delhi gang rape case and the accused of a separate rape, that of a young photo-journalist in Mumbai, came from do called urban zines of exclusion—Ravidas camp slum in New Delhi and Dhobighat slum in south Mumbai. Bhan further said, "gender-inclusive cities are not just sager for women, they are also more egalitarian for all citizens".

Moreover, apart from class-based segregation, India also faces the challenges of segregation on the basis of religion, with minority religious groups mostly, living in gutto-like neighbourhoods. Both the 1984 attacks on Sikhs in New Delhi and the 2002 communal riots in Gujarat were characterised by widespread sexual violence against women from Sikh and Muslim minorities. Kundu has pointed out, "Exclusionary cities wherein upper and middle class people create boundaries around their localities and thereby create a degenerated periphery tend to be extremely violent in situations of breakdown of law and order or outbreak of group violence. We saw that in 1984 when the Sikh neighbourhoods were attacked in Delhi and in the attacks on Muslim areas in Gujarat in the 2002 riots."

Thus, women of the world, especially India must unite and take up arms to fight injustices on them. Women must mobilise the women forces throughout the world to save their chastity!

References: websites of The UNO, The New York Times, The Guardian, The BBC, India Govt organisations and many more websites!

SUPREME COURT AND U.N PANEL CONCERNED OVER LAND GRABBING OF TRIBAL AND POOR IN INDIA FOR BUSINESS PURPOSES, VIOLATING LAWS: POSCO HALTED TO SET-UP STEEL PROJECT IN ODISHA BY U.N!

Sunday, 6 October 2013

IT HAS BECOME COMMON REFRAIN in the Globe that land must belong to tillers, labours, and peasants! But in India, it has different conceptions. Despite so many efforts since independence in India, Lands continue in the hands of landlords and rich people. Now gradually the lands are being shifted in the hands of new-type of landlords—corporates, industrialists, multi-nationals etc in the name of the economic development of the country, thanks to the faulty policy of the Indian government and its states! Over 85 percent dalits, poor, backwards etc have not even an inch of lands to construct even a roof to cover themselves—what to speak of tilling the lands! Much-hyped land reform measures are languishing in the last over 65 years because of 'vested interest and apathetic attitude' of the Indian and its state governments. After a long drawn controversy over the ticklish land acquisition procedures, the Union government had okayed an ACT— Land Acquisition, Rehabilitation and Resettlement Bill, 2013 to address 'the injustices involved in the land acquisition' by replacing colonial rule Act—Land Acquisition Act, 1894.

Notwithstanding the new Act, has brought some far-reaching changes in land acquisition process in the country, the new Act has included one of the strangest and finniest provisions in the new Act, providing to permit to the government to acquire the land for the corporate sectors. The colonial Land Acquisition Act, 1894, although have many drawbacks including the lack of provision for consent of those whose land was proposed to be acquired, did not permit the government to acquire land for the corporate sectors, industrialists etc in the name of so called economic development of India! Since the liberalization of economy in 1980s, a big quantity of land had been acquired by the government for creating 'Special economic zones' in different parts of the country as well as acquisition of lands for industrialists, corporates, capitalists etc in forest and mines and mineral areas in almost all the states of the country, violating Forest Rights Act and related Environment laws. These lands had been acquired on throw-away rate of acquisition and given to the corporates, industrialists, and capitalists on premium prices. Ultimately poor, dalits and tribal suffered whose small lands in forest and plan areas, were suffering.

At least my few essays and topics on the subjects—TRIBAL AND POOR BEING UPROOTED IN INDIA TO BENEFIT MULTI-NATIONALS, CORPORATES—on FEB.22, 2013, LACK OF LAND REFORM, BANE of POVERTY AND HUNGER IN INDIA— NOV.16,2012, another on Bihar, LACK OF LAND REFORM, BANE OF POVERTY IN BIHAR, DEc.04, 2012 and GREAT LOOT OF FARM LAND AND FOREST LAND IN INDIA—July 19, 2011 on www.kksingh1.blogspot.com have thrown light on the subject and the governments' in apathetic and callous posture over the burning issues.

The implication of the new land acquisition ACT will be known in time to come. But some of directives of the courts, particularly the Supreme Court and subsequent fall out in Niyamgiri forest areas in Odisha in the wake of forcible acquisition of Adivasis' land and given to a British mining company Vedanta as well as the report of the UNITED NATIONS ORGANISATION (UNO)'s independent human right experts, terming the forced eviction of the forested lands in Odisha and handing over to the South Korean steel giant—POSCO amid concerns that construction will displace large number people in the forested areas and disrupt the livelihoods of thousands more have created piquant situation. The Supreme Court, in a directive to Odisha government, had asked an independent panel, formed by the court itself, to visit major parts of Niyamgiri and call meetings of respective panchayat samitis— wheather they consented to give lands to Vedanta for mines and minerals production. Majority of panchayat samitis with overwhelming majority rejected the views of Odisha government and voted that they are not in favour of giving their lands to the Vedanta. Reports had been submitted to the Supreme Court recently and the SC will pass appropriate order on the issue soon.

POSCO HALTED:—Similarly, special rapporteurs of the UNO intervened in land acquisition to the Posco' $ 12 bn project in Odisha after allegation of forced evictions. UN experts have called for an immediate halt of the Posco steel project. Approval for the project— biggest single foreign investment in India—was permitted in 2011 after a six-year struggle between steel giant and environmental campaigners. However, Construction remained paralyzed and delayed because of a number of regulatory hurdles and public protests at plans to clear more than 600 hectares of mostly forested lands. Eight UN special rapporteurs have weighed in calling for the project to be suspended. The have said, "the construction of massive steel plant and port in Odisha, India by South Korean steel giant—Posco must not proceed as planned without ensuring adequate safeguards and guaranteeing that the rights of thousands of people are respected." Although India has primary duty to protect the rights of those whose homes and livelihoods are threatened by the project, the experts further said, "Posco has also responsibility to respect human rights and the Republic of Korea, where Posco is based, should also take measures to ensure that businesses based in its territory do not adversely impact human rights when operating abroad."

The UN experts intervened after allegations of human rights abuse. "Forced evictions constitute gross violation of human rights," said the UN special rapporteur on adequate housing, Raquel Rolnik, "and may only be carried out in exceptional circumstances and in manner consistent with human rights law, including after genuine consultation, without leaving people homeless or vulnerable to further human right violations." The UN special rapporteur on the right of food, Olivier De Schutter, warned that forcible removal of people from their; lands could be tantamount to depriving them of their means of subsistence. "People who would be evicted for the Posco project have relied on their lands for generations in order to obtain adequate food and sustain themselves and their families," he said.

Remarkably, in a development in July, the Posco, the world's fourth-largest steelmaker by output, dropped plan to build a $ 5.3 bn mill in the southern state—Karnataka—in India but said it would press ahead with the long-delayed and troubled Odisha project. On the website of, Posco India says it "has been highly sensitive to the humans of the local community" and strongly denies having abused rights. Posco has never infringed upon human right of any individual in the course of project implementation. Its policy has been inclusive and protective", the company said. And added "Posoco has therefore, always urged the government of Odisha to first safeguard the human rights and livelihood of innocent villagers and rejects/deplores any unlawful violence against them." The Plant to be based in the port city of Paradip was conceived in 2005 and is expected to create nearly 50,000 jobs. Posco says the plant has annual production capacity of 12 million tons and will include iron ore mine development over 30 years (total 600 million tons) at mines in the Keojhar and Sundargarh districts of Odisha as well as development of related infrastructures.

But things started moving otherwise! Houses of tribal and their farmings, especially betel vine were razed to the ground by Posco and Vedanta with the help of armed forces, provided by Odisha government. Not only that, the union government had announced in the last week of February 2013, that major infrastructures projects will be exempt from obtaining consent for forest clearance from tribal communities living in the forest, a decision that undermines the importance of the country's Forest Right Act—thus a big blow to the land tribal rights in India. "This is serious breach or trust and a huge step back in ensuring the dignity and survival of traditional forest-dwelling people across the country. Forests are going to be cleared to make way for a particular kind of economic development; it would adversely impact, communities and environments," said Dr Swati Shresth of the Ashoka Trust for Research Ecology and the Environment. the 2006 Forest Right Act "is a landmark piece of legislation recognising the rights forest-dependent communities have over the landscape they have traditionally inhabited. It mandates that forest dwellers cannot be resettled unless their traditional rights have been recognised. It is seen as the single most important piece of legislation protecting and preserving the country's biodiversity and the rights of tribal groups. By no longer gaining the consent of communities, the government stands accused of effectively overturning key provisions of the Act. "All traditional forest-dependent communities can be impacted including those who might have procured rights under FRA and those who are still struggling for its implementation in their areas," said Shresth.

In 2009, the union ministry of forest and environment (MoEF) made the consent of affected forest communities mandatory for all projects that would destroy forest. The move was in response to the attempt by British mining company Vedanta to clear swaths of forest in Odisha state belonging to the Dongria tribe. The government orders of February 1913 last effectively, surprisingly, revokes the 2009 order. The government, however, rejects claims that it is diluting rights in the name of streamlining big business, saying it will continue to enforce the provisions of the Act "where there is significant impact on the lives and livelihoods." The proposed changes will enable land grabbing and the violation of rights of traditional forest dwellers and sends a clear message that rights granted under the FRA are not inalienable but subjects to the whims of the government of the day," said Shresth and added that in a letter to the Prime Minsters office by the coalition of international forest rights movements "we believe that it is against the democratic principles to make centralised decisions about the extent of social impact worth considering while diverting forest over which individuals and/or village community may have inalienable forest rights vested through FRRA. Overriding of such process can lead to the danger of assuming that all rights can be mentioned and negotiated." Sanjay Basu Mullick of the All India Forum of Forest Movements has said, "The only objective is mining access. Mining companies need six road highways and optical fibre installations. Tribal communities do not want this, and do not want their precious forest replaced by these. The only beneficiaries of this amendment are the mining companies. This is about GDP and not about the rights of India's tribal communities.

LAND LOOT:—Story of land grabbing or loot is not new in India. Looters of land are more government, which confiscates lands of small holding-owners, as well as big land-holders like landlords! Throughout the country, lakhs of acres of land had been acquired by the government in the name of development. Also the governments are yet to implement land reform measures. Lakhs of acres of land of government lands, which are not traceable right now, are to be distributed to the landless for farming or for homes for homeless. But the net result remained big zero. Acquired lands by governments were diverted for some other purposes, violating the laws. Acquired lands changed many hands and the respective governments remained beneficiaries. It was provision in the Land and other related Acts that if the lands are not utilised for the purpose, it were acquired—in that case land must be returned to farmers. But respective governments of state and central never followed the provisions. The governments sold or resold lands to rich people after taking heavy premium money.

IN BIHAR:—For examples—Bihar has plenty of surplus lands on papers to be distributed or distributed to landless but the facts are otherwise or diverse. All these lands have been grabbed by vested and rich class people inconveniences with the Bihar government in successive years. The Nitish Kumar government has surpassed all governments in making land scams a big business. Hundreds of acres of land of industrial estates in different districts have been sold in the last few years. In the process, big politicians, cine stars, businessmen, industrialists, media houses etc were given lands of industrial estates on through away price by Nitish Kumar government, violating laws, rules and set principles. In turn, many of the beneficiaries including film producer Prakash ha, after constructing shopping complex, malls, multi-storey ed apartments etc had earned crores of rupees and left the venues, thanks to the laxity of the Nitish government. Various cases on these issues are pending in the Patna High Court and the Supreme Court. Both "Khash and AAM lands" were earmarked by the government but in both the cases, lands have been leased out to influential persons in the last several years on cheap "sallami" and at many places these types of lands had been encroached and unauthorisedly by landed classes and in many cases these lands are missing from the Bihar government records.

REFERENCES:—WEBSITES of The POSCO, The UNO, The India Government, The South Korea govt, The Guardian, The Odisha govt, The Supreme Court etc

GLOBAL WARMING CAUSING CONCERN BECAUSE OF CLIMATE CHANGE: ADVERSE AFFECT ON CHILDREN, BIRDS, REPTILES MAMMALS: FOOD SHORTAGE IMMINENT!

Wednesday, 2 October 2013

A recent report of the United Nation's Inter-governmental Panel on Climate Change (IPCC) on global warming has created stir in the minds of people throughout the GLOBE! Much controversy has been generated throughout the world, subsequent to the release of the report of the IPCC recently The IPCC report underscores that there are still significant uncertainties around climate science, including the role of understudied oceans, which have been absorbing much of the excess heat generated by global warming; the effect of warming on the animals and plants that live on this planet, including us; and perhaps most importantly, the 'actual level of warming we will experience as emissions continue to pile up in the atmosphere". It will be not out of mention here that the report says that scientists are certain that in term of percentage 95 pc "humans are the dominant cause" of global warming since the 1950s. There is physical evidence behind climate change as on the ground, in the air, in the oceans, "global warming is unequivocal" Increase and pause in the warming over the past 15 years is too short to reflect long-trend trends. The continued emissions of greenhouse gases will cause further warming and changes in all aspects of the climate system. Projected temperature increases under two scenarios and average rise in surface temperature by 2081-2100: Lowest Scenario—RCP 2.6 and highest scenario—RCP—8.5. Projection is based on assumption about how much green house gases might be released.

After a week of intense negotiations in the Swedish capital on physical science of global warming, the IPCC released 36-page document, which is considered the most comprehensive statement on our understanding of the mechanics of a warming planet. It all started badly since the 1950s, and many of us observing changes in the climate system, which are "unprecedented over decades to millennia". Each of the last three decades has been successively warmer at the Earth's surface and warmer than any period since 1850 and probably warmer than any time in the past 1400 years. My recent essays—PLUNDERING OF NATURE BOUND TO HAVE ADVERSE EFFECT IN THE GLOBE:—SEPTEMBER 20, 2013; THREAT TO LIFE ON THE EARTH VIS-A-VIS THE EARTH ITSELF THREATENED—JULY 06, 2013; UTTARAKHAND TRAGEDY DUE TO NATURE'S FURY-ULTIMATELY MAN-MADE TRAGEDY—JULY 03, 2013; DANGEROUS SIGNAL FOR NEPAL BECAUSE OF CLIMATE CHANGE IN HIMALAYAS: INDIA IS ALSO THREATENED and much more on www.kksingh1.blogspot.com amply substantiated the danger signal in respect of global warming and its repercussions on the EARTH!

PLANET UNDER THREAT:—While releasing the report UN'S IPCC, a co-chair, Prof Thomas Stocker, said that climate change "challenges the two primary resources of humans and ecosystems, land and water, In short, it threatens our planet, our only home" Another co-chair of the IPCC working group one, who produced the report, Qin Dahe said, "our assessment of science finds that the atmosphere and ocean have warmed, the amount of snow and ice has diminished, the global mean sea level risen and that concentrations of greenhouse gases have increased." Rajendra Pachauri was of the opinion confidently the report would convince the public on the global climate change. The IPCC, which is offspring of two UN bodies—the World Meteorological Organisation and the United Nations Environment Programme, has so far issued four strong-worded reports about the assessment of the climate condition on the Earth. These are commissioned by the governments of 195 countries of the world. The reports are critical in informing the climate policies adopted by these governments. The IPCC itself a small organisation, being run from Geneva, with only 12 full-time staff and all the scientists, who are involved with IPCC for doing scientific study on climate change, do so on voluntary basis.

It is almost man-made climate change. The scientific case for taking action to reduce greenhouse gas emissions and prepare for the effects of climate change remains clear, despite nagging doubts about the fact that global temperatures have risen more slowly in recent years despite continued increase in carbon emissions. More over the report has brought important facts to the fore by pointing out that exactly what and how much action should be taken and how politicians should balance tomorrow's threat of climate change against any number of present day challenges is some thing that would not be answered by another thick sheaf of scientific reports. Notably, IPCC report has formally endorsed a "carbon budget"—a red line for the amount of carbon dioxide created chiefly by burning fossils fuels and through deforestation, that can be emitted without warming increasing beyond an internationally agreed target of 3.6 F (2C). Think of it as a speed limit for the global economy—emit more than one trillion tons of carbon and we will likely to be in red. That should be worrying, given the fact that the are three trillion tons of carbon left on the ground as Bryan Walsh writes in the Time and adds, "energy companies are developing new technologies like hydrofracking and directional drilling, that are enabling them to find fossil fuels that were long considered uneconomical" An Oxford University researcher and one of the authors of the IPCC report Myles Allen. had spoken to New York Times, saying that limiting the warming to the agreed upon target is "technically doable, but at the moment we are not going in the right direction". Dr Allen said in an interview, "I do not think we will do it unless we bite the bullet and start talking about what we are going to do with extra carbon that we cannot affcord to dump into atmosphere."

CARBON EMISSION:—Notably, The U N Framework Convention on Climate Change (UNFCCC) is doing some think remarkable to contain extra carbon. Optimistically, many governments are doing more about their carbon emissions: Europe has long been a leader and in the US the Environmental Protection Agency just announced a new draft regulation that would make it all but impossible to build new coal plants without expensive carbon-capture technology. China, the world's biggest carbon emitter, is beginning to realise that it cannot simply keep burning carbon—heavy coal for ever—about more because of the local pollution it causes then out of fears of climate change. But truth is different, the globe countries are no where close to a path that would have the world essentially stop emitting carbon by about mid-century. No body, in realty, actually knows what exactly will happen if global atmospheric concentrations of carbon dioxide exceed 450 parts per million. Higher emissions mean higher temperatures and greater climate risk. Lower emissions means less. But one thing that appears to be virtual certainty is that emissions, which are rising faster than ever, are likely to go well past 450. The United Nations still hews to the conceit that we must stabilise global emissions below 450 ppm by 2050. But the reality is that world is on track to blow thresh-hold decade earlier. The IPCC report addresses the warming "hiatus" as it has been called, raising a number of possible explanations—the ocean absorbing the warmth, changes in the solar cycle, volcanic eruptions that causes cooling—without pointing the finger at a single one. Although scientists keep working on those question and others, the ball is in the politicians' court now—as it has been for years. Which means, really, that it is up to us!

But the so called pause in the increase in temperatures in the period since 1998 has been downplayed in the report. Scientists have described that the period began with a very hot EI Nino year." Trends based on short records are very sensitive to the beginning and end dates do not in general reflect long-term climate trends," the report says. Thomas Stoker, added, I am afraid there is not a lot of public literature that allows us to delve deeper at the required depth of this emerging scientific question—for example, there are sufficient observations of the uptake of heat, particularly into deep ocean, that would be one of the possible mechanisms to explain this warming hiatus."

CLIMATE SENSITIVITY:—The report, however, does alter a key figure from 2007 study. The temperature range given for doubling of CO2 in the atmosphere, called equilibrium climate sensitivity, was 2.0C to 4.5C in that report. In the latest document, the range has been changed to 1.5C to 4.5C. The scientists say this reflects improved understanding, better temperature records and new estimates for the factors driving up temperatures. In the summary of policy makers, the scientists say that sea level rise will proceed at a faster rate than "we have experienced over the past 40 years". Waters are expected to rise, the document says, by between 26cm (at a low end) and 82cm (at the high end, depending on greenhouse emissions path this century. Scientists further say ocean warming dominates the increase in energy stored in the climate system, accounting for 90 percent of energy accumulated between 1971 and 2010. For the future, the report states that warming is projected to continue under all scenarios. Model solutions indicate that global surface temperature change by the end of the 21st century is likely to exceed 1.5 degree Celsius, relative to 1980. Prof Sir Brian Hoskins, from Imperial College London told BBC news:" we are performing very dangerous experiments with our planet and I do not want my grand children to suffer the consequences of that experiment."

Twenty-five years of efforts to cap and reduce global emission have utterly failed. Two decades of heavy subsidies for renewable energy have not had any measurable success moving the needle on emissions or clean energy—thus we will be living on a hotter planet. How much hotter depends on what we do now! The only countries in the world that have moved to zero-carbon energy at the rapid pace that would be required to keep emissions close to 450ppm are FRANCE AND SWEDEN. To some extent USA and UK in 1990s have also achieved significant emissions reduction by switching from coal to gas. In deed since 1950, natural gas and nuclear re vented 36 times more carbon emissions than wind, solar and geothermal combined. Nuclear avoided the creation of 28 billion tons of carbon dioxide, natural gas 26 billion and geothermal, wind and solar just 1.5 billion. Surprisingly many of the scientists, conservative writers on energy and the environment, including Steve Hayward, formerly of American Enterprise Institute and Robert Bryce of Manhattan Institute are advocating nuclear energy even today despite many dangerous signals from the nuclear energy, mainly in Japan and other places of the world. Need of the hour for great powers like USA and China must step up efforts to develop safe natural gas and next generation nuclear technologies.

WORSE CONSEQUENCES ON CHILDREN:—Under such situation of alarming rise in global temperature as well as dangerous implication on environment, children of the world will bear the immediate consequences in the impact of climate change. Because of their increased risk of heath problems, malnutrition and migration, according to a new study. Food prices are likely to soar as a result of warming, undoing the progress made in combating world hunger. Climate change, almost caused by human actions and that it will lead to a global temperature rise likely to top 2C with related effects including the shrinking of the Arctic ice cap and glaciers, a rise in sea level by nearly one meter by the end of this century and more extreme rainfall in the parts of the globe. UNICEF argues children are most vulnerable to the effects of global warming. UNICEF UK executive director David Bull says in anguish, "we are hurtling towards a future where gains being made for the world's children are threatened and their health, well being, livelihood and survival are compromised . . . . despite being the least responsible for the causes . . . we need to listen to them." UNICEF points out children born last year will come of age in 2030 by which time the effect of climate change in the form of an increase in droughts, floods and storms are likely to be more in evidence in the ten most vulnerable countries including THE INDIA, THE BANGLADESH, THE PHILLIP INES where there are 620 million children under 18. UNICEF estimates that 25 million more children will suffer malnourishment because of climate change, with a further 100 million suffering food insecurity where they and their families are on verge of running out. Children among the 150-200 million people estimated to have fled their homes because of climate change will suffer more than adults because of their relative's lack of resources and higher vulnerability to disease. In heat waves likely to grow more intense and frequent under climate change, babies and small children are more likely to die and suffer heatstroke because they find it difficult to regulate their body heat.

ABNORMAL RISE IN FOOD PRICES:—Like wise a report of Oxfam says that global warming would cause rapid rise in food price, causing severe consequences in poor countries. Disputing the IPCC report, Oxfam listed recent examples of extreme weather condition that have caused food shortage and increased prices, quoting scientific estimates that these are likely to increase in number of warming countries. "Today one person in eight goes to bed hungry. Analysis suggests that the number of people at risk of hunger is projected to increase by 10-20 percent by 2050 as a result of climate change," the Oxfam study found. Tim Gore of Oxfam said, "We want a world in which everyone enjoys the right to affordable and nutritious food and we cannot allow climate change to throw us off course. Leaders listening to the latest findings from climate scientists this week must remember that a hot world is a hungry world. They must take urgent action to slash emissions and direct more resources to building a sustainable food system."

SPECIES LIKE BIRDS, REPTILES, MAMMALS THREATENED:—Australia is expected to experience a 6C average temperature rise on its hottest days, resulting into deaths of reptiles, birds and mammal species as well as the renowned wetlands of Kakadu by the end of the century, the IPCC report says. IPCC figures show Australia will experience an average overall increase of 2C by 2065, with the figure slightly lower at the coast. Beyond that temperature is expected to rise another 3C-$c by 2100. The number of days that do not fall below 20c is projected to rise to 100 a year, with most of the warmer days in the north and on the east coast. Rainfall patterns are set to change, with annual precipitation, humidity and cloud cover predicted to decrease over most of the Australia but for north of Australia and many agriculture areas, rainfall is predicted to get heavier. Soil moisture will decrease; mostly in the south of the country Australia will witness more and more deaths because of heatwaves. A 2C-4C rise in average temperatures will wipe out 21 to 36 percent of Australia's butterflies while the loss of nearly half of appropriate habitat of Queensland will spell doom for 7to 14 percent reptiles, 8 to 18 percent of frogs, one in ten birds and 10 to 15 percent of mammals.

EMERGENCE OF NARENDRA MODI FOR PRIME MINISTERSHIP IS THREAT TO INDIA'S SECULAR FABRIC?

Tuesday, 24 September 2013

Before I start writing on this ticklish issue, I think it proper to just refer the PREAMBLE OF THE CONSTITUTION, which says, "We, The People of India, having solemnly resolved to constitute India into a "Sovereign Socialist Secular Democratic Republic and to secure to all its citizens: Justice.

Is the emergence of the Hindu Right Leader and the Chief Minister of Gujarat Narendra Damodar Das Bhai as prime ministerial candidate of the Bhartiya Janata Party (BJP), a threat to the secular fabric of India? Much debate and discussions are taking place nationally and internationally over the issue. I am just putting the facts straight about the way; Narendra Modi is being projected as prime ministerial candidate of India, just seven months away of the Lok Sabha elections in 2014 by the depleted National Democratic Alliance (NDA), led by BJP as well as Modi's aggressive and militant postures in his speeches and interviews on the eve of elections. Narendra Modi, a controversial figure, represents an uncompromising stand of the BJP's Hindu Nationalist ideology.

To begin with only because of such militant approach of Modi, various coalition partners, particularly JD(U)), led by Bihar's Chief Minister Nitish Kumar has withdrawn as coalition partners of the NDA. Secondly, Modi, who is described as "HINDU HRIDYA SMARAT", is said to be one of the most divisive politician in India's history. He is an unapologetic Hindu chauvinist, who has been accused of mass murder of Muslims in 2002 communal riot in Gujarat during his chief minister ship of the state. Modi is known for dividing the society on communal and religious lines. Thirdly, with his projection as prime ministerial nominee

by the BJP and its father organisation—Rashtriya Swamsevak Sangh
(RSS), the entire country has been surcharged with communal tension.
Recent Hindu-Muslim riots, killing over 48 persons and injuring score
of persons as well as 42,000 people were displaced as their villages were
raided by rioters is biggest examples of communal divide with the arrival
of Amit Sah in Uttar Pradesh as BJP general Secretary In charge of UP,
the close protege of Modi and accused in several criminal cases, registered
by the CBI against him In Gujarat. And also Babri Masjid demolition
like misdeeds, committed by the BJP supporters led by senior BJP leader
Lal Krishna Advani in 1980, the Hindu Right Organisations including
Vishwa Hindu Parishad, trying to make "chaurasi Kosi parikarma" in
and around Ayodhaya to press for construction of "Ram Temple" on
the disputed sites of masjid. Such move definitely created surcharged
atmosphere in the entire Uttar Pradesh. Not only that, over a dozen states
of central and western India have come under the grip of communal
tension. And the union home minister has issued alert to all states of
the Indian union about the possibility of communal clashes in their
respective zones.

There are many more factors about Modi's decisive politics Although
Modi, who initiated anti-Muslim tirade in Gujarat initially, has tried to
replace them with message of development based on a record in Gujarat
that even worse critics acknowledge is impressive! But critics do not lag
behind that Modi and his party has been benefited from past violence
between Hindus and Muslims in Gujarat. It must be mentioned here
that India is vast and populous country in the globe and during election
campaign in different parts of the country, the campaigns result into
violent because of hate speeches by certain fundamentalist leaders. Under
the circumstances, the projection of Narendra Modi, who is considered
fiery Hiundutava orator mix with anti-Muslim slurs, the forthcoming
Lok Sabha election may be one of the deadliest elections in the decades!

According to the report; Hindus have 83 percent voters while
Muslims have 13 percent and remaining four percents are other minority
communities. Home ministry report has said that there had been already
451 cases of sectarian violence this year, surpassing last year's total of
410. The union home ministry has warned that violence was likely to
intensify as election approaches. During his speeches in the meetings
in different parts of the country, Modi appears to be darling of youths,
making the situation more hot up and surcharged. Modi never apologised
for the 2002 riots, killing over two thousands Muslims in Gujarat, now

he has shifted his focus recently to development and in the process, Modi ha become chums of business classes including corporates and multi-nationals. A recent report in the New York Times has quoted Talveen Singh, an author and commentator, in which she has made futile attempt to compare Modi with the first Prime minister of India Pundit Jawahar Lal Nehru and has said, "The reason why Modi needs a chance to lead is that he is the first politician since Nehru, who had articulated a clear economic vision".

Selecting of Narendra Modi as prime ministerial nominee, the BJP has also thought to implement its old Hindutva agenda vigorously as Modi represents uncompromising Hindu nationalist. But there are factors, which are troubling the BJP also like deepening of sectarian divisions. India is a home of world's second largest Muslim population Modi, who has questionable character during 2002 Gujarat riots, is accused of doing nothing while Gujarat burned and at worst of having helped to orchestrate the violence. Modi is also known for his arrogance, authoritarian and dictatorial style. In a recent interview to Reuter, Modi did say "I am Hindu nationalist" not Indian nationalist. Such version clearly reflects that Modi has more love for Hindu India than as a nationalist of secular India, as enunciated. Can it be not be described a slur on the Preamble of the Indian Constitution by Modi? Not only that when asked about the riots in Gujarat resulting into killings of hundreds of Muslims, Modi replied in strange connotation, apparently showing his deep-rooted aversion with Muslims. Modi told the interviewer of Reuter that his feelings of pain for the tragedy were similar to how he would feel if a puppy had been run over by a car in which he was merely a passenger. Shockingly in another interview to the Wall Street Journal last year Modi had strange justification over prevalent malnutrition in Gujarat. Modi appeared out of his depth when he diagnosed his state's high malnutrition rates as being a result of the vegetarian diet and the state middle class being" beauty conscious than health conscious".

Narendra Modi cannot be Atal Behari Vajpayee, whose years as prime minister from 1998 to 2004 were largely characterised by a consensual approach to governing. An opinion piece in the New York Times, written by Krishan Pratap Singh has written, "Vajpayee was like Ronald Regan: a true believer in the conservative cause, who packaged his ideological stridency into a narrative that depicted the BJP as a responsible party of governance, palatable to its core voters while allaying the fears of disparate coalition allies. But once Vajpayee left the scene, The BJP steadily drifted toward the far right. The promise of a Modi victory could prove to be mirage. Elections are still decided in rural India, where he is yet to give fully tested. Only L K Advani, the octogenarian—founder of the BJP and the Modi's mentor-turned rival, stands in his path ti leading the party. But Advani's failure as prime minister candidate in the 2009 elections, and the groundswells of rank-and-file support for Modi, may undermine his quest. YEt even if Modi is victorious, he would most likely lead an unwieldy coalition government involving decision making by consultation and consensus, a balancing act that is not his strong suit. With Indians begging for good governance, the BJP must decide whether to choose Modi's ideological path or to recalibrate to Vajpayee-like inclusiveness. On that question hinges the outcome of elections—and the future of India but Modi's message may well prove difficult to resist: From snake charmers, we are now a nation of mouse charmers. Our youngsters are shaping the world with the click of a mouse."

The son of a tea stall owner, Narendra Modi, 62, has spent most of his life in politics, joining the right-wing Hindu-nationalist Sangh Parivar organisation early on rising through its ranks by displaying impressive organising ablities. He moved to BJP in 1987 and was appointed chief minister of Gujsrat as a midterm replcement in 2001 without ever having fought an election. Like Gandhi-Nehru Gandhi family, Narendra Modi has no such tags. Apart from that, Modi had never been found in the company of his family members including his mother and deserted wife and brothers like Nehru-Gandhi family members, who are seen hobnobbing with each other in politics and other affairs in life. Modi is different metal and is self-made successful politician so far. Of course he brought drastic change in the development pattern in Gujarat. His focus on pro-investment policies, cutting red tape, extensive infrastructure development, while using his personal charm to woo foreign and domestic investments, has been marked contrast to most other state governments.

Today Narendra Modi has connected himself with the people of India, particularly youths and middle classes especially in towns and cities. Where ever one goes, he finds one name on every body's lip that is Narendra Modi! Huge crowds turn up to listen his speeches. Modi has succeeded in capturing cyber spaces and social media networks are full with Modi's supporters. Like V P Singh, who was once described "Raja nahi fakir hai; desh kaa taqdir d hai." while dethroning the then Prime Minister Rajiv Gandhi from power, Modi is also gravitating during election like him (V P Singh). But V P Singh, being a Jan Morcha chief that time, had stamina to unite all opposition to support the then Janata party, keeping their distinct identity. But following the path of V P Singh is different. VP had fought election on corruption plank that time. But Modi, although identifying with VP in removing the present UPA government on corruption plank like him (V P Singh), but Modi lacks acumen in uniting anti-congress parties on one front. Modi had of his own started claiming that BJP will win 272 plus seats in the forthcoming Lok Sabha elections. Modi must take one thing in his mind that without identifying anti-congress parties, will not be possible to garner such huge seats. Different pats of India have different characteristics. Southern and Eastern parts of the country invariably are not very enthusiastic with Modi or with BJP like earlier Lok Sabha poll. Narendra Modi's magic may move in central, northers and western India. The central and northern India, known as "cow belt" may have ground swelling support for Modi and BJP but there are many road blocks in these areas also like Bihar and Uttar Pradesh where regional straps like Nitish Kumar, Laloo Prasad Yadav, Ram Bilas Paswan (Bihar) and Mulayam Singh of Uttar Pradesh have tremendous support bases.

Apart from that Muslims, who are fearful of Narendra Modi and BJP, are likely to vote in the next election in tactical manner throughout the country. Muslims are expected to vote throughout the country this time on the perception that party' candidates, most suitable to defeat Narendra Modiu's candidates will get entire support of Muslims in the next elections as situation prevails today! When one compares victory of NDA led by BJP in previous elections on the basis of strong alliance partners, the victory in the forthcoming election of Lok Sabha by Modi all alone will be a difficult task. Being desperate over such ticklish issues, Taking into account such political scenario, the desperate Narendra Modi, who was initially wanted to contest elections of all alone, and his BJP have started approaching Chandra Babu's TDP as well as Babulal Marandi's Jharkhand Vikas Party in Jharkhand and expelled BJP leader Yedurappa in Karnataka to bring them in NDA alliance-fold. The BJP leadership has also recently appealed to former leaders of the party, who have resigned or expelled to rejoin the BJP. Making the situation clear the gradual growing of the BJP in election and forming union governments under the leadership of Vajpayee, Veteran journalist Vidya Subrahmaniam, in her opinion piece in the Hindu, under headline "The BJP's ak;la chalo challenge" has written, "In 2013, the RSS is not just back, it has decreed and ensured that Modi's elevation takes place. This, itself is hard to reconcile with the image that is being crafted for Modi. His national projection is of modern and aspirational leader but he seems ti exist at the pleasure of a mentor seen as a polar opposite to these ideas. The man, who changed the things around for the BJP was none other than L K advani through his Ayodhya's yatra and demolition of Babri Masjid till 1996 and subsequent Lok Sabha elections and had taken back seat to keep alliance partners intact and paved way for middle-roader Vajpayee." and BJP succeeded in keeping NDA intact. Today NDA led by BJP is torn, having only two allies—the Shiv Sena and Akali Dal, both in ideological sync with the party the calculation obviously is that Modi's early projection will trigger an infectious voting frenzy, enabling him to single-handedly pull off a BJP victory. If this happens Narendra Miodi will be the first since V P singh to set off a personality-induced wave. But for all the adulation he commanded, Singh was nothing without the political support he got—his own Janata Dal was formed by merging the Jan Morcha with the Janata party and two factions of the Lok Dal—formed National Front even supported by the BJP and left parties. So Singh's illusory single handed victory was a product in fact of support at every stage from a conglomerate of non-Congress parties . . . The truth is that there is no unified national vote today and for all the blusters of the RSS, the BJP will need allies and will seek allies . . . . seven months before the big fight, and notwithstanding the UPA's down-in-the-pit status, the political congregation is around the Congress alliance rather than the BJP alliance. If Modi's manages to win the election by him or even by winning over new allies, he will have beaten the odds and rewritten India's political history."

What ever the outcome of the next Lok Sabha elections, the scenario in the country is presently vitiated by communal frenzies being encouraged by the Hindu Right organisations, led by Narendra Damodar Das Bhai to become prime minister of India by any means?

PLUNDERING OF NATURE BOUND TO HAVE ADVERSE EFFECT IN THE GLOBE!

Friday, 20 September 2013

AMID THE THREAT to the fate of the Planet hangs in balance because of recurring changes in 'climate and weather' and also global warming as well as the over population on the earth in over hundreds of years, based on the several researches by the scientists throughout the world, a new set of expert opinion has emerged, ruling out misunderstanding of the ecology of human system and any threat to the, Planet! In a 'opinion essay', recently published in the New York Times, its author Erle C Ellis, an associate professor of Geography and Environmental Systems at the University of Maryland, Baltimore County and a visiting associate professor at Harvard's Graduate School of Design, has written that many scientists believe that by transforming the earth's natural landscapes, "we are undermining the very life support system that sustain us." Like Bacteria in a petri dish, "our exploding numbers are reaching the limits of a finite Planet with dire consequences". Disasters looms as human exceed the earth's carrying capacity clearly, this could not be sustainable. "This is non-sense. Even today, I hear some of my scientist colleagues repeat these and similar claims—often unchallenged. And once, I too believed them. Yet these claims demonstrate a profound misunderstanding of ecology of human systems. The conditions that sustain huminity are not natural and never had been. Since prehistory, human population have used technologies and engineered eco-systems to sustain populations well beyond the capabilities of unaltered "natural" ecosystems." Although I am not so qualified on such arguements, I have written an essay "Threat to Life on the Earth vis-a-vis the Earth is Itself Threatened" on July 06, deliberating the threat aspects, based on well researched subjects on the topics on www.kksingh1.blogspot.com

On the other hand, Book Review from the London Review of Books, by Thomas Jones, under the headline, "How can we live with it?" has different opinion on the topic! Jones has quoted a boy, telling his family members that "global warming is a load of codswallop", trying to explain the difference between climate and weather. "Global warming, he insisted, is load of codswallop" A "Nature Geoscience, published a paper showing summer melting on the Antarctic Peninsula at a level unprecedented over the past thousand years. The codswallop brigade say that even if the climate is changing, it is not our fault. 'We human beings, Boring Johnson wrote, in the Telegraph in January, 'have become so blind with conceit and self-love that we genuinely believe that fate of the planet is in our hands'. On the one hand, then, the modest mayor of London. On the other, a former head of the US National Oceanic and Atmospheric Administration (as paraphrased by Brian Stone): Only Newton's laws of motion may enjoy a wider scientific consensus than a human-enhanced greenhouse effect' effect. There is no consensus, however, either scientific or political, about the best ways to respond to the problem; in part because so many possible avenues of research are being explored, and it is still too early to say which, if any, have a reasonable chance of leading us out of the woods (or rather the desert or the flood plains).'

According to Jones; the green house concept, was first visualized by Joseph Fourier in 1814 and was proved experimentally by John Tyndall in 1859. In the 19th century it could be seebn as unambiguously a good thing: if carbon-dioxide and other trace gases did not trap heat in the atmosphere, the earth would not be warm enough to support life as we know it. But there is now far more carbon dioxide in the atmosphere than there has been at any point in the last 800,000 years (we know thus because researchers have analysed air bubbles trapped in the ice in Green;land and Antartica; the deeper you go, the older the bubbles). The concentration has increased from nearly 320 parts per million (high but not unprecedented) in 1960 to more than 390 ppm today, 30 percent higher than any previous peak, largely as a result of human activityNot even the most fervent climate change denier can argue with the fact that burning carbon dioxide levels were 280 ppm. Since 1850, more than 360 billion tonnes of fossil fuels have gone up in smoke. Average global temperatures have risen accordingly, for the last quarter century pretty much in line with the predictions made by the Inter-governmental Panel on Climate Change in its first assessment report in 1990. After every year since 1988, when the IPCC was established, has been the hottest ever recorded. The most opitimistic projections, which governments are nominally committed to (that is to say, the signatories of the Copenhaagen Accord in 2009 greed it would be nice) is that average global temperature will rise no more than 2oC by the end of the century. Sea level has six cm since 1990. The IPCC's fourth assessment report—2007—projected that it would rise between 18 and 59cc by 2100.

More over, the aim of the United Nations Frame work Convention on Climate Change, negotiated at the the Earth Summit In Rio de Janeiro in 1992, had decided to stabilize greenhouse gas concentration in the atmosphere at a level that would prevent dangerous anthropogenic interference with the climate system. Even after the elapse of 20, nothing tangible has come out. And the emission of carbondioxide in huge scale is going on, endangering the man-kind. Of the world;s eight biggest national emitters of carbondioxide, which between them account for more than 66 percent of global emissions, only Germany (2.4 pc) has agreed to legally binding reduction in the second commitment period (2013-20), Canada (1.7 pc) has withdrawn from the [rotocol; the United States (16 pc) never ratified it; China (29pc), India 5.9pc); Russia (5.4 percent), Japan (3.7pc) and South Korea (1.8pc) are still signatories but do not have binding target. China, which is generating energy through coal firepower stations and burn much of the black stuff as the rest of the world put together, is doing such things to manufacture goods for export to the west. Thus China is pumping as much carbon dioxide into atmosphere as it was 30 yeers ago. There is thinking that if China stops burning coal, everything will be OK. China, however, is trying to switch into renewable energy (hydroelectric, solar, wind, geothermal) as well as setting up an emission trading scheme like the one the EU had introduced in 2005.

All these haphazard emissoon of carbondioxide are making the life miserably of people throughout the globe and the time is not so far off when the entire globe will be perished under toxic exercises; researchers have predicted. Strange climate change and atmosphere have developed. Devastating heatwave that swept Europe ten years ago when temperature of 100oF was recorded for the first time ever in UK, are expected throughout the globe and similarly cold-like situation will prevail in the globe. In the EU alone over 70000 citizens of 12 countries died from heat wave in the summer of 2003. Similar heat wave had been recorded in different countries of the globe and over two lakh people die every year in different countries of the world. LBR suggests that the outlook may not be so bad for American and British cities. But the news that there are ways for the global north and west to adapt and to tolerate global warming is hardly reassuring for, say, the 12 million residents of Dhaka, which face a much greater risk of flofding and has far less money to spend on defences. A paper published in Nastural Hazards last year comparing the vulnerablity of flodding nine cities found-unsurprisingly, but is is useful to have quantified—that Shanghai, Dhaka and Calcutta, now Kolkata were far more vulnerable than Rotterdam, Marseille and Osaka. The director of the Research Institute of Global Climate and Ecology at the Russian Academy of Science has said that "it would be cheaper to resettle Bangaladeshis threatened by sea-level rise than to adhere to the kyoto protocol—and cheaper still to do neither. A recent report of UNICEF has also given warning signal about the impact of vulnerable climate change effect on children of the globe. Despite discussions in the Kyoto conclave on global changes and warming etc and subsequent commitments, global emissions are enormously higher than they were in 1990 and the climate change policy had achieved nothing.

While the entire globe is endangered with such alarming situation, Ellis is optimistic and says that earth would bear the burden of all these evil things in natural manner. He says, in his opinon piece in the New York Times, "The evidence from archaeology is clear. Our predecessors in the genus Homo used social hunting strategies and tools of stone and fire ti extract more sustenance from landscapes than would otherwise be possible. And of course, Homo sapines went much further, learning poor generations, once their preferred big games became rare or extinct, to make use of a far broader spectrum of species. They did this by extracting more nutrients from these species by cooking and grinding them by propgating the most useful species and by burning woodlands to enhance hunting and forging success. Even before the last ice age had ended, thousands years before agriculture, hunter-gatherer societies were well established across earth and depended increasingly on sophisticated technological strategies to sustain growing populations in landscapes long ago transformed by their ancestors. THe planet's carrying capacity for pre-historic human hunter-gatherers was probably no more that 100 million, but without their Paleolithic technologies and ways of life, the number would be far less—perhaps a few tens of millions. The rise of agriculture enabled even greater population growth requiring even more intensive land-use practices to gain more sustenance from the same old land. At their preak, those agriculture systems might have sustained as many as three billion people in poverty on near vegetarian diets."

Ellis, however, admits, and says, "There are no environmental reasons for people to go hungry now or in future. There is no need to use any more land to sustain huminity—increasing land productivity using existing technologies can boost global supplies and even leave more land for nature—a goal that is both more popular and more possible than ever"

Thus, I feel strongly, that while the nature with the man-kind in sustaining all the menaces, the problem created by ambitious countries to play cruel jokes with nature, is certainly wipe out the globe and its people.

REFERENCES:—New YORK TIMES, London Book Review's Books— namely Buy the Carbon Crunch: How We are Getting climate Change Wrong and How to Fix It, by Dieter Helm, BUY Earth Masters: The Dawn of the Age of Climate Engineering by Clive Hamilton, Buy the City and the Coming Climate:Climate Change in the Places We Live by Brian Stone.

USA, IN PURSUIT OF WORLD HEGEMONY, TRAPPING INDIA!

Sunday, 15 September 2013

THE UNITED STATES OF AMERICA, in its pursuits, of fulfilling the dream of global hegemony, since the days, of President Roosevelt, has an unending story. A recent book—"Strategic Vision::America and the Crisis of Global Power"—, written by Zbigniew Brazezinski, published by Basic Books, has highlighted many interesting points of growing ambitions of the USA. The book is thought provoking. In the process of of its hegemony, America is browbeating other super powers like Russia, China and many of even European countries and is aiming to strengthening its position by "capturing more slots in Asia" through its own "narrow self-interest". And India, which is developing fast in Asia, has become new target of USA to bring it in its fold! In my opinion recent closeness of India government of Manmohan Singh to USA in several aspects is point to be noted! Just I am subscribing below certain portion of the Brazezinski's book to substantiate my apprehension about India, being falling in the trap of USA!

Brazezinski has written in the book about India, "Contemporary India is a complicated mixture of democratic self-governance, massive social injustices, economic dynamism and wide-spread political corruption. As a result, its political emergence as a force in the world affairs has lagged behind China. India was prominent in sharing leadership of the so called non-alingned nations, a collection of neutral but politically wavering states including Cuba and Yugoslavia, all allegedly opposed to the Cold War. Its brief military collision with China in 1962, which ended in India's defeat, was only practically redeemed by its military successes in the two wars with Pakistan in 1965 and 1971. By and large, the prevailing view of India up til relatively recently has been one of a country with strong moralistic opinions about world affairs but without commensurate influence . . ."

The book further adds, ". . . . India's political elite is motivated by an ambitious strategic vision focused on securing greater global influence and a conviction of its regional primacy. A gradual improvement in U.S-Indian relations during the first decade of the twenty-first century has further enhanced India's global stature and gratified its ambitions. However, its simmering conflict with Pakistan, which includes a proxy contest with it for greater influence in Afghanistan, remains a serious diversion from its larger geopolitical aspirations. Therefor—the view held by its foreign policy elite—that India is not only rival to China but also already one of the world's super power lacks sober realism . . . ."

Brzezinski has also sharply commented on the domestic set-up as well as media;s hysterics on China! He writes, "The Indian political system has yet to prove that it can function as the 'world's largest democracy' . . . . That test will take place when its population becomes truly politically awakened and engaged. Given the countries very high-level of public illiteracy as well as the connection between privilege and wealth at the top of political establishment, India's current 'democratic' process is rather reminiscent of the British aristocratic 'democracy', prior to the appearance of trade unions, in the second half of the nineteenth century. The operational viability of the existing system will be truly tested when the heterogeneous public at large becomes both politically conscious and assertive. Ethnic, religious, and linguistic differences could then threaten India's internal cohesion . . . . In that potentially conflicted setting, the stability of Asia will depend in part on how America responds to two overlapping regional triangles centred around . . . ."

The author further writes in the book, "On India's side, the existing tensions and reciprocal national animosities are fuelled by the relatively inhibited hostility towards China expressed in India's uncensored media and in India's strategic discussions. Invariably, China is presented in them as a threat, most often territorial in nature and India's publications frequently make references in China's 1962 occupation by force of disputed borderline territories. China;s efforts to establish an economic and political presence in Myanmar and in Pakistan's Indian Ocean ports are presented to the public as strategic design to encircle India. The Chinese mass media, under official control, are more restrained in their pronouncements but patronise India as a not-so-serious rival, further inflaming negative Indian sentiments . . . .'

Brzezinski further writes in the book," To a considerable extent, such Chinese feelings of aloofness towards India are derived from China's superior societal performance. Its GNP is considerably larger that India's and its population is considerably more literate as well as ethnically and linguistically more homogeneous. In any case, both sides are the strategic captives of their subjective feelings and of their geopolitical context. The Indians envy the Chinese economic and infraststructural transformation. The Chinese are contemptuous of India's relative backwardness (on the social level most dramatically illustrated by asymmetrical level of literacy of their respective populations) and lack of discipline. The Indians fear Chinese-Pakistani collusion, the Chinese feel vulnerable to India's potential capacity to interfere with Chinese access through the Indian Ocean to the Middle East and Africa . . . .

". . . . America's role in this rivalry should be cautious and detached. A prudent U S policy, especially in regard to an alliance with India, should not, however, be interpreted as indifference to India's potential role as an alternative to China's authoritarian political model . . . . The unwise U S decision of 2011 to sell advanced weaponry to India, in contrast to the ongoing embargo on arms sale to China, while also enhancing India's nuclear programmes is already earning the United States the hostility of the Chinese by conveying the impression that America sees China as its enemy even before China itself had decided to be America's enemy."

Apart from Asia, particularly India, USA has similar approaches towards other nations of the world, looking China, Russia and many other many countries Middle East and Arab world, dangerous potentials and not allowing the global hegemony of America! Just I have mentioned the references in the book about India, falling in the grips of imperialist USA and it is upto people of India to decide!

SITUATION ALARMING IN JAMMU AND KASHMIR: MILITANCY GROWING PUTTING INDIAN GOVERNMENT ON TENTERHOOKS

Friday, 13 September 2013

Kashmir remains apple of discord! After a long spell of normalcy on security front in Jammu and Kashmir, militants have again pervaded the Kashmir valley, putting Indian government on tenterhooks. Kashmir, which was split controversially between India and Pakistan after the countries gained their independence from the Great Britain in 1947, are again in the news with violence and terror activities usually on India side. Recently seven towns in the Indian side were under indefinite curfew following sporadic clashes between local Hindus and Muslims. Apart from that Pakistan is accused of sending commandos to kill five of its soldiers stationed on the line of control, the defecto border dividing the two parts of Kashmir. Violence in Kashmir, launched by Pakistani army and its "jehadis", has become again matter of concern for the Indian authorities. Overall level of violence are lower side now in Kashmir than at any time since an insurgency that pitted groups of young Muslim Kashmirs enrolled in Islamists groups and later extremists from Pakistan too, against Indian security forces first flared more than two decades ago. In totality more than 50,000 militants, soldiers, police and civilians had reportedly been killed in the fighting in India's only Muslim-dominated state, Human rights abuses, perpetuated by all sides, had become order of the days At its height in 2001, 4,500 deaths were recorded, according to the Institute for Conflict Management, a Delhi-based think-tank. Lass year only, 117 people were killed.

Now, a new wave of violence has suddenly spurted. Notably matter of main concern is that in this new wave of violence, young and educated separatist militants have surfaced in villages, bordering with "Occupied

Kashmir" by Pakistan. Cluster of traditional homes and mosques amid green fields and woods in a fold of the dry hills in the south of the valley have become centre of activities by these elements. Experts on Kashmir have pointed out that these violent activities by militants are result of backlash after the hanging of Mohammad Afzal Guru, who had been sentenced to death in the Parliament attack case, as well as old scars on the wounds of Kashmiris have started etching again! Capital punishment to Afzal Guru of valley has also been condemned throughout Kashmir as Guru was not present to the site and time of Parliament attack. He was later arrested from Kashmir and made an accused in the case as a conspirator. The judgement giving death sentence to Afzal had drawn national and international criticism on the judicial system of India. Only criminal conspiracy and not being part of the crime cannot draw such harsh punishments, legal experts had commented.

"Fidayeen" (suicide) attacks on security forces at several places, especially in Srinagar, and encounters between militants and security forces have become routine affairs in Jammu and Kashmir! Here, again, according to annual union home ministry report, there was marked decline in the number of terrorist's activities and security forces causalities, compared with previous year. "The year 2011 witnessed a 30 percent decrease in the number of terrorist incidents and 34 percent and 52 percent respectively decrease in civilian and security forces respectively compared with the year 2010." the report said and added., "the level of infiltration from across the borders and the resultant terrorist activities in the valley of Kashmir showed a significant decline. The incident of terrorist violence declined from708 in 2008, 499 in 2009 and 488 in 2010 to 340 in 2011. The number of security forces killed declined from 75 in 2008, 79 in 2009 and 69 in 2010 to 33 in 2011. The number of civilians killed also declined from 91 in 2008, 71 in 2009 and 47 in 2010 to 31 in 2011. The number of terrorists killed declined from 239 in 2009 and 232 in 2010 to 100 in 2011; showing the effects of better domination of the Line of Control a d the resultantly lower infiltration." All these factors have brought changes in ground level, paving the way for the arrival of record number of 1.4 million tourists in 2012.

LIFE IS LIVING HELL:—Than why this spurt in terror activities? Perhaps because of new wave of active participation of well-educated, even professionally qualified, men in the recent terror attacks. This apart scars of old wounds of the atrocity and rape in the remote villages of Kunan and Pashpora in Kupwara district of north Kashmir on the night of February 23, 1991 by Indian security forces have also riminiscinced the people of Kashmir. The incident, in brief, was that soldiers of Indian Army, at around 11 pm raided the village and threatened to kill all villagers while hunting the terrorists. All men were told to come out and soldiers barged into the houses and attacked the women, molesting, raping them. Even today memories of women did not go away. Many of them became hysterectomies. Wounds have healed but scars are very much there. Enquiry after enquiry held. The then district magistrate of Kupwara S M Yasin, had visited the village and recorded the report with remarks that, "the armed forces behaved like violent beasts." The fact-finding team led by the then Chief Justice Mufti Bahauddin Farooqi, interviewed 53 women who had been allegedly raped and tried to determine why a police investigation into the incident had never taken place. Farpooqi had reportedly commented at that time, he had "never seen such a case in which normal investigative procedures were ignored as they were in this one," There were furore over the issue but nothing tangible came out. Life is living hell for them even today!

Another factor, responsible for sudden spurt in the terror activities are continuance of the Armed Forces Special Powers Act (AFSPA). The union government had enacted the Act when the entire Jammu and Kashmir was passing through critical phase of terror activities. The Act gives blatant power to security forces to cover the measures to filter terrorists by acting through their own modus-operandi. The Act is being misutilised by Armed forces and it has become a centre of criticism where ever the Act is implemented, particularly in the eastern states also. The Chief Minister of Jammu and Kashmir has also pleaded for revoking the Act. Security officials in the disputed province exaggerate the threat from extremism to justify wide ranging powers of arrest and detention—and a broad measures of immunity from prosecution for human right abuses—granted earlier in the the conflict. Large number of arrests has been taken place in Kashmir in recent months, creating stir in the state. Kashmiris are scared of arrest and tortures not deaths! Meantime, educated youths are being lured and encouraged by Pakistan based Lashkar-e-Taiba and many other terror organisations including Pakistan government's ISI. Another factor is declining official support for the extremists in Indian Kashmir from Pakistan over the past decade. Another one is growing disparity between the economies of the two neighbours, which have fought three wars over the state. Indian growth has undermined the argument for accession to Pakistan in Kashmir—though much rhetoric support for independence remains—and sapped enthusiasm for any return to a hugely disruptive violent struggle. Nawaz Shariff, who was elected in landslide victory in May, is keeping stony silence over terror activities added and abetted by Pakistan's terror organisations and Pak military wing ISI!

The situation has come to such a pass that Indian and Pakistan troops are indulging in unprovoked firings at each other on wire fencing borders, particularly in Kashmir. Violations of ceasefire have become order of the day by Pakistani army. Border is tense. The insurgency is supported by Pakistan began in Indian-administered Kashmir, seeking independence from Indian rule. Villagers on Indian side of border in Kashmir are compelled to hide in army's abandoned bunkers. Most of these bunkers were destroyed in 2005 earthquake. Echoes of despair fill the bordering villages in Kashmir. An escalating war of words between India and Pakistan over cross border attacks in Kashmir has practically tarnished hopes that the newly elected government in Islamabad will succeed in reviving peace talks between the feuding neighbours. Accusation and claims and counter claims over border dispute in Kashmir are aggravating the situation gradually.

Families of militants or terrorists in Kashmir blame security forces for pushing their wards to terrorism or militancy through constant harassment. Interestingly, a new trend has come to fore about the active participation of well-educated, even professionally qualified, men in the recent terror attacks. A recent article in Frontline fortnightly says "the profiles of militant killed in recent encounters with security forces are reason for worry. For instance, Saifullah Ahangar had a diploma in civil engineering; Musiullah Khan was a mechanical engineer; Sajad Yousuf Mir had an MA in Islamic Studies) he had not completed his MCA); Moar Ahsan had an M.Sc. Physics; and Hilal Ahmad, rather was a mufti (a scholar in Islamic Law) from Deoband. There are many examples that recent encounters have killed were not from less-educated sections of society. And these trends are continuing." Kashmir experts are of the opinion that in Kashmir educated youths, adopting extremism or terrorism, did not believe or tempt in monetary considerations, rather they say Islam is the biggest motivating forces for them to take up arms. They quote from Koran and Hadith (sayings of Prophet Muhammad) and one can see large number of people in Kashmir listening them on video with rapt attention. The Political scientist Gull Mohammad Wani, who heads the Institute of Kashmir Studies at Kashmir University, believes that stifling political environment in mainly responsible for this. For his "it is an alarming situation and I think repressive measures play a role in this as the place is devoid of accountability, a responsive administration and a regime of justice."

Indian government must initiate reopening dialogue with these elements taking into confidence the Jammu and Kashmir government to neutralise the ugly signs of separatism. Indian government must punish the personnel of army for indulging in rapes and perpetuating other kind of atrocities on Kashmiris taking the help of hated AFSPA!

REFERENCES: INDIA GOVT WEBSITES OF DIFFERENT DEPARTMENTS AND INDIAN ARMY, FRONT LINE FORTNIGHTLY, THE GUARDIAN, THE NEW YORK TIMES, WASHINGTON POST.

WAR OF BOOKS AND ESSAYS ON INDIA'S FAILING ECONOMY—AMARTYA AND BHAGWATI HAVE DIFFERENT OPINIONS!

Thursday, 5 September 2013

Down-turn in Indian economy is not only a subject of animated discussions but a war of books as well as essays in prominent Indian and international newspapers and journals by eminent authors and analysts has broken out in mis-judging or judging in correct perspectives about Indian economy! I am not qualified to assess and give expert opinions about the down-turn of the Indian economy and fall of rupee. in comparison to US dollar but simply analysing the facts, coming out from the books and essays, which, one section blames, global turbulence or mishandling of the economy by the Prime Minister Dr Manmohan Singh while another section finds fault-line in liberalisation policy in the vast India where over 70 percent of population are below the poverty line and hanker for food, health and education! I feel the Indian economy is revolving around "jholwallas" in the National Advisory Council (NAC) and "Davoswallahs" in the enlightened power circuit of capitalists, industrialists, multi-nationals, corporates, landlords etc and our economy will improve or not, it all depends how we handle the present crisis situation. Instead of massive welfare measures, the successive rulers since independence are wrongly diagnosing the things and they have brought 'unique and strange measures' for giving free hands to industrialists, capitalists, multi-nationals, corporates etc in the say of so called improving the Indian economy and plight of people in the country. In the process authors and essayists are harping on different models like Kerala model, Gujarat model, Bihar model, inclusive growth and exclusive growth, blame-game against each others etc. One fact is very much clear since the rise in GDP and so called claims of successive ruler that Indian economy is growing and India will be one of the biggest economic power in the globe by 2020—poverty has increased and rich have become richest and there appears hey-day for making maximum money among vested interests including political classes and poor in rural areas, who constitute largest chunk of population are facing agonising moment!

At least over half a dozen books—authored by prominent economists including Nobel laureate Amartya Sen and his co-author Jean Dreze (An Uncertain Glory:India and its Contradictions—Penguin Books—London), Jagdish Bhagwati and his co-author Arvind Panagariya (India's Tryst with Destiny-Harper Collins), another economist of the fame N K Singh, IAS retired and Rajya Sabha member of JD(U) (The New Bihar—Rekindling Governance and Development), another edited book by Akhil Gupta and K Sivaramakrishnan—The State in India after Liberalisation—Interdisciplinary Perspectives; and Globalisation, International Law and Human Rights, jointly edited by Jeffery F. Addicott, Md. Jahid Hossain Bhuiyan and Tareq M R Chaudhary as well as many essays and topics have thrown mixed views about Indian economy and instead of throwing lights to bail out India from economic morass, they have cited their views for their upmanship except a few!

In one of the Opinion Piece in the Times of India, senior journalist Vinod Mehta has thrown a new debate on welfare measures including Right to Education, RT Act, Food security bill, Land Acquisition Bill, MGNREGA etc through the initiative of AICC president Sonia Gandhi by exercising ground work in National Advisory Committee for poor and middle classes persons and how these measures will percolate to lower-level people of the country?! Mehta writes, "Her critics, starting from Jagdiush Bhagwati (will the Nobel Committee quickly give him the prize Amartya Sen got so that he can resume normal work?) And his domestic followers want us to believe that the mismanagement of Team Manmohan is directly attributable to the lady in 10, Janpath. She pulls the strings to promote her crazy schemes and the PM capitulates leaving behind all the good economics he learnt at Ox Bridge". (MY BLOG ESSAYS—BAD SHAPE OF INDIAN ECONOMY . . . . August 27, 2013, AMARTYA-BHAGWATI SPAT VIS-A-VIS INDIAN ECONOMY . . . . AUGUST 15, 2013).

The Books, written by Amartya Sen and his co-author and Jagdish Bhagwati and his co-author have different signals about Indian economy. While Bhagwati's book has stressed for "market" instead of "public action" in his book, Amartya Sen and his co-authrors' book, in lucid writings and public reasoning, have advanced the reasons for pain on seeing the pathetic pictures of human condition in India that has emerged gradually. Both Sen and Dreze do not denigrate the poor with contempt. They have humane approach! Bhagawati—Panagariya believes on free-market concept and have praised the Gujarat model of growth that has brought wide ranging progress. Both of them have discussed the pros and cons of Kerala Model and Gujarat model in totality. There are vast differences between the two models—while Kerala model stresses for redistributive and stare-driven development and Gujarat model mainly concentrates on growth and and private-entrepreneurship-drive development. Bhagwati and his co-author have mainly concentrated on lambasting Kerala model and praising Gujarat model without many thoughts over history and geography of both the states. A reviewer of the book R Ram Kumar in Frontline says, "a major section in the book is devoted to arguing that Kerala's developmental achievements are due neither to redistributive policies nor to state intervention. In a rather heroic effort to rewrite history, Bhagawati and Paniagariya argue that Kerala's achievements are due, primarily, to "economic growth."

Both Bhagwati and Panagariya, while concentrating on Kerala and Gujarat, have not threw light on overall economic situation in India—but both of them have justified the Gujarat model for shaping the economy of the entire country. There are many flaws about the truths in the development of Kerala in the book. Both of them have mainly concentrated on discrediting the historic process of as a change as "left wing populist fallacy" I do not want to tell more about well-known economist Bhagwati, who appears frustrated, mainly because that once his bosom economist-colleague Amartya got the Nobel prize and he missed that. Now in the fast changing political scenario in the country, Bhagwati seems to be getting closure to Narendra Modi, vastly criticising Sonia Gandhi and result of the down-grading economy of India under Manmohan Singh's stewardship.

More over, Amarty's books co-authored with Dreze are nearer to the ideas that independent India had promises to the people, especially for the vast majority suffering from poverty, ill health and illiteracy! And Amartya and his co-author believe the successive governments in India have lacked in this venture. Common men usually do not believe in the so "called gross domestic product (GDP)—they want measures for their welfare. Dreze is one of the best economist, born in Belgium and came to India in 1979 when he was 20. After ten years, he wrote with Sen a book—Hunger and Public Action and now he is Indian citizen. Sen, professor of Philosophy and Economics at Harvard, in my opinion, could be compared with one of the fathers of modern economics Adam Smith, who used to believe in moral economics! They have written comprehensively about Indian economy and other South-East Asian countries. They have also written about fault-lines like "societal reach of economic progress" in India has been remarkably limited. India is lagging behind in social indicators. Reforms are there in India than to perform. They have threadbare discussions on different aspects of Indian economy. The book says as against 55 percent of Indian households that have no option but to resort to open defecation. India and Pakistan is bottom ladder in literacy rates. Amartya has quoted Rabindra Nath Tagore on his preaching on education. Sen and Derze have also referred Mahatma's talisman. Chapter-wise analysis in the book has thrown light on all aspects of India and its people as well as their economy. The book must be considered a best book, written recently. With highlighting of a vast matter on Indian economy and people of India, the decision makers in India must take lessons from the book and try to improve the economy by applying inclusive growth and identifying all sections of society, especially poor!

These days, Bihar Model is also in news! And the book of N K Singh', co-authored with Lord Nicholas—The New Bihar-Rekindling Governance and Development, although I have not read the book, has also reportedly threw much light on the much-publicised inclusive growth by CM Nitish Kumar. Two edited books on globalising India, as referred above, have informed much about the globalisation, strongly influenced by the neoliberal ideology. The ideology of globalisation and liberalisation opposes an active role of the state in social and economic affairs, claiming that such intervention will negatively affect the economy of the country as a whole. In both the books much has been said about negative aspects like rise in poverty because of globalisation and neo-liberalisation of economy in India. Many essays and articles on Indian economy have their own perspectives including American Fed measures as well as scams after scams in stealing natural resources of the country, worth lakhs of crores of rupees in recent years, adversely affecting the economy of India.

Whether these books or essays or articles could be path showing for bringing the Indian economy to sound footings? But ray of hopes among common men is still there that situation for India's majority of poor will improve!

BAD SHAPE OF INDIAN ECONOMY HAS NOT ONLY DECLINED ECONOMIC GROWTH OF INDIA BUT ITS RUPEE HAS TUMBLED!

Tuesday, 27 August 2013

India's economy, growing fast in the last ten years, has taken worse down turn. Alarming bell is ringing in the entire country. The rupee is in trouble and no body is quite sure what to do about it. Today itself, the Indian currency has tumbled to Rs 65.35 paise against a dollar! There is widespread anxiety over the fact that the Indian government has yet to curb the currency's downfall since it started its down turn in May this year. Inflation and price rise are giving agonising moments to the people of India. Recently, the Deutsche Bank, in its report, says "Indian rupee may reach as low as 70 in the coming months" Echoing the similar sentiments, the Economist Jayati Gosh says, "This is big one. But it has been building up for a while due to many reasons: the growing 'current account deficit' (CAD), the industrial slow-down, the lack of infrastructure development, the negative investment in the country." She sees the crisis as evidence that "the model of development which focuses on only GDP growth" has run its course. What is needed now is "wage and employment-led growth".

Although, I have little knowledge of Economics, I have ventured to write on Indian economy in a number of essays on my sites—www. kksingh1.blogspot.com—describing about fault-line with our policy makers in shaping the economy of India since independence. In this very topic, I am just putting forward the alarming proportions of Indian Economy, based on the facts with Indian government as well as national and international newspapers, news magazines and websites!

In the last few years, Indian economy is going on bad shape, which has slowed from its rapid 9 percent growth rate to a forecast of between

5.5 percent and 5.7 percent for this financial year. After the 2008 world economic crisis, vastly affecting the USA, which had to pump huge money to banks from bankruptcy, India had recorded 9 percent GDP growth for at least two years but in recent weeks rupee have tumbled., losing a sixth of its value against the dollar this month alone, Share price have fallen, commodity prices are rising, investment is stalking, growth is slowing and the Indian government is under a huge balance of payments deficit. A sense of impending doom is building. Compounding the fears are signs that other emerging economies in Asia are also vulnerable, drawing inevitable questions as to whether this could turn into a repeat of the 1997 Asian financial crisis.

Opinions are badly divided for such beating of Indian economy! One section believes that part of the problem is not India's alone. With the U S Federal Reserve expected to start tapering off a stimulus programme that has pumped cash into global economy, investors have grown wary on the emerging markets they became so fond of in recent years. Countries running their own current account deficits have borne the burnt of the mood swing: currencies in India, Brazil and Indonesia, among others, have seen drops as investors—pull money out ahead of the Fed's anticipated tightening. Another problem of facts is that Indian economy has some home-grown structural problems has exacerbated the flight of foreign funds. An economist with the Capital Economics in Singapore, Daniel Martin has said, "If you are an investor, you want to put your money where there is going to be growth. The shine has come off India, It is not glaring success story it was a few years ago." Other experts trace problem to the failure of Manmohan Singh's government to push through structural reforms that could boost growth. The ruling UPA led by the Congress Party's emphasis on huge government subsidy schemes, such as jobs for the rural poor, has added to an already big fiscal deficit. Economist Surjit Bhalaa has said, "Just trying to accelerate growth from present low level (annual GDP growth is now down to five percent) will help the economy." More over India imports much more than it exports and so the current account deficit is at an unsustainable 4.8 percent. Until, it brought down, there can be very little hope of reviving investor's confidence in the economy.

The intensity of down-turn is so hard that apart from affecting poor and middle classes in the country, riches have also been badly affected. Mukesh Ambani, a towering industrialist and capitalist, who lives in a one billion $ 27-storey Mumbai skyscraper complete with swimming pools, three helipads and a 50-seat cinema, is down to his last 17.5 billion $ after the plunging value of the rupee wiped out a quarter of his fortune, in dollar terms. Mukesh Ambani, the chairman of the Reliance Industries, which operates the world's largest oil refineries, has lost 5.6 billion $ of his personal wealth since May one, according to the Bloom berg Billionaires index. Ambanies shares in Reliance Industries have dropped 15 percent since mid-July. Developing economies excluding China have seen an outflow of 81 billion 4 in emergency reserves since early May, as central banks try to prop up their currencies. Indonesia has lost 13.6 percent of its reserve, Turkety—12.7 pc, Ukraine—10 pc, according to central bank data complied by Morgan Stanley. Surprisingly, India's Finance Minister Palaniappan Chidambaram, who has tried to reassure investors that "there is no reason for excessive or unwarranted pessimism, failed to give any tangible result.

Core issues, slowing down Indian growth are now hurting currency—and by proxy, Indian consumers who want to buy, say, an imported phone or foreign car makers that need to import parts. Those fundamental weaknesses—poor infrastructures, unreliable power supply, difficulty in securing land and lots of sticky red tape—are all keeping foreign investments out of the country and that is problem for a country that imports far more than it exports and thus needs to finance a large current account deficit. When the CAD widens, the rupee's decline accelerates further. So even at a time when many emerging markets are looking risky to investors, India is looking riskier than most. In the process, gold is also a big problem in India. Gold has played an important role in skewing the trade deficit. A century ago, the Economist John Maynard Keynes wrote that India's irrational love for gold was "ruinous to her economic development" and the obsession still runs deep. India's annual production of gold is barely 10 tonnes, so last year it imported 860 tonnes, which were made into jewellery or stored as coins and bars in family safes! The government is now trying to stem the hunger for gold by increasing import duties. This has revived gold smuggling, a menace which in the 1960s led to creation of the Bombay now Mumbai, underworld. Not only that, it is estimated that households and Hindu temples are hoarding about 25,000 tonnes of gold bars and coins. Jewellers are lobbying government to implement a scheme that could unearth 10 percent of the hoarded golds.

Although there is growing anxieties about future, India's middle class may not have lost faith yet in the possibility of economic regeneration.

Just we Indian have become afraid of 1997-98 Asian economic crisis. The trigger for the run on the rupee has been news from Washington that the Federal Reserve is considering scaling back—"tapering"— its bound-buying stimulus programme from next month. This has consequences for all emerging market economies: firstly, there is fear that a reduced stimulus will mean weaker growth in the US, with a knock-on impact on exports from the developing world. Secondly, the high-yielding currencies such as the rupee have benefited from a search for yield on the part of global investors. If policy is going to be tightened in the US, then the dollar becomes more attractive and rupee less so. But while the Indonesian rupiah and the South African rand are also feeling the heat, it is India—with its large trade and budget deficits—that looks like the accident most likely to happen. On past from emerging market crises go through three stages: in stage one, policy makers do nothing in the hope that the problem goes away. In stage two, they cobble together some panic measures, normally involving half-baked capital controls and selling of dollars in an attempt to underpin their currencies. In stage three, they either come up with a workable plan themselves or call in the IMF. Thus India is on the cusp of stage three!

What ever may the facts of India's economy down turn, the country has also its own compulsions. Tribal population and their forest are facing dangerous situation as union and state governments have allowed multii-nationals and capitalists to open factories in the forest areas depriving them of their homelands by violating Forest and environment laws large number of poverty prevails in India. Education and health programmes are dismal in the rural areas where most of the people live in the country. I do not oppose economic liberalisation for the development of the Country. But there are certain basic things, which are best needed for the country like subsidies on food, housing, shelter etc. But subsidies are being gobbled up by rich people like subsidies on petrol, LPG, fertilisers and diesel. There must be some yardstick not to provide such benefits to affluent. Food Security Bill has been now enacted and it will definitely eliminate hunger. For education and health, there are many measures, it must be vigorously implemented. For employment, there is guaranteed job under MGNREG—it must be accelerated. For these welfare measures, need of hour is to stop leakage and corrupt practises! Huge amounts are given as subsidy or remission to the industrialists and capitalists must be stopped without any further delay. Law must be enacted to give 50 percent reservation in Parliament and sate legislatures to women to empower them completely. Women population is about 50 percent but they are being ignored in India. Large number of scams, which have come up with the entry of economic liberalisation, has also cost the country most. Money earned through corrupt practices must not only be stopped but confiscated. Black money stacked in foreign banks by Indian rich must be brought back—All these measures will bring India into a robust ECONOMY in The GLOBE

SCARS OF PARTITION STILL HAUNTS INDIA AND PAKISTAN!

Saturday, 17 August 2013

Scars of wounds, pains and anguish, even today, in the wake of partition in 1947 of greater India (Bharat) are giving agonising moments to the population of both India and Pakistan in Asia. Since partition both the countries—India and Pakistan—are indulging in only enmity, war, communal tension, bitter struggles for territories etc. On August 15, 2013 when the people of entire India were celebrating the Independence Day, strange thought started creeping in my mind, "if both India and Pakistan would not have partitioned, we would have "United India", most powerful country on the GLOBE, Recent border skirmishes and killings and counter-killings of army men of both the countries are not only pained me but old reminiscences have kept me wandering in my thoughts!

Finally, Britishers succeeded in dividing India into "India and Pakistan" by adopting divide and rule policy'. And both nations were freed from British rule in August 1947. Sadly, this partition resulted in killings of over two lakhs of people in both the countries another over 50 lakh people became homeless because of huge repartition of people from one country to another. Devastating tragedies had shaken both the countries. Exactly I remember the wordings of Mohammad Ali Jinnah, the main architect of partition in the wake his sidelining in the Congress party led by 'Mahatma Gandhi and Co.' had said, while making an aerial survey of the situation on the ground because of huge number of persons being killed by each other as well as refugees making their way away from their respective ancestral homes towards villages and towns, they had never seen or been to earlier, expressed pain and anguish and he (Jinnah) plunged plunged into shock. Jinnah had commented. "Oh what have I done?" that was the shock, he expressed—no one accompanying him answered! Within months, millions of Hindus and Sikhs would have their ancient homes in Punjab and Bengal and trek to an uncertain future across unknown geography. Millions of Muslims would make their way to Pakistan; convinced that it was there they would live in dignity as masters of their destiny.

Before discussing other aspects, I must mention the circumstances leading to the partition of the country by British Raj1 A study of the Jinnah papers, the literature that has grown around Jinnah and Pakistan give the impression that essentially an introvert and a narcissist with an insatiable craze for going to the top, Jinnah was given a raw deal as a congressman. He was only utilised and exploited and thrown away when not needed. He had been an ardent Congressman who had taken to be the ambassador of the Hindu-Muslim unity. A statesman like Gokhale had seen in him a front-rank born leader. Sarojini Naidu had said about Jinnah, ". . . . a naive and eager humanity, an intuition quick and tender as woman's, a humour gay and winning as a child's-pre-eminently rational and practical, discreet and dispassionate in his estimates and acceptance of life, the obvious sanity and serenity of his worldly wisdom effectively disguised, a shy and splendid idealism which is very essence of the man".

Jinnah's narcissism and interovertism had thrown a cloak over his core of steel that would not bend although lashed by the furies of circumstances. His domestic life was not very happy. He married late in life and after a short period of bliss the couple separated, His sister Fatima Jinnah sacrificed her life for her brother and looked after him. The brother and sister together weathered many phases in life-some times oblivion, occasional excitements, years of hard thinking and work, careful planning, cautious journeys in India ans abroad, parleys with Muslim Leagures giving up the Congress, planned interviews where Gandhiji and Sapru could cut no ice then frenzied advocacy of Pakistan, A quite man, who once denounced communal representation and who said he was proud of being a Congressman and an Indian and advocated partition as an inescapable solution of an Indian blazed as the champion of the two-nation theory in India and creation of the Pakistan, the toy-dream of a few Cambridge Muslim scholars as the panacea for the Musilms here. An ardent Congressite, who was not given his proper honour in the inner Congress coterie and who had to say at the Howrah station platform to a friend "—this is parting ways". Subsequently Jinnah had to leave India for a while and settled down in England to start as a lawyer.

But he was waiting, keeping himself abreast with the thoughts-current in India and in the right moment, he came back to India at the call of Liyaqut Ali Khan. The Muslim League crowned him. The many, who could hardly speak Urdu and seldom wore a sherwani and pyjama in the public over night, became the Messiah of Muslims. He had given that time strong confidence and warning to the millions of Muslims. He had his desolate days, exploited and neglected by the Congress. He started dictating terms to Gandhiji. And thus, after cabinet Mission plan had to go and independent Pakistan and India were created? Did he not through blood sheds, riots, arson and loot. Did Jinnah look for his revenge for all the ignomity poured on himl? Did he not outclass Gandhiji, Jawahar Lal Nehru, and Sardar Bhallav Bhai Patel? Mountbatten was out Gandhi Ji put on the shelf when he wanted to become Governor-General of Pakistan. Gandhi ji called him "Quaiad-E-Azam" in his parleys prior to the partition of India. Once only years before as a Congressite Jinnah had used the word "Mahatma" about Gandhi. In the later parleys he always addressed him as "Mr Gandhi" and would not listen to him but only as leader of Hindus. Nemesis works out through mysterious ways but with Jinnah he was clearly given raw deal which he nursed secretly and gave it back when the time came.

The metamorphosed Jinnah spoke and wrote in the following strains," India of modern conception with its so called present geographical unity is entirely the creation of British who hold it as one administrative unit by a system of bureaucratic government whose ultimate sanction is the sword and not the will or the sanction of the people behind the government so established. This position is very much exploited by Hindu Congress and another Hindu organisation, the Hindu Mahasabha. India is a vast sub-continent. It is neither a country nor a nation. It is composed of nationalities and race but the two major nations are the Muslims and the Hindus. Talk of Indian unity as one constitutional government of this vast sub-continent is simply a myth . . . . Muslims under the subjugation and hegemony of the Hindu Raj over the entire sub-continent of India which means that Muslims shall be merely transferring their bondage of slavery from the British Raj to Hindu Raj."

When one looks back Jinnah as Congressman from 1906 to 1920, he was actively associated with the Indian National Congress. At that time it was observed several times that Jinnah received his political training under Dadabhai Naroji whom he first met in England and later worked as his secretary for 14 years Jinnah had also close association with Surendranath Bennerjee and G K Gokhale and often referred to Gokhale as "a practical politician" Gokhale had also his regard for Jinnah. And had said, "He has true stuff in him and that freedom from all sectarian projects will make him best ambassador for of Hindu-Muslim unity". Jinnah had taken active part in Congress session of 908, 1910, 1913 and 1917 and he used to speak disapproving the scheme of communal representation in local bodies. Jinnah left the Congress on September 30, 1921 when he was convinced that the Congress was going wrong way with Gandhiji at its helm. Later he started giving fiery speech against Congress and Hindu Mahasabha as Muslim League chief. He had spoken for the safeguards for minority. He bitterly criticised Jawahar Lal, Gandhiji, Rajgopalachjari and the Hindu Mahasabha. Sir Tej Bahadur Sapru was described by Jinnah as "most subtle and plausible and therefore all the more treacherous." he asked the Muslims to maintain "complete unity and solidarity". Jinnah's tirade and resentment was so strong for creation of Pakistan that almost all leaders including Gandhiji, Subhash Bose, Jawahar Lal, Tej Bahadur Sapru, Mirza Ismail, Jayakar had failed cope Jinnah. In 1942, it was momentous year for Muslim League under the stewardship of Jinnah. Jinnah had become idol of Muslim League and Muslim-minded people. In between and independence and partition, many incidents happened and ultimately India was partitioned and India and Pakistan were created in August 1947 by dividing from brothers to brothers, fathers, sons, daughters, and eveybodies and every things. And partition left a greatest scar on the Indian sub-continent!

The Editor of the Daily Star, a newspaper published from Dhaka, Syed Badrul Ahsan, in a recent signed article—"The Legacy of Partition" has written," Sixty-six years after partition, one would do well to take stock of the ramifications of the vivisection of the land. Hindus and Muslims have only seen their relations worsen through the decades, to a point where communal ism continues to define life all the way from Pakistan through India to Bangala Desh. Hindutva undermines the secular vision that was once Pundit Jawahar Lal Nehru's legacy. In Pakistan and to certain extent in Bangala Desh, religious bigotry threatens to wreck liberalism of all sorts, India's Muslims remain largely backward, poor, and, in a very big way, less than well-educated. In Pakistan, Hindus are as good as non-existent; and the tiny Christian minority is always the target of blasphemy law peddlers in the Bangala Desh's Hindu population has been on sharp decline, despite the country's self-proclaimed secularism; its Christian community become smaller by the day; and after Ramu, its Buddhists are not sure this is their country any more. Post-partition Indian has thrown up the likes of Bal Thackrey, who thought all Muslims should be kicked out of the country. Today, it is controversial, none too Muslim-friendly Narendra Modi who dreams of being prime minister. In Pakistan and Bangala Desh, that a Hindu or Christian or Buddhist can not play leading role in politics and in the administration . . . ."

". . . . if India's BJP tout Hindu nationalism, Pakistan's political parties continue to see nothing beyond Islam, while Bangala Desh's right wing discovers, through 'Bangala Deshi nationalism', a clever way of repudiating Bengali nationhood in favour of a shrewd pursuit of religion-based politics. Secular politics never took roots in Pakistan. In India and Bangala Desh, it has been forced to the ropes. The division of India has led to a diminution of politics through the rise of dynasties across the old country. The Bhutto's in Pakistan, the Nehru-Gandhi in India and Mujib and Zia clans in Bangala Desh have created perfect conditions for mediocrity to thrive in politics. Behind these larger dynasties come the little ones—in politics, indeed nearly everywhere. The modern day republic is thus but another name for monarchies in new wrappings", Ahsan writes.

He further writes lambently, "Partition saw the best among the Hindu community—teachers, philanthropists, doctors,—leave Muslim Pakistan and make new home across the newly drawn frontiers. It was Muslim gentry, as in West Bengal; make the arduous decision to move to the new state of Pakistan in hope of better future. Both groups, as also their descendants, have remained trapped in nostalgia. Artistes and writers have seen their futures devastated by partition. The singer Noor Jehasn went off to Pakistan together with Saadat Hasan Manto, Khuswant Singh, Kuldip Nayar and Inder Kumar Gujaral, their homeland suddenly foreign territory for them, resettled in an India vastly different from the one they had known earlier. Sahibzada Yaqub Khan trooped off to Pakistan even as his parents and siblings decided to stay on in India, Jinnah, Liyaqut Khan, H S Suhrawardy and Buutto abandoned their homes in India and made new homes in Pakistan. Pakistan has seen democracy, to a great extent, minus the aberrations of the 1975-77 emergencies, thrive in in India. In Pakistan, army has undermined prospects of democracy four times and continues to wield unbridled influence over making of policy. In Bangala desh, the liberation of which was a revolt against Pakistan, military coups have led to the systematic murder of politicians and leading freedom fighters.

Louis Mountbatten and Cyril Radcliffe, who gave us, divided homes and villages and provinces. It gave us three wars. It gave the people of the sub-continent defence budgets that have left them impoverished.

And we are, after sixty six years after independence in 1947, in dark over the" legacy of partition remains questionable".

REFERENCES:—I have written many essays like Ominous Signal for Secularism in India (July 21, 2012); Muslims in Globe vis-a-vis in India (17 July 1912); Communal Harmony in India since Medieval Period (29 March, 2012); Why not Communal Harmony in India and Pakistan? (August 24, 2013); Why this Hate Campaign Against Muslims of the World? (16 October 2012)!

AMARTYA SEN AND AND JAGDISH BHAGWATI SPATS VIS-A-VIS INDIAN ECONOMY: BOTH WAITING FOR LAST LAUGH!

Thursday, 15 August 2013

The recent spat and criticism and counter criticism over eminent Economists—Nobel Laureate Amartya Sen and Jagdish Bhagwati is unfortunate! Both are distinguished economists. Both of them have worked on a broad spectrum of issues. Sen is best known for his work on public choice and development while Bhagwati for his work on trade. They are respected throughout the globe for their economic theories. Both are liberal, neoclassical economists, who support deregulation and disapprove of existing subsidies. Notably, in the recent past both Sen and Bhagwati have made their minor disagreements into slanging matches. Bhagwati has been repeatedly attacking Sen in public and in the print, while Sen expounding on his point through interviews and ope-eds largely without mentioning Bhagwati about his views!

Both Sen and Bhagwati have been in race in co-authoring books, available in the market. Bhagwati has long disapproved of Sen. On the other hand Sen, who has recently co-authored a book—"An Uncertain Glory: India and its Contradictions", co-authored with Jean Dreze, the Nobel prize winning Sen, has pointed out in an interview that he "does not understand why my book has received an angry reactions or why he is being called anti-growth and pro-redistribution." One of reasons of spat may be—Sen had spoken about food security, and fast space of controversial development in Bihar under Nitish Kumar chief ministership, while releasing a book on Bihar Economy in New Delhi, authored by JD(U) MP and Economist N K Singh (IAS retd) Sen had also voiced his reservation over Narendra Modi becoming prime minister of India. Such remark of Sen has blown up out of proportion in media, which is being termed a Congress view points!

On the other hand, Bhagwati's co-author Arvind Panigrahi, has praised Gujarat's growth in several pieces. Perhaps, that made Bhagwati, the Gujarat chief Minister Narendra Modi's best friend and these differences between Bhagwati and Sen escalated the 'tension' in the economic thoughts and principles between them. Now such differences have percolated to open fight between Modi and Congress, which are making headlines in the media. In his latest broadside against Sen, Bhagwati managed to mention his book frequently, insisting in it, he had proved how Sen was anti-growth, a point many reviweres, surprisingly failed to mention.

In my opinion, all these spats are unseemly and uninformative spectacles. Academics continue to be divided over simple mechanisms of growth and how it can be achieved in the India context—purely through deregulation, as Bhagwati would agree or with a simultaneous push to education and health as Sen wants. Sen has almost completely avoiding commenting on Bhagwati's views although Bhagwarti has become increasingly personal and petty in his attacks on Sen. Sen broke Bhagwati-as-Voldemort rule in recent letter to The Economist. The liberal British Magazine had run a review of Sen and Jean Dreze's new book; the reviewer happened to mention Bhagwati in passing without specifying that he, Bhagwati, was right and Sen was wrong. This was red rag to Bhagawati, who wrote Sen only paid "lip service" to growth. This was too much for Sen, who wrote explaining he did his PhD on how to stimulate growth and the first collection of essays he edited was titled "Growth Economics" In fact Sen is perhaps the greatest living scholar of the original philosopher of the free market, Adam Smith!

Bhagwati, then wrote an article for the Mint that basically returned, even more harshly, to his complaints about Sen. Bhagwati's books are littered with disparaging remarks about Sen; indeed, reading between the lines of his last book reveals even more such remarks, some of them from resentments that date back to the early 1960s when both were young professional economists in New Delhi.

LOVE TANGLE: A senior journalist and Editor of the Outlook India, Uttam Sengupta, in a lighter vein, have written, on the Facebook, Bhagwati is angry with Sen because Sen perhaps eloped with Bhagwati's girl friend! Another senior journalist commented and replied to Uttam Sengupta on the Facebook, it is possible for Sen as Sen has married third time with the wife of his one of the friends in US by eloping her friend's wife.

Sen won Nobel Prize for his work on social choice and welfare as also propounded by Prof Kedarnath Prasad, a former vice-chancellor of the Patna University. Bhagwati is path breaking trade theorists. Bhagwati's Ph D students included Psul Krugman, who propounded trickle down economy. Sen's PhD students included Kaushik Basu. But, in fact Bhagawati is called more an economist's economist than Sen., who at Harvard, for example had an office in the Philosophy department, not in Economics depatment. Sen is considered one of the unique and most respected living academic philosophers and a close associate and a fellow teacher of both the left-of-the-centre John Rawals, the leading philosopher of 20th century and liberation icon Robert Nozick.

Similar controversy had arisen in Great Britain in October 1932 and the two economists—John Maynard Keynes and Fredrich von Hayek—had exchanged letters in The Times, London! Both of them used to keep mutually in esteem." That was the only beginning of life time of public sparring between two individuals, who disagreed vehemently on economic policy. Echoes of their debate resonate even today in places such as the United States or Europe in shaping competing views of how best to combat the recession in which the global economy is still stuck"

What makes the Hayek-Kenes battle of ideas different from most distinguished intellectual controversies is that ideas of these two men had a profound impact on economic policy in the USA, Britain and elsewhere. The "Keynesian Consensus" that governments needed actively intervene to combat recessions by spending more became orthodoxy after the end of the Second World War and held sway for almost three decades. Then with the problems, known stagflation, a combination of high inflation and high unemployment, the faith in Keynesian economics broke down for a time and a new policies such as deregulation and privatisation came to the fore, In this, Hayek, as well as Milton Friedman, had a huge impact. However, Hyek might not have had the last laugh. Keynesian economics, which had been rubbished by many senior economists, has made a come back in the wake of global financial crisis and the battle of ideas is far from over.

Just the same Bhagwati-Sen debate has come after over 78 years, taken place in Great Britain! I strongly feel the Indian economy will have same impact as Hayek versus Keynes had on the West! Just We Indian will have to watch, who will have last laugh—Sen or Bhagwati with economic policy and development in India!

Although Both Bhagwati and Sen have had huge impact in different ways on economic liberalisation in India, many owed debts to Bhagawati's long advocacy, going back to the 1970s, that Indian economy needed open up. In the process slain Prime Minister Rajiv Gandhi had initially started efforts in the teleccommunication sector and other fields also by liberalising Indian economy amid stiff opposition. But the fact of realty was that the then union finance minister Manmohan Singh was a Cambridge classmate of Bhagwati. More recently, more over one can see the imprint of Sen's rights-based approach in many large schemes unveiled by the UPA, the most recent being the food security bill., Sen, who was critical of many details, was broadly supportive of the idea of creating an entitlement to food, which builds philosophically on the "capabilities approach" to well-being that he developed with philosopher Martha Nussbaum. As it happens, Sen was also at Cambridge in the days when Manmohan Singh and Bhagwati were there. In fact, all of them won Adam Smith prize in different years!

Notably, the direct salience might be the fact that Sen's long-time colleague, Jean Dreze, a former member of the National Advisory Concil, Sonia Gandhi's think tank for the UPA. But what about the Indian economy, which has turned down-ward trends, will the present debate on the appropriation of balance between growth enhancing policies on the one hand and social spending on the other side make a difference on actual economic policies of which ever government takes power next year?

". . . . The Keynes-Hyek debate of past provides some useful clues. The ideas of both were translated into economic policy, both because of historical circumstances and also because they were championed at crucial moments by politicians who carried conviction in their ideas, to put it crudely, the Soncond Workld War was a great natural experiment for Keynesian economics. Massive wartime spending—one type of government spending not exactly what Keynes in mind-essentially ended Great Britain Depression . . . . By the same token, Heyek's free market ideas were championed first in Britain by Margret Thatcher and than in the US by Ronald Regan. Whether one love them or hate them. Thatcher and Reagan had very definite clues on what they thought the right economic models for their respective countries."

A columnist of repute has said, "we are not in a war and nor do we have idea—driven politicians like Reagan and Thatcher The feud between

Sen and Bhagwati and their various disciples and collaborators is great fodder for newspaper columns and TV talk show, it is not evident that the niceties of this debate are going to resonate with the Indian electorate or have much impact on the election campaign to say nothing of the economic policy platforms of any of major parties. Ore likely, the impact of ideas of these two great economists will work indirectly as suggested by Keynes himself. By shaping the politicians not necessarily even today but in future think about economic policy, the different emphasis of Sen and Bhagwati might well have a longer term impact. In a shorter term, it is more likely the perspectives of both Sen and Bhagawati will colour the way see important economic news. The Sharp drop in the poverty rate during the tenure of UPA raises the question of what was responsible. Those sympathetic to Bhagwati will point to rapid growth during these years while those sympathetic to Sen will point to the large increase in programmatic expenditure and initiatives such as the Msahatma Gandhi National Rural Employment Guarantee Scheme."

In my opinion such debater on economic policy is good sign where great econoimc thinkers have been publicly discussing India's economic policies. It is shaping us as battle of ideas between those who see themselves more on the right versus those who see themselves on the left. Ideologically driven debates seem to have finally arrived in India like US and other European countries. It is not that only Indian politicians used to figure out economic policies of India!

Sen has often and publicly argued in favour of greater liberalisation, ending red tape, labour laws reform and cutting fuel power and fertiliser subsidies. Bhagwati has argued for second track of reforms in social sector areas though he would prefer public money are spent on say school vouchers that let poor parents pay for private schools. Both are little concerned about fall in India's growth rate. Sen argues it has fallen as much as its competitors; Bhagwati has blamed tight monetry policy and the freez-up in clearance following outrage over scams, adding government proposals could reverse the side. Both of these are, pretty much what the government also claims. Real differences between Sen and Bhagawati about Indian economy are: Sen wants more public funding (as distinct from public provision) of basic goods. Bhagwati argues this is secondary to focussing on growth. Sen says, growth depends on creating a dynamic work force capable of learning on the job, which needs health and education. Bhagwati wants laissez-faire growth will raise income sufficiently for the workforce to be able to invest in their own health and education. Both these mechanism can be true. In fact both probably are true, which means the differences are even smaller than is claimed—just a question of which can work faster and more effectively. One path can hardly be abandoned for the other; both mechanisms will need government attention. Nor is either major political party likely to act on only one mechanism, at the cost of other!

All these controversies are creation of media and the eternal quest in the India media to make absolutely everything relate Rahul Gandhi versus Narendra Modi!

Sources: NYTIMES, WASHINGTON POST, GUARDIAN, ECONOMIST, OBSERVER, THE TIMES OF INDIA, India govt websites and various other websites.

INDO-CHINA DISPUTES NOW SHIFT TO WATER GRAB FOR DAMS IN HIMALAYAN RIVERS, DANGERING ECOLOGICAL BALANCE!

Tuesday, 13 August 2013

It is dam building spree in Asian countries like China, India, Nepal, Bhutan, Pakistan etc, endangering the globe's most famous mountain range—Himalaya. Most of the Himalayan Rivers have been so far relatively untouched by dams near the sources. Now with the vast dam construction sprees, foot water resources have plunged into risk zone. In the process, all these countries have engaged themselves in a huge "water grab" in the Himalayas for constructing hydro-electricity generation units for boosting up their economy, At least Bhutan, India, Nepal and Pakistan has planned for constructing more than 400 hydro dams which, if built, could together generate over 160,000 MW of electricity-three times more than United Kingdom uses. Apart from that, China has alone planned for about 100 dam construction to generate a similar amount of power from major rivers rising in Tibet. A further 60 or more dams are being planned for the Nekong river, which also rises in Tibet and flows south through south-east Asia. Now, the two Asian giant power—India and China are competing each other to harness the rivers as they cut through some of the world's deepest valleys. It is estimated most of the proposed dams would be tallest in the world, for generating 4,000 MW, as much as the Hoover dam on the Colorado River in the USA.

Ecological and environment balance is already under tremendous pressure throughout the globe. Dam construction in Himalayan mountain and forest range will further disturb environment and ecology. Climate change will further warm the world and will trap millions in the world in poverty. A World Bank report has cautioned the people of these predicaments and says, "we could see a plus 20 C scenario in rise in temperature in 20 to 30 years and plus four C by the end of century". Amiya Kumar Bagachi in his book "Perilous Passage—Mankind and the Global Ascendancy of Capital has said, "Much of the advance of European capitalists and other members of the European ruling class was at the cost of the colonised and enslaved peoples of Africa, Asia, and Latin America. Capital expansion following the Industrial Revolution involved unmitigated exploitation of natural resources and world labour. The search for profit-led to the colonisation of the world and the pauperisation of much of what is today called the Global South. The over exploitation of the fossil fuels has meant that climate change has become an imminent threat. Underdeveloped nations will continue to bear the burnt." A scientific report commissioned by the World Bank, "Turn Down heart: Climate Extremes, Regional Impacts and the Case for Resilience" looks at the possible impact of global warming by 2oCelsius and 4o C on the most vulnerable parts of the world.

Recent haphazard construction of dams in Uttarakhand, a tiny state of Indian Union in Himalayan range has resulted into nature fury to worse scale, killing thousands of people and damaging property of crores of rupees. My three recent blog essays: Threat to Life on the Earth vis-a-vis the Earth itself Threatened; Uttarakhand Tragedy due to Nature's Fury and Also a man-made Devastation and Dangerous Signal for Nepal Because Of Climate Change in Himalaya . . . . Have dwelt in length about the shape of devastated globe because of climate change and disturbances in ecological balances in various region of earth, particularly Asia. www.kksingh1.blogspot.com

Further more, climate models suggest that major rivers running off the Himalayas, after increasing flows as glaciers melt, could lose 10-20 of their flow by 2050. This would not only reduce the rivers' capacity to produce electricity, but would exacerbate regional political tensions. The dams have already led to protest movements in Uttarakhand, Himachal Pradesh, Sikkim, Assam and other northern states of India and in Tibet. Protrsts in Uttarakhand, which was devastated by floods last month, were led by Prof G D Agarawal, who was taken to hospital after a 50-day fast but who was released this week. A member of Ganga Avahan, a group opposing proposals for a series of dams on Ganga, Mallika Bhanot has said, "there is no other way but to continue because the state government is not keen to review the dam policy"

More over, the governments have tried to convince and calm people by saying that many of the dams will not require large reservoirs but will be "run of the river" constructions which channel water through tunnels to massive turbines. But critics say that the damage done can be just as great. Shripad Dharmadhikary, a leading opponent of the Narmada dams and the author of a report into Himalayan dams the river flow, has said, "These dams will shift the complete path of the river flow." Everyone will be affected because the rivers will dry up between points. The whole hydrology of the rivers will be changed. It is likely to aggravate floods. A dam may only need 500 people to move because of submergence but because the dams stop the river flow it could impact on 20000 people. They also disrupt the groundwater flows so many people will end up with water running dry. There will be devastation of livelihood along all the rivers."

According to Ed Grumbine, visiting international scientist with the Chinese Academy of Sciences in Kunming; in next 20 years "could be that the Himalayas become the most dammed region in the world". Grumbine, author of a paper in Science has said, "India aims to construct 292 dams . . . . doubling current hydro power capacity and contributing six percent to the projected national energy needs. If all dams are constructed as proposed in 28 of 32 major river valleys, the Indian Himalayas would have one of the highest average dam densities in the world, with one dam for every 32 km of river channel. Every neighbour of India with undeveloped hydro-power sites is building or planning to build multiple dams, totalling at minimum 129 projects."

If the present pace of building multiple dams on all major rivers running off the Tibetan plateau by China is likely to emerge as the ultimate controller of water for nearly 40 percent of the world's population. Tashi Tsering, a water resource researcher at the University of British Columbia in Canada has said, "The plateau is the source of the single largest collection of international rivers in the world including the Mekong, the Brahmputra, the Yangtse and the Yellow Rivers. It is the head water of the rivers on which nearly the half the world depends. The net effect of the dam building could be disastrous. We just do not know the consequences."

Notably the border disputes between India and China appeared to have shifted from land territory to water. Water in rivers in Himalayas and other mountain range along Indo-China border is going to be apple of discord between India and China in the light of harnessing the water for electricity by constructing dams. Indian Geopolitical analyst Brahma Chellaney has said, "China is engaged in the greatest water grab in history. Not only it is damning the rivers on the plateau, it is financing and building mega-dams in Pakistan, Laos, Burma and elsewhere and making agreements to take the power. China-India disputes have shifted from; land to water. Water is new divide and is going centre stage in politics. Only China has the capacity to build these mega dams and the power to crush resistance. This is effectively war without a shot, being fired."

Chellaney has further said, "India is in the weakest position because half its water comes directly from China; however, Bangala Desh is fearful of India's plans for water diversions and hydro power. Bangala Deshi scientists were of the opinion that even a 10 percent reduction in the water flow by India could dry out great areas of farmland for much of the year. More than 80 percent of Bangala Desh's 50 million small farmers depend on water that flows through India. Bangal Desh is fearful.

In my earlier blog essays, I have written about disastrous consequences from dam constructions. Dam's construction will gradually increase the chances of flood as we have witnessed in Uttarakhand recently. Haphazard construction of dams without serious planning will not only make entire Himalayan range vulnerable to floods but also serious implications of earthquake in far and wide areas. Virtually, there has been no exercise prior to dam constructions by these countries. No attention has been paid on the human and ecological impact of dams. The Co-coordinator of South Asia Network on Dams Himanshu Thakkar has said, "We do not have credible environmental and social impact assessments, we have no environmental compliance system, no cumulative impact assessment and no carrying capacity studies. The Indian Ministry of Environment and Forest, developers and, consultants are responsible for this mess."

For dam constructions and other related projects, India and China have notoriety in displacing tens of millions of tribal and other persons by constructing big and giant dams like Narmada and Three Gorges over the past 30 years. Surprisingly both India and China are keeping silence over how many person have been affected or affected persons have been reallocated and how much land are being submerged after the construction of new dams in both these countries. Tsering has said, "This is being totally ignored. No one knows, either, about the impact of climate change on the rivers. The dams are all being built in rivers that are fed by glaciers and snowfields which are melting at a fast rate."

Thus—there is supremacy for water at the cost of crores of people of Asia. And Himalaya will be in danger!

Sources: Internet sites including The Observer, China and India, Universities other sites!

CREATION OF NEW STATES IN INDIA OPEN PANDORA'S BOX AS DECISION IS MADE POLITICALLY!

Saturday, 10 August 2013

Since Independence, it is invariably seen that successive political leadership take decisions, keeping in mind only 'politics and pressure tactics'. In this essay, I will put facts about creation of new 'States' since independence. Recently the Union government of the UPA led by the Congress, has given green signal to create "Telangans state" of the Indian Union, bifurcating the areas from the old Andhra Pradesh! Mainly the successive union governments have kept in their mind the 'political aspect' and language in creating new states spoke since independence. Thus people, who mostly spoke the same language, were brought together in one state. In the process, the successive governments ignored minority languages and dialects within the areas. Several north Indian states are all predominantly Hindi-speaking states! Demand for economic viability, regional autonomy and other factors were never considered in creating new states. Demand for separate state of Telagana, which has been merged with other Telgu-speaking regions to create the state of Andhra Pradesh in early 1950s despite vehement opposition, was never considered. And since than, agitation for creation of separate Telagana state continued unabated. At that time also the SRC, had not recommended merger in 1954 only because the areas was passing through communist-led uprising. The struggle of the Communist uprising for the first began in Telegana areas because of social and political discrimination of the merger of Telagana areas was completed. At that time, the then Prime Minister Pundit Jawahar Lal Nehru, while giving a note of dissent over merger of Telegana areas with Andhara Pradesh, has cautioned and said "this particular marriage should contain provision for divorce".

Now the pave for new Telagana state has come out, again on "political consideration," many, both of Telagana and Andhra regions have many reservations. At the time of merger of Telagana with Andhra for an united Andhara Pradesh state, the concern of the people of Telagana areas were mainly economic including distribution of resources—such as river water, as the headwaters of the Krishna and Godavari rivers were in Telegana but the planned irrigation projects at coastal Andhra. There were general apprehension that Telegana region was not so developed, especially in education sector, in comparison to other parts of the state—hence Andhra elite will usurp job and other opportunities in the united Andhra Pradesh. Such reasons continued to haunt Telengana people and they intensified their agitation for separate Telegana state since long. Eminent Columnist Jayati Ghosh has written in The Guardian, "The concern of the Telagana people have indeed been justified but the Telagana is by no means the part of the state that is struggling most—that dubious privilege rests with Rayalaseema region and some northern districts. The state capital—Hyderabad, which is emerging as modern metropolis, lies squarely within the region. While it is true, that locals have fewer of the coveted jobs in Hyderabad, in most other respects it is hard to make much of a case for economic discrimination of the region . . . ."

". . . . but the sense of injustice has remained to some extent, and has been periodically fed by political forces. The Telegana Rashtra Samithi Party was formed in 2001 when some leaders split from the Telgu Desam party to focus on the one demand. Since the TRS has been in alliance with the Congress party at the national level, the Congress in turn has blown hot and cold on this issue. The first United Progressive Alliance (UPA) government promised Telegana statehood but did not deliver. Many hunger strike and riots there, it seemed that this on-again-off-again state of affairs would continue, possibly indefinitely, comments Jayati.

But in the changed political scenario Congress led UPA government, in the recent past, started giving new thinking and gave go ahead signal for creation of Telagana state. Political calculation seems favourably to Congress in dividing Andhra Pradesh. The Congress party has currently 35 Lok Sabha seats from united Andhara Pradesh, thanks to charismatic leader but corrupt local leader late Y S Rajshekhar Reddy, who had later started behaving like feudal lord in the state. Realising its mistakes in giving long rope to late Reddy, the Congress started cutting to size his son and he is prison on various charges of corruption despite the facts that Reddy's son has huge mass following. Congress must have thought that the party will be routed in Andhara region because of late Reddy's influence—hence it created a new state of Telegana for rooting up the Congress in Telegana region.

Not only creation of Telegana, many states including Punjab, Haryana, Karnataka, Himachal Pradesh, Maharshtra, Uttarakhand, Jharkhand, and many eastern states were created on ethnic and languages formula as well as political consideration. Master Tara Singh of united Akali dal fought for creation of separate Punjab on language formula by separating Haryana and Himachal Pradesh and he succeeded in 1950s. Karnataka had also been created on language basis by carving out from the then Madras state, now Tamil Nadu. Likewise, Gujarat was created from taking away territory from old Maharshtra state. Even today there is fight for Chandihgarh for respective capital town between Haryana and Punjab. However, Chandigarh is governed as union territory. Such fight is bound to creep up over location of Hyderabad as joint capital of both proposed Telegana and Andhra Pradesh. Both the regions are harping for their respectve capital—Hyderabad. It will be appropriate for Hyderabad as a suitable capital site for Telagana because entire areas of proposed areas of new state are situated in and around Hyderabad. All round development of Hyderabad has become bone of contention for Andhra Pradesh and Telagana for their capital—ultimately a plan has been presently thought out for location of capital of both states at Hyderabad. And later, there is proposal to declare Hyderabad as union territory.

How the political considerations take place in creating new states? The best example is the creation of Jharkhand, which even after huge natural resources and small in size, is going down to the drains because of rampant corruption and instability. Originally, there was plan to create Jharkhand state following bifurcating tribal population as well as forest and mineral resources, by merging tribal-dominated areas from West Bengal and Odisha. The agitation for Jarkhand state by tribal population and their political wings were for amalgamating tribal areas of Odisha, West Bengal and Bihar for new Jharkhand state. But both Odisha and West Bengal government declined to part away their areas from their respective sides. And axe failed on joint Bihar, thanks rto weak political, leadership of the then chief minister of joint Bihar Laloo Prasad Yadav and his hunch that he will not remain chief minister if Jharkhand and Bihar areas remain united because BJP had upper hand in the number games. And Laloo added fuel to the fire and at a great loss, Bihar was divided.

During the NDA government of Atal Behari Vajpayee, a Jharkhand state was created only bifurcating parts of tribal dominated areas as well as mines, forest and mineral resources on political consideration because BJP had largest number of seats in Bihar assembly from tribal belt of Jharkhand. Bihar was left a poverty-ridden state because of weak leadership. Likewise, Uttar Pradesh was also divided at that time and a new state of Uttarakhand was created—here again the BJP had majority support in the areas. And both state—Jharkhand and Uttarakhand continued to be worse-governed states in the country because of instablity as well as immature leadership in both states. Uttarakhand, has been virtually perished in recent past because of unplanned decision on development and Jharkhand because inefficiency of political leadership and corrupt practices by all hues of politicians. People of both the states are languishing with no development in their economy at the sight.

It is said that creation of new states without any serious thoughts open Pandora's Box in India! Just with the announcements of creation of Telagana state, people of other parts of the country—Uttar Pradesh, Maharashtra, Assam, West Bengal etc have opened new agitation fronts for creation of new states by bifurcating Maharashtra, Uttar Pradesh, Assam, and West Bengal. Smart and concentrated agitations are going on in these states for harping for new states in their respective zones. The people of Darjeeling have started agitation for Gorakhaland, people of Assam for Bodoland, Maharashtra for Viudarbha, Uttar Pradesh for Harit Kranti, Purvanchal and also two other tiny states by bifurcating the present Uttar Pradesh.

All these agitation are getting momentum in the respective states by the regional separatists across the country and the Manmohan Singh government keeping mum over the issue. Property worth crores of rupees have been destroyed in the ongoing agitation in Assam, West Bengal, Maharashtra, Uttar Pradesh besides killing of hundreds of people in agitation in recent past.

Although, I do share the views that present states must be reorganised but not on this fashion, SRC must be revived for taking rationale decision in reorganising states as envisaged in the Constitution. Some academician have expressed their views that creation of new states will balk anise the India, some say smaller states should be created for good governance inclusively While justifying the creation of smaller states in India some of us have given examples of USA where there are as many as over 42 states and that country is doing well in all respects. China is also smaller in areas in comparison with USA. Similarly, some have cited the examples of China also, which have 34 provinces including municipalities, autonomous regions and two special administrative areas They must know that USA has vast areas (four times more) in comparison to India—the USA has land mass of 9629091 square km and 3717813 square miles where as India has areas of 3166414 square kms and 1222559 square miles. Like wise, China has 9706961 areas in square km and 3747879 square miles. Population of USA is 316418000, which comes to 4.45 percent of world population while India's population is 1232320000, about 17.3 percent population of the world, and China's population is 1359250000, about 19 percent population of the world. Amid these vast areas and population both USA and China time to time reorganise their states for good governance and development following the recommendations of legally constituted committees for the purpose. Jayato Ghosh has said, "Some argue that this is fine, because smaller states are easy to govern. And there may well be a case for another SRC to look into all of these issues. But the recent history of newly formed states such as Jharkhand does not suggest that things are always better in smaller states. What is clear is that created the Congress party, in its push for some immediate political benefit, has let the genie pout of the bottle—with very uncertain consequences. One again, we are reminded that we need to be careful what we wish for."

In India politicians must not take decisions on whims and dictatorial manner for the good of the country. There must be rationality in any decisions the governments takes!

A WOMAN DIES EVERY TWO HOURS IN INDIA BECAUSE OF ABORTION: INDIA SPENDS ONLY 3-9 PC ON HEALTH OF TOTAL GDP!

Saturday, 27 July 2013

NOTABLY, India has many wonders—evil wonders in malnutrition, poverty, illiteracy, health, education etc, what not, everythings! Politicians and Planning Commission are playing cruel jokes with poverty and poor in India. Instead identifying poverty and poor, who, in my opinion, constitute over 73 percent in India, by an independent and constitutional commission on the patters of the Election Commission of India (ECI), the union government is, sadly, banking on the data provided on poverty and poor by the so called economists and the Planning Commission, which have been misleading not only the union government but public also.

In this essay, I want to conststrate, one of the biggest 'wonder evil 'about women and their death from an unsafe abortion in the country and to some extend global scenario on this score. This essay has been based on the report of World Population Day, concluded recently. Each year 19 million to 20 million women risk their lives, globally, while undergoing unsafe abortions, conducted in unsanitary condition by unqualified practitioners or practitioners, who resort to traditional but rudimentary means. To substantiate the facts Dr Gilda Sedgh of the Guttmacher Institute, a U S sexual- and reproductive-health-and-advocacy centre, believes that "about half of all abortions world-wide are unsafe"—an appalling number when one considers that abortions are simple procedures when done correctly. Today, overcrowded planet of some 7.1 billion people marks World Population Day, and with an ever growing number of teenagers giving birth, the United Nations Organisation (UNO) has decided that the focus of this World Population Day will be adolescent pregnancy. Currently, highest concentration of young people is

113

found in India. With an average age of just 29, the country is home to 300 million people below the age of 25. Come 2028, it will also be world's most populous nation. For these reasons, there is need to highlight the state of sexual and reproductive health and rights in India!

In India, the problem of unsafe abortions is especially acute. There were 620,472 reported abortions in 2012; experts say the true number of abortions performed in the country could be as high as seven millions, with two-thirds of them taking place outside authorised health facilities. Not all of these are pregnancies out of wedlock. Many unsafe abortions are performed on married women unable to obtain contraception and unable to travel to a registered clinic, who for economic or personal reasons do not wish to have another child.

Notably, a woman in India dies every two hours because an abortion goes wrong. That seems like an extraordinary number until one visits the sort of locations where abortions take place—where it can be seen that possibility for some thing to go wrong is high indeed. India's expenditure on health care is only 3.9 percent of its gross domestic products, strangely, putting at par with Gabon or the Central African Republic. Rural government clinics are often nothing more that skeletal brick structures with tin roofs or no roofs and virtually no electricity supply. Women lie on old gurneys or beds if one is available, just so often, they bed down in dark rooms on mud floors scattered with bloody dressings. Less than 20 percent of these centres provide legitimate abortion facilities, compelling many rural women to seek alternative.

Because of demure saris and lashings of the Hindu religion, many have formed an impression of Indians as a sexually modest bunch. Even the country's most famous sexual text, THE KAMSUTRA, comes with singularly unsexy injunctions to self-improvement, portraying sex as means of spiritual enlightenment rather than physical gratification. But the country that has been in the thores of a development boom, social change has been exponential and attitudes to sex have been no exception—particularly among young. Three years ago, Tehelka, an Indian news website that specialises in exposes, found that "age was more than just a number to several young people—it is ticking stopwatch in the race to outdo each other in the bedroom". Reporters conducted interviews across urban India and "met terrifying sexual creatures of all shapes and size" from nine-year-olds who distributed porn in class to teenagers. Who had made sex tapes? Unwanted pregnancies are, meanwhile, on the rise, so are sexually transmitted infections (STIS).

A hospital based study done over a five year period and published last year reported a resurgence of syphilis in India and rising number of STIs. The study noted that all the evidence pointed towards a change in sexual practices. According eye-witnesses account teen young, in bold manner, are often found in medicine shops, openly asking for sex-simulating medicines like Viagra instead of contraceptives. Such scenes are variably seen in Patna town areas where the sales of sex simulating medicines demand have risen alarmingly high.

It must be noted that, there are barely any resources for young people curious about sex. Manak Matiyani of MUST BOL, Delhi-based group that works with youth on gender issues, is of the opinion, "sexuality is some thing a lot of young people want to learn about, not only because it is new but also because it is some thing that is talked about." Only 15 percent of men and women between the age of 15 and 24 reported receiving any sex education, according to another study on Indian youths a few years ago. Alarmingly, only 45 percent of young women and 37 percent of young men were aware of the possibility of pregnancy resulting from first intercourse. "Ignorance of sexual- and reproductive-health issues continues even after marriage" said one government report. More than three quarters of young women and 70 percent of young men "did not know what to expect of married life," the study noted.

More over, sex education came into spotlight after Delhi-gang rape incident in December 2012, when the report of a committee k headed by J S Verma pointed to dire need for greater gender-sensitisation among young in India. Due to lack of sex education are plain from the millions of unsafe abortions performed each year to a skewed gender ratio that sees widespread abortion of females fetuses owing to cultural preferences for boys. The 2011 census in India detected that there were 914 females age six and under for every 1000 males. Even after all these social evils, the politicians, teachers and parents continue to oppose sex education, fearing that such programmes would promote promiscuity and undermine social values. The Indian government is dithering over the matters for over 20 years. It's futile attempt to launch sex education programme, the Adolescent Education Programme (AEP, in 1999, could not take off because experts and policymakers continued to deliberate over which topics to include and whether these would offend any prevailing inhibitions in society. And the dilly-dilling attitude of the government continued unabated. A consultant on sexual education says "conservatives found that the course material allegedly featured offensives illustrations and class rooms exercise." The fear was that the programme "would ignite the curiosity of students about experimentation, resulting in teenage pregnancies and promiscuity. By 2007, many largest states of India including Gujarat, Madhjya Pradesh, Maharashtra, Karnataka, Rajasthan, Keral, Chhatishgarh and Goa had banned sex education and federal government dropped its support for it as well. A report of the Indian government committee came to the startling conclusion that "there should not be sex education in schools." and that previous attempts at such education had been "quite reprehensible in view of our sociocultural ethos." Indian youths, the committee, decided, needed nothing more than bracing doses of traditional medicines and yoga to cool their ardour.

Experts, however, say there are two possibilities for India. One is establishment of a sex-education programme that 'acknowldges the changing sexual landscape, parents accept that their children must know about safe sex, even if they are unwilling to communicate with their children on the subject and supplies and information are available to young people', says Dr Shireen Jajeeboy of the Population Council of India. The second option is maintaining status quo. Rates of infection will jump and unintended pregnancies will rise, Jajeeboy adds.

Notably, India already has the dubious distinction of being global leader in teenage pregnancy. Around the world, there are some 16 million girls under the age of 18 years giving birth every year. Almost four million of them are in India. Granted, adolescent pregnancies in India are culturally complicated, given the incidence of child marriage and therefore, early child bearing. study found that approximately 1 in 615 to 19-year-olds, "have already given birth or become pregnant, and about half of India's total fertility rate was attributable to those aged 15-24. "Nonetheless, early child bearing poses significant b health risks for mother and baby—young teenage bodies are not mature enough to bear children—and maternal mortality rates are high. But facts are facts—Reflecting a trend seen all over urban India, the city of Gurgaon, near Delhi is seeing a marked rise in cases of adolescent girls seeking abortions at government hospitals but then vanishing when asked to return with parents. These are the young women who end up in the back street clinics.

Public health experts promote contraception as protection against unintended pregnancies but it is not easily available in rural areas and where it is available, in the towns and cities, young Indians are either of embarrassed to ask for for it or do not know what to ask for. Because of lack of sex education ignorance is rife. A majority of young Indians do not use use protection during their first sexual encounter. At the same time as with any country that is developing rapidly, sexual patterns are changing and premartial sexual activity is increasing globally, women are not getting the contraceptives they need. The number of women with an unmet need for family planning is projected to grow from 900 million three years ago to 962 million by 2015. This increase, researchers, has noted will be driven by most developing countries. Studies have shown that 82 percent of unintended pregnancies in developing countries occur among women "who have an unmet need for modern contraceptives." Still there are some glimmers of hopes. a study last year estimated that 272,000 maternal facilities around the world prevented by contraceptive use and that India accounted for nearly a third of averted deaths. But the fact remains that India is home to the most maternal deaths in the world and that 50 percent of those fatalities are in the 19 to 24-year-old age group. With these sorts of numbers, sex education, contraception and greater health-care spending are simply desirable!

SOURCES: THE WHO, THE WORLD POPULATION DAY, UNO, THE ASIAN TIMES, GOVT OF INDIA HEALTH MINISTRY (Detailed facts on all these websites and their achieves)

'"MID-DAY MEAL OR MID-DAY DEATH" SCHEME: CHAPRA TRAGEDY RESULTS OF MISMANAGEMENT AND CORRUPTION!

Saturday, 20 July 2013

Very sad! It is "MID-DAY-MEAL (MDM)" or MID-DAY DEATH (MDD)" in Bihar. In many places in the country, particularly in Bihar, the MDM has turned into MDD because of corruption and mismanagement of the affairs of the scheme by respective state governments, which are implementing authorities. In mismanaging the affairs and corrupt practices in its implementation, less said is better in Bihar. DEATHS of 27 school children in village Gandaman in Saran district, just a neighbourhood village where the first President of India Dr Rajendra Prasad was born and brought up, of Bihar in India after eating poisonous food is worse tragedy and has turned into a full blown national crisis. The so called MDM, a policy conceived and launched by India government throughout the country to improve nutrition and school attendance. Recent outrageous deaths in Bihar have caused global outrage. Riots had broken out in entire Chapra district with distraught parents and relatives wrecking school kitchen and torching vehicles while the Nitish Kumar government in Bihar tried to insinuate that it is a political conspiracy to destabilise them in election year. Postmortems indicate the cause may have been adulterated cooking oil. This is terrible tragedy—awful, avoidable, unconscionable.

Instead of stern measures to streamline the scheme, the Bihar government continued in blame game—while its principal secretary Amarjeet Sinha shamelessly declining the statement of the union HRD minister M M Pallam Raju that Bihar government has been alerted Bihar government about irregularities like unhygienic food in MDM scheme specially in 12 districts of Bihar including Saran because of certain shortcomings in the implementation of the programme. Amarjeet Sinha, however, said, "For now this is confirmed that the oil used to prepare the meal was the major and immediate reasons behind the tragedy." The height of shamelessly shameness on the part of Sinha is that he had publicly told that no advisory had been received by Bihar government— now the question arises—who is liar Union HRD minister or Principal Secretary of Bihar's HRD department? Not only that Bihar's HRD MInister P K Sahi, who is protege of Nitish Kumar, is throwing blame game on opposition parties including BJP and RJD by declaring openly that there is political conspiracy behind the tragedy to defame CM Nitish Kumar. The inefficiency and callousness of Bihar government could also be gaused with a recent report that the Bihar government had returned to the Centre Rs 462.78 crore meant to built mid-day meal kitchen and buy utensils to serve cooked meals because Bihar government failed miserably to float tenders for the purpose, resulting into meal is prepared in open sky or in dingy rooms of respective schools.

There are diverse opinions about the utility of the MDM scheme because of harsh reality is that food provided to children all over the country, particularly Bihar, is often substandard and sometimes not even fit for human consumption. Snakes and worms have been reported in Mid-Day Meals and adulteration has been said to take place as well. A report has said that at another place in Bihar 15 children had been reported ill, after a lizard was suspected to have fallen into their lunch, the next day of Chapra tragedy such reports have become very common in many states of the country. In Maharashtra, 31 children contracted gastroenteritis after consuming their school meals. A few days back, such report has also come from Tamil Nadu. One section of the society were of the opinion that MDM scheme should be delinked from the school management and may be handled by a separate government agency while another sections are of the views that result of MDM scheme results are not very encouraging—hence an alternative arrangements must be made to save the children from malnutrition as well as to encourage poor children for education!

The Mid-Day Meal Scheme was introduced to ensure that a hot cooked lunch would be provided to government supported schools. The meal was meant to contain at least 300 calories per child, with 8-10 gram of proteins. The policy was initially welcomed as it would mean that the children, many of whom come from the most vulnerable sections of society, might attend school because of it and also receive some much-needed nutrition. It is estimated that approximately 100 million school children are fed through the scheme. But, unfortunately, the leakage and corruption in the system are said to be equally as large.

According to various studies in selected districts of Bihar and Uttar Pradesh; only 75 percent of the requisitioned food is usually doled out to the children. There are also issues of cleanliness. Often the cook hired for a task is some time not paid for months at a time. Even in particularly impoverished areas of Mumbai, school teachers have found that the children resist eating the food, because it is poor in quality.

A few years back, aware of the constant complaints, the central government had thought of replacing the hot food with prepackaged meals. But there have been instances when even biscuits given to the children have made them dangerously ill. Despite all of this, for some peculiar reasons, the government has not taken into account the views of the scheme's stakeholders: the children who are recipients of all this deadly state-run charity.

The recent MDM scheme tragedy in Saran district of Bihar has peculiar story. Children started complaining of stomach pain while eating food, the school headmistress allegedly snubbed them and rather forced them to finish the meal. She is now evading arrest along with her husband. Notably death figures rose by mani-fold because there were no medical facilities in and around the school on Chapra. Many children died on the way to Chapra Sadar hospital and Patna Medical College Hospital in the state headquarters in Patna. In Bihar medical system is also in disarray, you will find seldom hospitals in rural areas of Bihar and doctors also, thanks to lackadaisical approach of Nitish government!

Nitish Kumar, who claims good governance in Bihar and getting laurels throughout the country, is yet to speak about the gravity of tragedy. Kumar, however, announced freebies of a sum Rs two lakh each for every family of a child that has died, the facts remain that these underprivileged children have become victims of these free school meals, rather than beneficiaries.

More over the problem in India is that both in acquisition as well as in the delivery mechanism corruption is rampant. Most of the food is acquired from the Food Corporation of India, also in spotlight for its less than satisfactory role in in the Public Distribution System, which provides rationed grains at subsidised rates to those who live below poverty line. Now the government is getting ready to launch food security A ordinance, w under which over 67 percent of the population will receive food every month at highly subsidised rates, it is not sure how corruption free manner it will ever ensure a corruption free system where the food actually reaches to the targeted people who need it most. Can the government ensure food's quality? Even in Mid-DAy meal, there are little evidences to suggest that school children are actually getting any nutritional value from it all!

But another set of an essay in The Guardian, written by Abhijeet Singh, Research officer, Oxford University, Department of International Development and a doctoral student of Economics, has different opinion about MDM in India. He says Chapra tragedy is urgent topic for soul searching about neglect of basic services in India, particularly among political classes. Singh is opposite to the opinion of Kishwat Desai's essay on Chapra tragedy and unsuccessful handling of MDM scheme in India, particularly in Bihar! Singh's essay, particularly the tragedy in Bihar and scheme's success, gives possitive impression. For this assertion, Singh has quoted Farzana Afridi of Indian Statistical Instituter's. There have been large benefits of the scheme. In a paper in the Journal of Development Economics, She says, "at the cost of between 1.44 cents to 3.04 cents per child per school day the scheme improved nutritional intakes by reducing the daily protein deficiency of a primary school student by 100 percent, the calorie deficiency by almost 30 percent and the daily iron deficiency by nearly 10 percent."

In a paper in the Journal of Development Studies, she found that attendance rate of girls in grade one rose by 12 percentage points because of meals. Rashri Jayaraman and Dora Simroth at the European School of Management and Technology in Berlin said enrolment went up substantially as a result of the introduction of school meals, similar to evidence reported in other studies. In yet another recent paper co-authored with Stefan Dercon and Albert Park, forthcoming in Economic Development and Cultural Change in the Oxford university Singh found that children whose households experienced droughts when they were very young (under two years) had higher levels of malnourishment but if they had since been enrolled in a government school, the meals compensated for the early nutritional deficits— put simply, there was no physical evidence of worse nutrition by the time they were aged five to six years compared with children who had not experienced drought. In a country with high child nutrition and with agriculture often at the mercy of the monsoon rains, these are encouraging results there are other effects possible that are less easily quantified: on every school day, million of school children, from different castes and religions, eat meals from the same pot together—in a socially stratified society, this cannot be seen as being anything but good for social equality. Mid-day meals, which reach about 120 million children every school day, are probably the most successful of all interventions in education that the Indian state delivered in the past decades. On any school day, a quarter of teachers are absent from government schools, only 45 percent of those in school are teaching but in 87 percent of schools, a hot meal is served, Singh commented.

The Chapra tragedy has given signal to various state governments, particularly Bihar government as well as Union HRD ministry and govt for better monitoring and control to save the noble MDM scheme from mismanagement and corruption!

"USA, A CRIMINAL THUGS AND PAKISTAN, A FAILED STATE", SAYS JUDICIAL PANEL ON ABBOTTABAD RAID AND KILLING OF OSAMA BIN LADEN.

Saturday, 13 July 2013

IS THE UNITED STATES OF AMERICA act like "criminal thugs? Is PAKISTAN withering away as "dyfunctionmal institutions"? Both these big questions have been proved beyond doubt with the leaking of the report of the Abbottabad commission, probing the circumstances leading to the USA's NAVY SEAL raids in killing the world's most wanted man—OSAMA bin Laden—to al-Jazeera. While both Pakistan and USA have been facing much more criticism over the report of the commission, headed by a judge of the Pakistan Supreme Court and comprising three military and police officers thievery in raiding Pakistan territory without any information to the Pakistan government by American raiders and Pakistan government's notorious military intelligence apparatus—ISI—and police and civil machinery's failure to track the dreaded bin Laden, who was living in the military areas of Abbottabad for over six years. The commission was entrusted to trace the lapses of the Pakistan government as well as USA's unwanted raid of the sovereignty of the Pakistan by raiding and killing bin Laden in Abbottabad on the night of May 02, 2011.

Before I refer in detail the report of the commission, I must mention that I had written an essay on my blog—JINX of Osama bin Laden and Saddam Hussein continues to haunt America and Europe!—August 28, 2012 and another one—Why This Hate Campaign against Muslims of the World—October 16, 2012—www.kksingh1.blogspot.com And also some backgrounders about bin Lasen. Osama bin Laden, the man who has struck terror in the hearts of Americans, the man, who has dared to take on the might of the greatest super power, continued to remain a mystery and enigma for the world today!

Osama bin Laden was a dissident Saudi businessman, who had amassed a fortune in oil and construction business with his family fortune estimated at $ 5 billion during early 1990s of which he has access to an estimated $300 million. A graduate of Riyadh University's management economics department, he saw himself as a model businessman. But later on his products had been terrorists around the globe. Till his killing bin Laden enjoyed the unenviable position of being hated by one part of the globe and at the same time being worshipped by another part. Osama, who was once referred as "KING OF TERROR", had once declared jihad—a holy war—on America! His extensive Al-Qaeda network had spread over 35 countries in the world.

On September 11, 2001, terrorists dealt a devastating blow to the United States of America. They hijacked four air crafts of the United and American Airlines at roughly the same time. Two of them were used to hit and destroy the twin towers of the World Trade Centre in New York, the symbol of American capitalist power. One was used to hit and destroy a third of the Pentagon in Washington, a symbol of America military might. The fourth one apparently aimed At the White House or the Capitol, symbols of American democracy, failed to reach their destination and crashed in a field in Pennsylvania. It was said that such attacks were worse in the century and greater blow than the Japanese attack on Pearl Harbour. All suicide attackers, who carried the hijacking and attack, were trained as pilots in aviation schools within the US so that they could take over from pilots of the air crafts, which they had hijacked under the precision and planning of bin Laden!

The then President of USA George W. Bush, who had vowed to smoke out Osama and his Al-Queda group and get them dead and alive, could not succeed but his successor Obama not only traced out the hide-out of Osama in Pakistan but raided and killed him and his body was cremated at an unknown destination in the sea. Today in the world, Osama had been killed but his Al-queda networks of terrorists are still spreading terror in many parts of the globe. Laden had publicly issued his "Declaration of war" against the United States in August 1996. Osama bin Laden was one of the 53 children of the Saudi construction magnate Muhammad Awad Bin Laden. His mother was reportedly a Palestinian and the least favoured of his father's ten wives. After his holy war against Soviets in 1979 in Afghanistan on the secret support of the USA, It is said that USA had spent $500 million per year to arm and train the impoverished and outgunned mujaheddin guerrillas of Laden to fight the Soviet Union.

Finally, Laden was shifted to safe haven in Afghanistan by Talibans. From there Bin Laden had spread his extensive international network to effective use. Bin Laden told Qatar's Al-Jageera television in a rare interview in 1999 that even when he was on the same side as the United States—fighting the Soviets in Afghanistan—he always "hated the Americans because they are against Muslims . . . . We did not want the US support in Afghanistan, but we just happened to be fighting the same enemy." Following intensive hunts of Laden in mountain range of Afghanistan, Laden crossed to Pakistan border and aided and abetted by Pakistan military, secret service—ISI—and Pakistan government, Laden built a house in Abbottabad and started living there as an ordinary fellow but actively working through couriers.

Now the report of Abbattobad commission, which made startling revelation about the dreaded terrorist and connivance of Pakistan authorities. The 336-page report has said, "it is glaring testimony to the collective incompetence and negligence, at the very least, of the security and intelligence community in the Abbottabad areas", which criticised the Pakistan's military spy agency, the Inter-Service 1 Intelligence directorate (ISI) for having proximity "closed the book" on Bin Laden in 2005. Nor does the 336 page report rule out the possibility of involvement by rogue Pakistan's intelligence agency officers, who have been accused of deliberately shielding bin Laden by some commentators. Given the length of stay and the changes of residence of (Bin Laden) and his family in Pakistan . . . . the possibility of some some such direct or indirect and "plausible deniable" support cannot be ruled out, at least, at some level outside formal structures of the intelligence establishments.". It warns that the influence of radical Islamists inside the armed forces had been "underestimated by senior military officials whom the commission met."

Notably, the report of the commission's documents reflects official fury at the behaviour of the USA. It adds the US "acted like a criminal thug" when it sent the Special Forces or Navy Seal raiding party into Pakistan territory. The report further says, "The incident was a "national tragedy" because of the "illegal manner in which (Bin Laden) was killed along with three Pakistani citizens". It says the operation on May two, 2011 night was an" American act of war against Pakistan", which illustrated the US's "contemptuous disregard of Pakistan sovereignty, independence and territorial integrity in the arrogant certainty of its unmatched military might".

In addition to its scorching criticism of Pakistan institutions, the documents also points out begun soon after dramatic US raid, the judge-led enquiry by the Abbottabad commission heard testimony from some of the country's most important players including the ISI chief, Ahmad Suja Pasha (now retired), who shared much of the authors' despair about Pakistan, warning that "it is failing state". In remarks that will be seized on by critics of the CIA's use of drone strikes against suspected militants inside Pakistan, Pasha admitted to a "political understanding" on the issue between Islamabad and the USA—something Pakistan has officially denied. Pasha said there were no written agreements, and that Pakistan did subsequently attempt to stop drone attacks but added that "it was easier to say no to them at the beginning". Pasha was very much critical of the quality of Pakistan's civilian leadership, accusing his nominal boss, the defence minister, of failing to have read "the basic documents concerning defence policy there was simply no culture of reading among the political leadership and thinking process was non-existence."

The report also includes much more criticism of the US, in particular its CIA for its failure to share intelligence fully with ISI. At one point of time, the CIA gave Pakistan the phone numbers to monitor that would ultimately help identify Laden's personal courier—the all important lead that eventually brought the manhunt to al-Qaida chief's Abbottabad home. The CIA never explained the significance of the phone numbers and the ISI failed to properly monitor them. The Guardian, quoting al-Jageeera, said that but in striking echo of US unwillingness to share intelligence with its Pakistani partners, Pasha also said the ISI was reluctant to work with Pakistan's own law enforcement organisations because "there were too many instances where information shared with the police had been compromised". It may be mentioned here that with passing of time Pasha has become strong defender of Laden and has said to a TV channel that he was hero of Islam.

The report suggests that his evidence highlights the ISI's distrust of and anger at the CIA, which Pasha claimed deliberately, prevented Pakistan from claiming the glory for finding Laden, which he said would have improved Pakistan's international reputation. The "main agenda CIA was to have the ISI declared a terrorist organisation" he is quoted as saying. Pasha reports the words of a US spy: "you are so cheap . . . . we can buy with a visa, with a visit to the USA, even with a dinner . . . . we can but anyone."

The report asks whether the ISI had been compromised by CIA spies. One lieutenant colonel that "disappeared" with his family the day after the Abbottabad raid a profile that "matched that of a likely CIA recruits." The document repeatedly returns to what it describes as "government implosion syndrome" to explain the failure of any institution to investigate Laden's unusual hideout. The report further says, "how the entire neighbourhood, local officials, police and security and intelligence officials all missed the size, the strange shape, the barbed wire, the lack of cars and visitors . . . . over a period of nearly six years beggars belief."

Significantly, the report notes in disgust that the house was even declared uninhabited in an official survey of the area even though 26 people were living there at a time. The documents also gives fascinating glimpse into the day-to-day life of Laden: according to account given to the Abbottbad judicial panel by his wives, he wore a wide-brimmed cowboy hat to avoid detection from spy satellites above, liked to have an apple and a bit of chocolate to perk himself up when he was feeling weak, and encouraged his grandchildren to compete over who could tend best vegetable patch. The children one of Laden's trusted Pakistan couriers knew him as "Miskeen kaka" or "poor uncle"—after one asked why the tall Arab never went out on shopping expedition, the child was told he was too poor to buy anything. In tantalising moment when the car of Laden was riding in was stopped by police in the picturesque region of Swat. The policemen were not quick-witted enough to spot the then clean shaven bin Laden and the group were allowed to pass.

Moreover the report further point out that Laden must have required a support network "that could not possibly his couriers, security guards have been confined to the two Pasthun brothers, who worked as his couriers, security guards and general factotums." While expressing concern over non-existence of effective intelligence agency to contact, infiltrate or co-opt them and to develop a whole caseload of information, the report voices shock over US helicopters carrying members of Navy Seal team of six were not spotted as they swooped in over Abbatobad on May two night. A lack of operational radar meant the Pakistani Air Force only became aware of the attack from media reports after it was over! Thus report concluded that Pakistan failed to detect Osama bin Laden during six years he hid in Abbottobad because of the "collective incompetence and negligence of the country's intelligence and security forces."

SOURCES: al-Jazeera news website, a book-Osama bin Laden: King of Terror or Saviour of Islam? written by Luis S R Vas, The Guardian, The Time weekly websites.

GAYA TEROR ATTACK MAY BE RESULT OF ATROCITY ON MUSLIMS BY BUDDHIST MONKS?

Tuesday, 9 July 2013

Today the entire globe is shamed! There have been series of bomb explosion to damage the Boddh-Gaya or Gaya, Buddhist monasteries or Gaya in Bihar in India, about over 100 kms from the Bihar's capital—Patna, where the incarnation of the Almighty, Siddhartha Gautam, the Buddha, 2500 years ago got enlightenment under a "Boddhi (PEEPAL) tree to spread compassion, peace, kindness, non-violence throughout the planet. There are many theories of attacking the Buddhist monasteries by the "terrorists or extremists or militants"? But could we not call it a bloat on the man-kind?

Siddharth Gautam would have never imagined that his "apostle of peace" will turn into violence instead of peace and compassion. Perhaps because of his such hunch, Gautam after getting "enlightenment", had gone to Sarnath, in neighbouring Uttar Pradesh, to begin his pious journey of preaching his message of peace and compassion to the world. Boddh-Gaya or Gaya, which has historical importance since ancient days, and, has been always considered a region of feudalism and violence since the early days of the ancient period. It is based in MAGADH zone where only ruthless kings and kingdoms existed. The notoriety of Magadh is also described in famous, well-known and mythological book—Shree Ramcharit Manas, written by TULSI DAS, while depicting the noble character of 'RAM, and his "RAM-RAJYA". A verse in the book says, "Lagahi kumukh bachan subh kaise, Magahn (Magadh) nawadik tirath jaise; Ramanhi matu bachan sab bhaye, jimi surasari gat salil suhaye—(Step motherof Ram-Kakeiye's speaking resembles like notorious place Magadh where sacred 'Gaya' exists). Gaya or Boddh-Gaya has at least two golden feathers in its cap in ancient and historical parameters! Apart from Buddhist shrines, the

Boddh=Gaya is also famous and well-known for the "VISHNUPAD TEMPLE" for Hindu worship. This temple is visited by Hindu pilgrims for the performances of 'pindaddan' rituals for the final salvation of their ancestors' souls. Hindu during the rainy season, well before Durga puja, comes from different parts of the world for this performance.

Terror attacks and serial bomb blasts, although, could not make major damages to the Buddhist shrines of thousands years-old Boddhi (Peepal tree) under which Buddha got enlightenment, but it has sent strong signals for the followers of Buddhist religion! Again, I must put it probably, the recent happenings of damage of Buddhist shrines in Afghanistan and Middle east by Muslims as well as Buddhist monks, spreading terror and atrocity against Muslims in Burma (now Myanmar), Thailand, Sri Lanka and other Buddhist-dominated countries in Asia have been root cause of terror attacks and serial bomb blasts. Instead of spreading peace, compassion, non-violence, the Buddhist monks are indulging in violence and terror activities Forgetting Gautam Buddha's preachings in Gaya or Boddh-Gaya in Buddhist shrine a few days back. I must point out series of facts on Buddhist monks' terror attacks against Muslims—(MY blog essays— Dalai Lama has failed failed Buddha's teachings of compassion, peace, happiness by encouraging self-immolation in Tibet—May 25, 2013, Why this hate campaign against Muslim of the world?—October 16, 2012; Buddhism:What a wonderful religion in the world!—July 06, 2012—www.kksingh1.blogspot.com). Pundit Jawahar Lal Nehru, in his Discovery of India, has written, "Buddhism has started at the time of soul and spiritual revival in INdia—it infused the breath of new life . . . ."

A few months back, THE TIME INTERNATIONAL EDITION, had carried cover story on The Face of Buddhist Terror, depicting that straying from the middle way, extremist Buddhist Monks target religious minorities! It is proper to highlight the Buddhist terror tactics against Muslims, which might have resulted into terror attacks and serial bomb blasts in Bodh-Gaya, one of the most important places in the globe for the followers of Buddhism.

Buddhist monks' shaven heads and richly hued monastic robes; the swirls of incense; the pure expressions of devotees to a religion whose first precept is "do not kill" are being marred by radical strains that marries spirituality with ethnic chauvinism. In Buddhist-majority Burma, where communal clashes have proliferated over the past year, scores of Muslims have been killed by Buddhist mobs, while in Thailand and Sri Lanka, the fabric binding temple and state is being stitched ever tighter.

The godfather of radical Buddhism is a monk named U Wirathu, a slight presence with an out sized message of hate, who has taken the title of "Burmese bin Laden" around Mandalay in central Burma, as he preached his loathing of the country;s Muslims minority to school children and housewives alike. In March, tension detonated in the town of Meikhtila where communal violence ended dozen of lives, mostly Muslims. Entire Muslim quarters were razed by Buddhists hordes. Even today, anxiety churns. Muslim Rohingyas in Rakhine state in the west of Burma were subjected, once again, to atrocities by Buddhists and security forces. Last year alone, at least 192 people were killed and 1, 40,000 rendered homeless. An estimated 8, 00,000 Rohingyas live in Rakhine state. Many of them remain in camps which they are not allowed to leave. Burma's heroic freedom fighter for freedom Aung San Sau Kyi, who also appears to tell some thing about the atrocity of Buddhist monks on Muslims, simply said she was for the "rule of law", that is she is for virtue and against sin. However, she criticised the district government's policy to limit Rohingya families to two children—"this is against human right".

In southern Thailand, which was once united as a Muslims Malay sultanate, monks count on solders to shield them from harm. A separatist insurgency has claimed around 5,000 lives since 2004 and while more Muslims have died, it is Buddhists who feel particularly vulnerable as targets of shadowy militants. Wirathu, who is an abbot in the New Maesoeeyin in monastery, leading over 60 monks and having influence over 2,500 residing there, the Burmese bin Laden begins his sermon, inciting monks for communal clashes. According to the THE TIMES International cover story on Buddhist terror, in the reckoning of international extremism—Hindu nationalists, Muslim militants, fundamentalists Christians, ultra-Orthodox Jews—Buddhism has largely escaped trial. To much of the world, it is synonymous with non-violence and loving kindness, concept propagated by Siddharth Gautam, the Buddha, 2,500 years ago. But like adherents of any religion, Buddhists and their holy men are not immune to politics and on occasion, the lure of sectarian chauvinism . . . ."

When Asia rose up against empire and oppression, Buddhist monks, with their moral command and plentiful numbers, led anti-colonial movements. Some starved themselves for their causes, their sunken flesh and protruding ribs underlining their sacrifices of for the laity. Perhaps most iconic is the image of Thich Quang, a Vietnamese monk sitting in the lotus position, wrapped in flames, as he burned to death in Saigon while protesting the repressive South Vietnamese regime 50 years ago. In 2007, Buddhist monks led a foiled democratic uprising in Burma: image of columns of clerics bearing upturned alms bowls, marching peacefully in protest against the "janata", earned sympathy around the world, if not from the soldiers who slaughtered them. But where social activism end and political militancy begins? Every region can be twisted into destructive forces poisoned by ideas that are antithetical to its foundations. Now it is Buddhism turn!

Over the past year in Buddhist-majority Burma, scores if not hundreds, have been killed in communal clashes, with Muslims suffering the most causality. Burmese monks were seen goading on Buddhist mobs, while some support the authorities of having stoked the violence-a charge the country's new quashi-civilians government denies. In Sri Lanka, where a conservative, pro-Buddhist government reigns, Buddhist nationalist groups are operating with apparent impunity, looting Muslims and Christian establishments and calling for restrictions to be placed on the nine percent of the country that is Muslims. Meanwhile Thailand's deep sea, where a Muslim insurgency has claimed some 5,000 lives since 2004, desperate Buddhist clerics is retreating into their temples with Thai soldiers at their side. Their fear is understandable. But the close relationship between temple and the state ifs further dividing this already anxious region.

As the violence mounts, will Buddhists draw inspiration from their faith's sutras of compassion and peace to counter religious chauvinism? Or will they succumb to the hate speech of radical monks like Burma's Wirathu, who goads his followers to rise up against Islam? The world's judgements await! Apart from that good sense prevails ion Buddhist Guru Dalai Lama to stop encouraging Tibetans for self-immolation to protest Chinese presence in Tibet. Can compassion, non-violence not win Chinese for suitable welfare measures for Tibetans 'And Dalai Lama must initiate process for peaceful dialogues with China?

With these developments, my hunch goes that Gaya terror attack might be result of Muslims terrorists' anger against atrocity on fellow-Muslims by Buddhist monks in different parts of the world!

THREAT TO LIFE ON THE EARTH VIS-A-VIS THE EARTH IS ITSELF THREATENED

Saturday, 6 July 2013

Is life facing real threat on the EARTH? If population level continues to rise at the current rate, our grand children will see the Earth plunged into an unprecedented environmental crisis! This startling fact has come to light in a well-known well-researched book—TEN BILLION, written by the Computational Scientist Stephen Emott. I got a chance to see the book at a glance and complete review of the book in The Guardian. Apart from describing the real facts, prevailing on the Earth, the writer has enumerated various problems, being faced by the people on the globe! Notable among those are climate problems and growing population responsible for large scale of deforestation as well as water crisis.

Earth is home to millions of species. Just one dominates it. Us. Our cleverness, our inventiveness and our activities have modified almost every part of our planet. If fact we are having a profound impact on it. Indeed, our cleverness, our inventiveness and our activities are now the drivers of every global problem we face. And every one of these problems is accelerating. In fact, the writer says, "I believe we can rightly call the situation we are in right now an emergency-an unprecedented planetary emergency. We human emerged as a species about 200,000 years ago; there were one million of us. In geological time, that is really incredibly recently. 1800, just 10,000 years ago, there were one million of us. By 1960, just over 50 years ago, there were three billion of us. There are now over seven billion of us. By 2050, your children's children, will live on a planet with at least nine billion other people. Some time towards the end of this century, there will be at least 10 billion of us. Possibly more." (My Blog essay: "The World as '100'; Christians dominate the globe—Muslims come second—May 30, 2013—www.kksingh1.blogspot.com).

"We got to where we are now through a number of civilisation—and society shaping events, most notably the agricultural revolution, the scientific revolution, the industrial revolution and in the west—the public-health revolution. By 1980, there were five billion of us. By this point initial signs of the consequences of our growth were starting to show. Not the least of these was on water. Our demand for water—not just the water we drank but the water we needed for food production and to make all the stuff we are consuming—was going through the roof. But some thing was starting to happen to water . . . .

In 1984, journalists reported from Ethiopia about a famine of biblical proportions caused by widespread drought. Unusual drought and unusual flooding was increasing everywhere: Australia, Asia, and the US and the Europe. (My blog essay: "Hunger looming large over Globe"—June 19, 2012—www.kksingh1.blogspot.com). Water, a vital resource we had thought as abundant, was now suddenly something that had the potential to be scarce.

GLOBAL WARMING: By 2000 there were six billion of us. It was becoming clear to the world's scientific community that the accumulation of CO_2 methane and other greenhouse gases in the atmosphere—as a result of increasing agriculture, land use and production, processing and transportation of everything we are consuming—was changing the climate. And that as a result, we had a serious problem on our hands: 1998 had been the warmest year on the record. The ten warmest years on record have occurred since 1998 . . . . "We hear the term climate every day, so it is worth thinking about what we actually mean by it. Obviously, climate is not the same as weather. The climate is one of the Earth's fundamental life support system, one that determines whether or not we humans are able to live on this planet. It is generated by four components: the atmosphere (the air we breathe); the hydrosphere (the planet's water); the cryosphere (the ice sheets and glasciries); the biosphere (the planet's plants and animals). By now, our activities had started to modify every one of these components . . . . Our emissions of CO_2 modify our atmosphere. Our increasing water use had started to modify our hdrosphere'. Rising atmospheric and sea-surface temperature had started to modify the cyosphere, most notably in the unexpected shrinking of the Arctic and Greenland ice sheets. Our increasing use of land for agriculture, cities, roads, mining—as well as all the pollution we are creating—had started to modify our biosphere. Or to put it another way: we had started to change our climate . . . . There are now more than seven billion of us on Earth. As our numbers continue to grow, we continue to increase our need for far more water, far more food, far more land, far more transport and far more energy. As a result, we are accelerating the rate at which we are changing our climate. In fact our activities are not only completely interconnected.

CLIMATE PROBLEM: Moreover the emerging climate problem is entirely on different scale. The problem is that we may well be heading towards a number of critical tipping points in the global climate system. There is politically agreed global targets—driven by the Integrated Panel on Climate Change (IPCC)—to limit the global average temperature rise to 2C. The rationale for this target is that a rise above 2C carries a significant risk of catastrophic climate change that would almost certainly lead to irreversible planetary tipping points, caused by events such as melting of the Greenland ice shelf, the release of frozen methane deposits from Arctic tundra or die back of the Amazon. In fact, the two are happening now—at below the 2C threshold.

As for the third, we are not waiting for climate change to do this: we are doing it right now through deforestation. And recent research shows that we look certain to be heading for a larger rise in global average temperatures than 2C—a far larger size. It is now very likely that we are looking at a future global average rise of 4C-wand we cannot rule out a rise of 6C. This will be absolutely catastrophic. It will lead to runaway climate change, capable of tipping the planet into an entirely different state, rapidly. Earth will become a hellhole. In the decades along the way, we will witness unprecedented extremes in weather, fires, floods, heatwaves, loss of crops and forest, water stress and catastrophic sea-level rise. Large part of Africa will become permanent disaster areas. The Amazon could be turned into savannah or even desert and the entire agriculture system will be faced with an unprecedented threat.

More fortunate countries such as the UK, the USA and most of Europe may well look like something approaching militarised countries with heavily defended border controls designed to prevent millions of people from entering, people who are on the move because their own country is no longer habitable or has insufficient water and food or is experiencing conflict over increasingly scarce resources. These people will be climate migrants. The term climate migrants is one we will increasingly to have to get used to. Indeed, anyone who thinks that the emerging global state of affairs does not have great potential for civil and international conflict is deluding themselves. It is coincidence that almost every scientific conference that I go to about climate change now has a new type of attendee: the military.

WATER USE: There are increasing aspects of water use. Hidden water is water used to produce things we consume but typically do not think of as containing water. Such things include chicken, beef, cotton, cars, chocolate and mobile phones. For example: it takes around 3,000 liters of water to produce burger a burger. In 2012 around five billion burgers were consumed in the UK alone. That is 15 trillion liters of waters—on burgers. Just in the UK. Some thing like 14 billion burgers was consumed in the United States in 2012. That is around 42 trillion liters of water. To produce burgers in the US. In one year, it takes around 9,000 liters of water to produce a chicken. In the UK alone we consumed around one billion chickens in 2012. It takes around 27,000 liters of water to produce one kilo gram of chocolate. That is roughly 2,700 liters of water per bar of chocolate.

This should be surely be something to think about while you are curled up ion a sofa eating it in your payjama as there is bad news of pyjamas. Cotton pyjamas take 9,000 liters of water to produce. And it takes 100 liters of water to produce a cup of coffee. And that is before any water has actually been added to your coffee. We probably drank about 20 billion cups of coffee last year in the UK. And—irony of ironies— it takes something like four liters of water to produce a one-litre plastic bottle of water. Last year, in the UK alone, we bought, drank and threw away nine billion plastic water bottles. That is 36 billion liters of water, used completely unnecessarily. Water wasted to produce bottles—for water. And it takes around 72,000 liters of water to produce one of the chips that typically powers your laptops, Sat Nav, phone, iPad and your car. In short, we are consuming water, like food, at a rate that is completely unsustainable.

LAND FOR FOOD: Demand for land for food is going to double— at least—by 2050 and triple—at least—by the end of this century. This means that pressure to clear many of the world's remaining tropical rain forests for human use is going to intensify every decade because this is predominantly the only available land that is left for expanding agriculture at scale. Unless Siberia—thaws out before we finish deforestation. By 2050 one billion hectare of land is likely to be cleared to meet rising food demands from growing population. (My blog essay: World-wide poverty alarm man-kind—September seven 2011 and Poverty and starvation deaths-July 10, 2011—www.kksingh1.blogspot.com)

This is an area greater than US. And accompanying this will be three gaga tons per year extra CO_2 emissions. If Siberia does thaw out before we finish our deforestation, it will result in a vast amount of new land being available for agriculture as well as opening up a very rich source of minerals, metals, oil and gas, In the process this would almost certainly completely change global geopolitics. Siberia thawing would turn Russia into remarkable economic and political;l force this century because of its newly uncovered minerals, agricultural and energy resources. It would also inevitably be accompanied by vast stores pf methane—currently sealed under the Siberian permafrost tundra—being released, greatly accelerating our climate problems even further.

Notably, another three billion people are going to need somewhere to live. By 2050, 70 percent of us are going to be living in cities. This century will see the rapid expansion of cities as well as the emergence of entirely new cities that do not yet exist. It is worth mentioning that of the 19 Brazilian cities that have doubled in population in the past decades, ten are in Amazon. All this is going to use yet more land. (My blog-64 million urban population in major cities live in slums—March 26, 2013—www.kksingh1.blogspot.com)

Currently the globe has no means of being able to feed 10 billion of us at our current rate of consumption and with our current agriculture system. Indeed, simply to feed our selves in the next 40 years, we will need to produce more food than the entire agricultural output of the past 10,000 years combined. Yet food productivity productivity is set to decline, possibly very sharply, over the coming decades due to: climate change; soil degradation and desertification—both of which are increasing rapidly in many parts of the world; and water stress. By the end of this century, large parts of the planet will not have any usable water.

POLLUTION &DISEASES: At the same time, the global shipping and airline sectors are projected to continue to expand rapidly every year, transporting more of us and more of the stuff we want to consume, around the planet year on year. That is going to cause enormous problems for us in terms of more CO2 emissions, more black carbon and more pollution for mining and processing to make all this stuff. In transporting this stuff all over the planet, we are also creating a highly efficient network for the global spread of potentially catastrophic diseases.

There is a global pandemic just 95 years ago—the Spanish flu pandemic, which is now estimated to have killed up to 100 million people. And that is before one of our more questionable innovation—the the budget airline—was invented. The combination of millions of people travelling around the world every day, plus millions more people living in extremely close proximity to igs and poultry—often in the same room, making a new virus jumping the species barrier more likely—means we are increasing, significantly, the probability of a new global pandemic. So no wonder then that epidemiologists increasingly agree that a new global pandemic is now matter of when not if.

ENERGY OUTPUT: It is expected to have triple—at least energy production by the end of this century to meet expected demands. To meet that demand, we will need to build, roughly speaking, something like: 1800 of world's largest dams or 23,000 nuclear power stations, 14 m wind turbines, 36bn solar panels or just keep going with predominantly oil, coal and gas—and build the 36,000 new power stations that means we will need. Our existing oil, coal and gas reserves alone are worth trillion of dollars. Are governments and the world's major oil, coal and gas companies—some of the most influential corporations on Earth—really going to decide to leave the money in the ground as demand for energy increases relentlessly? Three is doubt!

OPTIONS AND SOLUTION: A planet of ten billion looks like a nightmare! The only solution left to us is to change our behaviours, radically and globally on every level. In short, we urgently need to consume less. A lot less. Radially less. And we need to conserve more. A lot more. To accomplish such a radical change in behaviour would also need radical government action. But as far as this kind of change is concerned, politicians are currently part of the problem not part of the solution because the decisions that need to be taken to implement significant behaviour change inevitably make politicians very unpopular—as they are too aware.

So what politicians have opted for instead is failed diplomacy. For example: The UN Framework Convention on Climate Change, whose job it has been for 20 years to ensure the stabilisation of greenhouse gases in the Earth's atmosphere: Failed. The UN Convention to Combat Desertification, whose job it has been for 20 years to stop land degrading and becoming desert: Failed. The Convention on Biological Diversity, whose job it has been for 20 years to reduce the rate of biodiversity loss: Failed. Those are only three examples of failed global initiatives. The list is depressingly long one. And the way governments justify this level of inaction is by exploiting public opinion and scientific uncertainty. It used to be a case of, "we need to wait for science to prove climate change happening". This is how beyond doubt. So now it is, "we need scientists to be able to tell to us what the impact will be and the costs" And "we need to wait for public opinion to get behind action" But climate models will never be free from uncertainties And as for public opinion, politicians feel remarkably free to ignore it when it suits them—wars, bankers' bonuses and heath care reforms to give just three examples. What politicians and governments say about their commitment ti tackling climate change is completely different from what they are doing about?"

TRADE AND BIODIVERSITY: What about business? In 2008 a group of highly respected economists and scietists led by Pawan Sukhdev, then a senior Deutsche Bank economist, conduxcted an authoritative economic analysis of the value of biodiversity. Their conclusions? The cost of of the business activities of the world's 3000 largest corporations in loss or damage to nature and the environment now stands at $2.tn per year and rising. These costs will have to be paid for in the future. By your children and your grandchildren. To quote Sukhdev, "The rules of business urgently need to be changed, so corporations comptete on the basis of innovation, resource conservation and satisfaction of multiple stakeholder demands, rather than on the basis of who is most effective in finfluencing government regulation, avoiding taxes and obtaining subsidies for harmful activities to maximise the return of stake holders. Do I think that will happen? No. What about us . . . ."

"I confess I used to find it amusing but now I am sick of reading in the week-end paper about some celebrating saying, I gave up my 4x4 and now I haver bought a Prius. Am not I doing my bit for the environment "they are not doing their bit for the environment. But it not their fault. The fact is that they—we—are not being well informed. And that is part of the problem. We are not getting the information we need. The sacale and nature of the problem is simply not being communicated to us. And we are advised to do something; it barely makes a dent in the problem. Here are some of the changes we have been asked to make recently, by celebrities who like to pronounce on this sort of things and by governments, who should know better than to give out this kind of nonsense as solutions. Switch off your mobile phone charger; wee in the shower (my favourite); buy an electric car (no, do not); use two sheets of loo roll rather than three. All of these are token gestures that miss the fundamental facts that the scale and nature of the problems we face are immernse, unprecedented and possibly unsovelable."

The behavioural changes that are required of us are so fundamental that no one wants to make them. What are they? We need to consume less. A lot less. Less food, less energy, less stuff. Fewers cars, electric cars, cotton T-shirts, laptops, mobile phones upgrade s. For fewer. And here it is worth pointing out that "we" refers to the people who live in the west and the north of the globe.

There are currently almost three billion people in the world, who urgently need to consume more: more water, more food, and more energy.

GLOBAL POPULATION: Saying, "do not have children" is utterly ridiculous. It contradicts every genetically coded piece of information we contain, and one of the most important (and fun) impulses we have. That said, the worst thing we continue to do—globally—is have children at current rate. If the current global rate of reproduction continues, by the end of this century there will not be 10 billion of us. According to the United Nations, Zambai's population is projected to increase by 941 percent by the end of this century. The population of Nigeria is projected to grow by 349 percent—to 730 million people. Afghanistan by 242 percent, Democratic Republic of Congo 213 percent, Gamia by 242 percent, Gautemala by 369 percent, Iraq by 344 percent, Kenya by 248 percent, Liberia by 300 percent, Malawi by 741 percent, Mali by 408 percent, Niger by 766 percent, Somalia by 663 percent, Uganda by 396 percent, Yemen by 299 percent.

Even the United States of Americca's population is projected t grow by 54 percent by 2100, from315 million in 2012 to 478 million. If the current rate of global reproduction continues, by the end of this century there will not be 10 billion of us—there will be 28 billion of us.

EARTH'S COLLUSION: If we discovered to morrow that there was an asteroid on a collusion course with the Earth and—because physics is fairly a simple science—we are able to calculate that it was going to hit Earth on June 3 2072 and we knew that its impact was going to wipe out 70 percent life on the Earth, governments worldwide would marshal the entire planet into unprecedented action. Every scxiuentist, engineer, university and business would be enlisted: half to find a way of stopping it, the other half to find a way for our species to survive and rebuild if the first option proved unsuccessful. We are in almost precisely that situation now, except that there s not specific date and there is not an asteroid.

The problem is "us". Why are we not doing more about the situation we are in—given the scale of the problem and urgency it needed—I simply cannot under stand. We are sending eight billion at Cern to discover evidence of particles called Higgs bosom, which may or may not eventually explain mass and provide a partial thumbs-up for the standard model of poaryicle ohysics. And Cen's physicists are keen to tell us it is the biggest; the most important experiment on Earth. It is not. The biggest and most important experiment on Earth is the one we are all conducting, right now, on Earth itself. ONLY an idiot would deny that there is a limit to how many [people our Earth can support. The question is, is i t seven billion (our current population), 10 billion or 28 billion.

Science is essentially organised scepticism. One can rightly call the situation is an unprecedented emergency. There must be some urgent measures to avoid a global catastrophe!

SOURCES:—POPULATION TEN BILLION By DANNY DORLING and TEN BILLION BY STEPHEN EMMOTT; THE GUARDIAN ARCHIEVES and other internet websites.

UTTARAKHAND TRAGEDY DUE TO NATURE'S FURY: ULTIMATELY A MAN-MADE DEVASTATION!

Wednesday, 3 July 2013

Any conflict with 'NATURE' results into huge tragedy. India has witnessed many disasters since long but some of the 'key' natural disasters since independence over 60 years ago appear to be fall-out of 'playing with nature' by We Indians as well as successive union and state governments. India is mainly a nation of 'water (sea and rivers), mountains including most fragile mountain Himalayan range and huge forest ranges, particularly Dandakaranya, which stretches from West Bengal through Jharkhand, Orissa, Chhatishgarh, Madjya Pradesh and parts of Andhra Pradesh, Maharashtra, Tamil Nadu and Kerala, now popularly known as "red corridor" and home to millions of India's tribal population. The naxalites are running parallel government in the entire Dandakaranya forest range!

The recent Himalayan tragedy in Uttarakhand and havoc followed by torrential rains has caused huge loss to life and property in the newly created tiny states, particularly to the Pilgrims of 'chardham' for the worship of Kedarnath and Badrinath (abode of the Lord Shankar and the Lord Vishnu). Over 10000 people are estimated to have perished besides huge loss of property and infrastructures of the state. Before this Nature has also played havoc in the form of earthquake in Latur in Maharshtra and Gujarat, sea tusmaniu in the coastal areas of sought India, huge flood of Kosi, originating from Nepal, in north Bihar and much-much and more-more.

Are the nature furies being caused by unnecessary interferences in the courses of nature in mountain, sea, forest etc? The hill state—Uttarakhand—is originating Point of Ganga River from Himalayan mountain range. These areas have 'chardham pilgrimage', which draws Hindu believers to undertake 'yatra' once in a life time. Since the liberalisation of the Indian economy in 1980s in the name of 'so called development' Uttarakhand has witnessed rampant construction and unmindful digging and explosion of hills, resulting into unbalances in the preserving ecosystem and the harmonious balance with human beings. Such practises are being adopted in almost all the states by disturbing forest, rivers, sea, mountain etc in almost all parts of India! (My earlier essays on my link—www.kksingh1.blogspot.com—Dangerous signal for Nepal and India because of climate changes in Himalayas . . . . June 04,2013; Beautiful Mount Everest . . . . April, 27, 2013; Tribal and poor are being uprooted . . . . February 22, 2013; Great loot of farm and forest land in India . . . . July 11, 2011).

The flash floods in Uttarakhand have caused damage in all the hilly districts and also parts of Nepal. But Rudraprayag, the home of Kedarnath shrine, which draws thousands of pilgrims every summer, has experienced much—much devastation. This disaster was much more beyond one's imagination. Floods and landslides washed out 41 roads and 28 bridges, both small and large and also damaged 188 state government buildings. Apart from unstimulated death figure of over 10000 people, many continued to be stranded and missing despite best efforts of Indian Army, Indian Air force, and paramilitary forces, who worked for continuous relief and rehabilitation iin the devastated Himalayan state of Uttarakhand. The calamity was caused by cloudbursts and unprecedented heavy monsoon rainfalls. Eminent journalist and writer Praful Bidwai, who has written an article in the Guardian under headline—India floods: a man-made disaster, says, "the true causes of the epic tragedy lie in the grievous damage recently wrought on the region's ecology by the runaway growth of tourism, unchecked proliferation of roads, hotels, shops and multistory housing in ecologically fragile areas and above all mushrooming hydroelectricity dams that disrupt water balances. Underlying the disaster are multiple government failures too."

In this way man-made ruins have converted the entire region into extreme weather event into a social catastrophe. It is a fact that the region experienced heavy rainfall of 340-370mm within 24 hours on June 16-17, resulting into flash flood. But such thing is not unprecedented. Cloudbursts, floods and rapid swelling of fast flowing rivers are not uncommon. Uttarakhand has had recorded single-day rain fall in excess of 400mm several times, including 450 mm in 1995 and 900mm in 1965. But this time the flood waters, laden with tens of thousands of tonnes of silt, boulders and debris from dam construction, found no outlet. The routes they took in the past including ravines and streams were blocked with sand and rocks. The water inundated scores of towns and villages submerging some buildings under several feet of mud, smothering life. Aggravating the devastation were downpours of water and rocks from higher mountain ranges in all probability caused by glacier lake outbursts and l floods, which deluged the Kedarnath temple, a major Hindu pilgrimage centre. Because of that the explosive bursting of glaciers lakes are thought to be a consequence of human-induced climate, which is causing rapid melting of glaciers in the Himalayas, themselves warming at twice the global rate.

If one take all these things into consideration, if an early warning system existed, such a massive loss of life could have been averted. There were no effective warning system and evacuation plan as well as a responsive disaster management system. Notably the comptroller and auditor general of India (CAG) had pointed out in April itself that Uttarakhand Disaster Management Authority, formed in October 2007, has never met or formulated: "rules, regulations, policies or guidelines" Modestly priced radar-based technology to forecast cloudbursts would have been saved lives. But it was not installed. Nor was emergency evacuation plans drawn up. Praful Bidwai again writes, "there was local-level governance failure, too. Haphazard, unregulated construction of roads and bridges was allowed on crumbling, landslide-prone ridges and steep slopes, ignoring the region's fragile geology and high earthquake vulnerability. Forest was destroyed on a large scale. Hundreds of buildings were constructed in the flood plains of rivers, their natural terrain, which should be no-go areas. Riverbeds were recklessly mined for sand. And construction debris accumulated, land contours and flows of streams and river changed."

More importantly, indiscriminate building of hydroelectric dams was the worst culprit, These involve drilling huge tunnels in the hills by blasting rocks, placing enormous turbines in the tunnels, destroying soil-binding vegetation to built water channels and other infrastructures, laying transmission lines and carelessly dumping excavated muck. Many dams have been built on the same rivers so close to one another that they leave no scope for its regeneration. Interestingly dam's water is stolen from local people. They alter the hydrological cycles and natural course of rivers. Uttarakhand's 70 completed large dams have diverted more than 640 km, equivalent to half length of major rivers. They have profoundly destabilised its ecology. Yet another 680 dams are reportedly in various stages of commissioning, construction or planning, mainly by private companies, which will be largely unaccountable.

A 2009 CAG report complained that the government was "pursuing hydro-power projects indiscriminately" ignoring the damaging "cumulative effect" of multiple run-of-the river dams. Technically, India's environment ministry follows and environmental impact assessment process but that badly compromised by the Indian elite's insatiable appetite for electricity and promoters' pressure. Boom in religious tourism and hydroelectric projects may have contributed to disaster in Uttarakhand. Hundreds of new multistory hotels, apartment blocks and religious centres have sprung up in Uttarakhand, often on the flood plains of the capricious Mandakinin and Alaknand rivers, in defiance of building regulations. Several were washed away. The Himalayas are relatively young mountain range with fragile geology prone to landslides. The deluge of June 17 destroyed towns, villages, roads and bridges for more that 60 miles along the bank of Mandakinin and Alaknanda, two important tributaries of the Ganga River. The glacier ruptured under pressure of water from a severe cloudbursts, raining tonnes of ice, water and rock on the Hindu pilgrimage town of Kedarnath on the left bank of Mandakinini. The boom in religious tourism in recent years has also put severe strains on the state's shaky infrastructures. Domestic tourism traffic has jumped up by 300 percent in a decade, to more than 30 million a year. This number is expected to be double by 2017.

Quoting a recent article in Science magazine, Mahraj K Pandit, Director of the Delhi University's centre for interdisciplinary studies of mountain and hill environment, says, "The magazine has warned against damage to the ecosystem from badly planned, poorly monitored projects. The region is known for its biodiversity—its flowers, butterflies and Mahseer fish. Science estimated that habitat degradation from dam building in the Himalayas could lead to the disappearance of 29 species of flowering plants and terrestrial and aquatic life. Nobody is saying there should be no dams—but the emphasis should be on securing the Himalayan landscape after understanding in fragility, not on uncontrolled development. The Himalaya is an earthquake-prone zone—so god forbids, if a major dam ever bursts the destruction it will cause will be unimaginable".

The Chennai-based think tank Tashkhashila Foundation Pawan Srinath remarks," the devastation would have been even more widespread if the reservoir of the region's biggest dam m Tehari had not contained a significant volume of the deluge. Dams can also prevent disasters—the critical issue is not dams but proper dam's management. In India we do not have a culture of public safety."

It is said that National Hindu leaders had appealed to the Prime minister not reallocate the shrine of Dhari Devi, a local 'Avatar' (incarnation) of the fierce Hindu Goddess Kali in Srinagar by a power company to construct reservoir as shrine will be submerged under the reservoir. But it was not heard! The power company stealthily reallocated the and moved 'black stone' of idol of the shrine on the night of June 16 to save it from the swollen dam reservoir and within hours, the disaster struck. According to local lore, the Goddess protected Uttarakhand from calamities so her shrine could not be touched.

As the Himalayan mountain range is youngest, highest and longest in the globe. Rock formation in the mountain range is yet to start. There are dense forests in the areas. But its denunciation in large scale is going on in both Nepal and India sides. If such trend trend continues further, the days are not so far off when entire India region up to Ganga River in both Bihar and Uttar Pradesh will be wiped out with huge deposit of silts from the rivers of Nepal, eroded from mountain range. Kosi and Gandak rivers in Bihar and other rivers in Uttar Pradesh will bring huge miseries of flood water from Nepal side and the region will be practically wiped out from the scene. There is urgent need for permanent solution of flood coming from Nepal Rivers to Indian rivers and plains, adjoining specially Bihar. A few years back when flood from Nepal in Kosi river had played havoc in entire north and eastern Bihar, the union and Bihar government had assured the people that there will be comprehensive talks with Nepal government for permanent solution of flood—but since than nothing tangible has been done and mater is where it lies! People of Bihar are especially on the mercy of God!

CORRUPTION AND SYSTEM FAILURES COST INDIA'S DEMOCRATIC FABRICS!

Thursday, 27 June 2013

Should the Indian citizen be silent over rampant bribery, scandal, and power-brokering? Of course not we as citizen of India must hammer upon these evils to eliminate the society for going into decadent stage! Now a days, bribery and scandals are dominating the headlines not only in India but in several countries in recent years, among them India and Nigeria figure most corrupt countries in the globe. A new survey of corporate officials and employees in 36 countries—in Europe, Africa and Middle East as well as India-indicates that there is plenty of corruption that needs deeper investigation. The survey was conducted late last year by Ipsos, a market research firm, on behalf of Ernst & Young, a major accounting firm.

The survey and responses of the people of various countries, however, indicated that corruption and bribery are rare in the Scandinavian countries, but common in some southern and Eastern European countries as well as in India, the Middle East and Africa. According David Stulb, the global leader of the group; it was growing in part because many countries were worried about enforcement of the American Foreign Corrupt Practices Act, which bars the bribing of foreign officials and of similar laws in other developed countries. The survey revealed what Ernst called a "corruption perception gap" in many countries where respondents said bribery and corrupt practices were far more common in other parts of their country than they were in their own industry. At the extreme, 94 percent of respondents in Kenya though corruption was widespread in the country, but only 34 percent thought it were a problem in their own industry.

In the last three years, in the wake of serious cases of corruption in corridor of power in Delhi, like telecommunication scam, coal allotment scams and corruption in government offices in Delhi and at every nook corner of state governments' offices etc, have made the life of Indian people miserable because ultimate fall-out of corruption falls on the general people of India. MY TWO BLOG TOPICS:— RAMPANT CORRUPTION IN INDIA SIGNALLING CIVIL WAR, written on December 11, 2012 and LOOT OF PUBLIC MONEY BY POLITICIANS, MEMBERS OF EXECUTIVE AND JUDICIARY, POWER BROKERS, written on August 10, 2012 on my site—www. kksingh1.blogspot.com have deliberated at length how India has gone down to the drains in corrupt practices!

Although the political corruption was there even during the primeministership of Pundit Jaewahar Lal Nehru, it has deteriorated because the political system is self-perpetrating and no party is accountable except a coterie of people that dominates all decisions— (recent example is sacked railway minister Pawan Bansal's nephew). Apart from that, there has been rapid erosion in the selfless dedication of leaders led to the growth of corruption in the entire body politic. National interest has become no body's concern. In India, welfare schemes turned the biggest source for sip honing off public funds and the poor are worst affected! Criminalisation of politics is also one of the main reasons in abnormal rise in corruption in India. Before deliberating the menace and its reason, I just want to mention major scandals and corruption cases in India since the independence of India. All the figures are converted to the 2011 price level to make them comparable. Thus Wholesale price index numbers are used for the period. In the post independence period, only six out of the 14 prime ministers had a term of five years or more: Nehru about 17 years, Indira Gandhi—16 years, Rajiv Gandhi—five years, Narsimha Rao—five years, Atal Behari Vajpayee—six years, Manmohan Singh—over eight years to date. Out of these six prime ministers who really matter, five were from the Congress, accounting for 51 years of Congress-led governments. Out of these 51 years, 38 years belonged to Nehru dynasty.

The following three scandals surfaced during Nehruvian period:— The jeep scandal (1948) Rs 80 lakh (Rs 36.52 crore); the Muindra scandal (1958—Rs 1, 20 crore)—Rs 47.73 crore and the Dharma Teja loans Rs 22 crores (Rs 785.32 crore). The Indira Gandhi tenure saw at least three scandals—totalling indexed values worth Rs 244.70 crores. These are Nagarwala scandal (1971)—Rs 60 lakh (Rs 11.10 crore); the Kao oil scandal (1976)—Rs 2.2 crore (Rs 22.80 crore) and the cement scam—Donation for the Indira Pratishthan Trust collected by A R Antulay Rs 30 crore (Rs 208.80 crore). Than comes the Rajiv Gandhi's prime minister ship. In his regime, Bofor scandal of Rs 64 crore in 1987 (Rs 313.72 crore). Thereafter Narsimha Rao's period when economic liberalisation policy in full n bloom, there were many scandals. They are: Lakhubhai Pathak pickles scam (1984) $ 1,30,000 equivalent at the conversion rate to Rs 22.75 lakh and indexed value Rs 7.79 crore; the sugar import scam (1994)—Rs 650 crore (Rs 1627.99 crore); the Sukhram telecom scandal (1996)—Rs 3.6 crore (Rs 12.33 crore); The C R Bhansali scam (1998)—Rs 1100 crore (Rs 2438.60 crore) and the fertiliser scam (1996)—Rs 133 crore (Rs294.85 crore). Thus total indexed value during Rao's tenure comes to Rs Rs 4,381.50 crore. Next ccomes to Atal Behari Vajpaye led BJP government at the centre. Scandals are Kargil coffin scabdal (1995) $ 1.87 lakh equivalent at the then conversion rate to Rs 80.64 lakh (Rs 1.87 crore) and the Barrack missile scabdal (1995) $ 80.64 lakh equivalent at the then conversion rate Rs 36.29 crore (Rs 66.13 crore). In this way, the total indexed value would be approximately Rs 68 crore. The last but not the least Manmohan Singh government led by Congress, although Singh's personal integrity is doubted by none but mired in cobweb of corruption! The scams are—the Scorpene submarine deal (2006)—Rs 500 crore (Rs 685.80 crore); the cash-for-votes scandal Rs 50 crore (Rs 59.95 crore); the 2G p spectrum (2010)—Rs 1,76, 000 crore (Rs 1,89,200 crore) and Coal scam totalling to Rs 1.87 lakh crore and and Commonwealth game scams Rs 8,000 crore (Rs 8,599.99 crore. The coal scam is latest one which I have not calculated in indexed value amount! Thus total scams and scandals, reach to over Rs 3, 00,000 lakh crores till date during Manmohan Singh's tenure. In all these scams and scandals ministers and the then as well as the present prime ministers are involved directly or indirectly.

Apart from that almost all state governments led by chief ministers of different political affiliations have ship honed off over Rs 50 lakh crores public money in different smas and scandals since independence. More over criminal cases were filed in all these cases but net results came out zero in all these years.

Not only that politicians, bureaucrats, smugglers, drug-traffickers etc have stashed huge amount of black moneypoutside India According to a White Paper brought out by the government of India black money stashed away in Swiss banks by Indians stood at Rs 9,295 crore during 2010 while FICCI figures; by July 2012 this figure stood at Rs 45 lakh crore. The then CBI director A P singh, in his address to the Interpol Global program on anti-corruption and asset recovery, said such amount stood at $ 500 billion. His statement came before in a case in the Supreme Court in February 2012. These estimates excluded money stashed away abroad as valuables in Safe Deposit Boxes, a recent innovation by Swiss Banks to overcome international treaties.

On the other hand, over 70 percent families are below poverty line, which do not have sufficient food, drinking water, shelter clothes to cover their bodies what to speak of health and education care in India! And these political classes, power brokers, capitalists, corporates are grabbing public money and the country's wealth in truckloads. Prof K C Mehata, former pro-vice-chancellor and professor of finance, MS University of Baroda has remarked, while elaborating these sordid facts, "unless people rise in revolt against this demon and punish the corrupt by refusing to vote for them, a time will come (if it has not already) when we get used to the debased public life."

Similarly the writer and activist Arundhati Roy, commenting on the corruption in India, has said, in an interview to a senior journalist Saba Naqvi "scams smaller than a few lakh crores will not ven catch out attention. In the election season, for political parties to accuse each other of corruption or doing shady deals with corporations is not new-remember BJP and the Shiv Sena's campaign against Enron? Advani called it looting through liberalisation. They won the election in Maharshatra, scrapped the contract between Enron and the Congress government and then signed a far worse one. Corruption is a symptom of a widening gap between the powerful and the powerless, which in India, is one of the worst in the world. Moral policing or even actual policing cannot be solution . . . . hence remove these filthy illegal slums, clear away these illegal vendors crowding pavements—and so on . . . . the point is how to define corruption? . . . . they can only be addressed if you know your people, if you have vision and ideology, not by just changing the props or costumes activists wear on stage when one or the other group accuses them of some thing or the other. Being against corruption is not in itself a political ideology. Even the corrupt people will say they are against corruption . . . . Pantomine is a harsh word. I see what happening now as psrt of the unrest, anger, and frustration that is building up in the country. Sometimes the noisiness of it makes it hard to see clearly. But unless we look things in the eye—instead of heading off in strange quixotic directions—we can look forward to the civil war, which has already begun, reaching our doorsteps very soon." My blog topic—RAMPANT CORRUPTION IN INDIA SIGNALLING CIVIL WAR—Written on DECEMBER 11, 2012—www.kksingh1.blogspot.com.

From 2010, in a span of just two years, as many as 10 anti-corruption bills have been tabled including the disputed Lokpal bill, the forfeiture of benami property, foreign bribery, money laundering and whistle-blowing bills plus five more—all aimed at deterring specific acts of corruption or uprooting to give corruption free public service as a right. None of these bills or laws addresses the fountainhead of corruption—the opaque management of political parties which includes sources and deployment of their funds. The Second Administrative Reforms Commission (ARC-2009 had noted that large scale f criminalisation of politics, noting that how participation by criminals in the electoral process was "the soft underbelly of the Indian political system" leading to "flagrant violation of laws, poor quality of services, protection from lawbreakers n political, group, class, communal or caste grounds, partisan interference in the investigation of crimes, the poor prosecution of cases, inordinate delays that last for years, high costs of judicial process, mass withdrawal of cases and indiscriminate grant of parole." Votes are fetched through large, illegal and illegitimate expenditure on elections, a starting point of corruption in public life. Money power controls vote in India. Poor are penalised for not obeying the dictum of feudal landlords and state power-police. Earlier criminals were envisaged by political parties to win the elections. In the last 20 years, criminals have tasted the blood and they themselves win election by utilising their muscle and money power.

According to annual report of the Association for Democratic Reforms (ADR among 543 elected members of Parliament, who were elected in the 2009 Lok Sabha elections, 162 (32 percent) have criminal records and criminal cases are pending against them. Five years earlier, the figure was 24 percent. Ethics in political life in India is laughed at. Illegal and indiscriminate expenditure in election by political parties and candidates in the elections ave become order of the day. Interestingly, the ruling of the Central Information Commission that political parties should also be termed as public bodies and they are liable for all information under Right to Information Act. The ruling was vehemently opposed by all political parties—even by left parties because they will be exposed by their huge expenditures and sources of funds for the elections!

More over there must be drastic change in our electoral laws even after some drastic reforms brought by the then Chief Election Commissioner T N Sheshan. This apart, elections are made state funding like other many countries. State funding may overcome clandestine collection of election funds. A bill called the Registration and Regulation of Political Parties (2011) has been drafted by a committee chaired by Justice M N Venkatachaliah, former chief Justice of India. The bill envisages a democratic process for selecting party office-bearers as well as those given the tickets. The committee has also spoke about limitation on donations by individuals and corporations and also recommends l penalties for non-compliance and addresses the vexed question of how to deal with with support groups that spend, money that remains unaccounted.

Another, most alarming issue is rampant corruption among judges right from lower courts to high courts and the Supreme Court. Mechanism for appointing judges is not full-proof. Supremer Court and high courts are appointing judges on their whims. Quality of judges has deteriorated. Sons and daughters of the judges, former judges, VIP politicians and officials have become very common. Judicial accountable bill is facing vehement opposition from the Supreme Court and high courts judges. Judges and government have no concern over pend ency of huge number of cases for years together. Approaching courts by poor has become impossible as they cannot bear the cost for getting justice Judges, by compelling their own mechanism for pay and perks, are today said to be leading most comfortable and luxurious life by getting extra money and facilities!

SOURCES: WEBSITES OF VARIOUS NEWSPAPERS, NEWS MAGAZINES, NEWS SITES etc.

JUDGES AND POLITICAL CLASSES ARE SENSITIVE TO CRITICISM IN INDIA!

Thursday, 20 June 2013

In India, these days, judges and political classes have become 'sensitive' to criticism of 'public interest'. Raising of voices by public, press, while expressing freedom of expression, etc have become crimes in the eyes of power-that-be and particularly judges of even of the apex court-Supreme Court—To suppress the voices of agitating people, suffering immense agonies of poverty, lack of education and health facilities, is going to be common refrain. Curb on freedom of expression has become rampant in India! Signals of the founding fathers of the Constitution and the Constitution itself are being violated by all wings of the Indian Union—the Legislature, the Judiciary and the Executive. Other 'misdeeds' of all these three wings, exposed by vigilant media and persons, are suppressed and ignored in this country. A recent example must be cited—the Central Information Commission has rightly called political parties, public institutions and these political parties must be brought under the preview of the Right to Information Act. But sadly, almost all political parties are opposed to this directive of the commission—perhaps being afraid of their being stoppage of muscle and money power in the elections!

In this nefarious game, direct responsibilities go to the mainly political classes except a few, who are law-maker and the judiciary, which interpret the Constitution so that no wrong is done in violating the Constitution, laws, rules etc. Strangely, when the interest of these sections come to fore, these two wings at least do not lag behind in subverting the Constitution. In case of politicians, they amend the Constitution, okays laws, frame rules as well as raise their salary and perks whimsically beyond imagination, ignoring the interest and prevailing poverty in India. With regards to judiciary and its judges, they think beyond the Constitution and laws. It is seventh wonder in the world while Supreme Court judges have framed their own mechanism to appoint judges in the high courts and the Supreme courts. Not only that Supreme court judges have managed to set-up their own commission to determine their pay-perks, which is highly exorbitant comparing the sad and deteriorating economic condition of over 73 percent of population in the country while other wings of services' salary and perks are determined the time-to-time setting-up of commissions and committees. As if there is no rule of laws for at least judges and political classes in the country.

A recent eye-brows by the Supreme Court judge Justice Gyan Sudha Mishra, through the registry of the court, in response to an article by the Senior Editor of The Times of India Dhananjay Mahapatra titled "IN VACATION, S C BENCH LATE BY AN HOUR "on June 15 edition of The Times of India, has created piquant situation as well as ripple among the freedom-loving persons of the country. I must mention here a few sentences of the letter from Gyan Sudha Mishra, bullying the prestigious English daily and its Senior Editor. The letter mentions " . . . . while the Court during the vacation resorted to some flexibility in fixing its time schedule for taking up the matters, it also functioned beyond court hours to cater to the heavy Cause List mentioned at the last moment by the counsels to take up matters out of turn in view of their urgency due to which it had to sit late in the evening daily at least up to 7 p. m in order to clear the orders for their dispatch as the orders were of the urgent nature. Therefore, the judges also had to go through . . . . In the process, if the court exercised some discretion by keeping the time schedule during the vacation . . . . devote beyond the working hours in the court and yet expect them to give an account of every single minute or else face derogatory publicity."

More over the arguments in the letter of Justice Gyan Sudha Mishra appears to be one-sided-report in the The Times of India had simply mentioned late coming of judges during vacation to attend the court matter, listed as scheduled. Host of litigants and their counsels, coming from far-flung areas had to wait long because of late arrival of judges to the office. Justice Gyan Sudha Mishra, perhaps, forgot such miseries of the litigants and their counsels. Apart from that, Justice Mishra also did not, perhaps, keep in mind the unannounced schedule of the "so called late coming of judges during vacation". In my opinion, if it is fact than court must publicise the matter well in advance. Why this emotional outburst on Mohapatra's report in The Times of India.? As far as my feeling goes, even the judges are public servants—if they have to work extra hour—they are paid handsomely. Apart from this, colonial hang-over still exists in the judiciary—Leave and vacations and other freebies for judges are beyond imagination in poor country like India.

In my opinion, the Supreme Court of India must, first, keep its house in order instead of swaying into emotion and sentiments. There are many judgements, delivered by the judges in recent years, are contradictory in nature, converting the Indian Constitution as "Pandora's Box". Cases of corruption among judges in various high courts, particularly in Allahabad and Patna High Courts, as well as some time among judges of the apex court have also surfaced. Appointment of judges in various high courts by the apex courts in recent years has been questioned. Is it not true that some incompetent judges have been appointed in recent years? Is it not fact that some judges, appointed, are put on further probation in view of their incompetency? Is it not facts that relatives of judges of the Supreme Court and various high courts have been and are being appointed judges in various high courts? It is a fact that certain sections of the society like backwards, SC, ST and other backwards and dalits are ignored in the appointment of judges even after the facts that many of them qualify for judgeship in the high courts—not only that many good persons, practising in various high courts and the Supreme Court are ignored for appointment as judges under the present system? Even a person, having criminal background have been appointed judges of the high courts? Why the judges of the apex court and high courts are opposed to parliamentary legislative on the appointment of judges and the judicial accountability? These are the big questions to be replied by only the Supreme Court!

Another opinion veering round is that a greatest blunder has been committed while reservation in services to backward classes under the V P Singh regime. Why this country and its dalits were deprived of such facilities in the appointment of judges in high court and the Supreme Court under Mandal Commission provisions? Majority of Indians belong to dalits category—than why this discrimination? The Country must reflect its citizens and system not pick and choose for a chosen few!

Now enough is enough—there must be way out in improving judicial system. End must come to an end over the so called supremacy of Supreme Court and Legislature in determining the criterion for the benefits of rich only—India lives in villages and rule of law must prevail to determine all these burning factors instead of silencing the people through bullying-respected Supreme Court must spell out the system beneficial to dalits and downbtroddens under the existing frame work of the Constitution.

USA EXPOSED FOR SWEEPING WORLD-WIDE SURVEILLANCE: INDIA AMONG FIVE COUNTRIES MOST AFFECTED BY AMERICA'S SNOOPING!

Thursday, 13 June 2013

While the Unitest States of America is struggling to contain one of the most explosive national security leaks in US history as world-wide public criticism of the sweeping surveillance state revealed by whistle blower 29-year-old Edward Snowden former technical assistant of the CIA and currently an employer of the defence contractor Booz Allen Hamilton, apart from the entire nations of the globe, India is among top-most countries in the globe, whose data have been compromised by the US National Security Agency (NSA) through various Internet networks like Microsoft, Yahoo, Google, Facebook, Paltalk, AOL, Skype, Youtube and Apple. Not only are that data of personal/individual throughout the globe connected with internet network being snooped by America!

The historic leak of the US's NSA surveillances of most secrets, first to the journalists, from the Guardian and Washington Post. The National Security Agency of America has been monitoring telephone calls and e-mails and even social media stuff of the sort, violating civil liberties throughout the globe. Snowden like Daniel Ellsberg, who had revealed the Pentagon papers to the Post and the New York Times more than four decades ago, has stirred the world by the current revelation of the facts by NSA of America. It may be recalled that Pentagon Papers proved that a succession of US presidents had lied about their intention regarding Vietnam—Lyndon Johnson above all. As the Times put it in a 1966 story, the Pentagon Papers "demonstrated, among other things, that the Johnson administration had systematically lied, not only to the public but also the Congress, about a subject of transcendent national interest and significance." A big debate has been sparked over surveillance and privacy among the people of the globe nations.

Snowden, an intelligence analyst and computer geek, who leaked some of the NSA's most precious secrets to journalists, is now on the lam, having checked out of the Hong Kong hotel where he holed up for several weeks as he orchestrated a worldwide media splash that shows no sign of ending. Snowden himself admitted that he has betrayed the consulting firm Boos Allen Hamilton and his promise not to divulge classified information. He paints what he did as an act of civil disobedience, but he has decided to seek political asylum abroad rather than surrender to authorities and accept the consequences. In published interviews, he comes across as grandiose to the point of self-parody, a legend in his own mind.

"Did you know that the NSA is compiling and storing a massive, comprehensive log of our democratic phone calls? I did not nor did I know that agency can access huge volume of e-mails traffic and other electronic data overseas—not just communications originating in trouble spots such as Pakistan but also in countries such as Germany and Britain. I would have thought that anyone who accused the US government of omniscient, automatic, mas surveillance, as Snowden did in exchange with the post contributor Barton Gellman, was being paranoid. Now I am not sure."

But here is a big issue. The NSA, it now seems clear, is assembling as unimaginably vast trove of communication data and the bigger it gets, the more useful it is in enabling analysts to make predictions. It is one thing if the NSA looks for pattern in the data that suggest a nascent overseas terrorist group or an imminent attack. It is another thing altogether if the agency observes, say, patterns that suggest the Birth of the next tea party or Occupy Wall Street Movement.

Political opinion was split with some members of the Congress in America calling for immediate extradition of a man they consider a "defector" but other senior politicians from both parties questioning whether US surveillance practices had gone too far. Daneiel Ellsberg, the former military analyst, who revealed secrets of the Vietnam war through Pentagon Papers in 1971, described Snowden's leak as even more important and perhaps the most significance leak in American History. British foreign secretary, William Hague, was forced to defend the UK's use of intelligence gathered by U S. Other European leaders also voiced concern. On the other hand, in Washington, Obama administration offered no indication on Monday about what it intended to do about Snowden, who was praised for privacy campaigners but condemned by US politicians keen on for him to be extradited from Hong Kong and put on trial. The White House, however, made no comments beyond a short statement released by a spokesman for the U S director of national intelligence on Sunday last, Shawbn Turner said Snowden's case had been referred to the Justice Department and that U S intelligence was assessing the damage caused by the disclosures.

After disclosures of the NSA secrets, Snowden chose Hong Kong because "they have a spirited commitment to free speech and the right of political dissent." In an explosive interview with the Guardian, published on last Sunday, Snowden revealed himself as source for a series of articles in the Guardian last week, which included disclosures of a wide ranging secret court order that demanded Verizon pass to the NSA the details phone calls related to millions of customers and a huge NSA intelligence system called Prism, which collects data on intelligence targets from the systems of some of the biggest tech companies. Snowden said he had become disillusioned with the overarching nature of government surveillance in the US. "The government has granted itself power it is not entitled to. There is no public oversight. The result is people like me have the lattilatitude to go further than they are allowed to." he said and added, "My soul motive is to inform the public as to what is done in their names and which is done against them."

Moreover, Snowden drew support from civil liberty activists and organisations. Esberg wrote to the Guardian, "In my estimation, there has been in Americans history a more important leak than Edward Sonowden's release of NSA material—and that definitely includes the Pentagon Papers 40 years ago." Thomas Drake, a former NSA executive who famously leaked information about what he considered wasteful data-mining programmer at the agency, said Snowden: "he is extraordinary brave and courageous,"

Meanwhile China watchers also wonder if Beijing would wish to become publicly involved in such a huge-profile case-particularly given China's doctrine of non-inter fence in other countries' domestic affairs and that it comes days after a meeting between Presidents Xi Jinping and Barack Obama, as the countries seek to improve bilateral ties.!

Interestingly, the Internet network—Google, Apple, Facebook, Facebook, Paltalk, AOL, Skype, YouTube, Microsoft, who are trying to salvage their reputation, are facing a battle to maintain their trust after disclosures that the US government was given access to their customers' data on line via the Prism programme operated by the NSA. The involved companies vigorously deny giving the Obama administration backdoor access to users' Internet information but the potential damage to their brand reputation has left the companies foundering for a way to respond. Victor Mayer-Schnbeger, professor of Internet governance and regulation at the Oxford Internet Institute, believes there could be serious consequences for the collective reputations of all Internet companies, who have meticulously built their trade and trust.

Thus what the NSA is doing in turning the US—and by extension, the rest of the world—into a Big Brother surveillance state. THE USA is spying the world! Julian Assannge, Wiki-Leaks founder, hold up in Ecuadorain embassy in London since June 19 last year, told in London to TNN India has been targeted in a big way, as alleged by whistle blower Edward Snowden while exposing the US cyber snooping programme. In view of Indian government and its data are being compromised by the U S A's NSA, the Indian government, which is in dilemma, is considering a new cyber security. A cyber security and protection umbrella coordinator will be named at the end of June for new security structures.

SOURCES:—THE GUARDIAN, THE WASHINGTON POST, THE NEW YORK TIMES and other Internet connected to the world!

BUMPER POPPY CROP IN AFGHANISTAN TO DISTRIBUTE POISON IN ENTIRE GLOBE!

Monday, 10 June 2013

Notwithstanding the US and its NATO forces are preparing for withdrawal of their forces from the war-ravaged-Afghanistan and hand over the security of the nation to the Afghan National Army under the president ship of Hamid Karzai, Taliban still continued to be a formidable force. Not only that, voter registration has begun in Afghanistan for general election in Afghanistan, scheduled for next year. Both US and NATO have promised support to the Afghanistan even if they withdrew from the country in near future. But the manner the US and NATO forces are fighting with Taliban to save Hamid Karzai and Afghanistan from Taliban has many important aspects.

One of the worst menaces in Afghanistan the abundance "illegal and unauthorised poppy farming during Karzai regime. Huge export of poppy to almost all countries of the globe in stealth manner has created big problems in developed and developing countries of the world. Young and old are being addicted to heroin, smacks etc, prepared from poppy. Thus Afghanistan is spreading poison throughout the globe nations!Twelve years after the fall of the Taliban, Afghanistan is heading for near record opium crop as instability pushes up the amount of land planted with illegal but lucrative poppies, according to a bleak UN report.

Just 14 of the Afghanistan's 34 provinces are now poppy free, down from 20 in 2010. In three provinces, the spring sowing was the first time this decade that farmers had risked an attempt at growing opium. If this year's poppy fields are harvested without disruption, the country would likely regain its status as producer of 90 percent of the world's opium. Afghanistan's shares of the deadly and illegal market of opium slipped to around 75 percent after bad weather and and a blight slashed production over the past two years. "Poppy cultivation is not only expected to expand in areas where it already existed in 2012 but also a new areas or areas where poppy cultivation was stopped," The Afghanistan Opium Winter Risk Assessment found.

According to UN report; the growth in record opium cultivation reflects both spreading instability and concerns about the future. Farmers are more interested in planting to plant the deadly crop in areas of high violence or where they have not received any agriculture aid. Opium traders unauthorised provide seeds, fertilisers and even advance payments to encourage crops, leaving farmers who do not have western or government agriculture help very vulnerable to their inducements.

"Opium cultivation is up for the third successive year, and the production is heading towards record levels," said Jean-Luc Lemahieu, Afghanistan head of the U N Office on Drugs and Crime. "People are hedging against an insecure future both politically and economically." Prices of opium rose to a record$300 a kilogramme. Prices have now slipped by over $100 but are still far above historic level, helping tempt more farmers to land over to poppy.

A report says the growth of poppy farming as western troops head home reflects particularly badly on Britain, which was a designated lead nation for counter-narcotics over a decade. But overall the government and aid community has not prioritised efforts to cut back a crop and trade that feeds global markets for heroin, Lemahieu said, despite its corrosive effect on security, corruption and trust in Kabul.

In this nefarious game, people close to power and even close relatives of Hamid Karzai are involved in this nefarious farming of poppy just to placate the defiant Talibans although the letters were at one time opposed to narcotics! Reasons are eradication programmes that do not provide farmers of Afghanistan with benefits such as health care and education and support for growing other crops will just push the Taliban or other insurgent groups that do tolerate or encourage poppy production, said Lemahieu. The increase in production and poppy farming has come despite a marked improvement in Afghanistan's specialised counter-narcotic units, Lemahieu said and added h fear of eradication has become a far more significant reason for farmers of Afghanistan to stick to legal crops than in the past, the report found.

In the meantime, Afghanistan continues to limp back to normalcy and reign of terror by Taliban and US and NATO forces continued unabated. The US war in Afghanistan has cost $4 trillion and Iraq—$6 trillion, taking into account the medicare of wounded veterans and expensive repairs to a force depleted by more than a decade of fighting, according to a new study by a Harvard researcher.

According to Harvard researcher and a public policy professor Linda J. Bilmes; Washinton increased military benefits in late 2001 as the nation went to war, seeking to quickly bolster its talent pool and expand its rank. Those decisions and the protracted nation building efforts launched in both countries—Iraq and Afghanistan—will generate expenses for years to come.

DANGEROUS SIGNAL FOR NEPAL BECAUSE OF CLIMATE CHANGE IN HIMALAYAS, ADJOINING INDIA REGION IS ALSO THREATENED!

Tuesday, 4 June 2013

NEVERTHELESS tourism is now Nepal's largest industry and the greatest source of foreign exchange and revenue as over seven lakh foreigners descend the country each year, mostly for trekking, mountaineering and adventure holidays; in the areas they frequent, (there tends to be little malnutrition, better housing and clean water), the entire Himalayan country is on the front line of climate change and is highly vulnerable to flash floods, landslides and droughts (As the entire Himalayan mountain range in said to be highest, youngest and largest in the world-rocks are yet to form in the mountains as well as large scale denunciation of forest). Glaciers are melting at an increasing rate and major climate changes are taking place today. Entire Himalayan ranges have become definitely warmer! Such changes are not seasonal change any more. It is rapid. Is is so apparent.

Narrating the story of Nepal, once among the world's poorest people, The Guardian, in a recent report, has said the Nepal has eight of the 10 highest mountains in the world—Khumbu, in north-eastern Nepal, is bustling region that earns millions of dollars a year from hundreds of expeditions, Mountaineering, a form of extreme tourism, has grown to point where Sherpas—the ethnic group, who mostly live in the infertile mountains and became load carriers for foreign mountaineers—now run their own businesses, contracting much heavy work to other Nepali ethnic groups. Sherpas are said to earn between seven and 10 times the average Nepalese wage. Significantly, many are able to send their children to the best schools. The new generation like Dawa, are likely to spend much of the year in Kathmandu or abroad; they aspire to start businesses or to become doctors, engineers or airline pilots. Mountaineering industry changed the face and brought real progress. Most of the Nepalese are not so fortunate. The country is unrecognisable from isolated Himalayan kingdom that the British expedition in 1953 found, and now at major trading crossroads with its mighty neighbours China and India. New roads are being bulldozed through previously isolated region, western influences are every where.

But the development has come at a huge price. The air pollution and traffic jams of Kathmandu are among the worst in the globe, the cities are chaotic, unemployment is massive, and the predominantly rural population remains mostly locked in subsistence farming. Tens of thousands of young men now work in Saudi Arabia and Gulf States as labourers and the Maoist revolution grew of deep poverty and worsening conditions in rural areas. Only about 40 percent girls and 45 percent boys go to secondary schools.

On the other hand melting glaciers and rising temperatures are forming a potentially destructive combination in the deep ravines of Nepal's Himlayan foothills and the Phulping bridge—on the Araniko Highways linking Kathmandu with the Chinese border—is a good place to see just how dangerous the pairing can be! A report in The Time says, "a bare concrete pillar stands there, little noticed by the drivers of the truck, laden with the Chinese goods, that rattle along at high speed across the bridge, about 111 km from Kathmandu. The pillar is all that's left of the original Phulping Bridge, which was swept away by flood waters in July 1981. The deluge was not caused, as in common, by monsoon rains, but by the bursting of glacial lake. The force of the raging torrent was strong enough to dislodge boulders 30 meter across. They still lie in the Bhote Koshi River."

Glacial-lake outbursts, as they are known, are not new. They occur every time the natural dams of ice or accumulated rock deposits that hold back glacial lakes give was because of seismic activity, erosion or simple water pressure. Millions of cubic meters of melt water can be released as a result, some time over course of a few days or—far more frighteningly—in a mater of minutes. During past century, at easy 50 glacial-lake outbursts were recorded in the Himalayas; according to data maintained by the Kathmandu-based International Centre for Integrated Mountain Development (ICIMOD). But what is new that the lakes are forming and growing much more quickly because the glaciers are melting faster than ever.

According to the programme coordinator of ICIMOD Pradeep Mool; the potential of Himalayan tsunami is a hazard of global warming that has yet to be given much attention by outsiders but it is a daily preoccupation. There were some 20000 glacial lakes in the Hindu-Kush Himalayan region, extending Afghanistan to Burma. In some parts of Himalayas like Dudh-Koshi are in eastern Nepal, the melt rate is alarmingly high.

Mool says, "Almost all the glaciers in Dudh-Koshi are retreating at rates of 10 to 15 meter annually—but the rate for some has accelerated during last half-decade to 74 meter annually." He explained that this had created 24 new glacial lakes in the area, which now had total of 34 such bodies of water. At least ten of them are considered dangerous.

Research papers by a team from the University of Milan, released this month, found that in the past 50 years glaciers in the Everest region had shrunk by 13 percent and snow-line was now seen about 180 meter higher up. Sandeep Thakur, a researcher with the team says the meeting was most likely caused by warming temperature and was certain to continue. Since 1992, premonsoon and winter temperatures in the Everest region has increased by 0.6_0C.

Earthquakes also add to the risk. Earthquake could act as major triggers for glacial-lake outbursts, Mool says. He feels that much better monitoring of the lakes is needed to get a proper assessment of the dangers.

Moreover, down in Bhote-Koshi valley, villagers now rely on text messages for warnings of potential floods, landslides and other hazards. The power station near village of Jhirpu Phulpingkatt will issue warning of a glacial-lake outburst, but people in the areas will only have a few minutes notice before flood waters arrive and only glacial-take outbursts in Nepal territory can be immediately detected. There are at least six glacial lakes close by in Tibet that lie outside the warning system and outbursts will be detected only when Waters enter Nepali territory; according to the plant's acting manager Janak Raj Pant. But regardless of where an outburst originates, he says, "all of us would have to run for our lives".

Apart from that the plain areas of Nepal, towards north, adjoining the land-locked border with mainly Bihar and Uttar Pradesh in India have become most vulnerable of flood devastation, coming from Himalayan range because of outbursts as well as major melting in glaciers due to climate changes and also large scale of forest denunciation by the Nepalese in the forest areas. Janak Raj Pant disclosed that all of "us would have run for our lives."

Seaborne tsunami has already unleashed enough devastation this century—let us hope that no comparable disasters dwell in the Himalayas' icy ravines!

THE WORLD AS '100': CHRISTIANS DOMINATE THE GLOBE —MUSLIMS COME SECOND!

Thursday, 30 May 2013

The World as '100'! An unique concept has been developed as "World as 100 people' in respect of almost parameters including population, health, education, community, religion, poverty, richness etc. That is 'if the world were 100 people"! Such concept has been developed by the website www.100people.org. The website beautifully illustrates each of statistics. These statistics are powerful learning tools, mainly on the ten areas of critical global concern that affect us all: water, food, transportation, health, economy, education, energy, shelter, war and waste. Currently the world population reached seven-billion marks. It is expected to cross nine billion by 2045. Can the Planet take the strain? The methodology of determining all these statistics have been wonderfully depicted. The main representing factors are gender, age, geography, religion, first language, overall literacy, literacy by gender, level of education and many others. Data and figure seems to be based on solid, well grounded and are less prone to bias.

The rising population raises serious concern, especially for the marginalised sections living in poorer countries. The richer nations have their own type of problems linked to industrialisation and supersaturated markets while the emerging economies such as India, Brazil and South Africa have been unable or unwilling to spread wealth generated over the past two decades or so equitably. The poor in Asia and Africa lead miserable life. Various studies have suggested that hundreds of millions of population in these countries have absolutely no access to food, water and shelter, leave alone health care and education. Survival rates of women and children are way below the global average. Men have played havoc on the planet by plundering its resources and leaving vast swathes of land polluted and uncultivavable. Huge rush is for urbanisation. The consequences of global warming have become serious in almost all nook and corners of the world. The world is marked with growing conflicts. Many countries spend their precious resources on weapons rather than food for hungry people. The wealth of the world continues to be in the few hands. And they are selling the false hopes that benefits of rapid growth will trickle down to the poor.

The details of 100 people concepts and statistics are mentioned herein:—Gepgraphical distribution is 15 would be from Africa, 11 would be from Europe, nine would be from Latin America and the Caribbean, five would be from North America and 60 would be from Asia. If the world were 100 people, the gender would be 50 percent women and 50 percent male. One thing in 100 people data and figure is very interesting and revealing:. Christians are majority population in the globe while Muslims are second to Christians in the world. That is followers of religion and their approximate populstion. Thirty-three percent in 100 concepts are Christian and Christinity; 22 percent are Muslims and followers of Islam, 14 oercent Hindu; seven are Buddhist and 12 percent believe in other religions (Twelve percent would not be identified themselves as being aligned with a particular faith).

100 peopler concepts have also deliberated literacy and poverty in the globe. 83 would be able to read and write while 17 would not be able to read and write. Seventy-nine percent females would be able to read and write while 88 males would be able to read and write; twenty-one females would not be able to read and write and 12 percent males would not be able to read and write. In other aspect of education sector, 76 percent of eligible males would habve a primary school education and 72 percent of eligible females would have a primary school education; 66 percent of eligible nales would have secindary school education and 63 percent of eligible females would have secondary school education. Only seven would have college degreee. About first language, 12 would speak Chinese, five would speak Spanish, five would speak English, three would speak Arabic, three would speak Hindi, three would speak Bengali, three would speak Portuguese, two would speak Russian, two would speak Japanese and 62 would speak other languages.

With regards to poverty 48 percent would live on less that two dollars per day as well as one out of two children would live in poverty. Out of 100, fifteen would be undernourished. With regards to infectious disease one percent would have HIV/AIDS and another one percent would have tuberculosis. Eighty-seven would have access to safe drinking water and 13 would use unimproved water.

Now urban/rural divide:—51 would be urban dwellers and 49 would be rural dwellers. On electricity front 78 would have electricity and 22 would not have such benefit. (In the meantime, the United Nations has launched ambitious programme to make sure that in the world, all will have electricity access by 2030. A progress report from the International Energy Agency 1.2 billion people around the world are still struck in the dark. Some 1.7 billion people have acquired access to electricity in the world since 1990. While 1.6 billion have access to cleaner cooking fuels) on sanitation: 65 would have improved sanitation and 16 would have no toi; tes and 19 would have unimproved toilets. Regarding technology 75 percent would be cell phone users, 30 would be active internet users and 22 would own or share a computer.

In 2006, only one person out of 100 would have had a college education—today that number has jumped to seven thanks in part to advances in higher education in Asia. Significantly if the world were 100 people, only one would be health worker. That one person might be a doctor or nurse in a developed nation or a midwife or traditional healer in rural community in the developing world.

This 100 people: Through lenss, prepared wonderfully by www.100people.org has described almost all parameters of people of the world in an authentic manner!

NGOS AND FOREIGN FUNDING: GOVT TIGHTENS NOOSE!

Wednesday, 29 May 2013

In the early 1980s, people of the world's largest democracy—India—had great hope of getting their condition improved with the entry of Non-Governmental Organisations (NGOs) in the social arena in big way. Both the state and union governments opened avenues for developments at grass-root level by opening flood-gates for NGOs. In the process, a huge number of NGOs came up and many of them started their work at the right earnest by getting huge amount of funds from India and various state governments as well as huge foreign funding. Later, many NGOs, concentrated on direct foreign funding as donations for developmental activities, especially at social and rural level. They got long rope in contacting various foreign governments and foreign social organisations for money to spend in India for the upliftment of the people, whom, they described, are in pitiable condition! And foreign donations and funding started rolling.

According to figure, compiled by the Indian government; the United States and its private institutions, is top donor nation to Indian NGOs, followed by Britain and German. In the year ending in March 2011, the most recent period for which data are available, about 22,000 NGOs received a total of more than $2 billion from abroad, of which $650 million came from the United States.

Curiously enough, in all these years, huge funds received specially from foreign funding by the NGOs, both the state and union government have practically no information about the ground-level work being done by the NGOs. People of especially rural areas for whose development, the foreign funds came also did not know about the utility of the foreign money. No social or government auditing was done about the utility of fund by the major NGOs.

In the meantime, founder-activists of the NGOs reportedly spent huge chunk of foreign fundings in the 'political activities, anti-government agitations'. In many cases rag to riches story also came out. Many NGOs owners became millionaires and started leading luxurious life. Many of them became vocal in political activities. Big NGOs holders including Ms Kiran Bedi, Arwind Kejariwal and his associates Shishodia have started participating in anti-government rallies and protest. No one knows their NGOs functioning and utility of foreign fund for development. Not only that these NGOs also started involving themselves in protest meetings for setting-up nuclear power plants. No doubts, installation of nuclear plants are not only harmful but detrimental to the interest of the people of the country. But for that, the matter is being tackled at political and social level. What is the need of NGOs being involved in these issues?

Trouble for NGOs started when Prime Minister Manmohan Singh blamed groups from the United States for fomenting anti-nuclear protests that have stalled the commissioning of India's biggest reactor, a Russian backed project in Koodankulan in power-starved Tamil Nadu state. NGOs also hobnobbed with protestors that delayed several important industrial projects. Officials including Peter Burkeigh, the American ambassador at that time, quickly moved to assure Indian officials that U S Government supports India's civil nuclear programme. Victoria Nuland, then the State Department spokeswoman, said the United States does not provide support for non-profit groups to protest nuclear plants." Our NGO support goes for development and it goes for democracy programme" Nuland said.

On the Indian government's moves against foreign-funded NGOs, a US State Department spokesman said the department is not aware of any US government involvement in the cases. The Spokesman said such civil society groups around the world "are among the essential building blocks of any healthy democracy." Situation in India is different in comparison to Russia where where similar situation prevails. Russia has enacted a law last year, which requires foreign-funded NGOs that engage in loosely defined political activities to register as "foreign agent" Further, the government's action appears to have led its desired effect." NGOs are too scared to visit Koodankulam or associate with us now," said anti-nuclear activist S P Udayakumar.

Because of all these developments, India government has tightened its noose on non-governmental organisations over the past two years, calling the NGOs engaging in activities that harm the public interest.

The government stepped up its campaign recently, suspending the permission that the Indian Social Action Forum (INSAF), a network of over 700 NGOs across India, had to receive foreign funds. Groups in the network campaign for indigenous peoples' rights over their mineral rich land against nuclear energy, human rights violations and religious fundamentalism; nearly 90 percent of the network's funding comes from overseas. In its letter to INSAF, the Home Ministry said the group's bank accounts had been frozen and foreign fundings approval suspended because it was likely to "prejudicial affect public interest." INSAF (in URDU its meaning is justice), has seen its portion of foreign funding increase significantly during the last 15 years. Now it receives funds from many international groups including the American Jewish World Service and Global Greengrants Fund in United States and groups in Germany, Switzerland and Netherlands. The top American donors to Indian NGOs include Clombo-based Compassion International, District-based Population Service International and the Bill and Milinda Gates.

A government official, who spoke on the condition of anonymity because of the sensitivity of the subject, said the government is not against criticism. But when an NGO uses foreign donations to criticise Indian policies, "things get complicated and you never know what the plot is", the official said adding that NGOs should use foreign donations to do development work instead.

On the other hand, Anil Chaudhary, who heads an NGO that trains activists and is a part of INSAF network, said "the government's action is aimed at curbing our democratic right to dissent and disagree. We dared to challenge the government's new foreign donation rules in the court. We opposed nuclear energy, we campaigned against genetically modified food and we have spoiled the sleep of our prime minister."

Indian officials say NGOs are free to use Indian money for their protests. But activists say Indian money is hard to find, with many Indians preferring to donate to charities A recent report by Bains &Co, said that about two-thirds of Indian donors surveyed said that NGOs have room to improve the impact they are making in the lives of beneficiaries. It said that a quarter of donors are holding back on increased donations until they perceive evidence that their donations are having an effect.

Meenakshi Ganguly, South-Asia Director of Human Rights Watch, said many NGOs are afraid to speak up about the suspension of their foreign funding approval, which "is being used to intimidate organisations and activists."

DALAI LAMA HAS FAILED BUDDHA'S TEACHINGS OF COMPASSION, PEACE, AND HAPPINESS BY ENCOURAGING SELF-IMMOLATION OF TIBETANS!

Saturday, 25 May 2013

Before Mahatama Gandhi became apostle of peace and non-violence in the beginning of 19th century, Gautam Buddha was harbingering of compassion, happiness and peace ten to fifteen thousands years ago. And his message spread throughout the world. Today Buddha is considered the incarnation of "god" and has followers in the very nook and corner of the globe! But Buddha's ardent follower and spiritual leader Dalai Lama, who is in exile in Dharmshala of the Himachal Pradesh of India, is running Tibet government from Dharmshala by 'proxy' against the so called 'illegal occupation of Tibet by China'. And an ugly turn of events is going on in Tibet and other parts of the planet where, Buddha's followers are indulging in 'self-immolation' to protest the Chineses 'occupation' of Tibet.

Curiously enough, Dalai Lama is keeping mum over these killings and violence in his own home land Tibet. Dalai Lama is such powerful spiritual leader that if he says stop, the self-immolation will stop. No doubt certainly the rest of the world is appalled by treatment of Tibetans by the Chinese, Dalia Lama is not realising the kind of power he has to stop such ugly happenings in the line of the teachings of Lord Buddha on peace and compassion! Most cultures are equally appalled by the suicidal self-destruction of protesting Tibetans. I strongly feel it does not look good for Dalai Lama. It does not look good for Dalai Lama. He talks about peace, happiness and compassion as propounded by Lord Buddha. Million dollar question arises—why has not the Dala Lama embraced the practice of 'Lhakar' rather than refusing to condemn self-immolation? A new form of protest has arisen among Tibetans, who feel that self-immolation is too violent. It is called 'Lahkar', which means 'White Wednesday' in Tibet. One day a week is set aside to celebrate all things Tibetans, including music, food and goods. This is a cultural rather than a religious protest and one on which it is much more difficult for the Chinese to crack down!

Recently the Dalai Lama was in Maryland for delivering Anwar Sadat Lecture of peace at the University of Maryland before over 15000 persons. According to the university website; Dalai Lama spoke about how "peace in the world must come from inner peace within individuals and the source of that inner peace is compassion for others". Compassion for others is at the root of the controversy over self-immolation of more than 100 Tibetans, who have taken their own lives since 2009 to protest China's occupation of Tibet. Those who burn themselves to death want to see the Dalai Lama return to Tibet. A Reuter report says why, people ask, would the Dalai Lama not put a stop to these violent acts of self-destruction in his name? Is not self-immolation the very antithesis of What Buddhism is about? How can it be moral or ethical to condone such behaviour? Yet Dalai Lama refuses to condemn it!

In an interview to Times Now, a major Indian news channel, Dalai Lama spoke about this practice. "If motivation (consists) too much of anger, hatred, and then it is negative, (but) if the motivation (is) more compassionates . . . . then such acts can also be positive. That is strictly speaking from (a Buddhist point of view). Any action, whether violence or non-violence, is ultimately (dependent) on motivation." Recently, while travelling in Japan, the Dalai Lama responded to the Chinese repression, saying, according to the Global Post that the incidents of self immolation are a "sign of deep frustration; Chinese leaders need to take a look into these incidents more seriously and not in isolation. Ruthlessness only will not be good for all." But still the Dalai Lama did not condemn such ugly incidents.

Moreover, as the number of self-immolation cases has risen, so too, have the mass protests. The Chinese government has cracked down on the protests, arresting and torturing many who speak out. Authorities are especially upset by the self-immolation, because they have caused a lot of bad publicity. Some Chinese police now travel with fire extinguishers on their back to head off the suicides.

According to a website report of Sally Quin, an e-mail writer; Matteo Pistono, the author of "In the Shadow of Buddha" and a Buddhist scholar, who lived and travelled in Tibet for a decade, says that in

Buddhism, there is a way to look at self-immolation that is non-violent. It can be seen as a great offering one is making and trying to become, literally, a lamp to lilluminate the darkness of the world." Pistono further says it is an act inspired "philosophically and emotionally, but some where in between is political activism trying to bring about changes. The differences, he says, between this kind of violence an d other kinds is that it does not result in violence against others. You are not blowing up buildings."

Pistono says that Mahatma Gandhi made popular the doctrine of non-violence or "ahimsa", a Sanskrit word meaning to do no harm. "Yet what is motivation here? To bring the Dalai Lama back to Tibet and to bring freedom to Tibet." Pistano says the position of some exiled Tibetan leaders on self-immolation is not that the world should ask why people are killing themselves but the world should ask China to desist from repression, which could stop the cause of the burning, Comparing the unsuccessful result self-immolation of Tibetans, Pistono points out that Arab Spring was started by a Tunisian fruit seller's self-immolation. So such action can produce results. Yet the Tibetans' self-immolation have not resonated with the rest of the world. It has been very frustrating to Dalai Lama that the United States has not taken a stronger position on the China-Tibet stand-off.

In "The Ethics of Self-Immolation"—from "into the Jaws of Yama, Lord pof Death: Buddhism, Bioethics and Death"—Tibetan writer Karma Lekshe Tsomo says that "there are cases of Buddhists, who have set their bodies afire as an act of generosity, renunciation, devotion or political protests" and that the MAHAYANA texts "extol the virtues of offering one's body to the Buddhas, often by burning" Later he says, "the spirit of a person who commits suicide out of despair or depression is believed to be intensely dissatisfied and therefore likely to wander as a hungry ghost, whereas self immolation is believed to be religious act committed with strong conviction and pure motivation."

Nevertheless spiritual leader Dalai Lama is drawing huge crowd for his spiritual sermons on Buddha through out the globe but his silence on Buddha's preachings of compassion, peace and happiness, related to barbaric practice of self-immolation by Tibetans, is drawing the fact that is Dalai Lama is fighting a losing battle against Chinese?

NOW HATE CAMPAIGN AGAINST CHRISTIANS: IN MIDDLE EAST CHRISTIANS ARE BEING CRUSHED BY MUSLIMS!

Sunday, 19 May 2013

Christianity and Islamic religions are at loggerhead throughout the COSMOS nations. Both Christians and Islams are not eye-to-eye, mainly after 9/11 Al Qaeda attacks against United States in 2001. And both the religions and their followers are after their blood against each other! Main reasons appear for supremacy in the globe. Muslims are being targeted by Christians by brandishing the formers being terrorists and they are being tortured and atrocity is being perpetrated in the areas of influences throughout the world led by the leadership in the United States of America. On the other hand, Christians are facing major threat in the areas of influences of Muslim countries, mainly in the Middle East countries where unnecessary military interventions by America have created problems. Apart from that, the natural resources like 'oil' is also one of the main factors of enmity because Gulf regions, dominated by Muslims, are the major oil producers, which once upon a time USA had harnessed and wanted its control by installing military bases in the region.

Nevertheless, the animosity between two—Christians and Muslims—has been taking definite shape since long despite contradictions in their own respective religions, While Christianity is marred by differences among Protestant and Catholic, Muslims are also poles apart from the divide between Shias and Sunnis throughout the globe. In my opinion, the secularism is gradually going down to the drains for co-existence on the earth? My two blog—www.kksingh1.blogspot.com—essays—"Why this hate campaign against Muslims of the world (October 16, 2012) and Muslims in the Globe vis-a-vis in India (July 17, 2012)—have depicted in detail the atrocity on Muslims and their Islam religion, by calling them 'terrorists'. In the current topic, just I want to narrate the retaliatory instances and measures against Christianity and their followers mainly throughout Middle East, Gulf, Arab and part of Europe by Islamics followers. Richard L Russel, Professor of the National Security Affairs at the Near East and South Asia Centre of for Strategic Studies has authored of books—Sharpening Strategic Intelligence, Weapons Proliferation and War in the Greater Middle East and George F. Kennan's Strategic Thoughts, and has detailed the sorry state of affairs among Christian Community in different parts of the world, mainly in the Middle East! The Washington Post and the New York Times have also carried various reports of atrocity on Christians in the globe.

Russel has said, "Americans of all political stripes have embraced the promotion of democracy as a centrepiece of U S foreign policy. But this American democracy crusade has caused huge and largely overlooked, collateral damage since 9/11 Al Qaeda attacks against United States in 2001. The fall of the authoritarian regimes throughout the greater Middle East has fuelled growing persecution of minority Christian communities."

More over, the Pew Research Centre has charted extensive government restrictions on non-Muslim religions in number of countries, including Egypt, Saudi Arabia, Afghanistan, Iran, Tunisia, Syria, Yemen and Algeria, The centre has found high social hostilities in Pakistan, Iraq, Yemen and Palestinian territories, Egypt and Saudi Arabia. Government of all these countries have imposed restrictions and social hostilities directed against Christians. Huge numbers of Christians are fleeing the region. Interestingly, in the beginning of the early twentieth century, Christians account for about 20 percent of the Middle East population, but now the figure is down to only five percent. In the aftermath of 9/11 and the 'Arab Springs', the Christians communities throughout the greater Middle East find themselves increasing under threat. Sadly United States administration is silent spectators of such naked drama against Christians by Muslims! Interestingly, the sieges against Christian's community have increased in the so called 'liberated' regions by the American Military in the recent years.

Reports suggest that democracy enthusiasts would anticipate that Christian community would be thriving now that a 'democratic' Afghan government was installed by the American Military power after the ouster in 2001 of the Taliban regime. Not only that Afghan Constitution, adopted in 2004, guarantees freedom of religion. But Afghan Christians are today deprived of worship and compelled to worship in secret lest they be accused of apostasy for converting to Christianity from Islam, a charge punishable by death, in neighbouring Pakistan, blasphemy laws are wielded more and more aggressively against Christians, who make up only about two percent of Pakistan's 180 million people. These Christians are living under tremendous mental agonies and economic discrimination. Barbarian attitude against Christian surpassed all cannons in Pakistan in March 2011 when only Christian minister in Pakistan, who bravely criticised harsh blasphemy laws that impose the death penalty for insulting Islam, was assassinated, exposing the so called secular and liberal Pakistan's approaches.

Iraq has, since starting open warfare from 2003 against Christian community, been forcing mass exodus of Christians although even the ousted Saddam Hussain was relatively hospitable to Christians. Iraqi Christians are severely embattled by Sunni extremists linked to Al Qaeda and are discriminated against by Iraq's Shiya majority, largely in control of the government. Incidents such as 2010 suicide bombing Our Lady of Salvation Church in Baghdad, which killed fifty Christians and two priests, have terrified Iraq's Christian population, which has dwindled to less than 5000,000 from 8000,000 and 1.4 million in the time of Saddam.

Situation in Egypt, dominated by Muslim Brotherhood, has posed far greater threat to large number of Coptic Christian community in comparison to its authoritarian predecessors under Hosni Mubarak. A Coptic church in Cairo was set ablaze by Islamists in 2011 and many Copts—an estimated ten percent of Egypt's 85 million people—live in fear that Egypt is on the path to being governed by Islamic laws or Sharia. Egypt police sided with an angry crowd of young Muslims in April 2013 throwing rocks and firebombs in a siege of Egypt's major Coptic Cathedral. Egyptian Copts, who have sought work in in neighbouring Libya, fared well in the chaos that has rained in that country since the fall of Muammar Gaddafi. Not only were that Christians shocked in December 2012 by bombing of a church in Misrata, Libiya. That attack has stoked fears that Libyans Islamists are growing in power and more such attacks against Christians are in store. Islamists also emerged powerful in Syria, generating fear that in the case they get power; they would persecute Syrian's Christian community. Over three hundred thousand Christians in Syrians have already fled the country and are refugees. Thus fate of Christian community in Syria is threatened by Muslims with the infiltration of uncontrollable fanatic fundamentalists groups of Muslims.

Syria's violence against Christian community have spread into neighbouring Lebnan. The Shia Islamists group Hazbollah is flexing military strength and lending support to embattled Syrian forces. Hundreds of Lebanese Christians have fled over the years due to civil wars and more recently, in fear that Hazbollah eventfully will control the country and turn it into an Islamic state. Christians were about 52 percent in 1932 in Lebanon and during the last national census, but now by some estimates suggest only 34 percent of the Christian population. A similar trend has long been under way in the Christian Palestinian community, caught in the middle of the conflict between Israelis on one side and secular and Islamist Palestinian on the other. The Catholic Patriarch of Jerusalem has lamented that the Holy Land is fast becoming a 'spiritual Disneyland' with holy sites as theme park attraction bereft of worshipping Christians.

In the rich Arab Gulf States, Christian communities formed primarily by Asian immigrate workers, quietly practise their faith but that is now happening in the regions powerhouse Saudi Arabia. Qatar for example, has allowed the construction of a catholic church in Doha for one hundred and fifty thousands Catholics. Churches in Kuwait, Bahrain, and United Arab Emirates are seen as a way to lure expatriate labour to those countries. These Gulf States have survived the political torrents of the Arab Springs but should they fall to street protests, successor's regimes likely would resemble Saudi Arabia today, which forbids Christian worship by the estimated eight hundred thousand Catholics in the kingdom. The Saudi government publicly lauds inter-faith dialogue, but Saudi-sponsored conferences take place outside the kingdom to avoid domestic religious-political backlashes from Saudi Arabia's Wahhabi religious establishment.

The tightening of nooses around Christian community in the Arab Middle East is running parallel to sieges laid against Christians by non-Arab Muslims elsewhere in the region. The Assyrian Christian population in Iran has plummeted from about one hundred thousand in the mid-1970s to about fifteen thousand today. More than 300 Christians have been arrested by Islamic regime since mid-2010. Churches operate in fear. And Christian converts safe persecution. In the meantime, Turkey is praised in the west as a democratic success story in the Muslim world and the government in Ankara often characterised in the media as 'mildly Islamic'. But the steady erosion of free speech rights in Turkey, as evinced by the increasing imprisonment of journalists and the government's aggressive purging of the secular Turkish military, raises doubts about future prospects for Turkish political and religious tolerance. Attacks against Christians living in a country of 71 million Muslims. A Catholic bishop was stabbed to death in southern Turkey in 2010 and several years earlier a Catholic priest was murdered in a Turkish town along the Black Sea.

All these hate campaign against Christians Muslims against each other have been initially started by United States of America and the then Soviet Russia now Russia. Initially both these big powers used Muslims and later threw them in waste paper baskets in the globe nations, calling them (Muslims) terrorists. Both USA and Russia used Osama bin Laden as well 'Taliban 'for their enlightened self-interest of hegemony in the world. After 9/11, the USA administration started vigorous campaign against Muslims in the name of eliminating terrorists, the so called Muslims. In between Muslims, to great extend, supported 'jehadi movement' under bin Laden and created tremor in the world solely to save their prestige and honour g;globally. Now the Muslim-dominated Middle East and Arab world have also started retaliations and creating reign of terror against Christians in their areas of dominance.

Will such action and reactions not destroy the secular fabrics in the democratic set-ups in the globe? Good sense must prevail both sides, especially America to diplomatically lessen the tension in the world especially among Christians and Muslims communities for everlasting peace globally by ending hate campaign!

3,009,000 LAKH CHILDREN DIE EVERY DAY IN INDIA ON THE FIRST DAY OF THEIR BIRTH!

Friday, 10 May 2013

It is sad and tragic! We cannot save our children and mothers. In India, babies die on the first day of their birth more and more than in many under-developed or developed countries on the globe. There are appalling condition of the Indian health care exists in India. Over three lakh children in India do not see the light of the day and do not survive the first 24 hours. Thus India tops in children mortality rate in the world, thanks to our health care system, envisaged by the successive union and state governments!

Sadly India is far ahead of Nigeria, Pakistan, and China on this score. According to a report "State of world mothers", released by the "Save The Children" India accounts for 29 percent of the deaths of the children on the first day they are born, globally. Each and every year 3, 09,000 children die in India on the first day of their birth. Nearly, 4, 20,000 babies die on the first day of their birth across South Asia. It indicates almost one in every one minute. It is all because chronic malnutrition among expectant mothers. One million children who die each year on the day they are born, almost 40 percent of these are from India, Pakistan and Bangaladesh.

In India one out of every 170 mothers face risk of their life while in Nepal the risk is one in 190. In Nigeria, 89,700 deaths take place every day followed by Pakistan—59,800, China—50,600 Congo—48,400, and Tanzania—17000. Loss of children in India is more rampant in rural areas. Odisha, Uttar Pradesh, Gujarat, Bihar, Jharkhand and Madhya Pradesh top the list of children death on the first day of their birth. Expectant mothers' delivery is not done properly. Deliveries of expectant mothers are done by untrained rural dais instead of trained midwives or nurses. It is only because there is no network of health system in rural region of India. However there is some solace in Tamil Nadu where health care system are under the hand of well trained nurses—hence Tamil Nadu has no such deaths because of safe delivery.

By and large the entire India, especially rural areas, is poverty-ridden where persons do not have two-square of meals. Over 78 percent of population does not have access to proper food, drinking water and health care system, such scarcity results into malnutrition. In many cases, it has been found that if the children or mothers are escaped deaths during pregnancy or delivery time, they subsequently die of many diseases or many of them never remain or lead life of abnormal human beings because of diseases.

INDIA IS PASSING THROUGH CRISIS AFTER CRISIS, THANKS TO MANMOHAN SINGH'S SILENCE!

Sunday, 5 May 2013

What are happenings in India? Everyday, one listens a new thing, worse from the earlier one! Apart from deteriorating relations with our neighbouring countries like China, Sri Lanka, Pakistan, Nepal, Bangladesh, Burma, the country is sick of present political dis pension at home fronts. Scams, corruptions, failure of governance etc have become order of the day. Still the people of India are tolerating all these non-senses. It seems that we have entered into a decadent society where nobody appears concerned about the ills in the country. Such deteriorating situation has camouflaged to camouflet the entire system in India by political classes of all hues! Poverty is growing fast. Education and health have gone down to the drains despite huge expenditures since independence. Simmering discords in eastern states like Mizoram, Nagaland, Assam, Meghalaya, Tripura etc are posing threat to the unity and integrity of the country. Southern states like Tamil Nadu, Andhra Pradesh, Puduchery, Goa have altogether different ways in running the affairs. In Tamil Nadu, atrocity on dalits is rampantly on the higher sides! With regards to central, north and western states in India like Madhya Pradesh, Chhatishgarh, Delhi, Uttar Pradesh, Gujarat, are working on altogether on different tunes as if all these above mentioned states do not appear parts of the Indian Union. Bihar and West Bengal are on different wave-length where politics is taking driver's seat instead of development.

India has one of the weakest leadership as Manmohan Singh in the last nine years. Prime Minister Manmohan Singh seldom speaks on the burning issues affecting adversely the country. An indecisive Prime Minister quitely watch uncertainty at almost every level. His ruling United Progressive (UPA-two) led by Congress has become silent spectators of all these naked drama. Opposition political classes, specially the National Democatic Alliance (NDA), led by Hindu front BJP are fishing in troubled waters. Instead of showing off and embracing the ruling UPA combine for messing up the situation, this opposition political classes appear more interested in grabbing power by any means. Fruitful discussions in Parliament never happen like earlier occasions. The current parliament has notoriety of minimum working days in the history of parliamentary democracy in India because of walk-outs and boycott of the session by the opposition leaders. In the last four years. Of all countrymen are watching the melodrama with keen interest but helplessly.

Almost, all organs of the government-legislature, executive and judiciary seem to have dithered away and crippled. These organs have no coordination among each other. Such signal is giving eminent threat of anarchy and chaos in India. Strangely, if any thing serious happens, only thereafter, a solution is found in jet-set speed on pressure from various quarters. There are many cancers in all the organs of the government.

Recent killing of the Indian RAW personnel in Pakistan jail Saranjit Singh is recent example of dithering approaches of the Manmohan Singh government. Except "jaan ka badal jaan", a Pakistani national Sanaullah Ranjay, languishing in Jammu jail, was injured by irate inmates and Ranjay is in critical condition in the hospital. Is it not being called anarchy in India? Eminent journalist M J Akbar has rightly said in the Times of India, "India has become a joke in Maldives, a foe in Sri Lanka, a doubt in Bangladesh, a shrug in Nepal, a snigger in Pakistan and a taunt in China. Every neighbour has tested India and discovered that this government walks on its knees, India has never seemed as helplessly weak as now Foreign Minister Salman Khursid thinks China's incursion into Despang is acne which will disappear—perhaps after an application of multinational creams."

Few ministerial colleagues of Manmohan Singh and their close relatives are involved in neck-deep corruption as well as misdemeanour. Every day there is one story of corruption. The latest one is involving the Railway Minister Pawan Bansal. Bansal's nephew and son have been raided by the CBI for giving favour in prize and moneyed postings in the Railway Board. Specific evidences have been found against Pawan Bansal for propping up such scandal in the railways! It all started in UPA-2 of Manmohan Singh with TWO-G scams by the then telecommunication minister Raja, gobbeling up over Rs 1.75 lakh crore. Thereafter, Commonwealth game scam was surfaced. Subsequently AUDITOR and

Comptroller General also examined various flagship programmes i like MANREGA and detected huge bungling of funds and finally selling off coal blocks, worth Rs 1.85 lakh crore was detected. All these cases are being investigated by the CBI and being monitored by the Supreme Court. Union government's interferences in the affairs of the CBI have also come to light. Union Law minister Ashawani Kumar reportedly poked his nose over the status report of the CBI to the Supreme Court. Kumar was caught napping by the court but politicking is going to bail him out huge uproar were witnessed in the country over all these issues but our Prime Minister is maintaining golden silence over the issue.

Thanks to the outside support of the left parties to UPA-ONE government, the first term of Manmohan Singh government made some remarkable achievements. People's angers are growing. A next Lok Sabha election is due early next year. People will have the last laugh. But the way, development is going on in the NDA over prime ministerial nominee of much-maligned Gujarat Chief Minister Narendra Modi and NDA is on the verge of split with JD(U) leader and Bihar Chief Minister Nitish Kumar opposing Modi's candidature, Citizens of India have been left on tenterhook without any alternative!

One quotable quote, the writer Chetan Bhagat has written in The Times of India about "the so called empowering of slaves" and has compared the CBI as slave of successive union governments in India. Bhagat sarcastically writes, "Once upon a time, a king committed a grave mistake. He stole the state's money and destroyed national wealth. Angry citizens clamoured for justice. The King agreed. He appointed his pet slave to investigate the matter. The pet slave felt the King had done nothing wrong. The case was closed. Life went back to normal." This is what is happening in the Indian system, likening CBI as 'pet slave!

Our executive branch is said to be one of the corrupts organs in the world. Nothing moves without bribe in the government offices. Not only the senior officials succumb to the political pressure for tailored-made opinion and decision of course on money considerations in connivance with their political masters.

The Judiciary in India has different story. Although, the Supreme Court of India has largely escaped systematic criticism, beneath the surface one finds an institution that many court—watchers believe has strayed from the mission and May even unintentionally be undermining the rest of judicial system. There are many examples of intellectual and corruptions by the judges of the high courts and the Supreme courts.

Least said is better about the worse scenario of corruption in lower judicial organs at the district and sub-divisional levels. The high courts and the Supreme Court disproportionately spends thousands of hours hearing the cases of wealthier litigants situated in and around Delhi and from more affluent states. None the other hands, dozen of vital pending Constitution Benches matters have waiting to be heard for decades. For instance, for many years the court has failed to hear a pending Constitution Bench case to examine the definition of 'industry' in the key piece of labour legislation, creating uncertainty for employers and millions of workers. There is no question that the courts continue to be the last resort of the poor in their quest for justice. But courts are not as forthcoming or responsive as they used to be in defending the causes of the poor.

Like much of the rest of the judiciary, it is overwhelmingly Hindu upper caste (roughly 60 percent of the Supreme Court judges today; but the average representation of Hindu upper caste tends to be higher— closer to 70 percent) with currently no member of the scheduled caste, only two women and very little representation of the Other Backward Classes (hardly ten percent).

Are we Indian are impotent in this decadent society?

JAMMU AND KASHMIR CONFLICT: WHY INDIA AND PAKISTAN FAILED TO RESOLVE THE ISSUE?

Monday, 29 April 2013

\

Now enough is enough! The Jammu and Kashmir issue has been hanging fire for over 67 years. Both India and Pakistan are claiming the territory of the J&K. Over half a dozen war between India and Pakistan have been fought, entailing huge expenditures to both the countries. Indo-Pak borders always remain tense. People of the Jammu and Kashmir have been marginalized in the process of resolution of the conflict. They always remain in agonizing moments. No sincere efforts have been initiated to resolve the conflict. Both India and Pakistan seem to have reconciled to keep their domination in retaining their respective "portions"—Jammu and Kashmir and Azad Kashmir. Terror activities in the Jammu and Kashmir have become focal points of conflict for both the India/and Pakistan.

Much water has flown under Sutlej since the ruler of Kashmir Maharaja Hari Singh was forced to Kashmir's accession to India. But the million dollar question still arises why and how Maharaja Hari Singh acceded the Kashmir to India in 1947? Historical facts have different opinions. One of them is that the Maharaja temporarily acceded to India on October 22, 1947 because Pakhtoon tribal population from Pakistan raided Kashmir. And the Maharaja sought help from India and acceded to India "temporarily". Another version was that the Maharaja never wanted Kashmir to accede with India or Pakistan, but after independence of the Indian sub-continent, wished an "independent and sovereign Jammu and Kashmir" It is also said that tallest leader Sheikh Mohhammad Abdullah's liking for acceding the Kashmir to India, rather, forced Maharaja for request of military help from India from the clutches of Pakhtoon raiders. New Delhi always legitimized the accession by projecting such theory.

A recent book—KASHMIR: THE UNWRITTEN HISTORY—
by the Australian politico-strategic analyst, author and academician
Christopher Snedden has added one more of many books on this ticklish
issue! But Sneeden's book appears a different one because the book gives
vivid descriptions of the causes of division of Kashmir in 1947 and
throws light on the solution of the problem! In the opinion of Snnedden;
three important factors that instigating the division of the state that
ultimately was responsible for the present status of Jammu and Kashmir
(FRIONTLINE FORNIGHTLY REVIEW OF THE BOOK). Many
political scientists feel that Pakistan was responsible for pushing the tribal
people to annex Kashmir. But Snedden highlights the three major actions
including the Muslim uprising in Poonch in western Jammu, serious
inter-religious violence throughout the Jammu region and the creation
of 'Azad Kashmir' government on October 24, 1947, which the author
believes was the final blow to the unity of the state.

While speaking to tales of woes of Jammu and Kashmir people,
the book has called the residents of the state "J&K-ites". Therefore,
"let the people decide" is the peg of his proposal to resolve the dispute,
although he adds a caveat that the "biggest challenge will be forcing
India and Pakistan to agree on the process." According to the Frontline
review of the book; Snedden also blames the disunity, as they constituted
77 percent of the princely domain. Snedden has also disclosed that the
Mahraja was quite unpopular with the "muslim subjects" and his armed
forces had lost control of the large parts of the state. "Had Muslims
been united, it would have been difficult for the Maharaja to take such
decision.

Snedden also suggests that the people of the state were desperate
to decide their fate. He cites two further actions to strengthen this
argument. "In late October-November, Kashmiris formed a people's
militia to defend themselves against the invading Pukhtoons which
intended, after looting, raping ad pillaging Kashmiris to capture Jammu
and Kashmir for Pakistan and in early November pro-Pakistan Gilgitis
rebelled to sought to join Pakistan." Such action was enough hints for
determining the region's international status that time.

The author is also of the opinion that people of the Jammu and
Kashmir are the main stake-holders in the unresolved Kashmir dispute.
Such factors, in the opinion of the author, suggest the need for people
of the state in confidence to resolve the dispute. One another important
aspect in the book is about "Azad Kashmir". He is of the opinion that

"Azad Kashmir" has virtually become an" integral part" of Pakistan and is completely dependent on Islamabad. Thus the book emphasizes a greater role of the people of Jammu and Kashmir (on both sides) and calls them the 'third party' in the dispute since India and Pakistan have failed to resolve the conflict. The author argues that the people of Jammu and Kashmir are at the centre of dispute in every way and they need to be taken on board and not marginalized.

BEUTIFUL MOUNT EVEREST FIRST CONQUERED FROM AIR IN APRIL 4 1933!

Saturday, 27 April 2013

The times have changed. Now it is easier for men-kind to go at as much height in sky like journey on Moon, Mars etc. But there was time even the best quality of aeroplanes could achieve as much as height as it could. But here is adventurous story of April 04, 1933 from the Achieves of The Guardian when the world's highest mountain has surrendered to aeroplanes, circling 100 feet above the summit. Before I put the essay of the Guardian as written and reported, I must mention some of the backgrounds of beautiful Himalaya mountain range including the MOUNT EVEREST in Asia.

In SANSKRIT language and literature, HIMALAYA has been called—HIMA (snow) + ALAYA (dwelling). Means 'dwelling of snow'. This HIMALAYA, with some of the highest peaks including the height of the MOUNT EVEREST, in Asia is the youngest, highest and the longest mountain range in the world. It criss-crises five countries of the PLANET—Bhutan, Nepal, India, China and Pakistan. Significantly, the Himalayan mountain range is youngest mountain range in the globe because ricks are yet to be formed. Still there are lots of sand and soils mounds in the mountain range. Because of large scale of forest denunciation, recurring threats of floods have made life miserable in parts of Bihar and Uttar Pradesh in India. Soil and sands are flowing during flood period from various rivers, originating from Nepal, mainly because of large—scale forest cuttings of trees in forest range, especially in Nepal areas. It spreads plans of the Indian sub-continent from Tibetan plateau. The range runs west-north ward to the east-south east. about 24 km long. Not only that Himalaya mountain rage incorporates 100 mountains exceeding 7200 meters or over 23600 ft. height. Several places in the Himalaya mountain range have religious significances in Hinduism,

Islam, Jainism, Sikhism and Buddhism. In Hinduism, the Himalaya has been personified as the GOD-HEMANT, the god of snow, who is mentioned in the Hindu mythological books and scriptures like GEETA. HEMAN, the god of snow, was father of GANGA and SARSWATI, the most pious and well-known rivers in India!

NO doubt many mountaineers have succeeded in conquering Himalaya's MOUNT EVEREST, in the last 25 to 30 years, the journey of HIMALAYA including mount-Everest by the Houston Everest Expedition on April 03, 1933 was wonderful historically as reported in the issue of the Guardian—"From Archive, 4 April 1933: EVEREST conquered from the air." The story of The Guardian, apart from mentioning many significant aspects of the conquering of Himalaya's Everest, has pin-pointed one of the oldest airbases—PURNIA in BIhar and FORBESGANJ in BIHAR for meticulating planning and taking off the related planes to conquer the MOUNT EVEREST. The mission was "full of thrills and passive dangers". Lord Clydesdale, Colonel Blacker and the Flight Lieutenant Mcintyre had been team members of the Westland planes expedition. The Guardian has also referred the wonderful and experienced role Indian meteorological officer of Purnea S N Gupta, whose information and advice about weather on April 03, 1933 had been of great value.

Just I a reproducing below The Guardian report about Everest Conquering:—

From the archive, 4 April 1933: Everest conquered from the air. The world's highest mountain has surrendered to aeroplanes circling 100 feet above its summit guardian.co.uk, Thursday 4 April 2013 07.30 BST.

Lord Clydesdale, Colonel Blacker, and Flight Lieutenant McIntyre set off early yesterday in the Westland planes on what was intended to be a trial flight. But the wind conditions turned out to be so favourable that they went on to Everest, circled the summit at a hundred feet above it, and were safely backed again at Purnea soon after eleven. It is a splendid achievement, and hearty congratulations must go out to the airmen and to all who have made it possible. It is a splendid achievement—not for any material gains, any additions to aeronautical knowledge that it brings, for it brings few or none, but simply because it was one of the few last great spectacular flights in aviation which remained to be done.

No one would attempt to compare these three brief hours of adventure, full of thrills and passive dangers, with the long months of arduous physical toil which those must endure who attempt to conquer

Everest by land, in the old way of the mountaineer. But to assert man's mastery of the air by flying over the roof of the world must make its strong appeal to everyone's imagination, none the less. What strange account will the adventurers have brought back of Everest and its great south face as no living eye has seen it? What strange photographs and film record may they have obtained—obtained for the rest of us to share—of the unknown Himalayas, looked at from a height higher than bird has ever gone?

"This morning (April 3) the Indian meteorological officer at Purnea, Mr. S. N. Gupta, whose information and advice has been of very great value to the expedition, reported from balloon observations that the wind, which previously had been unsuitable, had dropped to a velocity of 57 m.p.h. at 33,000 feet which altitude we had decided would be the most suitable working height for a photographic survey. Our two machines took off at 8 25 from Lalbalu Aerodrome in still air. The Houston-Westland plane contained Colonel Blacker and me, and the Westland-Wallace, piloted by Flight Lieutenant McIntyre, with Mr. S. R. Bonnett, who is the aerial photographer, as observer.

"Our direct route to the summit meant flying on tracks 342 degrees. This necessitated changing the compass course at intervals more to the west on account of increased wind velocity with height according to our weather report. We had relied on overcoming to some extent the difficulty of accurate compass navigation caused by this frequent change of wind speed by the good landmarks near and along our track.

"A heavy dust haze rising to a considerable height almost completely obscured the ground from Forbesganj to the higher mountain ranges. This made aerial survey work impossible. We climbed slowly at low engine revolutions to a height of 10,000 feet. By this height the crews of both machines had tested their respective electrical heating sets, and McIntyre and I signalled to each other that everything was satisfactory. After 30 minutes' flying we passed over Forbesganj, our forward emergency landing ground forty miles from Purnea, and at a height of 19,000 feet Everest first became visible above the haze."

INDIA SQUANDERING TO GALVANISE YOUTHS!

Tuesday, 23 April 2013

INDIA is squandering, one of the best opportunity, to galvanize its youths for nation building and emerging one of the best global power because of indifferent approaches of successive union governments and state governments towards health, education, employment etc India is expected to witness one of the best youth power in the cosmos by 2040!. The average age of Indian population will be 29 years by the end of the decade. By comparing other developed and developing power, such scenario in China and United States of America will be youths under age of average 37 years, Japan—48 years and western European countries—45 years. According to a report of the International Monetary Fund (IMF); India's youth power has the potentiality to produce additional two percent per capita GDP growths each year for the next two decades. Reacting to a detailed report, headlined, "Has India lost the 21st Century?" in TEHELKA, the Editor of the OUTLOOK INDIA UTTAM SENGUPTA, comments on the FACEBOOK," Political discourse and debate in the Parliament and on TV channels focus on the subjects? What need to be done? Political bloodletting and campaigns of oneupmanship do not address bread and butter issues. Time people demand answers from all political parties, not just the government."

But what is exactly happening in India? Indian youths are being misguided due to lack of proper education, human approaches etc. Large number of youths are being misguided in recent years and they are being trained and being utilized by non-ideological forces, mainly for extortion in the name of Naxal activities and other social activities. Their 'non-ideological mentors' pay them a small share of what they extort from businessmen and industrialists. Such practices have become attractive for unemployed youths in naxal-infested villages and crime-prone areas of the country. Another instances are unemployed and directionless youths, indulging in crimes besides, we see, million of angry youths and women taking to streets for some reasons or others to vent their frustration as Indian's growth story is gradually slipping away. They have their right perceptions that they have been let down by the government. In this game of venting their anger and frustration, they are again being misguided by many organizations, particularly political parties-whether they may be Swami Ramdev or Anna Hazare or anybody—they are not being trained to change the society and its system through ballot papers but by arson, loots and invasion on sheets of power like, Parliament!Bubbling youth power and its emerging trend in India must be utilized for the reconstruction and development of the country right from the days of being them in their mothers' womb to their health and education.

Ravi Venkatesan, former chairman of the Microsoft India, who has written a book "Conquering the Chaos: Win in India, Win Everywhere" to be published in mid-June in the United States by Harvard Business Review Press, has said in a recent interview to India Ink, "India is important not just because it is a big market. India is important because it is litmus test for the companies' success in emerging market. Most emerging markets look like India—they have uncertainty, corruption, poor infrastructures and chaos. It could be Brazil, Indonesia or Nigeria. But few have the same potential, so India is in many ways a lead case for emerging markets. Right now, multinational companies or corporations have two choices. They can either not grow, or they can embrace the chaos of emerging markets. Europe is not going to sort itself out anytime soon—they need to learn to deal with these situations. If you think you can escape chaos, you are sadly mistaken."

But the ground realities of India are multi-dimensional. India and its young men are" growing mass of largely undernourished, undereducated, unemployable, who aspire for a better life but do not have means to get their because they are not qualified for job market and even if they are, jobs do not exist," says Tehelka essay. India's present workforce (the 15-64 age groups) comprises 430 million people. Of them, only a few have received formal vocational training. Our organized sector, home to the jobs connected to aspiration, money and India's growth story, employs only 30 million people. This leaves 400 million people in the unorganized sector, feeding for them. Over 60 percent of our work force is engaged in agriculture, which contributes only 18 percent of GDP, indicative of the widespread disguised unemployment and low productivity.

As I have earlier said problem story of Indian people start in mothers' womb! Forty percent of children in India are malnourished. Forty-three percent in the age group of 12-23 months receive full immunization; forty-eight percent are underweight. Fifty percent of all deaths under age of five are related to malnutrition. Forty-five percent children are stunted. Seventy percent of children under age five are anemic. Thirty percent of adults have chronic nutrition deficiency. Fifty—five percent women are anemic. (Source: Cry Foundation). While detailing the impact of all these things, the World Bank (WB) has said the effect of undernourishment during first eight years after birth can be devastating and enduring. Its impact the individual health as well as the ability to learn, communicate, think analytically, socialize effectively and adapt a new environment and people. While more than half the deaths before the age of five are caused by malnutrition, for those who do survive past five and find their way into schools, shouldering the hopes of their parents, life does not get much better and the system sets them up for failure."

There are many strange things in India despite the tall claims of the successive union and state governments. According to the recent Annual Status of Education Report (ASER); 60 percent of the children in Class fifth cannot read at a Class second level and 75 percent cannot complete simple division sums. The government claims success on "Sarva Shiksha Abhiyan" by 96 enrolments in primary education, there is in fact an eighty percent dropout by Class twelve. Thus 27 million children who annually enroll in primary schools across the country, only 5.4 million make it to Class twelve. Shockingly, the quality of education is worse throughout the country. There are seldom quality teachers.

Ninety percent gross enrolment ratio in primary education with 27 million children entering primary education; two-one ratio of primary schools to senior primary schools; forty percent the dropout rates by class eight; eighty percent dropout rate by class twelve, 15 percent in college; fifty percent of children in rural India will go to private schools, i.e. pay for education by 2020; main reasons of female dropouts is lack of toilets and seventy-five percent, proportion of all children enrolled in class fifth who could not do simple divisions (Source:—ASER). India needs a huge number of teachers, numbering over 6.3 million to cater the need of children in the 6-14 age groups. Not only that there are need of brightest teachers from brightest five percent to ten percent of graduates like Singapore and Finland!

More over, another burning problem in India is employment. India needs to create 20 million jobs yearly. In the next 20 years, India will add 480 million people to labour market. India's formal sector comprises only 30 million jobs, which is only seven percent of total labour forces of 430 million. In the meantime, based on the figures provided in the Annual Survey of Industry report of 2010-11, there were 1,61,458 factories operating in the manufacturing sector, which employed around 12.3 million people and had a total investment capital of about 22 lakhs crore. There is urgent need to create 20 million jobs a year. If emerging economy of India does not take concerns of these factors, social unrest is bound to loom large over the country!

PAKISTAN ELECTIONS: IS IT 'DEMOCRACY' OR 'RELIGIOCRACY'?

Saturday, 13 April 2013

It is commonly said that democracy is the best form of government! This form of government has peoples' participation and ultimately power remains in the hand of people. But least said is better about this democratic form of government in various nations of the planet! One such glaring example is forthcoming elections, scheduled on May 10, in Pakistan. In the name of democracy, Pakistan, an Islamic country where Islam orthodox only prevails. People of the world are startled to find that under democratic system in Pakistan, politicians of that country are being tested on whether they are pious enough to face the elections. Only 'devout' Muslims' politicians are eligible to contest the elections, Judges from the lower courts, who are overseeing the elections, quizzed them on whether they could recite particular Koranic verses from memory or knew how to perform various Islamic rituals.

Interestingly one candidate was asked to pledge that from now on he would 'pray five times' and if participant-contestants are found lacking all these things, they are out rightly debarred from the contesting elections! The judges are drawing on vaguely worded clauses in Pakistan's Constitution that insist all members of the Parliament must be 'devout Muslims' it may be mentioned that clauses were imposed by General Mohammad Zia-ul-Haq, a former military ruler and religious hard-liner, as part of his sweeping "Islamization" programme during 1980s. In the past, election officials turned blind eye to the exacting religious standards set out by clauses. As many observers have quipped over the years, the stipulated demands that lawmakers be "sagacious" 'nonprofligate' observe all mandatory religious duties and abstain from 'major sins' would likely to lead an empty Parliament.

More over, the judges, conducting the Pakistan elections, won applause for standing up to lying politicians. But some question the wisdom of the move. "It is illegal, but there is a political context to it" says Ai Dayan Hasan, Director of the Pakistan Human Right Watch. A recent report in The Times World has said," when it comes to Pakistan's elections, many derive comfort from the fact that the religious right never wins more than 10 percent of the vote. But the political parties that neatly evade both laws imposed by Zia and Musharraf are from religious right. After being chastened at the last elections, they are back on the ascendants. When it came to degree requirement for contesting elections, as imposed by Musharraf, they madrasas education was mostly deemed equivalent to an advanced degree. And of course, they breezed through the piety tests." In 2002, Musharraf imposed a condition that all parliamentarians should be graduates.

The scrutiny process, critics say; could end up tilting the electoral field. "They are using a controversial overboard law imposed on the constitution by a dictator for precisely the purpose of arbitrary political screening"; says Hasan and adds," rather than allowing the voters to decided who's fit to sit in Parliament, the judges are arrogating that right to themselves. This is a form of pre-poll rigging against those who do not meet approval of these authorities on extremely flimsy grounds."

A leading lawyer Babar Sattar says, "It is impossible to decide who is and who is not a good Muslim—the language of Article-62 of the Pakistan Constitution, referring to the relevant clauses in the Constitution is not just enforceable. Are we saying someone who does not pray five times a day cannot be a Member of Parliament"? The wording is so misty as to be open to widely divergent interpretations. Part of problem is that judges can read into these words their own anxieties."

Many of the members of lower judiciary, who are scrutinizing the candidates, have inherited their religious views from the austere readings offered in standard Pakistani textbooks, says Raja, another lawyer. The attitudes on display also appear to reflect a growing sense of religiosity in Pakistan and disenchantment with the political class. A report issued this week by N British Council found that 38 percent of young voters between the ages of 18 to 29 think Sharia law is the best political system of Pakistan. Nearly a third said they would like military rule. And a paltry 29 percent said they wanted a continuation of democracy.

However, one factor that along with failing to persuade the youth of the merits of democracy, the politicians have also been unsuccessful in rolling back Zia's legacy. "These provisions should not be in the Constitution, the Parliament has clearly failed to take them out", says Sattar. Despite passing three constitutional amendments, the parliamentarians left the Islamic provisions untouched. Some ascribe the reluctance to fear of a religious backlash. In 2011, two major politicians were killed after speaking out against the country's notorious blasphemy laws.

Strangely, a well-known politician and long-standing newspaper columnist has even been disqualified to contest elections by Scrutiny judge because judges frowned him on a reference to alcohols in one of his weekly articles. No doubt alcohol is banned in Pakistan, though bootleggers discreetly do a brisk trade. Intense scrutiny being enforced for the first time in Pakistan. Much of it is focused on ethics and civil law. Recently for military ruler Pavez Mushrraf's nomination were rejected because judges said he subverted the Constitution when he mounted the 1999 coup that overthrow a civilian government. Strangely, nominations of many politicians have been rejected on the ground of variety of offences including defaulting in bank loans and failing to pay water bills.

However, right advocates and legal experts say judges are also reaching past questions of financial probity to arbitrarily decide who is a pious Muslim to sit in next Pakistan's Parliament.

INDIAN GOVERNMENT ENRICHING RICH AT THE COST OF POOR!

Wednesday, 10 April 2013

The way UPA government, led by Dr Manmohan Singh, is moving to reach the 'mirage' of the so called development of India, the time is not so far off when entire economy of the country will be drained out and controlled by the capitalist classes! Instead of bailing out the country from poverty, malnutrition, lack of education etc, the Indian government is building about 100 capitalists, corporate, political classes, industrialists and rich persons in the category of super rich by writing off government dues with them in respect of income-tax, duties on gold and diamonds, excise duty, custom duty etc since 2005-06 to 2012-13. The Forbes, the Oracle of Indian Business Journalism, which prepares a list each year of billionaires the world over, has named 55 Indians figure on the list (up from 48 last year) in 2013 with an average wealth worth around Rs 190.8 billion. Eminent journalist P Sainath in a recent essay in The Hindu, under headline "The Feeding frenzy of kleptocracy", says, "Since 2005-06, taxes, duties for the corporate world and rich have been written off at the rate of Rs seven million a minute average. Duties waived on gold and diamonds in the last 36 months equal the 2G scam amount."

More over, India ranks five in the world of billionaires on the Forbes List. The rank of the country in 2013, the ranking of India with regards United Nations Human Index (NHI) remains at 136 out of 186 nations. Over 78 populations, especially in rural areas hardly get even one meal a day. The India government seems more serious in waiving spree to rich people instead of strengthening and implementing welfare measures for poverty-ridden people of the country. Many countries in Latin America and the Caribbeans except one Haiti are ahead of us.

In 2005-06, the India government has waived corporate income-tax to the tune of Rs 34618 crore, in 2006-07 Rs 50075 crore, in 2007-08

Rs 62199 crore, 2008-09—Rs 66901 crore, 2009-10—Rs 72881 crore, 2010-11 Rs 57912 crore, 2011-12—Rs 61765 crore, 2012-13—Rs 68008 crore (Total—Rs 474359 crore). Excise Duty waiving has also similar tale! Right from 2005-06 to 2012-13, the total amount of waiving in respect of excise duty comes to Rs 1121122 crore. Year-wise break-up is 2005-06—Rs 66760 crore. 2006-07—Rs 75475 crore, 2007-08—Rs 87468 crore, 2008-09—Rs 128293 crore, 2009-10—Rs 16121 crore, 2010-11—Rs 192227, 2011-12—Rs 195590 crore and 2012-13—Rs 206188. In respect of custom duty waiving since 2005-06 to 2012-13, the total amount come to Rs 1515688 crore. In 2005-06, such amount was Rs 127730 crore; 2006-07—Rs 137107crore, 2007-08—Rs 153593 crore, 2008-09—Rs 225752, 2009-10—Rs 207949 crore, 2010-11—Rs 172740, 2011-12—Rs 232852 crore, and 2012-13—Rs 253967. Thus in eight financial years, the India government has waived Rs 3111169 crore in the name of so called encouragement for investments.

Before I further write about foregoing revenue in respect of gold, diamonds and jewellery from 2005-06 to 2012-13 as well as per capita availability of cereals and pulses daily in grams in different periods,. I must mention that the budget of the current financial year" has almost nothing worthwhile for say, health or education where there is a decline compared to allocation last year (in proportion to GDP). Ditto for rural development. And micro-rise in for food that will quickly be taken care of by prices." Sadly even the sub-Saharan standards would be an improvement. India ranks 65th in the 79 hungriest nations in the Global Hunger Index (GHI). The GHI score of India for 2012 was worse than it was 15 years earlier in 1996.

Here it must be noted the per capita net availability of cereals and pulses daily in grams. On and average, it is declining in every five years period of 'reforms' without exception. Significantly in the 20 years preceding the reforms—1972-1991—it rose every five year period without exception. Averagely from 1972-76, the availability of cereals was 383.9 grams, pulses—43.8 grams ore capital net availability. Like wise from 1977 to 1981, the availability was 407.5 grams cereals and pulse 40.4 grams, another average availability from 1982-86 was 420.2 cereals and 40.6 pulses and average such figure for 1987-91 was 440.7 cereals and 39.6 pulses. After reform years of 1992-96, the average per capita availability was 439.3 cereals and 35.6 pulses, average 1997-2001—these were 423.7 cereals and 33.6 grams pulses, another average for 2002-06 was 419.6 grams cereals and 32.9 grams cereals and last average of

2007 onwards 4068 grams of cereals and 37.8 grams of pulses on and average. Now anybody can imagine the plight of availability of per capita cereals and pulses per person, which have declined during economic liberalization years!

India government is paying full attention for benefits to capitalists and rich persons. Have anybody heard any middle class salaried persons or others' liability in respect of income-tax and duties have been waived? But the government of India is on spree of revenue forgoing on gold, diamonds and jewellery from 2005-06 to 2012-13. Total sum of Rs 314457 crore have been waived during these period on gold, diamonds and jewellery. Such figures are:—2005-06—Rs 16935 crore; 2006-07— Rs 25672 crore, 2007-08—Rs 25586 crore; 2008-09—Rs 27649 crore, 2009-2010 Rs 49164; 2011-12—Rs 65975; 2012-13—Rs 61035 crore.

In this manner, the flagship welfare programmes like MGRGM, Indira Awas, child and women welfare, education, health, subsidized food to poor are suffering in India due to lack adequate funds. But on the other hand, the government is helping with open heart the tax-payers money for the advantage of capitalists, corporate, and rich persons in the country. P Sainath says, "one of the biggest write-offs in this year's budget is the custom duty on gold, diamonds and jewellery—Rs 61035 crore. That is no more that what has been written off on crude oil and mineral oils, or even on machinery. The waiver on gold and diamonds in the just 36 months is Rs 1.76 trillion (or what we lost in the 2G scam). It is not as if we have not been generous with them in other secrets, though. The latest write-offs in corporate income-tax is even higher at Rs 68,006 crore. The total revenue foregone this year Rs five.28 trillion as others pointed out, is greater than fiscal deficit such write offs since 2005-06 is Rs 31.11 trillion. It also means we are writing off taxes and duties for corporate mob and rich at the rate of over Rs seven million every single minute on average."

Sources: The Hundu achieves, Successive union budgets, Statement of revenue receipts; Economic Survey of 2012-13 and Economic Survey of 2010-11 and various other websites.

RELEVANCE OF COMMUNISM!

Saturday, 30 March 2013

So many strange things are happening in the Cosmos! One of them is Communism. With the collapse of the Soviet Union and China's Leap Forward into capitalism, communism appears to be faded into the quint back-drop. It appears that the class conflict that Marx believed determined the course of history seemed to have melted away in the so called prosperous era of free trade and free enterprise. The Times Finance commented, "The far reaching power of globalization, linking the most remote corners of the planet in lucrative bonds of finance, outsourcing and border less manufacturing, offered everybody from Silicon valley tech gurus to Chinese farm girl's ample opportunities to get rich. But the global economy in a protracted crisis and workers around the world burdened by joblessness, debt and stagnant incomes, Marx's biting critique of capitalism—that the system is inherently unjust and self-destructive—cannot be easily dismissed. Marx theorized that the capitalists system would inevitably impoverish the masses as the world's wealth became concentrated in the hands of a greedy few. "Accumulation of wealth at one pole is at the same time accumulation of misery, agony of toil, slavery, ignorance, brutality, mental degradation at the opposite pole", according to Marx.

Notwithstanding like any form of government, Communism actually evolved over many years but the two philosophers, who captured and codified the basic concept of communism of a form of government that treated everyone equally, were Karl Marx and Friedrich Engels. Their ground breaking publication was "The Communist Manifesto" and it may surprise you to find that it has lot of ideas that are popular to our democracy (like schooling of children, not just the rich). More surprisingly Marx felt that there was natural evolution of political systems and that totalitarianism and imperialism naturally evolved into capitalism and that capitalism and that capitalist just a step along the way to an even, egalitarian society form of government that was communism. Karl Heinrich Marx was a Prussian-German philosopher and revolutionary. His ideas played a significant role in the establishment of the social sciences and the development of socialist movement.

Karl Marx is dead and buried but his philosophies of Communism and socialism have great relevance. With the new liberalized economic policy throughout the globe, particularly America, China, a big gap between the rich and poor has been created. Rich are getting richer while middle class and poor are getting poorer. Exploitation of poor is at its zenith."The income gap is producing a level of tension that I have never seen in my life time," says Richard Wolff, a Marxist economist at New School of New York. Tensions between economic classes in the US are clearly on the rise. Society has been perceived as split between 99 percent (the regular folk, struggling to get by) and the one percent (the connected and privileged super rich getting richer every day). Throughout the world strong to very strong conflict between rich and poor, particularly In China and India are taking explosive shape.

The Times Finance says, "A SEP study from the Economic Policy Institute (EPI) in Washington noted that the medium annual earnings of a full time, male worker in the US in 2011, at $48,202 were smaller than in 1973. Between 1983 to 2010, 74 percent of the gains in wealth in the US went to richest five percent while the bottom 60 percent suffered a decline, the EPI calculated. No wonder some have given the 19th century German philosopher a second look. In China, the Marxist country that turned its back on Marx. Yu Rongjun was inspired by world events to pen a musical based on Marx's classic Das Kapital, "you can find reality matches what is described in the book, says the playwright. One classic example of the US—"Trickle Down economics", which claims that the success of one percent will benefit the 99 percent. Such rhetoric of America has come under heavy scrutiny.

If one considers these inequalities throughout the planet countries, he will have to say Marx was entirely correct. His "dictatorship of proletariat" did not quite work as planned. But the consequence of widening inequality is just what Marx had predicted: class struggle is back. The Times Finance writes, "Workers of the wold are growing angrier and demanding their fair share of the global economy. It seems that from the floor of U S Congress to the streets of Athens to the assembly lines of southern China, political and economic events are being shaped by escalating tensions between capital and labour, a degree unseen since the communist revolutions of 20th century. How this struggle plays out will influence the direction of global economic policy, the future of welfare state, political stability in China and who governs from Washington to Rome."

Ferocity of new class struggle has penetrated deep with more revolution-type movement in France. and financial crisis and budget cuts for poor made the situation worse in France and the rich-poor divide widened to such an extend that citizens of France voted the Socialist Party's Francois Hollande, who had once proclaimed: "I do not like the rich". In China, Mao Zedong might have insisted that "political power grows pout of barrel of guns" but in word here Das Kapital is more and more mobile, the weapons of class struggle has changed. Rich-poor divide is perhaps most volatile in China. Newly installed President of China Xi Jinping faces challenge. Even in rapidly expanding emerging markets, tension between rich and poor is becoming a primary concern for policy makers. The Times Finance commented, "contrary to what many disgruntled American and Europeans believe, China has not been a workers' paradise. The 'iron rice bowl—the Mao-era practise of guaranteeing workers jobs for life-faded with Maoism and during the reform era, workers have had few rights. Even though wage income in China's cities is growing substantially, the rich-poor gap is extremely wide." Another Pew study revealed that nearly half of the Chinese surveyed consider the rich-poor divide a very big problem, while eight out of ten agreed with the proposition that the rich—just get richer while the poor get poorer in China. The report has also mentioned, "resentment is reaching a boiling point in China's factory towns and they say people from outside see our lives as very bountiful but the real life in the factory a is very different. Facing long hours, rising cost, indifferent managers and often late pay, workers are beginning to sound like true proletariat. Workers are organizing and uniting themselves to protest atrocities. Experts believe it has been on the rise, workers have become outspoken in their demand for better wages and working condition. Such tactics have left China's proletariat distrustful of their proletariat dictatorship. Social unrest is bound to creep in China to protest liberalized economic policy.

That is the ultimate fall-out in China. Class interest brings class struggle. by forcibly overthrow of existing social condition. Marx wrote: "the proletariats have nothing to lose but their chains" World labourers are increasingly inpatients with their feeble prospects. Ten of thousands have taken their streets of cities like Madrid, Athens, Delhi etc, protesting stratospheric unemployment and the austerity measures that making matter worse. Despite such volcanic situation throughout the world, the current economic policy, however, continues to fuel tension. In China, lip services have been adopted to narrow the income gap amid huge corruption. India government by its new economic policy not only growing rich-poor gap but encouraging rampant corruption. In Europe debt burdens have slashed welfare programmes even as joblessness has risen and growth sagged.

Thus communism, diagnosed by Marx, getting deeper to ameliorate the deplorable condition of poor and middle classes. If the policy makers do not discover new methods of ensuring fair economic opportunity, the workers of the wold may unite, and Marx will have last laugh!

64 MILLION URBAN POPULATION IN MAJOR CITIES LIVE IN SLUMS

Tuesday, 26 March 2013

Indian cities are said to be biggest slums in the planet! Over 64 million people in six major urban cities in India live in slums in degrading condition. According to country's first complete census of its vast slum population; over 64 million Indian live in most deplorable urban environment very much like much-publicized Oscar-winning movie—'Slumdog Millionare'. The first-ever nationwide report-prepared from data collated for the 2011 national census—looks at urban slums in about 4,000 towns across the country. (A slum is defined as a settlement of at least 60 households deemed unfoit for human habitation, but the report does not cover every towns and cities in the vast country like India).

The report gives alarming scenario of bleak vision of the future of urbanization in India. Ten towns with a population of around 5, 000 have been categorized as 'all slum towns' These towns concentrated in four states, namely Jammu and Kashmir, Uttar Pradesh, West Bengal and Sikkim. Mumbai has the largest absolute population of slum dwellers: 41 percent of its 20.5 million people. In percentage terms, India's commercial capital has been overtaken by two other megacities: the bustling port city of Vishakapatnam on the Bay of Bengal (43 percent of its 1.7 million inhabitants) and the central India cities of Jabalpur, (42 percent of its 1.3 million people). Open sewers and poverty are rampant in these slum clusters. At the same time it also shows many slum residents own mobile phones and televisions in their slum cluster respective houses. Both legal and irregular electricity connections are prevalent in these slum areas, the report said.

However, New Delhi, the capital of India, has comparatively low 15 percent households in slums, while the big cities of Kolkata and Chennai had 30 percent and 29 percent respectively, Bengaluru, formerly known as Bangalore, had only nine percent slum dwellers. A nation-wide survey has indicated that more than one-third of slum homes have no indoor toilets and 64 percent are not connected to sewerage systems. About half of the house-holds lived in only one room or shared with another family. Significantly, 70 percent have television and 64 percent have mobile phones. All these slums in major cities, especially in Mumbai are close to posh apartments complexes resided by millionaires and top officials. In these slum colonies, residents have to queue up for hours for toilets and also for drinking water from public hydrants.

After such alarming slum dwellers in Indian cities without any basic facility the Planning Commission has recommended urban clusters with as few as 20 house-holds should be classed as slums. The Registrar General of India Census Dr C Chandramouli said, "We will be analyzing the census data on the basis of the new definition also. This is likely to increase the number slum household's acrodss the country."

CHILDREN'S EDUCATION IN MESS IN INDIA!

Saturday, 23 March 2013

India's education scenario is worse. Less said is better about secondary and higher education in the country. Imparting education has become a trade in India for earning huge money under political and bureaucratic patronage. Whatever may be the government statistics, over 68 percent of children, particularly girl child, are deprived of education, especially in the rural areas, thanks to the lackadaisical approach of the union and the state governments. But for rich, education is easy because they could afford huge sum to educate their children! Four years ago, the World Bank upgraded India from "poor" country to middle-income one. Being alarmed over world-wide criticism over non-availability of education to children, specially in majority rural areas, and wide-spread illiteracy the India government awoke from deep slumber and enacted Right to Education Act in 2009, a free and compulsory education is guaranteed for all children aged between six and 14. To some extend primary education school enrolment is looking up! Earlier this year, the independent Annual Status of Education Report into rural schools found declining levels of achievements, with more than half children in standard five-aged around 10—unable to read a standard two-level.

According to Oxfam India's Anjela Taneja; going to school, as those monitoring progress on the millennium development goal of achieving universal primary education have increasingly realized, is one thing, the quality of education you get to another. Within government schools pupils face numerous challenges. Overcrowded class rooms, absent teachers and unsanitary condition as well as insecurity to children are common complaints and can lead parents to decide it is worth their child going to schools.

A report of the National Council for Teachers Education (NCTE) estimated that an additional 1.2 million teachers were needed to fulfill the RTE Act requirements and last year the RTE forum, a civil society collective of around 10,000 non-governmental organizations (NGOs) that only five percent of government schools complied with the basic standards for infrastructures set by the Act. Some 40 percent of primaries had more than 30 students per class rooms; and 60 percent did not have electricity, a report of UK-based Guardian newspaper says, quoting NCTE. The RTE Forum also reported official figures, showing that 21 percent teachers were not professionally trained. Taneja neither further points out nor do enrolment figures necessarily reflect who is actually attending schools. The number of primary age children not in school in India was put at 2.3 million in 2008 but other estimates suggest it could be as high as eight million. According to an Indian government report, the primary drop-out rate in 2009 was 25 percent.

More over to put the children in 'child labour' by their parents for livelihood is also one of the major factors of drop-outs in schools. Girl child and marginalized groups such as very poor and the disabled, are often left behind. While girls attend primary schools in roughly equal numbers to boys, the gap widens as they get older and more are forced to drop out to help with work at home or get married. Of the out-of school children in 2008, 62 percent are girls; they make up two-thirds of illiterate 15- to 24-year-old. And two-thirds of that not in school was from those lowest in caste system, tribal groups and Muslim communities despite those historically oppressed groups making up only 43 percent of India's children. Taneja is of the opinion that neighborhood 'low budget' private schools serving low income families desperate to provide children with a quality education have mushroomed. But they are unregulated and lack trained teachers and proper infrastructures.

Quality of teaching in government primary schools, especially in rural areas, is insufficient and poor. In many such schools, there are some of the gloomy bare-walled class rooms, having low benches and desks, the girls sit on the floor with books in their laps. The Global Campaign for Education (GCE), a coalition 26 NGOs and teaching unions wants all nations to allocate at least six percent of GDP on education, India has been promising that since 1968, but the figure has never topped four percent and currently it is 3.7 percent. Reacting over such deplorable manner of the Indian government Taneja says, "It is issue of political will, rather than a lack of cash. Education is not a vote widening issue in a system of frequent elections, where pledges need to be delivered immediately."

Political classes have no stake because they do not tend to send their children to government schools. As the 2015 deadline for the millennium goal of primary education looms, there are disappointments among parents for imparting education to their children in India, particularly girl child. Progress on the education, initially, was rapid but has stalled since 2008 and 61 million children remain out of education, resulting into marginalized citizens' children suffering in INDIA.

"CHINESE PARLIAMENT HAS 83 BILLIONAIRES"

Monday, 18 March 2013

ACCUMULATION of wealth in a few hands throughout the COSMOS is said to 'bad economy'. Such capitalist practice deprives the individual and society as a whole in sharing the fruits of nations' resources and they continue to be neglected! There are normally three forms of system in sharing wealth—accumulation of wealth in few hands, is called 'capitalism',; distribution of wealth equally to the society, is called 'socialism'; and distribution of wealth equally to all individual each is called 'communism'. Apart from these basic facts, there are many versions of economy, deliberated by economists throughout the globe.

A recent startling report, published in The Financial Times, has revealed that the Legislature (National People's Congress) of the World's major communist country—CHINA is wealthiest in the world, being a communist country. About 3000 elected delegates of the Congress had assembled recently on a 13-day session at the Great Hall of the People in Beijing. The session concluded on last Sunday with the installation of Xi Jiping as President of China in the capacity of the new General Secretary of the Chinese Communist Party. Li Keqiang has been elected as Premier of China.

There are 83 dollar billionaires among delegates to the China's Parliament. Indian Parliament has hardly four billionaire including Janata Dal (U) MP Mahendra Prasad from Bihar, Vijay Mallay of Karnataka. The United States of America, which is said to be world's richest and advanced nation, has not a single billionaire in the House of Representative or the Senate. Paradoxically the China, which is hard-core communist country, has, surprisingly huge wealth, accumulated in the hands of individuals.

The recently concluded delegates session of the National People's Congress (NPC) in Beijing, has seen the gathering of the wealthiest and richest people of the world. according to the China-based Hurun Global Rich List. Thirty-one delegates with more than $1 billion in personal wealth and assets were identified. The riches is Zong Qinghou, founder of Chinese drink maker Wahaha, with an estimated fortune of $13 billion, according to Hurun. Huge hidden wealth of many China's top leaders and their families have been detected by the analysts, say Hurun report. The number of dollar billionaires identified by the report was up 17 percent this year from the last year when 28 billionaires attended the NPC and 43 were the at the CPPCC. The average for tune among the 83 wealthiest NPC and CPPCC delegates is $ 3.35 billion, according to Hurun report, compared with average annual wage for Chinese urban worker less that $ 7000. Comparing the US house members, each of the 83 richest members of the US house and Senate has an average of $ 56.4 million, according to figures from the Centre for Responsive Politics.

More over, the NPC is tasked with approving legislation proposed by the ruling Communist Party of China, but in practice it plays a mostly ceremonial role. Another 52 billionaires are delegates to the Chinese People's Political Consultative Conference, a toothless advisory body that meets at the same time as the NPC for about two weeks each year in early March. At nearly 3,000 delegates, the NPC is the biggest legislative assembly in the world while the CPPCC boasts about 2,200 delegates.

In a communist country like China's authoritarian but nominally egalitarian system, the convergence of power and great wealth is highly sensitive topic and one that communist leaders regard as potentially destabilizing. The newly-appointed head of the party and military, Xi Jinping, has launched a campaign against extravagance and corruption immediately upon taking office in the last November. Xi Jinping has said, "It will make priority of social spending and other measures to spread prosperity more evenly and narrow a politically volatile gap between China's wealthy elite and poor majority as well combat endemic corruption. We must resolutely reject formalism, bureaucrat ism, hedonism and extravagance and resolutely fight against corruption and other misconducts in all manifestation."

This tone and tenor of Jinping's statement has reportedly sent a clear signal to the China's ultra wealthy that, now more than ever, they need to be inside the political tent. "Our government is a totalitarian one with an axe hanging over every body's head and the decision over whose head it will fall on lines with officials" said Fang Xingyuan Feng, a researcher at the Chinese an Academy of Social Sciences, a government think tank. "When business people amass fortune, they need to protect it—so either they find an agent to do so or they become an official themselves. Another popular choice is to acquire a foreign passport, and we are already seeing a lot of CPPCC members who have become foreigners."

The top three richest members of the CPPCC are all sons of Hong Kong tycoons, with Victor Li, the son of Asia's richest man, Li Ka-shing, coming in first with an estimated family fortune of $ 32 billion. Hong Kong's relatively smooth transition from a former British colony back to Chinese territory over the past 15 years has bee helped by support from the territory's richest citizens, who were mostly co-opted by the Communist Party in exchange for business opportunities on the mainland.

COAL-BASED POWER PLANTS ENDANGERING LIVES IN INDIA AND EUROPE: 1.20 LAKH DIE IN INDIA YEARLY BECAUSE OF POWER PLANTS POLLUTION!

Friday, 15 March 2013

Fast growing pace of industrialization, without any preventive measures, in India is creating more and more problems for inhabitants. Rampant setting-up of coal power plants is proving public health hazard. In India alone 80000 to 120000, premature deaths have come to light yearly and 20 million population have been suffering from asthma due to air pollution from coal-based power plants, specially in the region of West Bengal, Jharkhand, Delhi, Mumbai, western Maharshtra, eastern Andhra Pradesh and the Chandanpur-Nagpur region of Vidarbha. The first study of the health impact of India's dash for coal, conducted by the Greenpace under former World Bank head of pollution, says the plants cost hospitals $3.3-$4.6 in a year—a figure certain to rise as the coal industry struggles to keep up with the demands for electricity. Almost all regions of coal-based power plants were found to be most polluted but Mumbai, western Maharashtra, Eastern Andhra Pradesh and the Chandrapur-Nagpur region in Vidarbha were badly affected.

Not only that, lots of the world's attention has been focused recently on the 'startling high-level of smog' in China. But things are not too great in Europe, either, where the popularity of coal-fixed power plants is endangering the live of entire generations of people. According to a report, released late last week by the Health and Environment Alliance (HEAL), a Brussel-based nonprofit, which indicates that coal pollution causes more than 18,200 premature deaths each year in Europe—or 23,300 deaths, if one add in Siberia, Croatia and Turkey. The economic costs of burning coal totals up to $71 billion in dollars, equalling about four million lost working days every year.

Before I deliberate the dangerous impact of coal-based power plants in India, I must place here one important fact. Coal as power source has been a decade-long wane in Europe, but HEAL sees the potential for "short-term rebound" in the fossil-fuel's popularity due to high prices of natural gases. Actually, it is already happening: coal is gaining traction in part due to the action of Germany, which ditched nuclear power plants in favour of coal in the wake of the Fukushima disaster. And there are 50 more coal power plants in development in Europe, some designed to burn lignite (aka 'brown coal') that is cheap but especially foul for the environment.

The study of the Greepace, which data took from 111 major power plants in India, says there is barely any regulation or inspection of pollution. "hundreds of thousands lives could be saved and millions of asthma attacks, heart attacks, hospitalization, lost workdays and associated costs to the society could be avoided, with the use of cleaner fuels and stricter emission standards and the installation and use of technologies required to achieve substantial reductions in these pollutants, "the report says and adds, "there is a conspicuous lack of regulations for power plants stack emission. Enforcement of what standards (which) do not exist is nearly non-existent".

In India, there are general complaints that the power is mostly exported to large cities and heavy industries while local people, where electricity is generated, are left with pollution and toxic dumps. About 400 million people in India have no electricity and power outages are common. The pressure to generate power has led to tens of thousands of homes being moved to make ways for mines and plants. In the process, crores of people in Odisha, West Bengal, Chhatishgarh, Madhya Pradesh, Jharkhand, Maharshtra, Andhra Pradesh Karnataka etc have become homeless and landless as their living areas in forest and plan have been forcibly acquired by the government and the same have been handed over to multi-nationals, corporates, industrialists, neo-rich political classes etc for setting up power plants and industries in the respective regions.

India is the world's second coal burner after China, generating 210 GW of electricity a year, mostly from coal. But it is likely to become the largest if plants to generate a further 160 GVV annually are approved. "Thousands of lives can be saved every year if India tightens its emissions standards, introduces limits for pollutants such as sulphur dioxide, nitrogen oxides and mercury and institutes mandatory monitoring of emissions at plant stack", said the report's author, Sarath Guttikunda, a former head of the World Bank's pollution division.

Vinuta Gopal of GreenPeace says, "The ongoing coal expansion is irrational and dangerous. Coal mining is destroying forest cover, tribal communities and endangered species and now we know the pollution it emits when burned is killing thousands. Coal has failed to deliver energy security. We need a moratorium on new coal plants and ambitious policy incentives to unlock the huge potential India has in efficiency measures, wind and solar."

As regards, such menace in Europe, it is interesting to study the country-by-country breakdowns in HEAL's report as reported by The Guardian and the Washington Posts, which the group says is the first to comprehensively examine the medical-economic impact of coal on the continent. Some of the worst polluters are power-generation facilities in former Eastern Bloc countries like the imposing Maritsa Iztok lignite complex in Bulgaria and the quad-smokestacks Turcenia Power station in Romania. More than half of total health impacts that HEAL logged come from Romania, Poland, Germany, while runner-up countries with high levels of combustion include Bulgaria, Turkey, the Czech Republic, the France and the United Kingdom.

Experts say, "Coal pollution has been linked to chronic diseases of the heart and lungs and can trigger nasty stuff like bronchitis, emphysema, lung cancer, heart attacks and arrhythmia. A boom in coal could increase the amount of ozone and particulate matter over European cities where already between 80 and 90 percent of people are breathing air that is beyond dirty as defined by the World Health Organization (WHO).

The Guardian and the Washington Post have disclosed that HEAL is asking policy makers to consider putting a moratorium on new plants or use better pollution-scrubbing technology. At the very last says the group's leader Genom Jensen, the "startlingly high costs to human health should trigger a major rethink on EU energy policy".

HELPLESS CHILDREN AND EMPOWERED WOMEN!

Tuesday, 12 March 2013

Which one is more important—betterment of children's' life or measures for safety and security of women from atrocity? Both are essential in India! But in my opinion, children's' cause is more important because they are 'helpless' than the atrocity on women, who are competent enough to tackle the situation of their own because of their empowerment in the society.

Much hue and cry is being raised over atrocity on women, particularly much-publicized rapes in New Delhi. And the union government has also shown prompt attention by promulgating an ordinance amending various criminal laws for stringent punishment to rapists on the line of Justice Verma Commission report. Almost all political parties have also shown concern over the incidents of rape in the country. And the union government is taking extra measures to enact a stringent law for the safety and security of women in the country. And the genuine causes of lakhs of helpless children are being ignored!

Sadly, the same union government is showing little concern over enacting a radical law to improve the sad plight of lakhs of children, who are being trafficked, kidnapped and forced into child labour and sexual exploitation in India. The Indian cabinet led by the Prime Minister Manmohan Singh had last year decided to bring an effective law, which would make the employment of under-14s punishable by three years in jails. The current law bans the employment of under-14s only hazardous occupations. The Centre had decided in August 2012 to enact a new law—Child and Adolescent Labour (Prohibition) Act following reports of huge scale of children being trafficked for unlawful labour. Over 40 children were rescued and 20 traffickers were arrested from a train. Apart from that, 38 children were also rescued in other raids in Punjab and north-west Delhi.

More over the government had also proposed to introduce the criminal law amendment bill to include a ban on child trafficking and trafficked for forced labour. The proposed law has provision for sentence between seven years and life imprisonment for those convicted. But as the understanding goes that there had been serious attempts to water down the enactment of law on children. Anti-trafficking activists are alarmed over some hidden move to weaken the proposed law. Bhuwan Rhibu from the Bachpan Bachao Andolan (BBA) has said," it is very important for consumers in India and the west to speak-up. People need wise up and face the fact that many of the products they buy are made by child labour by children abducted from their homes and whose lives have been violated. It is important now for consumers to take action and demand change and for the authorities to then enforce the law."

The Guardian and The Observer of Great Britain have elaborated in detail about child trafficking in India, citing evidences of the trafficking and kidnapping of hundreds of thousands of children in India. Children are used to manufacture goods which end up on western high streets and have urged consumers to demand changes in the laws on children. Over 90000 children go missing in India every year. They are most neglected lot in India. (My two blog topics—CHILD LABOUR: A BIGGEST CURSE IN INDIA and 90000 CHILDREN GO MISSING IN INDIA EVERY YEAR, written on 25 September 2012 and November 30 2012—www.kksingh1.blogspot.com).

During raids at different places in India, some children were found hidden in sack. The youngest was seven-year-old. All these rescued children told their rescuers they had been working up to 16 hours a day for Rs 20 only (25p a week) A joint investigation between The Observer and BBA found goods being made for western brands in other backstreet workshop. A BBA spokesman said the children were found to be employed in embroidery work in a condition of forced labour and slavery in 11 workshops trucked away among the narrow lanes of the Delhi colony.

According to Indian government figure; there are currently about five million children working in the country (down from nine million in 2005). But activists say that is gross underestimate and that the true figure is closer to 50 million. Many of these children are trafficked by criminal's gang. At least 100,000 children go missing from their homes in India every year—274 each day—and only 10 percent are registered as officially missing. The Indian government's own National Child Labour

Project is reported to have rescued and rehabilitated 354,877 child labourers but mounted only 25006 prosecutions over the last three years. Other government records show that between 2008 and 2012, a total of 452,679 child labour and trafficking cases were reported. But the records also show that out of those 25006 prosecutions, only 3,394 employers or traffickers were convicted.

Recently, Minna Kabir, the wife of the chief Justice o f the Supreme court, has written an open letter to the Hindstan Times, English daily in which she has said," Every society is responsible for the well being and care of the children up to the age of 18 years, especially if they are marginalized, helpless and powerless to do anything for themselves."

POLITICAL CLASSES, JUDICIARY RESPONSIBLE FOR DESTROYING SECULAR FABRIC OF INDIA!

Wednesday, 27 February 2013

Our founding fathers of the Indian Constitution has given us an ideal resolution by declaring in the Preamble of the Constitution in 1950, "The People of India, having solemnly resolved to constitute into a 'Sovereign Socialist Secular Democratic Republic and to secure to all its citizens: . . . . But in the past over 60 years, the political classes as well as judiciary appear bent upon in subverting the Nobel Magnacarta—Indian Constitution. To begin with, the entire atmosphere in the country on at least secular front has been vitiated and general people of the India are mute spectators!

Communal harmony in the country is at the lowest ebb. Communalism has been aggravated with successive events in Ayodhaya in the last over 60 years as well as recurring of communal riots in different parts of the country. In such nefarious games, both Congress and Hindutva organizations like BJP in 'awatar (incarnation)' of Jan Sangh, Rashtriya Swambsevak Sangh (RSS), Vishwa Hindu Parishad (VHP) as well as judiciary appear equally responsible for destroying the secular fabric of the country.

It all started with "uncovering a wider plot to recast the Indian polity, of which the take over of the Babri Masjid on the night of December 22-23, 1949, was but a subplot" Since the inception of India as independent country, the politics is being religionised. A recent book—AYODHAYA—The Dark Night; The Secret History of Rama's Appearance In Babri Masjid—, authored by Krishna Jha and Dhirendra K Jha and its reviewer Eminent Jurist A G Noorani in the Frontline fortnightly, have depicted 'sordid episode' Resultant, the Sangh Parivar (Hindutva organisations) seem "all set to revive Ayodhaya issue and, as Noorani says, for the same reason for which it was seeking to make Narendra Modi its front man in 2004 Lok Sabha election and it is desperate because it had no vote getter. L K Advani's ambition has far outrun his abilities as a vote getter. Advani draws a yawn even in the Parivar." About the lies repeatedly to cover-up the crime of December—1949 in 'planting the idol of Ram Lala', Advani had said on August 01, 2003, by spreading a tale that idol of Ram "appeared" that night and no prayers were held at the mosque for years. The RSS organ, Organiser said, "It meticulously appeared—(March 29, 1987)."

Authors of the book have dwelt at length about planting of idol of Ram in the mosque on 1949 night. As per the record the testimony of the Babri Masjid's last 'Muezzin" Muhmmad Ismail, who put up a fierce "resistance to the intruders who had scaled the walls and were about to plant the idol. He was beaten up and forced to flee and he spent the remaining years of his life as a muezzin in a mosque in Pahraganj Ghosania on the outskirts of Faizabad. The Muezzin delivers the azan, the call of prayer and looks after the mosque.

Comparing the assassination of Mahatma Gandhi, the authors recall, "The hands that jumped bullets into the chest of the of the Mahatma were that of Nathuram Godse, but, as proved later, the assassination was part of a conspiracy hatched by top Hindu Maha Sabha leaders led by V D Savarkar, whose prime objectives were to snatch political initiatives from the Congress and destabilize all efforts to uphold secularism in India. It was in many ways a reflection of the same brutalized atmosphere that the surreptitious occupation of the Babri Masjid. Such act was planned by almost the same set of people about two years later-on the night of December 22-23, 1949. While Mahatma/was killed in full public view in broad day-light, the Babri Masjid was converted into a temple secretly in the dead of night. As a result, an event that so remarkably changed the political discourse in India continues to be treating as a localized crime committed spontaneously by a handful of local people led by Abhiram Das, a local sadhu".

And at the same time, there were deep divide within the congress between Prime Minister Jawahar Lal Nehru, the secularist and his Home Minister Sardar Ballabh Bhai Patel, the communalist. The Uttar Pradesh Congress was a house divided. Patel's supporters were led by the UP chief minister Govind Ballabh Pant and Nehru's by Rafi Ahmed Kidwai. Many political developments had taken place during the period, questioning mark the secular credential of the Congress! Being disgusted over the situation Pundit Jawahar Lal Negru commented ". . . . communal ism has

invaded the mind and hearts of those who were pillars of the Congress."
But Pundit Nehru because of divide in the Congress had soft approach."
There is a counter argument as well, which raises some pertinent
questions. Was it necessary for Nehru to remain mute spectators while
Govind Ballabh Pant and Purshottam Das played communal card to
finish off their opponents in UP—specially Acharya Narendra Dev—and
thus created ground conducive for the Hindu Mahasabhaites in Ayodhya?
Could it have been avoided? Would communalists still have succeeded in
taking over the Babri Masjid and retaining the in the face all hue and cry,
had Nehru opted for an uncompromisingly tough attitude towards right
from the beginning? Would not a harder attitude have forced the state
government to take effective steps to remove the idol from the mosque
and thereby, undo the wrong committed on the night of December 22,
1949? Could the Hindu Mahasabha have succeeded in going that far
in implementing its Ayodhaya strategy without Nehru's soft approach?.
Nehru's mass appeal was far greater than Patel's, who controlled the party
machinery and in this task Patel was aided by ranked communalists such
as Rajendra Prasad, Pant, Ravi Shankar Shukla and B C Roy."

As per records with Faizabad district police, the book has quoted
intensively about the incident of installing idol of Ram Lala in the
mosque in December 1949. The Book says, "The first information report
(FIR), lodged at 9 am on December 23, 1949, hours after the Ram
idol was installed, speaks for itself. Pandit Ramdeo Dubey, officer—in
charge, Ayodhaya police station, Faizabad, Uttar Pradesh, lodged this
FIR against Abhiram Das, Ram Sakal Das, Sudarshan Das and 50 to
60 others, whose names were not known under Sections 147 (rioting),
448 (trespassing) and 295(defilng a place of worship) of the Indian
Penal Code (IPC)—That at about seven in the morning when I Ramdeo
Dubey reached the Janmbhoomi, I came to know from Mata Prasad
(constable number—7 Ayodhaya police station) that a group of 50 to
60 persons have entered the Babri Masjid by breaking open the locks of
the compound and also by scaling the walls and staircases and placed an
idol of Shri Bhagwan in it and scribbled sketches of Sita, Ramji etc in
saffron and yellow colour on the inner and outer walls of it. That Hans
Raj (constable number—70, who was on duty at the time when 50 to
60 persons entered) stopped them (from doing so) but they did not care.
The PAC (Provincial Armed Constabulary) guards present there were
called for help. But by then the people had already entered the mosque.
Senior officials visited the spot and got into action. Later a mob of five

to six thousands gathered and tried to enter into the mosque raising religious slogans and singing kirtans. But due to proper arrangements, nothing happened. Committers of crime Abhiram Das, Ram Sakal Das, Sudarshan Das with 50 to 60 persons, names not known, have desecrated (naapak kiya hai) the mosque by trespassing the mosque through rioting and placing idol in it. Officials on duty and many others people have seen it. So the case has been checked. It is found correct."

To substantiate the facts, the then UP home Secretary Rajeshwar Dayal, made a shocking disclosure in his memoirs—A life of Our Times. "Officials brought to him a trunk load of plans for a holocaust obtained as a result of raids on the premises of RSS as well as intelligence report to assassinate Gandhi Ji. I pressed for the immediate arrest of prime accused Shri Golwalkar (the RSS supremo). Pant deliberately procrastinated. Golwarkar disappeared . . . ." Since then, the issue of Babri Masjid continues to be complicated. by political classes for vote bank politics—BJP from majority community—Hindu and Congress and other non-BJP parties for minority community Muslims! Not only that later in 1980 Indira Gandhi herself fouled the atmosphere in such a manner after her return in power following humiliating defeat in 1977, by encouraging Hindu chauvinism. After her assassination, her son Rajiv Gandhi took another strange stand and allowed 'shilanayas" and got opened the mosque for Shila Pujan in Ayodhaya. And ultimately, the Babri masjid was demolished when Narsimha Rao of Congress was the prime minister of India. Rao remained out of bound when masjid was being demolished. Babri mosque was demolished by Hindu parivar fascist and fundamentalist forces led by L K Advani.

Even the Judiciary also remained lethargic in giving prompt judgments about the authenticity of Babri Masjid and after a long gap of time; the Allahabad High Court had delivered a split verdict about Babri Masjid, complicating the case further. The case is right now pending in the Supreme Court. A number of civil suits are still languishing in lower courts on Babri Masjid and Ram Janmbhoomo issues. Verdict on criminal cases against Hindu fundamentalists Advani, Uma Bharati, many others involved in the demolition of Babari Masjid are lingering. In many cases even charge sheets have not been framed against the accused. There became many twists and turns in criminal cases against the big guns of Hnidutva parties!

Communal virus is spreading in India! Is India being pushed back into the dark ages by obscurantist, fundamentalist and fascist forces?

"Their appeasement . . . . has today given them strength and the audacity to seek to destroy the very basis of our nation state . . . . The secular forces will have to be united and determinedly meet this challenge if India is to survive as a democratic, secular, progressive, liberal and modern nation" Noorani laments and says, "Secularism demands not detachment but involvement in the entire range of nation's activities—economic, social, political and constitutional. The course they have followed in recent decades has furthered the fortunes of thugs in New Delhi, who claim to be their leaders, earned the favours and marginalized Muslims."

TRIBAL AND POOR ARE BEING UPROOTED IN INDIA TO BENEFIT MULTINATIONALS, CORPORATE!

Friday, 22 February 2013

It is amazing but painful. Tribal, poor and landless people have no say in India. Huge forest land as well as of poor farmers are being acquired forcibly for facilitating the industrial set-up by corporate, multi-nationals, industrialists and influential political classes Large number of adivasis are being uprooted from their homes and land in Orissa, Jharkhand, Gujarat, Chhatishgarh, Madhya Pradesh, Himachal Pradesh, Uttarakhand, Bihar, Maharashtra, Andhra Pradesh, Karnataka, Tamil Nadu etc for handing over the lands for industrial and mining purposes to multi-nationals, corporate like Korea-owned Posco, British-owned Vedanta, for mining and other industrial purposes. Trabal's betel vines and various crops farm land and houses in hundreds of acres and have been destroyed in the deep forest of Odisha by the Odisha government for handing over the lands to Posco and Vedanta. Similar situations are prevailing in various states.

More over, such forcible occupation of lands and forest areas are in violation of the provisions in the Constitution, laws and rules in India as well as international norms, laws and rules. Strangely, much-awaited, new bill for acquisition of lands—draft Land Acquisition, Resettlement and Rehabilitation (LARR) Bill is gathering dust for the last several years. This bill was supposed to replace the obsolete—Land Acquisition Act, 1984, enacted by the colonial British Raj following a lot of discontent over land acquisition and rehabilitation.

A recent circular of the union government has dwelt a new blow in acquiring lands and tribal rights in India. The circular was adopted at a recent meeting convened by the prime minister Manmohahan Singh and attended by the Environment minister Jayanti Natrajan and Tribal Affairs minister V Kishore Chand Deo, "which decided that that, subject to (the) Forest Rights Act, there will not be requirement of consent to each of 'gram sabhas' through which such linear projects such as roads, canals, pipelines, transmission towers etc pass" The government announced recently that major infrastructures projects will be exempted for forest clearance from tribal communities living in forest. Such decisions undermine the importance of India's Forest Act. The Forest Act, implemented after much hue and cry for restoring forest rights to tribal, has been ignored by the union government surreptitiously to please multi-nationals in the name of setting up infrastructural facilities in India. Tribal, who have been given enough power for utilization of their forest land under the Forest Act. Under new directive, originating from the PM secretariat; the power of 'gram sabha' has become meaningless. In accordance to the Act, the 'gram sabhas' of tribal has absolute rights in rejecting in building of roads, railways, transmission lines, canal system, pipeline or other projects that potentially violate their land rights.

This obnoxious directive, which would affect all traditional forest—dependent communities including those who have procured rights under FRA and those who are still struggling for its implementation in the areas, In 2009 itself, the ministry of forest and environment had made the consent of the affected forest communities for all projects that will destroy forest. Such thing happened in the wake of an attempt by the British mining Company Vedanta to clear swaths of forest in Odisha state belonging to the Dongaria tribe. Now the recent directive of the union government will definitely help Vadanta and Posco at least in Orissa.

Dr Swati Shresth of the Ashoka Trust for Research in Ecology and Environment has said, "This is serious breach of trust and a huge step back in ensuring the dignity and survival of traditional forest-dwelling people across the country. Forests are going to be cleared to make way for a particular kind of economic development; it will adversely impact communities and environment."

In the Opinion of the popular British Daily, the Guardian; the 2006 Forest Act is a landmark piece of legislation recognizing the rights forest dependent have over the landscape they have traditionally inhabited. It mandates that forest dwellers cannot be resettled unless their traditional rights have been recognized. It is seen as single mist important piece of legislation protecting and preserving the country's biodiversity and rights of tribal group. By no longer gaining the consent of communities, the government stands accused of effectively overturning key provisions of the Act.

However, the government rejects the claims that it is diluting rights in the name of streamlining big business, saying it will continue to enforce the provisions of the" Act" where there is significant impact on the lives and livelihoods." On the other hand Shresth further said, "The proposed changes will a enable land grabbing and violation of right of traditional forest dwellers and sends a clear message that rights granted under FRA are not inalienable, but subject to the whims of the government of the day." Such concerns were also expressed to the prime minister secretariat in a letter signed by a coalition of the international forest rights movements. The statement of the Movements said, "We believe that it is against the democratic principles to make centralized decisions about the extent of social impact worth considering while diverting forests over which individuals and/or village community may have "inalienable' forest rights vested through FRA. Overriding of such processes can lead to the danger of assuming that all rights can be monetized and negotiated"

Agitating activists are of the opinion that such free signal will allow industry to build roads or canal system for mining projects to transport extracted minerals to the refinery by exploiting tribal population. The only beneficiaries of the decision will be mining companies. This is about directive, which will threaten the area's biodiversity. Interestingly "this is for GDP, not about the rights of India's tribal communities" said Sanjay Basu Mallick from All India Forum of Forest Movements. Apart from that it will also discredit India's status as the current chair of the UN Convention on Biological Diversity and of the Nagoya protocol and the implementation of these international obligations on sustainable use and protection of biodiversity.

Sadly, although many "noble, and humane 'clauses in the proposed bill—draft Land Acquisition, Resettlement and Rehabilitation bill, awaiting for Parliament approval, in place of Land Acquisition Act, 1984, a concentrated attempt is being made to dilute and make it more private-investor-friendly; there will be compromises in the consent, rehabilitation and compensation clauses provided in the original bill. The contradictory views within various ministries, there have been attempts to water-down the present draft, which is inadequate in itself, under the pressure from the industry. Strangely, the provision in the draft bill in respect of PP projects, the consent clause has been reduced from 80 percent to 70 percent and only the consent of of the landowners, not all land losers, has been stipulated as being required. This apart, there is move to dilute in the original draft about compensation and resettlement and rehabilitation were to be given to both land losers and livelihood losers.

Considering the maneuverings at the government level to help vested interests to uproot tribal and poor and small land-holders, constituting over 70 percent in India, the government instead of taking strong and appropriate measures, it is creating more and more problems. Alas, there is no move from the government end to acquire land for dalits, tribal, poor homeless for a roof on their heads. Over 80 percent families in India have no houses of their own even after India achieving independence over 60 years back.

'FREE DEMOCRACY' (INDIA) VIS-A-VIS 'RESTRICTED DEMOCRACY' (CHINA)

Sunday, 10 February 2013

There are basic differences between two big emerging developing countries in the planet—India and China—and their progress and development. It is sad that world's largest and vibrant democracy—India—is lagging behind 'restricted democracy' in China. Apparently, it appears that China is growing because of 'disciplined approach' while India is lagging behind in the development parameters because of 'weak leadership' More over, poverty, corruption and inequality have gripped India as well as 'haphazard implementation' of liberalized economy. Apart from that 'prevailing feudalism' in India where landlords and big industrial employers behave like petty tyrants and almost all new papers except a few not reporting all these misdeeds as they depend on advertisements from government and industries and also judiciary, composed of friends and relatives of these feudal society, protecting the tyrants. Huge payment of pensions to retired employees and subsidies in the name of goodies to poor people, which hardly reach them, are also holding back the reforms in the economy of India. An economic measure in China is percolating to the common masses while in India such results are not going down to underprivileged and marginalized!

As recent Davos meeting has suggested that India is doing worse than China. Not only that almost all indicators like growth, inflation, output per capita, unemployment, budget deficit, corruption indicate that India is far behind China. A few years back, it was predicted by Davos men that India would emerge as most powerful and developed country in South-East Asia But that hopes are gradually belying. India, could achieve per capita GDP at $ 3,851 against China's $ 9,146. Official figures in India say that unemployment rate is double in comparison with China. On corruption front, the Transparency International's index

228

has put China 80th rank in the globe while India has been ranked 94th and it is growing rapidly. Apart from that military preparations and manufacturing arms and ammunition by China are increasing leaps/and bound, whereas India is yet to give full thrust on the security of its border although India is one of the top-most buyers of arms and ammunition for its defence preparedness. (My blog Topic: "Arms and Ammunition manufacturing and acquisition at the top among Globe Nations: US, China heading for manufacturing lethal and sophisticated weapons"— December 6, 2012—www.kksingh1.blogspot.com).

According to cross-sections of the society and various news and views reports; the" rural people are hardly better off than they were two or three decades ago." A former Supreme Court judge, Krishna Ayyer, a towering survivor of the progressive personality has expressed pain and anguish over prevailing situation in India and said, "more than 40 percent of the Indian children are malnourished—worse that in Africa, while detailing the report of the World Bank, depicting sad aspects on India. Over 17, 000 farmers have committed suicide in 2010 on the failure of their crops. Timothy Garton Ash has written in the Guardian in its issue on January 31, 2013, "Even the most superficial, privileged travellers cannot avoid seeing the shocking proximity of wealth and want, whether in the garbaged-piled slums of Mumbai or the medieval-looking peasant farms visible just off a brand new expressway."

Well-known economist and a former union revenue secretary, now JD(U) MP from Bihar N K Singh, who has recently returned after attending Davos's World Economic Forum meeting, has written in a national newspaper that Davos men felt bad over 'inefficiency of India government over economic development in India. "One European participant has said in the meeting that Indians are seen every where in the meeting but not India!" Singh said and added that GDP of India has sharply declined because of coalition government, resulting into political instability.

"Unlike China but like Europe, India expends a vast amount of energy simply coping with its incredible diversity. The French President Charles de Gaulle once exclaimed how you can you possibly govern a country that has 246 varieties of cheese? Well, how about a country with 330 million gods"? And when you say a country; a 19th century English observer once observed that Scotland is more like Spain than Bengal is like Punjab. A poetic exaggeration, no doubt, but the country is a continent, a commonwealth, an empire itself. And like Europe, it is trying to manage this diversity in freedom. China has diversity too, in vast its sparsely populated areas of mainly Tibetan and mainly Muslim population, but it cope with it mainly by repression." India lacks united powerful narrative. Unfortunately, if unsurprisingly, many of these stories in India are sectarian, regional, petty-chauvinist narratives, dividing rather than uniting.

Secondly, one of the main reasons of poor growth story of India is legacy of British Raj bureaucracy. Licensee and permit raj still exist in India indirectly. Captains of industry like Lakshmi Mittal and Tata's Ratan Tata prefer to invest elsewhere because it takes eight to ten years to get all permission in India to open industrial units. The Guardian essay by Ash says, "If the bureaucracy of a post-colonial state is the problem, more deregulation and economic liberalization should be answer; and so, in some respects, it is. This is, for instance, the only way that we will bet to an EU-India free trade agreement, which could bring great benefits to both sides. But the free market liberalization that was let rip in the 1990s is also part of the problem. Take the media, India's media now boasts a commercial, sensationalists, race-to-the-bottom culture that makes Fox News look fair and balanced and the British tabloid the Sun look like a new bulletin for the Salvation Army. A few quality papers such as Hindu are exceptions that prove the rule. Elsewhere paid news (corporations paying for favourable news coverage) is the order of the day."

More and more politicizing the things are also responsible for poor show in India. "Every one in Delhi but every where, there are general impression that business and politics in Delhi and elsewhere in India are cardinally inter wind like 'tantric gods and goddesses'. Besides the shrill name-calling, regional and religious identity politics and dynastic politics (witness the irresistible rise of Rahul Gandhi in the Congress Party), there is monstrous condescension to the two out of every three Indians, who are still dirt people."

Ash remarks, "Ruling political classes manly through to poor subsidies for basic foodstuffs, a few other cheap goodies, guaranteed low wage employment for a number of days a year—and buy their votes every election time. So is China bound to go on winning? No and again no, because while the Indian system is daily soap opera of small crises, the big crisis of China's self-contradictory system of Leninist capitalism is yet to come. And no, again because India is a free country, with the most amazing diversity of human talents, originally, personality and spirituality. Surely that free expression of human individuality must tell out in the end."

However, in his remarks on the essay of Ash on India, Prof James Manor of Institute of Commonwealth Studies says, "Ash is wrong about Indian politicians buying votes of the poor. Even illiterate voters of India are too canny to be duped and they have thrown out more moneyed parties at state and national elections on majority of occasions since the late 1970s." Craig Jeffrey of the Oxford University has rightly said in his comment, "Ash provides a timely reminder of the need for broader-based social development in the subcontinent but stops short of taking India's government to task. The state in India is engaged in a curious strategy of allowing schools, hospitals and other government services to atrophy while dispensing huge sums via populist development programmes. How this strategy will play out is unclear, but in the meantime the poor are taking things into their own hands, and it is interesting that on the day of this article in the Guardian, a huge demonstration against manual scavenging reached its climax in Delhi."

But growth rate in China also seems to be in long-term decline. According to National Bureau of Statistics (NBS), Chinese GDP growth, year on year, which had fallen from 8.1 percent in the first quarter of 2012 to 7.6 percent in the second quarters and 7.4 per cent in the third quarter, had bounced back to 7.9 percent in the last quarter of that year. But sign of survival appears to be weak. as growth spiked in China when the government launched a $ 585 billion stimulus package in response to the 2008 crisis, which drove the year-on-year quarterly growth rate from 6.6 percent in the first quarter of 2009 to 12.1 percent in first quarter of 2010. According to an article in the on line edition of The People's Daily, China's first release of the Gini coefficient for the past decade demonstrated the government's resolve to bridge the gap between rich and poor The director of the Chinese NBS Ma Jiantang, has said," The statistics highlighted the urgency for our country to speed up the income distribution reforms to narrow the wealth gap."

Slower growth rate may be upsetting Indian government, but it seems to be sign of achievement in China.

GAUTAM BUDDHA'S LIFE'S JOURNEY TOWARDS ENLIGHTENMENT AND SALVATION!

Monday, 4 February 2013

Before I begin on writing on Gautam Buddha's life journey towards his enlightenment and salvation, I must refer one quote of Geeta as Buddha was said to be the 'incarnation of Lord Vishnu'. Lord Krishna has said in the texses sixth and seventh in the Chapter four of Bhagavad Geeta, "Ajopi sann avyayarma-bhutanam isvari pi san; prakrtim svam adhisthaya sambhavamy atma-mayaya (6), yada yada hi dharmasya glanir bhavati bharata-abhyutthanam adharmasya tadatmanam srjamy aham (7). (Although I am unborn and my transcental body never deteriorates and although I am the Lord of all living entities, I still appear in every millennium in my original transcendental form. Whenever and where ever there is decline in religious practice, O descendant of Bharata and a predominant rise of irreligion—at that time I descend myself).

Facts about Buddha's are reasonably certain. Upanisads are of Brahimanic order, which is of orthodoxy and did not harmonized other 'teachings' of by 'heterodox sects.' For such change an yellow-robed followers led by Gautam Buddha came to the scene at the end of the sixth and beginning of fifth century B.C by establishing 'the enlightenment or Awakened'. If one considers the posthumous effects on the world at large, Buddha was certainly the greatest man to have born in India. The story of his birth and early life found places in 'Buddhst Scriptures. His sermon, "Turning of the Wheel of the Law", which is said to be the first sermon preached after the Buddha's enlightenment and which is the basis teaching of all. Buddhist sects, have great relevance in the present-day society, engulfed under violence and untruthness.

Story of enlightenment of Siddharth Gautam, at the age of 35 years old, has many facts. He was sitting beneath a large 'Peela tree' on the outskirts of Gaya town, under the regime of Bimbisara King of Magadh.

A L Basham, in his book, the wonder that was India, has referred, "Sujata, the daughter of a nearby farmer, brought him a large bowl of rice boiled in milk. After eating some of this, he bathed and that evening, again sitting beneath the peepal tree, he made a solemn vow that, though his bones wasted away and his blood dried up, he would not leave his seat until the riddle of suffering was solved. So 49 days Gautam Buddha sat beneath the tree. At first he was surrounded by hosts gods and spirits, awaiting the great moment of enlightenment; but they soon fled, for Mara, the spirit of the world and of sensual pleasure, the Buddhist devil approached. For days Gautam withstood temptations of all kinds. Mara, disguised as messenger, brought news that wicked cousin Devadatta had revolted, thrown Suddhodhana into prison and seized Yasodhara but Gautam was not moved. Mara called him demon hosts and attacked him with whirlwind, tempest, flood and earthquake but he sat firm, cross-legged beneath the tree. Then the tempter called on Gautama to produce evidence of his goodness and benevolence; he touched the ground with his hand and the Earth itself spoke with voice of thunder: "I am his witness."

". . . . Mara than tried gentler means of Gautama's resolve. He called his three beautiful daughter; Desire, Pleasure and Passion, who danced and sang before him and tried every means of seduction. Their wiles were quite ineffectual. They offered him Universal Empire, but he was quite unmoved. At last the demon hosts gave up the struggle and Gautama, left alone, sank deeper and deeper into meditation. At the dawning of the forty-ninth day he knew the truth. He had found the secret of sorrow and understood at last why the world is full of sufferings and unhappiness of all kinds and what man must do to overcome them. He was fully enlightened—a Buddha. For another seven weeks he remained under the Tree of Wisdom (bodhi), meditating on the great truths he had found. For a time he doubted whether he should proclaim his wisdom to the world, as it was so recondite and difficult to express that few would understand it; but the god Brahma himself descended from heaven and persuaded him to reach the world. Leaving the Tree of Wisdom, he journeyed to the Deer Park near Banaras (the modern Sarnath), where his five former disciples had settled to continue their panances . . . ."

Buddha's birth and upbringing up has also unique story. Gautam Buddha was the son of the King of Sakyas, a small Tribe of Himalayan foothill, namely Kapilvastu. One night Mahamaya, the chief queen of Suddhodhana, king of Sakyas and mother of Gautam Buddha, had a dream that she was carried away to the divine lake Anavatapta in the Himalayas where she was bathed by the heavenly guardians of the four quarters of the universe. Subsequently a great white elephant with a lotus flower in his trunk approached her and assimilated inside her. The next day dream was interpreted by wise men of the kingdom—she has had conceived a wonderful son, who would be either king of the universe or teacher of the universe, The child was born in a grove of sal trees called Lummbini, near the capital of Sakyayas, Kapilvastu while his mother was on the way to her parents' home for her confinement. At birth he stood upright, took seven strides and spoke: "This is my last birth—henceforth there is no more birth for me." He was named Siddharth. His 'gotr' name was Gautam, as he is known in Buddhist literature.

To prevent prophesy about Siddharth, the King Suddhodhan decided that the boy should never know the sorrows of the world and he was brought up in the Palace with all comforts, luxuries and facilities. From that place, the king removed all sign of death, disease and misery. He was trained in all aspects of life as a prince is taught. Gautam excelled in learning as students. Thereafter, he married his" cousin Yasodhara, who he won at a great contest at which he performed feats of strength and skill which put to shame all other contestants including his envious cousin Devadatta. But even after his success and vast knowledge, Gautam was not at all happy. So many efforts of his father did not deter him to take a path to shape his destiny. One day Gautam was moving around the royal park with his faithful charioteer Channa, he saw an aged man, in the last stage of infirmity and decrepitude—actually a god, who had taken this in disguise in order that Siddharth Gautam might become a Buddha. Siddharth asked Channa who this repulsive being was and when he learned that all men must grow old he was even more troubled in mind. This was the first sign. The second came a little later, in the same way, in the form of a very sick man, covered with boils and shivering with fever. The third was even more terrible—a corpse, being carried to the cremation ground followed by weeping mourners. But the fourth sign brought the hope and consolation—a wandering religious beggar, clad in simple yellow robe, peaceful and calm with inward joy. On seeing him Siddharth realized where his destiny lays, and set his heart on becoming a wanderer."

When the King could know all these developments, he stepped up his precautions to keep Gautam at a bay from all these evil things. Siddharth was virtually made a prisioner, surrounded with luxuries and pleasures of all kinds. But Siddharth never remained happy. One morning Siddharth was informed that Yasodhara had given birth to his son. But it gave him neither any pleasure nor any happiness to him. That night was night of festivities in the Palace. When everybody enjoyed and later slept in deep pleasure sleep, he awoke Channa, who was 'ghorsawar' of his horse 'Kanthaka' and he slipped in the midnight fro from the Palace. Surrounded by rejoicing demigods, who cushioned the fall of his horse's hoofs, so that no one could listen his leaving the Palace. "When far way from the city he stripped off his jewellery and fine garments and put on a hermit's robe, provided by an attendant demigod. Siddharth cut off his hear of head from his sword and sent it back to his father with his garments through Channa. The horse Kanthaka dropped dead from grief when he found that he was to be parted from his master, to be reborn in one of the heavens. Thus Siddharth started his "great going Forth" (Mahabhiniskramana) and became a wandering ascetic, owing nothing but the robe he wore."

To begin with Siddharth started begging for his food as a wanderer. There after he became a forest hermit. A sage named Alara Kalama he learn the technique of meditation and the "lore of Brahman as taught in the Upanishads; but he was not convinced that man could obtain liberation from sorrow by self-discipline and knowledge, so he joined forces with five ascetics who were practicing the most rigorous self-mortification in the hope of wearing away their karma and obtaining final bliss. He adopted very hard task that five quickly recognized him as their leader. For six years, he adopted rigorous and tortured himself. Just Gautam became walking skeleton. One day, worn out by penance and hunger, he fainted and his followers believed that he was dead. But after a while he recovered and consciousness and realized that his fasts and penaces had been useless. He again began to beg food and his body regained strength and started another round of meditation. The five disciples left him in disgust at his black—sliding.

After attaining enlightenment, Buddha, preached his first sermon or in Buddhist phraseology set in motion the "Wheel of Law." Five of his deserted disciples joined him and were so impressed with Buddha's new doctrine that they gave u p austerities and once more became his disciples. Later many more joined and Buddha sent them to different directions to preach the Buddhist Dharm. A few days later a band of sixty young ascetics became his followers and Buddha sent them to all directions. Soon his name got popularity in throughout the Ganges plain and greatest kings of that time favoured him and his followers. There are many stories about Buddha's long years of preaching.

Buddha returned to Kapilvastu and converted his father, wife, son Rahul as well as many other members of the court, including his cousin Devadatta, whose heart remain full of jealousy. At the request of his foster-mother and aunt," Krsa-Gautami, he allowed with much misgivings the formation of community of nuns. Devadatta grew so jealous of him that once he even tried to kill Buddha, by arranging for a mad elephant to be let loose in his path; but the beast, impressed by the Buddha's gentleness and fearlessness, calmly bowed at his feet. Not only that Buddha averted war between the Sikyas and neighbouring tribe of the Koliyas, by walking between the assembled armies and convincing them of the uselessness and evil of bloodshed. Buddha went alone to the camp of notorious bandit Angulimala and converted him and his followers from their evil ways."

Although his life was full of miracles and many wonders, the earliest traditions record few "miracles performed by Buddha himself. Once, indeed, he is said to have performed feats of levitation and other miracles at Sravasti, as a result of challenge from rival teachers, but he sternly forbade the monks to perform magical feats and there is no record of his healing sick by supernatural means. One touching story of the Buddha is interesting in this connection, since it contrasts strikingly with the Gospel stories of the miracles of Jesus. A woman, stricken with grief at the death of her only son and hearing that Buddha was in the vicinity, brought the child's corpse to his in the hope that he would restore it to life. He asked her first to go to the nearby town and bring a handful of mustard seed from a family in which no one had died. She went from house to house, but of course could find no such family, until at last she understood the inevitability of death and sorrow and became a nun."

Remarkably because of his growing reputation in over 40 years of his life, Buddha religious discourse made him a giant figure. And the Sangha (literally society, the Buddhist order) increased in number and influence. With the single exception of the conspiracy of "Devadatta, he suffered no persecution, though a few of his followers were maltreated by the religious opponents. His ministry was a long, calm and peaceful one, in this respect very different from that of Jesus."

The end of Buddha's life came at the age of eighty. Buddha spent his last rainy season of his life near the city of Vaisali (now in new Bihar) and after the rains he and his followers journeyed northwards to the hill country which had been the home of his youth. "On the way Buddha prepared his disciples for his death. He told them that his body was now like a worn-out cart, creaking every joint. He declared that he declared that he had made no distinction between esoteric and exoteric teaching, but had preached the full doctrine to them. When he was gone they were to look for new leader—the Doctrine (dharma) which had preached would lead them. They must rely on themselves be their own lamps and look for no refuge outside themselves . . . ."

At last the "D" day came and at the town of Pava he was "entertained by a lay of disciple, Cunda, the sinmith and ate a meal of pork. Soon after this he was attacked by dysentery but he insisted on moving on the nearby town of Kusinagara (Pali, Kusinara), now in Uttar Pradesh. Here on the outskirts of the town, he lay down under a sal tree and that night he died. His last words were: "All composite things decay strives diligently!" This was his "Final Blowing-out" (Parinirvana). His sorrowing disciples cremated his body and his ashes were divided between the representatives of various tribal people and the King Ajatshatru of Magadh."

Even today the Buddhist holy places—the Lumbini grave at Kapilvasti, where Buddha was born, currently in Nepal, the Tree of Wisdom at Gaya, now in Bihar, India, where g he gained enlightenment, the Deer Park near Banaras, where he preached his first sermon and the grove near Kusinagara, now Kushunagar in Uttar Pradesh in India, where he died—were visited by many pilgrims including the Ashoka the great himself, who spread Buddhism throughout the globe during his period of Kingdom.

Buddha's teachings relevance are gaining ground day-to-day year-to-year and Buddha is remembered throughout the Planet as a great saint and sage!

Sources:—Readers could get more details in Pali forms as used in the Sthaviravada Buddhists. Many writings on Buddha in Pali, The Discovery of India of Pundit Jawahar Lal Nehru, The Wonder That Was India, written by A L Basham and other rare manuscripts in Pali, available in Nalanda, Patna, Banars, Kushinagar and Kapilvastu. Etc.

USA AND ITS PRESIDENT BARACK OBAMA HAVE MILITARIST MINDSET FOR GLOBAL DOMINANCE

Wednesday, 30 January 2013

'Prematurely acclaimed' Nobel peace prize winner Barack Obama is gradually proving more dangerous and aggressive than any of his predecessors to create the America, a 'emergency state' as well as rapidly militarizing the country for moving towards destruction in the name of 'global dominance' of the country. In the process, Obama has been keenly 'eyeing' developing countries in the South-East Asia (SEA). A noted columnist A G Noorani, while reviewing the book in the Frontline, a fortnightly, published from Madras, "The Emergency state—America's pursuit of Absolute National Security at all Costs, written by David C Unger, has aptly said, "The United States Supreme Court, packed by successive Republican presidents, has often departed radically from its own earlier rulings. Those rulings bear recalling today because the records of the Supreme Court of India on the Terrorists and Disruptive Activities (Prevention) Act (TADA), the Armed Forces (Special Powers) Act (AFSPA), The Prevention of Terrorism Act (POTA) and the like issues have been worse than pathetic precisely because they are laced with eloquent rhetoric on freedom, while curbing freedom."

The Book David C Unger, editorial writer of The New York Times for over 30 years and teacher on the courses on American foreign policy at a prestigious university and a member of the Council of on Foreign Relations, has exposed the militarist mind-set based on foreign policy of Obama while accusing him for violating civil liberties. The America has always considered itself a 'super power' and its eyes were "set on global dominance" To spell—out the least about Obama, according to the book; he always carried "prosecuting the government whistle blowers" for speaking the 'truth'. All these actions of Obama have been very rare in the history of America. About the draft of the 'Defence planning Guidance'

Noorani has said, "The draft Defence Planning Guidance set ambitious goals in almost every corner of the globe. Rest assured the US will not countenance a powerful India." Thus US have never played any positive role in the world affairs!

'Barrack Obama is no better'. Unger writes: Three years into Obama administration, emergency state thinking and habit con5inues to damage our democracy, weaken our economy, and poison our international relationship. As candidate Obama talked eloquently about the importance of the Presidents acting in accordance with the Constitution and the rule of law and promised a new relationship with the world. But as President Obama has addressed only a handful of Bush's most flagrant constitutional abuses while building his core foreign policies around the familiar' emergency' state model. The assumptions and institutions of America's emergency state have been nurtured by 13 successive presidential administrations, Seven Democrats and six Republicans. Its practices and values have been sustained, and continue to be sustained by glib overreaching formulae for national security that politicians and foreign policy experts have trained voters to demand from all candidates for national office."

More over, Noorani has said that the state uses conflict for political mobilisation at home and the people inflamed by official propaganda and chauvinistic media develop a siege mentality. This is true of the US today for creating cold-war like situation to harm civil liberties and also of the states of South Asia., Noorani added. When one trace the history of America, a strange but logical thing have come out. The London Economists, representing influential opinion in Britain, wrote on September 16, 1944, "The American prejudice against imperialism—British, French or Dutch—has led many post-war planners to assume that the old sovereign ties will not be re-established in south-east Asia and that some form of international control or transfer of the imperium to local people, will take place of the old authority exercised by western nations. Since this attitude exists and is even backed by the most widely disturbed Americaan journals and newspapers, it is time that future intentions of British, the French, and the DUtch were frankly and fully explained. Since none of them has any intention of abandoning its colonial empire, but on the contrary regards the restoration of Mlaya to the British, the East Indies to the Dutch and the French Indo-China to the French as an essential part of the destruction of Japan's co-prosperity sphere, it will be inviting the worst sort of misunderstanding, and even accusation of bad faith, if the three nations allowed any doubt on the matter to continue in the mind of their American ally."

Pundit Jawahar Lal Nehru, in his Discovery of India, has rightly said, "America is a curious mixture of what is considered hard-headed realism and a vague idealism and humanitarianism. Which of these will be dominating tendency of the future or what will result from their mixing together?' Perhaps, the prophesy of Pundit Nehru about America has resulted into' hard-headed realism'! But one thing appears very clear that many of the western civilizations like America have 'fascism and Nazism' outlook. Pundit Nehru had also predicted, "whatever the future may hold, it is clear that the economy of the U S A after the war will be powerfully expansionist and almost explosive in its consequences The U S A and the Soviet union seem destined to play vital part in the future. They differ from each other almost as much as any two advanced countries can differ and even their faiths lie in positive directions. All the evils of a purely political democracy are evident in the U S A; the evils of the lack of political democracy are present in the USSR. And yet of them much in common . . . ."

In his Book Unger, has traced, "the emergency state 'in America took on its present contours in the days of Franlin Roosevelt, Henrry Truman and Dwight Eisenhower. I agree with the opinion of The New York Times of March 8,1992, titling "U S strategy Calls for Insuring No rivals Develop in a One-Superpower World" that the "US has no time for equals. It wants subordinates. Hence its resentment of China's rise". More over, the Obama administration's curb on civil liberties is taking a great toll to the Americans. Elimination of whistle blowers by the Obama administration is bound to result into keeping the American citizens in dark about what is happening in the country? People of America would have never known Abu Ghraib prisoner abuse scandals on the National Security Agency, warrant less wiretaps, and also about coming to surface Pentagon papers. Significantly personally vets papers, targeting assassination by Barrack has taken no action against officials under Bush administration for crime committed in that administration. On various fronts including Afghanistan, Libiya, affairs, the Obama administration has failed miserably.

Unger writes, "We Americans have built the world's most powerful military. Yet we now we live in greater fear of external and internal dangers than before the World War two. We have recorded the world economy to the American specifications. Yet globalization has fed out fears of outsourced jobs and inassimilable immigrants. We have filled our malls with more consumer products than previous generations could have imagined. Yet we enjoy less economic security than our parents, and we worry, with good reasons, that global competition will mean fewer good jobs and relentless downward pressure on our children's living standards. We have fought repeated wars to preserve the world's freest democracy. Yet the seven decades we have been yielding our most basic liberties to a secretive, unaccountable emergency state—a vast but increasingly misdirected complex of national security institutions, reflexes and beliefs that so define our present world that we forget that there was ever a different America. But there was and we could have it."

"America's emergency state was originally designed to wage hot war against Nazi Germany and cold war against Soviet-led international communism. Its institutions and the outdated world view they embody, are not good at protecting us against today's most dangerous international threats as the events of 9/11 and the wrongly targeted and disastrously mismanaged wars that followed painfully demonstrate, "Unger book informs.

And the USA is moving for 'absolute security' Henry Kissinger had said, "Absolute security for one state is absolute insecurity for all."

Obama's recent militaristic action has also exposed how he was selected for Nobel Peace Prize? Such selection has put big question mark over the 'authenticity and honesty' of the Nobel Committee in awarding Nobel prizes, which many persons of the globe have alleged that such awards are given under America and Europe influences! Instead of spreading peace and non-violence President Barack Obama is spreading hatred by initiating 'strong-arm-tactics' throughout the planet.

Not only that a recent report, emanating from Washington, Barack Obama, on January 7, 2013, Obama has made certain changes in the administration's foreign policy, against the spirit of the 'Geneva convention'. He has nominated Nebraska Republican Charles "chuck" Hagel as the new Defence Secretary to join a team that may also include the nominated Massachusetts Democrat John Kerry as the new Secretary of State. Both Hagel and Karry are said to be veteran war heroes during Vietnam War. Instead of making them "war criminals for their over doings and misdeeds as per Geneva Convention", Obama has made these unusual choices, signaling his intention for militaristic attitude. Apart from that, Obama has further stepped up extrajudicial assassinations using US Special Forces and drones since he assumed president ship of USA. Such measures of Obama will further escalate the conflicts in different pats of the globe like maintaining massive reach of US power through bases, utilize bases to strike countries with drone, bombers and Special Forces and use covert means (including sabotage and cyber attack) to send strong signal to adversaries in different parts of the planet.

This is how Brack Obama has changed himself from a "peace man to war monger"!

MAHATMA GANDHI AND SUBHAS BOSE VIS-A-VIS PRESENT DAY INDIA!

Sunday, 20 January 2013

If one makes objective appraisal of things or events historically, History definitely highlights 'truth' in shaping the destiny of a country like India! In these aspects, the' thoughts and philosophy' of Mahatma Gandhi and Subhas Chandra Bose during freedom struggle remained diametrically opposite. Gandhi wanted emancipation of the country from the grip of British Raj through 'obsolete, orthodox and conservative manners' while Subhash wanted scientific solution through 'revolution' coupled with the 'modern development approaches'.

Although India's road to Independence had started from Ram Manohar Roy (1722-1833), the first comprehensive man that India had produced. Roy was called' Father of Indian Renaissance'. Since than, so many developments had taken place and this road to independence had run through an intricate, chequered and often painful route. Gandhi did not work for India's independence in isolation. There were galaxy of his contemporizes who had nursed the trends in different ways. Many of Gandhi's contemporaries and close followers had fundamental differences with him over 'ideology, methods and strategy and as to concrete results'.

To begin with, Gandhi was great, very great, but he was not free from enigma and had his limitations. At least on two momentous occasions, Gandhi failed to take 'quick decisions' and 'failed India'. Many political thinkers and historians feel or think if C R Das had continued living for some more years he could have isolated Gandhi and with the help of Abul Kalam Azad and others won India's independence much sooner. Many are of the opinion that if Gandhi had not thrown a wedge between Subhash Chandra Bose and Pundit Jawahar Lal Nehru, when they came closer, India's destiny might have been fulfilled much earlier. Home Rule was almost within reach in 1920. Gandhi has taken up Home

Rule Movement from the hands of Annie Besant and had scuttled it. Lord Birkenhead had promised Home Rule in 1930 before his death But Gandhi sponsored the 'salt satyagrah' and set back the hands of the clock. Was Gandhi anxious to steal the thunder always and remain in the limelight?

More over Gandhi could also be impetus. He had described Ram Mohan Roy as a 'pigmy' in a meeting on the sands of Kathajuri River in Cuttack. Of all, Nehru was once much disillusioned and wrote to Gandhi, disapproving his 'style of functioning'! There were many things where Gandhi erred. When Subhash Bose won the presidential elections of the Congress, Gandhi at once smelt corruption in the election and isolated Subhas ultimately making him quit India. An ardent Congressmen Jinnah had to leave Congress in 1921 because he was not given proper place in the party. And because of that Jinnah, who was great nationalist and seasoned member of the Indian National Congress, had to change his track and became propounded of two-nation theory, ultimately resulting into division of the Country—India and Pakistan.

Not only that Gandhi described Subhas Babu as a 'misguided patriot' in a letter to Amrita Kaur on the death of Subhas. Referring to Pakistan, Srinivas Shastri had mentioned that Gandhi had 'sold' India but that Gandhi would not admit it and describe in some other way, In spite of great regards for him, Gopal Krishna Gokhale turned down Gandhi's application for the membership of the Servant of India Society. Many such instances had found places in the now defunct, The Sunday Standard, a national English daily, published from seven cities In India, The Hindu (Madras), now defunct Anand Bazar Patrika (Calcutta), Hindustan Standard defunct (Calcutta) and many other newspapers. At that time, almost all newspapers had highlighted for probe as to what had happened to the money and jewels Gandhi used to collect on tours!

Before analyzing the facts, one must give honest appraisal about Subhash Babu and his backgrounds as well as Mahatma's thinking about India during war of independence. After a brilliant career in Cuttack and Calcutta, which was marked by certain amount of tumult, Subhash Chandra Bose went to England and competed in the ICS examination in 1920, standing fourth in the order of merit. However, the heaven-born service had no charm for him and he came back to India in 1921 to take a plunge in the struggle of freedom. Bose met Gandhiji in Bombay. "Love at first sight may not be always true but mutual allergy at first meeting is possible. Bose had himself written that the meeting somehow did not hit and neither took to each other. This mutual allergy was a national tragedy," an eminent scholar and historian P C Roy Chaudhary had commented. On the advice of Gandhi Bose himself reported to C R Das in Calcutta and found Das as his political guide. From 1921 to 1925, Bose was the right hand man of C R Das., organizing the Congress Party. Subhash Babu's dynamic personality put him on the all India canvas as a born fighter, a man of steel but with an extremely soft heart. Bose crisscrossed the Indian sky as long as he was here and then became a legend abroad, fighting for India's cause according his concept. Bose had wonderful combination of idealism, dedication and realism.

It was Subhas's ideology that brought him a rift first and a chasm afterwards with Gandhiji. Bose had always high regards for Gandhiji, evident from his broadcasts from abroad on Gandhiji's birth day and Kasturba's death during his many exhort ions to the Indian people to revolt and await the arrival of 'Indian army' But Subhas babu thought very poorly about Gandhiji's as a politician and statesman. Bose never believed in Gandhiji's creed of non-violence. "give me blood and I will give you independence" Bose thundered from abroad. While contradicting Gandhiji's teachings of fighting for independence through a non-violence approach, Bose used to crank a joke that Gandhiji was more surrounded by "cranks and crooks". Bose was for complete revolutions and was in close touch with revolutionaries in India and abroad.

Before that Subhas was released from Burma jail in 1927. Jawahar Lal Nehru also returned from Russia full of advance socialist ideas verging on communism. Both joined hand to form leftist group within Congress under the m name of "Independence League". Subhash-Jawahar leadership gradually alienated the Congress old guards including Gandhi as the youth all over India flocked under its banner. At that time, taking into account the development in India, Bose had told the All India Youth Congress conference in Calcutta, decrying Gandhiji's philosophy ". . . . a feeling and impression that modernism is bad, large-scale production is an evil, wants should not be increased and the standard of living should not be raised . . . . that the soul is so important that physical culture and military training can be ignored". He further said, ". . . . Mystics would always hold honored place in India but it is not their lead, at once free, happy and great . . . . we have to live in the present."

Subhah Babu has also a grudge against Gandhij that C R Das was being kept in Bengal while Gandhi Ji has had pushed up Motilal Nehru more. The differences between Subhas and Gandhiji crystallized with the

Calcutta session of the Indian National Congress in 1928. In the session Bose refused to toe the line of the Gandhiji in favour of his principled stand. Interesting development took place in the session. Bengal wanted Moti Lal Nehru as president. But both Moti Lal and Gandhiji wanted Jawahar to become next president. From that point of time, it was made open that Gandhiji had wanted to create rift between both Jawahar and Subhash. Gandhiji succeeded in winning back Jawahar in his favour by making him next president of the party. Gandhiji had always soft-corner towards Nehru family. Subhash never forgot the surrender of Jawahar Lal to Gandhi Ji.

On his return from forced stay in Europe after continuous arrests and imprisonments from 1933 to 1936, while studying, contacting and pondering over the world problems and India's foreign relations, Subhas returned to India in 1936 and imprisoned under Regulation—three of 1818 but released in March 1937. In 1938, Subhash Babu was elected president of the Indian National Congress and presided Haripura Congress session. In the session, Subhash Bose, while giving "blue print" of "poorn Swaraj" Interestingly, for the first time in the history of India, Subhas Babu underlined the importance of phased planning for India. As president of the INC, Bose did not try to hide his allergy to many of Gandhi's ideas about how swaraj was to be won. He held that the adoption of village life and what he took to be watery type of politics and negation of scientific method of production would only help to perpetuate the conditions of servitude of the people. In a speech at the Indian Science News Association, Calcutta on August 21, 1938, Bose had said National reconstruction will be possible only with the aid of science and scientists and far reaching cooperation between science and politics was absolute necessary if India was to take its place with the advanced countries of the world. Such statements of Subhash Babu was open defiance of Gandhiji's philosophy and politics.

The dynamic personality of Subhash Bose and his pronounced socialist views were viewed with great deal of alarm by some of the ultra rightists like Vallabhbhai Patel, Rajendra Prasad, Rajgopalacari and others. Main thrust of Subhash Babu to pull out the Congress from what he thought was "Gandhian obscurantism and fascism." He was also of the opinion that capitalists had grip over the Congress. When Subhas Bose term of president ship was to expire, Gandhiji selected Dr Pattabhi Sitaramayya for next president ship. Bose decided to contest election opposing Gandhiji's nominee and won the election. Two days later, Gandhiji said, "Mr Subhas Chandra Bose has achieved a decisive victory over his opponent Dr Pattabhi Sitaramayya . . . . I am glad of his victory . . . . the defeat is more mine than his (pattabhi) . . . ." Both Gandhiji and Subhas Bose differed on ideological ground. Subhas made no secret of the fact that he thought Gandhiji was was' old-fashioned, orthodox and probably autocrat.' It is quite clear with developments Gandhiji worked for the ousting of Subhas from the Congress and Gandhiji's coterie fully supported Gandhiji. Subhas was practically driven to resign the president ship of the Congress. Later Subhas was expelled from the Congress.

In a letter, written to his brother Sarat Bose, Subhash Babu observed ". . . . If power goes into the hands of such mean, vindictive and unscrupulous persons when Swaraj is won what will happen in the country? If we do not fight them now, we shall not be able to prevent power passing into their hands. Another reason why we should fight them now is that they have no idea of national reconstruction. Gandhiasm will land Free India in a ditch—if free India is sought to be rebuilt on Gandhian non-violent principles. India will then be offering a standing invitation to all predatory powers . . . . The latest phase of Gandhism with its sanctimonious hypocrisy—its outrage on democracy and its queer and under-stand able formula for political ills . . . . is/ sickening degree. One is forced to wonder which is a greater menace to India's future—the British bureaucracy or Gandhian hierarchy. After such last pronouncements, Subhas Babu disappeared from India in the middle of 1941.

There can be no doubt that the work of Subhas abroad and the marching of his soldiers to Indian soil indirectly hastened India's freedom. Bose's voice through foreign radio was listened by lakhs in India and the progress of the march of Bose's Liberation Army was followed closely. It will be pertinent to refer to some of Bose's broadcast from abroad so far his relationship with Gandhiji is concerned. In his message to Gandhiji after the death of Kasturba, Bose, for the first time, addressed Gandhiji as "Father of our Nation" and wanted his blessings and good wishes in his 'holy war of India's liberation' He concluded his broadcast by saying, "the armed struggle will go on until the Britishers is thrown out of India and until our tricolour national flag proudly flies over Viceroy's House in New India." It may be mentioned here that It was Subhas, who named Gandhiji as "Father of The Nation", which is yet to be conferred formally by successive union governments after independence.

India achieved independence. And to some how, Pundit Jawahar Lal Nehru carried the leadership and under his stewardship, concept of "Modern India" on the line of Subhas's vision were taken up to some extend. In my opinion, Gandhiji's 'truth and non-violence as well as his philosophy of cottage and village industries' does not appear to have clicked. And only after adopting advanced scientific approaches, the concept of 'Modern India' as developed nation in the cosmos is gaining momentum. It is very difficult to understand the "real politics and philosophy' of Mahatma Gandhi and his 'cold attitude' towards revolutionaries like Subhash Babu and others under his (Gandhiji's self-styled leadership). His truth and non-valences might have succeeded in South Africa but as 'Leader' in India, Gandhi ji has failed! In one aspect, I strongly feel Gandhi and his philosophy and doctrines have become mascot of present days political classes to shield their 'deeds and misdeeds' in the name of 'truth and non-valences and other philosophies 'of Gandhiji and thereby creating political anarchy in India on almost all the fronts!

Sources:—National Archives, New Delhi, Sarpru House Library, New Delhi, Gandhi National Museum and Library, Rajghat, New Delhi, Sinha Library, Patna, National Library, Calcutta, Various books n Gandhi including Gandhi And His Contemporaries by P C Roy Chaudhary!

GROWING INFLUENCES OF RELIGION, CASTE, CREED, RELIGION, REGIONALISM IN INDIA; DANGERS FOR DEMOCRACY!

Sunday, 13 January 2013

Some say India is nascent democracy! But ruling elites and almost all political classes are subverting the democracy and the constitutional provisions under the 'garb of matured democrats'. Growing influences of caste, community, creed, religion and regionalism since independence of the country and more vigorous in the last 20 years, have put 'a big question mark over the survival of true democratic tradition and values in India!

In the name of carrying parliamentary democracy: Are not political classes cheating people of the country in the name getting support on the basis of mandate in the elections?; Have not they become authoritarians in imposing their views and opinions in running the affairs of the country in the 'so called democratic tradition?; Is the religion like 'opium' not dominating the Indian political scenes? These are the few points always rankle my mind and some time I become disappointed over the fate of 'India'!

Although British Raj 'legacy' had left us 'largely feudal society' because of neglecting the country on industrial fronts during Raj period, after independence political leaders led by Pundit Jawahar Lal Nehru made efforts to industrialize the country through 'modern democratic Constitution and contributions'. In the process, much had been done on 'industrial fronts'. But as the process started giving fruitful results, the 'ills like feudalism, religion, caste, creed and regionalism' hijacked our democratic system. And since than, most people in the country vote on caste and communal line instead of united secular and democratic India'. The process goes on!

To trace out such malfunctioning in our system, one must has to travel to acquaint themselves with 'political developments' in the country since independence as well as some books like The Indian Ideology, written by Perry Anderson., highlighting the 'flaws' in our system and leadership A quote of Gurramdas 'Alam', Azaadi, 1946—Kyun bhai Nihal, Azaadi tu hai dekhi. Na bhai Prava, ne kha de ne vekhi. Main Jaggu ti Sunni assi Ambala ti aaye si. (Listen brother Nihar, have yu seen Freedom? No brother Parva, I have not seen it nor eaten it. I heard from Jaggu—it has come up to Ambala.) Aptly described the fruits of Independence in India.

The reviewer of the book and an eminent writer, Vijaya Prashad has commented, "The Indian nationalism was stillborn. It had a very good run, but now finds itself on life support". The book surmises that there is a serious mistake within Indian nationalism that "dooms India's prospects for its ambitions to become a real power." The country has become vested interests of money and religion. In the present context, nationalism of yester-year has become tools in the hands of political leadership for encouraging religious thoughts, caste, and communal ism in the country to serve their own interest. Nationalism has far-sightedness! Anderson notes: "nationalism has become a discourse that fatally generates a culture of euphemism and embellishment, precluding and clear-eyed stock-taking of past or present." Conservatives and feudalism in the society dominate the Indian society in the garb of nationalism as their shield against criticism. And this Indian ideology is running the Indian democracy!

This perception has naturally came from 'Hindu Right' in India and the jehadi currents in Pakistan and according to Prashada; liberal elites in both the countries sought shelter in illiberal state repression and in alliance with U S primacy. Prashada further puts forward the views of Anderson and remarks, "It was Gandhi who injected religion into the arteries of of Indian Nationalism and forged Indian state with 'the particularists religion of his forebears', making Muslim 'second class citizens' and 'creating a caste-iron democracy'." What is hidden within India is Hindustan", Anderson writes. It appears that nationalism itself saturated with caste-Hindu concerns as if Gandhi were the true in charge of such nationalism! Much the same kind of censure came from Dr B R Ambedkar ("What Gandhi and Congress Have Done to Untouchables—1946).

But Prashada has point to say, "the arrival of Indian liberalism in the late 1980s and the 1990s is very significant—with the Congress setting aside its social democratic commitments, the 'Hindu Right' edging to mainstream of the political world and international situation shifting towards primacy of the United States." Exactly in these contexts economic liberalization (1991) and for a caste-Hindu character to the arriviste middle class (emboldened by Mandal protests of 1990; the Ayodhaya incidents of 1990-92 and Kargil war of 1999), a different situation emerged, which gave encouragements of to caste, creed, communal bias, encouragement of hardcore religion and regionalism in the country. Thus, in my opinion, the Congress's obstreperous ways have generated counter reaction and the Indian society was badly tilted towards religion, regionalism and communal line!

Another significant important factor for the threat of India's secular democracy is emergence of 'Hindutva' forces under Rashtriya Swamb Sevak Sangh (RSS) and Bharatiya Janata Party (BJP). It had started taking deep root with the demolition of Babri Masjid in Ayodhaya but the Hindutva forces has penetrated in the society with Gujarat pogrom under the headship of Chief minister of Gujarat Narendra Modi in 2002. Many reports and studies have suggested and exposed the so called development of Gujarat during Modi's chief minister ship. Such studies have pointed out that Muslims, labour classes, women, minorities, lower caste and Schedule Tribes have been marginalized and discriminated in Gujarat in the last ten to 12 years. But after his hat-trick in the last assembly elections, Modi's emergence at the national scene as prime ministerial aspirant could not be ruled out, again, a danger signal for already batter red India society communally.

Paradoxically, Hndutva, is gaining ground as 'New Right', a political accomplisher of the new liberalization economic order. Strangely, the Hindutva also combines neoliberal economic policy and authoritarian social and cultural policy and politics. Initially starting from upper caste groups of north India, Hindutva has started spreading far and wide corner of the country with its stress on new liberalized economic policy, which is changing the political landscape of India. In the process Congress declined as saviour as upper caste and middle caste while Hindutva parties as well as regional parties have started emerging as new harbingers of the 'new middle caste propertied to their upper caste counterparts in many states to create 'provincial propertied classes'(PPC)' as enunciated by late K Bal Gopal.

3 3 3 3

3 3 3 3 3 3 3

3 3 3 3 3 3 3

More over, the regional parties of Chandra Babu of Telgu Desam in Andhra Padesh, Navin Patnaik of BJD in Odisha, TC of Mamta Bannerjee of West Bengal, JMM of Shibu Soren of Jharkhand, Karnataka Janata Dal of H D Devegowda, Prakash Singh Badal's Akali Dal in Punjab, JD(U) of Nitish Kumar of Bihar, National Conference of Sheikh Abdullah in Jammu and Kashmir, AIADMK OF Jaylalitha in Tamil Nadu, Bahujan Samaj Party of Mayawati of Uttar Pradesh, DMK of Karunanidhi off Tamil Nadu and Siv Sena of Maharashtra have emerged time-to-time as strong forces in their respective states. They have got the notoriety of supporting BJP at the centre to form government despite their secular credentials. Some of these regional parties including of Mayawati, Karunanidhi are also supporting currently the UPA government led by the Congress Party. On the other had regional straps like Mulayam Singh Yadav of Samajwadi Party in Uttar Pradesh, and Laloo Prasad Yadav of RJD of Bihar kept their secular credential intact and had never supported BJP in forming governments in states or at the centre.

Significantly, all these regional parties have support bases among middle and intermediary caste people and to some extend the vote of minority community also. But in the case of Laloo Prasad Yadav and Mulayam Singh Yadav, apart from middle and intermediary caste support base, both have solid grass root support among minorities because of their intact secular credentials. But the gaining ground of regional parties in the country is also a matter of concern. Regional hopes and aspirations of all these regional parties are also harming the central political classes in maintaining equilibrium at the national level. But even than, the ruling political classes are keeping them in good humor and giving them 'undue favour politically to shield them from corruption charges and financial assistance to the respective states, violating norms and rules of the Indian Union.

Because of weakening of left parties in the country in the recent years is also not giving good signal for the common masses of the country. At least the left forces have some principled stand for the welfare of masses. Thus the polarization of class, caste, creed, religion and regionalism among the people of India between both UPA of Congress and Hindutva forces of BJP in recent years have preferred party of capitalist class into party with lower caste-classes and minorities as their electoral base has become matter of concern and it appears that country is heading towards 'authoritarianism' in the garb of parliamentary democracy. This is bound to create widening gap between 'minority powerful' and 'majority powerless'.

INDIAN POLITICAL CLASSES ALIENATING MAJORITY FROM NATIONAL MAINSTREAM!

Thursday, 3 January 2013

Is the India, the country of over 120 crore population, heading for alienating the majority of population from the national main streams? The facts appear very much like-the-same when I take a glance of the 'functioning' of the successive union governments as well as the 'say' of the people of States of the Indian Union like Uttar Pradesh, Madhya Pradesh, Chhatishgarh, Bihar, Rajasthan, Gujarat, Maharashtra, Delhi, Haryana, Punjab, Jammu and Kashmir, Jharkhand, Maharshtra, Uttarakhand, Himachal Pradesh etc on important matters of 'governance and policy decisions' at the national-level.

Not only that, reports, emanating from union government's in Delhi, are seldom taken into 'considerations seriously' by the people of politically alienated states in South India and Eastern States like Andhra Pradesh, Arunachal, Assam, Goa, Karnataka, Kerala, Manipur, Meghalaya, Mizoram, Nagaland Odisha, Sikkim, Tamil Nadu, Tripura, West Bengal, Andmand and Nichobar, Chandigarh, POndicherry, Lkshadweep etc! Rather the people of these states feel that they are 'not the citizens' of India. Their languages, culture and traditions are far different than the people of the mainstream states of 'cow-belt' like North India, Central India and West India. They consider their problems independently although mired in problem-galores. People of these states also 'consider' the people of the mainstreams states as 'of India'. They have their own 'India'. People of many eastern states 'want cecessation' from the rest of India because of their continued neglect.

Media bias from mainstream centres like New Delhi is also considered main factors for such 'story' of alienation of these states. After all India is country of Indians than why ignoring south and east in striking balance in the country in the dissemination of news and views!

253

However, respect of the Constitution in respect of adult franchise goes smoothly and after all these alienated states have 'faith' in parliamentary democracy. But taking into account the hegemony and supremacy of mainstream states over southern and eastern states will continue for how many years for the nascent democracy in India?

There are wide gulf between rich and poor in India. Over 78 percent populations of the country are under acute poverty. They have no house, no lands. Tribal, living in the forest areas are the worse neglected. Over 15 crore population living as 'khanabadiosh' in hills, ocean belts etc are yet to be brought under national mainstreams. They are yet to see the light of the day of Indian democracy! (My blog Topic:—over 15 crore population in India yet to come under national mainstream, September 06, 2012)

Considering the back-ground of these facts, I want to trace the history of India. I strongly feel that differences of opinion among the mainstream states and alienated states are mainly due to the 'Indus Valley civilisation' of Aryan culture in medieval and ancient Bharat'. This Aryan culture, which entered 'Bharat land' from the central Asia, had discriminated Dravidian population of Bharat. In this game, the aboriginal population of the India, mainly' black' living in hilly region and extreme south, who are said to be the 'original inhabitants' of the ancient India, were continued to be ignored to create supremacy of Aryan culture and civilisation. At the cost of a'aborginal', the 'foreigners-Aryans' are ruling the country although it is facts that Aryan culture also penetrated the south Deccan areas! Eminent historian A L Basham, in his book—The Wonder That Was India—has said, "While in northern India the standards of Hindu culture declined somewhat after the Gupta age, in the Deccan they flourished and advanced. By this time Aryan influence had penetrated the whole of the Peninsula, and the contact of Aryan and Dravidian produced a vigorous cultural synthesis, which in turn had an immense influence on Indian civilisations as a whole."

To substantiate further about the contribution of shaping 'Indian Nation' as a whole by Southerners, Pundit Jawahar Lal Nehru, in his book Discovery of India, has pointed out, "The repeated invasions of North India did not affect the south directly. Indirectly, they led to many people from the north migrating to the south and these included builders and craftsmen and artisans. The south thus became a centre of the artistic traditions while north was more affected by new currents which the invaders brought with them. This process was accelerated in later centuries and the south became the strongholds of Hindu orthodoxy."

In my opinion problem of north-south-east tussles mainly cropped up during the East-India Company domination of British Raj period Britishers played games to divide each other and without any substantial work of development and solving problems in India. The 'Raj" only ruled the country for their enlightened self-interest of imperialism. Real division and differences of opinions among Indians started from that point under the instigation of Britishers. In the process creation of Pakistan and "seed of discord' among Hindu-Muslim came into fore. And the country is facing a host of problems!

The political development in the Indian polity in the last 25 years should also be considered jolts after jolts in keeping the country united. It all started with demolition of 'Babr Masjid' demolition led by forces of Hindu Parivar of RSS, VHP, and BJP. Since the demolition of the 'masjid', a clear battle line has been drawn between secular and communal forces in the country. Bunch of Muslim population have also started feeling discriminated! Subsequent to Gujarat riots, killing thousands of people in Gujarat and other parts of the country, the so called 'icon of saffron brigade Narendra Modi' has aggravated the politics of communal ism, Hndu nationalism and the society in India has been badly divided. The 'hat-trick' winning of the Gujarat assembly election by Narendra Modi, who was an architect of eliminating Muslims in Gujarat 2002, is aptly reminds the 'demonstration' of Modi to formalise the electoral victory in the line Hitler, who too came to absolute power through ballot and later became a 'fascist'. A political analyst of Patna, Surendra Kishore has said, "Since the advent of policies of globalisation and liberalisation these sections of socially and economically advanced, who are active in social media networks such as Twitter and Facebooks, have been getting more and more vocal to protect their own narrow interests and at the same time deny the right of crores of the poor and the marginalised"

Thus, emergence of Narendra Modi is bound to have significant impact on the national political scenario in the wake of 2014 Lok Sabha elections. In the BJP circle Narendra Modi is widely expected to lead the BJP at the national level as prime ministerial candidate in the Lok Sabha elections. Modi's third victory has also proved that now a days, elections are not fought on issues like corruption, misgoverning, and administrative misdemeanours but stress is given on 'personality cult'— that happened with Modi, obviously to put Modi, a potential prime ministerial candidate. Modi is being considered in Hindu organisations, a potential leader to polarise votes on communal line throughout the country. The BJP leadership including national president Nitin Gadkari, party leaders like Sushama Swarajya, Lal Krishna adavani, have, however, certain reservation over the prime ministerial aspirations of Modi and they are opposed to bigger role of Modi at national level. Apart from that Sangh Praivar like RSS including its Sarsanghchalak' Mohan Rao Bhagwat are of the views that Modi will not make a good prime ministerial candidate.

But recent tacit move of Modi like his speech in Hindi (in Gujarat, Modi never speaks in Hindi but only in Gujarati, but on his election in recent assembly elections, he addresses huge crowds in Hindii) after his victory in assembly election appears a significant signal at the country-level. Modi's apology for 'mistakes' any during his rule in Gujarat also indicates his design to mend his ways in days to come. Not only that slogans, of party men at different places, notably in Delhi, for projection of Modi as prime ministerial nominee in the next Lok Sabha elections is also taken seriously in political circles. Projection of Modi as prime ministerial candidate is also signalling break-up in NDA because its major partner—JD(U) led by the Bhar chief minister Nitish Kumar has opposed Modi as prime ministerial nominee. Rather, Nitish has said that prime ministerial nominee must have secular credential! In all tussles in NDA and its partners, particularly in BJP circles are bound to be hot up in days to come over Modi issue. Modi's authoritarian way oif functioning had alienated RSS and host of party leaders. But general cadre in saffron groups are hell—bent to bring Modi at national level! Prof Ghanshyam Shah, an eminent social scientist, who has mastery on minority population of India, has commented, "It will be a disaster if Modi goes to Delhi. He has personified the RSS and VHP ideology. Given the cynicism in the country and the phenomenon of risng middle class, he will have support—this class looks for authoritarian personalities in leaders."

Thus nascent democracy is under serious threat. We Indian must for work unity and integrity of the country to alienate one section from another section in the name of region, culture and of all communal ism. India must remain like the Preamble of our Constitution," The people of India having solemnly resolved to constitute into a sovereign, socialist, secular DEMOCRATIC REPUBLIC AND TO SECURE ALL ITS CITIZENS: . . . .

CONCEPT OF WELFARE STATE DURING MAURYAN EMPIRE VIS-A-VIS NEOLIBERAL ECONOMIC POLICY IN THE PRESENT DEMOCRACY!

Friday, 28 December 2012

The rule of the 'New state"—that was Bharat—during 321 BC was more democratic and people-oriented than the present 'Parliamentary democrarcy' in the present-day India! That 'Bharat' of Mauryan period covered far the greater part of India, right up to Kabul in the north. In today's context, our parliamentary democratic system has deteriorated to such extend that over 80 percent of people continue to be in the grip of poverty and in dire need of proper health and education facilities! But history of the past depicts altogether different facts where people were happy although there was 'autocracy and dictatorship' at the top echelon of the governance. But at the local level, there was much 'autonomy' in the towns and villages units where elected representatives looked after these affairs. On the other hand, today's parliamentary democracy, existing right from panchayat to Parliament level in India, there are least concern over peoples' welfare. In the name of the so called majority, the successive ruling dispensations in India are initiating measures, detrimental to the people of the country. Present day political classes are more interested in amassing huge wealth as well as conniving with 'nations and groups 'to further their enlightened self-interest The. Mauryan empire reminds one of the most successful 'state' on the scores of peoples' welfare.

Pundit Jawahar Lal Nehru in his book—Discovery of India, who has deliberated in length about successful rules of the 'Mauryan Empire', has said, "There could have been then, in a purely agricultural age, nothing like the control of the individual by the state which we see today. But, in spite of limitations an effort was made to control and regulate life. The state was very far from being just a police state, interested in keeping external and internal peace and collective revenue. There was a widespread and rigid bureaucracy and there were frequent references to espionage. Agriculture was regulated in many ways, so were rate of interest. Regulation and periodical inspections took place of food markets, manufacturers, slaughter houses, cattle rising, water rights, sports, courtesans and drinking saloons. Weight and measures were standardised. The cornering and adulteration of foodstuffs were rigorously punished. Trade was taxed, and, so also in some respects, the practice of religion. When there was a breach of regulations or some other misdemeanour, the temple monies were confiscated. If rich people were found guilty of embezzlement or of profiting from national calamity, their property was/also confiscated . . . . The state give relief to widow, orphans, the sicks and the infirm. Famine relief was special care of the state, half the stores in all the state warehouses were always kept in reserve for time of scarcity and relief . . . ."

The village communities were autonomous during Mauryan period. When we look the present-day India, apparently every things are there but of practically no use and people are suffering! Like our 'Magnacarta-like Indian Constitution' there was Chanakya's Arthashastra, which provided a variety of subjects and covered almost every aspects of the theory and practice of the government. Like our 'Indian Constitution', the Arthashastra had defined the duties of the King, of his ministers and councillors, of council meetings of departments of government, of diplomacy of war and peace. Chnakaya had stressed the enforcement of strict discipline. More over, we have the Constitution, mentioned 'all good' but it seldom comes to surface. The Constitution, laws, rules, conventions etc are manipulated and mutilated by present-day ruling and opposition classes! Interestingly, there are huge arguments against subsidies on welfare measures to poor during the current neo-liberal economic policy but during the Mauryan regime, there were wide-scale relief to widows, orphans, the sick and the infirm.

There were references that at the time of the coronation of the King, he had o take the oath of service to the people—'May I be deprived of heavens, of life and off springs if I oppress you'. 'In the happiness of his subjects, lies his happiness, in their welfare what ever pleases himself he shall consider as not good but whatever pleases his subjects, he shall consider as good . . . .'. And if the King misbehaved, his people have right to remove him and put another in his place. But misdeeds of present day 'democratic' rulers in India appear rule of law do not exist in India as the entire governance machinery including executive, legislature and judiciary are suffering from policy-paralysis.

Before I end up describing 'golden period' of India during Maurayan empire, I must mention that there were many wonderful cities in that vast empire. But the capital of the Mauryan empire—Pataliputra (the present day Patna and capital of Bihar state under Indian union) was magnificent. The city, even today, is spread out along the banks of Ganga River, where the Sone River meets in the modern Patna. Magasthens, the Greek ambassador describes Pataliputra as thus:" At the junction of the of this river (Ganga) with another is situated Palibothra, a city of eighty stadia (9.2 miles) in length and fifteen stadia (1.7 miles) in breadth. It is of shape of a parallelogram and is grided with a wooden wall, pierced with loopholes for the discharge of arrows. It has a ditch in front for defence and for receiving the sewage of the city. This ditch, which encompassed it all round, is 600 feet in breadths and thirty cubits in depth, and the wall is crowned with 557 towers and has four and sixty gates."

Significantly, all the great walls were made of wooden structures. Many houses were of wooden structures. Even today in the old Patna city areas (now called Patna Saheb), many old wooden houses are in existences. Apparently, the wooden houses were preferred at that period, as the entire Pataliputra zone even today is considered most vulnerable to earthquake. Not only in Patna city areas, in many parts of Bihara (now Bihar), houses were structured with woods. The worse earthquake of 1934 in Bihar reminds us the facts that fewer houses were damaged because houses were comparatively constructed with wooden structures!

Another revealing aspect of Pataliputra was best-administered local—self government. In the capital of Maurayan empire, Pataliputra had a 'municipality', elected by the people unlike the present-day Patna Municipal Corporation, messing up the present-day capital of Bihar-Patna!. The Maurayan Empire Capital Pataliputra has a 'Municipality'. It had thirty members, divided up into six committees of five members each, dealing with industries and handicrafts, death and births, manufacturers, arrangements for travellers and pilgrims etc. The entire municipal council looked after finance, sanitation, water supply, public buildings and gardens. Today's Patna Muncipal Corporation has rather worsened the situation in the vast growing up city!

I feel that there were only good during Maurayan Empire and bad after bad have emerged in our present set-up of democracy. Have the systems failed or political leadership failed?

PRACTICE OF POLITICAL OPPORTUNISM AMONG POLITICAL CLASS IN INDIA IN IMPOSING NEOLIBERAL POLICIES!

Tuesday, 18 December 2012

Perhaps, it is not the policy paralysis in India but policy adventurism among Indian political leadership against the public interests while striving for neoliberal economic policies in the name of economic development of the country! Many things including foreign direct investment (FDI) in the multi-brand retail trade are being initiated at the highest-level of governance to liberalise our economic system right from the time of the minority-ruled prime minister ship of Narsimha Rao and his union finance minister Manmohan singh (now prime minister). Country's interest is being compromised not only by the ruling United Progressive Alliance(UPA), led by the Congress but also by the NDA, led by BJP as well as regional parities like DMK of Karunanidhi, RJD of Laloo Prasad Yadav, BSP of Mayawati, Trinamul Congress of Mamata Bannerjee, BJD of Navin Patnaik, Janata Dal (U) led by Sharad Yadav and Nitish Kumar and Samajwadi Party of Mulayam Singh Yadav All these stake-holders on the Indian political scenes are manipulating the things in the practise of opportunism to serve their enlightened interest.

Happenings of the last six to eight months, particularly in the run of governance and parliamentary proceedings, for carrying the government business in the Parliament and throughout the country have aggravated the situation—not only deterioration on the economic front of the country but mainly widening the gap of social and economic disparities. Political classes are making "democratisation of corruption". Corruption has become a symptom of a widening gap between the 'powerful and powerless'. Political classes as a whole are indulging in anarchy. Pantomime like situation is prevailing in the country! Thus the country is sitting on subdued volcano. India has been passing through worse phase in the world. Both the houses of Parliament-Rajya Sabha and

Lok Sabha—have virtually turned into political theatrics, unmindful of meaningful discussions for the upliftment of poor classes in the country!

In this game of manoeuvring politics by both major political players—Congress and BJP—appear conniving each other to divert the attention of people from burning issues like corruption right from high-level to rural panchayat level in the country as well as lack of food to poverty-ridden poor, education and health measures throughout the country. The political players are playing their own games. Congress and its partners are engaged in criticising the Comptroller and Auditor General of India (CAG), which has exposed the UPA government over wrong doings in 2-G spectrum, coal block allotment and other financial irregularities. Not only that they rushed through in managing the resolution of FDI in the both the houses of Parliament and also hinting other liberalised economic measures, detrimental to the majority of poor living in India.

Likewise, the main opposition—BJP and Rashtriya Swayamsewak Sangh (RSS)—led Sangh Parivar have been trying hard to hush-up corruption charges against the national president of the BJP Nitin Gadakari despite the facts that many senior BJP leaders including Ram Jethamalani, demanding the resignation of Gadkari. Sign of party with a difference—BJP—has also done the same thing in covering up Nitin Gadkari. Such harakari by the BJP and RSS have adversely affected the opposition onslaughts against corrupt practices by the Congress and other UPA ministers. In this way, it appears that BJP and the Congress appear on the same wave-length despite their tall talks in at least recent parliament session on various issues of public interest. With regards to regional outfits, which virtual keep lever of power, have also grown weak. Many of its leaders like Mayawati and Mulayam of Uttar Pradesh, Laloo Prasad Yadav of Bihar and Karunanidhi of Tamil Nadu are involved in neck-deep corruption and the ruling UPA led by Congress is controlling them by whipping the 'CBI stick'. Recent dramas in the Parliament over passage of FDI resolution have exposed the entire political classes in the country.

Situation in the country is heading towards the one that existed in 1989 when the Rajiv Gandhi, who was allegedly involved in Bofor scandal and HDW submarine scam, was humbled in the Lok Sabha elections by the Jan Morcha led by Vishwanath Pratap Singh. Corruption is becoming the issue second to only price rise. Lamentably, there is no leader of V P singh stature on the Indian political scene. Singh had vision and organisational statures to unite the people of the country for a change and biggest issue of that Lok Sabha election was corruption. Apart from vacuum in almost all political parties because of lack of strong and efficient leadership, there are general perceptions that all political leaders are corrupt. The recently formed Aam Aadami Party by Arwind Kejariwal, has, however, evoked mixed response and the party is attracting attention, mainly from urban middle classes. A ray of hope has also arisen some significant performances of Jan Sambad by a group of civil society activists led by Aruna Roy and P V Rajagopal the Jan Samwad is holding fruitful discussions and peoples' participation in the proposed movement. In this endeavour, the recent Ekata Parishad—led padyatra of P V Rajagopal on land reforms has also noticed political awareness among masses, who are fighting for "jal, jungle and zameen", Apart from that gatherings and agitations, launched by left parties and its trade union movement, farmers and agriculture organisations have also shown a significant development during the critical hour in hte country because of failure of entire system. But for all these changes in the prevailing rotten system, there is need of charismatic leadership, which the country is lacking in today's context.

A Patna-based eminent columnist Surendra Kishore has said "present situation could be compared with 'art of the possible' regime of Narsimha Rao. There are several similarities between that regime and the present one. Both are minority governments in formal sense, but both have survived on the basis of a value—neutral pursuit of power using questionable means. During Narsimha Rao's regime, one saw the blatant cash votes scam, where in members of of the Jharkhand Mukti Morcha (JMM), a regional party of tribal state now Jharkhand, were literally bought with money transferred to their accounts to ensure survival of the government. Now we see other carrot-and-stick ploy being used to bring regional parties in line. On the one side, you have the bait of special packages for states in which regional parties have roots. Then there is ploy that broadly term as CBI consent, which involves beating down leadership of regional parties by periodically showing them the stick of various investigate and punitive agencies."

Prakash Karat, general secretary, Communist Party of India (Marxist), who also shown concern over prevailing political scenario in the country, has told the Frontline in a recent interview, "To cope with the present situation, the challenge is how to build an alternative politics which is not influenced by big capital and money and to build an alternative platform, which can rally all sections of the working people. As far as the left parties are concerned, we cannot rely on some of the non-congress alternative policies. The vote in the Lok Sabha, disapproving FDI in retail is an example of the opportunism of some of these parties. We do not think a third alternative is possible with such parties as there cannot be a common platform of alternative policies. The only way an alternative to the present set-up will emerge is through developing movements and struggles and building a left and democratic alliance in the process."

Now before I further discuss other aspects of the present situation, I think it better to highlight about neoliberal measures. Prabhat Patnaik, a prominent social scientist, has said, "Neoliberal measures include, above all, an opening of the economy to free cross border movements of capital, including in particular, finance capital. In a country like that is open to such free movements of finance capital, if the state pursued measures that are disliked by finance, then finance would pull out of the country and more else where: and since such movements can be quite large, the economy would find in itself in and an acute crisis. In a neoliberal economy, the state is forever caught in the attempt to retain the confidence of the investors in the economy (a euphemism for keeping finance capital happy). For this it has to bow to the caprices of globalised finance capital (with domestic big capital is closely integrated) and adopt only such measures as finances likes, that is, measures that promotes its interest. This fact itself constitutes a negation of democracy. In a democracy, the state is supposed to pursue policies that benefit the people, who are sovereign and on the basis of whose electoral verdict the government is formed. But if the government elected by the people must follow policies that are not in the interests of the people but in the interests of finance capital, then we have negation of democracy."

Corruption is bane of neoliberal economic policy. One must be watching that since the implementation of neoliberal economic policy from Narsimha Rao regime, corruption started touching a new height in India. New policy compels the dictum of globalised country to put persons on the helm of economic affairs not traditional politicians but technocrats from the world finance, former employee of the World Bank, the International Monetary Fund (IMF) or other international financial institutions. All of them implement the policies of neoliberal to the hilt where globalisation of economy has taken place. In the case of Narsimha Rao, he had appointed Manmohan Singh, well-known World Bank employee as finance minister and since then such technocrats were appointed on key position by the respective union governments. Currently Montek Singh Ahluwalia, World Bank and IMF person has been appointed deputy chairman of the Planning Commission and his views on economy in the context of India is well known and some times his statements become matter of joke. Many other top ranking posts in the economic affairs wing are filled up with such technocrats during Manmohan Singh regime. To substantiate the facts; one example must be cited for prevalent corruption among political classes. There becomes conflict between traditional politicians as ministers and liberalised trained officials. And for solving the situation, and to win over traditional political-ministers, a price is tagged and that price is 'corruption' in that price. One must have observed that only political rulers like ministers are involved in corrupt practices not the persons of international finance bodies, who had brought political-ministers under the trap of corrupt practices!

With such bending of rules and laws in India, the country is slowly moving towards fascism. There was a time when Hindutva forces, used to be of adopting fascist style of functioning. Now, such fascism has developed every where in the union and state governments. University professors in West Bengal are arrested for circulating a cartoon of the chief minister Mamta Bannerjee,; a man is arrested for posing a problem to Mamta Bannerjee at a public meeting; at many places leaders of political parties tortures dalits openly; two innocent girls were arrested for making comments on the Facebook, entire city is closed down on the death of a local politician, known for arms-twisting methods; a man who had presided over and possibly winked at a communal carnage being openly touted as the next prime ministerial candidate; a prolonged communal carnage inflicted upon a minority border state; the widespread glee surrounding the hanging of a young man who had indulged in, no doubt, in horrendous acts of terrorism but who was a mere minion of little consequences. Are not these incidents are symptoms of creeping fascism in the country? The haste in pushing up "reforms" by the Manmohan Singh government is bound to bring further miseries for poor, particularly tribal, dalits and other weaker sections of society as the capitals will be accumulated under the hand of a few detriments to the general people of the country.

It is high time for progressive Indians to unite for a long-drawn agitation to resist the policies against the general masses as well as erosion in democratic values in the country!

RAMPANT CORRUPTION IN INDIA SIGNALLING CIVIL WAR!

Tuesday, 11 December 2012

EVERY where there are corrupt practises in India! Common masses are worst affected because of pervading corruption every where. Unrest, anger and frustration writ large among the masses. Evil of corruption is not only confined to political classes only it has deeply entrenched in government businesses. Situation has gone down to such extend that entire government machinery is afflicted by this evil. Even in small matter in remote rural areas, none could carry their government business without paying underhand payment in the entire country. Poor like adivasis, dalits, minority community etc are the worst sufferers! They cannot taste the fruits of welfare measures without paying bribes to government officials. On the other hand brokers, neo-rich classes, contractors, corporates, multinational companies, industrialists, capitalists, bureaucrats, political classes except a few are amassing huge wealth through corrupt practices. Deprived lots of margins continue to suffer!

There have been strange perceptions of corruption being floated by vested interest. Some say it is international phenomena; some say bribery is not new things; but no body come with any concrete measures to eliminate the corruption menace. In India, political corruption has started deeply entrenching just after the independence of the country over 65 years earlier. And now such menace has taken bigger dimension. India has been ranked 94th out of 176 counties of the world in Transparency International's 2012 Corruption Perception Index (CPI). The Transparency International's CPI has, in a recent report, says that India earned a very low score of 36 points on a scale from 0 (most corrupt) to 1000 least corrupt. The Transparency International India has attributed the low scores to the recent scams and incidents of corruption in the public sector involving government officials, private officials and private companies. As per Transparency report, two-thirds of the 176 countries recorded a CPI score below 50. Denmark, Finland and Switzerland topped the index with a score of 90 followed by Sweden with a score of 88. Afghanistan, North Korea and Somalia were perceived as the most corrupt countries scoring, just 8 out of 100. However, India has been ranked below neighbouring Sri Lanka and China, while it feared better than Iran, Nepal, Pakistan and Bangladesh. From this year, the CPI methodology has been updated allowing for year-over-year comparisons from 2012 on onwards. India was ranked 72 among 180 countries in 2007 and since the country's ranking fell to 87 in 2010 and 95 in 2011. (www.kksingh1.blogspot.com LOOT OF PUBLIC MONEY BY POLITICIANS, MEMBERS OF EXECUTIVE, JUDICIARY AND POWER BROKERS IN INDIA, written on August 10, 2012)

The Transparency International further says that the data from 10 independent sources specialising in governance and business climate analysis including the World Bank and the World Economic Forum were used to arrive at India's CPI score. India head of the Transparency International P S Bawa has said, "Corruption is hydra-headed monster and governments have to make efforts to tackle it from all sides. This can only happen if all stakeholders work together."

Because of rapid erosion in the self-less dedication of leaders has led to increase in corruption in India. National interest has become no body's concern. Even during Pundit Jawahar Lal Nehru's Prime Minister Ship, a number of corruption cases had come to the surface! These corruption cases were geep scandal (1948) of Rs 36.52 crore; the Mndra scandal (1958—Rs 1.20 crore and Rs 47.73 corore); Dharma Teja loans of of Rs 22 crore. Total indexed value in 2011 would be Rs 869.57 crore.

During Indira Gandhi prime minister ship—there were Nagarwal scandal (1971—Rs 60 lakh, indexed value Rs 11.10 crore; the Kuo oil scandal (1976—Rs 2.2 crore—indexed value Rs 24.80 crore); the cement scam: Donations for the Indira Pratishthan Trust collected by A R Antulay—Rs 30 crore—indexed value Rs 208.80 crore;—thus During Indira tenure scandals indexed value would be Rs 244.70 crore.

Rajiv Gandhi's tenure as prime minister ship witnessed the much-maligned Bofor scandal of Rs 64 crore in 1987 (Rs 313.72 crore indexed value).

The prime minister ship of Narsimhaha Rao saw many scandals:— the Lakhubhai Pathak pickles scam (1984—$ 1,30,000 equivalent at the then conversion rate to Rs 22.75 lakh(Rs 7.79 crore); the sugar import scam—(1994—Rs 650 crore-indexed value Rs 1627.99 crore; Sukhram telecom scandal (1996—Rs 3.6 crore-indexed value Rs 12.33 crore); CR Bhansali scam (1998—Rs 1100 crore-indexed value Rs 4,381.60 crore and Fertiliser scam—(1996—Rs 133 crore-indexed value Rs294.85 crore). Index value of this scam during Rao's regime comes to Rs 4381.56 crore.

Atal Behari Vajpayee's Prime Minister Ship also did not lag behind in corrupt practices. During his regime, the Kargil coffin scandal (1995—$ 1.87 lakh equivalent to at the then conversion rate to Rs 80.64 lakh— Rs 1.87 crore indexed value and Barak missile scandal $ 80.64 lakh equivalent at the then conversion rate to Rs 36.29 crore-indexed value Rs 66.13 crore—thus total indexed value would be nearly Rs 68 crore. Vajpayee period's scams does not include telecommunication scandals in which "first come-first serve basis" for granting licences includes, which have been deprecated by Supreme Court •as well as adoption of such system by Manmohan Singh government, which entailed loss to the exchequer to the tune of over Rs 1.85 lakh crore as audited by Comptroller and Auditor General of India.

During Manmohan Singh's prime minister ship, corruption in government deals has touched a new height:—the Scorpene submarine deal (2006—Rs 500 crore-indexed value Rs 685.80 crore; the cash for vote scandal Rs 50 crore-indexed value Rs 59.95 crore; 2G spectrum—2010—Rs 1,76,000 crore-indexed value—Rs 1,89,200 crore and the Commonwealth Games scam—Rs 8000 crore—indexed value Rs 8,599.99 crore)—thus total indexed value during Manmohan Singh's regime comes to Rs Rs 1,98, 546 crore.

Moreover all these scams and scandals involved ministers and prime ministers as well as bureaucrats! Black money stacked in foreign banks has different story. The white paper of government of India says that black money stacked in Switzerland stood Rs 9,295 crore during 2010. FICCI version is different and says black money figure stacked in foreign banks stodd to Rs 45 lakh crore on the other hand the then Director of the CBI A P Singh has said that such amount stood to rs $ 500 billion. Singh has given such statement to the Supreme Court.

Apart from that over Rs 1000 lakh crore, meant for welfare measures and other development schemes are being pocketed by greedy politicians, bureaucrats, middle men, contractors, neo-rich classes every year. And the helpless poor people of the country are watching such naked dramas helplessly!

Anna Hazare hammering the issue of corruption but he has become helpless. Now on the same plank, Arwind Kejariwal has launched a new party, "AAm AAdami Dal" and entered the politics in big way. In my opinion, there is anarchy in the country on the corruption front. In the last two years, as many as 10 anti-corruption bills have been introduced in the Parliament including Lok Pal Bill, the forfeiture of benami property, foreign bribery, money laundering and whistle-blowing bills plus five more—all aimed at deterring specific acts of corruption or purporting to give corruption-free public service as a right. Apart from that Bihar Odisha, Rajasthan, and Jharkhand have enacted laws, which could result in attachment of ill-gotten property of public servants. But nothing tangible is appearing on the surface to eliminate the corruption menace.

I share the views of Arundhati Roy, who in an interview to the Outlook weekly magazine has said, "What our economists like to call a level playing field is actually a machine spinning with a centrifugal force that funnels the poor out like disposable residue and concentrates wealth in fewer and fewer hands, which is why 100 people have wealth equivalent to 25 percent of the GDP and hundreds of millions live on less than 2Rs 20 a day. It is why most of our children suffer from malnutrition, why two lakh h farmers have killed themselves and why India is home to majority of the world's poor . . . . it is absurd situation for a country to be in. Unless mega corporations are reined in and limited by legislation, unless the levers of such untrammelled power (which includes the power to buy politics and policy-making, justice, elections and the news) is taken away from them, unless the cross-ownership of businesses is regulated, unless the media is freed from absolute control of big business, we are headed for a shipwreck. No amount of noise, no amount of anti-corruption campaigns, and no amount of elections can stop them. Unrest angers a frustration that is building up in the country. Some times the noisiness of it makes it hard to see clearly. But unless we look tings in the eye—instead of heading off in strange quixotic direction—we can look forward in the civil war, which had already begun, reaching out our doorsteps very soon."

Likewise, Prof K C Mehata, former vice-chancellor and Professor of Finance, MS University of Baroda has written in an article, recently published in The Hindu, has said, "Unless people rise in revolt this demon and punish the corrupt by refusing to vote for them, a time will come (if it has already) when we get used to the debased public life."

ARMS AND AMMUNITION MANUFACTURING AND ACQUISITION AT THE TOP AMONG GLOBE NATIONS: US AND CHINA HEADING FOR MANUFACTURING LETHAL WEAPONS IN THE WORLD!

Thursday, 6 December 2012

Perhaps, the world nations have forgotten the consequences of use of lethal weapons used in Hiroshima and Nagasaki, killing lakhs of people and destruction of the unprecedented scale. Not only that, recent wars in Iraq, Afghanistan, Middle East countries etc, spearheaded by imperialist America, have killed thousands of people and destroyed the economic structures of the affected countries. Moreover escalations of tensions on the borders of many countries are giving ominous signals of further loss of human beings. Manufacturing of sophisticated weapons like Drone and targeted missiles have become very common for world countries apart from having nuclear bombs, chemical bombs like hydrogen etc. Will the manufacturing, acquiring and of all exporting of destructive weapons by various nations, particularly U S, China, Russia, France and others to various developing and developed countries put the entire globe under perpetual threat of destruction throughout the world?

China's military spending has been rapidly spiralling and the growing amounts are unnerving the Beijing's Asian neighbours and policy planners in the Pentagon. And they are wary about the China's long-term 'intention'. On the other hand, the United States of America have significantly increased the manufacturing and sales of arms in the 'world arms bazzars'. In both the cases, such heinous tendencies of these two big powers have been exposed in various newspapers, periodicals of the world including Washington Post, New York Times and various periodicals of India! (My three blogs in the last one years—Scar of Sino-Indian War!, October 22, 2012; US; World's biggest arms manufacturers and India, globe's biggest arms importers—September 08, 2012 and Fight for expanding territorial boundaries in Sea, Island and Islets in Asia—August 13, 2012, have dwelt about weapons race globally)

According to a report of the annual survey of the U S Congressional Research Survey (CRS); a policy research arm of the U S Congress; quoted by eminent columnist John Cherian in tte Frotntline; American arms manufacturers sold a staggering $ 66.3 billion worth of weaponry in 2011. Most of sold arms went into the disturbed countries in the West Asia region. The CRS survey has put the "U S far ahead of other major arms exporters such as China, Russia and France."

To assess the massive manufacturing and exporting weapons by the China is difficult because much of it is "the opaque and off the books", such as "the People's Liberation Army's spending on research and space exploration", say reports of the Washington Post and New York Times. Although the United States still spends four times as much on its military. But if one looks by same account, China is on course to surpass the United States in total military spending by 2035! China's military programme spending increased as allowed by the PLA and it has embarked on a sweeping modernisation programme that in cluded new long-range cruise missiles, a new fleet of J-10 and S-11 fighter jets, an experimental stealth J-20 plane, a refurbished Soviet-era aircraft carrier and a growing space programme, which includes China's own satellite navigation network. The PLA has also launched on a long-term campaign to improve the inter-operability of its various grounds, naval and air forces—long a weak point for the Chinese military power.

Significantly, Washington has signed 77 percent of arms agreements globally last year. US weapons sales have registered phenomenal growth in 2011 compared with $ 21.4 billion in 2010. Russia has globally, imported 5.6 percent arms sales last year. Quoting Russian President Valadimir Putin, John Cherian has said that his country's arms sales in the first half of 2012 had crossed the $ 6.5 million mark. This is 14 percent more than the sales in the corresponding period last year.

More over, India, which was until recently imported most of the defence requirements from Russia, has interestingly turned towards the U S and Western Europe. In 2011 alone, Russia used to fulfil the defence requirements of India for more than 50 percent India's arms imports. Such figure was around 80 percent in the previous decades. Russia has now found new 'arms bazzar' in Latin America and also other parts of the world. Iraq has issued new orders of weapons supply and military hard wares. Russia has inked a deal of worth $ 4.2 billion with Iraq in October 2012. In this way Russia will be counted as second biggest arms supplier to Iraq after U S. During Saddam Hussein region, Russia was the biggest arms supplier to Iraq. Not only that, Russia is also supplying arms to beleaguered Syria., Algeria and Iran. They buy significant of weapons from Russia. After the ouster of Muammar Qaddafi, the lucrative Libyan arms market is being monopolised by U S.

Meantime, China's critics, specially its neighbours, are definitely alarmed over huge expenditures of China on weapons, which, the critics describe, China's more assertive stance over long-disputed, unhindered islands in the South China and East China Sea. Especially Japan and Vietnam are more disturbed over such weaponry tactics of China because, they, call, unauthorised interferences of China in Japan's sea territory. Some of them also say China's growing military might shift the balance with American armed Taiwan, which Chinese leaders consider a renegade province to be reunited with the mainland! Apart from that, India also seems disturbed over growing military strength of China! The scar of 1962 war of China against India is still haunting India because the China has been persistently claiming more and more territories like Arunachal and NEFA region. Of late some visa action of China to Arunachal Pradesh, a state of Indian Republic, has also been giving agonising moments to India. Chinese map shows major parts of Himalayan areas, particularly Arunchal Pradesh of India as their territory! The Chinese buildup has caused Japan and some South-East Asian countries to seek assurance from the United States that they would not be abandoned, although Chinese diplomats have accused the U S of meddling in what are essentially regional disputes.

Major-General Luo of the China Military Science Society has said outsiders need not be concerned. China's military spending only "reflects the newly booming economy". He further added that the country's "is simply playing catch-up after years of neglect." Actually, our rapid spending increase in recent years is more like compensation for the past", Luo said and added, "second the huge increase our budget is because China faces a lot of threats, traditional and non-traditional. We have a lot of land occupied by other countries. We are also one of the countries in the world with the most neighbours." Luo also said "while other sectors are enjoying the fruits of reforms, the armed forces should not be neglected. It is important that a person not only grow his bones, but also his muscles and the military are the muscles."

Both the China and United States are criticising each others for military build-ups. India, which is the biggest weapons importers in the world, has pacted a deal with United States worth over $ 6.9 billion for weapon supply and more such deals are under pipelines. Beijing has criticised a deal of U S with Taiwan for purchasing Patriot anti-missiles batteries for over $ 2 billion, China has signalled that such deals will escalate tension in the region. China is entangled in territorial disputes over marine boundaries with many of its neighbour. Military tension is increasing in South-East Asian countries because of abnormal increase in the sales of weapons in Indonesia, The Philippines, Vietnam and Malaysia. China has been wishing the reunification of Taiwan with China since 1949.

Andrew Shapiro, the Assistant Secretary of State for Political-Military affairs, told U S media in August 2012 that 2012 "is already a record-breaking year for foreign military sales. We have already surpassed $ 50 billion in sales in fiscal year 2012." (The fiscal year of America is from October 01 to September 30). Such bulks of weapon shipments have gone to developing countries. Shapiro, however, said that the earnings from the sale of military hardware are estimated to be only around one-eleventh of the total American expenditure, totalling around $ 766 billion Major buyers of American weapons are Gulf monarchies of Saudi Arabia, United Arab Emirates.

According to a latest report of Globalisation Militarisation Index (GMI), released by the Bonn International Centre for Conversations (BICC), Israel is the top most militarised nation. Israel is attacking blatantly hapless people of Gaza. The second place in militarisation is of Singapore, a close ally of the West. Six of the nations in the GMI list of ten top militarised nations are Syria, (3); Jordan (5), Kuwait (7), Bahrain (9) and Saudi Arabia (10) in the West Asia. Militarisation is gradually spreading to the central Asian countries also.

India, which is also militarising itself, has been at the rank of 71 while China is ranked 82. The US is ranked 29. Thus rapid militarisation by the countries of the world is giving sleepless nights to peace loving people of the earth.

RAM KA NAM BADNAM NA KARO-BABARI MASJID DEMOLITION IN AYODHAY 20 YEARS BACK BIGGEST SHAME FOR INDIA: JUDICIARY FAILED IN ITS DUTY!!

Monday, 3 December 2012

It is not that I am not a believer and exactly remember the fanatic crowds, belonging to Hindu organisations, led by former union home minister and Bharatiya Janata Party Leader, Lal Krishna Advani, demolishing the Babari Masjid in Ayodhaya, 20 years back on the noon of December 06, 1992. Top Hindu leaders including Advani, Murali Manohar Joshi, Uma Bharati, Ritambhara, Ashok Singhal, Vinay Katiyar, inciting the huge crowds to demolish the Babari Masjid, adjacent to Lord Ram temple. And they succeeded in demolishing the structures of Babari Masjd! Had these Hindu leaders taken inspiration from the Lord Ram to demolish Babari structures? or they were ought to ruin the secular fabric of India in the name of 'politic'? As far as, the epic—Ramcharitmanas (RAMAYAN)—written By Tulsi Das on the direct 'inspiration' of Lord RAM and SHANKAR—is concerned, the MAHAKABYA, praising the character of Lord RAM had no where differentiated between religions of the world; it only teaches us 'adarsh grahsath jeevan, adarsh bhratprem, supreme bhakati, knowledge, sacrifice, vairag and sadachar'. But today in the name of Lord, they (Hindu) leaders ruined the masjid and striving hard to consolidate Hindus against the MUSLIMS—my humble submission to them, "RAM KA NAN BADNAM NA KARO".

No doubt, the demolition of Babari Masjid 'under planned conspiracy' is the greatest shame for India since its independence!In the after math of of Babari Masjid demolition, hundreds of people had also been killed in communal riots in different parts of the country! In the process, such fanatic action of the Hindu organisations is gradually destroying the democratic and secular fabrics of India. TWENTY years of

273

the heinous crime elapsed and the perpetrators of the crime led by Advani are moving free, thanks to the incompetence and inefficiency of Judiciary and government machinery! Villain of the pieces Advani, a shamelessly shameless politician on the Indian political horizon, is still keeping prime ministerial aspiration as shrewed operator in the BJP! Are we Indian are really shameless? (MY blog—www.kksingh1.blogspot.com)

Advani had hatched conspiracy to demolish Babari Masjid as back as in October 1990, which culminated in ultimate demolition of the masjid in 1992. Hindu organisations have srange connotation and they say that Babari Masjid was constructed on RAMJANMBHOOMI by Meer Baki about 1500 years ago. In the process of creating hatred towards MUslims in the country, Advani had toured throughout the country, particularly from Somnath to Ayodhaya to create atmosphere of hatred and ultimately destroying Babari Masjid in Ayodhaya. While touring the country, Advani had asserted before the huge crowds led by Bal Thakare in Dadar areas of Bombay, now Mumbai that on Babari Masjid site, they would construct 'RAM TEMPLE'. After touring on his so called "Rathyatra" Advani finally came to Ayodhaya in Uttar Pradesh where Kalyan Singh government of BJP was in power. On December 05, 1992, Advani held a secret meeting at the residence of his another colleague Vijay Katiyar in Ayodhaya and hatched conspiracy to demolish the 'masjid'. Moreover Advani announced at the Masjid site that 06, December, 2012 will be the last date of' Karsewa' by Hindu fanatics. Not only that Advani incited the fanatic Hindu crowd to block Faizabad road from where the central para-military forces were moving to stop untoward incidents. Ultimately, they blocked the highway and did not allow the central forces to enter Ayodhaya. Advani, even, called them to become martyr to construct 'Ram mandir' at Babari Masjid disputed site by demolishing masjid if the central forces advanced towards at masjid site! Such action was openly floated by Advani to make 'secular India", a Hindu Rashtra! Kalyan Singh government even after undertaking to the Supreme Court, to save the situation, did not act and left the field scot-free to demolish the masjid!

Ultimately, amid inflammatory speeches by Advani and other Hindu leaders, the 'karsewaks' demolished the masjid in no time on December 06, 1992. Thereafter, legal formalities started and altogether 49 cases were registered by the police. Apart from special cells of Uttar Pradesh CID, the CBI also took up the cases. Charges sheets were filed February 1993 against Hindu leaders led by Advani under Sections 153A, 153B, 105,

147, 149 of IPC and many other Sections of the Cr. P.C. And from there, all criminal cases under various sections of IPC and Cr.PC entangled in the judicial cobweb right from lower courts in Rai-Barailey and Lucknow to Allahabad High Court and Supreme Court. In between, 10 accused persons and over 50 witnesses have died. And now finally, the admissions for the starting of proceedings in all these cases against Hindu leaders led by Advani are pending in the Supreme Court for the last few years. Incidentally, the Supreme Court has fixed on December 06, 2012, the same day of demolition of Babari Masjid in 1992, to hear the appeal of the CBI. All the cases are lingering and culprits are scot-free! This is what our judicial system-Judges, right from lower courts in Uttar Pradesh to Allahabad High court and Supreme Court, are playing games with such serious nature of cases in the annals of the history of the country. From the very beginning, all these cases are shuttling between Lalitpur lower courts to Barailey and Locknow lower courts and subsequent stays after stays by the benches of Allahabad high court and the Supreme Court.

Advani and other accused pesons are taking advantage of loop-holes in instituting cases and transferring it one lower court to other courts. The Allahabad High court and Uttar Pradesh successive governments, especially of Mayawati had faltered in clubbing the cases and start proceedings against the accused persons even after taking cognisance against the culprits. In the continuation, one judge of Allahabad High court had stayed proceedings against Advani and others on May 20, 2010. One judge, in a separate appeal, on July 06, 2005 had remarked that there were prima facie evidences against Advani and others and criminal cases hearing must start at the earliest. Ultimate, the CBI hasd moved Supreme Court on February 09, 2011 for its directive to start proceedings against Advani and others without any further delay.

Are these things not posing million dollar questions on our judicial prudence and efficiency of our government in the country? I strongly feel the judiciary and government are saving the culprits from such heinous crime-but Lord is witnessing the naked drama of Indian politicians and judges in the Babari Masjid demolition cases. And a time will come when—"hohi yohi jo Ram Rachi Rakaha—"

CHILD LABOUR, A BIGGEST CURSE IN INDIA!

Friday, 30 November 2012

It is common refrain that children are messengers of the God; they are the future of the country! But in India, children among the marginal and middle classes, totalling over 87 percent particularly are most neglected lot in the country! Prevalent of child labour is highest in India. If we take into account the census data of 2001, in every 10 workers in India, one is a child. These children are in the age-group of the 5-14 years. Children are abducted, kidnapped and allured in a big way in the country according to an International Labour Organisation (ILO) report and a revealing story in the Washington Post. They are forced into labour and sexual exploitation. In the process over 90000 children are missing for the last several years in India—(My blog Topic—headlined, 90000 Children missing in India! written on September 25, 2012). Instead of shaping the destiny of the children by providing them food, health provisions and education, they are forced into child labour. Worse is the scenario among children below the age of five years. They are malnourished and die every year in huge number because of absence of medical facilities despite the facts that both union government and state government have been claiming large number of measures for the welfare of children in the country!

In 2004-05, the National Sample Survey Organisation (NSSO) had put the figure of child labour 8.9 million. Since than there have been no significant change in the situation for improvement. Hosts of non-governmental organisations (NGOs) have assessed that the child labour over 60 million in India. What ever may be case, India is the largest employer of child labour. Over 80 percent of child labour is not visible as they work in the unorganised sectors including within family or in house-hold work. As per the NSSO survey in 2004-05, six percent children work in dhabas. restaurants, hotels, motels etc; 15 percent as domestic workers; construction—17 percent; ceramic—two percent; auto-work-shop and vehicle repiars—four percent; carpet making—three percent; gem-cutting and jewellery—three percent; brick-klin and tiles—seven percent;; spinning and weaving—11 percent;; pan biddhi and cigarettes workshops—21 percent; agarbatti, dhoop and detergent making—one percent and others—11 percent.

If one sees the poor plight of children world-wide, in the context of India as particular; poverty is the main cause of child labour. More than one billion people globally live on less than one$ a day! Number of poor are greatest in the South-East Asia. Over 186 million child including India in the world under age 15 years are engaged in child labour. The Asia-Pacific region is most notorious on this score. About 150 million children in 5-17 age group are engaged in the worse-type of work globally. Apart from that decreasing trend in providing education to children is also one of factors of child labour in the world. One hundred three million children of elementary school age are out of school. Of them 60 percent are girls. In sum and total, world illiteracy population is 799 million. Lack of employment avenues throughout the world is also one of the major factors of engagement of child labour. An employment potentiality is decreasing even in most advanced countries of Europe and America. Over 184.7 million people are unemployed in the globe among adult, resulting into forcing children in doing work in unorganised sectors for the livelihood of the family members.

Child labour has strange connotation in economic term. Children participate in the work, that is called economic activities as their participation results in the production of goods and service that grows the economy! In India Child labour is mainly due to acute poverty among 78 percent of population mainly in the rural areas. About 90 percent of children, engaged in child labour, are from rural areas of the country. Children from lower caste and minority community are majority in child labour because of their exploitation in the country. They are mostly from illiterate section of society. Girl child are also engaged in such work in rural house-holds of big and landed class people. More over a survey of NSSO has indicated that in India 32 percent children, who are considered "no where" in government record of schools nor at identified work places or at their homes are actually working as child labour, hiding their identity. In the country like India where facilities for education is at minimum level from government side at cheap rate, education is bought on high premium. Thus, their parents allow them for child labour for earning in unorganised sectors because they cannot afford education of such high cost. To some extend, similar situation prevails in other South-east Asian countries. A UNICEF report has said, "International trade appears to be associated with lower incidence of child labour. Some studies indicate that globalisation may increase the demand for unskilled labours in the countries that specialise in labour-intensive industries. In this way, such demand of unskilled labour may increase in the child labour throughout the globe, particularly In India where globalisation and neo-liberal policies are being implemented indiscriminately."

The Bachpan Bachao Andolan, which is doing wonderful work for the welfare of the children in India, is of the opinion that a profit of around Rs 1, 20,000 crore is made by employers of child labour annually in India. These incomes are not on records to evade taxes." Six crore child labour substitute a similar number of adults in the job market. As per government estimates, Rs 15 is spent on child labour a day while as per the national floor wage, an adult labourers must be paid Rs 115 per day. For 250 working days, the wage cost work out to Rs 18,000 crore for child workers and Rs 1,38,00 crore for adults. The differences of Rs 1, 20,000 crore is undeclared profit." the Andolan paper says.

Not only hat there are instances of coersive measures by ownerss of work places on chilren for work more and moee even during odd hours. In many cases children have become sick and died while working. Such reports are rampant with Bihari child labours engsaged in Delhi, Punjab, Haryana, many towns of Uttar Pradesh, Madras etc. In some cases, children have been rescued from these places. Surprisigly, even at the houses of urban elites, inavriably the instances of child labour are found. One may find that small children serving the guests and house-hold owners their meals, tea etc after preparing in the kitechens. In many cases, exploitation of these child labours is at the height. They are beaten mercilessly by the house-hold owners. In rural areas, child labour is in abundance. Both male and female child labour are found working at the houses of rich and landowing class's people. Girl child labour are sexually abused and sold to brothel owners at many places. Regretably the child Labour Act covers only in organised sectors. Whereas child labour are engaged in unporgansed sectors. No doubt the Union government has taken many measures like enactment of the Child Labour (Prohibition and Regulation) Act, 1986 and the Right to Education Act to curb child labour but nothing tangible appears on the surface to eliminate the child labour in the country!

SOURCES: International Labour Organisation, Bachpan Bachao Andolan, The Economics of Child Labour by Kaushik Basu and and Hoang Van Pham, The Economics of Child Labour by Xinye Zheng National Sample Suvey oginisation, National Commission for Protection of Child Rights, Childline Foundation of India, Economic and Political Weekly, Frontline, International Centre on Child Labour and Education.

NEED TO ABOLISH CAPITAL PUNISHMENT AND CONSTITUTIONAL IMPROPRIETRY IN HANGING AJMAL KASAB!

Monday, 26 November 2012

Lamentably, over 60 years of the independence of India, we carry the retrograde burdens like death sentences in our statute book! We Indians are moving in the beginning of 21st century when the entire nations of the world are striving hard for progressive measures to enter new culturally, and humane society as well as advanced technology. And in India old and ancient fashions and orthodox, mixed with feudal thinking contiunes to take driving seats! We have miserably failed to adopt a humane approach towards-men-kind and death penalty is existing when there are needs of reforms of guilty people for heinous crimes. Why a culprit for death is not confined in jails for whole life in the process of reforming him? And instead of that in India, there are craze for violence in the form of death penalty. No doubt the Pakistani terrorist Ajmal Kasab had committed heinous crime and killed many persons and his capital punishment is justified. But Our Constitution has many provisions to complete the paraphernalia before the hanging could take place to any person, guilty for murder or even for worse type of crimes. Only after exauhstation all legal formalities, extreme step of death penalty could be considered!

Recent instance of hanging of Ajamal Kasab in hush-hush and secret manner has left behind many unanswered questions! Such secret hanging of Kasab is injustice. Ajmal Kasab, a terrorist and a killer was hanged to death in Yerwada jail in Pune on the morning of November 21, 2012 in secret manner following the rejection of his mercy petition by the President of India Mr Pranab Mukherjee. The operation of hanging Kasab was code named "Operation-X" by the Maharshtra government.

Kasab was young and belonged to a poor family of Pakistan and had only primary education to his credit. Society in Pakistan made him a terrorist and killer and in despair, Ajamal moved to the crime and terror world. And his guilt in 26/11 round of murders of innocent people in Mumbai landed him to such pathetic end of his life. There are many loop-holes in hanging Kasab. At one point, the administrative lapse in hurried and secret hanging of Kasab has pointed out the "constitutional impropriety" of the entire procedures of hanging Kasab! Not only that the union government and Maharshtra government have ignored many well-established procedures, conventions as well as traditions of culturally ancient civilisation of Hindustan in last thousand years. At least, we must have remembered the non-violence peaceful solution of ills from Gautama Buddha and Mahatma Gandhi.

Despite so many voices of people against death penalty, why we are keeping the provision of capital punishment? In the last 60 years many thoughts have been given on the subject without any fruitful result. More over over half of the world nations including Great Britain, United States of America have abolished death sentences. In Great Britain, where Lord Mountbatten was killed brutally, had not awarded death sentence to the culprits! Even in India, right from the very beginning of freedom movement, Mahatma Gandhi remained all-opposed to capital punishment. The first prime minister Pundit Jawahar Lal Nehru also had spoken openly against death sentences in India. And lamentably in Gandhi's country Ajmal Kasab was hanged!

In his 'angush remark' the former Judge of the Supreme Court and a champion of liberty, Mr V R Krishna Iyer, who is striving hard for abolishing capital punishment right from 1950s, has said, "It is or not that Ajmal was Pakistani terrorist, but he was humane being. I have no doubt in my heart that Gandhi's country should not have killed Ajmal Kasab-he was after all young and belonged to poor family—Pakistan or not, he was a humane being." Justice Iyer has further said, "In my humble view, all humane societies, especially a society that swears by the Indian Constitution—that is deep-rooted in compassion, should abolish judicial executions. Mahatma Gandhi was opposed to it and so was Pundit Nehru."

I must refer here the wonderful and remarkable gesture of the president of the Congress, Ms Sonia Gandhi, who had written to then President of India K R Narayanan spelling out her views against hanging of her husband's murderers following death penalty to the persons, who killed Rajiv Gandhi brutally, She wrote, "The Supreme Court had confirmed the death sentences on four persons, who were responsible for the assassination of my beloved husband Rajiv Gandhi—our family does not think that the four held responsible for the heinous murder of my dear husband must be hanged. My son, Rahul Gandhi, daughter Priyanka or I do not wish that the four murderers be hanged. In particular we do not wish Nalini, mother of an eight-year-old child, to be hanged. I am aware that how my children miss their father and we do not want another child to loose its parents to get her orphaned. As you are well aware my children Rahul and Priyanka and myself are suffering untold mental agony day in day out due to loss of our beloved Rajiv. But neither my children nor myself would like the persons, responsible for my husband's tragic end to be hanged-hence I humbly request you to stop their hanging and grant them pardon when they seek your clemency."

Now apart from discussing constitutional impropriety in hanging Kasab, I musr mention here the views of Justice Iyer in abolishing death sentence in India. When he was minister in Kerala in 1950s, Iyer had tried to minimise the death sentences with the consultations of then Governor of Keral. And such move had clicked in early 1950s for carrying a campaign to abolish death sentences in India.

About constitutional impropriety, it is not out of place to mention here that there are many administrative lapses in hanging Kasab in secret and hurried manner. The President has also erred in not making public his decision to reject the mercy petition of Ajamal! If the President would have made public his decision, the country could have known the reasons behind the rejection of Kasab's mercy petition. In executing Kasab, all legal formalities have not been adopted by the administration. Questions are: Why Ajamal was not informed about his constitutional rights to seek judicial review of his petition's rejection by Pranab Mukherjee?, Second—The judiciary has all power to review the ground on his petition has been rejected by the President!, Third;—Article 21 of the Constitution guarantee the right to life equally applicable to the Indian as well as foreign nationals,; Fourth:—Article 19 says that a person cannot be deprived of life or personal liberty except according to established procedures! Fifth: The Constitution empowers the citizens the right of judicial review of even President's decision to examine reasons of rejection of mercy plea by the President.

Not only that, the Supreme Court has had ruled in Kehar Singh vs Union of India case landmark judgement (AIR 1989SC-653) that citizens cannot be deprived of any eventualities like judicial review of rejection of mercy plea by the President like in Ajmal Case. The bench headed by then Chief Justice of India R S Pathak, had observed and gave written directive that the Constitution of India had every check and balance while finally implementing the judgements of any case!

Taking into account such lapses, hanging of Ajmal has left behind much and much as well as more and more things of questioning about the propriety of his hanging in secret and hush-hush manner. Mudabhushi Sridhar, professor and Coordinator, Centre for Media Law and Public Policy, NALSAR, University of Law, Hyderabad, while questioning the hanging of Ajmal before exhaustion of all the formalities, has said, "Darkness and secrecy not only breed disease and corruption but also hide them"

IN OUR DECADENT SOCIETY, INDIA HAS MANY SHAMES!

Saturday, 24 November 2012

Among our countrymen, particularly writer, political classes, intellectuals, intelligentsias, academic, it has become a common refrain to refer about many prevalent "shames" in India! When we live in a decadent society where all systems have failed, there are bound to be many "shames" in the country. In the present day India, successive political classes and fanatics have subverted the Constitution, laws, rules etc for their enlightened self-interest. Political classes of all hues except a few, have mainly one aim—that is to remain in power or grab power solely to earn as much money by anyhow. In the process, they are bending the instrumentality of the Indian Constitution. And we have become a part of decadent society and bearing the burnt of ills being perpetuated by political classes and their cohorts-bureaucrats! Thus, India after over 60 years of its existence, has been manufacturing only "shames" everywhere. Apart from many "shames" including corruption, inequality, poverty, illiteracy, lack of health facilities, power brokering, criminalisation of politic etc one of the great shames is "untouchable, and manual scavenging", still prevalent in every parts of the "Bharat Mahan or India shining".

We have failed to eradicate the "manual scavenging". This has further intensified the "practise of untouchability", right from south to north and east to west in our country of over 120 crore population. Particularly in rural India, conservatism and feudal mindset persists. Persons of lower caste are not allowed to sit on chair before feudal people as well as these lower caste people are not allowed to share, ponds, wells, tube wells, temples with people, belonging to upper caste. These practises and being exercised well before the eyes of government and so called messiah of poor and down-trodden, violating the Constitutional provisions are prevalent in India, adding more and more "shames" to India. And we, as part of decadent society are tolerating injustices after injustices and inequalities after inequalities towards lower caste 'silently and shamelessly'!

It is strange that merely because of birth in lower caste family; they clean sewers, septic tanks, open drains, flowing with excreta in the house-holds, streets and railway lines and platforms. To substantiate these lapses, one will invariably find that even in the government records—for these works persons of lower caste are appointed and in their service roll, they are described "mehtars"!

More over, after 43 years after its prohibition in the Constitution, a law was passed by the Indian Parliament in 1993, prohibiting such practices. Strangely, this law remained on the statue book without any effective control of such evil practices. Even today lakhs of men and women manually engaged themselves in this barbaric rituals of disposing human excreta, entering the manholes and nullahs for cleaning drains flowing with dirty waters mixed with excreta. These paractices ruin the health, dignity and honour of lakhs of lower caste people. Despite so many assurances and promises of successive Presidents and prime ministers, the union government continues to move in dark to free the country from manual scavenging. Thus this nation has failed in its duty as per constitutional provisions for providing a life of dignity to lakhs of citizens.

In 2010, the Safai Karmchari Andolan (SKA) had filed a petition in the Supreme Court, highlighting their miseries and had informed the court that as many as 252 districts of the country are in the grip of such 'shameless" work. The case is still pending in the Supreme Court where it has been reported that 7, 94,390 dry latrines across the country where human excreta is cleaned by humans. Of these 73 percent is in the rural areas and 27 percent in urban localities. In another 13, 14,652 toilets, human excreta is flushed into open drains. And here again to clean these channels fall on scavengers, employed by the union government and state governments.

A few years back on the directives of the Supreme Court, the union ministry of social justices and empowerment had constituted task forces to indentify the prevalence of manual scavenging. After some discussions, the union finance ministry allotted Rs 35 crore to identify scavengers across the country. But nothing moved and the union government dropped the idea, initiated for the first time in the country for identifying the manual scavengers. Many men also clean sewers, septic tanks, open drains into which excreta flows. People trapped by their birth in this vocation are shunned and despised. It clearly infers that government failed miserably in announcing comprehensive time-bound action plan to get rid this country from its "shameful casteist legacy". We must remember the spirit of final words of Dr B R Ambedkar in the context of liberation of manual scavenging. Dr Ambedkar had said, ours is a battle not for wealth or for power. It is battle for freedom. It is battle of reclamation of human personality."

In the last 40 years, some thing tangible has been done by Sulabha International, pioneered by Dr Bindeshwar Pathak to eradicate manual scavenging Dr Pathak worked hard in Bihar and other parts of the country to eradicate manual scavenging by developing a new technology of soil-based pit. Pathak's technology clicked not only in different parts of India but in under-developed and developing countries of the South-East Asia. Now his International has become a corporate in this venture. I exactly remember the feudal mind-sets of Bihar and how Dr Pathak, a Gandhian strived hard and dedicated his life to the mission. I remember at one occasion, a few Orthodox Bihar people had laughed at the idea of Dr Pathak and called him "Paikhana-Pathak". But this discouragement did not deter Dr Pathak and he carried his mission successfully throughout the globe!

Now the Union government has also awoke from deep slumber following the snubbing of the Supreme Court.! The struggle of Safai Karmchari Andolan has compelled the union government to bring an effective bill to strengthen 1993 law on this score. The 1993 law had outlawed the practice. But the law was bundle of toothless provisions. Some thing good in the preamble o f the new proposed law," it is necessary to correct the historical injustice and indignity suffered by the manual scavengers and to rehabilitate them to a life of dignity." The provision in the 1993 law had defined "manual scavengers as a person engaged in or employed for manually carrying human excreta." But the proposed 12012 law has proposed more effective parameters and had elaborated, "a person engaged or employed . . . . for manually cleaning, carrying, disposing of or otherwise handling in any manner, human excreta in an insanitary latrine or in open drain or pit into which the human excreta from the insanitary latrines is disposed of or on a railway track . . . .". The expanded definition in the proposed Bill has completely undergone by previous proviso that a person, who cleans" excreta with the help of such devices and using such protective gear, as the central government may notify in this behalf, shall not be deemed to be manual scavengers.".

Not only that a prominent columnist Harsh Mander, has said, "the proposed bill of 2012 strictly prohibits construction of dry latrines and employment of manual scavengers as also the hazardous cleaning of a sewer or a septic tank. But the cleaning railway tracks has not been included and hazardous cleaning is defined not by employers requiring workers to manually clean sewers or septic tanks but requiring them to do so without protective gear. Our objection is manual cleaning of sewers and septic tanks is not just of compromising worker safety—which is no doubt important—but of human indignity, which would continue even if such manual cleaning is done with protective gear. And it is unconscionable to let the railways off the hook."

It must be noted that liberation from such condemned pratices must come from the invention, discovering as well as use modern technology. The Application of modern technologies, which are globally available, will make the occupation humane, dignified and safe and also ensure that human beings do not have direct contact with excreta. Both railways and local bodies could procure such technologies for the purpose! But the both union and state government appear helpless for spending huge amount to implement renovating ideas because human beings are available in abundance to perform this work cheaply. This is manly because that lower caste people are propelled by their birth in most disadvantaged castes and lack of other livelihood options. This appears to be the real shame for the country and its rulers, who have failed to provide proper employment to weaker sections of society by providing them proper education and medicare! The proposed bill must ensure adequate provisions to punish the officials, who fail to implement the measures including for not identifying, reporting and ending manual scavenging, as well as demolishing dry latrines, rehabilitating manual scavengers and other unjust and unlawful social practices.

This is what shamelessly shameless India and we Indians!

LACK OF LAND REFORMS, BANE OF POVERTY AND HUNGER IN INDIA!

Friday, 16 November 2012

What has gone wrong in our system? None has care about prevailing poverty and hunger as well as wide-scale disparity In the Bharatvarsh, which is called India and Hindustan! Now it has become fashion to speak about corruption in our decadent society's system. Hardly, political leaders of all hues and the representatives of the so called civil society and Non-governmental organisations (NGOs) speak about sorry state of affairs among rural poor and adivasis, agriculture, education, health etc. Of course corruption is one of the main reasons in derailing welfare and development measures also, but voices of deprived lots, constituting over 78 percent population, are big deal. Corruption can be tackled by streamlining the rotten system under existing laws under the Constitution but hunger and poverty, lack of education; health could be faced with determination by launching welfare measures! Vision among the political leadership is lacking to face the alarming situation in the country. Are we moving towards worse scenario in the country where there will be no takers of peoples' voices?

Neo-liberal economic policy in the last over 20 years, I strongly feel, is aggravating the situation. It is surprising that in India, there are no land records. Land reforms are hanging fire. Lands are accumulated in the hands of 10 to 15 percent population. Old feudal order is continuing! Many Acts and Laws for land reforms by almost all successive state governments and union governments were framed in over last 60 years but poor and landless increased by over 85 percent. Over 80 percent populations are homeless and landless. What ever lands remained under their control especially in tribal belt are being acquired forcibly for setting industries by corporates and multi-nationals. In plain areas, also similar situation is prevailing! Apart from other states in India, Bihar is an example of bitter feudal and communal massacres in the country only because of wide disparity between rich and poor and 'no land and home to poor' although the Jawahar Lal Nehru government at the centre had made drastic amendment in the Constitution to abolish 'zamindari system' in the country. The then chief Minister of Bihar Dr S K Sinha was all opposed to abolition of 'zamindari system' and land reforms along with many chief ministers of the country, the dynamics of the then Bihar's Revenue Minister Krishna Ballabha Sahay impressed Pundit Nehru to go whole hog for land reforms in the entire country and in the process visionary Pundit Nehru had prepared road maps for equitable distribution of lands and houses to poor in the country! An amendment was carried out in the Right to Property under the Constitution and Zamindari system was abolished. But the time passed and nothing tangible was made for land reforms in the country!

In between, some thing tangible was made by the then Revenue Minister of Bihar K B Sahay on land reform fronts. Thousands of acres of land were taken away from land-owing classes and to little aspect lands were given to the landless and homeless. After some years, the land problem further aggravated in Bihar. The so called 'surplus lands' were given to the Bhoodan Bhumi Jagya Committee, led by Vinoda Bhave for distribution among landless and homeless. From there situation, worsened. Lands were distributed to them but sadly taken back forcibly by influential land-owing classes from poor people! Since than, massacres after massacres are being taking places between poor and feudal land-owing classes in Bihar. Naxal movements came to the fore because of atrocity of feudal land-owing classes towards poor and dalits in the successive years. (Please see my blog topic—Bihar is Known for Bitter Feudal-Communal Massacres in India, detailing deaths, killings and destruction's). However, a ray of hope came out when the present chief minister Nitish Kumar came to power and announced distribution of lands to poor on the basis of the report of the Bandopadhaya committe, which Kumar had constituted just after assuming power about eight years back. Moreover, on the influences of his alliance partner—Bharatiya Janata Party (BJP) and vested interests among feudal land-owing classes as well as many other political compulsions, Nitish Kumar retracted from his promises. And the situation remained where these were during successive rules in Bihar. On the other hand, huge lands are accumulated in the hands of a few thousands land-owners, neo-rich-political classes and intermediary castes people in Bihar. The same Nitish government had forcibly deported the President of Ekata Parishad P V Rajagopala from the state when during his year-long Jansamwad yara highlighting issues relating to land reforms, particularly the plight of the landless. Rajagopal was described a Maoists by Nitish government a few months back when he had visited Nawada district a few months back!

But land reforms had taken some roots earlier in Uttar Pradesh during the regime of the chief minister Hemvati Nandan Bahuguna and later during the left front government of the West Bengal led by Jyoti Basu. Some tangible reforms are even today are witnessed and landless have at least land for constructing home and some lands for farming under share cropping pattern in West Bengal. But the situations in other states are not encouraging. Feudal Andhra Pradesh has also failed to take any initiatives for land reforms. Worse position prevails in tribal belts including Odisha, Chhatishgarh, Jharkhand, Madhya Pradesh, Gujarat, Maharashtra and also many eastern states where tribal population are being forcibly evicted from their land, forest rights, water in the name locating industries by multinationals and corporates as well as neo-rich political classes.

Sadly, the law to acquire lands during British Raj is still under vogue. Many local restrictions in Adivasi belt about forest rights under various Laws under the Constitution are being violated by the government to acquire lands of tribals. During the year-long yatra and jansatyagrah by Rajagopala has found that government's policies have accentuated the plunder of agriculture and forest lands for corporate interests. The Yatra had begun from Kanyakumari on October 2 in 2011 and journeyed across the country and finally culminated into a foot march of over 50000 people in Gwalior on October 2, 2012. At least after several rounds of talks between Union Rural Development Minister Jairam Ramesh and the representatives of Ekata Parishad led by its president P V Rajgopala signed an agreement at Agra during the period, which envisaged that the government will fulfil the promises to complete the land reform process. But a sense of caution among the senior activists was also witnessed taking into account the past experiences of similar negotiations. Five years ago, the Ekata Parishad had organised similar agitation with thousand of landless. At that time also, the government had taken notice of the agitation. Prime Minister Manmohan Singh had himself initiated deliberations and had announced the formation of National Land Reforms Council, led by prime minister himself and consisting of chief ministers, sociologists and actvistists. But that body is yet to see the light of the day.

However, a ray of hope has arisen from the present agreement. The agreement stipulates that the ministry of rural development will initiate talks with all state government immediately and put out a draft of the policy for public debate and discussions in the next four to six months. Thereafter the draft will be finalised. The agreement has mainly stressed the need of statutory backing of the provisions of agricultural land to the landless poor in the backward district and home stead rights to the landless and shelter less poor in rural areas across the country. At least ten cents of land homestead lands to every poor, landless and shelter less rural households. It also focused effective and time-bound implementation of various laws enacted by the legislatures aimed at protecting the land rights of dalits, adivasis and other weaker and marginalised sections of society. Fast track courts to speed up of disposal of the cases pending in revenue and judicial courts. Legal aid must be provided to socially deprived persons. The rural development ministry will coordinate with ministries of tribal affairs and panchayati raj to ensure effective implementation of the Panchayats (Extension to Scheduled Areas) Act, 1996 (PESA), which will empower gram sabhas to function more effectively in the implementation of the Act. It must be noted that the ministry of tribal affairs put a comprehensive guidelines for the implementation of revised rules and directives for the effective implementations of forest right and the states will be actively supporting them. There must be advisories to the state governments to undertake thorough survey of forest and revenue boundaries in order to resolve disputes. Gram panchayats and gram sabhas will be fully involved in the survey and settlement process as well as updating of records governing common property resources.

Land reform is a big problem. Effective implementation of the land reform is the need of hour—otherwise the country, which is still dominated by poor, landless, and homeless, who may rise in revolt along with Maoists and Naxal elements, sympathising them.!

AMAZING STROY OF GROWTH RATE IN INDIA AND HUNGER AND POVERTY RISING!

Saturday, 10 November 2012

It is amazing! India has lagged behind in GLOBAL HUNGER INDEX (GHI) notwithstanding its story of substantial rise in growth rate. A latest study by three organisations—the International Food Policy Research Institute, Concern World-wide, and Wealthungerhilfe—have revealed that the progress in reducing the proportion of hungry people in the world has been tragically slow. The study has highlighted that in as many as 20 countries, particularly in India, the levels of hunger are extremely alarming. (Please refer my topic—Hunger Looming Large over Globe—on my blog—www.kksingh1.blogspot.com on June 19, 2012 referring global food crisis).

In the context of India, hunger and poverty have taken alarming proportion in between 2007 to 20012 amid the much-hyped story of dramatic increase in the growth rate in India. Since than over 155 million people have been fighting back to wall because of hunger and poverty rampantly in India in the wake of neo-liberalised economic policy. Exactly, after 1996 disparity between economic development and progress in the fight against hunger have widened and India is slipping towards bottom-line gradually, the report says and adds China lowered the level of hunger and under-nutrition through a strong commitment to poverty reduction, nutrition and health intervention and improved access to safe water. In the case of India all these measures seem to be a distant dream!

The report—"2012 Global Hunger Index", mainly highlights on—"The Challenge of hunger, ensuring sustainable food security under land water, and energy stresses". Simultaneously, the reports also points out the identification of of the main challenges of an impending global food security—drought, scramble to invest in farm-land around the world, shifts in energy prices, and also shocks in energy supplies.

Apart from that there are many worrying facts like persistent poverty, the current consumption pattern of industrialised countries, and profligate consumption by the elites in the developing countries. As per reports, there are three dimensions of hunger: undernourishment, child underweight and child mortality.

Sadly, India has taken backward trends among the countries like neighbouring Sri Lanka, Pakistan and China in the South-East Asia even-after strong economic growth. More over, India as per the parameter on a 100-point scale (the lower the GHI values, the better ranking country), is ranked 22.9 in GHI whereas its land-locked neighbours—Nepal is better by having 20.3 and, Pakistan—19.7. However, the Bangla Desh is on 24.0 in GHI ranking despite the facts that the country has broad-based social progress, vibrant non-governmental organisations and public transfer programmes that has reduced child under-nutrition. As regards, Sri Lanka, the country in the South East Asia has tremendously achieved high rate of literacy and life expectancy through welfare-oriented policies, investment on public health care and education system and commitment for gender equality.

India has many hicuups! Bad governance are prevailing throughout the country. Although public transfer programmes are being explored in India, there are apprehensions and misgivings about their efficacy and the reach to the grass-root level. The report has mentioned a study to say that poor design, low coverage and insufficient monitoring are the main challenges to reducing under-nutrition levels in India, which is as incomplete way of approaching the problem. One more factor is responsible for poverty and hunger in India—that is higher food prices. Food prices are increasing in recent past: it rose by 40 percent in 2007 and further 2008, resulting into hunger and poverty everywhere in India! Even the sub-Saharan Africa has done better progress in many points on this score in comparison to India. Over 43.5 percent children are underweight in India whereas only 23 percent children in Sub-Saharan Africa were found in that category. If we compare the GHI of ten countries with India, there are vast gaps of poverty and hunger in India. The report has mentioned the countries like Azerbaijan—5.0, China—5.3, Malaysia—5.2, Paraguay—5.3, Trinidad and Tongo—5.4, Mauritius—5.7, B Salvador—5.8, Kyrgyz Republic—5.8 and South Africa—6.9 in global hunger index parameter.

The report has also underlined that food security is mainly linked with developments in water and energy and scarcity of land, particularly the scarcity of farm land because of short-sighted policies. Huge foreign investments in developing countries are wiping out land rights of residents, specially in forest areas in India. It is fact that high-instances of hunger and poverty are found in the countries where the rights on land and energy, and water have been curbed by the respective governments. Here also India tops the list as our union government and almost all state governments have indiscriminately allowed foreign investments in different parts of the country especially in Jharkhand, Odisha, Chhatishgarh, Madhya Pradesh, Maharashtra, Andhra Pradesh, Karnataka, Gujarat etc. Following such measures, lands and water are being deprived from villagers and tribal in India. And more and more hunger and poverty are pushing the people to live without adequate foods.

The Food and Agriculture Organisation (FAO) has also admitted food deprivation to the people, resulting into undernourishment. As per FAO, 1800 calories a day—the minimum that most people require to live a healthy and protective life. The case of India is considered more serious on poverty and hunger fronts notwithstanding the entire globe is expected to land in serious food crisis because of various reasons like comparatively low and less stress on agriculture fronts.

SOURCES:International Food Policy Research Institute, Concern Worldwide, Wealthungerhilife, FOOD AND AGRICULture Organisation, The Frontline, Websites of Various affected countries and Human Index parameters of different organisations of the World and India.

REFLECTION OF ECONOMIC DOWN-TURN IN EUROPE AND AMERICA VIS-A-VIS ECONOMIC CRISIS IN INDIA AND CHINA!

Tuesday, 30 October 2012

The recent economic down-fall in the two most emerging economy in Asia—India and China—appears the result of rescuing America and European countries as well as Japan—"the old World" from economic turmoil! The implication—Brazil, Russia—India—China (BRICs), coined by veteran economist Jim O'Neill of Goldman Sachs symbolises the rise of once poor countries (emerging markets) into "economic power houses". It may not be out of place to mention here that Europe, America and Japan must have thought that economic turmoil will prop up the global demand for industrial goods and commodities (oil, foodstuff, metals). During the 2007-2009 economic down-turns in the developed countries like America, European countries, the economy of some BRIC countries, particularly China adopted large stimulus programmes and others just grew rapidly. The economy of China in 2010 expanded by 10.4 percent, India 10.1 percent and Brazil's 7.5 percent. But in the fast changing economic scenario in the world, the situation seems different and economies of these countries have started declining. In 2012, the economy of China is expected to grow by 7.8 percent, India 4.9 percent and Brazil 1.5 percent. These are the latest projection of the International Monetary Fund (IMF). While the IMF predicts a little bit improvement in 2013, noted economists forecast further decline!

The Recent World Economic Outlook (WEO) of the IMF, titled "coping with High debt and sluggish growth", has dwelt with analysing examples from the past to compare if there are lessons for today. Results are quite interesting. During the heyday of the "Washington consensus" the World Bank, the IMF and other economic agencies of the imperialist order dispatched economic teams to every countries that was desperate for money. Hankering was the same: privatisation, welfare state

295

squeezing, union bashing and so on. Dark-suited guys of the respective teams seemed in convincing that urgent need of globalisation and liberalising economy. Entire world order—from Africa to South America, from Eastern Europe to Central Asia, the same policies was propounded! Globalisation celebrated its triumph: poverty, malnutrition and curable diseases were celebrated too. The IMF begins by remembering that" public debt in advanced countries has climbed to ts highest level since World War-two". Debts are growing, previously because of world wars now since 1980s debt has been growing apace without a major war and even during strong periods of growth. Debts have become permanent cancer that affects senile capitalism. The IMF has shown its helplessness and has given no explanation for this plague. The WEO has simply said, "the episode . . . .—during the 1980s and 1990s ave their genesis in the breakdown of the Bretton Woods System, when government policy struggled with social issues and the transition to current economic systems". This is hardly an explanation. Bretton Woods collapsed. In the last 40 years, so many countries are in transition. The solution to reduce public debt: "The largest debt reduction followed the world wars, usually as a result of hyperinflation". The IMF must understand that the problem is that restoring to hyperinflation is like using a flame-thrower to eliminate dust from a house. Such solution will destroy many other things in the process, even possibly the house itself. Moreover, the grip of finance capital on the world economy is much stronger than in the 1940s.

As part of the "sorry we have no clue approach" of the IMF' today, the document explains that debt and economic growth have no direct links:sluggish growth is bad for public finances, of course but generally speaking growth rates appear to be unrelated to debt level. The problem, however, is to explain why since 1980s public debt is growing everywhere. That is the key issue that bourgeois strategists do not want to address. Capitalism as a whole is less and less productive. Debts are the result of this simple fact, very well known to classical economists like Smith and Ricardo and thoroughly explained by Marx. Capitalism is doomed to drown in debt. There are many examples like Korean War to help American economy, Japan in 1997, Italy in 1992, etc. Strangely IMF always harps on structural reform, which is about market without unions, rules, and other obstacles to exploitation. Such situation appears crisis of regime. Lenin has rightly said that one of the conditions for a revolution is the crisis of the regime!

Taking into account all these facts, the economy of India and China notwithstanding America would celebrate China's and India's growth rate in 2012; the US economy will grow by two percent. But this proportionate misleading comparison because China and India still benefit from "catch up economy". These two countries are poor and expand rapidly by raising workers' skill and adopting technologies and management practises pioneered else were. Describing BRIIC advances, Ruchir Sharma of Morgam Stanley has said these are economic bubbles; sooner or later, reality picks them! In his book "Brakout Nations: Pursuit of the Next Economic Miracles" Shrama does this for BRIC bubble and write" The perception that the growth game had suddenly become easy—that everyone could be winner—is built on the unique results of the last decades when virtually all entering markets did grow together. Story of growth rate is same for China and Brazil. With regards to India, the country faces comparable problems. Some reflects the hangover from recent booms. India has highest inflation rates in the globe. Economist Arvind Subramaniam of the Petreson Institute has said, "The budget deficit is around 10 percent (of the economy). Investor's confidence has slumped. To spur growth the government is trimming subsidies and has liberalised foreign investment in retailing, airlines, broadcasting and power generation.

In the meantime, the RBI has predicted that India's growth rate expected to drop to 5.7 percent. Current inflation rate of huge proportion is likely to increase from 7.3 percent to 7.7 percent and under present circumstances; the inflation may be inching further in India. The IMF and ADB have also put the growth rate in the range of 5.6 percent to 6.7 percent.

More over, India continues to be toughest place for doing business even as the country has improved regulator processes for starting enterprises and trading across borders, according to World Bank and IFC. In terms of doing business, India is ranked 132nd among 182 countries. Singapore is at the top position, followed by Hong Knong SAR, China at second place, and New Zealand at third spot. Other top ten nations are US(Fourth), Denkmark (fifth), the UK (seventh) Norway 9sixth), Korea (8th), Georgia (9th) and Australia (tenth). Surprisingly, India is the lowest among BRIC nations—Barazil (130th), Russia (112nd) China (91th) and Taiwan—China (16th). Interestingly, India is also below the rank of neighbouring Pakistan (107th) and Nepal (108th)! The report, namely doing business 2013 smarter regulation for small and medium-sized enterprises, has said that the local entrepreneurs in developing countries are finding it easier to do business than at any time in the last ten years. The ease of doing business in the developing world reflects, the significant progress that has been made in improving business regulatory practises world-wide" the report added and said "India focused mostly on simplifying and reducing cost of regulatory processes in such areas as starting business, paying taxes and trading across borders." The ranking is based on various factors—starting a business, dealing with construction permits, getting electricity, registering property, getting credit, protecting investors, paying taxes, trading across borders, enforcing contracts and resolving insolvency." Thus in my opinion, the Indian economy is grappling with sluggish growth amid European debt turmoil and high inflationary pressure. Such thing has also been reflected in the report of the World Bank and its group entity International Finance Corporation (IFC) on doing business.

Every where, the global economy is weak or weakening. Against this dismal backdrop, it was tempting to think that resilient BRICs would act as a shock absorber. They will buy more European and American exports; they send more tourists to Dismay World and Eiffel Tower. This would provide the world more time to make adjustments. Just to opposite occurred. The weakness of advanced economies transmitted itself, through export markets, to the BRICs. The World economy is truly interconnected. What was hoped happen was wishful thinking! But In India's GDP story is strange in the last several years with the opening of liberalised economy. Rich have become richer and poor more and more poor. Human index on health, education, malnutrition, hunger etc are increasing by leaps and bound and wealth is being accumulated in few hands!

SOURCES: World Bank, IMF, IFC, India's Finance ministry, China government, Economy of Marx and Lenin achieves Washington Post websites as well as books on World economy.

SCAR OF SINO-INDIAN WAR!

Monday, 22 October 2012

Although the scars of the wounds of the humiliating blow from Sino-Indian full-fledged war fifty years ago are yet to heal up, our countrymen are still to know the exact causes of such war in Asian continent! I, personally, still remember the horrible situation throughout the country when the troops of both India and China were fighting pitched battle. At that point of time, I was a student of honours graduation degree and was living in a student lodge! The administration had issued strict directive to put off light during night hour and if lighted the windows of the rooms must be covered with black clothes so that light could not be sighted from outside. All these precautionary measures had been taken to avoid air attacks during nights. In the process, there were huge runs for donations to the government for strenghtening the defence needs by general people. My reminiscences goes that the then Maharaja of Darbhanga and his trust had alone donated nine mounds of gold to the government of India to recover and manage the battle at the front in the extreme parts of out northern border.

Both China and India were close allies under the stewardship of Pndit Jawahar Lal Nehru from India and Chou-in-Lai and Mao-Tse-Tung of China in the Asia. Apart from historical ties between both the countries, people of both China and India were enthusiastic to respect each other. There were popular slogans—like "Hindi-Chini Bhai-Bhai". But some provocations from the both the sides resulted into beginning of full-bloom war between China and India from October 20, 1962. The war continued for over one month, inflicting heavy damage to Indian troops and grabbing of huge Indian Territory. At last China unilaterally declared ceasefire and Peking in a statement said, "Beginning from November 21, 1962 (midnight) Chinese Frontier Guards will withdraw to position 20 km (12.5 miles) behind the line of actual control which existed between China and India on November 7, 1959." Battle cry of Chinese troops was so swift and sudden those Indian governments were found in helplessness situation. Fear stalks countrymen!

As authentic stories go, it became imperative for China to launch attack on India. Thousands had been killed by Red Army in China. There were sharp differences of opinions between Mao and Chou. Poverty had gripped China beyond imaginations. And last but not the least, to express their anger towards India for giving shelter to Dalsai Lama, who raised the bogey of Tibet for its independence although Tibet had become part and parcels of China in accordance with the UN Resolution! All these factors compelled China, perhaps, to attack India. Situation became so frightened during war that nobody knew when the Chinese forces will stop as they were facing very little resistance from unprepared Indian Army. At that time N J Nanporia, who was editor of the Statesman had told Pundit Nehriu" Chinese would offer a ceasefire unilaterally, citing reasons" Chinese has attacked to punish India not to occupy it". Much drama and hype were created just on the eve of China declaring unilateral ceasefire. None of the senior government functionaries including Pundit Nehru were aware of cease fire declaration by China!

Subsequently, the then Defence Minister V K Krishna Menon resigned owing moral responsibility. Later, Menon had said openly about the sketchy story of such sudden attack by China, "My story must die with me because I would have to lay the blame on Nehru, and I do not want to do so because my loyalty to him." Many senior army officials head rolled. Sadly Pundit Nehru had to face hostile anger for debacle during China and he continued to smart under the criticism by his key cabinet ministers on China policy and opposition leaders till his death. Alas, visionary Pundit Nehru could not live long and died under the shadow of back-stabbing by Chinese leaders, whom Jawahar considered true friends of India!

Notwithstanding both India and China are leaping forward economically and harping on cooperation to each other, there are many constraints between friendly ties of both the countries. Apart from legal trade between China and India getting boost, unauthorised and illegal entry of goods, especially electronics, have flooded Indian markets through Nepal, jeopardising the developing economy of India. Main hurdles have centred on the status of Tibet and sheltering of over one lakh Tibetians in India as refugees under the leadership of Dalai Lama!

Dalai Lama slipped to India along with huge number of Tibetans with huge movable property! They have their full-fledged Tibet government in exile in Dharmshala in Himachal Pradesh of India! A long shadow has casts over Tibet and Tibetan staying here. Such situation is proving a million dollar question over the India and China relation! They live here as sheltered people—this generosity, as India clarifies very often, was out of respect for Dalai Lama and his spiritual eminence.

According to a recent Report in the Time Magazine; many in China, however, deem this as meddling in the internal affairs. As early as in May 1959, Mao Zedong, a top Chinese leader, in his "The Revolution in Tibet and Nehru's Policy" had accused Nehru of encouraging Tibetan rebels. And as recent as last year, Chinese Foreign ministry spokesperson Hong Lei had said China opposes "any country that provided a platform to the Dalai Lama" whom they consider a separatist. Last year, China also cancelled border talks with India in protest over a speech by Dalai Lama in New Delhi. That may be rote, predictable picture at this point but it speaks of an intractable problem dogging ties between the two Asian giants. "The issue of Tibet is a core issue between India and China" Lobsang Sangay, the prime minister of Tibet government in-exile told Time. "We want India to have productive relations with all its neighbours including China."

Now the question of significance for both the countries marking October 20, 2012, 50th anniversary on China-India border war of 1962. Sadly month-long war between India and China, which the Chinese had given crushing blow to India, because of defence unpreparedness by India. Chinese's fight witnessed its soldiers attacking across disputed McMahon line, a boundary through Himalayan terrain, earmarked in 1914 by the British Colonial authorities and Tibetan officials. The Beijing refuses to recognise this earmarking of the border. The main motive of China appears that it desires to secure hold over Tibet played a significant role in its decision to raid into India. The Chinese had unilaterally declared ceasefire on November 21, 1962 and withdrew from much of the land it conquered save the strategic barren territory appended to Kashmir known as Akasai Chin.

Despite all these hicuups, the relation between China and India has achieved significant economic changes between these two countries. In 2005, China and India pacted to agree to a strategic and cooperative partnership between Chinese Premier Wen Jiabao and India's Prime minister Manmohan Singh. Again in last July both the countries led by Chinese vice-premier Li Keqiang and prime minister of India Manmohan Singh proclaimed that Indo-China relations would prove most significant and important mile-stone in bilateral relationship in the 21st century. Dr Manmohan Singh said in 2009, "India and China are not in competition—there is enough economic space between us both."

The Times report says; but where does Tibet fit into picture? China's annoyance at India sheltering the Dalai Lama has surfaced regularly and India has often made concessions to the trade partner's sensitivities. In 2009, Beijing raised a stink when Dala Lama wanted to visit Tawang, a historic monastery town in Arunachal Pradesh—a state the Chinese still claim as 'southern Tibet'. While New Delhi did not stop him, it restricted coverage of events by not allowing foreign journalists to accompany him to the country's remote north-east,. In 2011, the Chinese consulate in Kolkata sent a written protest when the governor of West Bengal met Dalai Lama while he was in city on a speaking tour, ruffling feathers in India. "They have no business doing that publicly", Sangay says referring to written protest. "That is interference in India's sovereignty and internal matters."

On the other hand Beijing disagrees and said, "Dalai is terrorist with a separatist agenda. I do not think that China's protest against the Delhi's movements for Tibet independence in India is interference in India's internal matters, but just the opposite that if India allows Dalai to engage separatists activities in India is interference in China's internal affairs, the so called autonomy of Tibet (that) the Dalai Lama claims to be seeking is actually the independence of Tibet, which is definitely forbidden," Wang Dehua, Director of the Sanghai-based South Asia Research Centre at Tongji University said.

According to Uday Bhasskar former director of the Delhi-based Think Tank of the Institute of for Defence Studies and Analysis; India never used the Tibet card—in a fragile geo-political neighbourhood, New Delhi better knows than to use its small leverage in a contest it cannot win.

Despite recent visit of from high profile Chinese dignitaries including President Hu Jinto and defence minister General Liang Guanglie, the issue of Tibet continues to be a point of discord. Chinese still fears that India will leverage the might of more that one lakh Tibetan exiles on its soil and fuel tension in Tibet. Uday Bhaskar said "Tibet issue is is one of the China's historical fears."

But there are certain trends of animosity (in China) towards India. Mohan Guruswamy of the Observer Research foundation says, "And we have to live with just the way they have to live with our growing friendship with other countries and the Tibet issue. But 1962 will never happen."

In totality, India's debacle in the Indo-China war of 1962 still continues to be mystery! Cause and reasons of Indo-China war of 1962, enquired by the two army officers—Lt. Gen Henderson Brooks and Lt. General Pre Bhagat is still gathering dust with union government eevenafter 50 years of war. The government kept the report under wraps. The government got way under cover of "public interest". Strangely no where in the world has the army been able to deprive the public on facts on such an important in India's history for such a long period under the cover of secrecy. When the Central Information commission did not allow to make the report public, the eminent journalist Mr Kuldip Nayyar, has filed an appeal before the the Delhi High court for directing the government to make the report public in their interest even after long gap of time. But the case is hanging fire in the court!

Worse and humiliating defeat of India in the hand of China in 1962 will continue to haunt the Indians and coming generations in years to come!

WHY THIS HATE CAMPAIGN AGAINST MUSLIMS OF THE WORLD?

Tuesday, 16 October 2012

Recent uprising and protests among Muslims of the globe is justified in the wake of the release of the hate video, "INNOCENCE OF MUSLIMS". Such protests have virtually engulfed the West Asia and North Africa and the entire Muslims community in India and the globe. More than 20 countries including Tunisia, Yemen, Egypt, Iraq, Algeria, Yemen, Jordan, Morocco have recently witnessed street fight and protest, killing many of the Muslims while trying to enter US and other Western embasies to protest blasphesy of Islam. India also did not remain untouched from such protests by Muslims throughout the country. Many of such countries, which had recorded serious protest over the issues, are close to imperialist and authoritarian America! Sadly, such hienous crimes against Muslims and their religion are not new in at least Africa and Latin Amnerica as well as some countries of the Arab world where articles, cartoons etc have appeared lampooning the Islam and the Prophet. There appears virtual war cry against Muslims in the world including in India when we go through the records of the Indian government towards treatment to Muslims in the name of being terrorists! I had written a comprehensive story on July 17, 2012 on my blog www.kksingh1.blogspot.com under headline, "MUSLIMS IN THE GLOBE VIS-A-VIS IN INDIA", depicting atrocity on Muslims in the pretext of being them terrorists in the world. Are the Muslims of the world not human beings; do not have they cultural and literary history as well as do not they make the world, place for peace and prosperity?

The President of UNITED STATES OF AMERICA (USA) Barack Obama, has, sadly no words of remorse over these ugly happennings including killings under his open eyes because of US drone missiles attacks in Muslim—dominated countries. Obama had, in his speech in the United Natation General assembly had said, "US protect the right of all people to express their views that we profoundly disagree with". Obama cotninued to delivering threats to Muslim countries, particularly Iran. About recent violences, Obama used the language of his predecessors George W Bush, who had initially started smear campaign against Muslims of the world! Tension between US administation and Muslim countries appear to be escalating in view of insult to Islam and the Prophet. Fear and hatred towards Muslims, who are one of the largest populations in the world! The US is creating Islamophobia in the Indian sub-continent, which is directly influencing the Indian government to victimise innocent Muslim youths.

Least said is better about successive Indian governments in recent years about treatment towards Muslims, the Islam and their religious places in India. It all started from 1980s when a fanatic mob led by the senior BJP leader and the party's prime ministerial aspirant Mr Lal Krishna Advani demolishing the Babari Masjid in Ayodhaya. In India Muslims are fear-ridden because of the continued neglect of Muslims towards their poor socio-economic status. The Sachar committee, appointed by the Union government of India, has pointed out the reasons of backwardness among minority community and had suggested many measures to uplift them.

Moreover, in India, a strange development is taking place. Muslims are framed in criminal cases because of their alleged involvement in terror activities! Many Civil Society organisations have complied facts about their innocences in the terror activities. Intrestingly, it has been fond in most of the cases that Muslims, framed in terror and sedition charges are released after living behind bars for months together because of non-substatiation of charges against them. A fortnightly Front Line in its recent article," STRAINING TO BE HEARD" has written, "At a time when Muslims across the world have been taken aback by the hate-inducing depiction of the Prophet MUhammad in the derisively tilted film, "INNOCENCE OF MUSLIMS", such fabricated cases point to a larger trend of anti-Islamic propganda, perpetuated particularly by the United States and its allies." In India context the Frontline article has further said," The community's socio-political environment is marked by its own insecurity and the Indian state's indifference to such fabricated cases."

To substantiate the evil design of India governmet under the patronage of U S Administration towards Muslims of India, just I am pointing out the few glaring instances of concocted and fabricated cases against Muslims and mainly their youths in terror activities related cases. While protesting anger against film, hoodwinking and lampooning Islam and the Prophet, the agitationist-Muslims have aptly incdicating the American influences on Indian government's policy. Such indication amply cleras that India is sadly deviating from its non-alingmenment policy and in blatant manner following the footsteps of imperialist America in its foreign policy.

While poining out many fabricated cases against Muslims, a New Delhi based, the Centre for Policy Analysis, which conducted public hearings, has submitted instances of many fabricated cases, involving a number of Muslims in terror-related cases. The centre, in a statement, has said, "there is rising concern across the country about the large-scale arrests and harassments of Muslim youths by the security forces of the state. Young men are being picked up without explaination, taken into custody, beaten and tortured and eventually thrown into jail awaiting trial for years to end. Several have died in custody; the latest case being a Darbhanga based Qateel Siddiqui who died in mysterious circumstances in the Yerwada jail in Pune. He was arrested last November and killed in a high-security prison for a case in which his complicity had still not been established. There has been silence about the disappearance of another Darbhanga-based engineer FasihMahmood, picked up from in Saudi Arabia. Except for denying any knowledge of his whereabouts, there has been no response from United Progressive Alliance (UPA) government about efforts to trace an Indian citizen whose family is now running from pillar to post in search of justice. Urdu journalist Syed Kazami remains in jail on charges of terrorism, with the police still to file charge-sheetd against him." The Supreme Court, hearing the pleas of Fasih's family has shown its helplessness in rescuing Fasih!

Another recent report of a civil society group, Jamia Teachers Solidarity Association (JTSA) has also revealed that accused Muslim youths in 16 cases, in which the government police had been arrested and charged Muslim youths terrorism, sedition and treason have been acquited by the court. THe report of the JTSA is titled as "framed, damned, acquited:Dossiers of a very special cell has come on the eve of the fourth anniversary of the Batla House incident, which has been described many persons as fake encounter." The JTSA had also released two such reports in the past on "Encounter at Batla House: Unanswered questions (2009) and the case that was never: The SIMI trial of Jaipur

(2012). In both the reports, the JTSA says the Delhi police and the Intelligence Bureau had connived to frame innocent youths.

In a series of third report, JTSA says, "When human right activists or families of those arrested in the charges of terrorism, allege foul play on part of the investigating agencies, the usual response is this: Surely, there must have been some involvement or else why should the police arrest him, and not me?" The evidences that the report, presents show clearly that the acquitals were not simply for want of evidence (a common reason cited by the polce when it loses the case). What judgement after judgement comments on is the manner in which the so called evidence provided by the police and the prosecution was tampered with and fabricated, how story afer as presented by the prosecution was unrealiable, incredulous and appeared as concocted." The JTSA, in the process of making its report public, has described manoeuvring by the special cell for spreading Islamophobia following 9/11 world. The JTSA futher comments, "To those who say that there is no smoke without fire . . . . the reason behind the police—the special case in this case, but this could be true for any othe inverstigating agency as well-framing innocents can be many; to settle scores, to teach a lesson, to buy favours, to dispose of petty informes past their usefulness to help out colleagues in other parts of the country." The JTSA has also disclosed that in most of the terror related cases between 1992 to 2012, a large number of accused persons from amongst the Muslim youths had been acquitted and these facts had been revealed through right to information petitions!

Over enthuasiatic police and intelligence officials concot these cases against Muslims for terrorism with sole purpose to please their successive political bosses as well as for getting gallantary awards. Apart from this, the present judicial suystem in India had also many hicuups. Judges feel helplessly helpless. Huge time is taken by the police to file chargesheets against the accused persons in all these cases, resulting into victimisation and liguishing in jail of the Muslim youths in the country.

Now, the way hatred is being created in India against Muslims in the name of terrorism, obviously to please US government by the UPA government led by Dr Manmohan Singh will rebound in destroying the secular fabrics of the country. Not only that there is million dollar question about deviating from our much-cherished non-alingment policy! Just US wants to create its hegemony on the Indian subcontinent when the India is growing economically. The US needs us not we need US! Surprisingly, why UPA government is suspicious about Iran, Cuba, and other South-East Asia countries, which have been India's age-old friends in pleasure and pain? The America believes in imperialism and is in search of market in Asia and Africa to sell their junk goods and is showing us lolly pops!

Sources: Various websites including union Home ministry, New Delhi-based Centre for Policy Analysis, Jamia Teachers' Solidarity Association, The Hindu, The Frontline and some websites of Muslims countries as well as US president and US administration website, UNITed Nations website:

ILLITERACY IN INDIA VIS-A-VIS CANADA TOP MOST EDUCATED COUNTRY IN THE WORLD!

Sunday, 7 October 2012

India is the most uneducated country in the world! Its literacy rate is 74.04 percent. Kerala is the most literate state in the country with 96 percent of that state are literate while the Bihar, which was once place of ancient learning and education, has lowest rate of literacy with 63.8 percent people are literate. In over 1.20 cores population in India, hardly two to three percent population has college or university degrees in the country.

While the nations of the globe are spending more that 25 percent to 35 percent on education in their respective countries, the successive governments of the union and the states in India hardly earmark three to four percent budget on the education! Much-publicized fund for literacy programme are going down to the drains with rampant corruptions at every level and illiteracy is increasing year to year what to speak of college and university education to the students.

Sadly in India the most important components—education, health and food are practically not subsidized while subsidies are given on with open heart on kerosene, diesel, LPG and petrol, which mainly concern the upper strata of the country. It is a fact that entire world countries understand that poor must be subsidized but not in the manner, the Indian people are subsidized on diesel, petrol, LPG and kerosene oil. Instead of subsidy on kerosene to poor in India, the Indian government must subsidies, the poor should be given solar lantern to light up their houses and help the poor children educate themselves in evening hour by providing electricity charge at important points in the rural areas! Paradoxically, the two important political parties in the country—the Congress and the BJP are undergoing a geographical shrink because of their wrong policy to run the affairs of the country and regional parties are taking definite shapes and there appears to be upsurge to run the affairs of the country by adopting proper policy to educate people and other upliftment measures to wipe out regional imbalances and poverty in the country.

Now I must place some instances about the world nations, which are doing tremendously well for educating their respective countrymen. Despite ongoing financial crisis throughout the globe, p[particularly Europe and America, the investment of adequate money for college education is still worth investment. Developed countries are most educated countries and there are chains of high learning centers.

Based on a study conducted by the Organization for Economic Cooperation and Development (OECD) and displayed on 24/7 Wall St., the 10 countries are with the highest population of college educated adult residents. Topping the chart of most educated country in the world is Canada—the only nation in the world where more than half of residents can proudly hang college degrees on their walls. In 2010, 51 percent of the population have completed a tertiary education, which takes into account both under-graduate and graduate degrees. Canada also commanded the top spot in the last study in 2000 but even still has shown serious improvements. A decade ago, only 40 percent of the nation's population had a college degree—thus Canada is most educated country in the world!

Surging the number two most educated spot was the Israel, which neared the Canada by five percent increase, the Japan, the US, the New Zealand, the South Korea, the UK, the Finland, the Australia, the Ireland. All ranked more than 40 percent citizens having a higher education degree. College graduation rates continued to surge despite world during recession. The percentage of adults with the equivalent of a college degree rose by more than 30 percent in 2010. In U.S, more than 40 percent, which is the highest in the world, population have college and university degree! However, the improvement in higher education is higher to achieve in developed countries. Most developed economic courtiers have most educated population.

OECD—education at a glance—2012 report calculated the proportions of residents with a college or college equivalent degree in the group's 34 member—nations and other major economies; based on the report 24/7 Wall St. identified the ten percent with the highest population of adult with a college degree. The majority of countries that stand the most on education have the most educated population.

In an interview with 24/7 Wall St. OECD chief media officer Matthias Rumpf explained that educational findings appear to have a strong relationship to how many residents pursue higher education, private spending on educational institutes relative to public expenditure is much larger in the countries with the highest rates of college equivalent education—OECD says further average private spending is 16 percent. In the US, 28 percent of funding comes from private sources.

But in the case of India, what to speak about college and university degrees, even literacy is worse aspect. Children, who start education at infant level, hardly reach primary level and if they reach, do not complete middle education! Question of secondary does not arise in most of the cases. College and university education are far cry for them because of acute poverty in India! Apart from that, government spending on education is lowest in the world in India. Over 30 years back, most of the college and schools were managed by private persons and teaching were high class—But the day union and state governmements nationalized the colleges and schools, teaching had gone to the drains. None of the union and state governments is paying adequate attention on education! But now with leliberalisation in economic policy, some very good educational institutions have come up and those institutions are providing learning of excellence!

Today in rural India, one has to walk for two to three miles for even primary, middle and secondary education. There are no networks of schools. Besides acute shortage of teachers, appointment of semi-literate teachers have made the situation beyond imagination in India's rural and ur, some NGOs are working good work in rural areas for imparting education to rural folks!. Students-teacher-school ratios in India are awfully low.

90,000 CHILDREN GO MISSING IN INDIA EVERY YEAR!

Tuesday, 25 September 2012

It is amazing. Over 90000 children go missing in India through abduction, kidnapping, allurements etc. Many of them sold in forced labour on farms and factories. Globally, trafficking of children for forced labour and sexual exploitation remain a "largely hidden crime" says the International Labour Organisation (ILO), with no reliable data even existing on the scale of the problem. The ILO makes a "conservative estimate" that 5.5 million children around the the world are trapped in forced labour, but in India alone the government uses estimates of five million to 12 million children forced to work.

Sadly such social evil are ignored by the mainstream media in India by and large! The general media trend of giving primacy in coverage to life style and leisure over livelihood issues, sex surveys' over falling sex ratio, and the socialist concern over social issue, thanks to the neoliberalism and imperialism and their impact ON the ground, literally and figuratively Apart from that general trend among elite classes, particularly politicians, has to sideline increasing poverty and welfare issues to ameliorate the condition of poor in India! Significantly, poverty in India is defined in terms of food and their intake availability norm: People unable to access2, 100 calories a person a day in urban India and 2,200 calories a person a day in rural India (initially 2,400 but late rescaled down) are counted "poor" in India. By this criterion, the percentage of "poor" in urban India, in rounded figures were 57, 65, 73 respectively in 1993-94, 2004-2005 and 2009-10: and in rural India 59, 70, 76 respectively (by Utsa Patnaik from basic consumption and nutritional intake data provided in the National Sample Survey (NSS) for these years). Thus, over 73 percent of people, who are not getting prescribed calorie intake, are under the bracket of poor both in urban and rural India by and large. More over the union government is more concerned about GDP growth—during the same period when GDP growth rate was unprecedented, around eight percent, absolute poverty increased in the country!

I though to bring to the attention of the readers and people over such deplorable scenes in the country, before going through in detail over children trafficking in the country. Such practises have taken alarming proportion in India. The Washington Post has in a recent article has threw light ion child trafficking in India and I feel strongly that this should be an eye opener for both print and electronic media to pay more attention on welfare measures to uplift poor in the country than to sway their pens in highlighting neoliberal model in the country. What has gone wrong with our "Swadeshi model and socialistic pattern of society"?

The Washington Post has based its article on the basis of children's rights group Bachpan Bachao Andolan, which showed the problem, was far greater that previously thought. The Andolan has compiled the data and released late last year, which has said that 90,000 children are officially reported missing every year. "up to ten times that number are trafficked, according to group—boys and girls, most of the poor families, torn from their parents, some times in return for cash, and forced to beg or work in the farms, factories and homes, or sold for sex and marriages," the Washington Post report said adding that it is an epidemic that until a few years ago, remained unreported and largely ignored by the authorities!

But years of tireless work by activists, a few crucial victories in court—and the shocking discovery of the bones of 17 slain girls and young women around a businessman's house in a suburb of New Delhi called Nithari in 2006—have gradually push the issue on national agenda. The media frenzy surrounding the Nithari killings was a watershed, reminiscent of the way the disappearance of Etan Patz in Manhattan in 1979 helped spark the missing-children's movement in the United States, the Washington Post commented.

Sadly in recent times, footage from surveillance cameras—a new phenomenon in modern India—has also repeatedly broadcast on television here, showing infants being brazenly snatched from train stations and hospital lobbies as parents slept nearby. "A couple of decades ago, there was no understanding of the issue of missing children or trafficking for forced labour—child labour was not even considered a crime" said Bhuwan Ribbu., an activist for children's right group. "Though things are slowly changing, the biggest issue is the lack of political and administrative will to enforce the law, which is often outside the reach of the common person."

The Washington Post report has further said that In India and many other developing countries, children often work in agriculture. What is only now becoming apparent is the huge trafficking industry that has grown up outside the law. The sad tale of Irfan, a resident of Nangloi district of Delhi, son of, Iqbal Ali, abducted and subsequently recovered after a long time and six-year son of a rickshaw puller from Patna town are tips in the iceberg of children trafficking in India.

Thus kidnapping represents just the tip of the iceberg of a vast child-trafficking industry in India. Many young children are sold by their parents or enticed from them with the promise that they will be looked after and be able to send money home. Never registered as missing, many simply lose touch with their parents, working long hours in garment factories or making cheap jewelry. On a recent raid with activists and police in a mohalla in Delhi, 36 children were rescued from a series of tiny rooms where they were making bangles for 10 hours, some for just $4 a month. One of them was a Patna boy.

Only recently, The Union Government has proposed a blanket ban on the employment of children younger that 14, building on a new law that established a child's right to education until that age. Activists have hailed the proposal, which now needs Parliament's approval, as a major step forward, but warned that enforcement will remain a significant challenge. However, parents of several missing children in the past month have grievances of their own—they complained that that they received little or no help from the police, largely, they said, because they were poor. "The police are very cold. They just keep saying: a lot of kids are missing. What can we do?, said Kanwar Pal (48), whose son Ravi, was missing when he was only twelve years old about two years ago. After going to ride bicycles in a Delhi locality. May be if I had money to pay a bribe they would have found my my kid."

Nearly 450,000 cases of children trafficked for labour were reported in the past three years, but prosecution were launched in just 25,000 of those cases and 3,394 employers were convicted, official figure show. Even the US State government has given left handed compliments to Indian government by saying that India is "making significant efforts" to comply with minimum global standards for the elimination of trafficking but notes challenges and the "alleged complicity of public officials in human trafficking".

UNITED STATES OF AMERICA, WORLD'S BIGGEST ARMS MANUFACTURER: INDIA, GLOBE'S BIGGEST ARMS IMPORTERS!

Saturday, 8 September 2012

Sadly India, which was once considered a nation of peace and non-violence in the Globe, thanks to the principles of "Satya-Ahimsa" propounded by Mahatma Gandhi as well as vision of disarmament of the former prime minister of India Pundit Jawahar Lal Nehru, has gone for huge arms and ammunition in the name of so called security of the nation while its crores of people are dying without bread, medicines, home etc.

Not only have that people of the world also forgotten the devastation and destruction, created by America in Hiroshima and Nagashaki at the end of Second World War On August 6, 1945, American B-29 flew from north of Tinian island and after three and half hours, the fighter plane had dropped an 8900 pounds atomic weapons from its specially modified bomb from 2000 feet above the ground. The bomb was dubbed "Little Boy", destroying 90 percent of everything in Hiroshima. Again on August 9, 1945 B-29 Bockscar was dropped on Nagasaki. Killing of over one lakh forty thousand and injuring millions of people in both the bombardments apart from destroying every thing in and around Hiroshima and Nagasaki. Highly enriched uranium and plutonium, grinned in the bombs had many side-effects and generations after generation of both the cities of Japan are still under the effect of such devastation of bombardments.

Not only that, Americans in their miles stones after miles stones to spread their influences in the entire world, particularly in the Middle East and Arab World, have created devastation and killed thousand of persons in the name of restoring peace in the areas. Vietnam, Iraq, Afghanistan and many other countries especially Cuba had to face rough weather in many years and these countries lost their leaders and huge number of populations in the so called operation of America, mainly to spread its (U.S) imperialism in the globe through its "dadagiri"!

A recent report on various news websites including Yahoo and a comprehensive report in the Washington Post have pointed out how the world nations are acquiring sophisticated weapons, arms and ammunition including nuclear arms and chemical weapons and America has "evil design" to arm its allies and friendly countries to keep its hegemony intact in the world. Such tendency of America reflects its "super power dadagiri" in the world. Instead of growing food produce and bring agriculture revolution in its vast areas, six and seven times more than India, the America's economy is mainly based on manufacturing and sales of arms. Among the ten largest arms manufacturing countries in the world, United States tops the List.

According to a report of the Stockholm International Peace Research Institute (SIPRI), in its report published 2012 year book on armaments, disarmament and international security, the America's Lockheed Martin, an American Global Aerospace, defence, security and advance technology company heads the list of arms manufacturers in the world followed by BAE Systems UK. The SIPRI has categorised in its 2012 year book the arms manufacturing companies like Boeing, Northirop Grumm an, General Dynamics, Raytheor, EADS (trans Europe), Finmeccanica (Italy), L-3 Communications, and United Technologies. These arms manufacturing companies are vying each other to export deadly arms and am munitions including chemical weapons and arms to various countries of the globe!

A report in the Washington Post has said that legacy of decades of mistrust, together with lingering barriers to technology transfer between India and US "continues to dog defence trade between two allies whose relationship President Obama said would be one of the defining partnerships of 21st century." The report quoted Ashton Carter, U S Deputy defence secretary "we want to knock down any remaining bureaucratic barriers in our defence relationship and strip way the impediments."

Perhaps India is suffering from fear psychosis in the South East Asia and thinks itself a weak nation in respect of acquisitions of arms and ammunition to counter growing influence of China in the continent. The Washington Post report has said, "With a wary eye on China's military build-up, India is in the midst of an ambitious defence acquisition programme—worth about $100 billion over more than a decade—to replace its ageing Soviet-arsenal and but new fighter aircraft, maritime patrol aircraft, infantry combat vehicles, helicopters, assault rifles, under water submarines and tanks, because India's own defence production industry is relatively small, much of that equipment has to be imported."

India's strategic defence partnership between the United States and India has alarmed the peace-loving country throughout the globe particularly in the South-East Asia. India had to face economic sanction from America for many years after nuclear explosion by the Vajpayee government. As part of strategic partnership with India, U S has opened in Adibatla aerospace, near Hyderabad major of that country Lockheed Martin and Indian company Tata Advanced Systems and producing wing parts and tail sections for the American SuperHercules military transport aircraft. Sudden interest of America with India appears an ominous signal for India and Indian as whole because of well-known imperialistic design of U S, defence experts feel, adding that India must move cautiously.

The Washington Times report has said, "India is expanding market for us and by building our industrial foot prints here, we are trying: we are not here to sell and walk away. We have got our skin in the game we are here to stay," Abhay Paranjape, national executive for India at Lockheed Martin Aeronautics said in an interview. Defence trade between India and United states grew from almost nothing to generate $ 8 billion since 2005, marking definite shift on India's part towards buying American equipment. But Russia continues to be the top arms supplier to India, with the United States and Israel vying for second."

US, however, felt disappointed last year when even after several rounds of fierce competition, the contract for 126 fighter aircraft went to French Company Dassault. Washington Post report has further pointed out that the 2005 civil nuclear energy deal helped cement the United States's relation ship with India as a counter to China's rise in Asia. The U S plans to move 60 percent of its naval fleet to the Asia pacific by 2020 makes the partnership vital for with India.

However, the Washington Post has put a rider about all these things has said, "In India, though, the vision is some what different. New Delhi closely guards its strategic freedom and is reluctant to get too closely alingned militarily with Washington" The Post has also quoted S Amer Latif, visiting fellow of the at the Washington-based centre for Strategic and International studies, "there was a lot of scratching of heads in New Delhi when the U S lost the contract, given that the U S had invested such a lot of political and diplomatic capital into this relationship".

Indiscriminate arming of India at the cost of huge expenditure is expected to adversely affect the welfare measures and programmes of poor people, constituting over 60 percent in the country! No doubt, India's security should also be considered primarily but not in such large scale!

HUGE POPULATION OF INDIA YET TO COME UNDER NATIONAL MAINSTREAM: SUCCESSIVE GOVERNMENTS ENGAGE IN SHOWCASING THEM!

Thursday, 6 September 2012

Over 15 crore population of India is yet to be brought under national mainstream—they live life of vagabonds, moving from one place to another; many of the tribes are yet to know that they have a homeland or nation of country—that is called"—INDIA, A SOVEREIGN, SOCIALIST, SECULAR DEMOCRATIC REPUBLIC . . . ."

Before I deliberate on this topic about sad plight of huge number of population, I exactly remember two quotable quotes of the first Prime Minister Pundit Jawahar Lal Nehru and Editor of the well-researched Literary monthly magazines—Dowab, published from New Delhi and retired professor of English and former member of Council of States Prof Jabir Husain . . . .

Pundit Nehru had said on the night of 14/15 August, 1947 after India had achieved independence from British Rule, "Long years ago we made a tryst with destiny and now the time has come when we will redeem our pledge, not wholly or in full measures, but very substantially. At the stroke of the midnight hour, when the world sleeps, INDIA will awake to life and freedom . . . . A moment of comes which but comes rarely in history, when we step out from the old to the new, when an age ends and when the soul of a nation long suppressed finds utterances. We end today a period of all fortune and India discovers herself again . . . ."

Prof Husain has written in a purview of his article in "Khanabadosh (nomads)" in Dowab . . . . "Jaab mein aaya tha meri koyi jaat nahi thi; Aur jaab mein ja raha hun tab bhi meri koi jaat nahi hai; Aakash ko aisa hin khula rahne do; Dharati ko bhi mat bandhi; Tumne jo bich bich mein diwaren khara ki li hai; Unhen gira do kyonki wah tumhin ne

319

banai hai; Aapne purkhon ke kewal gaurav ko lo; Unki gati ka samman karo; Undino ki yaad karo jab pahiye nahi the; Par purbaj chalana Chahte the . . . . (When I had come then I had my no caste; And when I am going then also I have no caste; Allow the sky to open like this; Do not bind even earth; You have raised walls in between; Demolish them because you have raised them, Let take your ancestors pride; Allow normalising their speed; Let remember those days when there were no wheels; Even than ancestors wanted to walk . . . .")

Is India running of its own or some body is pulling the nation? India as a nation achieved independence exactly over 62 years! We have adopted a well defined Constitution, enunciating Justice, social, economic and political; Liberty of thought, expression, belief, faith and worship; Equality of status and of opportunity; and to promote among them all; Fraternity assuring the dignity of the individual and the [unity and integrity of the Nation]. Then why discrimination galore prevailing everywhere in the country?

To begin with, one must take into account, the burning question of deprivation of over 15 crore population of nomads in the country. They are yet to identify in the social and national set-up. Prof Husain has taken a lead to highlight the plight of nomads in the country. Apart from that, huge number of Adivasis and primitive population, living in the deep forest areas of Jharkhand, Chhatishgarh, Madhya Pradesh, Orrissa, Andhra Pradesh, West Bengal, Karnataka, Tamil Nadu, Maharshatra many eastern states as well as remote islands of south India nearing Sea shore are yet to see the light of independent India. Sadly primitive and ancient tribes in Andmand and Nicobar islands, Puducherry, Lakhshdweep, Dadar—Nagar Havelis as well as many deep forest areas of adivasi-populated Jharkhand, Orrissa, Chhatishgarh, Madhya Pradesh, Andhra Pradesh, West Bengal etc have not been identified so far—they live in island forest and tribal forest, unknown nobody knows their living—Some random survey have found that they move naked and their population are dwindling because of diseases and natural calamities. In this way, our successive union governments had been showcasing these rare population of the country and made them exhibition subject matter, ridiculous of being their ancient and primitive living away from the civilisation and culture of India as a whole!

Stories of cursed nomads, published in various issues of Dowab, (I think Dowab is a Persian word ant it means conjunction of two rivers) reflect the indifference of successive governments towards sad plight of over 15 crore such population in the country. They have no home, no shelter etc—they move one place to another right from their ancestors to present youths, old, women and children. The British Raj, which had enacted a law in 1871, considering nomads a bunch of thieves and female population prostitutes, used to punish them under such black law. After independence Pundit Jawahar Lal Nehru could know the sad plight of nomads and after the repealing the black law of British enacted a new law—Habitual offender Act—1952. That law still today in vogue has proved more darocian in humiliation terms of nomads! The issue got momentum when Prof Jabir Husain raised in Parliament the plight of nomads—but sadly government remained silent over such important issue! Prof Husain has pointed out in his Article—"Delli mein Khanabadosh" in Dowab monthly, that nomads have many sub-caste. They are Kureri, Kureriayar, Kurori, Dhami, Dhamin etc. They move different places in live in tents on road side streets away from life of urban and rural habitats in rural and urban areas. They are held most neglected community in Indian society. Reports of their killings pour from different places. A few years back in September 2007, nomads of Kureri sub-caste, numbering ten, were killed mercilessly on the concocted charges of thievery by villagers of Rajapakad-Delphoswan in Vaishali district of Bihar. Such incidents in different parts of the country with nomads have become order of the day.

Prof Husain has also referred about a commission, constituted by the union government, to identify nomads and suggest measures for puting them in Schedule Tribes list. The Commission under the chairmanship of Balkrishna Renke long back submitted the report to the union government—but the union government is putting them in cold-storage. Interestingly, the report has not been placed in the Parliament in the last several years., resulting into rampant rise in atrocity and violence against them. In yet another revelation of facts in another issue of Dowab, Prof Husain has put startling facts about the recommendations of the commission and the union government's indifference towards them. Balkrishna Renke commission report, submitted interim report and final report in 2007 and 2008 respectively to the union social Justice ministry. But the report was not presented before Parliament! In the meantime, the report was any how reached to the much-publicised National Advisory Council 1 (NAC) led by the AICC president Ms Sonia Gandhi. To the hopes and aspirations of nomads, the NAC referred the report to the working group, comprising Ms. Aruna Roy, Mr Harsh

Mander, Mr Madhaw Gadgil, and Mr Narendra Jatav, for suggestion to uplift the plight of nomads in the wake of Renke Commission report. However working group studied the report and put them on website for public suggestions to bring them on national mainstream. Even there remained many shortcomings on the suggestions of working group— but in one aspect, the working group admitted that present law of 1952 appears more darocian and wanted its repeal. But thanks to Ms Sonia Gandhi, she voiced many objections over working group suggestions. she lamented that the suggestions are limited to 200denotified communities and pointed out that about 1400 nomads tribes and sub-tribes have not been referred in the working group suggestions, Prof Husain said and added that even today thousands of above mentioned tribes and sub-tribes have not been provided any right so that they could be brought under national mainstream!

More over, Prof Husain has disclosed that the British Raj had declared 200 communities, mostly travellers, moving from one part to another and had put them under "criminal tribal" under 1871 Act. British thought them they are criminals and had considered travellers moving from one part to another as possible criminal. After Nehru's intervention in 1950s a new Act was enacted—that also not at all suitable and considered nomads, indulging in thievery and other crimes. Both NAC working group and Renke commission made many suggestions but all of them are yet to draw the union government's attention to bring nomads under national mainstream!

In the meantime, an article by Malini Bhattacharya, a former member of the National Commission for Women in the Frontline fortnightly has also mentioned many things about nomads in the wake of a raid conducted by the police in well-known brothel areas of Uttam Rampur, Ward Number-3, and Forbesganj in Araria district of Bihar written. The writer has said that she was shocked to find the name of one Md Kalam mentioned as person the person who had been arrested following the testimony given by one of the rescued girls. Md Kalam, had first met Ms Maninin in Uttari Rampur as a member of the marginalised Nut community, which provided women for brothels of Rampur for generations. Kalam has been raised by two elder sisters, who had been themselves been inducted into the trade at an early age but had vowed to make sure that their brother never become part of the vicious network of traffickers and pimps. Both the sisters had sent Kalam for education and in time, Kalam took opportunity and became the first graduate from the Nutta community in the areas. Kalam also acquired a degree of law and returned to his birth place as a social activist fighting against the exploitation of women. Kalam succeeded in his venture and started schools for marginalised community. But he was got involved in the case on false charge when he was doing social work to bring back nomads girls from the clutches of brokers. And knowing all these things, Maninin has added in her article, "But what is more unfortunate is that the social and political forces outside Nutt his own community also seem to be inclined towards perpetuating the fate of the Nutts."

Ms Manini has reminded in a foot note in his article, "The Nutts are a marginalised community of tribal origin, now settled in parts of Bihar and Rajasthan. From whatever mythical memories of their past they retain, one learns that they were nomadic and possessed exceptional acrobatics skills. The half-forgotten bardic songs of "Alha-Rudal" note that Nutts had shown great bravery as contingents in the army of Rana Pratap in his battle against Mughals. They never took up agriculture. They are settled on homestead lands in some parts of Bihar and Rajasthan by their feudal overlords who used their military prowess for their own purpose. Perhaps, even in pre-colonial times these feudal lords' extracted sexual services from Nutt women, which would explain the evolution of the so called custom prevalent in the community even today. It is closed and largely endogamous community. Many of them have Muslim and Hindu name, suggesting that they have been on the margins of both the religious without being accepted by either. Poverty and underdevelopment, even after they gave up their nomadic ways, combined with the uneven power structures in society, helped perpetuate among them the so called custom of pressing their girls into prostitution and eventually some of their settlements turned into red light areas and centres of trafficking."

Here I must discuss the primitive tribes living in interior fo deep forest of Andmand Nichobar Islands. Because of dense forest and non-accessibility in the areas, rare tribesmen, belonging to Great Andamanese, Oges of Little Straight Island, Jarawas south and middle Andmand, Sentinelese of Sentinent Island, Shom pens of Great Nicobar and Great Andamanese remains neglected and joining of them in national mainstreams appears quite impossible and a distant dream, thanks to the lackadaisical approach of the union government. Population of many these tribes are declining. They remain quietly naked in deep forest. They feel unsecured as soon ssas they see people from the developed areas, moving on helicopter. Either they ran away in deep forest or fire arrows and bhallas on flying helicopter. They are far away from the culture and civilisation of India. Large numbers of their population have perished in the last Tsunami. By random survey and census, the union government has determined their population! There are only 19 Grat Andmanese, who were 24 in 1971, 25 in 1901 and 10000 in 1789. Another Tribe Onge is considered most primitive tribe. They are semi-nomadic tribe-fully dependent on food provided by nature. It population have no record—but negligible in the Forest island. Jarawas tribes are only 341 inhabitants. Sentinelese are world's only tribes without any contact with any other group and community. They are said to be very hostile and never leave the island. Very little is known about this tribe. Shopens Mongoloid race and they are very shy. This tribe's major groups are hostile. Populations of all these tribes are decreasing because of hunger and various diseases. They are gradually becoming physically weak! More Over in this age of advance technology, successive union governments are yet to rescue and rehabilitate these primitive tribes what to speak of identifying them in national main streams.

Just only not these facts, even adivasis in remote and deep forest of Jharkhand, Odisha, Chhaitshgah, Madhya Pradesh, Andhra Pradesh, West Bengal and eastern states are already away from national mainstreams. I had been Saranda forest range in Jharkhand state about a few years ago and many deep forest areas of Orrissa and West Bengal, Chhatishgarh, Madhya Pradesh along with some of my Naxalite friends, I personally found tribal running away in deep jungles perhaps being afraid of us!

SOURCE: Issues of DOWABA, monthlyliterary magazine, FRONTLINE, a fortnightly magazine, Constituent Assembly Websites, Chhatishgarh, Orrissa, Jharkhand, West Bengal government websites as well as websites of Union Territories and eastern states government websites, Tribal Achieves of many organisations etc.

JINX OF OSAMA BIN LADEN AND SADDAM HUSSEIN CONTINUES TO HAUNT AMERICA AND EUROPE!

Tuesday, 28 August 2012

The recent revelation in details about circumstances leading to spotting of Osama bin Laden and Saddam Hussein and subsequently the killing of Osama in the raid and execution of Hussein by American security forces has not only created flutter in entire America and Europe but has put a big question mark over capability and actuality of successive administrations of United States of America (USA) in eliminating these two big names in the Globe!

The Guardian, UK and the Washington Post have recently prominently carried out stories about these leaders and the circumstances they were apprehended and killed subsequently. A report from Dawr (Iraq) dateline in Washington Post has given vivid description about the capture of Saddam Hussein and tortures to his saviours in "The Hole", known to the world as the "Spider hole" in the tiny underground bunker on Alaa Namiq's farm! In another report, both The Guardian and the Washington Post have vividly described the capture and killing of Osama bin Laden in air raid on Abbottabad residence of the fugitive. While the report in Washington Post from Dawr (Iraq) is in conversion of the man, who gave shelter to Saadam in "The Hole" with an American journalist, the report both in The Guardian and the Washington Post have dwelt at length about Osama bin Laden on the basis of a book—"No Easy Day: The First hand Account of the Mission that killed Osama bin Laden written by a U S commando involved in the Navy Seal raid"—to be released on September 11, 2012, creating stir in US administration and politics just on the eve of the Presidential elections.

Both these incidents were held in piquant situation in the respective sub-continents in the world. Both the capture of Saadam and subsequently his hanging and capture and killings of Osama bin Laden had given much relief to America on terror front as well as revenge of 9/11 attack on World Trade Centre and Pentagon by Osama bin Laden and company terrorists although both the incidents also drew sharp reactions on human right fronts in the entire globe!

Sipping tea in the modest little restaurant he opened this summer. a couple of foot-ball fields away from" the hole" Alla Namiq seems "willing to say American reporter some thing about the capture of Saadam by American security forces. Washington Post report says," Alaa Namiq narrates, he (Saadam) came here and he asked us for help and I said yes. He said, you might be captured and tortured, but in our Arab tribal tradition and by Islamic laws, when some one needs help, we help him. I dug the whole for him", he says his eyes, burning with pride. The hole known to the world as the" spider hole" is the tiny underground bunker on Namiq's farm where former Iraqi dictator Saadam Hussein was captured on December 13, 2003. Namiq and his elder brother Qais have rarely spoken publicly about how they helped hide most sought—after fugitive for nearly nine months after the US-led invasion," the Washington report said.

"But now, sipping tea in modest little restaurant, Alaa must have felt may be enough time has passed. May be a few have asked. But for what ever reason, Namiq now folds his tall, broad-shouldered frame into plastic chair, tugs on a cigarette and talks about hiding the his family had known for decades. Hussein was born in a village near Tirkit, just north of this little town on the banks of Tigris River. When the US military was searching for him, it became convinced, correctly, that he would find shelter among his Tikrit clansmen in these lush green orchards of date palms and orange and pear trees, The Washington Post report added.

On the flutter on book on Osama bin Laden's capture and killing, the Guardian said, "the book recounting Osama bin Laden raid surprises in U S military. The book will be finally released on September 11, 2012, coinciding the 11the anniversary of the Al-qaida attacks on the U.S, caught Pentagon and intelligence napping. The publisher, a subsidiary of the Penguin, less said—no easy day. The first had—six who was one of the first men through the door on the third floor of the terrorist hideout and was present . . . . A blow-by-blow account . . . . of the assault, beginning with helicopter crash that would have ended author's life straight though the radi o calls contrary the bin Laden's death, the Penguin and its subsidiary, publisher of the book said the account is an essential piece of modern history . . . . No easy day is to be published under Pen name, Mark Owen. But Fox News said it was established the identity of author,—he is 36 year-old from Aska, who also took part in SEAL raid in 2009 that rescued the captain of American merchant ship by Somali pirates—he retired from military last year—What ever its tone, the account is likely to be caught up in the attempts by a group of right wing former military and intelligence officers with ties to Tea Party movement and the Republican Party accuse Obama of claiming much credit for hunting down bin Laden. The group, the special operation OPSEC education fun, last week released a 22-minute video accounting the president of taking intelligence and military secrets—including the role of Pakistani doctor in providing the al-Qaida leader, details of virus attacks on nuclear programme ands Obama's pact in deciding a "kill list" of targets of Drone strikes in Pakistan-for political gain. In the video many of military and intelligence retired officers say of Obama is wrongly taking credit of bin Laden's death although there is no evidence that they have special knowledge of the situation . . . . Abbotabad raid was one of the most important in the United States of America's history . . ."

While expressing apprehension over final release of the book, The Guardian has said, "In 2010, the defence department had stopped the circulation of of a book written by a former intelligence official in the interest of national security. The Pentagon paid $47000 to destroy 9500 copies of the book, called Operation Death Halt Skycraft and special operation on the frontier of Afghanistan and the path to victory, written by Anit Shaffer . . . ."

The Washington Post has also written by and large similar report and has written "If the description is true, the book would shatter the secrecy maintained by members of the team of Navy SEALs involved in the bin Laden's compound in Abbotabad, Pakistan. It could also raise legal and political issue for the Obama administration, which has carried out an aggressive crackdown on leaks even while it has been accused of offering access to journalists and movie makers to exploit the success of the bin Laden operation. The raid was carried out by the elite and the secretive U S Joint Special Operation Command under the authority of the CIA, Pentagon and CIA officials appeared to be caught off guard by a spokeswoman of Dutton's announcement of the forthcoming book The book is titled "no Easy day: The Firsthand Account of the Mission that killed the Osama bin Laden. The author's name is listed as Mark Owen, which Dutton acknowledges is pseudonym. The author has pledged to donate the majority proceeds to charities that support families of slain Navy SEALs. Officials indicated that neither the author nor the publishers had cleared the book's content with Defence department or the CIA, a step ordinarily required by former service members or spies seeking to write about classified information operations. THE CIA spokesman Preston Golson said as far as we can determine, this book was not submitted for pre-publication review. Pentagon Spokeskesman Goerge Little said he as unaware of that anyone in the department has reviewed it. White House officials said they knew nothing about the book.'" the Washington Post report concluded.

The Washington Post has also written very very interesting things about Saada Hussain arrest operation. The report has said, "Namiq says, over and over, during the course of a couple of hours. Some day I will say all I know. May be I will write a book, may be a movie. But I will not tell you every thing. However Namiq says his family, mainly he and Qais (who declined to be interviewed) helped move Hussein among various houses in the area after the March 2003 invasion. Hussein never used a phone, he says, knowing that Americans were listening for his voice. Namiq says that Hussein read and wrote extensively, prose and poetry, and that his writings were confiscated by the U S troops, who captured him. Namiq says Hussain wrote to his wife and daughters but he never saw them. His only visitors were his sons Uday and Qusay-Namiq says he helped arrange their secret meeting trip to the farm. Hussein released several fiery speeches during the time he was hiding, exhorting his supporters to fght the Americans. Namiq says he and Hussein recorded them on a small tape recorder. Knowing that Americans would be analysing the recordings for clues to Hussein's whereabouts, Namiq says he once drove 10 miles to the city of Sarmera, parked on the side of the road and recorded the sounds of urban traffic. I wanted to feel Americans feel dizzy and confused; Namiq quoted Saadam as speaking and doing! Namiq clearly still reveres Hussein, who was hanged in 2006. Namiq says Saadam knew there would be a day that he would be captued and executed. In his heart, he knew every thing was gone and he was no longer president. So he started some thing knew-Jihad against the occupiers. He sacrificed evetry thing he had, including his two sons, for the sake of the country. Namiq says that when he was held at Abu Gharaib, U S soldiers—including a female interrogator who told him he looked like actor TomSelleeck—questioned him daily about weapons of mass destruction and the hiding places of of top aides of Hussein. He says that cell was kept dark 24 hours a day and that guards threw in buckets of water to keep it constantly wet. He says he was hooded and beaten, and bitten by guard dogs. He was submitted to mock execution, he says, and constant, deafening rock music. I endured the dogs and the torture, but I could not stand that music, Namiq says, without a trace of humour in his deep voice . . . . "

The Washington Post further elaborated the interview of Namiq and has said, "Hussein's attorney, Khalid Dulaimi, quoted the former director dictator in a 2009 book as saying that he had known the Namix family since 1959 and that they had hidden him. In the book, Qais Namiq is accused of eventually tuning Hussien in thew US troops, which Alaa Namiq vehemently denies . . . . The Namiq family has become some thing like royalty in Dawr for sheltering a local tribesman who is still ido lised by many here. We consider it a heroic act, the report quoted Col. Muohammad Hassan of Iraqi National Police, who is stationed in Dawr. This act does not concern his family only but it represents all the citizens of Dawr because this ciity embraced Saddam. Now Nmiq family commands respects and appreciation even more than before . . . . Hussein was buried just up the road of Auja, the village where he was born. Aware of the former dictator's enduring popularity around here, Prime Minister Nouri al—Maliki has ordered his grave site closed to the people to keep it from becoming a shrine . . . . On the farm where Hussein was captured, the spider hole sits at the base of a date palm tree, covered with a four-foot-square concrete cap largely forgotten beneath dirty cages filled with doves and park parakeets. Chickens and dogs roam the grounds, the huge orange carp swim in two ponds on a midsummer evening, and the trees are so full that with every storng breeze, small yellow pars fell like rain drops. Namiq finally says he and his brother Qais were arrested along with Hussein and spent a miserable six months in Abu Ghraib prison. Once a driver and aide of Hussein, he has spent the past few years driving taxi, finally saving enough to open hisfamily restaurant a few weeks ago . . . . "

These reports in important dailies including The Guardian and the Washington Post have practically nerved the Americans and Europeans. It is said that the US President Obama was not so serious about capturing and killing Osama despite reports intelligence reports and it was Ms H Clinton, who pressed Obama to take the drastic steps to capture and kill Osama in Abbottabad in Pakistan. In Iraq also Americans and Europeans are bearing the burnt, the peace still eludes Iraq and US 's hegemony is still there and people of Iraq are unwillingly tolerating Americans!.

WHY NOT COMMUNAL AND ETHINIC HARMONY IN INDIA AND PAKISTAN?

Friday, 24 August 2012

Even after the partition of India and Pakistan over 65 years ago in the wake of the independence of the Indian sub-continent from British Raj, Hindu and Muslim of both Pakistan and India continue to live in anger and revenge against each other! Was the partition of India and Pakistan as separate country was wrong step or the the seed of divide and rule of the British Raj of population of both the community continue to seething in anger of killings of over three lakhs both Muslims and Hindu in both the countries just after the independence? The incidents of the last 65 years in both the countries have brought only miseries to Hindu in Pakistan and Muslims in India!

The demolition of Babari Masjid in Ayodhaya led by Hindu fanatics from BJP, RSS, Hindu Mahasabha, RSS etc and subsequent killings of huge number of Muslims in India because of scores of communal riots including Mumbai communal riots, Narendra Modi Gujarat government-sponsored communal riots in Gujarat and Bhagalpur riots in Bihar etc, killing over ten thousands of Muslims has added new dimension to the deteriorating relations between Hindu and Muslims in the sub-continent.

Not only that in Pakistan, Hindu, Sikh and Christian—minority, which consists about three percent population of Pakistan have also suffered a lot—apart from killing of many of them for not converting to Islam as well as rape, abduction of Hindu women, specially girls and forced them to marry with Muslims and convert to Islam have also worsened the plight of Hindu-Muslim relation in both the countries. Comparatively Muslims, who were around 12 percent of total population of India at the time of partition, have increased to nearly 18 percent in India!

More over India have been facing persistent threats from fanatics Islamic organisations and their terror activities in different parts of India. In this connection, one must recall the Muslim invasions on India during Medieval period when the Hindu had to suffer because of barbaric and atrocious acts of Muslim rulers in India—those days witnessed demolition of many temples and religious places including Vishwanath Temple in Varanashi, Somnath temple etc by Muslim rulers and Muslim fanatics. Even after these things, relations between Hindu and Muslims remained cordial when British India Company and later British Raj enslaved the entire Indian sub-continent.

The recent ethnic clashes between Bodo, an aboriginal tribe in Assam and Muslims, mostly migrated from Bangaladesh, killings over 100 and over three lakhs people flee their home and stationed in refugee camps in Kokarjhar areas of Assam have stunned the people of the world and particularly of India. In a recent article The Times of America has commented, "In the world's largest democracy, fears of pogroms and ethnic violence have highlighted just how fractious febrile India's social make up is . . . ."

Here it will be proper to mention the social and political structures of Assam in eastern states. Earlier, Assamese had problem with Bengali speaking people and Bangles and in the process Bengals settlers in Assam had to suffer a lot. Thereafter, the Bodo and other tribes of Assam had made targets to of Muslims. And the time is getting on. And the recent ethnic riots Muslims were made real targets in the name that they were Bangala Desh settlers—although both Bodo tribes and Muslims suffered in the ethnic clashes, but Muslims are more sufferers in comparison ot Bodo persons! Bodo indigenous tribe clashed with Bengali Muslim settlers. Thousands of Muslims fled away from their houses. Such clash and attack on Muslims in Kokarjhar areas of Assam gave rumours of Muslim reprisal attacks on North-easterners in Banglore, Mumbai, Chennai and other big cities in the country.

Taking into account these developments in the last 65 years, I reminiscences three quotable quotes of three stalwarts—South Asia's iconic poet Faiz Ahmed Faiz, the founder of Pakistant Mohammed Ali Jinnah and the chief architect of gruesome partition of India and Pakistan, exercising the policy of divide and rule and the then prime minister of Great Britain Winston Churchill.

In an article in the Pakistan Daily Times, a progressive international writer Lal Khan, has mentioned, "South Asia's iconic poet Faiz Ahmed

Faiz had termed the independence of the sub-continent in August 1947 as blighted dacon to his famous poem—Morro of Independence . . . . Blood massacres during partition on religious line . . . . It was perhaps biggest genocide in modern history. Independence became harrowing nightmare for the oppressed masses of the sub-continent sixty five years on . . . . today the condition of the masses in India, Pakistan, Bangla Desh are atrocious . . . . the celebration of formal independence by the ruling classes and their toady petty bourgeoisie are an insult to injury for the millions chained in capitalists slavery . . . . the region contains more than one/fifth of human population yet almost half of the world's poor reside in this region . . . . misery, poverty and deprivation have worsened since 1947 . . . health and educations are luxury for a few . . . ."

The second quote of Winston Churchill also reminds us about the the real truth of a New India and Pakistan after independence! Churchill had written, "Power will go into the hands of rascals, rouges and freebooters. Not a bottle of water not a loaf of bread shall escape taxation . . . . these are men of straw . . . ." Although the sayings of Churchill are very objectionable, in some extend the affairs of India and Pakistan sub-continent are being run by the successive rulers in messy situation!

Last but not the least, the anguish feeling and sentiments of Mohhmed Ali Jinnah in the wake of thousands of people killed in Hindu-Muslim riots in India and Pakistan as well as huge number of people fleeing from each other countries had put people of the world aghast! A recent book released—BEYOND THE LINES: AN AUTOBIOGRAPHY OF veteran journalist, Kuldip Nayar, has referred, "One day When Jinnah was in Lahore Iftiikhar-ud-din, Pakistan's rehabilitation Minister and Mazhar/Ali Khan, editor of Pakistan Times, flew him in Dakota over divided Punjab. When he saw streams of people pouring into Pakistan or fleeing it, he struck his hand on his forehead and said despairingly" "What have I done??" Both Iftikar and Mazhar vowed not to repeat the remark. Mazahar took his wife Tahira into confidence and told her what Jinnah had said, and she communicated Jinnakh's comment to me long after her husband's death . . . ." Again it has been cleared that Jinnah was architect of partition of India and Pakistan sub-continent because of so many reasons, particularly the obstinacy of Pundit Jawahar Lal Nehru not to allow Muslim League to join UP government in 1937 following the conspiracy of Purshottam Das Tandon.

Another reference in Beyond the Lines depicts the Jinnah's version! The book says, "Louis Heren, South-Asia Correspondent of Times, Landon, who was stationed in Delhi in 1947-48 had told me (Nayar) that Jinnah was not willing to accept the onus of partition . . . . Heren recalled Jinnah's words:" Had he (Nehru) agreed to the Muslim League joining the U P Government in 1937, there would have no Pakistan . . . . Jinnah's allegation, according to Heren, suggested 'that Nehru's judgement was impaired by Pushottam Das Tandon, a Hindu nationalist, who was a senior Congress leader in Uttar Pradesh' . . . . More or less Azad Maulana Abdul Kalam Azad said the same thing in his book, "India Wins Freedom" (1988) . . . ."

Ethnic clashes in north-eastern states, a conglomerations of seven states, has strange story, especially in Assam. Most of the people of the north-eastern region usually migrate to big cities for earning livelihood. Especially the Bangala Deshi infiltrators, after entry into India, opt for big cities like Mumbai, Delhi, Banglore, Kolkata etc. They are lakhs in number—but nothing tangible is being made to send them back to their Bangala Desh country by various political parties obviously to garner support among minority community. Infiltrators are given voting right and almost all facilities knowingly or unknowingly by the north-eastern states, particularly Assam government. Now they have become gradually liability for the country as infiltrators have moved thorough out the country! Only because of that Mumbai has recently witnessed vast protest meeting by Muslims in in Azad Maidan to speak atrocity against Muslims by aboriginal Bodo tribes. Following incidents of ethnic strife in north-eastern state of Assam, mass SMSs e-mails, and posts on Facebook and Twitter warned of (and in many cases encouraged) Muslim reprisals attacks on north easterners in the holy month of Ramdan. Indian Officials predictably pointed fingers at Internet trouble-makers across borders in Pakistan. Some Hindu fundamentalists also shared in the nefarious games to encourage spread of communal riots in the country! Disillusionment has set in through out the northeastern, living out side their native lands! And heavy exodus of northeasters took place from big cities.

On the Current ethnic situation, the Times, America, has written, "Every one says that central government is on right track to bring stability to the region, albeit belatedly. Its potential for hydro carbon could go a long way in addressing India's long-standing energy short-falls. New planned roads and rail lines could restore colonial era trade tracks that once threaded India with South-East Asia, turning remote back water into continental cross roads. But beyond development, Ninong Erinmg, a Member of Parliament from Arunachal Pradesh, other steps can be taken to better integrate the north-east with rest of India. We all go to schools and learn about Indus Valley and the Mahabharata; he says referring to south Asia's first urban civilisation and the ancient Hindu epic. But there should be some thing more in our education that makes people understand that Ok, the people of the north-east may look Chinese of Korean or what ever but they are Indians. And their stories are India also . . . ."

Nayar in his recent book has said, "The Muslims felt cheated, not having realised that they would have to pay the price of partition; a pronounced bias against them and the Hindus' demand that they go to Pakistan. Even today the same thing echoes in the ears of some of them. Muslims were afraid and confused, yearning to turn a new leaf but the Hindus were too bitter and too hostile to allow them any quarter . . . ."

There are many things to tell about Hindu-Musklim animosity in the Indian sub-continent. Even today efforts should be made to make a confederation of India, Pakistan, Bangal Desh, Burma, Afghansitan to restore confidence among Hindu and Muslims of the Indian subcontinent. This confederation should be in line with European Union for prosperity and communal harmony in the sub-conitent!

LOOT OF PUBLIC MONEY BY POLITICAL CLASS, MEMBERS OF EXECUTIVE, JUDICIARY, AND POWER BROKERS IN INDIA

Thursday, 16 August 2012

In India, every where there are loot of public money. Mainly political class in all political parties and their henchmen are robbing the money and resources of the Nation! Officials, judges and holders of constitutional posts are also not lagging behind in the naked drama. Hardly ten percent of allotted money for a project and schemes are spent at ground level. Estimates of big and small projects are inflated or crafted in such nefarious manner that major chunk of money are gobbled up. People of the country are silent spectators!

Wealth of politicians, contractors, neo-rich class, bureaucrats, and judges are increasing rhetorically. Honesty among them is in microscopic minority! Entire system has collapsed and misuse and misutilisation of funds have become order of the day. If one goes by the only reports of successive years by the Comptroller and Auditor general of India (CAG) into the accounts of union government and different state governments, peoples' money to the tunes of Rs 4000 lakh crores have been looted and such generation of black money has resulted into serious set back to the economy of the common masses and ultimately the country. Ultimately this money is stacked in the foreign banks and investments in different sectors by these thieves and looters!

More over, thousands of corruption cases registered against politicians, bureaucrats, judges and many others are languishing in different courts of the country for the last several years. Hardly one-five percent such corruption cases have proved and many of them have been convicted and are languishing in jails—but in many cases, they are let off by higher echelon of judiciary in the entire country. Not only the legal system is blamed but the old laws and rules of Cr.P.C and IPC are also proving big stumbling bloc to reach the corruption cases or any other criminal cases to the logical conclusions.

A recent essay on corruption, written by eminent writer Mr A G Noorani, on loot of public money by political class in India, in The Hindu has said, "The Penal code of 1860 and the Cr. P. C of 1895 were enacted when there were no" ministers". They came much later. The sanctions provisions in the Cr. PC were designed to protect minions of the Raj. Today they make the government, judge in its own cause if a minister comes under a cloud. No other democracy has it . . . . Changes of government been no more than reshuffles among political cliques and politicians were primarily motivated by venality and self-interest. Clashes within parties are more real that the ones between them. The start will proceed apace and all will faithfully disclose their assets to an admiring public—while India is being looted by this political class . . . ."

Bribery has become a menace—It is in defence, telecommunication, power generation, investment deals in union government and the state governments as well as delivering choice judgements in courts right from lower courts to high courts and the Supreme Court. Judgements are purchased. In many serious corruption cases, many political leaders, officials, judges, involved, have been acquitted either from lower courts to Supreme Court. On the patronage of political class, bureaucrats and government staff discriminate in giving just order and on payment of bribes, the works are done. Political class specially ruling party or alliance bend or subvert the rules and laws to give favours with sole purpose to mint money. Recent instances are telecommunication scams and many other defence deals in union government and various such corrupt practises in various state governments.

Sadly power-that-be involving their rivals in different scams bypassing the involvement of their own leaders. One such instance is multi-crore-animal husbandry scams in the joint Bihar. the former chief minister and Rashtriya Janata Dal national president Laloo Pradad Yadav and his wife and former chief minister Ms Rabari Devi were got involved in various cases of AHD scams while despite statements in the court by big mafia of AHD that they have also paid crores of rupees to the present Bihar chief minister Nitish Kumar and his companion and former minister as well as national general secretary of the JD(U) Shivanand Tiwari, MP, the CBI did not think it proper to even investigate the matter. Recently on the directive of the Ranchi High court, the Special

CBI court has taken up the matter and is investigating the allegations levelled in the court records about involvement of Nitish Kumar and Shuvanand Tiwari by examining the matter himself and also through CBI. Such discrimination is very much common among the ruling political classes against their rival's politicians throughout the country!

This apart there many loopholes in our laws and legal system and judicial Prudence. Taking advantage of these loopholes, many scamsters are acquitted. For example—Laloo and his wife were acquitted a few years back in a Disproportionate assets case in the wake of AHD scam; recently an IAS official Sajal Chakrovartoy, who was neck—deep involved in the AHD scam, was let off by the court recently. Fate of all these AHD scam cases, registered by the CBI are gradually falling like house of cards!

Cases of corruption against the chief minister of Tamil Nadu Jaylalitha, which has been pending since long and had been transferred to Banglore court by the Supreme Court, are at stand still for the last over nine years. Recently, a government advocate, pursuing the case on behalf of government, has resigned citing several reasons including political pressure. One more example is failing flat the corruption cases against the former chief minister Mayawati. Noorani has commented in his Hindu article," consider but one instance, the judgement must be with hold till the court pronounces on it, but which nonetheless cannot raise a suspicious eyebrows. It is the case of that champion of the down trodden, Ms Mayawati of Uttar Pradesh. The Central Bureau of Investigation (CBI) had claimed that her assets increased from one crore to in 2003 to Rs 50 crore in 2007. Its affidavit in the Supreme Court talked of 96 plots, houses, and orchards acquired by her and her close relatives between 1998 to and 2003. The affidavits filed along with Ms Mayawati's nomination for the Rajya sabha seat a few months ago contains an estimation of of her wealth: Rs 111.64 crores . . . . This is by no means an unusual case. Prosecution of for possessing assets disproportionate to known sources of income is rare and the CBI's conduct is not above suspicion . . . ."

Recently a number of judges of lower courts in Karnataka have been booked under anti-corruption cases for allowing bails to BJP leaders including Reddy brothers in illegal mining, to the tunes of Rs five hundred crore. Not only that some judges of different high courts including Justice Dinakaran and a few of Delhi and Calcutta high courts are also involved in corruption cases and are facing criminal charges. Many senior judges of Supreme Court have stated that many judges of Allahabad, Patna and Calcutta high courts are most corrupt and they are giving bad name to the respective high courts and judiciary in the country, but the circumberance procedures of impeaching high courts and Supreme Court judges are only eluding because of dishonest intention of the political class. A recent revelation of favourable judgement in favour of Vodaphone case, to the tune of Rs 12000 crore by the Supreme Court has created furore about the impartiality of the Supreme Court and its Chief Justice Mr Justice Kapadia. The judgement has revealed many startling facts. Civil Society activists including senior advocate of Supreme Court Prashant Bhushan have openly criticised the Chief justice of Supreme Court for giving anti national judgement ignoring the pleas of the union government as well as for favouring Vodaphone out of way because the London-based son of the chief justice is legal consultant of Vodaphone! Similar are the many allegations against some judges of the Supreme Court. (My earlier blog topics have detailed the Vodaphone case a few months ago: Please read).

Now there are some apparent instances of political class becoming from rags to riches in few years of their being in active politics through amassing huge wealth. The rhetoric rise in their property shows how they have looted the state exchequer in few years! Almost all of them have rag to riches stories.

Chief Ministers of almost all states including Bihar have opened shops in their respective headquarters through their touts to collect huge money on transfers and postings as well as awarding contracts and implementing cash-rich schemes, being financed by union government. Such shops are being looked into in Bihar by Nitish Kumar; s close lieutenant R C P Sinha, who has resigned from IAS ship and joined Rajya Sabha on JD (U) nomination from Bihar.

Our founding fathers of the Constitution led by Dr B R Ambedkar had smelled such facts at the time of framing of the Constitution. Members of the Constituent Assembly including K T Shah and H V Kamath had informed the Constituent Assembly that there should be a provision in the Constitution of ministers declaring their assets before they assume office. Reacting on the proposal, Dr B R Ambedkar on December 31, 1948 has informed similar to the present situation, "One is this, namely, that we should require by law and the Constitution—if this provision is to be effected—not only that the ministers should make a declaration of their assets and their liabilities at the time when they assume office, but we must also have two supplementary provisions. One is that every minister on quiting office shall also make a declaration of his assets on the day on which he resigns, so that everybody, who interested in assessing wheat her the administration was corrupt or not during the tenure of his office should be able to see what increases there is in the assets of the minister and wheat her that increase can be accounted for by saving which can make out his salary . . . . The other provisions would be that if we find that a minister's increase in his assets on the day on which he resigns are not explainable by the normal increases due to his savings, then there must be a third provision to charge the minister for explaining him he managed to increase his assets to an abnormal degree during that period that period. In my judgement, if you want to make this clause effective, then there must be three provisions as I stated. One is declaration at the outset; second is declaration at the end of the quitting of this office; thirdly, responsibility for explaining as to how the assets have come to be show so abnormal and fourthly, declaring that to be offence, followed up by penalty or by a fine . . . . the legal sanction is inadequate. Have not other sanctions at all? In my judgement, we have a better sanction for the enforcement of the ourity of administration and that is the public opinion as mobilised and focused in the Legislative assembly."

Abnormally high rise in wealth of political class and public servant has been giving anxious moments in real polity of the nation. For the income-tax authorities should be on high alert how these persons have increased their wealth in short span of time like the Election Commission of India keeps on tabs on the expenditure of hundred of candidates in the elections!

Corruption among political class is not new in independence India-Corruption we have inherited from the British Raj. According to the the records based on the materials in the National achieves, the corruption among the congress started just after the formation of ministries in provinces in 1937. Before that, in 1926, Pundit Moti Lal Nehru being disgusted with corrupt practises, bitterly complained to Pundit Jawahar Lal Nehru on December 2, 1926, "heavy bribing of voters was the order of the day. I am thoroughly disgusted and am now seriously thinking of retiring from public life . . . . The Malviya-Lala (Lajpat Rai) aided by by Birla's money is making efforts to capture Congress. "As per achieves records, quoted by Mr Noorani, very many Congress candidates spent lavishly on their campaigns. Ministers like Syed Mahmud in Bihar were pestered with demands of congressmen "to provide posts for them whether it is possible or not. They seem to think that I have power to give them government money." On 13 January 13, 1948, Gandhiji read out a letter at the prayer meeting from his one of the friends, who had written mounting corruption. Thereafter many committees and commissions were formed including Sanathan Commission in 1964 on prevention of corruption, which reported "there is widespread impression that the failure of integrity is not uncommon among ministers and that some ministers, who have held office during the last 16 years, have enriched themselves illegitimately . . . ."

Above all there are loot of public money at one hand and on the other hands there clamours among political class and government officials and staff for more and more privileges and perks as well as special treatments—this is how corruption is eating into vitals of India even after 66 years of independence despite so many announcements by successive political class to end corruption menace!

Sources: Constituent Assembly Debates on websites; National Achieves, Congress and other websites including The Hindu Achieves; Books like the Indian National Congress and the Raj by B R Tomlinson; ;kept in the NA; the then Viceroy G F de Montmorency records in the National achieves ETC.

FIGHT FOR EXPANDING TERRITORIAL BOUNDARIES IN SEA, ISLAND AND ISLETS IN ASIA!

Monday, 13 August 2012

Now the time has completely changed. Once upon a time there used to be battle for expansion of landed territory in their respective favours, now almost all countries of Asia are battling to expand their territory in the seas, islands and islets in their respective zones. Mainly the fight has grown for creating infrastructures for natural resources off the shores.

Sadly India, which is engrossed in implementation of neo-liberal economic policy, the country's leadership perhaps is forgetting the utility of sea shores at a time when the economy of a country could go to a new zenith by utilising natural resources from sea-shores, islands etc, which are considered lighthouse for creating wealth by harnessing natural resources, mainly for energy in the shape of hydrocarbon from its shores!. Various reports in the media suggest that Indian sea shores territory have become most vulnerable right from west sea-shores adjoining Maharashtra and Gujarat, eastern sea-shore territory in Bengal and in and around Burma and southern extreme of Tamil Nadu, Andhra Pradesh, Karnataka, part of Odisha. Surprisingly all these zones are unprotected and negligible deployment of coast guards are not coping with the extreme situation, created by neighbouring countries in the sea-shores, islands, and islets falling under the jurisdiction of Indian Territory! More over, strange situation prevails in India right from its independence; warring political classes continue to be of their views that certain parts of even our disputed land territory might be surrendered to neighbouring countries to buy peace! But majority of Indians are opposed to any such concessions.

A recent report in the Washignton Post has interestingly highlighted the fight for sea territory, islands, and islets among various countries of Asia. Apparently all these unimpressive bunch of the zones are rocky, windswept outcropping far from the respective mainland of countries of Asia. The writer of the report in the Washington Post Chiko Harian from Tokyo date lined has mentioned, "these tinny territories, sweeping from south-east to north-east Asia, are fiercely contested among countries that are buoyed by nationalism and by a growing thrust for the natural resources off the shores. The territorial disputes involve nearly a dozen of countries at least three major seas and they have set off a chaotic crisscross of conflict in some of the world's most trafficked shipping lanes. The disputes are not at all connected, but analysts say that several of Asia's key countries—China, Japan, South Korea and the Phillippines—have in recent months followed a similar pattern, turning old historical squabbles into national priorities, escalating tensions and raising the chances of a small armed conflict . . . ."

All these Asian countries are bent upon in claiming these far flung off-shore territories because of their growing need for oil and gas reserves in the under the waters around them in the seas. Japan, which has biggest electricity shortages as it had decided to abandon nuclear power generation due to mishaps after mishaps in the nuclear power plants, wants to switch from this method of power generation by harnessing energy from its seas. The China, which is known for one-fifth of energy consumption of the world, is also looking for more and more electricity generations from sea shores.

The Washignton Post has quoted Sydney-based Lowy Institute Director of the International Security Rory Mecalf, who has said, "particularly from a Chinese and Japanese point if views, there is new sense of the need for energy security. None of these countries want to categorically give up claims to territory where there could be large hydrocarbon deposits. Both China and SouthKorea, which are set for change in leadership this year, are strongly putting their claims for their sovereignty of sea, island etc territory expansion. Again the Washington Post has quoted the version of a senior researcher and a North-East Asia expert at the Heritage Foundation Bruce Klinmgner, "we have seen over history countries to go to war over territory—are that seems to be meaningless, but it is soil of the country—even if it would appear illogical for countries to risk conflagration over rock . . . . that is what is occurring."

More over to counter the Chinese move to its claim on sea territory with sole purposes to strengthen its growing economy, several South-East Asian countries have tightened their alliances with USA and are conducting joint military drills in their respective zones, posing danger to China and also forcing China to engage in fight to retain its control over sea territory. The WP has mentioned that the most notable current disputes over sea territories involve Japan and South Korea, China and Japan, and China and a host of South-East Asian countries most vocally the Phillippines and Vietnam. In July Phillippines President Benigno Aquino-third asked his country's Congress to approve a massive military upgrade involving new planes and combat helicopters for deploying in the contested areas in South China Sea, Which the China claimed since long that South China Sea are theirs. On the other hand, Aquino said, "If some one enters your yards and told you he owns it, will you allow that? It is not right to give away what is rightfully ours" The WP POST quoted Phillippines President in its report.

Similarly South Korea also claims Japanese controlled sea territories. South Korean President Lee Myung-bak has pointed out to the Washington Post that Dokdo" is genuinely "our territory" Japanese Foreign Minister Koichiro Gemba, while countering the claims of South Korea, has said, "why did he (South Korea President) visit there at a time when we need to consider issues from a broad view point?—It is extremely regretted." Incidentally both these countries are strong allies of Washington in Asia.

But the situation appears explosive in the areas claimed by China. The Report of Washington Post has quoted a recent findings of Brussel-based International Crisis Group, which depicted" how China is patrolling the sea with "nine dragons", a tangle of conflicting government agencies, many of them trying to increase their power and budget." The findings further said, "the People's Liberation Army navy tends to take a background role in sea disputes, allowing a greater role for civilian law enforcements of para-military agencies. An increasing number of Chinese fishing vessels are operating in the contested areas, as seen in an April stand-off between Beijing and Manila that started When Chinese fishermen were caught poaching near a disputed Sacarborough Shoal. Eventually China won the stand-off and the fishermen made off with their catch."

In this way the tension is escalating in most of the Asian countries over disputed claims of bound sea and island boundaries. To fish in the trouble water, The USA has wished to base a nuclear-powered aircraft carrier on the Australian coast, allowing the USA a second carrier strike group in the region. But Australian Defence minister declined to allow such facilities to USA, saying the Washington that the Australian does not want to antagonise China, its largest trading partner.

With regards to India's coastal areas, the union government has completely failed to even deploy adequate security forces and coastal guards with modernised appliances! The result was that three or four terrorists came from sea routes to Mumbail from Karanchi and created not only panic but killed many persons and made the prestigious Taj Hotel destroyed as well as many historic and archaeological sites and inhabitants destroyed. This is what happening in India when most of the Asian Countries are engaging themselves to protect their coastal areas and sea-shores for utilising more and resources!

MAMATA IN BENGAL: ATROCITY ON WOMEN ON RISE!

Friday, 10 August 2012

Bengal is land of revolutionaries!, sage, saints, academics, culture and what not? Gaur Mahaprabhu, Ram Krishna Pramhans, his disciple Swami Vivekanand had brought revolution in spiritual field throughout the world. In literature, Kaviguru Rabindranath Tagore brought laurels to Bengal in particular and India in general by winning Nobel Prize in early 19th century. Many great things and deeds are cited as examples to put West Bengal at the top. First left front government in Bengal under dynamic leadership of Jyoti Basu for the welfare of the masses although some wrong measures brought the down fall of the left front government after over 30 years. The well-known and prestigious college of Calcutta-Presidency College—has produced finest quality of political leaders and literatureure as well as pro ponders on Marxism and also many progressive thoughts in once decadent society of Bengal!

Now the Bengal is known for the first woman chief Minister Mamata Bannerjee in West Bengal after much-publicised the so called misdeeds or deeds of the left front government. Now Mamata is seen in Bengal for all the wrong reasons with curbing freedom of media to her level to fulfil the high expectation to the masses to make in a new Bengal and her government is aggravating the poverty since she had taken over the chief minister ship of the state.

Latest one is horrible picture of the West Bengal with regards to atrocities on women including rape, kidnapping, abduction, dowry deaths, molestation, sexual harassment and trafficking under the stewardship of women chief minister Mamta Bannerjee! A recent revelation of atrocity on women in West Bengal by the union minister of state for home affairs Jitendra Singh in Rajya Sabha while replying to a question has shocked the people of entire country. While citing the figures, released recently by the National Crime Records Bureau (NCRB), the union minister has informed the house that the West Bengal has topped among the states in the country in crime against women. The west Bengal has reported 29133 crimes against women—the highest number of cases registered among 28 states in 2011. Just after West Bengasl, Andhra Pradesh has registered with total 28246 cases of crime against women and Uttar Pradesh has followed by 22639 case of crime against women. The NCRB, in its report, has revealed that West Bengal has surpassed all states in registering crime against women with regards to rape, abduction, kidnapping, dowry deaths, molestation, sexual harassment and trafficking etc.

Is not this figure about West Bengal on crime against women during the chief minister ship of a woman chief minister Mamata Baneerjee shame to Bengal and particularly to Mamata? More over instead of regretting and controlling such menacing increase of crime against women in Bengal, Mamata is placing strange logic beyond imagination. For every wrong deeds of her government, she puts blame of on left parties!

Such statement of Mamata Baneergee has made women most vulnerable in west Bengal. cities of Bengal are being compared with five worst states of United States of America-Kentkucky, West Virginia, Arkansas, Oklahome, and Mississippi, which have been described worst state in America in atrocity against women in America in latest reports and published in the New York Times, Washington Post and Times (America) recently.

Will Mamata take a lesson from such serious issues like atrocity on women in Bengal or she continue to adopt her mercurial behaviour and fickle style of functioning in running her government in her own fashion or she would be known as women baiter in the annals of Bengal?

STATE POWER IN DOCK FOR KILLINGS OF INNOCENT ADIVASIS IN CHHATISHGARH VILLAGE!

Sunday, 5 August 2012

The rampant and indiscriminate killings of 29 Adivasis including men, women and children in a combined operation in the name of counter insurgency against Maoists in India by the Central Reserve Police Force (CRPF) and Chhatishgarh Police at Sarkeguda village in Bijapur district of Chhatishgarh state of India reminds at least two quotable quotes—"thousands of criminals may be let off but not even a single innocent should be killed (in the context of judgements delivered by our judicial system in the country)" and another by E N RAM MOHAN, former Border Security Force (BSF) chief with years of counter-insurgency experience, who had conducted enquiry into the April 2010 killings of 76 CRPF troops in Chhatishgarh, had said in his report, "Give land to the tiller and forest back to the tribal people with the help of a strong-willed and honest administration. Plus bring down the vast gap between rich and poor . . . . and the Maoists would be on the wane"

Moot point of aggravating the Naxalism upsurge, mainly in tribal belt and in poor villages in different parts of the country, which initially began with the outbreak of Naxalwari upsurge in West Bengal in 1967 with large scale agrarian disputes not only in Bengal but in many other states, are lack of land reforms and wide gap of poor and rich devide in rural India. While confirming such anamolies, the Research and Planning Division of the Union Home Ministry in the "Causes and the Nature of Current Agrarian Tensions (1969)" has said:" The basic cause of unrest, namely the defective implementation of laws enacted to protect interest of the tribals, remains:unless this is attended to, it would not be possible, it would not be possible to win the confidence of the tribals whose leadership has been taken over by the extremists. Although the peasant political organisations in most parts of India are relatively weak, the tension in the rural areas, resulting from the widening gap between the relatively few affluents farmers and the large body of small land-holders, landless and agricultural workers may increase in the coming months and years." The division had emphasised for land reforms and other various welfare measures for weaker sections of society.

Even after, all these cautious approaches, the union home ministry has stepped up anti-Maoists campaign in nine states of the country. The anti-Maoists campaign has been named as "Operation Green Hunt". Apart from severe criticism of the campaign by general people, even the Planning Commission of India expert group note on "Development Challenges in Extremists-Affected Areas" has taken serious note of the campaign and has said," The methods chosen by the government to deal with the Maoists phenomenon (have) increased the people's distrust of the police and consequent unrest, Protest against police harassment is itself a major instance of unrest . . . . The response of the Maoists has been to target the police, which in effect triggers a second round of the spiral . . . . One of the attractions of the Naxalite movements is that it does provide protection to the weak against the powerful and takes the security of and justice for, the weak and socially marginalised seriously."

Instead of brining the Naxalites in the mainstream life by approaches of law and order and development in the affected areas to redress popular grievances, the government realises in the practice of brute force to suppress militants. Moreover, the perception of the government thinkings that the Maoists in India are greatest internal threat is misconstrued Maoists are never for ruining the unity and integrity of the country and undermining security of the country—they are for overthrowing the system by creating law and order problem to support poor people and adivasis, which the government could tactfully tackel by development orientation in neglected areas. The government must take lesson from the counter-insurgency experts like Robert Thompson, who says:" Hardly if ever has a counter-insurgency campaign been won strictly by waging war. Military action has an important role in overcoming guerillas, but the philosophy espoused by the guerillas must also be defeated and this requires a well-reasoned combination of political reforms, civic action and education of the population."

In the context of brutal killings of tribals in Chhatishgarh village para-military forces, killing of 20 civilians including ten children—girls and professional drum players—in the name of encounter with Maoists must be called a terror activities by the government forces. It must be called black spot in the name of counter—insurgency by the state power. The CRPF has advanced many strange arguements and logic to support its action in Chhatishgah village right from some of the killed have bad records with the police to the logic of the CRPF has not developed any system to segregate guerillas from civilians during a gun-fight. Strangely the chief minister of Chhatishgarh Raman Singh's logic that civilians like Adivasis become human shield of Maoists—hence they were killed in the encounter has drawn much criticism. Raman Singh is a known baiter of Naxalites, supporting tribals in different parts of Chhatishgarh against volley of atrocities against them. Tribals of Chhatishgarh are being deprived of their habitats, land and access to forests as well as terrorised by forest contractors and timber mafia and the mining industry in conniviance with the administration, Raman Songh's these mafia gang work in close cooperation with his (Raman Singh) sponsored the much-maligned Salwa Judum militia, who rampantly killed tribals, raped tribal women and burned tribal population houses, resulting into running away of thousands of adivasis from their homes in Chhatishgarh state. In Chhaitishgarh tribal are being isolated by the government through continuing push of distructive mining and industries. The state government has failed to trace the reasons of Adivasis' alienation of which Maoists thrive!

However, the government has agreed to constitute judicial enquiry into the killings under public pressure throughput the country. More over, following the decision of abandoning combat operation if militants use civilians as human shield and to raise reward for those who surrender their weapons at the, the meeting of security forces in the "Left-Wing Extremism-Affected States" on July 13, 2012, a high hope has arisen that the union government must be realising its mistakes and would engage themselves with some concrete measures to take up the situation a fresh to deal with naxalites and innocent tribals in different parts of the country. While dealing with the subject eminent Columnist Praful Bidwai in his Column "Beyond the Obvious" in the Fortnightly Frontline has written, "Our internal security apparatus, from the home ministry downwards, has cultivated a deplorable larger mentality which compulsively forms a protective ring around the self-imposed paramilitary encampment, mush like appartied-era South Africsn Whites did 'Politically, the incidents is a huge triumph for Maoists' argument that the Indian state is structurally and irredeemably anti-people, anti-Adivasis and brutal. Democracy is mere facade. The state must be overthrown through an armed revolution or people's war—in keeping with the Communist party of India (Maoists) agenda."

Rightly after much hue and cry over the issue the them Union home minister P Chidambaram has voiced haly-apology in case "any excesses were committed by the state power"

SOURCES: UNION HOME MINISTRY AND OTHER WEBSITES; WEST BENGAL GOVERNMENT WEBSITE ON NAXALWARI MOVEMENT; FRONTLINE FORNIGHTLY ETC.

RECENT POWER TRIPPINGS IN INDIA VIS-A-VIS SEXUAL APPETITE IN DARKNESS

Wednesday, 1 August 2012

IN LIGHTER VEIN: MY CLUMN:—

Recent power trippings in 21 states and union territories in India, affecting over 648 million Indians, said to be the one-tenth population and one of the biggest blackouts of the world bring me back to the memory lane of about 30 years back. One of the magnificent cities of the globe—New York in the United States of America plunged into darkness, unexpected in America, because of serious power trippings for hours together.

However the electricity was restored after long hours of wait in New York, Americans; basically believe in research and studies. Some reputed organisations started research on power trippings and subsequent affects on human beings.

In the year-long research and studies on these subjects, researchers found that darkness gives sexual stimulation among male and female! To substantiate their studies, the researchers found that on the day electricity failed in the New York City, sexual appetites were at the highest level among both male and female.

Hundreds of women gave birth to their babies after conception on that night sexual engagements as per the records of the almost all hospital records of birth of babies after nine months. Apart from that, almost all hospital records show the abnormal increase in abortions by girls, particularly teen-aged in subsequent months in New York City.

This not for comparing the situation of New York City with recent grid failure in as many states, resulting into complete darkness for hours together in India. But of course for unmanageable and irresponsible management of electricity production, its transmission, supply system to consumers in India!

Although in India, that is Bharat in ancient period had based their researches in the famous book—KAMSUTRA—that darkness stimulates sex among male and female, which is most practical in India. By nature male and female cohabit during night in India!

One trippings of electricity because of grid failure in northern India had occurred on Monday late night, which remained till noon on Tuesday—another failures of north, east and north-east grids simultaneously tripped around one pm on Tuesday, plunging the major parts of in darkness, which remained till late evening. Now the people will guess about the sexual appetite among persons of the affected areas because of remaining a few hours in darkness. Only researchers of India like America could find out exact fall-out of these sudden and surprise black-outs!

WOMEN ARE NOT SAFE IN INDIA!

Saturday, 28 July 2012

Little less than half of the total population of India (1.22 crore)—Women—are passing from shocking phases! Crime against the women in the forms of rape, dowry killings, abduction, Khap and caste panchayats dictum to women, honour killings, harassment at work places, molestation, human trafficking, incidences of crime against female children, tortures etc, have practically made the life of women horrible in the whole of India. Gender bias is gradually is eating into the vitals of the country. All these incidents against women have exposed the lackadaisical manner in which these crimes are taken up by the authorities throughout the country. Such incidents give us the views on the so called globalised India's economic reforms since 1992. Crime against women has escalated as per figures of complaints received with National Women Commission (NWC). Against the 122 complaints to the NWC in 1992, coinciding the beginning of economic reforms, the complaint petitions to NWC have gone up to 13,190 in 2008. With regards to much-publicised equal partnership of women of all classes in the governance and administration as well as fifty percent reservation to women in the Parliament and state assemblies are also hanging fire for the last several years, thanks to the gender bias attitude of male-dominated political class in the country. In respect of atrocity on women, India is even surpassing the records of Islamic countries' restrictions on women, wave of violence including killings of women in Ciudad Juarez in Mexico and UN intervenes (My blog—Wave of Violence Swallows Women in Ciudad Juarez in Mexico). In China women are being forced to abort (My blog: Women of The Globe Becoming Most Vulnerable).

Besides many incidents of atrocity on women, the recent one in Assam that a 17-year-old girl was molested by about two dozen men outside a pub in Guwahati''s main shopping area for 30 minutes on July

09, 2012 in full view of the public has shocked the nation. Such heinous crime reflects that there are no law and order and the constitutional provisions prevail in the country. Strangely in the hub of areas, police came after half an hour. It is said that the reporter and camera crewmen of a local news channel of Rinki Bhuyan Sharma, wife of the health minister Himanta Biswa Sharma in Tarun Gogai government had incited the mob to target the girl. The statement of the Assam Director General of Police J N Chaudhary that the police could not be expected ATMs over the incident has also surprised the people.

Not only that, the role of the NWC, which had sent a two-member fact-finding team to Guwahati, led by the novice former youth Congress leader of Delhi, Alka Lamba has also created piquant situation. The team members, especially Alka Lamba had disclosed the name of victim girl, which is strictly prohibited in practise. More over, Lamba narrated all these things before filing any report to the chairperson in charge of the commission Mamta Sharma. Interestingly, the post of chairperson is vacant for over six months and the union government instead of appointing chairperson of the commission has made Mamta Sharma, who is a former MLA of Rajasthan, as acting chairperson of the commission. Later Mamta on behalf of the commission apologised for revealing the name of teen-aged victim girl.

The commission, which has assumed pro-active role over the last one decade in term of conducting several facts findings and enquiry committees against violence against women, is a statutory body, set up two decades ago to strengthen the legal apparatus to protect women. But the commission has failed to perform its core functions to protest the women. Even its chairperson in charge Mamta Sharma has been criticised for suggesting women should dress carefully. Later she denied making that statement. Under the circumstances, many suggested disbanding of the commission. Instead many suggested to strengthening existing laws to stop atrocity against women throughout the country.

Highlighting the enquiry into murder of Sister Valsa John in November last year in Pakur district in Jharkhand, allegedly by the mining mafia, a fortnightly has reported," encountered with a senior police officer, who said, in connection with the rape of a tribal women, who was an associate of the nun and perhaps a witness to the murder, that police frequently did not register first information report in such cases. Worse, he said that rape was common among tribal people, the commission took an adverse view of the officer's comments and recommended that its observation be entered in the confidential service reports." But Jharkhand government led by BJP's Arjun Munda is yet to take any measures on this score.

The way entire thing happened in Assam has become a blot on the face of eastern states' cities like—Guwahati. As per Crime Records Bureau figures, Assam has witnessed 11,503 crime against women—domestic violence—5,745, abduction—2,998 and rape—2,011. A young Congress MLA Rumi Nath of Assam Assembly was assaulted by a mob in June 2012 in full public view only because she had married second time with her government appointed assistant. Another glaring instance has been reported from Gujarat where a woman member of Parliament from Dahod was mercilessly beaten up for raising her voice against police atrocity. Any was this is fiefdom of Narendra Modi, who does the things on his own whims!

According to the latest figures of the Crime Record Bureau (CRB), which is keeping a record of all crimes committed in India including those against women and children since 1953, released in June 2012 has disclosed that crime rates of all kinds have increased sharply, particularly against women and children in India. There have been 7.1 percent rises of crime against women from the year 2010. In 2011 alone, as many as 2, 28, 650 cases of crime against women had been registered in India. Of these numbers of crime, rape cases alone have 24,206, an increase of 9.2 percent from 2010. Maximum number of crimes against women have been reported from Triupura—37 percent, Assam—36.9 percent and Kerala—33.8 percent, Andhra Paredesh—33.4 percent, West Bengal—31.9 percent. Thanks to the efforts of Nagaland government, the state has lowest crime rate against women—1.9 percent. Only 38 cases have been reported in Nagaland.

Khaps and caste panchayats in western Uttar Pradesh, Haryana and a few parts of Punjab have different stories of atrocity on women. Recently a caste Panchayat in Baghpat district of Uttar Pradesh has declared a "farman" that the movement of women, specially young girl must be restricted within the village and also banned the use of mobile phones by them. Surprisingly a highly educated MP from the areas Jayant Chadhary of Rashtriya Lok Dal justified the dictum. It may be recalled that this district is represented by union minister Ajit Singh. Many of the political class demanded amendment in the Hindu Marriage Act to ban marriages in same gotra.

Women are also forced to die in the name of honour killing in India. The Prevention of Crime in Name of Honour and Tradition Bill—2010, prepared by Law Commission is still pending with the union government for enactment in the Parliament besides a host of bills, proposing several amendments to the Code of Criminal Procedure (CrPC) and the Indian Penal code (IPSC) for widening the ambit of the Acts relating to rapes and other atrocity on women are languishing. However, the Parliament has passed a bill—Protection of Children Against Sexual Offences Bill, raising the the age of consent from 16 to 18 has been enacted but many such bills to give equal right to women as well as protection against atrocity are still languishing. Although the Supreme Court had issued a guidelines against sexual harassment of women at their work place, the government is yet to enact the Bill—the Protection of Women Against Sexual harassment at Workplace bill, 2010. Because of such lethargic attitude of union government and different state governments, crime against women, filed under IPC and SLL, have gone up by 7.1 percent over 2010 and 23.4 percent over 2007. Economically advanced states are recording high rate of crime against women in comparison to poor states in the country.

Sharp increases of crime against women have been reported from West Bengal and Andhra Pradesh. Rise in rape cases is monumental in Madhya Pradesh, accounting for 14.1 percent of the total cases. In all India contexts, rape on girls under 14 constituted 10.6 percent of the victims and 19 percent are teen-aged girls between 14 to 18 years. Major victims, 54.7 percent are women in the age group of 18-30 years. At least 141 victims of rape are over 50 percent years kidnapping and abduction cases of of women and girls are highest of 19.4 percent in Uttar Pradesh. Dowry death figures are also increasing by leaps and bound in 2011 and of which major numbers are from Uttar Pradesh and Bihar. Torture case by cruelty of husband s have also increased by five percent—West Bengal has reported highest number of such cases in 2011. Incidents of molestation have also considerably risen—by 5.8 percent and Madhya Pradesh again has topped in such crime. Importation of girls have jumped by 122 percent—Madhya Pradesh has topped in this nefarious game followed by Bihar and Karnataka. Crimes under dowry prohibition have also increased by 27.7 percent while Andhra is at the top of the list, Karnataka comes in second ranking. Odisha leads in dowry killings—26.4 percent. In witchcraft killing Karnataka—has registered 32.1 rises. Dowry deaths have raised considerably-up by 25.8 percent over 2001. In 2011 Uttar Pradesh has registered highest number of cases while Bihar came second in dowry related deaths in the country.

Last but not the least abnormally low sex-ration has made the situation worse in the country, resulting into all kinds of crime against women in the country. But killings of girl child in womb have become common in the country. The Preconception and Pre-Natal Diagnostic Techniques Act is not being implemented strictly and also because of weak provisions in the Act, Out of 1165 cases filed across the country, only conviction have been awarded in 102 cases. No stringent law has been framed in this regards. Under such tardy manner almost all cases crime against women are being handled by the successive governments. Most vulnerable is dalit and adivasi women in the country. Comprehensive laws to deal against crimes on women are the need of the hour!

SOURCES: NCRB, Parliament and government Websites, NCWI websites, Assam and Jharkhand governments Websites, Women Organisations' Websites, Achieves of Rajya Sabha and Lok Sabha, Weekly—The Week, Fortnightly—The Frontline.

DEMOCRACY IN THE WORLD: RECENT CONTROVERSY OVER PRESIDENTIAL ELECTIONS IN INDIA!

Tuesday, 24 July 2012

No doubt democratic system of government is considered best form of government in the globe. Al least, even minority population has taste of power in the system—they rule their respective countries on the basis of majority share of votes—even less than stipulated qualified electorate get opportunity to exercise their franchise, Nowhere in the world countries hundred percent qualified electorate exercise their franchise. Even in the United States of America, vote percentage during elections remains terrible low. In India it is by land large 50 to 60 percent exercise of franchise! Therefore the democratic systems of governments throughout the world are called the government of minority of people in the respective countries—that is so in India also! But there must be safeguards to implement democratic system in true spirit—it should be matter of debate discussions throughout the Planet. But the system has many loopholes and demerits because present system lacks safeguard throughout the world where the democratic system prevail. But the system gives adequate opportunity to the people to speak about the government openly because of freedom of expression and also by misusings their rights and duties towards the respective Constitutions of the countries in the globe!

In the background of the recent elections of the President of India, many controversial things have come to the surface. Supporters and political class of the two respective contestants—Pranab Kumar Mukheerjee and Puran S Sangma have utilised their lungs power to malign both the contenders to their hilt.

Amid all these mud-slinging Congress—supported UPA candidate Pranab Kumar Mukherjee won the race by defeating Bhartiya Janata Party (BJP)—supported P A Sangma by the huge margins of votes of the electoral college, formed under the basis of the Indian constitutional provisions. But the controversy is yet to die down. Under Indian Constitution, the President is supposed to be custodian of the Constitution as titular head of the country. Mukherjee's road to magnificent Raisana hill, residential-cum-official residence called Rashtrapati Bhawan, constructed by British Raj has been cleared and now apart from best luxury and life style in the Rashtrapati Bhawan, Mukherjee will be entitled to use luxariest life-styles materials including one of the best luxury car—Mercedes Benz S600 (W221), Pullman guard crafted in Stuttgart, German, which is said to be the epitome of luxury. Thus from travelling in Ambassador Car, manufactured in Uttarapara in West Bengal during his tenure as minister in the Union government to the Mercedes Benz, epitome of luxary. Also from a mud house in a small village of Birbhum district in West Bengal, Pranab Kumar Kumar Mukherjee alias Paltu, will enter the best and luxuariest place on the earth—Rashtrapati Bhawan as first citizen of India in the next few days after his swearing in sprawling Parliament house to take over the titular post of Rashtrapati of Bharat from the outgoing President Pratibha Devi Singh Patil.

Much firework has been created on the Indian political scenes in the last two months. This is the way in India where lakhs of people die without food, medical assistance, proper education etc runs under so called democratic system of government and tax-payers and general public have to bear the burnt of their lively-hood at the cost of the comfort and luxury of President of India and also other class of ruling and opposition elites of the country.

In the process of the elections of the President, the credibility of political class has gone down to the drains. Both the candidates for the Presidential fights lack credibility, taking into account their past history of political life. Mukherjee's candidature has drawn much controversy because of his four-decade long political life, his role and priorities in political life. It first started with his controversial forged signature of Mukherjee on the resignation letter from holding the post of the Chairman of the Indian Statistical Institute before filing the nomination papers for the election to the post of the President. Non-congress opposition including BJP challenged his nomination paper on the ground of forged signature on resignation letter from the post of profit post and pressed for its rejection. Sangma, his rival also reiterated that

Pranab's nomination must be quashed and even threatened to challenge Mukherjee's election in the Supreme Court.

Notwithstanding many controversies had been witnessed since the elections Dr Rajendra Prasad as the first President of India, the ongoing controversies and stalemate over the candidature of Pranab Kumar Mukherjee has added new dimension of such things in the recently concluded Presidential elections. Various question marks were raised over Pranab's political career, which have captured the attention of media and public. These finger raising questions range between his decisions and actions during the Emergency (1975-77) to his oblique support to an industrial house, which has become a big corporate.

The Shah Commission, constituted by the Janata Party government at the centre to enquire into affairs during emergency of the Prime minister ship of Indira Gandhi, has, in clear term, indicted Pranab for "Cronyism" during emergency and not for cooperating with the commission. Mukherjee's action during emergency has raised doubt over his democratic credentials. The BJP leadership, while opposing his candidature, has alleged that Mukherjee had played active role in cooperating with Indira Gandhi for declaring emergency and also throttle democracy in the country. The Shah commission report, still in the achieves of the Union Government, said, "Although Shri Pranab Mukherjee assisted the commission at the preliminary stage of the fact-finding enquiry, he did not file any statement in the case, as was required to be done under Rule 5(2)(a) of the Commission of Inquiry (Central) Rules 1972. He had responded to the summons us 8B of the Commission of Inquiry Act, 1952. But he refused to take oath and tender evidence."

It is said that Pranab refused to depose before the commission on the directive of Indira Gandhi, showing disrespect to the law of the land. The Shah Commission dwelt at length about the "misdeeds" of Mukherjee right from his role in shacking T R Varadacharya as Chairman of the State Bank of India (SBI) without noting any reasons and appointing K C Puri as Chairman of the SBI, who was close adviser of Sanjay Gandhi. Pranab also indulged in harassing and targeting people, who were anti-congress during emergency as minister of state revenue under Indira Gandhi prime minister ship. Pranab was instrumental in raids on the houses of trade union leaders Prabhat Kar, D P Chadha, general secretary and president respectively of the All India Bank employees Association. Pranab's directive as union minister of state revenue in the Indira Gandhi government to arrest Gayatri Devi, former Rajmata of Gwalior, and Rajmata Vijaya Raje Scndia are still exactly remembered in political and administrative circles. Most criticised raids on Bajaj and Mukund groups in May 1976 on the instruction of Pranab are stll considered breach of power by him. Both the groups had openly supported anti-corruption campaign and movement of Sarvodaya of Jay Prakash Narayan, the Shah commission noted and added, "while these raids were being pursued by the ministry of revenue for tax evasion, no action was taken against two women, who were registered as shareholders in Maruti Limited, a Sanjay Gandhi venture, as their addresses could not be verified despite their names being in the defaulters list. Not only that enquiry against Maruti Limited were stopped abruptly during the emergency by Mukherjee,"

More over, after return to power by Indira Gandhi after the fall of Charan Singh government in 1980, Pranab was made Union Finance minister as a reward for his loyalty. Thereafter he shown undue favour to to a particular business house, Differential taxing system was introduced; practically ruining the Bombay Dyeing at the cost of some unknown business houses, which later on became the industry leader in 1980. Surprisingly, while defending UPA—two government when opposition charged it with inaction against the flow of black money recently, Pranab also tried to justify the controversial raids during emergency for curbing flow of black money outside India. His recent white paper on economy was simply a tokenism, which did not give any estimate of black money. Eminent journalist and researcher Pranjoy Guha Thakurta criticised Pranab and said, "The Finance minister acknowledges that the report was presented to comply with an assurance given in Parliament and that he would have been happy if he could have included the conclusions of reports of three premier institutions that have been tasked to quantify the magnitude of black money reports which are likely to be received by the end the year. The institutions include the National Institute of Public Finance and the policy that prepared a study on the black economy of India in 1985, which suggested that illegal income generation in India was not less than 18 percent of the country's gross domestic products (GDP). These findings were criticised by by the economists Suraj B. Gupata and Arun Kumar, both of whom suggested that the proportion was much higher at around 40 percent."

Not only that Team Anna has also launched tirade against Pranab and its one front-ranking leader Arwind Kejariwal has openly called Pranav "a thief" and described that victory of Pranab "shows black chapter of corrupt politician, taking over as President of India" Team Anna has also referred different deals during the defence minister ship of Paranab from 2004 to 2006. During his period, submarine deals are still being investigated by Central Bureau of Investigation (CBI). During his external affairs minister ship, rice scandal had taken place in which Ghana had accused Indian officials and ministers of corruption in export of rice. Pranab always worked to promote relations with imperialist and capitalist—United States of America during nuclear deal and forcing direct investment in the retail sector, many academics and economists have charged Pranab with supporting big corporate at the cost of livelihood of farmers and small businessmen.

Odisha chief minister openly spoke against the candidature of Pranab Mukherjee and charged him with distributing huge finances to Bihar, Uttar Pradesh and West Bengal governments with sole purpose to garner support from Bihar's chief minister Nitish Kumar, Mulayam Yadav's party Samajwadi Party and West Bengal's chief minister Mamta Bannergjee.

On the other hand, much mud was also thrown on Sangma during the electioneering. Many congress leaders described him "opportunist-remaining in Congress, deserting the party and joining Nationalist Congress Party and finally turning into anti-Congress parties like BJP, Biju Janata Dal and AIADMK" to put himself as Presidential candidate. Sangma has claimed that he is a candidate representing tribal interests but he never championed the causes of tribal during his political career. Interestingly his daughter Agathat Sangma, who is a NCP member of Lok Sabha, is minister in Manmohan Singh government. Interestingly she campaigned for her father during elections and voted to him defying her stature of being a minister and also NCP directive! Sangma's primary aim appears to join NDA in the 1914 Lok Sabha elections run-up because of his being a candidate o f BJP, Biju Janata Dal and AIADMK. Sangma is trying for a new political space by becoming unsuccessful presidential candidate.

Significantly, Presidential elections this time, although described most pitched fight and controversial, such controversies have not left previous President Elections untouched on the political scenes of India. First Presidential elections had also a lot of confrontation and controversies among ruling political leadership. Sardar Ballabh Bhai Patel had sponsored Dr Rajendra Prasad's name as first President of India while Pundit Jawahar Lal Nehru wished C. Rajgopalachari as first President. But Pundit Nehru had to succumb to majority views and Dr Rajendra

Prasad was elected first President of India. Like wise, serious rift emerged at the time of contest between V V Giri and Neelam Sanjiv Reddy in 1969 presidential elections during Indira Gandhi's regime—there were fight between "syndicate and indicate (syndicate led by old guards of Congress and Indicate led by traditional and progressive Congressmen led by Indira Gandhi)" Sanjeev Reddy, being the official candidate of the ruling Congress party had to lick the dust and V V Giri, who was independent candidate, unofficially supported by Indira Gandhi had won that elections. Subsequently the ruling Congress split-Congress led by Nijlinggappa ad Congress led by Indira Gandhi. Later Congress led by Nijlinggappa vanished and Indira Congress became official Congress party led by Indira Gandhi.

Finally, Mukherjee will be 13th President of India amid much-much controversy. In view of 1914 Lok Sabha elections, which appear to be hung Lok Sabha in view of resentment of against UPA led by Congress against corruption and price rise, role of Pranab Mukherjee will be keenly watched. Apart from that over 17 mercy petitions including of Mumbai bomb blast accused Kasab, waiting for death sentence, pending before the President and their disposal are also eagerly awaited During Pranab Mukherjee presidency although President has not much say over the matter as only after the advice of President can act and will have to ditto the government recommendation as per the Constitutional provisions. Of course people are afraid over neo-liberal views of Pranab Mukherjee?

Although Pratibha Devi Singh Patil's tenure did not have any political turmoil like earlier occasions, the controversy did not leave her untouched l. Her frequent foreign trips had attracted much criticism on which over Rs 700 crore were spent during her tenure. Apart from this her defence land wish in Pune from military lands also raised much resentment in the country and later she dropped the idea of taking such land from defence ministry for constructing post-retirement house in Pune.

SOURCE: Parliament proceedings, Shah Commission Report, Day-to-day newspapers and weekly magazines and fortnightly including Frontline, Achieves of South Block and North Block, Various sites on Internet.

OMINOUS SIGNAL FOR SECULARISM IN INDIA!

Saturday, 21 July 2012

Recent happenings in "Sangh Parivar", led by Rashtriya Swambsewak Sangh (RSS) exactly bring back to the memory of horror in India in the wake of Babari Masjid demolition and subsequent massacres of Muslims in riots throughout the country in late 1980s. Intense infighting, power struggle in the Bharatiya Janata Party (BJP) and its cohorts in the Sangh Pariwar, a strange development are taking place in the saffron party—BJP—a political wing of the RSS! There is a strange craze for bringing the Gujarat Chief minister and a Hindu fanatic Narendra Modi on the national forefront as prime ministerial candidate in the forthcoming Lok Sabha elections in 1914. It is a fact that Narendra Modi is capable of creating stir in uniting Hindu, particularly its youths throughout the country, thanks to the RSS—the BJP's progenitor, ideological mentor, political master and organisational gatekeeper. All these happenings will remind us how the Babari Masjid was demolished under the patronage of senior BJP leader Lal Krishna Advani in Ayodhaya, giving bad name to the secular fabric of India as well as insecurity among minority communities, particularly Muslims.

Only because of these developments, the BJP succeeded in uniting Hindu votes throughout the country and remained in power for over six years in the shape of National Democratic Alliance (NDA). Following the sad demolition of Babari Masjid in Ayodhaya, not only thousands of Muslims were killed in different places of the country but also rampant rise in terrorists activities, spearheaded by fanatic Muslim organisations in collaborations with the fanatic Muslims of the world resulted into killings of hundreds of persons in different bomb explosions in the country in the last 15 years. India continues to be a sensitive and has become more and more prone to terror activities.

Notwithstanding Narendra Modi cannot be forgotten for his dubious role and stigma of 2002 Gujarat riots in which thousands of Muslims were butchered with the tacit support of Modi as chief minister of Gujarat, the Hindu and Sangh Pariwar is giving weight to Modi because of his ability to encourage and incite party cadre as well as other wings of Sangh Pariwar through his demagoguery, his martial image and his vicious war-mongering rhetoric. An eminent columnist Praful Bidwai, in a recent article in an English fortnightly, has said, "Modi has become the BJP's membership's biggest hero to whom everyone must knot ow. But Modi has also proved himself petty-minded, parochial, egotistic, viciously self-serving and vindictive. Whether or not this is compatible with the stature of a national leader, the RSS seems to have decided that Modi is the winning horse; he must be backed."

More over May-24 and 25, 2012 meeting of the national executive of the BJP in Mumbai saw some emergence of "second generation" leadership in the BJP following the eclipse of Atal Behari Vajpayee and Lal Krishna Adavani's hold over the organisation. And the Mumbai meeting ended with Narendra Modi emerging as strong leader in the party, obviously for managing next general elections of the Lok Sabha. Taking into account the image of Modi among Hindu fanatics, the RSS has to digest many abnormal situations to placate him. If anybody goes by unprecedented welcome of Modi in Mumbai meeting, Modi's emergence as undisputed and uncontested leader of the BJP in recent past. The absence of L K Advani and Sushama Swarajya from the public meeting in Mumbai after national executive session, obviously to exptress their reservation over encouragement of Modi by Sangh Pariwar, particularly RSS remained symbolic and ineffectual.

Modi's gradual emergence at the national scene is not because of his exoneration by the Supreme court-appointed Special Investigation Team (SIT) under former director of the Central Bureau of Investigation (CBI) R K RAghavan for the massacre of 69 people including former member of Parliament Ahsan Jafari in the Gulbarg Society case or the so called hype about development in Gujarat under the stewardship of Modi. Rather many more hidden things are behind his propping up by Sangh Pariwar.—mainly that is internal dynamics, electoral calculations based on bulk of Hindu votes and also the Modi's ability to raise maximum funds for the party for spending in the next elections. Modi has rewarded the capitalists and industrialists with open arms in the recent years. Almost all industrialists and capitalists including Ambani Brothers,—Anil and Mukesh Ambanis, Sunil Bharati Mittal, Ratan Tata as well as home-grown businessmen—such as Gautam Adnani and Karsan Patel besides some big multinationals including Maruti Motors of Japan etc have welcomed Modi and praised him for giving them opportunity to set-up flourishing industrial units in his state In getting support from Modi, at least these big capitalists and industrialists have forgotten Modi's hands soiled with blood in communal carnage in Gujarat because Modi led Gujarat government have given them free hands, ignoring rule of law in the state! "They rather consider Modi most" ideal, next leader of India", Prafulla Bidwai said and added "these industrial magnates consider Modi as an inspiring leader with whom Gujarat is blessed, whose flawless execution of Gujarat development model."

Interestingly the scenes in Gujarat are not like that what are being painted. The official human development Report (2004) has said that the Gujarat has achieved only 48 percent of the targets set for human development. Gujarat's achievements on the front of illiteracy, education, health, nutrition, welfare and social security are much lower that than its gross domestic products growth rates. It has gone down in many sectors even the state is fourth rank of all states in percapita income in the country—, it has gone down at number-six in education and number nine in health care as well as its sex ratio is much below the national average. On malnutrition and hungers, the Gujarat has worse rankings. Amid tall claim of plenty of power, the electricity crisis is there in many parts of the state. Praful Bidwai, who has visited to Mundra in Kutch, where a huge 4,600 MW private power station exists and another 4000 MW is coming up. He has said that the zone have frequent power cuts.

In Mumbai's meeting, Modi was called "Gujarat Ka sher" (lion of Gujarat) and glorified as greatest leader of India. Praful Bidwai has said, "the Sangh Pariwar is looking for a quasi-fuehrer, the Supreme Leader, behind whom BJP cadres can rally in war-like formation—no matter how incompatible such bellicosity is with democratic process and how it vitiates India's social and political climate."

In my opinion such impending political scenes must be antagonising everybody; beieving secular, socialist, democratic republic in India. But the gambles of RSS goes how far depends on the maturity of the Indian electorate? It is definite facts that with the energence of Modi on the national political scene and his so called ability to mobilise Hindus of the country—there are many if and buts in giving him chance to rule the nation. Chances of a number of political allies like JD(U) led by its national president Sharad Yadav and Bihar chief minister Nitish Kumar alienating from Modi could not be ruled out.

But their past records have different story. If the past history of BJP-RSS combine's refusal to act against Modi for his role in carnage of Muslims in Gujarat during last NDA rule at the centre led by Atal Behari Vajpayee, is taken into consideration, except Lok Jan Shakti Party of Ram Bilas Paswan, who quit NDA to protest Gujarat riots, the JD(U) of Nitish Kumar, who is currently keeping Narendra Modi at a distance in his home state Bihar being BJP, a coalitoon partner of his government, had failed to speak against Modi or Gujarat riots or hold an enquiry into Godhara train burning as railway minister during those period. Now let us hope, this time Nitish Kumar is in stroneger position and to woe Muslims, his JD(U) may desert NDA if Narebdra Bhai plunges in national politics as Sangh Pariwar's prime ministerial candidate in next Lok sabha elections. Nitish Kumar himself claims as prime ministerial nominee on behalf of NDA for next Lok Sabha elections.

But for that Sangh Pariwar may make alternative arrangements like aligning with AIDMK of Jayalalitha, Biju Janata Dal of Navin Patnaik, TDP of Chandrabanu Naidu, Bahujan Samajwadi Party of Mayawati, TC of West Bengal chief minister mercurial Mamata Bannerjee and floating parties like National Conference of Adbdulla and Assam Gon Parishad, Janata Dal (Secular) of Deve Gowda as they had been in the NDA rule in 1998-2004 led by the BJP or alingned with Sangh Pariwar this way or that way in case Narendra Modi succeeds in emerging Sangh Pariwar's BJP as largest party in the next:Lok Sabha elections!

But strong secular parties like left parties including CPI, CPM, etc as well as Rashtriya Janata Dal of Laloo Prasad Yadav, Samajwadi Party of Mulayam singh Yadav, which had been all opposed to NDA during its rule in the country, are already there to counter such move. And the Congress is itself gear its loins to face Narendra Modi's onslaughts lock, stock and barrel. And of all there may be polarisation of votes of minority communities, particularly Muslims against Hindu fanatics' mobilisation in the country under the leadership of Narendra Bhai Modi.

Muslims account of 13.4 percent votes of total population of the country. All minorities together constitute 18.4 percent— (Christian—2.3pc; Sikh—1.90 pc, Buddhist—08 pc, Parasi—0.00/pc. Over 100 districts have Muslims largest population. Will these populations will remain silent spectators in case of fire-balling of Narendra Modi during next elections under the patronage of Sangh and Hindu Pariwar? Will not Narendra Bhai Modi be isolated for destroying secular fabric of the Indian democracy? How far RSS gamble to put Narendra Modi will succeed in view of ignoring top-ranking BJP leaddrs in the country?

WOMEN OF THE GLOBE BECOMING MOST VULNERABLE!

Friday, 20 July 2012

There are many sad tales of women in India! But women of the world are also not safe in many countries. Atrocities, harrassments of women are gradually increasing in many nations of the world. Recently, I have put a topic on my blog, headlined "Wave of Violence Swallow Women in Mexico" where rate of attacks and killings of women have risen sharply. Women are killed indiscriminately in Mexico out of gelousy and gang-warfares, aflicting by drug menace. But the pictures are not so rosey in other parts of the world. In India, women are still considered second class citizens whereas the Constitution of India provides equal right to all human beings. Rapes, murders, dowry deaths, denigeration of women in India have become order of the day. Recent example is in Gauhati in Assam where a girl was raped by some influential people after abducting her from busy thorough-fare in full view of the public. Such incidents in different parts of the India are not new. One must be aware about bull-dozing of reservation to women in Parliament and state assemblies. Definitely the women reservation proportion must be on caste basis. Deprived women of deprived caste and community must be given quota in reservation to women in the Indian context. In some countries, women are tortured and harrassed for not giving births to more than one child. And in India such situation is gradually being forced upon and women are being told to give birth to only two child otherwise they will be deprived to government facilities including representing the prople in panchayat, local bodies, Parliament and state assemblies. Male dominance in India is still forcing the women to lead their lives under the thumb of males!

A recent harrowing tale of forced anbortion in to a seven-month-old fetus in a hospital in Shaanxi Province has practically shocked the men-kind. Not only that, under one child policy in China, women are forced to abort the second child with tacit pressure of Chinese government and its officials. According to a recent report in The New York Times;as well as score of internet surfings; it has come to light how cruelty in forcing abortion are taking deep root in China. Women of China are under lot of pressure and they are guard by officials and security forces when they come for delivery of child in different hospitals of the country. The women—Fen Jiannei had been in a country hospital in Shaanxi province since her a girl child was stillborn after officials induced labour pains on June 02, 2012. Her sister-in-law said that her brother Ms Feng's husband—was beaten last week by loca l officials on some flimsy pretext and described him "traitor", obviously for second child. The reported harrassment came despite the fact that local officials were punished for the forced abortion after a photograph of bed-ridden mother and bloody fetus was posted on the internet in mid-June.

Xinhua, the strate news agency of China, had reported that after investigation, two-conutry level or lower officials were fired and five others received warnings or demerits, The New York Times report said and added that however the woman was provided subsidy. Even than, the topics of forced abortion became matter of intense discussions on the internet. Hu Xijin, chief editor of the Golabal Times, a state run newspaper that often prints nationalistic editorials wrote on his microblog on June 12, 2012 that what Ms Feng had endured was "barbaric. We should promote civilised fsamily planning. However, I am against using this one incident to reject China's family planning policy. Family Planning has saved China rather than harmed it."

The New York report says, "In a telephonic interview Ms Feng, whose voice filled with exhauaution, says, my body is slowly recorvering. I still have headaches. I am not allowed to leave hospital. The hospital is bringing food three times a day, the food is okay. But I feel I am under lot of pressures." Ms Feng is in the hospital with her five-year-old daughter and sister-in-law Deng Jicai-her husband is missing since a few days back to talk to officials. Family is from Yuping in Zengijia, township of Zhenping country.

CicChinese state media has reported that local officers had visited Ms Feng and apologised to her. On the opther hand Mr Deng, who tried to go to Beijing to see a cibil right lawyer, sat for an interview, he was stoppedby men in cars and beaten up Ms Deng alleged.

After forced abortion, Mr Deng opened a microblog account and began recounting family's ordeal. In between, he was abducted by the family planning officials after he refused to pay fine $6,300 for the second pregnancy to his wife.

ICELAND TOPMOST PECAEFUL COUNTRY IN THE WORLD: INDIA RANKS 142 POSITION OF 158 NATIONS SURVEYED!

Wednesday, 18 July 2012

Mahatma Gandhi's truth and non-violence has still a big meaning a small country in the Planet!, known as Iceland, is the "most pecaeceful country in the world". Whereas Afganistan, Sudan, Iraq, and the Democractic Repoublic of Congo are most crime-prone and violent countries in the world. India ranks 142 worse than China, Italy, United Kingdom, Cuba, Indonesia, Nepal, Bangla Desh, Iran, etc, according to an authenticated survey under Global Peace Index (GPI), published by the Institute of Economics and Peace (IEP).

According to GPI; peacefulness has returned to approximately the level seen in 2007 butmeasures of peacefulness have improved, There has been rise in "internal conflicts". This is particularly noticeable in the rise in fatalities from terrorists'acts which have more than trebled since 2003 in many of the 158 nations surveyed. The indicators range from a nation's level of military expenditure to its relations with me neieghbouring countries and the level of respect for human rights. The index has been tested against a range of potential "driven" determines of peace, including level of democracy and transparency, education, and national well beings. The index also finds the monetery cvalue of peace, they estimate that if the world had been completely peaceful in 2011—equal to the size of Germany and Japan's economic combined!

The smallest population of any NATO member state—Iceland is elusive country, which state of affairs known as peace on the earth. Iceland is one of the best progressive nations on the Planet: its welfare system offers health and higher education for each of its 320,000 citizens. Significantly Iceland is the fiirst country in the world to legalise gay marriage. While the country has hit some thin ice—in 2008 it basically went bankrupt, promoting public riots and in 2010, an unprecedented

Icelandic volcano wreked travelchaos across the north Atrlantic—its general repetation as a pleasant environment put it number one on the list. Iceland is followed by Denmark and New Zealand, which tied best second place in peacefulness in the globe.

Out of 158 countries listed, the war-torn East Africaan nations of Somalia came in dead last while Syria, which the UN says has developed into civil war, dropped more than 30 places in the rankings. "Iceland is once again ranked the most peaceful country in the world followed by Denmark and New Zealand while Suyria has biggest drop in margin failing over 30 places to be placed at 147th. The UK has fallen three places behind to the 29th position, meaning it is the first year the U K placement has not risen in the list. The top fallers are Syria, Egypt, Tunisia, Oman and Malawi. The Middle East is now amongst one of the least poeaceful countries reflecting the turbulence and instablity created by events of the Arab Springs.

Sri Lanka, Zimbabe, Bhutan Guyuna and Phillipines are the top five risers on GPI—2012 including three of the top five rises. Asia's pacific region's overall score improved by the greatest extent from 2011. However India has slipped to 142 positions from its earlier score of 136, 128, 122 in the preeeding years in respect of peacefulness and at the same time rise in criminal activities!

Accotding Steve Killilea of the IEP; Afganistan, Sudan, Iraq and Democratic Republic of Congo make up the bottom five. Sub-Saharan Africa is no longer the least peaceful region in the world for the first time GPI began. Situuation in China is also not good. Currently, the China is at 89th position in comparision to its earlier rankings in the preeedings years.

A crime rate in the United States has also increased sharply. Currently it is ranked 88 positions. But reports, emanating from the US; the killing rises sharply in its prestigious city—Chicago by 38 percent per year. Chicago is considred third largest cities in the US-there homicides are up by 38 percent a year ago and shhoting incidents have also risen considerably. However, killing is steady or dropped in New York, Los Angles and some other important cities. As of June, 17240 people have been killed here in the United States this year, mostly in the shooting incidents, 66 more than the corresponding period in the same period in 2011. Chicago is located magnificently near Magnificent Miles near the Lincon Park. All these criminal actvities in Chicago are because of gasngwarfare!

While Iceland is number one peaceful country in the world, Japan's rank five, Austria—sixth Czech Republic—13, German—15, Bhutan—19, Malaysia—20, Australia—22, Singapore—23, UK—29, Italy—38, France—40, South Korea—42, United Arab Emirates—46, Kuwait—47, Indonesia—63, Cuba—70, Greece—77, Nepal—80, Barazil—83, US—88, China—89, Bangala Desh—91, Saudi Araboia—106, Egypyt—111, South Africa—127, Iran—128, India—142, Syria—147, North Korea—153, Iraq—155, Afganistan—157, Somalia—159 (These figures of rankings do not include all 158 surveyed nationss).

MUSLIMS IN THE GLOBE VIS-A-VIS IN INDIA!

Tuesday, 17 July 2012

I must talk about Muslims! Sadly, Muslims in the world are called terrorists in view of large scale terror activities in a number of nations in the world. Strange situations are prevailing in the world countries, the entire Muslims community are feeling themselves isolated and unsafe despite the facts that Islamic religion has best tenants in the globe as well as their cultural and literary contributions have great impact. There are general perceptions that the community is being used for enlightened self-interests throughout the globe, particularly in India!

In this nefarious game, the super powers of the world have played sinister games for using and misusing Muslims countries in the world. And after their enlightened self-interest, these super powers have discarded them and given them bad names. It all started about one hundred years ago when Europe and America had come in the Gulf and Arab World as well as Muslim-dominated countries to discover oil. In the process, they grabbed not only their prime natural resources but also imposed upon them their supremacy. America has surpassed in these misdeeds! Except Iran most of the Muslim-dominated gulf and oil countries of the planet had fallen in the traps of America and Europe!

Later they started playing each other Muslim countries against each other. Such story is old—but happenings of about 20 years exaggerated the problems for Muslim community in various nations, dominated by them. To gain economic power bases in the oil countries, America and Europe did not lag behind in maligning the community. In the process, they played their games to instigate Iraq against Iran, Pakistan against India and Afghanistan, Afghanistan against Russia, formerly USSR and many other Muslim countries against each other. Osama bin Laden was made a king-pin by America to create anarchism throughout the world.

And later after serving its interest, America sent Osama in the waste paper baskets.

One must know that unethical and bad practise do not exist for long. Osama finding himself and the Muslim community in lurches as well as being disgusted with the attitude of Europe and America definitely incited their community for revenge mainly because of denigratin their community in the eyes of the world. From there Taliban, a dreaded terrorists' organisation was formed and its activities spread in the entire world. America was taught a lesson. Taliban under the leadership of Osama Bin Laden meticulously planned attacks on important centres including WORLD TRADE Centre in America and not only ruined these centres but gave warning signal to US and Europe that Muslims community are not going to tolerate denigration of community more now. Thereafter many terror activities, initiated by Muslim terror organisations were given shapes and many nations including India and even Muslim countries like Pakistan were made targets. Much have happened in different parts of the globe.

Such circumstances made Muslims as a whole suspicious in the eyes of the world. Although Muslims are considered one of the largest contingents in respect of populations in the planet, natural resources as well as cultural heritage in the world, today they are finding themselves in helpless situation and crazing for space to spread their influences And because of that, I strongly feel, they have adopted the path of terror to show their might and also in an effort to restore their glorious past.

A recent two parts write up, published in the fortnightly of India— The Frontline, by an independent Pakistani writer Raza Naeem on the 100th birth anniversary of well-known Pakistani Urdu writer Saadat Hasan Manto has dwelt at length not only the contributions of Manto but also exposition of America by him to the Muslim world, particularly Pakistan in the past years. For elaborating his points on Manto, the writer has referred beautiful few lines written Majjeed Amjad in Manto, "I have seen him; on the cleanest roads in a dust covered amazement; in the gathering storm of blind, overturned cups; when he says throwing away the empty bottle: O World! Your beauty is ugliness; then the world stares back at him."

Discrimination to Muslims is reminiscent since long. Here we must mention, Raza Naeem, who has written about Manto for his plain speaking and writings. Raza says, "A collection of Manto's stories, essays and sketches translated into English, by his nephew Hamid Jalal just a year after his death was quickly censored and withdrawn from circulation. Looking at the list of some of the luminaries who received the Nobel Prize in Literature between 1936 and 1955—the period of Manto's intellectual efflorescence—one can feel sorry that some unknown such as Roger Martin du Gard, Frans Eemil Sillanpaa, Johannes Vilhelm Jensen, Par Fabian Lagerkvist and even Francois Mauriac received the award and Manto did not. It would have been a different story had Jalal's translations reached the Nobel Committee samizdat (and Manto would surely have heartily approved if the long arms "Uncle Sam had taken some time off from something democracy in Pakistan to help smuggle these to Oslo, as happened later in Aleksandr Solzhenitsyn's case. But may be Manto was on the wrong side of the Cold War). Surely, Winston Churchill, one of the history's greatest warmongers and 1953 Nobel laureate in Literature, might have been overlooked in favour of Manto that year for it was the irresponsible policy instituted under Churchil's leadership that led to blood bath of Partition and deaths of close to 1.5 million people and which Manto the consummate artist he was; he was perfect example how poetic justice would have ideally been served. And Manto would have been a worthy successor to the only prior winner from the subcontinent of the Nobel Prize in Literature, Sir Rabindra Nath Tagore . . . ."

Such discrimination to Muslim, in the words of Manto himself, in a satirical short story titled "Progressive", in which Manto assailed the notion of progressive writing as not having any relation to real life, he elaborates on his definition in the follow-up following words: "Amrit Kaur asked," what is this dreaded progressiveness? Joginder Singh gave his head slight movement along with his turban and replied:" Progressiveness—you wont understand its meaning straight way. A Progressive is one who likes progress. It as a Persian word, In English a progressive is known as radical; those short story writer who want progress in story writing; they are known as progressive story writer. At this moment in India there are only three or four Progressive story writers, of whom, I am one . . . ."

Not only that Manto lamented in his Letters to Uncle Sam" depicting about creating hegemony by Europe and America in the Muslim world to destroy their culture, history, economy as well as using Muslims to serve their interest!Manto has also blamed Pakistan and Muslim countries Mullahs, who were openly and shamelessly adopting pro-American. Manto, in critical but straight forward writings, had offered some of equally subversive remedies for America's financial crisis, remarkably prescient if one look at the state of affairs of that country today as well as of Europe . . . ." Raza adds.

Without shedding light on horror of India-Pakistan partition on the eve of independence, now one must see the plight of Muslims in India. In both partitioned countries—India and Pakistan—minority community, Hindu in Pakistan and Muslims in India are continuous victims of atrocity by the majority people in their respective countries. In India, Muslims are always used as vote banks by almost all political classes. After vote, they are neglected like anything and nothing tangible is done to improve their deteriorating living condition! Here I must elaborate a few facts about discrimination to Muslims in India, pushing them to terror activities under the umbrella of various terror organisations. In India, there were many commissions and committees were formed since independence to ameliorate the living conditions of Muslims. Last but not the least we must refer the Sachchar Committee report, from which many measures were implemented by India and various state governments to salvage the pitiable conditions of Muslims in India without any fruitful results.

Even today Muslims are worse neglected lot in India! They even lack basic humane facilities—what to speak of education, health etc. For this reasons appeared divisive forces in India like Saffron brigade led by Rashtriya Swawm Sevak Sangh (RSS). After independence it all started with demolition of historic Babari Masjid in Ayodhaya led by senior Bhartiya Janata Party leader and prime ministerial aspirant Lal Krishna Advani and subsequent Hindu-Muslim riots in different parts of the country. There are a nother gruesome communal riots in Gujarat under the chief minister ship of Narendra Bhai Modi (he continues to get heroes welcome by majority sections of fanatic Hindu led by saffron brigades). Practically various towns and cities as well as urban areas and rural areas of India witnessed bloodbath. In Mumbai alone, the attack was organised by Shiv Sena, a Hindu organisation under the patronage of RSS. Truth and non-violence preached by the Father of The Nation Mahatma failed to click!

Since 1967, 58 major riots were witnessed in different parts of India in which Muslims remained the worst victims. It happened like this: ten communal riots in south; 12 in east, 16 west, and 20 north India. Total death toll in these communal riots remained 12,829 (official figures— but unofficial figures count them over 25,000) death figure region-wise are like this:—south—597, west—3426, east 35 81and north—5274. In Gujarat alone over 2500 Muslims were butchered under Modi's patronage!

For all these killings of Muslims, one must blame Hindu fanaticism!

As I belong to Bihar—I think I must mention communal riots in Bihar also. First communal riot took place in Bihar in August 1967 (183 illed); Jameshedpur—April 1979—120 killed; Biharshariff—August 1981—80 killed; October 1989 Bhaglpur—1161 killed, October 1990—Patna, state capital of Bihar—18 killed, October 1992—Sitamarhi—44 killed, March 200—Biharsharif—(Nalanda)—eight killed. These are official figures of killings—but unofficial figures count the death of more than 3000. Except a few most of the killings were of Muslims. Moreover Muslims, perhaps of their neglect and isolation among world community, are becoming terrorists under Muslims' fanatic organisations either to restore their condition or to grab their lost supremacy, once mattered in the world!

BUDDHISM: WHAT A WONDERFUL RELIGION IN THE WORLD?

Friday, 6 July 2012

"Buddhism had started at a time of social and spiritual revival and reforms in India. It infused the breath of new life in the people, it tapped new sources of popular strength and released new talent and capacity for the leadership. Under the Imperial patronage of Ashoka it spread rapidly and became the dominant religion of India. It spread also to other countries and there was a constant stream of learned Buddha scholars going abroad from India and coming to India. This stream continued for many centuries. Buddhism influenced Indian life in hundred ways, as it was bound to, for it must be remembered that it was a living, dynamic and wide-spread religion in India for over a thousand years. Even in the long years of its decline in India, and when later it practically ceases to count as a separate religion here, much of it remained as a part of the Hindu faith and in the national ways of life and thought—"Pundit Jawahar Lal Nehru in his book Discovery of India, written in 1940s in the Ahmednagar fort Prison Camp.

With these few lines about Lord Buddha are not only the faith and relevance of Buddhism in India and the major parts of the Planet but are shining for salvation of human beings. To supplement the contention of Buddhism, I must refer about Mahatma Buddh as narrated by A L Basham, in his book The Wonder That Was India—"one night Mahamaya, chief queen of Suddhodhana, king of Sakyas, dreamt that she was carried away to the lake Anavatapta in the Himalayas, where she was bathed by the heavenly guardians of the four quarters of the Universe. A great white elephant with a lotus flower in his trunk approached her and entered her side (pl23c) Next day the dream was interpreted for her by wise men—she had conceived a wonderful son, who would be either Universal Emperor or a Universal Teacher. The child was born in a grove of Sal trees, called Lummbini, near the capital of Sakyas, Kapil Vastu, while his mother was on way to her parents' home for her confinement. At birth he stood upright, took seven strides, and spoke, "This is my last birth—henceforth there is no more birth for me" The Boy was named Siddhartha at a great ceremony of his fifth from his birth. His gotra name was Gautam (in Pali Gotama by which he is commonly referred to in Buddhist literature).

It is said that Gautam was born and brought up, lived and died as a Hindu because much of his thoughts, which could not be found in one or other orthodox system and a great deal of morality could be matched from earlier or later Hindu books. Pundit Nehriu had said in his book Discovery Of India, "The Buddha story attracted me even in early boyhood, and I was drawn to the young Siddhartha, who, after many struggles and pain and torment, was to develop into the Buddha. I liked to visit the many places connected with the Buddha legend, some time making a detour for the purpose. Most of these places lie in my province or not far from it. Here (on the Nepal frontier) Buddha was born, here he was wandered here (at Gaya in Bihar) he sat under the Boddhi tree and gained enlightenment, here he preached his first sermon, here he died—"

His wonderful preachings captured the imaginations of intellectuals and it went deep down into hearts of people "go unto all lands", Buddhas had said to his disciples and preach the gospel. Tell them that poor and lowly, the rich and the high are all one and that all caste unite in this religion as do the rivers in the sea. "Buddha's message was one of the universal benevolence, for love for all. For "never in this world does hatred cease to hatred; hared ceases by love." And "let a man overcome anger by kindness, evil by good. One may overcome a thousand men in battle but he who conquers himself is the greatest victor. Not by birth, but by his conduct alone, does a man became a low caste or a Barhmin" Even a sinner must not be condemned for who would willingly use hard speech to those who have done a sinful deed, strewing salt, as it were, upon the wound of their fault? Victory itself over another leads to unhappy consequences—"victory breeds hatred, for the conquered is unhappy."

What ever may be the reasons all these preachings are not at all based on any religions as well as without any references to God or another world. His teachings are based on reasoning and logic and experience. Buddha had asked people to find exact truth from his own heart. Ignorance of truth is cause of all the miseries. In my opinion and experts view on Buddhism religion, Buddha has referred about pain and suffering in life and given us "Four Nobel Truths", which mainly concerned with sufferings and its causes, the way to end it and the way to do it. Once Buddha has reportedly told his disciples, ""and while ye experienced this (sorrow) through long ages, more tears have flowed from you and have been shed by you, while ye strayed and wandered on this pilgrimage (of Life) and sorrowed and wept, because that was your portion which ye abhorred, and that which ye loved was not your portion, than all the water, which is in the four great oceans."

On such preachings of Buddha, Pundit Nehru has described in his book, "—Discovery of India," Through an ending of this state of sufferings is reached Nirvan. As to what Nirvana is, people differ, for it is impossible to describe a transcendental state in our inadequate language and in terms of the concepts of our limited minds. Some say it is just extinction, a blowing out. And Buddhas is reported to have denied this and to have indicated that it was an intense kind of activity. It was the extinction of false desire, and not just annihilation, but it cannot be described by us except in negative term. Buddha's way was the middle path, between the extreme of self-indulgence and self-mortification. From his own experiences of mortification of the body, he said that a person, who has lost his strength cannot progress along the right path . . . . Buddha told his disciples what he thought they could understand and live up to. His teaching was not meant to be a full of explanation of everything, a complete revelation of all that is. Once, it is said, he took some dry leaves in his hand and asked his favourite disciple, Anand, to tell him whether there were any other leaves besides those in his hands. Anand replied: "the leaves of autumn are falling on all sides and there are more them than can be numbered." Then Buddha said: "in like manner I have given you a handful of truths, but besides these there are many thousands of other truths, more than can be numbered."

Thus Buddha's teachings spread far and wide in the globe thanks to the efforts of Maurayan empire—ChandraGupta's grand son Ashoka, Ashoka, being disgusted by killings of thousands of people in Kaling war; he decided to abandon warfare in the full tide of victory. His mind turned under the influence of Buddha's gospel and he embraced Buddhism. Ashoka got carved numerous of edicts of Buddha in rock and metal and they conveyed his message not only to his people but to posterity. Ashoka himself devoted himself to the spread of Buddha's teachings. Buddhism spread rapidly from in India from Kashmir to Ceylon. It penetrated into Nepal and reached to Tibet, China and Mongolia. During those days, one of the consequences of this was the growth of vegetarianism and abstention from alcoholism drinks. Animal sacrifice was forbidden. There are many Ashoka's famous many-pillared hall in his palace at Pataliputra in Patna in Bihar was partly dug out by archaeologist about thirty years back.

A l Basham has referred in his book, "for over 40 years the reputation of Buddha grew and the sangha (literally society, the Buddhas Order) increased in number of influence. The end of Buddha came at the age of eighty years. He spent the last rainy season of his life near the city of Vaishali and after the rains he and his followers journeyed northwards to the hill country, which had been Buddhists home of his youth. On the day he prepared his disciples for his death, he told them that his body was now like a worn-out cart, creaking at every joint. He declared that he had made no distinction between exoteric and exoteric teaching but had preached the full doctrine (dharma). At Pawa he was entertained by a lay disciple, Cunda, the smith and ate a meal of pork. Soon after that he was attacked by dysentery but he insisted on moving on to the nearby town of Kusinagara. Here on the outskirts of the town he laid down under a sal tree and that night he died. His last words were: all composite things decay strives diligently!" to them.

Buddha died but his religion still is far and wide in the world although some deformities had come out at later stage. To counter Buddhism, Shankaracharya, one of the greatest of India's philosopher, reportedly started religious order of or math for Hindu sanyasis or monks to counter Buddhiosm!. According to Pundit Nehru in his book; this was an adoption of old Buddha practise of the Sangha. Previously there had been no such organisatons of sanyasis in Brahminism although small group of them existed. Some degraded form of Buddhism continued in East Bengal and in the Sind in the north-west. Otherwise Buddhism gradually vanished from India as a widespread religion. But before his death Shakracharya also admitted the importance of Buddhism and reportedly excused to counter the Buddhism.

Hardly, three to four percent populations of Indian are Buddhist religion followers. On the other hand, the teachings of Buddha and Buddhism religion are spreading not only entire South-east Asia but entire Asia and many parts of Europe and America. According to an Opinion piece, written by famous author of "My life in the middle ages: A survivor's Tale: James Atlas in New York Times recently; Buddhism is the fourth largest religion in the United States of America.

More Americans converts to Buddhism than to monrmonism (think about it Mitt). Dr Paul D Numrich, a professor of the World Religion and Inter-religion Relations, conjectured that there may be as many Buddhist as Muslims in the United States by now. Thomas A Tweed in "the Anerucaan with Buddhism," refers as "nightstand Buddhists"—mostly catholics, Jews (yeah I know Juddihists) and refugee from other religion who keep a stack (Prema choldron books besides their beds). Perhaps Buddhism is our current mind-body obsession. Dr Andrew Weil, in his book, Spontaneous Happiness, establishes a relationship between Buddhist practise and the developing integrative model of mental health". This connection is worth documented at the laboratory for affective neuroscience at the university the Wisconsin, researchers found that Buddhist meditation practise can change the structure of our mind—which we know from numerous clinical studies, can change our physiology. The mindful awareness research centre, at UCLA is collecting data in the new field of "mindfulness-based cognitive therapy" that shows a positive correlation between the therapy and what a centre co-director, Dr S Daniel Siegel, calls mind sight. He writes of developing an ability to focus on our internal world that "we can use to re-sculpt our neutral pathways, stimulating the growth of areas that are crucial to mental health."

"I felt this happening during my four-day retreat. Each day, we sat for hours as bees hummed beyond the screened windows of the meditation room, it was hard to concentrate at first, as anyone who had tried meditating knows: it requires toleration for the repetitive, inane—often boring—thoughts that float through self-observing consciousness (Buddhist the word use the word "mindfulness to describe the process; if it some times felt more like mindlessness). but after a while, when the brass bawl was struck and we settled into silence, I found myself enveloped if only for a few moments in the calm emptiness of no-thought." the opinion writer said The writer has narrated experiences of attending a four-day meditation camp at Buddha religion camp at Vermont-Sakyong's "turning the Mind into Ally," about four hour drive from Manhattan. END

NITISH, MODI CRAZING FOR IMAGE BUILDING NOT DEVELOPING BIHAR AND GUJARAT?

Thursday, 5 July 2012

At least two chief ministers—Nitish Kumar of Bihar and Narendra Modi—in the country appear past-masters in building their own image not only in the name of the "so called development in their respective states but are reportedly projecting themselves as "so called real messiah of poor", obviously with their eyes fixed on the prime ministership of India in the wake of the Lok Sabha elections, scheduled in 2014. In the process, both of them were engaged in the war of attritions to malign each other. While Modi is blaming caste leadesrship mainly resonsible for Bihar's backardness, Nitish Kumar, accusing Modi of creating communal divide in the country, specially in Gujarat.

Amid the shrewdness of both these regional leaders, there are certain crude facts about their role in their respective states, which could raise eyebrows of people of the country. Both of them are claiming themselves as "vikash purush (Development men)" for bringing their respective states to new zenith. But recorded facts and statistics smashed the myths of "Vikash purush".

According to official records, the GDP growth increase rate in the country during the period between 1994-95 to 1999, which was 06.09 percent, was rose by on and average 07 percent during the period between 2001-2010.

Taking into consideration the average of national GDP increase in the past several years of India as a whole, the growth rate increase durng the same period like 1994-95 to 1999, the growth rate of Gujarat, which was eight percent, had increased to average 8.68 percent between 2001 to 2009-2010. Although Gujarat is considered a rapid developing and developed state since its bifurcation and inception from greater Bombay state, now Maharshtstra. Clearly during the rule of Gujarat chief Minister

Narendra Modi, the GDP, on and average, has increased by only point 68 percent in comparision to such figures of previous regime. Such is the one aspect of the so called "Vikash Purush" of Gujarat Narendra Bhai Modi.

More over such figure of Bihar under the stewardship of another so called "vikash Purush"—chief minister of Bihar Nitish Kumar—is also astounding! In between the period, the GDP of Bihar had clearly and definitely jumped to attractive level between the period 1994-95 to 1999, on and average, the GDP of Bihar was 4.70 percent. The GDP of Bihar surprisingly jumped to 8.02 percent during the period between 2001 to 2010. However these period should be shared by five years each by both Laloo-Rabari regime and the present chief minister Nitish Kumar.

During the same period, GDP of other states of the countryt also started jumping—Chhatishgarh (2.88 percent to 7.98 percent), Haryayana (5.96 percent to 8.95 percent), Uttarakhand (3.22 percent to 11.84 percent), Odisha (4.42 percent to 7.95 percent), Maharashtra (6.30 percent to 8.13 percent).

When this growth rate is taken into considerations, economic performances of other states were not bad in comparision to the "so called majic figure of GDP of Gujarat and Bihar". It does definitely mean that other states of the country are also developing at good pace but not like faster pace in Bihar and Gujarat. But Gujarat has long history of adequate development in the country unlike Bihar, which was considered a "Bimaru state" in the country.

According to Anand Pradhan, associate professor of the Indian Institute of Mass communication; the myth of Gujarat development is that its economic development and per person SDP, "sakal Gharelu utpad" had remained at the top in the country since long—not during the period of BJP of Narendra Modi's regime. Gujarat remained among the top of ten states in the country in the SDP zone per person in the last 40 years in the country. At some time Gujarat remained on fifth or sixth position and once at fourth places in comparison to top ten developed states of the country! Modi has not initiated a magic wand to improve Gujarat's GDP to beat Haryana, Punjab, Maharshtra, and Tamil Nadu like developed states in the field of the SDP per person. There are many instances of such myths of GDP growth in Gujarat.

With regards to Bihar, GDP increase during Nitish tenure, the increase rate is 2005-06—0.92 percent, 2006-2007—17.75 percent, 2007-2008—7.64 percent, 2008-2009—14.58 percent, 2009-2010—10.42 percent, 2010-2011—13.37 percent definitely looked like magic band—but these figures and statistics appear to be attractive art of presenting datas of GDP! In fact, according to Pradhan, Bihar's economic management had remained at the most small level, which is called "base effect" in Economics. Bihar's economy was at lower level and its increase level was also minimal as soon as the economy started looking up in Bihar; it started showing attractions in sudden increase level of GDP.

According to Pradhan; the economic management of Bihar and recent spurt in GDP appears to be unitary and have many anomalies— it meant that economic development in certain sectors has brought big jump in the GDP of Bihar. For example it must be noted down that sudden increase in the GDP in Bihar has taken place because of sudden boom in the construction of roads-bridges-real estate. Sharp increase in GDP has not toughed upon core sectors like agriculture, industry etc. Notably per capita income of in Bihar per person, which was Rs 8341 on and average in 2005-2006, has also sharply risen in 2010-11 by Rs 20069 per person!. If such per capita income is compared with developed states like Haryana, which has percapita income per person is Rs 92387, Punjab—67473, Maharshtra—Rs 83471, Tamil Nadu—Rs 72993, Bihar is far behind to these developed states. If such trend continued in respect of GDP growth anamoly, Bihar will take 20 years to reach at the level of developed states.

Sadly, Bihar has not developed in its GDP because of lack of industries, particularly manufacturing, primary sector agriculture, and creation of basic infrastructures in the field of electricity, which is in worse position presently. Farm sectors' economy is not upto mark because the Nitish government is reportedly not paying proper attention to this sector in view of its importance in rural areas and masses dependent on this serctor, economic experts lamented.

Lowest human index ratio in at l;east two states—Nitish Kumar's of Bihar and Gujarat's of Narendra Bhai Modi—have made little impact. Mascs in both states are still groaning under starvation, lack of proper fruits of poverty elimination programme, health, education, housing, employment etc Malnutrition and hunger are rampant in both Gujarat and Bihar as per reports of various international and national bodies like WHO, UNO as well as reports of union government. In this respect, Bihar is at the lowest ebb of three worse affected states in the country on these scores.

Pradhan, in his report to Hastak-kshep, has painted 'shameless situation on these scores in Gujarat". In the instances of hunger, Gujarat, which whose "Raja Narendra Modi "claims shining Gujarat, is on the lowest ebb as human index reports incomprision to other developed states. Gujarat is bracketed with Bihar and Odisha, where hungers among poor class are common. Gujarat is not better than even Uttar Preadesh where such incidents are very common with regards to human index figures!

Inequality and creation of regional imbalances as well as discrimination towards Muslims and adivasis dominated areas in respect of spreading development network. are said to be the main reasons of not reaching the fruits of development to these majority sections of society in Gujarat, the hman index reports of WHO and UN say., adding that in respect of malnutrition, Gujarat and Bihar surpassed all records to tackle hunger and malnutritions incomparision to other developed states. Thus the situation is far worse in both Bihar and Gujarat on these scores! Friuits of development are not reaching to Muslims and Adivasis in Gujarat because of discriminatory attitidue and "undeclared economic discriminatory economic policy of Narenbdra Bhai Modi government in Gujarat", said Pradhan.

Pradhan further highlighted the lacunae of both Nitish Kumar and NarendraModi and alleged that both the "self-styled stalwarts are encouraging no-liberal policy bypassing poor in their respective states, resulting into not percolating the fruits of GDP increases in their respective states to common masers. And both of them are engaged in putting the blames on union government to divert the attention of general masses towards these maladies".

While Nitish Kumar, who is said to be the main beneficiary of central assistance as per reports of India government in successive years, is harping continuously on "special status to the state", Modi is well set and accusing the union government of the UPA and its leadership for" ignoring the masses of the country and self-praising his extraordinary role in developing Gujarat to score his points among masses"! END

JUDICIAL ACTIVISM OR JUDICIAL ENTHUSIASM

Monday, 25 June 2012

Judicial activism and enthusiasm right from lower courts to the Supreme Court while delivering judgements have pushed the democracy and its legislatures and executive at the wit's end as well as loss to public exchequeres and as well as peoples' diminishing faiths in the judicial system!. Before I deliberate recent judgements of the Patna High Court, and lower courts ignoring the serious points of law and falacies in judgements, I must visit the the few overreach action of the Supreme Court in delivering judgements in the recent past.

At least some recent examples like Supreme Court pronuouncements of judgements in the interlinking of rivers and remission to Vodafone of over Rs 12000 crore as tax liabilities on the basis of an equally unprecedented transaction between Vodafone and Hutch, with a clear nexus to the sale of latter's assets in India. Like wise the Supreme Court judgement on interlinking of rivers is said to be direct interferences on the exective powers of the State. The old debate on the inter-linking of river idea revived by a February 27 directives of the Supreme Court of India to the central government to set up a special committee to ensure its implementation as priority. To many, this sounded like a clear case of judicial overreach, one setting a wrong precedent of the judiciary entering the executive domain!

The judgement of the Supreme Court, comprising the Chief Justice of India S H Kapadia, Justices Swantra Kumar and K S Radhakrishnan (Chief Justice Kapadia and Justice Swantra Kumar delivering one and Justice Radhakrishnan authoring second), in Vodafone case has recent ly set aside the Mumbai high court judgement in the case, which had directed with ample of reasons and law points the Vodafone to pay tax liability of Rs 1200 crore. In the back drop of Vodafone judgement by theSupreme Court, I want to mention a judgement of the the then

Supremecourt Judge O. Chinnappa Reddy in the MCdowell and Company Limited vrscommercial taxes officer (1985). Justice Reddy had referred, "We now live in welfare state whose finamcial need, if backed by the law, have to be respected and met. We must recognise that there is behind taxation laws as much moral sanctions as behind any other welfare legislation and it is pretence to say that avoidance of taxation in not unethical and that stands it stands on no law less moral plane than honest payment of taxations."

In my opoinion tax revenue are main sources of government's development initiatives currently when the government is in the grip of serious fund crunch, depriving citizens the right of to an adequate means of livelihood and to lessen the inequalities in income. Thus Supreme Court judgement in the Vodafone case on January 20, 2012 is an instance of lapses on the part of our judicial procedures and ignoring the interest of the country. There are many other things behind the scene judgement of the Supreme Court in between! Fingers are being raised on the partiality of judges in delivering judgement in the Vodafone case. Chief Justice Kapadia's son Hoshnar Kapadia was with Ernst and Young—a firm which advised Vodafone on its tax dispute after Vodafone's deal in 2007. He had joined E&Y India and not E&Y UK. It is also pointed out that that income tax depatrtment used the E&Y UK's report as evidence against Vodafione.

Prof Mohan Gopal, Director of the Rajiv Gandhi Institute of for Contemporary Studies (RGICS), New Delhi, has voiced concern over the likely implication of the Vodafone judgement for governance citing several well placed law points. Gopal, however, said that about the references of son of Chief justice Kapadia must be avoided at this stage in linking the judgement as chief justice Kapadia has a well deserved and hard-earned reputation for the highest integrity. On the other hand Prashant Bhushan senior advocate of the Supreme Court has also questioned the Judgement of SC in Vodafone case. Bhushan has put many facts about the integrity of judge's right from lower courts to apex court!

More over the Supreme Court judgement of on interlinking of rivers has also raised many eyebrows in the country. Interlinking of rivers will have many ill effects including environment, huge cost of over five lakh crore on the project and many hicuups by different state governments over their agreement in interlinking rivers of the country. Many of the legal experts have pointed out that judgements apart from usurping executive powers of the state, has also ignored the facts of many reports and diocuments of the past pros and cons in interlinking rivers. Intrestingly the SC judgement has itself pronounced reservations on interlinking of rivers by different state governments including Bihar, Karnataka, Punjab, Assam, Sikkim and many states like Kerala, Assam, Sikkim have have raised protests over interlinking of rivers on many grounds.

Significantly, the cost, which has been analyesd in the SC judgement on the project varies from Rs 4,44,331.20 crores and Rs 4, 34, 667 crore at the 2003-2004 price. Now it would escalates in over several crores if the project is implemented for inter-linking of rivers. It appears "dadagiri" of Supreme Court to implement the project and constitution of special committee, bypassing the union and state governments over the issues, many legal experts commented. The former secretary of the union ministry of Water resources Ramaswami R Iyer has criticised the interlinking of rivers. Iyer said, "It is pity that union government has not made its reservation clear to the Supreme Court.—if it would have stated opposition, the judgement would not have come in such manner. But it has not been done by the government because of political compulsion." Iyer has referred the reports of many committees including of K L Rao came up with Ganga-Cauvery linkk canal projects in 1972, Captain Dastur's Garland Canal project etc. The Centre for Science and Environment (CSE), New Delhi, a leading environmental organisation, has also opposed the idea of interlinking of rivers and has said, "This is delicious idea where water from flooded river basins can be divereted to dry river basins through canals and storage. While it may sound really good on paper, it is technically implausible." Since I will write further detailed story on all these issues later on. But taking into account the at least two recent judgements of the Supreme Court, I want to mention a few facts of judicial activism and enthusiasm in Bihar also. First I will deliberate the recent judgement of the Patna High court on Bathani Tola massacres of Dalits, which is well known facts.

A division bench of the Patna High court, comprising Justice Navneet Praad Singh and Justivce ashwani Kumar has set aside the judgement of the Arrah additional judge judgement, which had awarded capital punishments to three and life imprisionment to 20 accused persons on the ground of lack of evidence. The case of murdering 21 dalit persons including children and women in Bathani tola village under Bhojpur district by forward caste people is well known. It was in the knowledge of everybody. The Patna high court, which had found fault in evidences, should have instead of acquting all the accused persons, would have duirected the state government and its police for reinvestigation the case. But the court had failed and in extra enthusiasm, acquited all the accused persons, allegedly involved in the ghastly murders of youths! Another case in point is the recent judgement of the fast track—court of Judge Ram Darash for acquitting influential persons including Maharjganj MP Umashankar Singh of the Rashtriya Janata Dal and his son Jitendra Swami in a murder case when the matter of transfer of the case from the Ram Darsh's court was already pending in the Patna High court. Earlier the court of Darash had rejected the transfer plea. Thereafter, an appeal was filed in the Patna High court and it was under process of hearing. In the meantime, Fast track Court-1 Ram darsh has pronounced the judgement, acquitting the MP and his son. The Patna High court, however, took cognizance in the matter and directed the Judge to file a show-cause it appears a clear case of miscarriage of justice by the lower court! As regards other such judgemnents right from the district courts to the Patna high courts are very common in Bihar.

WAVE OF VIOLENCE SWALLOWS WOMEN IN MEXICO'S CIUDAD JUAREZ

Monday, 25 June 2012

When the entire planet is well set to give equal rights to women, a sad story about violences on women—killings, rapes etc have shocked international community. Such gruesome crimes are being taken place in Ciudad Juarez in Mexico for the last three years—wave of attacks beginning in the 1990s that left hundreds of women dead over the course of decades.

According to a report published in the New York Times recently; international attention moved on but the killings continued—the second wave larger than the first. Clusters of slain women are continuously being discovered. Roughly 60 women and girls have been killed so far this year—at least 100 are missing over the past two years. At least 304 were killed in 2010. More women killed in 2012—than any earlier year so called feminicide era.

"People have not reacted with the same force as before," said Gustavo de la Rosa, a human right investigator for Chihuahea—"they think it natural." In the wake of international pressure, authorities revealed that more of these killings are being solved. But arrest and conviction are exceedingly rare. For the victims found in mass grave in the Juarez valley—most details are still mystery—none knows how many women were buried there.

State authorities amid heaps of files of violence against women led by Helter Hawley, charged with documenting the crime scenes of the most of the women killed in Ciudad Juarez, the forensic investigator suggest, "it is more vulnerable group—these are the people we expect to see killed.", the New York Times reported.

Hawley has been working murder cases since 2003. He started specialising in women lkilling recent years, and in his views, the stunning tally of women killed is mostly caused by the increased local involvement in gangs and drugs, and jealous men. Often both gangs and jealousy come together in a single case. He opened a file on computer showing one of the 18 women killed in April photographs showed that she had been dumped in a public street and fund around 8 am "she was stabbed 63 times", Hawley said. Her pink shiort, featuring an image of heart, was stained with blood. Based on the number of stab wounds, he said, "The killer had to be on drug." He opened another file showing a woman shot dead at bottom of garbage pile." she was pregnant we think she owned her bosses money for something drug may be." He clicked through several other cases showing women young and old, mostly shot and killed at close range. He and his two of ingvestigators in his office said, they did not have any specific information about women found in the mass grave but they warned against seeing their deaths as the product of single cause. In Juarez, there is everything", Hawley said. There are jelous husbands, jelous father-in-laws—there are women killing women."

While exposing such heinous criminal activities, the Ney Yok Times points out that a government committee found a similar array of causes for the earlier wave of killings. Aftyer surveuying 155 killings of women out of 340 documented between 1993 and 2003, the committee found that roughly half of them were prompted by motives like domestic violence, robbery and gang wars while a little more than a third involved sexual assault.

Victims advocates, however, argue that the klilling of women found in the Valley fall on the more bizarre. Francisca Galvain, a lawyer, who has been working with the parents of missing girlss, said that Ms Gowaler's daughter, Parlo, 15, was last seen down-town talking to a middle-aged man around lunch time. Several other girls from the grave, along with some still missing have also disappeared from location thereby, Ms Galvain said.

First, there were just few bones and body parts found in valley beyond the sprawal of this wild city—at least four women killed and dumped, the authorities said. Dozen more bodies of women and girls were found. Most of them disappeared in 2009 and 2010; many were teen agers and good students. Idali Juache's mother still insists her daughter is missing although police inked her DNA to l fragrnments in the valley's grave. Elvira Gsnzalez said she felt what seemed like her daughter's spirit at home, before finding out she had been dumped in the grave. "I always believed she would be given back to us alive, I never believed this was how she would be brought back to us" she added to Ney York Times writer Damen Cave.

All were around same age and several looked very similar, posters hanging all over the city shows that they had long, straight dark hair and skimmy features." The authorities, they do not want to see the truth, she said, adding, "Life have just has so little values." Her own theory run the gamut; may be girls targeted for organs thefts, may be killers arrived as part as part of the surge in deportation that has sent through immigrants—criminals to Ciudad Juarez from America. Though it is unclear if the victims had been raped, she added, may be killing started as sexual assaults.

American officials in El Pavo said they were stalling their heads, too when during gangs were involved in high profile killing paid in firmness without call with tips. But not in the case the Juarez Valley grave.

Several mothers of missing girls said the prosecutors have refused to let them visit morgue, even as officials offered up complicity tallies for how many female bodies were held there. "They are liars," said Norma Laguna Labra, Idali's mother.

The incidents of killings of women in Mexico appear without any justice in ananarchy like Nation in the conteninet my opinion.

The New York Times report sums up the gruesome story with one liner conclusion—"all depends of justice on Law of God."

BIHAR IS KNOWN FOR BITTER FEUDAL-COMMUNAL MASSACRES IN INDIA!

Saturday, 23 June 2012

In the wake of the killing of known Rashtriya Swaymsewak Sangh supporter and the founder of dreaded Ranvir Sena, private militia of upper caste specially Bhumihars, Brahmeshwar Nath Singh alias Mukhiya in the Ara town by unknown assailants recently and subsequent violence in most of the districts in central Bihar and in Patna town areas by majority sections of Bhumihar caste men, if one remembers the conservatism and feudalism mindset in Bihar, right from the days of the British Raj to independent India, he will shiver how gruesome murders, atrocities, injustices etc have been inflicted on Dalits, backwards, Muslims, poor among forward caste etc in the last several years, specially after independence and in 1990s with rising backward caste movements as well as for their assertions of right under the Indian Constitution against the conventional feudal orders!

Organised violence and crimes by upper caste landlords are very common in Bihar. And it became a fashion in 1990s to eliminate as much of Dalits, Muslims, backwards and poor among upper caste in 1990s in Bihar! All these started when upper caste people felt threatened by the assertion of Dalits, Muslims, backwards, and poor during the regime of the Laloo-Rabari in Bihar, initially know pro-poor government, which gave voices to dalits, Muslims, backwards and poor etc. As these sections of deprived society started asserting for their rights and have raised voices against their suppression for long, the upper caste landlords raised their ugly heads to silence them for retaining their age-old supremacy in Bihar.

All these nefarious activities including a number of massacres and subsequently communal pogroms else where in the state were carried in Bihar under Ranvir Sena, militia organisation and saffron brigades under the patronage of Barhmeshwar Singh and the RSS leadership respectively. Most of them were taken place in 1990s, attracting the attention of countrymen and also the global community.

To make the point straight, I must point it out that land have remained' moot point of all these massacres Apart from that wages and social dignity to dalits as well as mobilisation of radical groups on these issues under constitutional frameworks have started giving agonising moments to feudal classes and they want to deprive the deprived lots from all these things to keep their hegemony intact! Prof Anand Chakarvarty, retired professor of the Delhi School of Economics in a a lecture on Bathani tola massacre accused acquittal by the Patna High court in New Delhi felt that real "reason for the massacre was the assertion of the under class was viewed as an act of defiance against the hierarchical class and caste order.". Prof Chakravarty is of the opinion that Bihar government today, for all its rhetoric, was actually deeply inimical to the economic, social and political entitlement of the oppressed classes that that there, the prospects of justice for the latter were quite bleak.".

Land owing feudal upper caste do not want to leave their land and the dalits want genuine shares in the land for at least for their home!Anand Chakravarty, has also spoken about deep divergence between the rule of law and justice at a convention held against Bathani tola judgement of the Patna High court. (All the accused were acquitted by the Patna high court upsetting the judgement of the Ara district and session judge, who had awarded death sentences and life imprisonment to all the accused for killing 21 persons, most of them children and women in Bathani tola village of Ara district in 1996). Prof Chakravartay has stated that justice should" be understood not just in a judicial sense but in wider sense of economic, social and political justice."

While voicing concern over instances of judicial injustices against dalits and adivasis agrarian labourers, Prof Chakravarty cited the Tamil Nadu High Court verdict in Keezhavanmani massacre of 1969, which had found it "astonishing" and "difficult to believe", one whom even "possessed a car" could be guilty of burning alive 42 dalits. In the context of Rupaspur in Purnia district of Bihar carnage, massacre of 14 adivasis sharecroppers in 1971, he quoted the words of a well-known advocate, who had justified the massacres: "it is because of me (that is, the landlords) that he had the land, it is because of me that he had a livelihood . . . . Now he is violating that relationship by refusing to share the crops; this is breach of a trust which cannot be tolerated." Prof Chakravarty thus spoke about principal social contradictions of Bihar that resulted in the massacres by Ranvir Sena in the 1990s.

Reminiscences of massacres' lists of dalits, adivasis, Muslims and poor are long at different places, mainly in the central Bihar districts including Gaya, Jahanabad, Arwal, Aurangabad, Rohtas, and also at few•districts of north and east Bihar. It all started in village Rupaspur under united Purnia district in 1971 where 14 adivasis sharecroppers were burnt alive by feudal Rajput landlord. No one knew the fate of cases and all accused persons were perhaps let off because of lack of substantial evidences. The 1990s massacres galore began with the mobilisation of upper caste under Ranvir sena and various other upper caste militia of in the central Bihar under Brahmeshwar Singh. After Bathani tola massacre, the upper caste militia went on rampage, killing people in Laxamanpur—Bathe, Shankarbgha and MIapur and many other villages. Finally the massacres ended with the arrest of Brahmshwar Singh in 2002. But incidents of violence against dalits and Muslims continue even after those fearful days of worse massacres.

Sadly people still remember the open admission of Barhmeshwar Singh, who had during his underground days, had openly told different media persons that Ranvir Senas kill children and women of Dalits, Muslims, backwards and poor because children after growing youth will become naxalites and women will give births to children, who will become naxalites.

According to a report published in the Frontline, a fortnightly; in order to understand the Bathani Tola massacre, a brief account of the history of Bihar is necessary. Land has been the crucial issue in the politics of Bihar. Because of fertile land irrigated by Ganga, Sone river system, the districts of Bhojpur, Gaya, Patna and Arwal in central Bihar have historically been a hub of political movements. During the colonial era, Bihar was the heart of the zamindari system, which drove deep wedges between dalits and backwards classes and upper castes, which had a major share of the zamindari. Even after it abolition in 1950 and the introduction of the Land Ceiling Act in 1961, the landlords worked their way up in politics to retain most of their lands, to the extent that Bihar has the worst record in the implementation of land reforms.

According to a 2009 report, among the landowners in the state, 96.5 percent are marginal farmer's poor small farmers. They own about 66 percent of total land. Medium and large farmers comprise just 3.5

percent of the land owing community, but they own roughly 33 percent of the total land. Northern Bihar has bigger landlords, but the value of their land is much lower than that in southern Bihar because northern Bihar is flood plain. It is because of this that the landlords of southern Bihar are much more aggressive about possessing land. Most of the upper caste leaders come from southern Bihar. In 1971, Bihar witnessed its first feudal massacre when 16 santhals were killed in Rupaspur village in PURNIA district. In the years to come, private armies such as Kunwar sena of Rajputs, the Brahmarishi sena, Savarn Liberation Front, Pandav gang and Sun Light Sena emerged to fight for upper caste landlords.

Encouraged by this trend, a few backward castes landlords also formed private armies such as the Bhumi Sena, the Kisan Kranti Sena and Lorik Sena run either by yadavas or kurmis. In 1995, the politically powerful Bhumihar caste landlords brought all the upper caste armies under the Rranvir Sena umbrella. They declared that the Ranvir Sena was formed to wipe out communists from Bihar so that the tradition of feudalism, given to them by their ancestors, was maintained. The Ranvir Sena under the leadership of Brahmeshwar Singh organised youths among upper caste including minors and created violence to a new height against dalits, Muslims and backwards, and poors. And the first case of a big massacre was given by Ranvir Sena in Bathani tola village of Bhojpur district.

More over, the upper caste organised violence started increasing by leaps and bound eliminated over 500 dalits, Muslims, backwards and poors from other caste and community by 1995, the ultra-left militants under the banner of CPI-ML killed 93 upper caste landlords between 1994 to 2000. CPI-ML activists killed eight ranvir sena members at Nadhi village in Bhojpur district. In 1997 and 1999 CPI-ML had also raided Jahanabad district and kjilled 16 landlords. The biggest such attack was conducted by Maoist coordination centre (MCC), which along with other naxalite outfits, merged into CPI (Maoist) in 1999, emerged forces in south Bihar, and apart from killing about 50 Rajput landlords in Aurangabad district in its previous MCC form in 1987, killed 35 Bhumihars in Senari village in Jahanabad not only to show its strength but also revenging the killings of dalits, Muslims etc by Ranvir Sena men in different districts of the south Bihar.

I exactly remember before that, first naxal operation was carried in Musahari village of Muzaffarpur district against upper caste landlords in early 1970s by the then naxal organisation of Charu Mazumdar and

Kanu Sanyal of Naxalwari fame and pro ponders of the first left ultra forces to end exploitation of weaker sections of society. Three landolrds were killed at that time besides two in Darbhanga town itself! Before that some socialist leaders of north Bihar led by Socialist leader Suraj Narayan Singh and CPI leader Bhogendra Jha had also launched movement of land grabbing of big landlords in the old Darbhana district comprising Madhubani and Samastipur. The agitation succeeded to some extent and landless poor grabbed lands of landlords in Pandoul and different places in Madhubani and Samstipur and Darbhanga areas and at least constructed their huts on the lands of landlords.

Even after all these developments, feudal mindsets of land owing classes, particularly ex-landlords have not changed and they continue to create reign of terror against dalits, adivasis, Muslims, backwards and poor among forward caste. Land continues to be the bone of contention and the successive Bihar governments did not bother to implement land reform measures although first land reform measures like abolition of zamindari system had started in Bihar under the chief minister ship of Dr Sri Krishna Sinha. His revenue minister later chief minister of Bihar Krishna Ballabh Sayay had played pivotal in implementing land reforms including abolition of zamindari system for nationalising their lands to give them to landless in Bihar. Even the matter as challenged right from 1 C lower court to Supreme Court, which upturn the decision of the then Bihar government on the ground of Right to Property in the Fundamental Rights, guaranteed under the Constitution. Later the Jawahar Lal Nehru government in Del;hi carried first amendment ton the Constitution and Zamanidari system of holding huge land was abolished The ACT subsequently put in the 10th schedule so that matter could not be challenged in any court of Law!

INDIAN POLITICAL CLASS IN HURRY?

Thursday, 21 June 2012

It is strange why Indian political class is in so much in hurry to become prime minister or president or ministers or chief ministers by projecting themselves for respective posts? Elections to the next Lok Sabha are due in 2014! But almost all political parties or politicians have started projecting prime ministerial candidates or politicians themselves to become prime minister after the next elections where there are least signs of which political parties or comologeration of smaller and regional parties will get how much seats in the forthcoming elections to the Lok Sabha! Such tendencies are clearly indicative to influences the mood of electorate, who will participate in the next Lok Sabha elections.

The UPA led by Congress, the NDA led by Bhartiya Janata Party (BJP) and many other regional outfits and parties, whose leaders have been immensely benefited to get prized political position in the coalition era of the last 25 years are vying each other for the prime minister position as well as other important assignments in the government in India.

The race is on. The BJP, a partner of National Democratic Alliance, is more in hurry to project the Gujarat chief minister Narendra Modi, allegedly involved in the carnage of Muslims during Gujarat riots (investigation in many cases of the carnage against Modi are under the investigation stage) as the prime ministerial candidate. The Rashtriya Swamsevak Sangh (RSS), supreme operator of the saffron wings in India appears hell—bent to consolidate Hindu votes throughout the country in favour of its political wing—BJP by projecting Narendra Modi as prime ministerial candidate in the next elections although there is cleavage in the party over the name of Modi.

In the line in the BJP are former Deputy prime minister Lal Krishna Advani, former union minister Sushama Swarajya, national president

399

of the party Nitin Gadkari, Madhya Pradesh BJP chief minister Shivraj Chauhan etc. But the majority of leaders of the BJP from majority of states seem to favour Narendra Modi as prime ministerial candidates because of his Hindu consolidation capacity as well as deliverer of good governance in Gujarat in the last over ten years. But there are exceptions also like Bihar a senior leader of the BJP and the deputy chief minister of Bihar Sushul Kumar Modi, who is said to be very close to Nitish Kumar has serious reservation on the name of Narendra Modi.

On the other hand ambitious and shrewed Chief Minister of Bihar Nitish Kumar, who himself want to be projected as prime ministerial; candidate, has vociferously objected to the projections of NarendraModi as prime ministerial candidate. Kumar has recently made clear that prime minister of the country must be above from any controversy, obviously indicating that Narendra Modi's hands are drenched in communal bloods. His ministerial colleague Sushil Kumar Modi, a senior BJP leader from Bihar has also dittoed the line of Nitish Kumar and has pointed out that his party (BJP) must project a prime ministerial candidate like former prime minister Atal Behari Vajpayee, who was above from any controversy and acceptable to even opposition leaders—what to say—NDA (Both the Janata Dal (U) of Nitish Kumar and BJP are alliance partners in Bihar's NDA government.). Nitish Kumar has even threatened to leave NDA on the issue of prime ministerial candidate of safforn wings as Narendra Modi. More over, his senior party colleague, former union minister and convenor of the NDA Sharad Yadav is maintaining golden silence over the issue. Sharad has refused to support and oppose the Nitish Line in the party, saying that he is busy in presidential election candidates' issue in tthe NDA. Thus it appears that everything is not well even in Nitish's JD (U).

Not only that there are serious differences of opinions in Bihar's BJP. The Animal Husbandry minister Giriraj Singh, who is minister from the BJP quota in Nitish government, has openly revolted against Sushil Modi and Nitish Kumar for their statements, objecting Narendra Modi as prime ministerial candidate. Giriraj has not attended the cabinet meeting a few days back and also meetng of important BJP leaders at the residence of Sushil Kumar Modi. Many such ministers from BJP quota including Ashawani Choubey, Chandra Mohan Rai, Prem Kumar, Gautam Singh, Sukhda Pandey, who have serious grudges against Shusil Kumar Modi are secretly supporting the stand of Giriraj Singh, who has openly said that Nitish Kumar and Sushil Kumar Modi are not competent to give secular certificate to Narendra/Modi as he has emerged a as a tallest leader of the BJP in the country by supports of all sections of society in Gujarat in successive elections. With such activities in the BJP, Sushil Kumar Modi appears to be on back-foot in the Bihar BJP!

The latest statement of the RSS chief Mohan Bhagwat that there is no harm in the BJP to project Narendra/Modi as prime ministerial candidate has boosted the stand of Giriraj Singh and other BJP leaders in Bihar. Bhagwat has made crystal clear that Narendra Modi is a staunch Hindu and Hindu have all right to become prime minister of the country The statement of senior BJP leader Balbir Punj and other party functionaries in Delhi that NarendraModi is right choice to be projected as prime ministerial candidate in the next Lok Sabha elections has also created upheavals in the BJP right from state level to national level. Dissident BJP leaders, opposed to Sushil Kumar Modi for hijacking organisation to serve the interest of Nitish Kumar, have started felt boosted with encouraging statements of RSS chief!

Controversy is going on over the fate of NDA government led by Nitish Kumar in Bihar. At one place, Nitish is determined to consolidate his Muslims and most backward votes by showing his secular credential and opposing Narendra Modi as prime ministerial candidate. BJP leader Sushil Kumar Modi and many other BJP functionaries as well as party's grass root support base, supporting Nitish Kumar, have been put in wrong box It is rumoured that Nitish Kumar may split BJP in Bihar to save his government as well as consoling Sushil Kumar Modi and many other BJP leaders that door for them are opened in the JD(U)!

The Congress is also fishing in troubled waters in the NDA and reportedly started move to bring Nitish Kumar in UPA fold. More over the congress is also delved in similar circumstances. The Congress party has already announced that the party would fight next elections under the leadership of AICC general Secretary Rahul Gandhi, who will be the next prime minister after UPA comes to power in the next Lok Sabha elections although the UPA government led by Congress has created mess in the country like price rise, inflation, encouraging corrupt practises as well as scams after scams in the country during the tenure of Manmohan Singh government at the centre. For this Congress is also making arrangements with allying with left parties, Samajwadi Party of Mulayam Singh Yadav, Bahujan Samajwadi party of Mayawati, Rashtriya Janata Dal of Laloo Prasad Yadavetc.

The chief ministers mercurial Mamta Bannerjee of West Bengal (Trinamual Congress) and of Tamil Nadu (ADMK) Jaylalitha and former chief minister of Uttar Pradesh Mayawati (Bahujan Samaj Party) are respectively also reportedly dreaming for prime ministerial post, having political ambition in view of coalition era in the country with the emergence of regional parties in the country. Role of Odisha chief minister Navin Patnaik is being considered pivotal because his regional; outfit—Biju Janata Dal is also gaining ground in Odisha. Unlike dithering role of NDA in the race of presidential elections, Navin Patnaik and Jayalalita have already announced their suport to the former speaker of Lok Sabha P A Sangama as their presidential candidate, which in all expectation BJP of the NDA will also support Sangma against UPA and other oppositon candidate for the president ship Pranab Mukherjee. But the million dollar question about Nitish joining UPA led by Congress because his arch rival and RJD national president Laloo Prasad Yadav is already alingned with UPA and Congress!

Left parties, which are expected to do better performances in the next Lok Sabha elections because of vigorous protests and agitation by these parties on price rise, inflation, discrimination to working classes as well as opposition to multinationals, are obviously opposed to NDA, particularly BJP for its communal tinges, may throw weight in favour of UPA with common minimum programme of governance after next Lok Sabha elections.

Amid all the controversies in at least in Bihar, it appears the handiwork of Nitish Kumar, who has miserable failed in his efforts of the so called development of Bihar and his good governance, has created unnecessary controversy to divert the attention of masses on prime ministerial candidate. Nitish reportedly of the opinion that he would get political mileage from this move—but it appears his move would boomerang or has boomeranged with the clarity over the issue by RSS chief!

HUNGER LOOMING LARGE OVER GLOBE?

Tuesday, 19 June 2012

Recently, I was just going through pages of the Washington Post. Suddenly my eyes went on a opinion piece in the newspaper about the global challenge of food and nutrition scarcity! I was amazed to find that entire planet, particularly India, China; Nigeria will become most populous countries by 2050 and will face food and nutrition scarcity in considerable manner! In this respect the opinion piece on the basis of the statements of Paul Pol man, Chief Executive officer of the Unilever, one of the world's largest consumer goods companies and Daniel Sorvitje, chief executive officer of the Group Bimbo, the largest baking company in the world, who are authoring of B-20, the food Security Task Force for the G-20 nations, has highlighted some of the major factors of food and nutrition scarcity in the globe.

The planet is already stressed, about waters particularly and most of its next two billion inhabitants will form in areas where the stress is greatest. The UN expert team has identified India, China and Nigeria, which will become world's most populous nations in 2050. More over in my opinion danger signal for food and nutrition scarcity as well as instances of hunger expected to be more alarming in these populous countries!

Both Paul Pol man and Daniel Sorvitje are of the opinion, "Imagine all the food mankind has produced over the past 8000 years. Now consider that we need to produce that the same amount again—but in just the next 40 years if we are to feed our growing hungry world."

The Opinion piece based on the statements of both the experts has pointed out that seven billion people live on earth and the population is growing by 77 million every year. That is country like size of Indonesia every three years. By 2050, nine billion people live on the planet.

Amid this rapid growth, more than 850 million people go to bed hungry. An additional billion do not get sufficient nutrients in their diet although both the speakers have made it clear that the data appears high and a stain on our collective conscience! These are life time health implication for these unfortunate people as well as considerable negative impact on economic productivity and significant cost of health care.

Notably based on the statements of two experts, the Washington Post has points out, "To alleviate this situation, global food production must increase 70 percent by 2050."

And things are not getting easier. The agriculture sector account for 70 percent water use and up to 30 percent of global greenhouse gas emissions. Climate change could reduce yields more than 20 percent in many areas within developing countries—think of the floods in Thailand and droughts in Horn of Africa. Changing temperature also contribute to food price volatility, which has a direct impact on the poor and on child nutrition.

Moreover, agriculture faces dual challenges; being more sustainable on a dwindling resources base while having to feed an increasing number of people. To provide food and nutrition security in the coming decades will require a major sustained effort by all stakeholders including business. Both the co-authors of G-20 on food security have said, "we believe that this require a new vision for sustainable and equitable growth. We have food security task force as co-chairmen of the B-20 food security Task Force, We have led a group of CEOs and other stakeholders to provide affordable recommendations for the G-20 to achieve, a 50 percent increase in products and productivity by 2030 to boost agriculture by 50 percent by 2030—some stakeholders committed to invest $ 15 billion to help boost agriculture productivity. We have identified five priority areas: increasing investments in agriculture productivity; improving market function; ensuring more sustainable food production (including water resources management); and integrating and prioritising nutritional needs."

This productivity growth must develop food and nutritional security for all in an environmentally sustainable manner while ensuring improved livelihood and income for farmers, going forward, and farmers will have double annual yields increase—and we need reach out to 500 million small-holders farmers or two billion people, who produce most of the agriculture output in developing countries. Women make up 43 percent of developing world farmers. We need targeted programme to help them to increase their productivity and earning potentials. The problem of land tenure rights and access to finance including risk management tools will be key enables.

The statement has lamented that thirty to forty agriculture produce gets lost between the farms and consumers. We need strengthen capacity along the value chain to reduce waste while improving the nutritional value and food safety for consumers to optimise productivity. Considerable areas of the globe are clearly food-deficient. We need to make easier to transport goods from suppliers and promote the development of local survey, which helps develop local markets and reduce urban migration. We need trade policies that increase the exchange of sustainable agriculture goods. Reducing trade support and protection would provide significant opportunities for farmers while expanding consumers' access to affordable foods.

Resources for food production will become scarce. Sustainable response to global challenges is the acid test for company's everywhere—not just producers but also suppliers and retailers as well as international organisations, governments of the nations, NGOs and citizens!

AMID CRAZE FOR DEISEL CAR, WHO SAYS DIESEL FUME CAUSES LUNG CANCER

Monday, 18 June 2012

With the petrol price sky-rocketing in the recent past, thereare virtual cries in India, particularly in. Patna for disel cars! For diesel cars, the manufacturers will have to maintain the technology and guidelines, propounded by the Global Diesel Technology Forum, which represents car and truck companies and others that make diesel engines, such technology is already under implementation in the United States and other wealthy countries, introduced in 2000 in America.

According to a report published In the New York Times, the World Health Organization (WHO), at its meeting in Lyon, France, at scientific meet; on Tuesday (June05, 2012) declared diesel fumes cause lung cancer. The WHO experts said that they were more "car cinogenic than second hand cigarette smoke", which is said to be the main reasons of lung cancer in the planet. The report of the WHO said that the diesl fuel emition is "known carcinogen" level, which eventually affects the mines workers as they are heavily exposed to exhausts diesel fumes! The WHO said that it is partcular relevant to poor countries, whose truckers generates and farm and factory machinery routinely belch clouds of sooty smokes and fill the air with sulfurous particulars, the New York times report said. Adding that United States and wealthy nations have fewer problems because of they require modern diesel engines to burn much cleaner than they did even a decade ago. Most of the industries in these countries like mining, already here limits on the amount of diesel fumes to which workers may be exposed.

The New York Times report suggests that the medical director of the American Cancer Society Dr Otis W. Brawley praised the signal of the WHO's international agency for research on cancer, saying "his group has for a long time had concerns about diesel" The Cancer society is expected

THE INDIA AND THE WORLD

to come to the same conclusion the next time its scientific committee meets, Dr Brawley said to NY TIMES. She fuhrer stated, "I do not think it is bad to have a diesel car and at the same time I do not think it is good to breathe its exhaust. I am not concerned with the people, who walk past a disel vehicle, I am little concerned about people like toll collectors and I am very concerned about people like miners, who work where exhaust is concentrated. Government of the globe countries must declare diesel exhaust a carcinogen, she added to the New York Times.

The WHO, as quoted in the New York Times, also said that disel exhaust is a probable cause of bladder cancer. They require modern diesel engines to burn much cleaner than they did even a decade ago. Most of the industries like mining already have limits on the amount of diesel fumes to which workers may be exposed. The New YORK Times report said that WHO researches indicated that occupational disel expenses was far greater lung cancer risk than a passive cigarette smoking but a much smaller risk than smoking two packs a day. The diesel Technology Forum reacted cautiously to WHO report noting that modern diesel engine had in USA and other wealthy countries burn low sulfur fuel, so new trucks and buses emit 98 percent less particulars than old ones did and 99 percent less nitrogen oxide, which adds to ozen build-up. Such technology in vogue in U S, the New York Times report added. According to Indians and particularly of Biharis for diesel engine cars; amid craze for diesel cars and running of trucks, and buses, having diesel engines in India in the wake of rampant increase in petrol price will have to adopt the new technologies to lessen the risk of lung cancer, prevalent in India. Because of fumes of diesel engines in this country For this fool-proof arrangements, Indian manufacturers of cars, buses, trucks and for other purposes unsing diesels like mining, India must develop modalities of US in view of WHO report, warning spread of lung cancer because of diesel burn emotions, causing lung cancer!

407

INDIA PARTICULARLY BIHAR MOST DANGEROUS PLACES TO GIVE CHILD BIRTH!

Monday, 18 June 2012

India Including Bihar most dangerous to give child Birth! a: India as a whole and Bihar and Uttar Pradesh in particular are most dansgerous places to give birth of children as per reports and studies by Harvard School of Public Health; Save Children India, Lancet and U N Study Reports. India lacks basic maternity care and worse scenario exists in Bihar; according to a report published in the American Time magazine website on June 08, 2012.

The write up has quoted a study report of India particularly Bihar and Uttar Pradesh has put India as a whole worse than Nepal among the developing countries on this score. Pregnant women die eitherat the time of giving birth or during pregnancies in India, mostly in Bihar and Uttar Pradesh due to lack of basic infrastructures both in urban and rural areas. A pregnant woman of nearby Delhi, who somehow, was saved at the time of giving birth to a child, told the writer of the story Nilanjana Bhaumick, "Giving birth is not at all safe in India. But may be easy if taken to a hospital to give birth or a competent dai (midwife) was there, it would not have so traumatic and my other child would have been saved in the past."

The write up in the Time suggests that basic maternity care, if, would have been in India and particularly Bihar many life in India would have been saved. The Time has quoted a 2010 study by Harvard School of Public Health, which has said that 1,50000 deaths would have been prevented by 2015 if Indian women have aceess to better family planning and health care during their pregnancies and deliveries. The Times has quoted another report by Save Children India, which suggests, "that despite of India's booming economy, the country is still one of the most high-risk places in the world to give birth. It ranked India as the fourth country among 80 less developed countries, in its survey, with nearly half of births taking place without a traned heath professional. Even though

India has made effort to improve level of maternal health by encouraging institutional deliveries and taking other measures;" says Thomas Chandy of president of the Save the Children India. He has furtjer informed the Time, that the benefits have not yet appeared to bring about a pradigam shift.

The Time website has further states that although figures show national maturity rate dropped by 66 percent from 1990 to 2010, in India, particularly Bihar and Uttar Pradesh have so far highest number of women dying during child birth on the planet. The U N Report on maternal and mortality trends has revealed that 56000 deaths in 2010 have taken place whereas such figures remain 6000 in China during the period!

India's maternal mortality rate in 2010 was 200 women per year of 100000 live births, which are slightly better than Bangla Desh (240 deaths per year on 100000 live births). Intrestingly the Nepal, considered a poverty-ridden and less developed country, adjoin India has tremendously just 170 deaths per 100000 births!

The Time website report, headlined, "Why India is still one of the Most Dangerous places to give Births"? has further stated that lamently India and its states including Bihar and Uttar Pradesh has launched many welfare programmes for women like Janani Surakhsha Yojana, food for malnuritioned pregnant women and children but these welfare measures are yet to percolate grass-root level, aggravating the deaths of women and children at the time of deliveries and pregnancies. Although there is strict provisions to carry pregnant women through government transports to nearby hospitals and health centres, food, medicines and even cash rewards of upto $30 for giving birth, such facilities remained on papers only in Indian states including Bihar and Uttar Pradesh. Facilities are not available due to lack of infrastructures in both urban and rural centers.

However, The Time magazine website has lauded the efforts of Kerala and Tamil Nadu and has said that these two states have already reached U N Millennium development on this score by bringing their mortality rate down to 100 women per year on every 100000 live births While ther states like Anbdhra Pradesh, west Bengal, Gujarat, Haryana are close to chasing the figures of lowest casualties during births and pregnancies!

The Time has pointed out that spread of literacy is crucial factors for stopping casualities. In this respect, the Time has referred about Kerala where literacy rate among women is 92 percent and by adopting various women welfare measures, the state has brought down such figure to 81 deaths per every year of 100000 births in the state. About Bihar and Uttar Pradesh, worse said is better on these scores!

RETROGADE BIHARI YOUTHS AMID PROGRESSIVE YOUTHS OF ONCE UPON A TIME!

Monday, 4 June 2012

I strongly feel that the recent invasion on India to ruin our political and social cultural fabrics and progressive thinkings as well as economy of India, based on socialistic pattern of society through imposition of new economic policies of imperialists, are destroying our youths Europe and United State of America in the shape of multinationals and corporates culture have practically brought brinkmanship among our youths. Today's youths of India are described the future rulers under our democratic system.

In the past few years, youths of India have become untouched with progressive thoughts for the benefit of the country! There were time, sons and daughters of rich and big people as well as from middle class families used to get good education and they visited foreign countries including United Kingdom, America and other foreign lands for higher studies in Oxford, Cambridge, and other top-ranking universities of the globe. From there, they brought many progressive ideas like communism, socialism and other revolutionaries theory for the upliftment of downtroddens etc.

In this categorey, we cannot forget the names of Pundit Jawahar Lal Nehru, B R Ambdkar, Subhas Chandra Bose, Jyoti Basu, and many others. For radical and political thinkings we cannot forget the contributions of revolutionaries like Saheed Bhagat Singh, Chandra Shekhar Azad, Ram Prasad Vismil and many other, who sacrificed their for the political emancipation of the country.

RADICAL AND PROGRESSIVE:—They all brought new ideas of revolution and became instrumental in shaping the destiny of India in the last several years. About ten years back, prestigious colleges like St. Stephen College under Delhi University, the Jawahar Lal Nehru University, Presidency colleges in Calcutta, Madras and Mumbai, Shanti

Niketan University and many other top ranking educational institutions in the country used to be hub of progressive thoughts. And many of their students excelled in different aspects like politics, revolution, Marxism, socialism etc. These institutions once upon time were described hub of political and social thoughts! Many of the products from these institutions are excelling in different fields including some in politics, journalsm, top ranking government jobs, NGOs, social services and even in private sectors. Their progressive thinkings are beng reflected in their good deeds. In government services, many of such scholars are doing excellent jobs in premier services like IAS, IFS, IPS and senior rank-central services. In many instances, they never succumb to political pressure and work on the basis of strict rule books as well as going to rural areas during their postings to listen to the grievances of rural people, who are supposed to be worse sufferers and also deprived lots in the present political system.

I mustt mention of name of Arwind Narayan Das, a Bihar and product of St Stephen, who was a research scholar in the AN Sinha institute, Patna, had joined journalism. Later he left journalism and founded a NGO, namely Asian Development Research Institute (ADRI) in Patna for socio-economic development of the state with Prof Saibal Gupta. While Prof Saibal is looking after the institute more as close advisor of the chief minister Nitish Kumar, Arwind died prematurely about ten yars back. Arvind had bubbling ideas of progressive thinkings and he was sympathisers of Naxal movement in India for the upliftment of poor, dalits, adivasis etc.

Of late these tendencies among our youths are lacking and they are concentrating more on materialistic approaches. Instead of sentiments of services to people, they are making them selves machines of money minting. They seldom care for the interest of the country. Their approaches have become narrow-minded. Instead of progressive thoughts, they are shaping themselves in the format of feudalism. Some time, I feel disappointed and desperate over their attitudes throughout the country. I will rather call some thing very serious fault-line in our education system right from primary level to university level.

RETROGADE TENDENCY:—Instances of the last few days in Bihar among mainly youths in a large number in the wake of killing of dreaded founder of banned Ranveer Sena at Ara Brahmeshwar Mukhiya and his funeral procession at Bansghat in Patna have shocked the people. Youths in the age group of 16 years to 40 outnumbered the people participating in the funeral processions. Right from Ara to Patna and other districts of central Bihar, they indulged in vandalism, violences, burning of police and private vehicles, beating of people moving on roads, damaging public and government property. I feel that this shows the decadent thoughts among youths in majority in Bihar. For whom, they were protesting—for a man, like Brahmeshwar Mukhiya, who throughout his life indulged in loot, arsons, killings of over 300 dalits, muslims, poor among forward, backwards for establishing the hegemony of their landlordship on the lands, manily in central Bihar. Sadly these youths behaved like lumpens on the street of Patna, the state capital!

Moreover elder politicians of JD(U), BJP, Congress etc rather allegedly encouraged them for creating ugly scenes on the street of Patna and other districts of Bihar. I must mention the names of a few politicians including Akhilesh Singh, former union minister (Congress), Lalan Singh, Lok Sabha member from Munger (JD-U), Dr CP Thakur, state unit chief of BJP Bihar unit, and BJP MLA Ms Usha Vidyarathi (both BJP). They allegedly created scenes to restore feudalism and landlordship in Bihar and eliminate poor, dalits, muslims, backward caste, poor among forward caste in Bihar!The arsonists chased the police and raised slogans in support of banned Ranveer Sena openly.

PROGRESSIVE YOUTHS:—There were time in Bihar. Many educated and brriliant youths in their educational career entered left and socialist movement to protest atrocity on dalits, backwards, poor, adivasis etc in Bihar itself. They also joined naxal movement setting aside theuir luxurious life with their parents as well as brilliant technical educations in 1960s and early 1970s. In course of their political activities, they joined the founder s of naxal movement from Naxalwari in Darjeeling district in West Bengal Charu Mazumdar and Kanu Sanyal. By the time Indira Gandhi, the then premier of India declared emergency, and many of these reformists and Naxal leaders were tortured and killed at many places, particularly in Bhagalpur jails.

In this connection, I will point out a few families, whose wards, sons, had sacrificed their lifefor justices to poor in Bihar. One such falmily is of an eminent historian late Prof Radha Krishna Chaudhary. Prof Chaudhary and his wife Shanti Devi lost his one MBBS doctor son Dr Prashant Kumar Chaudhary, who was shot dead in Bhagalpur jail on May 04, 1976. Dr Prashant Kumar Chaudhary's guilt was that he wanted to give medical treatment to fellow jail inmates after he was put in jail in a drive against naxalites during emergency. Dr Chaudhray was shot dead in

jail premises from point blank range by jail and armed police personnel
in Bhagalpur jail. Dr Chaudhary died instaneously. News of his killing
was censored for months together during eergency. His body was not
handed over to the Professor family. His elder brother, Prabhat Kumar
Chaudhary, who was topper in matriculation and I sc. in Scince College,
Patna, had joined Sindri Institute of Technology. There also he took lead
in academic activities—but his zeal for helping poor did not resist him
and he joined Charu Mazumdar and Kanu Sanyal of Naxalwari-fame. He
was imprisioned for several years and tortured by police. He, however,
later on released. Currently, Prabhat is setteled in Delhi and as being
CPI-Ml central secretariat member, is doing social services! His third
brother Prasanna Kumar Chaudhary continued to be an active naxalites
sysmpathisers and he and his wife moves in tribal areas of Jharjkhand
and meets adivasis for ameliorating their condition. Pranava Kumar
Chaudhary, the youngest son of Prof R K Chaudhary, has naxalites
leaning and is sympathisers of Maoists, is currently Special correspondent
in The Times of India. Pranava had also to pass through many ups and
downs in life and struggled for survial after the sudden death of his father
Prof R K Chaudhary and the entire family plunged in pall of gloom with
the death Dr Prashant and other tragedies in the family. Shanti Devi, wife
of late Prof R K Chaudhary, who lives with her son Pranava in Patna,
still shivers in pain and angusish first on the killing of his doctor son in
Bhagalpur jail and death of her professor husband during his service of
professorship. Tears rolloing down on her face, she could not reply my
few questions and only wept uncotrobaly!

In this connection, I must mention the contribution of one former
naxalites, a hardcore follower of Charu and Kanu, Umadhar Prasad Singh
of Darbhanga town. Umadhar, a brilliant stiudent f economics, later
during jail period perhaps topped the list in post-graduate in Economics
from Bihar University. Umadhar is lone member of central committee
of nine of the CPI-Ml formed after split from CPM is surviving.
An architect of the first naxalite operation in Bihar in Musahari in
Muzaffaropur district alongwith another senior naxal leader Raj Kishore
Singh, Umadhar singh become later MLA from Hayaghat assembly
constituency of Darbhanga district three times. Umadhar, who was
tortured in brutal manner in different jails, particularly in Hazaribagh
central jail, is still struggling between life and death at his Darbhanga
residence. As long as Kanu was alive, Kanu Sanyal was regular visitor
to see the condtition of Umadhar in Darbhanga. Surrounded by books,

magazines, newspapers, documents on his bed, Umadhar is leading a life of loner and bewildred with the present state of affairs in the country! Umadhar also had given other naxalite operation in Darbhanga district when he shot dead for instant justice to a landlord Balani of Dilahi, a village in Darbhanga town suburb. Umardhar also symbolised naxal operations in a few places in Bengal, Champaran and Sasaram region of Bihar in his prime youth under the direct control of Charu and Kanu when he was hardcore naxal leader in 1960s and 1970s.

I have already written about well known Naxal leader of high-ranking from an Ara village Satya Narayan singh, who was architect in organising Telegana movement in Andhra Pradesh and remained underground till he died in Telegana forest areas in 1979.

DREADED JWALA SINGH: Another dreaded landlord of an Ara village Jwala Singh, for whom life of weaker sections of society was play for him. Jwala was more dreaded than founder of of the Ranveer Sena, a private army of landlords Brahmeshwar Mukhiya, whio was killed a few days back in Ara town, raising a hall of protsts by conservative's upper caste! Jwala, a holder of over 1000 acre of land in Ara village, was not only monster but used to taste the blood of weaker sections after their killings. Jwala was a congress leader, whose writ ran in entire central Bihar. One woman Congress legislator was practically his kept. Jwala himself used to tell people that his first task is to rape, murder, loot and violences like burning of houses of dalits and other weaker sections of society in entire central Bihar. Police and administration during the days of Congress were under his thumb. A day came in 1980s perhaps, and Jwala was killed and shot dead while he was travelkling in his car near his village home like the killings of Brahmeshwar Mukhiya. Today in the changed political situation, Jawala's sons are thriving on lands and other huge property, acquired by Jwala himself. In between, there was lull in his family but in the changed situation; huge lands of killed Jwala are being managed by his sons. And some time, Jawala's sons also grabbed the lands of dalits, Muslims and backward s and poor among forward caste.

Such is the tip of ice berg story of feudalism in Bihar and naxal activities. The degenration of youths from upper caste mainly in Bihar and their feudal outlook instead of progressive and radical views has created piquant situation in the state. If proper education and training of well beings are not imparted to our youths particularly in Bihar, the situation would go down to the drains and the dream of good governance of the Chief minister Nitish Kumar would continue to remain a distant dream.

FEUDALISM VIS-A-VIS LEFT MOVEMENT IN BIHAR IN THE WAKE OF DREADED MUKHIYA'S KILLING

Monday, 4 June 2012

For the last four days, Bihar, which is well known for feudalism and atrocity on weaker sections of the society, has once again gained more and more notoriety with the killing of the founder of the Ranveer Sena, a private army of landlords, conservative people and their upper caste tags, Brahmeshwar Singh Mukhiya in the suburb of Ara town by unkown assalaints. Apart from violences in Ara, damaging public property, arsons, loot and assaulting poor and weaker sections of the society, the trouble spread to the state capital—Patna—where his body was cremated nearby Bansghat funeral site where the first President of India and apostole of peace and non-violence Dr Rajndra Prasad was also cremated over 45 years back.

The long processions of a particular sections of society, added and abeted by their caste's senior leaders, with the body of Mukhiya, known for murders of over 459 dalits, muslims including children and women, specially in Bhojpur, Gaya, Jahanabad, Ara, Arwal, Aurangabad district in late 1970, 1980s, 1990s reached Patna and created vandalism, violences, loot, anti-government slogans, and strangely glorifying banned Ranveer Sena and Mukhiya.

FREE FOR ALL AND WHO ALLOWED CREMATION IN PATNA?—It was free of for all of them. Police were no where to prevent any untowards incident. In the process, the arsonists with the body of Brahmeshwar Mukhiya spared none, burnt police and private vehicles, assaulted pepole on the main streets of Patna without any rhyme and reasons. And the police, under the command of the Director General of Police Abhayanand remained silent spectators! Entire government machinery was found cripilled. In this critical hour, the chief minister of Bihar Nitish Kumar was away from the scene in the state capital on his

415

sewa yatra tour of Bhagalpur and Kishanganj districts. His deputy chief minister and a senior Bharatiya Janata Party (BJP) leader Sushil Kumar Modi and other ministers and senior officials on whom Nitish Kumar bank for so called good governance were conspicuous by their absence to control the situation!

With all these developments, a big question arises, "who allowed the funeral procession and cremation of Brahmeshwar Singh Mukhiya, who was killed at Ara, about 60 km from Patna, at the bank of Ganga River at the Bansghat cremation ground"? Is he Abhayanand to appease the banned Ranveer Sena activists and their political associates including rebel JD(U) member of the Lok Sabha from Munger Lok Sabha seat Lalan singh, the former union minister Akhilesh Singh, of then Rashtriya Janata Dal, now of the Congress, state unit chief of the BJP Dr C P Thakur?

FEUDALISM IN BIHAR:—Feudalism and caste war are not new for Bihar. It all started in late 1960s vogorously in the state, in which it is said that over 20000 people, majority of them from dalits, Muslims and poor among firward caste were killed. Initially it started with socialist movement in Darbhanga and Madhubani under the CPI leader Bhogrendra Jha and Socialist leader Suraj Narayan Singh. Both Socilists and Communist parties fought for land to land less in these two districts by capturing forcively Darbhanga Raja lands and distributed them among landless. Later ultra left movement in Bihar started raising voices against atrocity by feudal upper caste people and finally culminated into caste and calss war by private armies of almost all upper caste people to suppress the voices of haves-not. Resultantly, at least two private armies—Ranveer Sena and Bhoomi Sena were formed in late 1970s by land-owing fedal Bhumihar and backward Kurmi caste "in the name of protecting lands and farming from ultra left and dalits in central Bihar districts including Patna, Nalanda, Nawada, Gaya, Jahanabad, Ara, Rohtas, Aurangabad, Arwal ditricts etc Kurmis' bhoomi sen wasmainly to protect their lands from ultra left and upper caste landloards! Subsequently intense fighting between these senas of vested interests in one hand and MCC (Now CPI-Maoists), and IPF (now CPI-ML) and other naxal organisations started in these districts! By that time ultra left organisations had launched agitation for lands, home for homeless and stopping of atrocity on weaker sections of society by feudal land-owing classes and caste.

Feudal mindest of upper caste grouped and regrouped under the over-all leadership of Ranveer Sena, formed by Baramhshwar Mukhiya. Under the gangloard ship of Mukhiya, upper caste people engaged in mass annihiliation of dalits, Muslims, backwards, poor from upper caste in central Bihar districts. And Ranveer Sena activists under the direct leadership Barhmeshwar Mukhiya started genocides in central Bihar districts and killed over 600 dalits, Muslims, backwards, poor among upper caste to revenge the armed revolution of ultra left parties and killings of upper caste landed atrocious and feudal landlords and their family members in old Gaya and Arungabad districts.

KILLING SPREE:—Thereafter, killing sprees of dalits started and over 300 of them were killed in massacres by Mukhiyas and his army members in late 1980s and in 1990s in Bathani toila, Lakshmanpur-Bathe, Nagari, Sidani, Ekwari, Haibashpur, Miyanpur, Panchkouli aaAkopur and various other villages in the central Bihar districts.

It all started from Congress rule and Laloo-Rabari rule in Bihar mainly. Mainly because Laloo Prasad Yadav, who on his height of mass populariity, had given voices to the weaker sections of society to resist and protest atrocity on them by rich, feudal upper caste in Bihar. Thus gravitation of killing spree by Ranveer Sena and his founder in central Bihar Barhmeshwar Singh took full form, Laloo Prasad Yadav had banned Ranveer Sena and a serious hunt to arrest Mukhiya was started during his regime. Laloo-Rabari tenure in Bihar had also constituted a judicial enquiry commission led by Justice Amir Das to enquire into role of private armies; particularly Ranveer Sena led By Mukhiya in giving results of massacres after massacres in BIhar.

The commission had spotted many active politicians of BJP, Congress etc of particular sections of society in encouraging Ranveer Sena and its head Mukhiya. Being affarid of exposition, many such politicians had demanded scarapping of Amir Das commission. And at last, with the installation of Nitish Kumar of NDA rule in Bihar, the chief minister Nitish Kumar, without assigning any reasons, had scrapped the commission, to utter surpricse of the people of Bihar! Its head and founder Brahmeshwar Mukhiya went underground and remnained elusive for over eight years. Ultimately Brahmeshwar Mukhiya was arrested from Exihibition Road house in Patna and put on trial in over two dozens massacres cases.

Even during underground period, Brahmeshwar Mukhiya used to meet mediapersons and secretly mainly in Kankarbagh areas. Once during morning walk, this writer had by chance meeting with Mukhiya through common acquintances, morning walkers! I asked him why he is killing children and women of dalits. His instant reply to me during morning walk was that "our Sena and I eliminate children as after growing they will become naxalites and raise their voices against upper caste". About women, his reply was, I and my sena activists target them as they give birth to children, who would become naxalites to teach lessons to upper caste landowners." I was stunned with his statement in early 1990s when Brahmeshwar Mukhiyta had surfaced during morning walk in Kankarbagh areas with some of my and his common acquintances!

KILLING OF MUKHIYA BECAUSE OF GANGWARFARE:— Latest killing of Brahmeshwar Mukhiya, in my opinion, is the result of gangawrs among activists of banned. Ranveer Sena as well as fight for political supremacy among higher caste, especially dominant Bhumihars among the legislators of NDA coalitoon government, comprising JD(U) and BJP in Bihar. Apart from that, one more reasons could be cited recent acquital of all the accused persons in a massacre case of 23 dalits including women and children in Ara district including Mukhiya, who were awarded capital punishment and life sentences by the district and session judge of Ara, had been declared null and void by the division bench of the Patna high court. Instead of appealing the case in the Supreme Court, Nitish Kumar government showed dithering attitude to appease a particular upper case and his dominant alliance partner—BJP. I think this must have antagonised concious and elightened people and they would have thought to give instant justice to Mukhiya by killing him.

ORIGIN OF NAXALWAD IN BIHAR:— In 1970s, over a dozen instances of killings of landlords and feudal forces had taken place in north Bihar. It all started from Musahari village in Muzaffarpur district where four landlords were killed by naxalites while carrying out their direct annihiliation theory, propunded by top—ranking naxalites— Charu Mazumdar and Kanu Sanyal. There after a seriors of murders of landlords and feudal people, having vested interests had taken place in Darbhanga district, especially in town areas. The then dreaded naxalite Umadhar prasad Singh, who was product of Naxalbari movement under the leadership of Charu and Kanu, killed a landlord Balani, who created atrocity among weaker sections of society in Darbhanga town suburb, and one Prasad of Mirzapur areas of Darbhanga town, and known for investing money on high interest rate to poor and torturing them in case of non-payment, were killed by Umadhar Singh in direct action of Naxalites. Later Umadhar Singh had told mediapersons in late 1980s that ultra left had now chanmged their strategies because they could not get peoles' support for whom naxalites are eliminating feudal and landloards. Umadhar Singh later became three times MLA from Hayaghat assembly constituency and even today he is formewr naxalite but working for success of naxal movementin the country leaving lonely at his Darbhanga town residence where on a few uyears ago before his death Kanu Sanyal was a regular visitor. Recently, I personally went to meet Umadhar Singh out of courtsey and sauw a host of present and pastMaoists at his residence chalking out strategies over a cup of coffee! Umadhar Singh was also key organiser in giving result to Musahari killings in Muzaffarpur district!

BHOJPUR TURF:—More over later, war of turf shifted to Bhojpur and Gaya zones of Bihar where under the stewardship of Veteran Naxalite top ranking leader Satya Narayan singh had given shapes to annihiliation theory of Naxalites at many places in these areas. Satyanarayan Singh, a resident of a nearby village of Ara town, had spent his whole life in Telegana/areas in Andhra Pradesh for harbouring the naxal activities in that state. In his early 50s, Satyanarayan, who remained underground in Telegana areas, fell ill in the deep forest of Teleganana while underground and before he was gven treatment, he died. It must be recalled that his body was brought to Calcutta just after emergency during the regime of Morarjee Desai and his cremation took place on the confluence of Ganga-sea in Calcutta. His funeral procession was unique in the sense thar being from Bihar, worked whole life for ultra-movement throughout the country, especially in Telegana areas, was well attended. Thousands paid floral tributes to him. His funeral procession was four-kilo meter lomg.

After that mantel of ultra-left movement in central Bihar went to IPF, led by Vinot Mishra and MCC, now CPI-ML (Maoists). Their presence was significant in late 1970s and 1980s and 1990s in Bihar. But at later stage, the IPF, who had gained most popularity among masses, were converted into a political Party-CPI-ML. Practically the CPI-ML had beeen left lone voices of masses in Bihar as one of the viable communist parties in the state. CPI-ML (Maoists) are also concnentrated in Bihar's Gaya, Jahanabad, Muzaffarpur, Champrans, Aurangabad, Jamui, Nawada, Sitamarhi, Raxoul, Purnia, Saharsa, Darbhanga etc areas in Bihar. Of late these naxal organisations are giving shape to spread the movement in different parts of Bihar by spreading its network. Earlier Laloo Prasad Yadav had sympathetic corner with Naxals and Maoists now Nitish Kumar has also applied same theory although during Nitish regime, many hardcore and senior naxal leadrs had been arrested and put behind bars!

In the background f of all thse developemnets in Bihar, the killing of Barhmeshwar Singh Mukhiya must not be taken seriously. But Nitish Kumar will have to answers many questions with latest developments in the wake of killings of Mukhiya and vilolences and vandalism in Ara, Patna and other placres of the state with tacit support of his administration. Nitish Kumar, who is striving hard to build new Bihar and during his stewardship Bihar has started looking up on almost all fronts, must bev facing the worse challenges of his political life. Nitish will must to take final call!

MAMTA IS MASS LEADER, NITISH IS A MANOEUVRER

Monday, 28 May 2012

In the last recent years, two regional straps—Mamta Bannerjee (West Bengal) and Nitish Kumar (BIhar)—have emerged powerful politicians in eastern India out of" negative votes of the electorate in both the states, being disgusted with the misrule of left front government led by Buddhdeo Bhattarya in west Bengal and also Laloo-Rabari "so called Jungle Raj" in Bihar". But there are differences in "negativism" in West Bengal and Bihar. Mamta Bannerjee had been fighting continuously in West Bengal in the last several years of her own and alone while in Bihar Nitish Kumar was working against the Laloo-Rabri misrule along with Hindu saffron party—Bharatiya Janata Party (BJP).

In one aspect Mamta Bannerjee had started anti-left campaign mainly through principled stand of land acquisition from poor farmers mainly in Singur areas for Tata motors as well as atrocity by left brigades in West Bengal for the last 34 years. In the process, she took support of "negative votes" of urban middle class". One thing also went in her favour in dethroning left front government, her clean image and honesty and at the same time wide support base among common masses including Muslim community, which constitute overr 28 percent in West Bengal and alliance with Congress in the last assembly elections in west Bengal about one year back.

Moreover, Nitish Kumar, who upset Laloo-Rabari regime of Rashtriya Janata Dal (RJD) over seven years back and took over the rein of Bihar government, had only "negative votes" against RJD Situation in Bihar had gone bad to worse. But some how or other major chunk of vote banks of national president of RJD remained intact. Laloo was mainly defeated over seven years back with the support of upper caste votes consolidating against him and also militant attitude among upper caste to get Laloo anyhow humiliated. In the process, Laloo lost the support of

421

dalits, poor, other backwards and muslimsas as well as even some chunk of votes of upper caste like Rajputs, who remained with him earlier. Practically, there were outbursts against Laloo Prasad Yadav for creating mess in Bihar during his rule in 15 years in Bihar. Nitish proved more tactful in managing these splinter votes along with bulk chunk of votes of miltant upper caste in both the assembly elections with the support of his alliance partners—BJP.

Like Mamta Baneerjee, Nitish could not be described as mass base leader! On the front of proven integrity, Mamta Bannerjee is at high pedestal—there having been no finger raised against her for accepting money or creating corrupt bureaucracy. In this sector, Nitish excelled many political leaders. During his regime of over seven years, corrupt practises have increased mani-fold in Bihar. Rather people of Bihar are groaning under corruptions right from panchayat and block level to secretariat level of Bihar government.

Not only that, there are no complaints against Mamta Bannerjee that she had given seats to industrialists or capitalists for Rajya Sabha on the consideration of money. But in Bihar, it is open secret that Nitish Kumar and his alliance partner—BJP have sold seats to industrialists and money mafia. In the process, Nitish Kumar from his JD(U) quota has given Rajya sabha seat twice to one King Mahendra of Bihar, a medicine producer allegedly in lieu of money. A retired controversial IAS official Mr N K Singh was admitted in JD(U) fold and made Rajya Sabha member from Bihar by JD(U) of Nitish Kumar, reasons best known to him. Singh was in no way connected with JD(U) any time in the past! In this respect Mamta had given her party nomination to a few journalists of proven integrity.

Mamta, having all political qualities, is not so shrewed like Nitish Kumar. Once Laloo had described Nitish Kumar that "Nitish has teeths in his stomach (Nitish ke pet mein daint hai)"! Mamata, who has become targets of media in west Bengal because of her frankness while Nitish kumar has controlled the media by practically declaring "undeclared censorship on news papers and news magazines as well as electronic channels" through his manoeuvrings in distributing advertisements indiscriminately and also through pulling up owners of newspapers and electronic channels!

One factor is also marring Mamta's prospect in West Bengal despite her mass support base, Mamta appears all alone in carrying the responsibility of running her government without any vocal support from her party leaders in Trinamula Congress as well as Ally-Congress party, whereas Nitish Kumar has array of leaders both in his party—(JDU) and alliance partner—BJP to highlights the things unnecessarily. I find while Nitish Kumar making only announcements of developments in the last over seven years more and his colleagues in alliance partner and his own party more vocal in highlighting achievements and developments in Bihar—that are not true!

Unlike Nitish Kumar, Mamta has strong base among Scheduled Caste, Scheduled Tribes and Minority Muslims (Muslims alone constitute around 28 percent of the West Bengal electorate). Although Nitish Kumar in Bihar has also initiated certain measures among Muslims, particularly Pasmanda (backward and dalit Muslims) to woe the minority, the muslims are still feeling not so secured in the hands of Nitish because of saffron party—BJP, being his alliance party in Bihar and at the central level also. Muslims as a whole are not happy with Nitish Kumar for dividing Muslims as backwards and forwards Derfinitely; Nitish Kumar has implemented reservation for women and mahadalits for their upliftment for having biggest share of chunk of development measures. But these measures are already in vogue in West Bengal well before the installation of Mamta Bannerjee government in West Bengal! In this respect Mamta is in advantageous position because she has been beating left front from their sticks in the changed political scenario.

On land reforms measures and stopping of forcible land acquisition, Mamta Bannerjee had long back pulled up the carpet from left front government led by CPI-M in West Bengal. Before coming to power Mamta had vigorously opposed the land acquisition move in Singur and Nandigram against the left government policy of land acquisition for industrial purposes. She put the left front on wrong box as harbourer of industrialisation by snatching land of poor land owners, she presented herself as fighter for the right of farmers, after assuming power in West Bengal she outmanoeuvred the left at its own game. She adopted firm stand against foreign direct investment (FDI) in retail, creation of special economic zone (SEZ) in West Bengal, She also opposed Pension Fund Regulatory development authority bill at union level, which the left parties had made their own agenda. Similarly she had opposed Lokayukta clause in the Lokayukta bill and has practically held to ransom the move of the centre on the National Counter Terrorism Centre notification under Unlawful Activities Act. She had been harping seriously on a three—year moratorium on the interest on loans taken by the west Bengal government in successive yrears from Union government.

On these scores, Nitish Kumar had lagged behind in vocally raising the issue. On land reform measures for implementing bataidari right and surplus land to landless, Nitish is yet to fulfil his promises despite the facts that he had constituted Bandopadhaya committee on much fan-fare. Bandopadhaya committee's recommendations on land reforms if gatherinmg dust. To please upper caste vote banks and his alliance partner-conservative BJP, Nitish put the entire land reform measures in cold storage just on the eve of the last assembly elections to please the vested interest vote banks! Unlike Mamta, Nitish is gradually acquiring lands for setting up industries for investors in Bihar.

Both have similarity in at least one aspect—that is wiping out opposition voices through political violences. In Mamta regime in the past one year more than 90 persons have been killed in political violences, mainly from CPM rank and file. Nitish Kumar also weakened the opposition voices in Bihar and has become allegedly instrumental political violences, over 200 persons were killed in the last two years In Bihar—recent one is a liquor trader in Gopalganj district by his party MLA Pappu Pandey, against who a case has been registered for murdering the liquor trader a few days back. Opposition voices and suggestions are ignored by Nitish Kumar and practically thrown into waste papers baskets right from Assembly proceedings to government level.

Mamta had different approaches from Nitish to refute her failures in governance. She used to tell entire thing has been "shajona (staged)"— right from Park street rape case to attacks on media, suicides of framers and agriculture labourers. On the other hand Nitish Kumar government in Bihar does not take notices of all these failures in authoritarian style although Mamta Bannerjee also believes in tackling her failures in authoritarian style. Mamta always sees the spectre of the CPI(M) behind any embarrassment to the government. In this game Nitish Kumar has unique style of silencing vocal opponents like Ram Bilas Paswan and Laloo Prasad Yadav, by reminding the people the past misdeeds of both these leaders.

Both Mamta and Nitish have to some extend achieved success in tackling Naxalite or Maoists problems. While Mamta, who had got maximum support in dethroning left front government by Maoists, had forgotten all those things in "realpolitik". She discarded them after coming to power. she successfully combined armed forces operation against naxalites militants, fighting for advasis along with promise of development in the naxal-infested zones of Pachim Midanapore, Bankura and Purulia etc in the zone where Maoist violences, prevalent since 2008. Nitish Kumar, who is also in agonising moments because of intermittent naxal violences in different parts of Bihar, specially in Champaran and Juamui region, has also played his card very cautiously and like Laloo Pradsad has made naxalites and their organisation his friends for temporary truce. His government, although, has even failed ro modernise the police forces and initiating development measures in naxal-infested areas in Bihar despite the facts that union government has pumped huge funds on this score.

Mamta has interestingly faced Gorkhaland problem by signing an accord with Gorkha Janmukti Morcha for the establishment of a larger autonomous Gorkha Territoral administration and in initiating anti-land acquisition for industries through a move to put on the investors themselves for acquiring land for setting up industries themselves, who have promised investment proposals of over Rs 80,000 crore in the first nine months of her tenure. In Bihar Nitish Kumar had has not succeeded in preparing any blue prints for setting up industries in Bihar by investors although the Bihar government has received such proposals worth over Rs 60000 crore in the last two years.

On the moratorium of interest on loans from union government, Mamta is fighting tooth and nails with the centre and also for adequate fund for the development measures for West Bengal and she has been given patience hearing by union government on this score, Nitish Kumar, who is raising persistent campaign for special status to Bihar, has been rebuffed by the Planning Commission that Bihar could not be put under special category quota. However, the long fight of Nitish has extracted assurances from union government and planning commission that special assistance's might be arranged to Bihar from central government!

Now the question is of mass appeal of both the regional stalwarts from eastern states. Mamta has clean image!

There used to become many ups and down for Mamta in West Bengal—but when I visited the many parts of West Bengal in March-April, I found that Mamta Bannerejee has definite mass appeal throughout the West Bengal! Even her worst critics, never deny her courage, fortitude and financial integrity! She has proved that she is the credible leader in West Bengal against left parties. She is the lone face among women leader, who without any tacit support of anybody, particularly male politicians, has succeeded in ending the 34 year rule of left front government in West Bengal. Many political obituary and epitaph have been written on Mamta but she proved that she is the mass leader of West Bengal without any black-spot. And After Jyoti Basu, Mamta Bannerjee has only appeal among masses of West Bengal. Here I must compare her with Laloo Prasad Yadav of Bihar, who had such tremendous mass appeal in touching the hearts of rural poor and in giving the poor the voices in Bihar in late 1990s and early 2000s. Like Laloo Mamta, in her oratorial skill, speaks voices of people in West Bengal like Laloo in his typical style, used to speak the voices of poor in Bihar.

Nitish Kumar of Bihar, who had given hopes and aspirations to the people of Bihar for rebuilding a new Bihar, has developed many ifs and buts. Enlightened people had seen in Nitish Kumar, an able and efficient administrator like first chief minister of Bihar Dr Sri Krishna Sinha! But hopes and aspirations are bellying! His authoritarian and dictatorial style apart from his dependence on bureaucracy have cost him heavily and dented his public image. His image has taken down-turn especially in rural areas because of non-implementations of his promises at the time of elections. Situation has come to such a pass that now the people have stated demonstrating against him and pelting stones on him during his various yatras in rural areas!

WELFARE PROGRAMMES AND LIFE OF DALITS AND ADIVASI IN INDIA!

Saturday, 28 April 2012

For the last few days, my mind is being agonised to see the reports about the plight of poor, dalits and Adivasis in India even after the facts that the Union government and various state governments pumping huge resources for their upliftment through various flagship programmes and implementation of laws stringently for their welfare. Instead of development in poor, dalits, and adivasis zones in the country and improvement in their life-style, they are getting more and poorer and these people are being exploited more and more! Just this reminds me one of the statements of Dr B R Ambedkar," My final words of advice to you are educated, organise and agitate. Ours is a battle not for wealth or for power. It is battle for freedom. It is a battle for reclamation of human personality."

Since the Independence of the country in 1947, it appears that some things tangible are being made to uplift the rural poor, tribal, and dalits, but on the ground realities, we find very insignificant impact of all these measures; exploitations are there; untouchablity and hatred towards dalits and adivasis are prevalent; Feudals' conservative attitude towards them continue—and what not? Slight changes are there in exploitation—earlier it was by and large by landlords, moneyed people, upper caste people, bureaucrats—now a different class of neo-rich class in the shape of influential political class, corporates, capitalists, industrialists, multinationals has emerged. Attitude of upper caste, landlords, conservative people have also added new dimensions to the present state of affairs.

Socio-economic rights of people through "flagship" programmes like Sarva Shiksha Abhiyan(SSA), Mahatma Gandhi National Rural Employment Guarantee Act (MANREGA), National Rural Health Mission (NRHM), Integrated Child Development Scheme(ICDS),

Indira awas Yojana(IAY) for houses to homeless as well as semblance of equality before law like removal of untouchablity, continued hatred of sons and daughters of lower caste in different spheres of life, particularly in educational institutions are gradually being trampled in India because of politicians—bureaucrats—upper caste—vested interest nexus! Same tales are with various state governments' welfare schemes to uplift poor, dalits and tribal! Amount for all these flagship programmes of government of India as well as welfare schemes of different state governments are being spent but fruits of benefits hardly reach to them in rural areas. In Human Development Index, deprived people are at the lowest level on almost all fronts.

Teams of social audits of implementation of all these welfare measures by various organisations even of the Sample Survey Organisations of India (SSOI) and also by the international organisations like World bank and its subsidiaries, International Children Emergency Fund (ICEF) have exposed the hollow claims of the union government and state governments about benefits and improvements in their life. Particularly, ICDS programme implementation throughout the country is marred by corrupt practises and the benefit to poor under the scheme fail to reach at the ground level.

A recent book," the Integrated Child Development Services: A flagship adrift" by K R Venugoapal, Konark Publication highlights important insights into functioning of the scheme In Andhra Pradesh and other parts of the country. Apart from that, audit reports of Audior and Comptroller General of India (CAG), specially in Bihar has pointed out various irregularities and corrupt practises in the flagship programmes of the centre and also welfare mare programmes of the Bihar government. Under NDA rule led by chief minister Nitish Kumar. Non-utilisation of fund on various flagship programmes of the centre by the Bihar government have been rampantly pointed out as per recently released CAG report on Bihar. The report has came down heavily on the Bihar government for financial indiscipline. The report has commented that Rs 10309 crore were transferred by the centre directly to the state implementing agencies, but the Bihar government hasd failed to submit proper documentation and status of expenditure by these implementing agencies. Fate crores of rupees spent by the Bihar government are not known, the report said, adding that out of Rs 25331.05 crore drawn on 83542 AC bills, only 9425 DC bills for Rs 2755.68 crore were submitted to the Accountant General of Bihar. As on September 14, 2011, DC bills in respect of 74117AC bills for Rs 22575.37 crore drawn between 2003 to 2010-11 were not submitted despite repeated requests. Under one flagship programme—Indira Awas Yojana—The Bihar government due to carry over of funds in excess of the prescribed norms, resulting into non-release of Rs 794.14 crore by the central government. Over 10000 crore of central fund on MGNREG, ICD, NRHM etc have not been utilised, Utilised amount of over Rs 3000 crore on these scores have been misappropriated at different level of Bihar government in the last two financial years!

Venigopal's book has given much food for thoughts how the major chunk of ICDS have been misappropriated in Andhra Pradesh districts, especially Anantpur of that state and other districts of of other states. The book of Venugopal has covered a wide range of issues including immunisation, health check ups and referral and the form it takes (locally cooked or prepared ready to eat) pre-school education, maternal health, nutrition education. In all these aspect, the book has described the situation dismal and disappointing. Under the ICDS, even supply of iron and folic acid tablets to pregnant women and vitamin A tablets to children are not distributed in rural areas. All these have resulted into unsafe pregnancy and defects in birth. There are no centres, formally opened in the rural areas of the country. Anganwadi Sevika, workers and helpers have lack of inadequate training for such activities. Venugopal has suggested in the book "all aganwadi centres be converted into creches that function from 8.30 am to 5.30 pm, retaining all the current services with additional provision for serving supplementary nutrition thrice a day, doubling the strength of anganwadi workers and helpers, utilising voluntary services of trained and willing adolescents girls and raising the honourarium of anganwadi workers for the longer hours of work." Apart from bungling of funds meant for ICDS under Aganwadi being misappropriated by government officials inconvenience with aganwadi workers, there is wide scale social discrimination. Upper caste children and women do not attend aganwadi centres, located in dalit tolas. They do not take food prepared by dalits anganwadi workers under ICDS. Upper caste men do not allow their children and women to mix with lower caste children and women in aganwadi centres. Thus centre's major flagship programme is in deep sea like other programmes including MGERGS in rural areras of the country.

Such point has shocked me when I further analysed the facts about social discrimination and untouchablity practise in educational institutions, particularly of national repute like AIIMS, where dalit and advasis students are tortured, resulting into their deaths in many cases. Such incidents have taken place with Angita Veghada, a first years students of B Sc. Nursing, Institute of Nursing, Ahmedabad, Jaspreet singh, final year MBBS, Government Medical college, Chandigrah, S Amravathi, national-level young women boxer, Centre of Excellence, Sports Authority of AP, Hyderabad, Senthali Kumar, Ph D School of Physics, University of Hyderabad, Malepula Shrikant, Final year B Tech, IIT, Bombay, G Suman, Final year M Tech, IIT Kanpur, Ajay S Chandra, integrated PhD, Indian Institute of science, Banglore, D Shyam Kumar, First year B Tech, Sarojinin Institute of engineering and Technology, Vijayawada, Anil Kumar Meena, First year AIIMS, New Delhi, Sushil Kumar Chaudhary Final year MBBS, Chhatrapati shahuji Maharaj Meducal university (former KGMC), Luchknow, Manish Kumar,3rd year student of B tecxh, IIT Roorkee, G Varalakshmi, B Tech first year, Vignan Engineering College, Hyderabad, Linesh Mohan Gawle, PhD, National Institute of Immunology, New Delhi, Madhuri Sale, Final Year B Tech, IIT Kanpur, J K Ramesh, second year B Sc. University of Agriculture Sciences, Banglore, Bandi Anusha B Com final year Villa Marry College, Hyderabad, and Pushpoanjali Poorty, First year MBA, Vesvesvaraih Technological university Banglore. Lists are long!

A recent Opinion piece by S Anand in Outlook India, has pointed out, "Most children of from Disadvantaged caste end up as maids, child labourers or drop outs. In most of rural India Dalit students are asked to sit apart, sweep the school veranda or clean toilets. Omprakash Valmiki, the Hindi Dalit writer in his autobiography JOOTHAN, recalls the humiliation of being forced to perform his caste occupation by his head master, who told him,' Go sweep the whole playground. Otherwise, I will shove chillies up your arse and throw you out of school" Almost every first generation formally educated Dalit has such horror stories to share. For every youth who manage to persist with the skewed education system for members of the family skip a meal; sibling work as farm labour to help one person hope for and dream of a life of dignity. For a Dalit girl, the odds were worse."

Following a report in the Telegraph, UK: "fewer than one in 100 students beginning courses at Britain's two oldest universities in 2010 were Black, including just 20 of the 2617 British students accepted to Oxford, a fall from 27 in 2009" A Black Labour Party MP collected data using freedom of information and wrote a column in The Guardian, "lamenting, The Oxford whitewash." S Anand further wrote in his Opinion piece, "the debate in Britain is in sharp contrast to the silence in India. In 2006, following reports of discrimination in internal evaluation (especially practical and viva), segregation in hostels, mess rooms and in sports and cuiural events, A three-member committee headed by Sukhdeo Thorat, then chairman of the University Grants Commission, conducted an enquiry into the state of affairs in the AIIMS. The 77-page report of the Thorat committee indicted the administration on many counts and offered recommendations but it was dismissed as prejudiced and no action was taken."

There is no murmur when dalit students are murdered in campuses, Anand says, what makes Indian society so shameless as to not just deny but even justify such prejudices against Dalits that lead to murders?" Anand further argues, "Just imagine the repercussions if Black students were to die half as routinely in Harvard or in Oxford as Dalits and Adivasis students die in AIIMS, IITS and IISCS."

Are you we not living in primitive retrograde society?

ARE THE PUBLICATIONS OF BOOKS ON 100TH YEAR OF BIHAR BY BIHAR LEGISLATIVE COUNCIL UNTRUE AND BEYOND HISTORICAL FACT?

Wednesday, 18 April 2012

One cannot ignore the historical facts based on true events, learning and historical records. And if one does that, he will have to put himself in ridicule. There is a phrase or proverb, "for hiding one truth, one has to speak thousands of lies to justify his stand and ultimately he becomes ridiculous in the eyes of history, culture and many other aspects".

Such unprecedented stories are being planted by the Bihar government as well as the Bihar Legislative Council for celebrating the so called 100th years of the state. While the chief minister of Bihar Nitish Kumar is cashing on image building by holding centenary celebrations of Bihar here and in different parts of the country, the chairman of the Legislative Council Pundit Tara Kant Jha has gone a step further in celebrating 100th years of Bihar throughout the year-1912 as part of the centenary celebration programme of the Legislative Council and origin of Bihar. Over a dozen books, narrating Bihar and its people, culture, participation of people of Bihar in freedom movement etc, have been published in multi-coloured glossy papers in book forms. Contents in many books have ignored the facts on Bihar, based on history!

(I have written two articles on March 5, 2012 and March 14, 2012 on my blog-www.kksingh1.blogspot.com under headlines "Hype over Bihar Diwas vis-a-vis Facts about Bihar and Strange political development in mid 1950s to merge Bihar and Bengal as joint state.)

Exactly, the Bihar government and Legislative Council have based that the origin of Bihar was on March 22, 1912. It appears that both Bihar government and Legislative Council have erred in establishing of the exact year and date of creation of Bihar. As per historical facts, it was in 1912, a state of "Bihar and Orrisa" was created after carving out of the greater Bengal by British Raj—than how could anybody say that Bihar was created in 1912—it was both Bihar and Orrisa was separated from Bengal and made a separate state. Exactly Bihar was finally came into shape as separate state in 1936 through an Act passed by the British Parliament. The Act was named as British India Act-1935 on which our Constitution is mainly based!

If one go into detail and admit the contention of Pundit Tarakant Jha and Mr Nitish Kumar's, sponsored books and statements, that Bihar was created in 1912 and its origin was in 1912 and that is 100th years of Bihar—than one has to peep into the historical facts since East India Company days much, much before when our country was slaved by British Raj snatching the rule of slavery of India from East India Company. In 1764, East India Company, which had initially come here for trading, had started taking interest in the rule of India. At that time, a battle, namely" Battel of Buxar" had taken place between Nawabs of Awadh and other small rulers one side and Birtish India Company on another side. Ultimately, the British East India Company had won the battle. The Company got raiyati rights of Bihar, Bengal and Orrisa and started ruling over them. The company formed "Presidency of Bengal", comprising Bihar, Bengal and Orrisa after ruling for several years the company handed over the suzerainty to British Raj and India along with entire south, and west, east was slaved by British Raj.

Historians and History books have such orientation about creation of Bihar. Only Mr Nitish Kumar and Pundit Tara Kant Jha could tell the justification of exact date of origin of Bihar state in India. Facts are crystal clear! Facts need broader debate over exact date of origin of Bihar although Bihar is ancient old and formerly named as Behara Books on centenary celebrations on glossy coloured papers with aggrandisements of present day political rulers have hardly referred the historical facts about the origin of Bihar, published by Legislative Council and also by the Bihar government.

However, the legislative Council has engaged on at least one historian, Prof Nihar Nandan Sinha, a professor of Patna university, who had has mainly written on the contributions of people, engaged in the freedom movement instead of digging up historical facts about origin of Bihar except at one point he has mentioned about creation of Bihar and Orrisa as separate state by carving out Bengal in 1912. Other persons engaged in the publications of the books, published by Legislative

Council, come from general walks of life and they have no connections with historical facts about origin of Bihar.

In my opinion Pundit Tara Kant Jha and Mr Nitish Kumar should hold broader debates by historians Bo, expert ON both ancient and medieval period to come the conclusion of exact dates of origin of Bihar! Both owe explainations from the people of Bihar!

COMMUNAL HARMONY IN INDIA SINCE MEDIEVALPERIOD!

Thursday, 29 March 2012

Apart from some unfortunate incidents like demolition of Babari Masjid a few years back and killings of thousands of people of Muslims and Hindus in the wake of partition of the country as well as some serious Hindu-Muslim riots in independent India in past years and also before that some destruction of religious places by Muslim rulers in the medieval period, communal harmony has remained by and large an important factor in the country amid tremendous diversity in India! Only because of that, we are holding our country together in secularism and giving equal respect to all communities.

I must begin with a quote of the eminent scholar and former judge of the Supreme Court Markandey Katju, before deliberating more facts on the secular fabric of India. Justice Katju has said, "Since there is so much diversity in India the only policy which will work is the policy of secularism and giving equal respect to all communities. Otherwise India will break up into a hundred pieces since there is so much diversity." Justice Katju has made this remark while delivering his speech to non-residents Indians in California in June 2011.

We must remember about our modern India. In Katju's opinion, two people—Emperor Akbar and and former prime minister Pundit Jawahar Lal Nehru can be said the creators of present day modern India.

Emperor Akbar has no parallel in the world as ruler of honesty and integrity. In the 16th century Akbar had proclaimed the doctrine of Suleh-ekul, which means "universal tolerance of all religion." At that time there were upheavals in Europe. Exuropeans were massacring each other in the name of religion, Catholics massacring Protestants, Proteststants massacring Catholics and both massacring Jews. Similarly In India, religious passions were inflamed after partition in 1947 and people of both Hindu and Muslim communities behaved like animals. Both of them were butchering each other. Pakistan had declared itself an Islamic state. We can imagine tremendous pressure on the then prime minister Pundit Jawaghar Lal Nehru at that time to declare India as Hindu state! But Pundit Nehru kept cool and declared that India will not be a Hindu state but will be secular state and provided such Constitution to India! Katju has further commented, "For this reason, we are relatively more stability as compared to our neighbouring countries.

More over, initially Muslim invaders including Mahmud Ghazani had demolished a lot of temples including Somanath temple. But their descendants, who were Muslim rulers in different parts of India, did not disturb the secular equilibrium of India. In many cases, historically we find that they used to give grants for upkeep and maintenance of temples. They celebrated Holi and Diwali festivals together. One example, Babar was an invader but Akbar was not invader; he was born in India and was very much an Indian. These descendants of the invaders ruled India, having population of 80 to 90 percent Hindus. If they continued in demolishing temples, there would have been turmoil and in their interest, they fostered communal harmony; they gave grants to temples, they celebrated Hindu festivals. Another example" Nabab of Awadh used to organise Ramlila and celebrate Holi and Diwali. Tipu Sultan used to give annual grants to 156 temples, his prime minister was a Hindu called Purnaiya and his commander-in-chief was a Hindu, called Krishna Rao. Tipu Sultan sent 30 respectful letters with grants to the Shankaracharya of Sringeri."

Surprisingly British had always played games to divide Muslim and Hindu—In history of that time, you will find mention of communal tinges in the society between Hindu and Muslim but will not find communal harmony, spread by Muslim rulers in the form of "land grants for building Hindu temples, celebrated and organised Hindu festivals etc".

Our history books, influenced by Britishers, have depicted many nasty stories of communal disharmony! One instance is about a book written by Professor of Sanskrit in Calcutta university Harprasad Shastri, in which, 'it was mentioned that Tipu sultan told 3000 Brahimins to covert to Islam or otherwise they would be killed and those 3000 Brahmins committed suicide rather become Muslims. On reading this, Professor of History in Allahabad University Prof Pandey said that when he asked Prof Shastri about the source of such write up, Prof Shastri replied that that the source of information was the Mysore Gazetteer. again Prof Pandey wrote to Prof of history in the Mysore University

Srikant-Prof Srikant wrote back to Prof Pandey that this was totally false—there is no such mention in the Mysore Gazetteer; rather correct version was just reverse namely the Tipu Sultan used to give annual grants to 156 temples, he used to send grants to the Shankracharya Of Sringeri."

Justice Katju further spoke in his lecture, "It is time we rewrite our history books and show that in fact upto 1857 there was no communal problem at all in India. A composite culture had been developing in India. Hindus used to participate in Eid and Muharram celebrations and Muslims used to participate in Holi, Diwali etc festivals. There were some difference no doubt, but they were becoming narrower."

He further said, "In 1857, the great mutiny took place. Hindus and Muslims jointly fought against the British. After suppressing mutiny it was decided by the British rulers that that the only way to control country was to divide and rule. In other words, Hindu and Muslims must be made to fight each other. Communal riots started in 1857. English collector would secretly call Hindu pundits and give him money to speak against Muslims and similarly he would secretly call the Maulvi and give him some Maulvi to speak against Hindu. A racket was started in this way and and this resulted ultimately into partition in 1947."

After we achieved part independence, there were many Hindu-Muslim riots were reported and it started from Ranchi and Jamshedpur in joint Bihar. There after, many more were reported in the country, killings of thousands of people exact figure of killings in Hindu-Muslim riots since independence have been carried out in the Outlook India recently. Worse communal carnage was reported in Gujarat and the chief minster oif Gujarat Narendra Modi was allegedly main conspirators in eliminating Muslims from Gujarat. Many killings of Muslims in riots were reported from Gujarat under the leadership of Narendra Bhai Modi. Demolition of Babari Masjid in Ayodhaya by Hinduvata forces, particularly Bharatiya Janata Party, led by Lal Knrishna Advani has become another blot on the secular fabric of India!

Justice Katju has cautioned Indians and said, "India is passing through transitional phase from feudal agriculture society to to a modern industrial society. In my opinion the duty of all patriotic people is to help in shortening this transition period, in reducing this pain . . . . there is going to be turmoil in this period since the vested interest of old feudal order will not give up their vested interests without a fierce struggle—we must combat caste ism, communal ism and superstitions in order to get over the transition period faster and with less pain."

ORIGIN OF COMMUNISM IN INDIA VIS-A-VIS COALITION ERA IN INDIA!

Sunday, 18 March 2012

In my earlier blog, I have reasoned in detail importance of regional parties in coalition government in India at a time when both national parties—Congress and Bharatiya Janata Party (BJP) waning its influence and importance in the country's political scenario!

Communism has their origin lies before the independence of the Country. Communists had initially split from the Indian National Congress and subsequently from a pressure group within the Congress-Congress Socialist Party (CSP). Many books have been written on the origin of Communism in India (Whilch I will name later on), mainly on the communists' split with the Congress Socialist Party; the CPI's stand on the second world war; the second party congress in 1948; evolution of tactical line, the leaders' historic meeting with Joseph Stalin in Moscow; the Telengna struggle and the Andhra Thesis. Eminent writer A G Noorani has threw light on communism and communists. In my view, communist plays important role in this coalition era in the country!

On the basis of an interview with towering communist leader of India, Jyoti Basu on behalf of NMMLby, Shikha Mukherjee and Usha Prasad on December 18, 2001 on some in depth facts about communism and its role in formation of coalition governments at the centre and states have come to light. Apart from speaking about lack of proper policy with regards to giving autonomy and more powers to the Kashmiris, ways to put down militancy and solution of problems politically etc, Jyoti Basu had said to the interviewers, "It was not just once that he was invited to become prime minister. The full accounts bear quotations in extenso. You see, when the United Front was there, we got a majority and the Congress said that it would support us so as to keep the BJP at bay. So we got together, but who would be the prime minister? VPSingh would be the best person, but he was ill. So they all, 12 parties, said: you must be the prime minister. Why did they say it? It was not because I am God's son, but because, as you said, I have got experiences of running a United Front government and the left Front government. That is why they thought that our party should join the 12-parties government, and I should become prime minister."

Basu had further said, "Then what happened was that because before the elections, we had no common programme although we were fighting together against the Congress. We said in the election meetings—I had spoken in many election meetings: We should help to form government but we will not be part of it (That had been our View). Now since you are requesting 12 parties, including CPI, whose representative Indrajit Gupta became the home minister, we have to call a meeting of the central committee of the CPI-M. That is the way we function; it is democratic functioning. So we called a meeting of of the central committee on their request:: This new situation has arisen and so we have to have a programme that they want us to enter the government and I become the prime minister. In voting there was division. I think by 8 or 10 votes we lost—our general secretary and I were in the minority. We thought politically it would be excellent thing and the right thing to do so to join this government and head it, try to lead it. Even though it may be for few months, it would be politically advantageous. But the majority thought otherwise that it would be a great risk for us to join with these people but we said: Already we had worked out common minimum programme for West Bengal United Front government. Now we will have common minimum programme at the centre. As people saw in West Bengal united Front government, similarly, on an all India scale it will help our party, it will help the left forces. Other said: nothing can be done with leading the government but we can support 12 of them. Some of them, that are true also, were very much against our policies like the then Finance minister, he was very much against our policy but our argument was: In the centre, the prime minister is unlike what we have in West Bengal, in Kerala. In the centre the prime minister wields a lot of influences and we can for the time being influence them***********the people would have new experience; within these limitations so many things could be done. Then if we are thrown out we shall leave a new experience for the people cannot last for five years. The Congress is supporting us. When they will withdraw support, people will judge who is to blame. If it is breaks up, then we could leave some thing behind for the people***** but my argument was not accepted by the majority. Again a second meeting was called. This time also we failed. Among the comrades of West Bengal also there is also division******".

"When 11 non-communist parties, VPSingh and others asked the CPI(M)—the CPI had decided to join the government—to join the government will with me as prime minister, it would be correct step. In parliamentary democracy, never in the world has such situation arisen. Again I say this is a historic blunder. Historic, why, because such opportunity does not come, history does not present you with such opportunities. But anyway that was that . . . ."

AS regards BJP coalition working, Basu had said, "all these state parties and groups want to become ministers. We cannot form such coalition. According to us, if there is not minimum understanding sincerely pursued, we should not have a government, but the BJP does not believe in any principles or politics, it wants to rule and Hinduvata and all this business are there; they are guided by the RSS (Rashtriya Swayasevak Sangh) and the VHP (Vishwa Hindu Parishad)," Basu added and cited several examples when he was requested by Congress including Arjun Singh, Pranaba Mukherjee and Samajwadi leaders like Chandra Shekhar and the then Samajwadi Yashwant Sinha, now in BJP, Mulayam singh Yadav had requested me to become prime minister!

Now I will shift on history of Communist movement in India. To begin with I must refer towering EMS Namboodirpad and his interview to Hari Prasad Sharma. EMS had said, "Actually I first came in touch with the communist groups in Andhra about February 1935 when M RMasani and I were returning from Nagpur where a meeting of the national executive of Congress Socialist Party (CSP) was being held. We both went to Guntur to address a meeting of the (CSP). There there was a group of communists; they were putting questions to Masani and he was answering them. Persons, who were asking questions on behalf of e M Basavapunniah of Communist Party. I did not know them and had no interactions with them. The actual personal contact that I had with communist with South India or with the communists anywhere in India was some time in October 1935 and that was at Madras with P Sundarayya. Again the opportunity was meeting of Indian National Congress in Madras in which I had gone there to participate as Congress delegate. There a radical conference was being held, a forum in which all the radical groups like the Royists, the CPI, the CSP and unattached individuals and trade unions had been participating. The meeting was attended by Krishna Pillai and me. One of the delegates was also P Sundarayya. And I met him and that the first real discussions held between authorised representatives of the Communist Party and us in 1935."

EMS had further said to interviewer, "a nucleus of Communist Party was formed in Andhra. From there my journey to communist party began. There after I met Jayaprakash Narayan, actively involved in CSP and told him that I was keeping contacts with communists. CSP led by JP wanted to unite all revolutionary forces including the communists. From there I spread the network of communist party in Kerala and other parts of the country. EMS added.

P Sundaarayya was legend in his own life time in Telengana. He had told HDSharma in his interview, "JP and Acharya Narendra Dev and certain other sections were definitely for a united movement though they did not want this full-fledged communist approach. One accusation against us that the communists will always follow the instruction they got from the communist international or what they call the Soviet leadership. Majority was with JP, naturally, did not accept some of the issues that were raised and knowing that we could not get through we also did not insist too much on it. Congress socialism was contradictory in words and would pave way to fascism," he added and continued for ultra communist movement in Telengana region of Andhra.

Another senior Communist leader Basavapunniah told his interviewer Sharma about the Telengana revolt in detail. After war in 1945, this movement in Nizam's areas had taken a very militant form. When we had to fight against Nizam, his Razakars, his army, his police and all that, then we were compelled to go far guerrilla warfare, armed warfare and with all these ideas we had go through Mao's theory of partisan welfare, guerrilla warfare and peasant warfare etc. The Andhra unit took the lead in this respect because it went into action first, a militant form of struggle and faced police bullets, repression by armies of theNizam and all that. The second phase of revolution was after the Indian government had come in. The alternative that had posed before us was either to abandon the whole struggle and leave the land and leaves the peasantry to its fate or to organise the peasantry and resist and demand that these lands must be with us and not allow landlords to reoccupy the land. The Government of India was trying to suppress it with arms. We decided to that we must resist the maximum. So this resistance went for on for three years. Whereas Sardar Patel was thinking that in 30 days everything will be finished but it took three years. Meanwhile Sardar had finished himself but the movement it was not finished."

In between Communist party faced many splits in its rank and file! But the communism have not died down. Of all communist leaders SA Dngeh proved a villain of the piece in weakening the communism in India. In 1920s Dange, of fascinating character man, a brilliant pamphleteer, orator and a supple tactician had apologised to the British government and released from Sitapur jail where he was serving four-year-sentence in Kanpur conspiracy case, eminent columnist Noorani has said.

Ultimately united Communist party split and CPI(M) and CPI remained on in existence as well as communist, having hard lines design, also split and continuing in various factions like CPI-ML, many groups, CPI (Maoists) etc. But these communist parties have their regional standings and winning elections of both Lok Sabha and state assemblies in the country and raising the voices of poor against exploitations.

STRANGE POLITICAL DEVELOPMENTS:
MOVE TO MERGE BIHAR AND WEST BENGAL!

Wednesday, 14 March 2012

Some Time strange political developments take place in India. Bihar, Bengal, Orrisa were part and parcels after Buxar battle in 1764 and the British's East India Company had created Presidency of Bengal, merging these three regions in one part. Thereafter, during British Raj, the Raj separated Bengal and created Bihar and Orrisa a separate state in 1912. Again in 1935, after creation of India Act, enacted by British Parliament, Orrisa was separated from Bihar and Bihar became new state! Orrisa was also born separately. Subsequently many developments had taken place and India got independence in 1947 and we got a New Constitution of Independent India.

Notably, some portion of Bihar like Purulia areas of Bihar was transferred to West Bengal under the recommendations of the State Reorganisation Commission. Much hue and cry were raised over the transfer of parts and districts of Bihar to West Bengal. Matter took serious turn with animosity between the people of Bihar and West Bengal. Amid sentimental atmosphere, the Indian National Congress had approved a resolution merging Bihar and West Bengal in its Anmritsar session. The then chief Ministers Dr Sri Krishna Singh (Bihar) and Dr Bidhan Chandra Roy had signed on an agreement for merger of Bihar and West Bengal on January 23, 1956 and for carrying the resolutions of merger in their respective Legislatures. Remarkably, Dr Sri Krishna Sinha held a press conference in Delhi and announced to utter surprise of the people that by May 1956, a bill will be introduced in the Parliament to formalise the merger of Bihar and West Bengal. Later on Orrisa will also be merged with the merged state of West Bengal and Bihar!

Amid politically surcharged atmosphere during those days, the then Governor of Bihar Dr R R Diwakar, while addressing the joint session of

Bihar Legislature on January 31, 1956, informed the legislators the desire of the SKSinha government to bring a resolution in both the houses of the Legislature for merging both Bihar and West Bengal into single state. While narrating the sequences of events in the wake of bifurcating some areas including Purulia from Bihar and merge with West Bengal, Dr Diwakar had told the joint session" lack of far sightedness, gravity of political situation, such resolution of merger of two states would have rarely come out in this Legislature:. He cautioned the Legislature about far reaching political developments in the wake of coming up such resolution of merger of these two states: the merger could not be easy; it should be very cautiously think over and opinion of people should also be sought over such ticklish issue—such decision must not be taken in casual manner—approach for such discussion must not be hatred and competitiveness but harmony and cooperation of the people of both the states."

Both the houses of Bihar Legislature discussed in detail on the Thanks Motion to Joint address of the Governor over the issue from February 01, 1956 to February 06, 1956 intensively and passed the motion of Thanks.

Even after, such subtle approach of Dr Diwakar and members of both the houses of the Bihar Legislature over merger of Bihar and West Bengal, both the chief ministers Dr S K sinha (Bihar) and Bidhanchandra Roy (West Bengal) brought the merger resolution in their respective Legislature. Dr S K SInha put formal resolution to merge Bihar with West Bengal on February 24, 1956 in the Bihar Legislature. After intensive discussions over merger issue for two days, Bihar Legislature passed the resolution for merger of Bihar-Bengal in single state on February 25, 1956 by 156 votes in favour and 25, opposing the motion! One of the strangest aspects of the Bihar Legislature was that had it approved the resolution in the interest of people of Bihar? And history wants reply of this question! Such resolution was passed in West Bengal Legislature also between the same time. But Bidhan Chandra Roy withdrew the resolution of merger on March 13, 1956. But clash of interest over territory of Bihar did not end there!

According to detailed compilation of records of the Legislature proceedings of those days, anchored from the Legislative achieves, the then Chairman of the Bihar Legislative Council Prof Jabir Hussain, who edited the proceedings of the houses and other reports, kept in gathering dust in the Legislative council secretariat, has quoted at least two vital quotable quotes on September 15, 1998; Prof Hussain, known for his scholarship, had quoted the then Pioneer (now defunct), over the issue kept in the secretariat having gathering dust! The Pioneer, which had written these topics when movement of separating Bihar from Bengal was at its zenith, had said, "Behar has always been Bihar, Bengal. The people and the nobles of Behar are justly proud of their country and will doubtless rejoice to see it severed from a common rule with Bengal, with which in climate, in crops, in manners and morals, it has nothing in common."

Before I continue on another such quotable quotes, edited by Prof Hussain of Jonh Malchom, based on Max Muller, I strongly feel to refer most important aspects of merger resolution of Bihar and West Bengal and subsequent developments. Amid all these fast changing political developments over the issue, there was a great political personality. His name was Jay Prakash Narayan, who strongly protested the merger of Bihar and West Bengal. In Delhi Jay Prakash Narayan met the then Prime Minister Pundit Jawahar Lal Nehru and spoke to him expressing his strong protest and anguish and dismay of the people of Bihar over merger of Bihar with West Bengal.

In another records in the Legislative Council, according to Prof Hussain, Sir John Malchom, who had based his statement to Max Muller on Bihar, had said, "—but from the moment you enter the districts of Behar, the inhabitants are a race of men, generally speaking, not more distinguished by their lofty stature and noble frame than they are for some of the finest qualities of the mind. They are brave, generous, and humane and their truth is as remarkable as their courage."

It will be proper to refer at least as passing references of debate on Motion of Thanks on Governor address to the joint session and also on the resolution of Dr S K Snha to merge Bihar with West Bengal. The Debate was hotly discussed in the Legislature. To begin with, a legislator, Shree Nayan Jee had moved amendment over the references of merger of Bihar and West Bengal in the governor's address and said, "—but deeply regret the reference to the proposal of merger of the two states of Bihar and West Bengal as the proposal if given effect to is bound to affect adversely both the states and unity of the country." Another interesting speech of another legislator in the council Shri Abdul Hayat Chand, who while expressing his dismay over the issue, had said "na tarapne ki ijajajt hai na fariyad ki hai; ghut kar mar jaun yah marji mere saiyad ki hai." Chand, while criticising Dr S K Sinha had said, "—and lastly regret that

Governor's address fails to bring in its true light the highly authoritarian and partisan and manner in which the chief minister has sought to wipe out the very existence of Bihar from the political map of the country." Similar interesting views had been expressed in the proceedings over merger of Bihar and West Bengal.

Noted legislators of that period like Ram Charitra Sinha, Jamuna Prasad Sinha, Ignesh Kujur, Rana Shivlakhpati Singh, Yogendra Ghosh, Basawan Sinha, Binodanand Jha etc had raised many aspects over mereger of both the states, by points of order, amendments and other legislative modes for stalling the resolution. However the resolution was Okayed by majority votes.

Now when I reminiscence the past, I find the quality of leadership in India was not as perfect as we used to think about statures of political leaders of during during those days. With the withdrawal of the resolution by Dr Bidhan Chandra Roy, the matter ended and merger plan of the then Congress party did not succeed!

NATIONAL PARTIES VIS-A-VIS REGIONAL PARTIES IN INDIAN DEMOCRACY!

Wednesday, 7 March 2012

In 1966 Dr Ram Manohar Lohia, while lambasting Congress Party for creating regional imbalances and exploitation of poor as well as rampant price rise in India, had commented in a public speech in l historic and sprawling Gandhi Maidan in Patna that in years to come democratic process in India will be strengthened with a host of regional parties, having secular and socialist credentials rooting in the election arena in the process of capturing power from national parties like Congress in states and at the centre. By that time many socialist thinking politicians, who were part and parcels of the Congress, had left Congress and started launching regional parties of socialist orientation under the present democratic structures in India. In the process, the present Hindu party—the Bharatiya Janata Party, which was originally Jan Sangh and had considerable support in the country, had also faced the tune of revolt. From Jan Sangh, number of leaders also resigned and had joined conservative and bourgeoisie party like Swatntra Party and many other outfits, having communal credentials.

Churning process in democratic system in India, which had started after independence of the country in 1947, continued. As regards united left party, number of communist leaders, who had formed the communist party, could not go together and splits after splits in Communist party, made the left forces weaker. But in few states like Kerala and West Bengal, the communist forces grew gradually. Rule of left front government led by CPI(M) stalwarts Jyoti Basu and later by CPI(M) leader Buddhdeo Bhattacharya continued for over 30 years in West Bengal and Left parties continues to be strong o in Kerala in extreme south India More progressive communist leaders, separated from mainstream communist party, had started revolution in Telegana region of Andhra Pradesh and many other states, who were later termed Naxalites and now they are called mainly Maoists. Some of them differ with the present democratic forces and wanted direct revolution against feudal forces to revenge exploitation of poor, dalits, tribal etc. Influences of Naxalites or Maoists have also to some extend lessened exploitation of poor in Naxalite-influenced parts of the country and the union government and respective state governments have started launching progressive measures in neglected areas.

The prophecy of Dr Ram Manohar Lohia came true. Even before his such statement, for the first time, CPI, having no national status so far because of differences of opinion overt Marxism and Leninism among socialists and communists, a first non-Congress government of Communist Party of India got victory in the Assembly elections of Kerala during the premiership of Pundit Jawahar Lal Nehru in 1950s. First Communist government led by E M S Namboodaripad was installed in 1950s. But in the middle of 1960s, numbers of state governments were formed by non-congress parties. Coalition arrangements of smaller regional parties remained key factors in installing non-congress governments in various states including Bihar, West Bengal, Uttar Pradesh, Gujarat etc. In this game because of numerical lesser strength of the so called Jan Sangh, now Bharatiya Janata Party, had also joined the anti-congress forces.

More over in many states, particularly in Bihar, the then Jan Sangh remained coalition partners and its legislators were ministers with communist and other socialist parties. Currently in new avatar—BJP is a coalition partner in governments in Bihar and Punjab. Likewise, Congress being national party is also coalition partners in West Bengal government led by Mamta Baneerjee. Congress also remained coalition partners in Rabari-Laloo government in Bihar. Now taking into polarisation of Hindu votes, the Bharatiya Janata Party also become national party and joined the tags of Congress in such term.

Strengthening of coalition era proved successful when under the leadership of Lok Nayak Jay Prakash Narayan all non-congress parties except Communist parties merged into a single Party—Janata Party— and succeeded in defeating the Congress led by Indira Gandhi after much-maligned emergency in the country. Morarjee Desai was installed prime minister, first—ever non-congress government in Delhi.

Thereafter, numbers of coalition governments have survived including the present one—UPA government led by Manmohan Singh in Delhi. Some of the government remained short-lived at the centre but democratic system continued as usual!Congress leadership led by Sonia Gandhi of Nehru clan, who were dithering over joining coalition politics, had to realise the truth and only after that Congress could get some strength and won maximum seats and formed UPA government under the leadership of Manmohan Singh twice.

In between national politics had seen many twists and turns! Demolition of Babari Masjid in course of Somnath to Ayodhya rathyatra of the BJP leader Lal Krishna Advani also changed the political scenario of the country mainly because of consolidation of Hindu votes. But the influence of BJP among masses had started also declining in view of recent assembly elections results. The BJP is gradually losing its grip over masses and except Karnataka in south India, it continues to be party of Hindi heartland and cow belts. Although as the voting pattern in entire country shows, the Congress continues to be national party as the party gets votes in each and every parts of the country, but its number of seats in Lok Sabha, Rajya Sabha as well as state assemblies are declining sharply, posing a big question mark whether the BJP and Congress will remain national parties!

During all these years of coalition era, regional parties had trumped. These regional parties had important says in forming governments at the centre and different states. In coalition politics, masses have to great extend benefited and fruits of developments have spread in states also. It was moribund during one party rule of Congress in successive years because of lack-lustre regional imbalances, created by it in the country. Says of states have gradually pushed the centre and its Planning commission to flow of funds for equal development of the states. It was because of the pressure of coalition partners, dynamic and progressive programmes like quadrilateral communication network in the country during Atal Behari Vajpayee regime and Right to Information Act, employment guarantee schemes, right to education etc by UPA government of Manmohan Singh had been implemented on the basis of common minimum programmes of both the coalition governments at the centre as well as by different state governments, having coalition arrangements.

Notably, Congress and BJP should also accept the reality of facts and find path of coalition politics, which is rather strengthening the democracy and also fruits of developments are reaching to the grass-root level. Unity and integrity of the country as well as politics of development not the path of confrontation should be motto of these so called national parties. The days of single party rule at national and states level are gone. Many regional leaders have emerged and they appear capable to handle the affairs of the country under democratic process. It also appears the liking of Indian electorate in the country!

The latest results of assembly elections in Uttar Pradesh, Punjab, Uttarakhand, Goa, had again proved that national parties—Congress and BJP—cannot control the country single-handedly. Although in some cases, it was a fractured verdict, theory of consensuses could form the government in Uttarakhand specially.

HYPE OVER BIHAR DIWAS VIS-A-VIS FACTS ABOUT CREATION OF BIHAR!

Monday, 5 March 2012

Much hype is being created over the Bihar and its 100th year's anniversary by the present government led by the chief minister Nitish Kumar in next one week! People of Bihar and the Nitish government first must know the exactly the real birth day of Bihsar!

The British East India Company, which was instrumental in slaving the entire India in the hands of Great Britain, was first to get Diwani right (collection of revenue and governance) after the battle of Buxar in 1764 for "Bihar, Bengal and Orissa" many ups and downs were witnessed since then. The Great Britain had taken the India under its control! During the British India period, the Great Britain had created "Presidency of Bengal (PoB)". And Bihar and, Orissa had become part of the PoB after the East India Company handed over the governance of slavery of India to Great Britain. Bihar was ruled by PoB from Calcutta now Kolkata.

Again, the Great Britain separated Bihar and Orissa from Bengal in 1912 and made Bihar and Orissa a joint and separate province! Whole Bengal including present Bangla Desh was made a separate province under British Raj and finally Province of Bihar came into existence in 1935 under Government of India Act, 1935, of British Raj. And Orissa became a separate state. After separation from Bengal, Bihar and Orissa was government from Patna, having headquarters of top civil servants of British Raj as well as Council (Legislative wing) here in Patna. In my opinion now it is people to decide when Bihar was born in 1764 or 1912 or 1935!

Before deliberating the other aspects of Bihar before and after independence, I feel it is necessary to bring the people to down the memory lanes about importance of Bihar and its people right from ancient India to advanced India. Bihar has wonderful history. During ancient time, Bihar was centre of learning since 5th and 8th century. The name of Bihar was probably derived from Sanskrit and Pali word as well as of Devanagari scripts. Bihar means in Hindi and Sanskrit "abode". It may be abode of Buddhists monks! Great and famed rulers like Chandragupta Maurya, Ashoka, Samundragupta, Vikaramaditya etc remained finest rulers of the entire country from Bihar and Pataliputra or Patna. As per historical records, Bihar was important place of power, culture, education in the last one thousand years. Spiritualism was its core. Sanskrit scholars like Panini had given new doimension to our culture, civilisation, language and literature. Gautam Buddha got enlightenment in Boddh-Gaya and spread the message of compassion and brotherhood brotherhood in the entire world. Apart from many others, the last and tenth Guru of Sikhism Guru Govind Singh was born here in Patna city areas. Once upon a time, the ancient Nalanda university had attracted students of far-lung countries including China, Japan, Thailand, Indonesia, even some European countries. Since it was destroyed by despotic ruler Bahkhtiyar Khilji, who committeed massacxre In Bihar Shariff and ruined the ancient Nalanda university!

About wonder of Bihar and about Bihar, I must quote one quotable quotes of A L Basham in his book—The Wonder That Was INDIA—," "The age in which true history appeared in India was one of the great intellectual and spiritual ferment. Mystics and shophisists of all kinds roamed through the Ganges valley, all advocating some form of metal discipline and asceticism as a mean to m salvation, but the age of Buddha, when many of the best minds were abandoning their homes and profession for a life a sceticism, was also a time of advance in commerce and politics. It produced not only philosophers as ascetics but also merchant prince and Men of action—."

Although Dr S K Sinha was first chief minister under the British India Act, 1935, he continued even after the India achieved independence in 1947 till his death in 1960. Dr Sngh's regime notwithstanding considered one of best governed states in the country, it was he who under his golden regime brought some tangible things like Heavy Engineering Corporation (HEC), Bokaro steel, IOC oil refinerry in Barauni, Rajendra bridge on Ganga in Mokemah, many other heavy and power industries in united Bihar before its bifurcation and dividing Bihar and creating Jharkhand about ten years back. One glaring mistake Dr S K Sinha committed that was not constructing high dams on rivers originating from Nepal although under an treaty with Nepal during British Raj, a sum of Rs 40 crores were sent to India by Great Britain government for final construction of the dams on rivers after independence. Reluctantly the then Prime Minister Jawahar Lal Nehru had to hand over the sum to Punjab for constructing high dams on Bhakhara Nangal. And today Punjab is feeding the entire country because of construction of high dams and irrigation network in that state as well as industrial hubs in that state.

Alas after his death, practically a lull was created in Bihar and the state started deteriorating.

Another remarkable feature was achieved in Bihar during the regime of Krishna Ballabh Sahay, Kedar Pandey, Karpoori Thakur and Bhagwat Jha Azad. While Sahay to some extend implemented land reform measures and given land to landless for basgit and agriculture after enacting law to take over surplus lands from the then rajas, maharajas, landlords and big land holders, Kedar Pandey streamlined the higher eduction in the state to great extend and during his regime, universities in the state started funtioning well and marvelously.

Karpoor Thakur was considered messiah of poor and imlemented reservation for dalits and, backwards, who were deprived off of jobs and education and exxploited by higher caste people in the state. Last but not the least Bhagwat Jha Azad, during his short tenure, started war against corruption in the state for the first time substantially. It was during his regime big politicians particularly from cooperative sectors and big officials were booked on corruption charges in the state, which had brought tagible results later on.

In between successive chief ministers of the state proved ineffective, and the Bihar started going down to the drains and its backwardness aggaravated miserably.

I do not want to name any other chief ministers, who had brought all the ills for Bihar during their respective tenures. One chief minister institutionalised corruption in the state during his rule in 1980s. Another one and his family member, who also become chief minister, shiphonned off over Rs 850 crore from state treasury. Many criminal cases are pending against him.

Situation started down hill turn from 1980s. Corruption has adversely affected governance in the state and now the situation has reached to such height during Nitish Kumar regime that poor continued to be neglected and corruption has percolated right from state headquarters to panchayat level in the state. Since 1980s, specially in during Laloo-Rabari regime to Nitish Kumar rule from late 1990s to 2000s corruption and deterioration in law and order situation have become worse. Some definite improvement in law and order and development sectors had taken place in the beginning of Nitish rule, but common masses are passing through agonising moments.

Nitish failed to implement much-publicised land reform measures despite his promises and reports of Bandopadhaya committee. Before coming to power Nitish had announced implementation of land reform measures but under the pressure of big land holders and BJP leaders, he dithered to implement the measures leaving the lands in the hands of holders and depriving the landless their right of lands Development funds, specially central schemes, are not percolating to rural poor. Government officials and ruling class politicians comprising JD(U) and BJP have created havoc with peoples' life. Big announcement of Nitish government have become order of the day. Curb on freedom of press in the form of undeclared censorship have posed a big question mark over freedom of expression. Authoritarian attitude of Nitish Kumar and bureacratic cobweb remind the people of how Hitler in the garb of democracy had imposed the dictatorship in Germany!

Only hope appears on youths of Bihar. Bihar has 58 percent youths below 25 years of age. Such data of youths is highest in comparision to other states. As regards sign of development, Bihar is agriculture based state. Its soils have highest fertility. Rural masses are trying their best to produce maximum from their lands. One more thing is remarkable factor in Bihar and its residents. They are definitely developing but not at the cost of assistance and help "rahmo-karam" of government of Nitish Kumar but of their own by dint of hard labour.

Now youths of Bihar could give a new road of development overthrowing present decadent politicians, who are exploiting the people in the name of shining slogans o in Bihar. Lot of youths is also getting specialised education in other parts of the country. Many Biharis are working in other states and sending money to their kiths and kins here. And development is taking shape!

SANSKRIT-HINDU NUMERALS AND SCIENTIFIC ACHIEVEMENTS!

Thursday, 23 February 2012

Sanskrit is most scientific literature of the world! Once upon a time, we Indians were leading the entire globe in science and technology. The concept of zero was invented by our ancestors. The Arabs borrowed it from us and the European borrowed it from the Arabs. Our numerals is expressed in numbers in astronomical terms.

Markandey Katju, a former judge of the Supreme Court, in his lecture delivered to non-resident Indians in California in June 2011, has dwelt at length these scientific terminology of numbers and alphabets, discovered by our ancestors. Remarkably Katju's explanations about the zero is wonderful—for example, Katju has said," one thousand requires 1 with three zeros, add two more zeros it becomes one lakh, add two more zeros it becomes one arab, two more zeros one kharab, two more zeros one neel, two more zeros one sankh, two more zeros on mahasankh etc. Each of these large numbers has names."

Notably, Arabian, Persian and Urdu are written from right to left, but you ask any of writer of these languages to write any number randomly, say, 152 of 1,085, he will write it from left to right. What does it indicate? It indicates that these numbers were taken from language that was written from left to right, and now it is accepted that decimal system was invented by Indians, who could conceive very high numbers unlike the Romans, Kattju has said.

One more example will substantiate the arguments and logic of Katju. It is believed that Kaliyuga, in which we are living, has 4, 32,000 years; according to Vishnu Purana. The Yug (age) before Kaliyuga was Dwapara yug, in which Krishna lived. That was twice as long as Kaliyuga, therefore it was of 8, 64,000 years, before that there was Treta yuga, in which Ram lived. It was thrice as long as Kaliyuga.

And before that there was Satyyuga, which was four times as long as Kaliyuga. One Kaliyuga+one Dwapara yuga+one Treta yuga+one Satyuga is known as Chatiuryugi and one Chaturyugi is hence ten times as lons as one Kaliyuga (1+2+3+4=10). Katju has said that that means one Chaturyugi is 43,20,000 yerars long. Seventy-two Chaturyugis make one Manvantara. Fourteen Manvantaras make one one Kalpa, and 12 Kalpas make one day of Brahma. Brahma said to have lived for trillion of years. When traditional Hindu do their sankalp every day they have to mention particular day, the yuga, the Chaturygi, the Manvantara and the Kalp and the date changes daily. It is believed that out of 72 Chaturyugis, half have passed and we are in the second half of the Vaivaswsata Manvantara."

While concluding the topic, I must mention that one must look at the flight of imagination of our ancestors about Sanskrit language and literature. In the various field of Science, for instance medicine, we made great advance. Shushrutu did plastic surgery 2000 years ago but the westerners discovered it only 200 years back. Indians are far ahead of the westerners in medical science. Similar is the case with the astronomy, which I have dwelt in my earlier write-up in the blog. END

SANSKRIT-URDU CULTURE IN INDIA!

Sunday, 19 February 2012

After discussing about the India and Indian, mainly a nation of a group of hundreds kinds of immigrants as well as the original or aborginal Indians, believed to be pre-Dravidians tribal people, called Adivasi like Bhils, the Mundas, the Gonds, the Todas etc, currently about seven to eight percent of the total population of India in my previous write-up in my blog, now I want to highlight about the Sanskrit-Urdu culture of India, which had continued to adhere secular character of the country!I have tried to base my write-up on the opoinions of the eminent historians, sociologist, reputed scholars including the speech of the former judge of the Supreme Court Markandey Katju, delivered to the non-resident Indians in California in June 2011.

Both the Sanskrit and the Urdu languages in India have been misuderstood. While there misconception about Urdu that it is the language of Muslims and of foreigners, people think that Sanskrit is a language for chanting mantras in temples and religious ceremonies. About Urdu false propganda is being made after 1947. Likewise, I must make it clear that only five percent of Sanskrit literature is mantras and used in religious ceremonies. Ninety-five percent of Sanskrit literature is no way connected with religion. Sanskrit deals with varied ranges of subjects like philosophy, science, law (including astronomy, mathematics and medicines), grammar, phonetics and literature. About Urdu, I must say that the language was not only for Muslims alone but of Hindus, Muslims, Christians, Sikhs and others. It was propganda spree after partition by certain vested interests that the Urdu is the language of Muslims and Hindi is language for Hindus. Before 1947, almost all the educated people in India used to study Urdu also. For many government offices, documents were written in Urdu scripts! Sucha canard had been spread among Hindus and Muslims for deviding and ruling and also makes Muslims and Hindus fight each other. All efforts were made to eliminate Urdu language and literature in India. But a lanuguage, which comes out from hearts cannot be crushed as long as people have hearts.

The Sanskrit lkanguage and literature is for enquisitive minds of people. An inquisitive mind means inquiring minds, who want to know about everything and Sanskrit has whole range of subjects, which have been discussed in this language and literature. "Sanskrit is a language of science", a paper in which everything in details have been discussed. For this, we would have to mention the constribution of Sanskrit Scholar Panini and also Nyaya Vaisheshik philosophy. Teaching of these days Sanskrit is Paninin Sanskrit, which is called classical Sanskrit or Laukik Sanskrit. There are many earlier Sanskrits. Earliest Sanskrit book is the Rig Veda. It was composed between 2000 and 1500 BC later it was passed on orally. With the passage of time language and literature changes—so there has been little change in Sanskrit also.

Panini, a greatest grammarian the world has seen, had fixed the rules of Sanskrit in his book "Ashtadhyayi" in the fifth century BC. There after no further changes in the Sanskrit were allowed except some slight changes made by two other grammarians—Katyayana in his book "Vartika" about 100-200 years after Paninin and Patanjali. Patanjali had written his book "Mahabhashya" about 200 years after Katyayna. Except these slight changes, what is taught in schools and colleges is Panini's Sanskrit. Panini had reformed crude sanskriyt prevailing in his time and meticulously systemised and liberalised it to make Sanskrit powerful vehicle of profound and abstaract not only that Panini had made the sanskrit a powerful language in which scientifc ideas could be flowed with precision and clarity for making the language mainly uniform all over India. Thus the Sanskrit language had become interactive not only in the entire India but for thinkers in one part of the sub-continent to ineract easily with thinkers of another parts of the globe and region. Panini had scientifically arranged the consonants of the Sanskrit language unlike English alphabets in a haphazard manner. Arrangements of letters in the alphabet in Sanskrit is carefully confirmed and has been done on the basis of scientific study.

Sanskrit has great contribution in such manner and second of that is the development of rational and scientific thinking. It was based on Nyaya Vaisheshik philosophy. The India philoshophy has six classical systems—Nyaya, Vaisheshik, Sankya, Yoga, Purva Mimansa and Uttar Mimansa and three non-classical systems,—Buddhist, Jainist, and

Charvaka. Among the nine systems eight are atheistic as there is no place for god in them. Only Uttam Mimansa, which is also called Vedanta, has a place for God in it, according to Katju.

Vaisheshik was the physics of ancient times (the atomic or parmanu system). Katju has said, "Physics is part of science, hence at one time Vaisheshik was part of Nyaya philosophy. It was the Nyaya Vaisheshik philosophy, which provided the scientific background and gave great encouragement to our scientists to propound scientific theories. Nyaya Vaisheshik philosophy, which says that nothing is aceptable unless it is in accordance with reason and experience. "At one time we were leading the whole world in science and technology."

There are much advancement of our scientific knowledges like medicines, surgery, astronomy, calculations in comparision to Europe and America. Indians are far ahead iof the western countries in medicines. In astronomy, the calculations, which were made 2000 years ago, are still the basis of predicting with great accuracy the day and time of solar eclipseor a lunar eclipse by reading a "patra." These predictions were made 2000 years ago by our ancestors, who did not have telescopes and modern instruments; by sheer oibservation with the naked eye and power of intellect they predicted what is going to happen 2000 years in future, Katju said.

According to Katju; with regards to Urdu, there is no match to Urdu language poetry. Urdu poetry is voice of the heart. It is none in other languages. Unlike Arabic and Persian, which are foreign languages, Urdu is an indigenous language and loved by people of India. Urdu has a dual nature. It is combination of two languages, that is, Hindustani and Persian, which is why it is called Rekhta, which means hybrid. Since it is combination of two languages, the question arises: it is special kind of Persian or a special kind of Hindustani? The answer is that it is speciasl kind of Hindustani not a special kind of Persian. Why? Because the verbs in Urdu are all in Hindustani. The language is to which a sentence belongs is deterimined the verbs used in it, not the norms or adjectives. In Urdu, all the verbs are in simple Hindi (which is called Hindustani or khadiboli).

Urdu has dual nature because it is a combination of Hindustani and Persian. Hindustani is the language of the common man, while Persian is the language of aristocrats. Now the question arises, Persiaian is the language of Persia, how it came to India? To explain this it has been noted that it often happens that the elite or upper class of a society speaks a foreign language. For instance, In India and Pakistan, the elite speak in English. In Europe, elite upto to the end of 19th century, the European aristocrsats often spoke each other in French though they spoke to their servants in the native languages. French was the language of the elite in large parts of Europe for many centuries. Elite wants to distinguish itself from the common people. In India Persian was the language of the court and the elite for the centuries although Persian originated in Persia, it spread to much of South Asia including India. Akbar's foreign minister Todarmal had passed an order that all court records throughout the Mughal Empire shall be maintained in Persian, Katju said.

Katju has added further that Urdu is the common man's language, "awaam ki zubaan" because part of of it is Hindustani and, the common man's language. It is also the aristocrats' language because another parts of it is Persian, which as the aristocrat's language. The content of Urdu, that is, the feelings, emotions etc. in it are of common man. But the form, the style, the andaaz-e-bayaan is that of an aristocrat. That is what gives Urdu such great power.

According to Katju, Urdu places more reliance on emotion and Sanskrit more on reason. We requere both of our country's progress. Urdu and Sanskrit complement each other, and in fact Sanskrit is the grand mother of Urdu because 70 percent of the words in Urdu are from Sanskrit. Katju has said, "Since there is so much diversity in India the Only policy which will work is the policy of secularism and giving equal respect to all communities. Otherwise India will break up into hundred of pieces since there is so much diversity." Katju has said in his lecture.

INDIA AND INDIAN!

Monday, 13 February 2012

About six month back, I had read a judgement of the Supreme Court about who are the initial aboriginals and Indian in our vast land? The judgement had clearly mentioned that the pre-Dravidian tribal people people such the Bhils, the Santhals, the Gonds, called Adivasis or Scheduled caste were the original inhabitants of India. Time changed fast, they are now hardly eight percent population of India today—that also neglected, discriminated, oppressed etc. Thereafter I have gone through an interesting article of the justice Markandey Katju in an English fortnightly, based on a speech delivered to non-resident Indians in California in June 2011 and other sources like various articles on the website, kgfindia. com, under the title "What is Urdu—, Great injustice to Urdu in India" and "Sanskrit as a Language of Science" about initial and real inhabitants of India, its language and culture, roles of successive rulers, immigrants' invasion to India, communal harmony etc.

All these facts and opinion of Kataju and various other writers have left my mind wandering that real and aboriginal Indians were put in the background and India now remained a country of immigrants like North America. Thus over 92 percent of populations of India are not original inhabitants of India. Their ancestors gradually came from the outside, mainly from the north-west. Only because of that India has become country of diversity, having many religions, castes, languages, ethnic groups. Despite all these diversities in India, a common culture gradually had developed, called the Sanskrit-Urdu culture.

Before deliberating Sanskrit-Urdu culture in India, I want to put forward the present state of affairs in the country. India is passing through transitional phase, mainly from feudal agriculture society to a modern industrial society. Such situation in India, as per opinions of various historians and academicians, are very painful and agonising period in the history of the country. Such situation is expected to continue for some more years and only thereafter India will emerge as a stable and powerful country. For examples, history of Europe had also similar churning during 17th to 19th centuries. Many ups and downs were witnessed In Europe during those periods. There were wars, revolutions, turmoils, intellectual ferment, chaos, social upheaval etc. Only after passing through such agonising periods, Europe emerged modern society! In North America, mainly immigrants came from Europe in over last 400 to 500 years.

India is country of old immigrants. In India people have been coming in for 10,000 years or so. Only on two occasions, the Indians had migrated to other countries. During British Raj, huge number of Indians migrated to South Africa, Fiji, Mauritius, West Indies, and different islands etc as indentured labourers in 19th century. On an another occasion after independence in the last 30 to 40 years, b brain drain had happened in India and highly qualified engineers, scientists, doctors etc had migrated to Europe and America in search of better life! Except these two periods, hardly Indians had migrated to other countries as immigrants. Instead people continued to come to India as immigrants since long.

Usually people migrate from one place to other for greener pastures or comfort or earn livelihood. Justice Katju has rightly said, "The reason is obvious. People migrate from uncomfortable areas to comfortable areas, obviously because everybody wants comfort. Before the industrial revolution which started in Western Europe from 18th century and then spread all over the world, there were agricultural societies every-where. Agriculture requires level land, fertile soil, plenty of water for irrigation, etc. All this was in abundance in the Indian subcontinent from Rawalpindi to Bangladesh and to the Deep South up to Kanya Kumari. Why, will anybody migrate from to, say, AAfghanistan, which is cold, rocky and uncomfortable and covered with snow for four five months a year? For an agricultural society, India was really paradise; hence everybody kept rolling into India, mainly from the north-west and to a much lesser extends from the north-east."

Now the main crux of the facts about the original inhabitants of India! Originally, it was said that Darvidians were the original inhabitants of India. Gradually, this notion was faded away. Presently it is said that even Dravidian were also outsiders. Historians have cited certain proof

462

like there is a Dravidian language called Brahui, spoken in western Pakistan even today by over three million people.

Now a new theory has come to light. The original inhabitants of India were the pre-Dravidian tribal people. They are called Adivasis or Scheduled Tribes in India. They are Bhils, Santhals, the gonds, the Tedas etc—"that is, the speakers of Austric, pre-Dravidian languages like Munda and Gondvi. They are hardly seven to eight percent of the Indian population today. They were pushed into the forest by the immigrants and treated badly. Except them We are all of us are descendants of immigrants, who came mainly from north-west of India", this references have been quoted by Justice Katju, referring articles "Kalidas Ghalib Academy for Mutual Understanding" on the website kgfindia.com.

There are vast difference between China and India on this score. There is homogeneity in China—they have Mongoloid features, they have one common written script called Mandarin Chinese. Ninety-five percent population of China belonged to one ethnic group where as in India there is tremendous diversity, because which ever of immigrants came into India brought in its own culture, religion, language etc. Thus India is a nation at all or is it just group of hundreds of kinds of immigrants. However the immigrants, coming to India in phases in the last over 10000 years or so by their interaction and intermingling, created a common culture, which can be by and large be called the Sanskrit-Urdu culture, by far the present culture of India!

BEHIND THE SCENES DRAMA IN CORRIDOR OF POWER VIS-A-VIS JOURNASLISM: LUCKNOW BOY!

Sunday, 15 January 2012

Apart from misdeeds in the corridor of power and journalistic ethincs as well as criminal-politicians nexus in the wake of March 1993 Bombai blast, masterminded by then underworld don and now international terrorists Dawood Ibrahim, The LUCKNOE BOY, A MEMOIR OF VETERAN JOURNALIST AND EDITOR OF THE OUTLOOK VINOD MEHTA has thrown light on some Bihari politicians and persons including widely anacknowledged as figure of immense moral authority, Jayprakash Narayan, former IAS officer and now JD(U) MP N K Singh, former union minister Raghubansh Prasad Singh, Rashtriya Janata Dal national president Laloo Prasad Yadav, former union minister and Congress leader K K Tiwari, scavengers mobiliser Tiliya Devi for their deeds and misdeeds in the political arena of the country! Intresting reading book has touched every aspects of politcs and bureacracy in Delhi and has cautioned the mediapersons of "dos and donots" in carryig their harazdous professions. The book has also singalled out the mean temperament of senior journalists, indulging in power-brokerings in the corridor of power. The book highlighted almost all the topics right from Indira Gandhi's turbulent emergency to present day corrupt practices in the political and officials' corridor in Delhi! The book in detail has referred about wheeling deelings of N K Singh alias Nandu Babu from Bihar. Son of an ICS T P Singh and respected and popular Congress MP from Purnia Mrs Madhuri Singh, said to be confidant of Mrs Indira Gandhi, N K Singh's role during NDA rule of Atal Behari Vajpayee has priominently figured in the book!

I think it my duty to write about the role of Biharis in their endevoure in unscrupulous work in the corridor of power in Delhi as referred in the book. To begin with, I must start with Jay Prakash Narayan and his disciple Raghubansh Prasad Singh. The protest of Jayprakash Narayan, started as a students' movement turned into a peoples's movement in 1970s, had given the call of for smpoorn kranti (total revolution) throughout the country. The book referred, "JP, a friend and admirer of Pundit Jawahar Lal Nehru—his relationship with Indira Gandhi, unfortunately, was bitter and confrontational. When Mrs Gandhi called JP's Bihar stir an insult to the people, JP accused her of being the foundation head of all corruption in the country." Referring to the JP's agitation Raghubansh Babu, a student follower of of JP has explained in the book, "The reasons were closed to his heart:corruption, unemployment and inhumanity. One particular protest remains in my mind:JP leading hordes of students on a silent march through the streets with everyone's mouth covered and their hands tied behind their back."

The book further revealed, "The political landscape in 1974 was dominated by JP, with the prime minister merely reacting to the serial challenges he threw at her. Ironically, Jayprakash Narayan's offensive against Indira Gandhi came at a time when she was basking in the glow of several trtriumphs. In the 1971 general elctions, Mrs Gandhi's party Congress (R) won an emphatic victory on a simple yet unbearable slogangs—Garibi hatao! Soon after, the historic military victory in East Pakistan electrified the nation and even BJP (then Jansangh) and RSS leaders hailed Indira Gandhi as a modern Durga."

The book has many interesting tit-bits and secret revealation about Bihar leaders like Laloo Prasad Yadav and K K Tiwari! Vinod Mehta has described all these things in very interesting manner in his memoir. While referring wheeling deelings under the rule of P V Narsimha Rao, the book has said, "Rao's political opponents within the party (Congress) found the excerpts a golden opportunity. A congress MP K K Tiwari described P.V as a sex maniac." Vinod Mehta while referring to his talks with JRD Tata has written that "the other person who exasperated Tata was Laloo Prasad Yadav, Seven chlidren.' Can you imagine seven children? What short of example is he setting?' Family Planing was an obsession with Tata. He believed the future of the country depended on putting place strong deterrent measures for birth control. JRD's irritation with Laloo might have had something to do with the facts that, he (Tata), despite the best medical intervention, was unable to produce even one child.(In this respect Mehta did not even spared JRD for his remarks against Laloo)!"

Mehta has mentoned even the minute things in his book: I had invited many persons,—whose contributions matter in welfare measures on the completion of the ten years of The OUTLOOK INDIA as news weekly under my editorship—. "Tiliya Devi for mobilising scavengers from Bihar was invited to speak"—and she spoke!

The book has referred Patna boy N K Singh, like Lucknow Boy as the title of the book—but in some other aspects! Mehta, in his book has referred Atal Jee's Man Friday, BRajesh Mishra, in company with NK Singh had become" deteriorating BJP environment caused by internal squabblings that threatened the Atal's job, is not an open question. "The book says, "Atal Jee was no saint. He liked to drink moderately and eat non-vegetarian food less moderately. Being a bachelor and a political star (Henry Kissinger: power is the ultimate aphrodisaic), he was never short of female company. When he became India's prime minister, he juggled a strange domestic life. A Mrs Kaul, whose husband was a clollege professor and had passed away, moved into 7, Race course, alongwith her daughter Namita and daughter's husband Ranjan Bhattacharya. Namita's official designation was foster daughter and Ranjan Bhattacharya became foster son-in-law. Vajpayee, to his credit, made no effort to hide the menage a quatre. "The same Ranjan Bhattacharya, Mishra and Singh, a senior bureaucrat and officer on special duty for economic affairs in PMO were trio virtually in complete charge of the PMO!" The husband and wife team of Ranjan and Namita were the other power centres in 7, Race Course Road. Vajpayee may have certain reservation about his foster son-in-law. However, the foster daughter could do no wrong in his eyes. Namita and Ranjan began assiduously cultivating in Delhi media. They had unconcealed contempt for what they called knickerwala journalists; they mingled with Vir Sanghvi, Barkha Dutta, Shekhar Gupta—even me."

"The activities of Trio (Brajesh Mishra, N K Singh, and Ranjan Bhattacharya) had found cursory mention in the media. Nothing more. Our reporters came back with the full chronicle: the three were running riot. We put two senior reporters on the job and in March 2001 published our cover story," Rigging the PMO. "It provided details of numerous decisions taken by the PMO, brazenly favouring a select group of business houses, specially the Hinduja and the Reliance. With the former, Mr Vajpayee had long-standing personal relations; he had even written an indiscreet note to Prime Minister Narasimha Rao, seeking his indulgence on their behalf in the Bofor scandal.", the book has revealed.

Mehta says in his book, "once Rigging the PMO came into public domain, consternation and panic set in the PMO. Outlook and its editor could be dismissed as congenitally biased. The revealation of E A S Sarma, widely known in the civil service as outstanding officer, honest to a fault, on the other hand, were not easy to dismiss because of his widely acknowledged reputation for probity and professionalism. None of his specific instnces of wrongdoing could be denied or contested. His testimony was rich in detail."

The writer further says, "Vajpayee summoned me on tea. It was an unhappy meeting. N K SINGH, Vajpayee conceded, could if necessary be shown the door. Brajesh and Ranjan were another matter. I had got it wrong, Vajpayee mildly scolded, those two were pure as snow. I refused to get into a wrangle with the PM. Suddenly; he changed the subject and launched an attack on Outlook Correspondent Saba Naqvi, who was covering BJP.' I do not know what has gone wrong with her lately; she is always writing against me. 'He suggested she had been covering the BJP for too many years. Perhaps she needed a change of beat."

Another clout of N K Singh in the book," In the last week of March, our second expose—Vajpayee's Achilles Heel—appeared. It began—,'ever since Atal Behari Vajpayee became prime minister and consolidated his hold over NDA, the whisper in the corridor of power have been about the formidable clout Brajesh Mishra, N K singh, and Ranjan Bhattacharya enjoy'. Later in the report we were more specific:' over the last couple of years Bhattacharya's influence has grown—a cross section of people Outlook spoke to including bureaucrats, industrialists and politicians, say Bhattacharya if powerful yet invisible force which drives the PMO. His primary conduits, say all, are Mishra and Singh".

"—trooping the lists was Rs 58000—crore national highway project—, theRs 20000—crore Reliance-Hirma power projectetc", the book revealed and added another huge sum of Rs 3179 crore under telecommunication sector—the defaulters included Birla, Reliance, Tata Essar. These influential corporates pressed the PMO for extension of payment deadline. They succeeded. Further, they pushed through the draft of new telecom policy heavily tilted in their favour. The Samata Party (of Nitish Kumar and George Fernandes), a vital ally of the NDA, in a stinging letter to Vajpayee on 16 m March, demanded a probe into various corruption charges against Mishra, Singh and Bhattacharya. A couple of days after our second expose, Brajesh Mishra and N K Singh held a press conference. Without mentioning Outlook even once, they denied outright all the charges as'mischievous and 'baseless'. It was commanding performance."

(The same Samta Party now Janata Dal (U) has nominated N K Singh as its party candidate for Rajya Sabha elections from Bihar and under the leadership of the so called Mr Clean—Nitish Kumar, Singh was elected to Rajya Sabha! What a double face of the JD(U) leaders Nitish Kumar and Sharad Yadav—my comment).

The book has also referred much-maligned Neera Radia tape for brokering during the prime ministership of Manmohan Singh for huge scandal namely telecommunication scandal, shiphoning lakhs of crore rupees. Apart from invoolvement of over half a dozen jornalists, N K Singh has also figured in the tape conversions with Neera Radia for power brokering!

Lucknow Boy, the book of importance by Mehta, has told about NK Singh, "JD(U) Rajya Sabha MP N K Singh, a former Bureaucrat, describes the UPA (second) cabinet as "Shivji ka baratat", a reference to the creatures that danced at Loard Shiva 's wedding. Referring to Murli DEora's second innings as petroleum minister, N K Singh says'—Murli (Deora's) incompetence is proverbial. Every time a question comes up in Parliament, he is busy trying to appease the questioner. Perhaps Mukesh (Ambani) has swung for it for him—but Murli is an incompetent minister' Taklking to Praful Patel, the civil aviation minister, Singh says more than the Indian Arirlines,'I think he worked for Naresh Goyal (Jet Airways)."

THUS THE "LUCKNOW BOY", WRITTEN BY VINOD MEHTA, REVEALS HAPPENING IN CORRIDOR OF POWER IN DELHI! ETHICS OF JOURNALISM IS ALSO HIGHLIGHTED IN THE BOOK! (SOURCES: LUCKNOW BOY WRITTEN BY VINOD MEHTA)

US BLIND APPROACH IN WEST ASIA, PARTICULARLY IRAQ!

Monday, 9 January 2012

Now the world must have taken a sigh of relief from American imperialist approach in West Asia, particularly in Iraq in the last nine years. US army have left Iraq lock, stock, barrel last month (December 16, 2011). But even today, the intention of America is not honest! Several thousands US forces are even today stationed in Iraq even after withdrawal. But many bases of America now appear deserted look. But protests of Iraqis continue against America and the American armies are under tremendous pressure to quit the country for all time to come.

But a million dollar question will continue to haunt the globe—what America gained from this misadventure in interfering in the affairs of Iraq in the last several years?! They have left behind a ghost country like Iraq and have practically destroyed the country. They left behind thousands of widows and orphans. And educational institutions and big factories have been ruined by Americans, according to a letter of Vijay Prashad to the Frontline, a fortnightly of India.

US war operation in Iraq began in 2002, continued till 2011. Over 4000 US personnel killed in Iraq than Americans killed in the attack on 9/11. Successive US governments right from Bush to Obama had faced rough weather in America for killings of Americans in the war. Not only that Although the death figures of Iraqis in the war are astronomous (some count a million dead), The Lancet has put figures slightly smaller number—nearly 7000000. The New York Times, which was in possession of 4000 pages papers of US military investigation on the 2005 massacres at Haditha, where US marines killed 24 Iraqis including 76-year-old man in wheel chair, children and toddlers: Results: Most of the US troops had been acquitted by their justice system,.."

Apart from that US faced worst-ever down trend in its economy. Entire America and Europe are under tremendous economic crisis because of American wars not only in Iraq but in other countries of West Asia. Vijay Prasad has said, "The Bush war on Iraq alone cost at least $ one trillion if not more. It was to make Iraq a model private sector country. All this failed as Iraqis refused to utterly plaint. The US miscalculated the neighbourhood. The assumption was that the US forces would be able to create a satellite in the area that could checkmate Iran's ambition in the region and provide some relief to Israel. Instead the wave of democracy that swept the region was was not inclined to US power but against it. Even Iraq government was not docile as hoped."

It all started in 2001; The Bush administration had practically invaded Iraq in his bid to end global war on terror Afghanistan to Iraq. Bush had decided to hit Saddam Hussain for so called "connivance with Osama bin Laden in the wake of 9/11 attack on Washington. It was gradually intensified. In this war, Bush had apprehension that Iraq had biological weapons. Bush had gone to United Nations and informed that Saddam Hussain had prepared for biological warfare and had instructed his field commanders that to use chemical weapons. Saddam had vehemently denied that Iraq had biological or chemical weapons. Even the Director General of IAEA Mohamed Elbaradei had cautioned the UNO that Iraq had such weapons. Thereafter the UN Secretary General Kofi Anna, who had also enquired about biological or chemical weapons existence in Iraq through Swedish politician Hans Blix, had come to the conclusion that Iraq had no such weapons. Blix had told to The Guardian," there are bastards who spread things around of course, who planted nasty things in the media, not that I cared much.": Subsequently many developments had taken place in Iraq and butcher machines of US Army continued to break the back-bone of Iraq." Guardian had further commented, quoting Blix" a massive media blitz orchestrated by the White House and conducted enthusiastically by the Murdoch machine (At Devas in 2007, Charlie Rose asked Murdoch if News Corp. has shaped the agenda for the Iraq war "No I do not think so," replied Murdoch. "We tried. We basically supported Bush policy in the Middle East (west Asia)"

Vijay Prashad has said, "US occupation of Iraq continued even after it became clear that all the reasons of launching war against Iraq by Bush administration had been false. As US troops had withdrawn from Iraq, there are little discussions about: that no chemical or biological weapons or weapons of mass destruction (WMDs) were found, that no link between Saddam Hussain and Al Qaeda could be established and that Saddam Hussain had no plans to attack US."

Now I must point out the villain of the pieces for initiating this war against Iraq. In my opinion the vice-president Dick Cheney, Defence secretary Rumsfield and state department head Collin Powell and national Security adviser Condoleezza Rice. The mo moires by the main players in Bush Administration" haave appeared with Cheney and Rusfeld defending their roles and Powell and Condoleezza puting the onus on Cheney and Rumesfeld" But in US every body is aware that all these villain of the pieces were in agreement of war against Iraq. Sadly "no body has taken responsibility for Iraq fiasco. At most of the leaders of the country simply blame each other for poor execution of the war (too little planning, say some, too few troops say others)", the memoirs of these people recalled.

There are many other sad tales of barbaric and torturous scenes enacted by US army in Iraq. Another villain piece to encourage the war in Iraq is no more less than media baron Rupert Murdoch!

However, the present president Obama, who gave a well regarded anti-war speech in Chicago in October 2002," "I do not oppose all wars. What I opposed to is a dumb war. What I opposed to is a rash war. That I opposed to is cynical attempt by Richard Perle and Paul Wolfowitz and other armchairs, weekend warriors in the administration to shove their own ideological agendas down our throats, irrespective of the cost of lives lost and in hardships borne. What I opposed to is the attempt by political hacks like Karl Rove to distract us from a rise in the uninsured, a rise in poverty rate, a drop in the medium income, to distract us from corporate scandals and a stock market that has just gone through the worst month since the Great Depression. That is what I am opposed to. A dumb war, a rash war. A war not based on reasons but on passions, not on principle but on politics."

Now let us hope for the best—the globe must be freed from Americans evil imperialists design!

MAHATMA GANDHI AND BIHAR!
(ONE HUNDRED YEAR OF GANDHI'S FIRST VISIT TO BIHAR)

Wednesday, 4 January 2012

In next five years, it will be one hundred year (1917-2017) when Mahatma Gandhi had first visited Bihar to take up the sad plight of indigo planters (oppressed tenant farmers) of Champaran in the Himalyan foothills of northern Bihar. Although much has changed by now, the exploitations to oppress and scar of untouchablity still persist even after the country achieved independence in 1947 from the yoke of British Raj. We Bihari will celebrate the centenary celebrations of Gandhi's visit to Champran but we many have forgotten the ideals of great Mahatma.

Down the memory lane, the Champaran region, which was once cleansed by Gandhi, has been facing so many upheavals after Independence. Being land-locked areas on Indo-Nepal border, the land of Champaran continued to have notoriety in excess holdings of lands with influential persons, crime prone-areas, called Chambal of Bihar, and also centre of smuggling and last but not the least, the division of society between high caste and low caste, aggravating untochablity. Let us hope for the best—good sense prevails among us!

Mahatama's Champran visit had many stories of ups and downs. It was in early 1916 when Mahatama Gandhi had come to Lucknow to attend the Congress conference. There Gandhi could know about exploitation of indigo planters and Champaran. An exploited farmer Raj Kumar Shukla (as Gandhi had quoted in his autobiography) caught holds him there and persuaded him to speak to Vakil Babu and he will tell him everything about the distress of farmers of Champaran. Raj Kumar Shukla also requested Gandhi to visit Champaran. Mahatama had also written in his autobiography that Vakil Babu was none else but Braj Kisore Prasad, who had become esteemed co-worker of Mahatama

472

Gandhi during his "Champaran satya garah" for months together (unscheduled programme). In Lucknow itself, Shukla brought Braj Kishore Babu in his tent and had explained the situation of Champaran farmers. But Gandhi appeared unmoved and asked in turn to move a resolution in the party session in progress on this score. Subsequently Barj Kishore Babu moved a resolution expressing party's sympathy with the people of Champaran and it was unanimously passed in the Congress session. Even after that Gandhi was reluctant to visit Champaran despite requests by Raj Kumar Shukla. Gandhi, however, told Shukla that he would let him know about his visit later on. Helpless Shukla started following Mahatama Gandhi and pursuing to him to see the plight of farmers. Reluctant Gandhi later promised Shukla that he would visit Calcutta and thereafter decides about Champran visit. But ignorant, unshophisticated but resolute agriculturist did not leave hope and met Gandhi in Calcutta. Ultimately Gandhi had taken up a train of Patna from Calcutta in early 1917 along with Raj Kumar Shukla.

Mahatma reached Patna for the first time. Gandhi had idea that Shukla would be an influential person and knowing Patna people and from there he would move to Champoran. But Gandhi's illusions about Shukla soon over. Raj Kumar Shukla, hiowever, had taken Gandhi to Kadamkuan residence of Rajendra Prasad. But Rajendra Baby was away in Puri. At Rajendra Babu's residence, Gandhi tasted for the first time untouchablity and feudalism tendency among the people of Bihar. Gandhi has said in his autobiography, "there were one or two servants at the bungalow, who paid no attention. There was strict untouchablity in Bihar. I might not draw water at the well whilst the servants were using it, lest drops of water from my bucket might pollute them, the servants not knowing what caste I belonged. Although Raj Kumar pointed me indoor latrine but servants promptly directed me to the outdoor one. All this was far from surprising or irritating to me, for I was inured to such things. The servants were doing the duty, which they thought Rajendra Babu would wish them to do. These entertaining experiences enhanced my regards for Rakj Kumar Shukla, if they enabled me to know him better." Such treatment of Rajendra Babu's resdence to Mahatma Gandhi had also been written in the autobiography of Dr Rajendra Prasad in later years.

Taking into account the helplessness of Shukla, Mahatama Gandhi contacted Maulana Mazharul Huq, who in turn rushed at Rajendra Babu Residence to fetch Gandhi to his residence. But Gandhi resisted and asked Huq to guide him the way of Champaran. Huq talked to

Shukla and suggested Gandhi should first go to Muzaffarpur and from there he should take train for Champran after reaching Muzaffarpur, Gandhi met Principal Kripalani of Government College, Muzaffarpur as Gandhi was knowing him for long. There Kripalani also explained to Gandhi the desperate condition of farmers and rather gave the idea of difficult task for him. From there final journey of Champaran began for Gandhi. In the process, leaders like Rajendra Prasad Brajkisohore Prasad, Ramnavi Prasad, and Gaya Babu had reached to meet Mahatma. All these illustrated sons of Bihar were Gandhi's helping hands in launching Chapmparan satyagrah by him. Gandhi decided to avoid court procedures to end exploit ation of farmers.

From there Gandhi's face to face with Ahimsa began. "tinkathiya" system was in vougue in Bihar, specially in Champran. An informative book on Gandhi, ""Great Soul-Mahatma Gandhi and his Struggle with India", written by Joshe Joseph Lelyveld, winner of the Pulitzer Prize has dwelt at length Gandhi's Champran satyagrah. About the exploitation, the writer has said," Farmers were forced by a corrupt combination of local law, taxation, chronic indebtedness and crude force to devot a portion of the land they farmed to growing indigo plants on which they seldom earned a meaningful return. The indigo, in demand In Europe as a dye for fine fabrics, went to class of British planters, who leased the land, including whole village, from large Indian landlords called zamindars with the land came to tenants, who then had little or no bargaining power against the planters. State of these peasants called ryots was any better than that of indentured labourers of in South Africa; in many cases, it was probably worse. The system had grown up over near a century." "Lelyveld has also quoted the write up of a British official, who had described exploitation of Champaran farmers, "Not a chest of indigo reaches England without being stained with human blood."

Non-violent agitation, launched by Gandhi, by one estimate had spent 175 days in Bihar in 1917 working on the Champaran struggle. Gahdi had later described his Bihar visit as "birthplace", meaning it as his first immersion in rural India. In Champaran Gandhi was ordered by the collector, the local representative of colonial British Authority to leave but Gandhi politely defied the order, then sent nightlong missives in all directions until the national movement and everyone from the viceroy on down knew he was facing arrest. Llyveld has written, "Crowds of rough unlettered tenant farmers gathered to protect him; youthful nationalists made their way to Champaran as would-be satyagrahis; and the viceroy intervened to cancel his expulsion from Champaran region. Within weeks Gandhi himself was appointed official commission investigating the complaints of the tenant farmers—it would recommend they be freed from any compulsion to grow indigo."

In the wake of Champaran satyagrah, Pundit Jawahar Lal Nehru has described Gandhi, "the see essence of his teaching was fearlessness and truth ad action allied to these. This voice somehow different from others. It was quite and low and yet it could be heard above the shouting of the multitude; it was soft an gentle, and yet there seemed to be steel hidden away some where in it . . . . Behind the language of peace and friendship there was power and quivering shadow of action and a determination not to submit to a wrong."

In between his champaran visit, many things happened. Ganbdhi had to pass through many experiments—rights from court cases to satyagarkh to free the farmers from the clutches of exploitation. His method of satyagrah was unique. And after full-fledged enquiry by Gandhi himself and the Raj agreeing to his recommendations, the tinkathiya system, which was in vogue of for over a century, was thus abolished and with planters' raj came to an end. In his autograph, Gandhi had commented, "the ryots, who had all along remained crushed, now somewhat came to their own and the superstitions that the stain of indigo never be washed out exploded."

Mahatma had desire to do more for Bihar, specially Champran but it could not materialise ansd Gandhi has concluded in his autobiography about Champaran satyagrah, "It was my desire to continue the constructive work for some years to establish more schools and to penetrate the more effectively. The ground has been prepared, but it did not please God, as often before, to allow my plans to be fulfilled. Fate decided otherwise and drobve me to take up work elsewhere."

Successive rulers after independence in Bihar have failed to root out social evils like untouchablity, inequality, and land to landless, food to poor, education to all without any discrimination. At least remembering Gandhi's role to end exploitations through non-violence means in Champaran in Bihar although we have voluminous Constitution and laws to tell the world that there is democracy in India!

LACK OF LAND REFORMS: BANE OF POVERTY IN BIHAR!

Sunday, 4 December 2011

Dream of land reform—and to poor and landless—continues to create Herculean task for successive state governments since independence: Result:—rampant rise in poverty, no home for homeless, and no land to cultivate by poor. Because lands continue to be accumulated in the hands of feudal landlords, neo-rich classes, politicians of all hues. Even the government lands (aam and khas lands, vacant since the time of British Raj), have been grabbed by influential political class and big land holders in the successive years. It appeared that there are no land left now even for poor to construct their houses under much-hyped ambitious schemes of the union government and Bihar government.

Except the first government of Dr S K Sinha after independence and mid-way governments of both the Congress and anti-Congress formations have had taken half-hearted measures for land reforms. And in the process, some lands were distributed among landless by the successive governments and state sponsored non-governmental organisations like Bhoodan Yagya Committee of Binoba Bhave. But the distributed lands were again grabbed by vested interests like big land holders and feudal forces. Matter in Bihar stands where it was long back—Raj of British Raj and landlords. More over here in India, Kings, and Nawabas are still being crowned after the death of elder kings and Nawabs—like that of Sindhia family and Nawab of Pataudi family. Such practises have been abolished long back under the Constitution. But thanks to government, these practises are continuing in almost all parts of the country, especially Bihar, Rajasthan, Madhya Pradesh, Bihar etc.

The present government of the National Democratic Alliance(NDA), comprising of JD(U) and Bharatiya Janata Party, led by Nitish Kumar was installed over six years back. Poor and land less had have great hopes from Nitish Kumar for emphasis on the land reforms under the laws and rules, spelt out in the Constitution. Nitish Kumar, as promised to the people, has started on right direction, knowing fully well that unequal distribution of lands are the bane of poverty in Bihar. Kumar took some lessons from the West Bengal government of the left Fronts where land reforms measures were taken much headway and landless got title of lands, distributed by the government and also effective laws in that state to implement Barga law (bataidari law) on the basis of Bandopadhaya committee report. Nitish wanted to make West Bengal land reform measures as replica for Bihar. Bandopadhaya was called by Nitish Kumar and entrusted him for suggestions for land reform measures in Bihar. Bandhopadhaya had recommended to Bihar government a comprehensive measure for the land reforms.

Nitish Kumar was well set to implement the suggesstions of Bandopadhaya committee report in Bihar for land reform everything was on to take up the matter. But by the time, assembly an election of 2010 was round the corner. Decision of Nitish Kumar started facing hurdles after hurdles. Conservative party like BJP and big landlords, neo-rich classes, upper caste majority, having big chunk of lands, opposed the much-publicised land reform measures of Nitish Kumar it may be mentioned here that these sections are said to be the main vote banks of NDA. Reluctantly Nitish Kumar side-tracked the issue and under the pressure of dominant alliance partner—BJP and land owing classes put the matter in cold storage. Land reforms measures got yet another set back.

Recently, Nitish Kumar has again opened the Pandora's Box. While releasing the report cards of his one year rule of his second term, Nitish Kumar announced yet another schemes for the so called land reforms. He announced that all land will be surveyed and consolidations will be made in the next few years. Such utterances of Nitish Kumar are again being resented by the major coalition partner—BJP as well as big land holders. Nitish has very surreptitiously raised the issue of land survey and consolidations, which may prove an uphill task and it will take a long time. Again the process is likely to be landed in the political cobweb! No doubt these measures of Nitish Kumar have some tangible hopes among the landless. Over 94000 square kilo meters of land, mostly in rural areas, has not been surveyed in the last over 100 years, and land records in the state is not at all updated.

Here I must tell about successive land reform measures. Late K B Sahay was the first Revenue minister in the Dr S K Sinha government of the united Bihar. Right to property was incorporated in out Constitution by which anybody could keep as much of property specially lands. K B Sahay under the shadow of the directive principles of state under the Constitution, started aquiring lands of rajas, maharajas, landlords and big holders for distribution among landless for cultivation and homes. The Move of Dr S K Sinha was challenged in the higher court in the name of right to property, enunciated under the Constitution, by Maharaja of Darbhanga. Move of Dr S K Sinha government were defeated as court verdict had gone in favour of Drarbhanga Maharaja. But progressive leadership of the then prime minister Pundit Jawahar Lal Nehru intervened. First amendment to the constitution was made and the entire right of land holdings was put in seventh schedule of the Constitution. And hurdles, preventing land reforms measures ended. And Different state government had taken measures and lakhs of acres of land throughout the country were taken and acquired by the almost all states in the country. Bihar at time topped the list in acquiring surplus lands from land holders. But half-hearted measures could not fecilitate to distributea surplus lands to land less. Thereafter, the SanyuktaB Vidhayak Dal government of non-congress parties in mid sixties and seventies also initiated some measures. During those days, many agitational programmes were launched by non-congress parties specially Communist Party of India and Socialist party to grab lands of big land holders and distribute them among landless. And to some extend, it succeeded also!

More over big land holders, especially zamindars, started playing a different game. Many of them in Bihar, especially in Purnia, Darbhanga, Hazaribagh, Ranchi, Palsamu, Bhagalpur, Saharsa, Champaran etc got their lands transferred in the fake names like their dogs, cats, as well as trusted men to escape the surplus land holdings. And Bihar government remained silent spectators. In successive years, lands distributed to poor and landless had been grabbed after they were evicted from their possession by big land holders and neo-rich classes, particularly politicians of all hues in Bihar. These big shark land holders, did not even leave "aam and hkhas lands" of the government and by making laws by the successive governments in Bihar simple, not only in the rural areas but in the urban areas. In urban areas, particularly big politicians and other rich sections of society in Patna have got the khas land in Patna in their names and have built multi-storey buildings in different parts of Patna, particularly on Fraser road and Buddha Marg, Kadamkuan etc.

All these slackness of the successive government to bring on effective laws on land reforms have aggravated poverty, which have gone 80 percent in the state, especially in rural areas. Over 70 percent people have no land for constructing even their houses in the state what to talk of cultivating the lands. On the other hand, big land holders, feudal s, neo-rich class and political class are thriving on lands in almost all parts of the state.

If we take into account, the global Hunger index (GHI), the poverty in India is on rise. Out of 81 countries, which have been taken into consideration in GHI, India ranks 67 and Bihar state is at the lowest ebb. Surprisingly, India is below Sri Lanka (rank-36), Nepal (rank-54) and Pakistan (rank-59) in the global hunger index chart, released in 2011. More over, on the other hand, India is advancing when it comes to dollar billionaire in the country as per recent figure, released by the UN Human Development Report (UNHDR). There are totall 134 billionaires in 2011 in India. UNHDR says that over 55 billionaires have grown their wealth at an astonishing rate in since 10991 because of new economic liberalisation police of the union government. India's multidimensional poor now exceeds 612 million as per report of the UNHDR—such inequnl India. In Bihar, less said is better, while poverty has increased. Over 80 percent poor are poverty-ridden bin Bihar. Many of them hardly get two meals a day what to talk of medical facilities, rise in malnutrition and education in both ur rural and urban areas of Bihar while neo rich, contractors, politicians, businessmen, industrialists are thriving on huge property, earned through foul means!

OLIGARCHY-INDIAN STATE?

Sunday, 6 November 2011

We have democracy. India is state or nation or country being governed in the name of so called democratic, socialist, secular Republic parliamentary system under a well defined Constitution. But elections come and go. We exercise our franchise in the successive general elections. But the country is being governed in successive years not by politicians and political classes, we choose but by an microscopic enlightened people, acquiring huge wealth and control over every things including natural resources of the country. Over 80 percent of population of the country of over 120 crore in India have hardly tasted the power in the last over 60 years of the inception of country. Inequality has widened in menacing proportions in India. Entire wealth have been accumulated in the hands of less than 20 percent people like capitalists, industrialists, corporates, brokers, political class of almost all hues except left parties' politicians. Even the natural resources like forest, water, land etc have come under the control of these sections of people. Fundamental laws land for landless remained on paper only in India!

Many people may have different opinions over the widening gap between few wealthy people, influencing the democratic system in India and ocean of vast population, leading miserable life throughout the country! Some enlightened people of United States, which is also inflicted of such scenarioo attribute such problem between wide gaps of educated and non-educated in that country. I strongly feel that it is not such that at least in India. Here is a growing income disparity between few wealthy and majority of poverty-ridden people.

When we look the entire scenario in India, it is evidently cleared that in our society money are being increasingly concentrated in the hands of few people—hence the gap between equality and inequality is getting wider gradually. Mainly because of such economic imbalances, general

480

masses, numbering over 80 percent of population in India, only manages their things by earning less than Rs 25 a day each! There have been sharp decline in the earnings of lower and middle classes.

Remarkably it is only because of that agitation, dharnans, protests, crimes and criminal activities, naxalites' activities, fight for justice and equalu rights etc, enshrined in the Indian Constitution, have become order of the day throughout India. Hardly a day passes when such things do not happen from east to west and north to south in India. Mainly Maoists are waging relentless war to protest atrocity on poor and tribal, who are being uprooted from jungles, their lands and houses in different parts of the country in the name of industrialising the country, ignoring economic condition of poor and ecological balances. Such situations could be compared with different political upheavals in European, Middle East and other Arabian countries in the globe in recent years. Recent movement in America to occupy Wall Street and other vital installations in America as well as few month's back protest agitation in Great Britain, mainly because of non-availability employment in that country. Such movements may be usual for advanced countries like US and European countries because they are considered high class society where educated and rich people are doing well and capitalists are churning economy for getting more and richer.

But when we think of India, such scenario is ominous signal for the parliamentary democracy and people are in majority illiterate. Time is not so far there may be mobocracy in India taking into account the sufferings of majority of perople and existence of the country may be jeopardised. Indian political system is entirely being influenced by wealthy people. Successive ruling class appear helpless in tackling the deteriorating situation because of corruption have entrenched their body politico! All these ills have are being reflected in India since the country's ruling elites have shifted to new economic policy of liberalisation from early 1980s by ignoring socialistic pattern of society for the welfare of the people of the country. Gradually wide gap between rich and poor is growing rapidly in India. Political system is being influenced by big money wallah. And they have corrupted the whole system, particularly of political class and bureaucracy!

Before I conclude my piece on oligarchy—Indian state, I must quote Paul Krugman, a nenowned and Nobel Laureate Economist of America, who has in a recent article in the context of US economy in New York Times said, "But why does this growing concentration of income and wealth in a few hands matter? Part of answer is that rising inequality has meant a nation which most families do not share fully in economic growth. Another part of the answer is that once you realise just how much richer the rich have become, the argument that higher taxes on high income should be part of long run budget deal becomes a lot more compelling—. The larger answer, however, is that extreme concentration of income in incompatible with real democracy—the whole nature of our society is at stake."

Just we can also put such perspective or paradigm shift in Indian context also?

INDIA, PAKISTAN VICTIMS OF TERRORISM IN WAKE OF 9/11 ATTACKS IN AMERICA!

Friday, 28 October 2011

After 9/11 devastating terror attack on the World Trade Centre, killing over 2000 Americans, the course of history and political scenario not only changed in US and Europe but the entire globe, particularly India and Pakistan in South East Asia. In both these countries, terrorist's activities have increased many-fold in the last ten to 13 years. Both countries have become victims of their own follies in supporting openly against the terror attacks on America. Hate Muslim community campaign throughout the world and also to capture oil in gulf and other Muslim-dominated countries by US in the name of fight terror activities and in the process attacks on Iraq, Afghanistan and Muslim countries in Middle east and Arab world by US security forces and other allied defence forces, the situation had impacted very much the world countries, specially in India and Pakistan. While Pakistan is being considered in the world as a stooge of Washington on every sphere of developments, India, which had glorious history of non-aligned country and for adopting socialistic pattern of society policy in the globe, has been carrying with the pro-US policy and has gradually surrendered to US interests by signing agreement with America on nuclear deal and civilian nuclear liability bill under the prime minister ship of Manmohan Singh. Foundation of such nefarious deal with US was laid during the NDA government led by Atal Behari Vajpapee to teach Pakistan a lesson by aligning with US—but it could not materialise that time. Now US surreptitious and strategic support to India reflected in black and white during the present UPA government led by Manmohan Singh. Now US is encouraging each other by its patting and economic power, furthering more animosity.

Strangely on the eve of commemorating the 9/11 tragedy, the Pakistan government placed an advertisement in the Wall Street Journal of America to show its solidarity on rooting out terrorism such advertisement of Pakistan has detailed that Pakistan had to pay heavy price to counter terrorism along with America. The advertisement said, "Since 2001, a nation of 180 million has been fighting for the future of the world's seven billion. Can any other country do so? Only Pakistan" the advertisement also cited many examples of sacrifices the Pakistan has made on war on terror. Over 21,672 Pakistani civilians have been killed since September 11, 2001. In the process 3,486 explosions including 283 suicide attacks have taken place in different parts of the Pakistan. Over 3.5 million people have become homeless and economically Pakistan lost $68 billion apart from 2,795 Pakistan army men killed and 8,671 injured. The Editor of The Dawn, a popular daily of Pakistan, Rafia zakaria has said that Pakistan suffered more than half tragedies in comparison with America during fight against terror. Many Pakistan people lament that Pakistan was totally a different country ten years back but with open support to US, the country has slipped into death traps as this country is now being considered most dangerous nation in the globe. It economy has gone down to the drains. People are in secured. Government expenditures of Pakistan has showed that Pakistan has spent rs 1500 in the first half of the last financial year, which has increased by 31 percent since 2001 when the figure was about rs 163 billion. Economic survey report 2010-11 of Pakistan said, "the event that trans[pired after 9/11 worsened the security envioronment. this has affected paakistan's exports, prevented the inflows of foreign investments, affected the pace of privatisation programme, slowed overall economic activity, reduced import demands, reduced tax collectin caused expenditure overrun on additional security spending and domestic tourism industry sufferred."

On the other hand India has different terminology to support America on war of terror. Terror in India appears to be mainly becuase of American Support by the country on various matters, forgetting its past history of non-alingned spcialiostic psattern of society. apart from this, discrimination in society is also said to be only of the main causes of resentment and increase in terror acivities—whether it may be Islamic terror attack on vital instalments of India or Maoists or Ultra Marxists attack s on state power and feudal to protest atrocities on poor and tribal in different parts of the country. Minority community Muslims are being discriminated and randomly called terrorists if any attacks took place in

India. Apart from that bad governance, encouragement of communalism by certain Hindu based organisations are also likely causes for rise in terror activities. One of such examples is demolition of Babri Masjid in Uttar Pradesh's ayodhaya by communal elements over ten years back and worst-ever communal riots in Gujarat state of India in which thousands of Muslims were killed by Hindu fanatics in connivance with Hindu fundamentalitalist chief minister of Gujarat Narendra Modi. Such happening had hurt the Muslim Sentiments and some time they become revengeful.

More over there were 25 major terrorists' attacks in the country in the last ten years. apart from major attack on Indian Parliament in house in December 2001, bomb explosion in busy Sarojinini naganr market in New Delhi in October 2005, Mumbai blast in in July 2006, Mmalegaonbomb explosion in September 2006, samjhauta express bomb explosion in February 2007, Hyderabad mecca masjid attack of may 2007, ajmer dargah blast of octber 2007 and attack on mumbai in most heinous manner in november 26, 2008 had taken place in different parts of india. Curiously in all these incidets muslims were arrested and held responsible for attack, which later in course of deeper investigation tuned untrue all thse were result of anti-Muslim mind sets of the successive governments at the union and state level. There were many cases in which it was later found that Muslims aware not at all associated with many such incidents, one of such incidents is Hyderabad mecca masjid attack initially over 60 Muslims were arrested and out on trial but later on intensive investigation resulted that it was the handiwork of Hindu fundamentalists. Maharashtra police had detected that Hindutva groups had committed this crime in retaliation of jehadi terrorism by Muslims. Many Hindu fundamentalists including Pr Ms Pragya singh thakur, Assemanand of Hindu fundamentalists organisation were later charge sheeted in the case. Demolition of Babari Masjid was an eye—opener when thousands of Hindu fundamentalists mob led by the former deputy prime minister of India Lal Krishna advani demolished the masjid in ayodhaya and criminal cases were under progress against them. Case of Gujarat riots had different tales—many Muslims were butchered by police and Hindu mobs under the direct supervision of the chief minister Narendra Modi. Many cases were pending in different courts of the country. Muslims of India have genuine complaints that discriminatory treatment of government and majority Hindu fundamentalists m have made life miserable to minority community in India. Not only that poor and tribal in India were being deprived of equal right and they were being uprooted from their lands and houses in the name of setting up industries in the wake of new economic liberalisation policy. In this manner India's rulers were serving the interest of America, resulting into rampant increase in terror activities in the country.

GROWTH RATE VIS-A-VIS TRICKLE DOWN THEORY, AN EYE WASH!

Sunday, 16 October 2011

"GROSS DOMESTIC PRODUCT(GDP)" growth has become strange connotation in the globe, particularly in India and its different states with the advent of new economic liberalisation policy, implemented in India in 1991 under the union finance minister ship of the present prime minister of India Manmohan Singh during the regime of Narsimha Rao government at the centre. Such measurement of this growth rate had for the first time came in United States of America and Europe under a policy—"TRICKLE DOWN ECONOMY", formulated by Nobel Laureate in Economics Kuznitis of America during the period 1974-75. Under this "Trickle down policy" of economy, as per theory of Kuznitis, the real development of any country will grow in the head of GDP with vast richness of corporates, industrialists, capitalists etc. and when these rich sections will touch highest point of richness, the welfare from such rich economy will automatically percolate to downward trends at the bottom and all sections of society will be benefitted. Such theory had become major economic policy formulation in America and Europe. In the entire US and Europe, wealth concentrated in the hands of rich, corporates, capitalists, industrialists etc following boosting of Trickle down policy in their respective countries. They became rich and poor became poorer. Economy from rich is yet to percolate from the top, resulting into widespread down trend economy in entire America and Europe.

Significantly this economic policy did not click and instead of success trickle down economy theory has failed. Noted economists of America Joseph Stieglitz and Pal Krugman, both Nobel prize winners in Economics had vehemently opposed the trickle down economy and had cautioned the US men that such policy will result into disastrous policy not only for America but for Europe also. "This economic theory had no practical approach and was just imaginary that wealth will percolate to downward for poors' welfare when the rich will have enough wealth and would reach at centurion point!

Significantly, the new economic liberalisation policy of India has also copied the trickle down theory of economics—hence richer getting richer and poor getting more and more poor in the last 20 years. Present measurement of GDP is the same indicator which indicates that India's economy like GDP is rising and rising and the country is getting stronger and stronger. Because of heavy boost to corporates, multinationals, industrialists, capitalists by the Indian government the production were increasing but it fails to percolate employment generation and core agriculture sectors, on which even today over 67 percent depend for their livelihood. The India government in the rat race of encouraging production of goods and materials had withdrawn subsidies on agriculture sectors. And farmers are crying for help and assurances—many social sectors are suffering while corporates, capitalists, industrialists, multinationals are being given concessions after concessions.

BIHAR: If entire gamut of growth rate are taken into consideration, India is failing to mitigate the sufferings of common and poor masses and on the another hand concentrating on helping big business houses so that GDP of the country continue to increase to obviously show the people that India is developing—, this is completely an eye wash, said Uamadhar Singh, ex-MLA and former naxalite leader and associates of late Charu Mazumdar and Kanu sanyal and also pioneering and researching on economic policy in the globe, particularly in india and Bihar. Taking pot shot on the so called increase in the GDP of Bihar, Singh said that in actuality economy of Bihar for benefitting poor and farmers are sharply declining. In the last several years no investment had come in Bihar, unemployment is mounting, agriculture main items in Bihar is suffering—only growth in non-viable sectors including oil mills, hotel business, richness of capitalists, rise in building construction sectors have been taken into consideration—than it was obvious that GDP of Bihar will definitely rise to over 14 percent as per figure released by union government, singh added.

About the increasing economy of Bihar, the figure of 14.15 percent (GSDP) has been released by the union ministry of programme implementation and statistics. The report has said that annual Gross state domestic product (GSDP) of Bihar is more than developed states including Tamil Nadi, Maharashtra, Punjab, Haryana and Andhra

Pradesh, which have recorded 11.75, 10.74,7.21, 9.69, and 9.22 percent GSDP growth respectively. Significantly Bihar's GSDP rate is better than mineral rich states like Orrisa, (5.87 pc), chhatishgarh (11.57pc) and Jharkhand (6.01pc). Big states like Rajasthan (9.69pc) and Uttar Pradesh (8.08 pc) are also lagging Bihar in the growth parameters.

Economic experts are not entghuisiatc over the increased growth rate of Bihar. Patna university professor of Economics N K Chaudhary said that agriculture, which is backbone of Bihar, has shown no growth in the last two years. Growth is only in non-viable sectors and tertiary sectors. Such growth generally does not sustain unless the growth in made in primary and secondary sectors." I do not feel optimistic over GSDP in Bihar", Chaufhary lamented. And added that present growth rate was not pro-poor as evident that poverty is rising.

Senior economist and the Director of Asian research development research institute (ADRI) P P Ghosh is also apprehensive over present growth rate in Bihar. He said that it was only because of low base of economy was one of the factors for such a high growth rate. If the increase in poverty and almost no attention on primary agriculture sector in Bihar were taken into consideration, such high growth bound to be rebound, Ghosh added.

However, national general secretary of JD(U) Shivanand Tiwari patted the Nitish government for stressing on development of the state, resulting into rise in GSDP. With regards to rise in poverty Tiwari put blame of union government and said that Bihar needed maximum m support of union government to overcome the problem.

In this way this trickle down economy, adopted from US and Europe is giving ominous signals for Indian economy when look into down-ward trends of economy in the US and Europe. For eliminating poverty, agriculture and social sectors must be given priority—only than fruits of development and employment percolate to common masses in India. It will be foolish to undermine the level of life of masses in India and encourage rich and capitalists to get richer!

Exactly I remember one of the statements of eminent writer Arundhati Roy in which she had ironically commented about this trickle down economy and had said that like rich in abundance percolates benefits to poor from new height of richness like wise naxalites will reach in their revolution from trickle down to trickle up manner for achieving their goals!

Journalist, Analyst, Columnist based at Patna my blog www. kksingh1.blogspot.com.

MISDEMEANOR OF PROF AMARTYA SEN WHILE CALLING BIHAR A PAROCHIAL STATE IN INDIA WHILE GB-CUM-MENTOR GROUP MEETING OF NU IN BEIGING!

Sunday, 16 October 2011

I strongly feel Prof Amartya Sen has become senile because of his old-age as told by him in a New York meeting recently that he wants to opt out from the active functioning of the Nalanda University as NU governing board-cum-mentor group chairman and instead want advisory role in the university. Later addressing a meeting in New Delhi, Sen changed his pats and blamed officials for delay in releasing fund for smooth functioning of the university. In the same meeting Sen had also said that the former President of India Dr A P J Kalam has not dissociated from the university during his talks in Delhi while he (Sen) met him. Sen did not speak even a single sentence about controversy in the appointment of Gopa Sabharwal as Vice-Chancellor of the university, unauthorised opening of the university office in Delhi instead of at Nalanda where theuniversity is to be located, did not give any inkling of meeting of the GB-CUM-Mentor group in Beiging in next few days, about the statement of the minister of external affairs E. Ahmed in Rajya sabha that no V-C has been appointed in the NU etc. Sen came and vanished, telling the people that he was going back to New York, putting a million dollar question over the fate of the NU, which was to be set up as world standard university on the ruins of the ancient Nalanda university, in Nalanda in Bihar!

Now the meeting of GB of the university and discussions over allied matters concluded on Saturdayiin Beiging. There Sen's misdenmur had tuched a new height at a meeting in the Peking university, he used abusive languages against Biharis and Bihar not giving any definite and substantive arguments and logic over the appointment of Gopa as vice-chancellor of theuniversity. Academicians pointed out to Sen that petty Gopa, who speaks good English, that might not be the criteria for appointing her as V-C. In trun Sen spoke in his arrogant style when Indian academicians in the audiences wanted to know the controversy surrounding the appointment of Gopa Sabharwal as the V-C of the university as well as dissociation of the APJ, who had concieved the idea of the university initially in Nalanda, according to newspapers reports, published in the indian newspapers.

Reports say that Sen appeared flaggerbasted and told the audiences that local media should be blamed for this controversy. Local media reports are not correct," sen told the gatherings and in the process Sen did not even spare Gopa Sabharwal while replying to the questions of the audiences. Sen further told the audiences that among top 200 universities in the world, Indian and its state-Bihar state figure no where. He furrthjer said that Bihar is a parachial state. "We wanted to give Bihar NU of the world class but if the people of Bihar want to live parachial life than we cannot help." About APJ dissociation from NU, Sen pointed out that He talked to APJ during his recent visit to Delhi on phone (Not met APJ personally as told by him in Delhi meeting) and APJ told him that He (APJ) is ready to guide us. Sen further blamed the External affairs ministry of India government for not contacting him (APJ) in the last six months. APJ advised me to send Gopa for further discussion on NU. Sen admitted that Gopa is handpicked V-C because of various reasons including carrying university affairs in smooth manner. Moreover, earlier Sen had humiliated eminent historian Prof D N Jha and many other eminent scholars on NU affairs. Sen, however, said that surreptiously Gopa shifted the office of the university in New Delhi. Earlier Sen had called the Bihar acdemicians hierarchia and caste ridden at a meeting on NU in New York when some of them had raised the issue of appointment of the vice-chancellor and the manner in which funtioning of the university were being carried out!

Now I consider the union government is mainly responsible for all the ills in the NU. Enacting an Act for developing a wrorld class university in Nalanda on the pattern of theancient Nalanda University and constituting a mentor group-cum-governing borad of the university do not mean that centre has no responsibility—definitely It has all the responsiblities to frame guidelines under the ACT to start the university with the cooperation of Buddhhist intrest countries like China, Japan, singapore etc. Prime Minister Manmohan singh and union external affairs minister S M Krishna are keeping mum over the issues and Sen not only blatantly humiliating officials but the media and people concerned over the setting up of NU in Bihar. At least Centre should ask explaination to the mentor group led by Sen that the group had to submit report on infrastructures and other thinfs in nine months—why the group has taken such a long time of over five years in not submitting the repor? Lapses on the part of union external affairs ministry have also come to surface in the recently concluded meeting of GB in Beiging. Embassy of Indiain China has depicted in its credentials that Gopa is V-C of the university when the union external affairs ministry does not consider her V-C of the universityas he had stated recenty in the Rajya sabha that no V-C has been appoiintedin in the Nalanda university! Such types of falacies have created worse type of confusion.

Many loopholes in the NU affairs have come to surface as per replies of the union external affairs ministry under Right to Information Act on various applications of Indian citizens. Gopa has appointed one of her saheli Anjana Sharma as officer on special duty and has appointed many officials and staff for the university in illegal manner. One of appointees Parwez as coordinator of the university at Nalanda is a mediocare and has been appointed under the influences of one of the JD(U) MPs of Rajya Sabha. Parwez is just a typist and does not know abc of university affairs. Parwez appeared helpless when I visited the site of NU a few days back. Parwez told the mediapersons before me that he has not even a register to write about any thing—just he has been appointed and sent here without any work. Parwez appeared to be a mental case—he was more concerned about his newly wed wife which he had married recently at the ripe age after divorcing his earlier wife and deserting grown up childrens.

Such things are not new for NU. Even Prof Sen has three or four marriages—divorcing his earlier wives and childrens and married again and again in United States of America. And this Prof Sen is giving us lecture on the culture and civilisation of Biharis and Bihar and calling us parachoal. I do not like to react on the statement of Sen on Bihar because of our culture and civilisation but I must say one thing to Prof Sen he is himself a great parachial. ignoring the claims of the Indian academicians of repute and Sen became instrumental in appointing as many as his close men including one of his relations "one Sen" working with Amartaya in the same university as member of the GB—cum—mentor group pressurising uninion government and keeping other foreign members in dark. Sen has also succeeded in appointing handpicked V-C Gopa of the university, violating the Nalanda University ACT, enacted by the Parliament and also keeping in dark other foreign members of the board.

Intrestingly there is surprise among people of India, particularly Bihar over the silence of the Bihar chief minister Nitish Kumar over the entire issue. Nitish used to be very sensitive over the lapses of the centre and used to be past master in criticising union government over drop of hats. But centre's lapses and Amartya sen's humiliating approach towards Bihar have been surreptiously silencing Nitish Kumar. Kumar must intervene so that Bihar must not be deprived of prized opportunity of a world class university. More over his close party colleague and MP N K Singh, a seasone d former bureacrats and efficient politicians mustrspeak about the misdeeds in the university. N K Singh, pouplarly known as Nandu Babu in his close circles had replied my email and informed me that he would raise the issue about controversial appointment of Gopa as VC in in the next board meeting. But wheather Singh had raised the issue or not—I am waiting for his reply. Let us hope for the best from Singh, who is the loner r from Bihar in the governing board-cum-mentor group of the NU.

Perhaps Sen is after keeping secret his mistakes in all these matters and get provoked and abuses Bihar and Biharis. Sen has not explored opportunity for right candidate of V-C taking into account academic excellences etc. Sen's suspicious approach towards APJ also raises many questions as APJ is considered one of ther top stalwarts on the Indian scene for right action throughout the country. But one thing is appears very strange, Sen does not lag behind in praising Nitish Kumar and Bihar government on the university affairs instead finding some time to meet Manmohan Singh to apprise him of all the related problems and bottelnecks at central level to start work promptly for the university infrastructures in Nalanda. It is on records that Sen had started many NGOs including Pratchchi, which have been assigned lot of jobs and research work by Nitish government worth over Rs 50 lakhs. Such works have been provided by another NDA government led by the BJP government led by Arjun Munda in neighbouring Jharkhand.

DOWN THE MEMORY LANE: ADVANI'S RATHYATRA OF 1990 TO CONSTRUCT RAM MANDIR!

Monday, 10 October 2011

Today's event of beginning nation-wide "Rathyatra" of the senior Bhartaya Janata Party(BJP) and prime ministerial aspirant for next general elections of Lok Sabha Lal Krishna Advani from Chapra instead of Sitabdiara in Eastern Uttar Pradesh to protest corruption and misgoverning in the country, has put me into down the memory lane of similar "rathyatra" of Advani from Somnath to Ayodhaya to p ress for construction of Ram Mandir in Ayodhaya at the site of Babari Masjid in 1990 and halting of his yatra and arrest him (Advani) at Samastipur in Bihar by then chief minister Laloo Prasad Yadav of Bihar on the advice of the then Prime minister of India Late Vishwanath Pratap Singh and "gospel truth mantarana" of trusted colleague Nitish Kumar of Laloo., who (Nitish) was that time minister of state for agriculture in the union government Chief minister of Bihar Nitish Kumar, who was in the Janata PARTY THAT TIME and close confidant of Laloo, was the main architect of halting the yatra of Advani and arresting him, is incidentally the alliance partner of the bJP and heading the coalition government in Bihar.

Coincidentally Nitish Kumar, once bitter critic of Advani and BJP to maintain his (Nitish) secular credential will today flag off the yatra of Advani from Chapra Kumar was that time key advisor of V P Singh and Laloo to stop yatra of Advani in Bihar obviously to save the country from communal flare-ups. It was 21 years back when I was eye-witness of the entire "arrest operation Advani and stop his rathyatra right from Darbhanga to samastipur" as journalist in the Times of India, covering the incident.

Before going to cover the flagging off the yatra of Advani by Nitish Kumar to Chapra, now as a freelance journalists at the age of 67 years as I have retired from the active services of the Times of India, I want to mention few facts—first I salute the then Resident Editor of TOI Sumant Sen for giving me free hand to cover the yatra and related incidents amid communally surcharge d atmosphere during those days and published my all stories, related to Advani and his rath yatra in Biharon national hook-us. Second—my most valuable sources in government quarters, the then Inspector General of Darbhanga range late R R Prasad(later promoted to the rank of DGP and remained DGP of Bihar for several years) and the then Divisional commissioner of Darbhanga V. Jayshankar(a senior IAS official of the Bihar cadre now retired) and other officials and staff of both the districts gave me ample inputs time to time to write factually correct stories and analysis, related to halting of Advani yatra and arresting him.

Entire atmosphere was that time were surcharged with communal tension in entire north Bihar Protest, rallies, burning of trains, beating of minority ccommunity members here and there, blocking of roads had marked the days following the arrest of Advani and halting of his rathyatra, which remained lying abandoned for day together later on in the sprawling Samastipur Circuit House after the administration in a swift operation arrested Advani in the early morning and airlifted him to the luxurious guest house in Masan Jore, now in Jharkhand state at that time Bihar was united state. In the process, scores of people were seriously injured in entire north Bihar in police lathicharges, brick batting etc— but major incidents of communal flare ups did not take place because of strict handling of situation by Laloo prasad Yadav government and in next few days calm was restored in entire joint Bihar. Nitish, at that time, had been camping here to give valuable advices to Laloo to face the situation. More over entire country in next few days flared up with communal incidents killing thousands of people of minority community and subsequently demolition of Babari Masjid by frenzied Hindu fundamentalists in Ayodhaya. But Bihar remained calm and quite!

Since the demolition of Babari Masjid by huge mob of frenzied Hindu fundamentalists in the presence of senior BJ leaders including L K Advani, Murali Manhar Joshi. But instead of controlling the crowds— they encouraged them to demolish the masjid in no time. And this has happened in three hours and entire masjid was razed to the ground by the Hindu fundamentalists. Incident was condemned throughout the globe and since than India's graph as secular country was being questioned in the world countries. Apart from that ongoing unstable atmoshper in the world, particularly in the India is said to be the result of the fall outs of Babari Masjid demolition. Such fall out had also resulted into terrorists activities in India where thousands of innocent people had been killed in the last 15 years.

Operation arrests Advani and halting rath of advani were meticulously planned with many alternatives. Darbhanga aerodrome base of the Indian air force was kept ready to land big plane in case of emergency even in night hour by lighting with "masals" by army officials. Hectic activities were seen at the Circuit house in Samastipur where Advani was to stay overnight after his departure from Patna on his rath. At about two pm Advani and his rath conclaves reached Samastipur. All of them leisurely slept without any inkling what is at store. All the telecommunication network of entire Darbhanga zone especially with Samsastiur was jammed on the instruction of the Darbhanga divisional commissioner. Jayshankar was seen personally camping in telecommunication centres, monitoring the situation of jamming network. It resulted quite delay in submission of new reports to my editor Sumanta Sen after the arrest of ASdvani there.

Early morning a senior IAS official that time registrar of the cooperative societies R K Singh (now union home secretary) and a senior IPS official Rameshwar Oraon (now retired and two times Congress member of Lok Sabha from Jharkhand) were drafted by Laloo to give final show-down to the enactment of arrest Advani and stop his rathyatra". Both the senior officials reached Patel Maidan, in the centre of Samastipur town by a helicopter at about 5 am and straight rushed to the Circuit House where advani was styaing. Both of them awoke advani and armed with arrest warrant under National security Act, p plainly told Advani that he was being arrested, advani asked for time to get ready and requested Singh and Oraon to allow another BJP leader late Pramod Mahajan to accompany him. Later both the officials granted such request of Advani. In the meantime Advani wrote a letter to the President of India, informing him to withdrawing support to V P Singh government and handed it to senior BJ leader Kailashpati Mishra to deliver the letter as soon as possible to the President. And in next few minutes both of them were taken out and straight taken away to Patel Maidain where the helicopter was ready.

After sleepless whole night Amitab of Navbharat Times and I were there at the Circuit house whole night as I had strong hunch that some thing serious was cooking up at the administrationand government level in Patna. Here I must mention that over 300 hundred journalists were accompanying advani during his rathyatra some on the cost of BJP and some on the cost of their respective newspapers but significantly none of the journalists except two—I and Amitiab were present at the time of the arrest of Advani. Later I could know that almost all journalists had preferred to stay at Patna and had planned to accompany advani at Samstipur next morning for his advance jurney. I asked a few question to advani and he readily replied and said that his arrest will create further problems for both union and state government. R K Singh was angry with me while I was talking to Advani. Any way Singh and myself were old acquaintances at least he did not misbehave with me at that crucial moment. In next few minutes advani andMahajan were airlifted and brought to Masanjore after his arrest as earlier Planned by Laloo government.

With the arrest of Advani not only communal rights were witnessed in several parts of the country, but whole comlexion of Indian political scenario changed and it is continuing right now also. Coalition era started since then after a few midterm poll many union govts came but did not last long. Finally with many political developments in the country, NDA, comprising of many coalition parties, mainly of BJP came to power and stayed in for more than six years if terms were taken into consideration.

Much avowed rathyatra of advani could not succeed to construct Ram Temple in Ayodhaya at the site of demolished Babari Masjid, becauuse of coalition compulsion but NDA, particularly tasted the share of power and luxury under the stewardship of Senior BJP leader Atal Behari Vajayee as prime minister of the country.

Paradoxically the same Nitish is today with Advani in his rathyatra. People have serious apprehension that advani's yatra throughout the country might turn violent and communal clash es are not ruled out, political observers are of the opinion.

I just wanted to put the facts before the people, especially young generation as far as my experience goes and the things which I had seen with my naked eyes during my journalism profession.

US NEFARIOUS DESIGN IN WORLD CASTING ITS OWN DOOM?

Monday, 3 October 2011

NEED OF CAUTION TO INDIA!

America's so called GLOBAL War on Terror (GWOT) is not only creating instability to the entire Globe but eating into the vitals of its own viability as super power in the world! After 9/11, terror attacks on the twin towers of the World Trade centre and Pentagon ten years back, there have been many changes in the political dimension in the entire world. America, once considered the super power and its exconomic bases at its zenith is passing through one of the most critical phase of its political and economic survival. Its economic downtrend is posing a big question mark—"will US survive the set back?" America and its major allies in Europe are under severe economic strains.

Like his predecessor Bush of Republican Party, the president of America of Democrat Obama is also following the same dangerous foot-print in waging war against terror and creating panic in the entire globe. Although such step of the American government on GWOT is giving to the people of dangerous signal to entire America and Europe, they appear helpless. Gradually once known for the "sense of belonging among Americans", the US perhaps appears to have deviated from its cherished path. From hindsight view, it appears that US is fighting for its security in view of 9/11 terror attack, killing over 3000 people in Washington, living in and around the twin towers of World Trade Centre as well as the targeting of Pentagon building, housing important offices of the American government. Exactly in the aftermath of the attack, the US has developed more of its imperialistic design to spread its influence in the world, particularly West Asia and Arab world. By such thinking among American leadership, US are alienating the Muslims and their Islamic tenants at all cost particularly in West Asia and also to capture the oil resources of the world under its influence. Such attitude of US has changed the course of geographically, economically and historically trends in the present day world.

Apparently it appears that GWOT of America is to finish its enemies. a recent of Pew Research Centre's opinion poll, released on September 01, 2011 has indicated that vast majority of people of America are of the opinion that war on Iraq and Afghanistan have aggravated the threat of terrorism. Many of them have also objected the internal censorship by the US government about checking their mails and also monitoring personal calls. Only 25 percent people of America admit that war on terror in Afghanistan and Iraq have decreased the threat of terror.

War against terror by America has witnessed enough blood-letting in different countries and peoples' miseries have aggravated. After 9/11 attack, the US has failed to analyse the things after 9/11 attacks and its indiscriminate war against terror in Arab world, Middle East other major parts of South-East Asia have resulted into alienation of the Muslims population of the whole especially Arab world.

On economic front alone US has suffered much because of prolonged war against terror and economic down trend started. War on Afghanistan has been costing America 8$ billion a month. Apart from that, cost on war on America in both Afghanistan and Iraq have cost $ 5 trillion so far. Many noted economists in US have termed that because of expenditure on war have become cause of decline in its economy. The Nobel Prize winner in Economics of America Joseph Stiglitz has studied the war expenditures of US on Iraq and Afghanistan and has cautioned the American government in 2003 that war on these two countries would adversely affect the economy particularly on education, health, research and environment in the US. He has pointed out after about seven years, in an article in 2010 In Washington Post, that after military action in both the countries oil price has increased by $140 a barrel in 2008 incomparision to $25 a barrel when the war on terror was started in Iraq eight years ago. It has not only hit the economy of US but almost all countries of the globe. Result:: The latest figure of American government, released in the second week of September, has stated "one out every six American today lives below the official poverty line."

According to US Census bureau report, a record 66.2 million Americans are living in poverty. Expenditure of US on defence and homeland security has increased to $6.7 trillion. All these things have added collapse of American economy.

Historically, the last major civil war occurred in America in 1861-65. Over half a million people had died in that civil war. Impact of that industrial civil war was immense. Columnist Vijay Prasad in his recent article in the Fortnightly-Front Line has said,"no such large-scale bloodletting took place within the territory, apart from the wars against the Amerindians in the American west in the last few decades of the 19th century. Henceforth, the US took its battles to other peoples' land, the Philippines, Cuba, Puerto, Rico, Central America, west Asia, the long war in Europe (1914-1945) and the wars of the Pacific and Africa. The shock of the Japanese attack on Pearl Harbour (December 7, 1941) has to be understood in this context. No wonder that President Franklin Roosevelt called it "a date which lives in infamy."

More over, apart from GWOT, the real motive of US has come to surface when foreign policy wing of neoconservatives created the Project for a New American Century (1997-2006), on that basis, released in 2000 a report, "Rebuilding America's Defences" for increasing "military spending and using the massive US military power to capture political and physical resources around the world". The project has requested the US government "to build up a military and construct a foreign policy to spread American values around the planet—thus called "a new Pearl Harbour" policy of US. "Significantly between September 11, 2001 and May 2011, the national priority project shows the US exchequer spent $7.6 trillion in defence and homeland security. Economy of the US has been rightly and comparatively down graded by Standard and Poor's (S&P), reflecting that the "views that effectiveness, stability and predictably of American foreign policy and political institutions have weakened at a time of ongoing fiscal and economic challenges. "The net effect of 9/11 for the US economy has meant downgrading in the US federal debt to AA plus from the risk free rating of AAA.

Significant aspect of GWOT is that in the name of fighting terrorism, the human rights, rule of law, the liberty have been compromised drastically all over the world. According to confirmed and authenticated report, the death figure because of GWOT, have reached over 150,000 in Pakistan, Afghanistan and Iraq. Over 7.8 million have become refugees because the war by America on terrorism. "War on Iraq cost more than $3trillion," says Stiglithas in his piece in Washington Post. He has observed, "the global financial crisis was due, at last least in part, to the war higher oil prices meant that money spent buying oil abroad, was money not being spent at home." Significantly US is under heavy debt

—even China and India had given monetary loan assistance to America in this critical juncture.

The 9/11 attack and subsequent fighting terror throughout the globe put its economy at the lowest ebb while China remained engaged to build up its own economic power. The prolonged and unnecessary war by US, knowingly and unknowingly continued to siphon off American economy. On the other hand China progressed well to maintain its economic strength in the global, economy on the global arena, sitting on trillion of $ in surpluses. It may be recalled here tht in view of might of China among world power, US compromised from its stand of open hostilities with China. in July 2001 secretary of stae Colin Powell had visited Beijing and assuaged the hurt feeling of China because of some uneasy calm wityh US and said, "we are not enemies, we are looking for cooperation********" The Chinese premier Wen Jiabao, while addressing world economic forum meeting in Dalian in September 2011 says about economic Crisis in US and Europe on asking by audiences, "the two advanced economies in the world, the European union and the US should adopt promptly amend resolutely responsible fiscal and financial policies and push forward policy adjustment and institutional reforms as soon as possible so as to cut budget deficit and ease debt pressure."

International Monetary Fund (IMF) has reported that by 2016, China will have the largest economy in the world. Being separated from the so called war on terror by US, the China is progressing well while India is engaged in hobnobbing with America in many ways although its economy is progressing well in the last few years. Indian must be cautious of America's evil design and take a lesson or two from China to continue its march towards development unmindful of American imperialist theory.

POVERTY, PUBLIC MONEYLOOT, EXPLOITATION: NEED TO CHANGE CONSTITUTION PREAMBLE!

Saturday, 24 September 2011

Some thing very serious in my mind and compelling me to express some serious thoughts over what is happening in the country (India) of over 1.20 crores population? I remember Cherukuri Rajkumar, known to his comrades as Azad, a member of the Politburo of the banned Communist Party of India (Maoist), who had been nominated by his party as its chief nnegotiator for the proposed peace talks with the government of India, and while coming for initiating negotiations was surprisingly and sadly killed on July 02, 2010 in the remote forest of Adilabad by the Andhra Pradesh police. In the process, a Young journalist Hypochondria Pandey, who was travelling with Azad, was also killed after his arrest, perhaps to wipe out evidences of fake killing in the so called encounter with Azad!

Before his death few months earlier, Azad had replied the eminent journalist B G Verghese, in a piece, probably last before his killing, "In which part of India is the Constitution prevailing, Mr Verghese? In Dantewala, Bijapur, Kanker, Narayanpur, Rajnandgaon? In Jharkhand, Orissa, in Lalgarh, Jangalmahal? In the valley of Kashmir? Manipur? Where was your Constitution hiding for 25 long years after thousand of Sikhs were massacred? When thousands of Muslims were decimated? When lakhs of peasants are compelled to commit suicide? When thousands of people are murdered by state-sponsored Salawa Judum gangs? When advasis women are gang raped? When people are simply abducted by uninformed goons? Your Constitution is a piece of paper that does not even have the value of a toilet paper for the vast majority of the Indian people." Azad had just replied Verghese following his article in the Outlook, in which he had written, defending the state and big corporations. Verghese had further written, "The Maoists will fade away, democratic India and the Constitution will prevail despite the time it takes and the pain involved".

Apart from that. there are several aspects of misdeeds of political class, bureaucrats, capitalists, industrialists, multinationals, taking advantage of new economic liberalisation policy, are rather shaking my conscience to look other hand the sad tales of majority of population of this country. To be precise here, I must refer the report of National Commission for Eenterprises in the unorganised sector, headed by reputed economist late Arjun Sengupta, who had reported that 836 million people people in India live on Rs 20 a day or less. Rrecently the Planning commission of India has filed an affidavit before the Supreme Court in the case of determining poor in India, detailing that percapita expenditure Rs 20 a day as a viable cut off line for determining poverty in urban India and in rural India as Rs 15 per day!

On the other hand wealth is being concentrated in the hands of over 20000 capitalists, political class, landlords, company holders, industrialists, corporates and multinationals, operating in different parts of the country. Sstrange are the ways among political class of all hues. As per recent reports of Aassociation for Democratic Reforms (ADR) and Election Media watch(EMW); politicians of a particular set-up make by and large half million rupees a day while in office and serving the people of India. Number of crorepatis have increased by leaps and bound in almost all legislatures of states in the country and both houses of Parliament. In Maharashtra Legislature alone, they were upto 108 in 2004 to 186 in 2009. Over three-fourth of union council of ministers of Manmohan Singh government is crorepatis. Much of this new wealth had been acquired by them while in office. Senior journalist P Sainath has rightly remarked that the union cabinet "is getting healthier and wealthier".

Reports have further revealed that one union minister Prafulla Patel, having assets of more than Rs 79 crore, has added on and average, over half a million rupees every day to hs assets in the last 28 months of his minister ship between May 2009 and August 2011—average of Rs five lakh a day! Patel is the richest cabinet minister.

Average assets, worth over a union minister increased from Rs 7.3 crore to Rs 10.6 crore in the last 28 months. Minister of state in Information and Broadcasting ministry S Jagathrakshakan of DMK has taken big jump in accumulating assets while as minister and serving people of India. His assets have grown by 1092 percent in the last 28 months in comparison to Patels growth of assets 53 percent. Patel, s assets grew by Rs 5.9 crore in 2009 to Rs 70 crore this year. Minister of state for communication Millind Deora has doubled his assets from Rs 17 crore to Rs 33 crore between 2009 to 2011 adding almost a lakh every day taking into account his election affidavit in 2008 his worth at Rs 8.8 crore. Ssimilarly the union Science and technology minister Vilasrao Deshmukh has added Rs 1.73 crore since 2009. Union minister of state for Parliamentary affairs Rajeev shukla has added over Rs 22 crore in the last 28 months to his total assets worth over Rs 7 crore in 2009 to over Rs 30 crore this year.

Political class out of power are also not lagging behind in accumulating huge assets during their office in the state legislatures and Parliament the rebel congress leader and MP Y S Jagmohan Reddy of andhra Pradesh has added Rs 357 crore to his just Rs 72 crore in 2009. Strangely, the former Andhra Pradesh chief minister Chandrababu Naidu, who was considered one of the richest politicians in the country, has strangely grown poor. He is not even worth Rs 40 lakh, thanks to fuzzing the figures. Thus Jagan of Andhra is on rise and Naidu is on decline. Surprisingly the Jubilee hill house of Naidu, which was worth Rs nine crore in 2009 in his affidavit in 2009, has not been declared as per present market value of that houses and other wealth, acquired by him in the last several years in his political life.

These are the stories in nut and shells of wealth being acquired by a section of political class. The government is yet to declare assets of crores of rupees of capitalists, industrialists, company holders, corporates, multinationals operating etc in the country. It is said authenticated by facts that over 90 percent of wealth are concentrated in their hands!

Atrocity on poor and tribal population by state terror and feudal forces and so called system in the government are increasing by rapid scales and Maoists are only forces in the country are fighting for their interests and for this they are called anti-nationals! The sale of tribal lands to non-tribal in the Schedule five are prohibited in states. However transfers of land continued in during post-liberalisation period rampantly. Besides tribal are being forced in Jharkhand, Orrisa, MP. Chhatishgrah, Maharashtra, Gujarat, Bihar to vacate the forest lands, violating laws of the lands for making rooms for multinationals and corporates for installing industrial units in mineral-rich areas. Not only that even in plan areas of the country, farmers are forced to part away their fertile lands for public purposes only to develop the lands by private entrepreneurs for constructing malls, shopping complexes, and developing the areas for earning huge amounts in different parts of the country. Here I think necesasary to quote Saheed Bhagat Singh, who had in last petition to the Punjab Governor, before he was hanged by the British Raj government in 1931, the celebrated revolutionary—and Marxist—had said, "let us declare that the state of war does exist and shall exists so long as the Indian toiling masses and the natural resources are being exploited by a handful of parasites. They may be purely British capitalists or mixed British and Indian or even purely Indian—all these things make no difference."

All these murky affairs in India remind me a story and version of Che Guevara over half a century ago before he died. Che wrote, "When the oppressive forces come to maintain themselves in power against established law, peace is considered already broken." Strangely after Azad was killed, several media commentators tried to "paper over the crime by shamelessly inverting what he had said, accusing him of calling Indian Constitution a piece of toilet paper," remarked eminent writer Arundhati Roy and added that "if government won't respect the Constitution perhaps we should push for an amendment to the preamble of the Constitution," we, the People of India, having solemnly resolved to constitute India into a Sovereign Socialist secular democratic Republic**********, could be substituted with, "we the upper caste and classes of India, having secretly resolved to constitute India into a Corporate, Hindu, satellite state******" Such situation has arisen in India only because "the Government of India's only answer has been repression, deviousness and the kind of opacity that can only come from pathological disrespect for ordinary people." Arundhati further said.

Time is not so far off if the situation continues the union government would "enact a model so called Act on the pattern of the Uunlawful Activities (prevention) Act (UAPA) and Chhatishgarh Special Public Security Act, which criminalise every kind of dissent—by word, deed and even intent". The UAPA is enforced in Kashmir, Manipur, Nagaland and Assam depriving the people of their civil rights while the dreaded Chhatishgarh act is enforced in that state to create terror among poor, particularly tribal in Forest areas in the name of checkmating naxal activities by forming Salwa judum, which had been declared invalid by the Supreme Court recently as well as silence the voices of advasis against forest land acquisition of for installing industrial units by uprooting them from their houses and lands in forest areas. War of nerves and supremacy of naxalites and state power will continue to grow in time to come as long as poor and tribals are continued to be exploited and gap between rich and poor in India continue to create disparity in the society!

THERE ARE TWO INDIAS—POOR AND RICH?

Wednesday, 21 September 2011

Just I am presenting a few hard facts and truths prevailing in our Hindustan—that is called Bharat—"Before that I must remind you all about the preamble of the Constitution: We, The People of INDIA, having solemnly resolved to constitute India into a SOVEREIGN, SOCIALIST SECULAR DEMOCRATIC REPUBLIC AND TO SECURE ALL ITS CITIZENS: JUSTICE, social, economic and political; Liberty of thought, expression, belief, faith and worship; EQUALITY of status and of opportunity; and to promote among them all FRATERNITY ASSURING the DIGNITY of the all INDIVIDUALS and the UNITY and INTEGRITY of the NATION; (In our CONSTITUENT ASSEMBLY ASSEMBLY THIS TWENTY-SIXTH DAY OF NOVEMBER, 1949, DO HEREBY ADOPT, ENACT AND GIVE TO OURSELVES THIS CONSTITUTION:

DAYS are passing by since our independence in August 1947 and adoption of the Constitution. Successive governments have assumed power in all these years—but for WE are going to dark age in all the spheres instead of implementing the dreams of an independent Hindustan!We continue to have a part of the 836 million people inthe country, living on less than twenty rupees a day, "the ones who starve while million of tonnes of foodgarins is either eaten by rats in the government warehouses or burnt in bulk (because it is cheaper to burn food than to distribute it to the poor people." Not only that there "are the parents of ten of millions of malnourished children in our country, of the 1.5 million who die every year before they reach their first birthday. They are the millions who make up the chain gangs that are transported from city to city to build the New India. Is this is known as enjoying the fruits of modern development?"

One must think, they are these people, about a government that sees fit to spend 240 billion rupees of public money (the initial estimate four billion rupees) for a two week-week-long sports extravaganza which, "for fear of terrorism, malaria, dengue and New Delhi's new super bug, many international athletes have refused to attend?" from these huge amount, enormous amount have been siphoned off by politicians and games officials—like eminent social scientist and and a well-known writer, ArundhatiRoy, feels that that "is why corrupt politicians in India never have a problem sweeping back into power, using money they stole to but election! Instead of thinking about their misdeeds, these political classes say, who MAOISTS NOT PARTICIPATE IN election to to protect poors interest?"ll these action of misdeeds of political classes are being reflected in Bhumkal (earth-shaking like celebrations) among Naxalites or Maoists in deep jungles of Chhatishgarh, Jharkhand, Orrisa, west Bengal, Bihar, andhra Pradesh, Maharashtra etc states o the country.

Dignity of the poor is at stake in India! thanks to naxal comrades for their courage and wisdom in fighting for years, for decades, to bring change or even the whisper of justice to their lives and sufferings masses, being exploited for years after independence of the country. "Whether people are fighting to overthrow the Indian State or fighting against Big dams or only fighting a particular steel plant or mine or SEZ, the bottom line is that the. Are fighting for their dignity, for their right to live and smell like human beings. They are fighting because, as far as they are concerned the fruits of modern development stink like dead cattle on the highway." says Arundhati roy in her recently published book, "BROKEN REPUBLIC"

Interestingly, this is a story of a country—that is some time called Bharat, as mentioned in the Constitution instead it should have been called "Hindustan" as being demanded by some quarters of learned people of the country. Despite having the second highest economic growth rate in the world, has more poor people in just eight of its states than in the twenty-six countries of sub-Saharan Africa put together, dreams of workers, artisans, farmers have brought the country where it is today. Instead of stakes of every citizens in building new India, majority chunk of people are living without life of honour and dignity and environment of peace and good will are elusive them.

More over, we the fellow citizens of the country, who are building a new India, in which "our 100 richest people hold assets worth over one fourth of our GDP". Wealth of the country are being concentrated in a fewer hands in our present system. That is why the real democracy flows through the barrel of guns", as being propounded by naxalites and Maiosists, who are fighting for poor and tribal. Prime Minister Manmohan Singh has very surprising background of reaching to the height of his career. India's economy was at the lowest ebb. according to an autobiography, "A prattlet's Tale" by Ashok Mira, the west Bengal's finance minister during left front regime, has his story of how Manmohan rose to the height of his political career To sum up the facts, Mitra has said in the book that in 1991, when foreign exchange of the country's reserve were acute state of affairs, The P V Narsimha Rao government had approached International monetary Fund (IMF) for an emergency loan. The IMF put forward two conditions—the first was "structural adjustment and economic reforms; the second was the appointment India's finance minister of its choice—that man, says mitra, in his book was manmohan Singh from that point Manmohan started so called economic reform at the behest of IMF in India and gradually corporatised every things like water, power, mineral, agriculture, land telecommunications, education, health—no matter what the consequences. Later Vajpayee government, which was called pro-US, left no stoneunturned to formalised rest of the formalities for a free run of free economy in the country. After the ouster of Vajpayee in the Lok sabha elections, AICC president Sonia Gandhi, got instrumental in bringing back Congress in commanding position and formed UPA government under the leadership of Manmohan Singh, knowing and unknowingly that Manmohan is pro-capitalists and he would wipe out socialistic pattern of society a dream Pundit Jawahar Lal Nehru. She wasat that time mired in controversy that she cannot be prime minister because she is not India in original form! Later his son Rahul Gandhi also could not realise the follies of Manmohan and both mother and son are tolerating Manmohan at the cost of their earlier mistakes. In between Manmohan, who is himself honest man and politician of proven integrity, was put in dock for defalcation of crores of rupees by his cabinet colleagues and this government was called "most corrupt government ever have in the country".

Now after enough is enough, both mother and son are on fire—fighting modes and Rahul became the first politicians among Congress leaders, who started fighting for tribals' forest right in Orrisa and opposed Vend ant move to set up bauxite factory and other multinationals setting up such factories for steel, power generation in forest areas uprooting the tribal population. Rahul declared that he was a 'soldier for tribal people". He also raised voice for farmer's right in Uttar Pradesh and his campaign is going on in almost all parts of the country—let us for the best? Change of leadership in the UPA led by Congress after the next general elections cannot be ruled out!

I have presented a few facts about the state of affairs in the country and plight of over 80 percent population living in rural areas and activities of Maoists and naxal comrades in fighting for poor and tribal. I have also questioned the preamble of the Constitution, which has shown many dreams to toiling masses but these are yet to be implemented, depriving the poor their basic rights of dignity and honour.

OMINOUS SIGN FOR NALANDA UNIVERSITY: KNOWLEDGE BROKERING BY AMARTYA

Tuesday, 13 September 2011

KNOWLEDGE AND INTELLECTUAL BROKERING OF AMARTYA SEN!

Will Bihar miss yet another golden opportunity of setting up Nalanda International University in Nalanda on the ruins of aancient Nalanda University? The ambitious university, which is to be established in Nalanda, Bihar, under the aegis of East Asia Submit, mainly comprising China, Japan, Singapore, Thailand etc, as a regional initiative, is gasping at its infancy stage because of "knowledge and intellectual brokering" by the chairman of the mentor group of the university, Amartya Sen, professor of Harvard universityty! With the idea conceived by the former President of India, Dr APJ Abdul Kalam, was deeply interested in opening of the university, the union and Bihar government completely agreed to revive the old civilisation and culture and set up the university of international standard nearby the ruins of the ancient Nalanda university, existed in Nalanda from 5th century CE to1197CE. The union government enacted a law for setting up university and Bihar government also provided lands, measuring over 443 acres of land for the university and handed over to the centre about one year back. The Bihar government also informed the mentor group for starting office of the university temporarily and for which a government building was also provided to the mentor group for office of the university at the nearby site. Sadly, today in reply to my e-mail APJ has said that he was now in no way connected with the proposed university!(pls see bihar times.com)

Ssubsequently, the union government constituted a mentor group in 2007 under the chairmanship of Sen. Other members of the group are Sugat Bose, Professor, Harvard University, Wang Bunwei, professor of Beizing university, Meghnath Desai, professor of London School of Economics, George Geo, ex-minister, Singapore, Tansen Sen, AP. Baruch, CUNY, and N K Singh, a former IAS and MP of JD(U) from Bihar. The mentor group, which was entrusted to examine the frame work of international cooperation and proposed structures of partnership, for governing and establishing the university as an international centre of education and learning. The group was to submit report within two years of its constitution and recommend the start of functioning of the university by 2013. But even after the lapse of nearly four years, the mentor group led by Sen is yet to submit the report to the union government despite over a dozen meetings of stake-holders' countries in different parts of Asia!

The university, a dream project of APJ, is being funded by stake-holders' countries. Japan and Singapore are financing for construction with contribution of over US$ 100 million. China donated US$ one million with assurances and promises of more and more assistance for the university. Over US$ 500 million will be required to create new faculties. Another US$500 million will be spent to sufficiently improve surrounding structures. Everything was going on smoothly over nine months back.

Suddenly and surprisingly, the mentor group chairman Sen appointed glamorous one Gopa Shabarwal, who is reader in the Lady Sri Ram College, Delhi, as the vice-chancellor of the university in illegal manner and also opened office of the university in one of the posh colonies of Delhi when Bihar government was ready to hand over building to locate temporary office at nearby site of the proposed university!. Has Sen ignored members of mentor group in appointing Gopa as V-c of the university?Here I am not throwing blame on other members of the mentor group as one of the important members of the group N K Singh has e-mailed me,"—certainly bring its contents to the notice of the next meeting of governing board." I had e-mailed Singh the copy of my open letter to Amartya Sen about his unjustification in appointing a reader as V-C of the international university, violating all norms, rules, laws, UGC guidelines etc and also drawing Singh's attention on critical fate of the proposed university in Nalanda in Bihar! Only a professor of ten years experiences of professorship can be V-C of any university in India not a reader like glamorous Gopa Sabharwal.

More over, Gopa has also appointed one of her close friends and "sakhi" from Delhi university one Ms Sharma as officer on special duty. Sen is so kind and magnanimous that he has allowed monthy salary of over Rs five lakh to Gopa and over Rs 3.5 lakh to Ms Sharma. Not only that Gopa is allowed frequent tours of foreign countries on so called university work—currently she is perhaps in Japan on so called university work. Anybody can imagine the clouts of Gopa and her mentor Amartya Sen in the corridor of power in Manmohan Singh govt in Delhi and Nitish Kumar Kumar government in Bihar!

All these facts have come to notice with a reply to Right to Information Act petitioner from human resource and external affairs ministries. Apart from that the union minister of state for external affairs E Ahmed has also informed the Parliament recently that no V-C has been appointed for the proposed international university. Apart from resentment among people of the country, particularly from Bihar, every body is stunt over such nefarious game of Sen and "golden silence of Bihar Chief Minister Nitish Kumar over the issue". Strangely, the state national and international media are also silent surreptitiously over the issue. However a news website Bihar Times.com is keeping posted the people of all related development on Nalanda University. Is it really the fact that media are under under declared censorship in Bihar under Nitish Kumar regime"?

The proposed university was to start with seven schools of learning and more to be expanded later on. Before I conclude my story about nefarious design of vested interests to torpedo in the opening of proposed world-fame university, I must recall the facts about ancient Nalanda University. Historically, the university was initially established during the reign of a King, called Sakradityas. This ancient university in Nalanda attracted the students from Korea, Japan, China, Indonesia, Turkey, Greece, and Persia etc The Tang dynasty Chinese pilgrim and scholar Xuanzang had studied and taught in the ancient university for 15 years. He had depicted the detailed account o f the university in the 7th century!The gradual destruction of the university, which used to impart learning and teaching to over 10, 000 students with 2000 teachers from different parts of the globe during those period, started firstly by Huns under Mihirkula in the reign of Sakandgupta(455-467AD), second attempt to destroy the university was made by Goudas in early 7th century and final blow to destroy the university completely was initiated by Afghans invaders by Bakhtiyar Khilji—1193 and finally the ancient university was converted into ruins in Nalanda. Currently, the ancient university sites are under excavation by ASI and unique things are being discovered from dug up earth at the sites!

Now the dream project is being ruined nearby the site of ruined ancient university by our own men, led by Sen before it becomes a reality! Thanks to the Manmohan government and Nitish Kumar government, a silent spectators of naked drama of destruction!

WORLD-WIDE POVERTY ALARMS MEN-KIND!

Wednesday, 7 September 2011

Poverty, hunger, malnutrition, unemployment are not confined to a particular country on the globe! Almost all countries of the continents are afflicted by these dreaded pproblems, and crores of people in the world are in the grip of such evils. America and European countries are worst sufferers and people there are mainly groaning under poverty and unemployment in the wake economic upheavals in the regions. Less said is better about other parts of the world countries! Crores are dying because of non-availability of food in different parts of the world. Bane of poverty is not only in the poor countries—it has spread its tentacles in rich and capitalists countries also. There are wide gaps in equality in America. Economic growth is powered by and large consumed by the wealthy few. Federal tax money continues to be siphoned off to pay for wars from Libiya to Afghhanistan. An IANS report, quoting United Nations, published in various websites including Yahoo news today has said that over 7.50 lakh people in east Africa are on virtual death traps due to famine. UN report has said that 12 million people of across the region and four million in Somalia are alone in need of food. Over 60 percent are malnourished in southern Somalia because of violence, drought and famine. Kenya, Ethiopia, Djibouti are badly affected because of famine in the region!

Exhaustive reports and expert comments in Washington Post, NY Times, the Economist, BBC news and its electronic channels, Frontline Hindu Business Line, Economic Time s, Business Standard, different news agencies in international media are full with reports of poor economy and poverty in the countries of the world!Apart from richest America and European countries to developing countries including China, India are badly affected by rise in poverty and unemployment in the respective countries. Situation has worsened to such great pass that communist countries like China, Cuba, Vietnam are also facing strange situation on poverty front and they have been compelled to deviate from their principled stand and principles of Marxist economy because they failed to implement Marxist economy in proper and suitable manner.

An Opinion column in the Washington Post, published on August 19, 2011, by Joel Berg, Executive Director of New York City Coalition Against Hunger and author of "All You Can eat: How hungry is America", has said that after Clinton regime in US, welfare measures are gradually being restricted—only thing that care is middle class and rich people. He has further said in the article that 44 million Americans are badly affected because of poverty. Over four million people are receiving cash welfare each month—now do not exist. Welfare reforms have become forgotten goal in America after the regime of Clinton. From 2005 many more restrictions are being put on welfare. People, receiving cash assistance nation-wide declined from 12.3 million in 1996 to 4.4 million in 2010. In 1990s, during strong economy in America—both overall poverty rate and child poverty rate had decreased in Clinton's regime. Gradually from 2007 economy of America worsened and between 1996to 2009, number of people in severe poverty climbed 36 percent from 14 million to 19 million-highest in decades—now 50 million Americans live in food insecurity zone and also in homelessness. Like India ultra rich flourish in America.

Various other articles in Washington Post, New York Times, The Economists etc have exposed the claims of America, specially conservative and status-quoits of Republican party for poverty aggravation in US. Unnecessary wars by America in different parts of the world have broken the back-bone of economy of that country and people are sufferings because of poverty and unemployment. Similar condition prevails in entire European countries. In America and European countries—no concrete new jobs have been created to tackle unemployment. In an another articles by various writers in the same Washington Post-Writer Greg Jaffa has said that radical ideologies, new technologies, cheap and powerful weapons have led to persistent conflict in entire Europe and America—a decade after constructing a common currency, Europe has been unable to build an integrated economy to match, said Anthony Fariola in the Washington Post. On September two 20011 issue of the Washington Post, it has been pointed out that it is for the first time since February 1945, the government has reported a net job change of zero and the unemployment rate is 9.1 percent. A detailed report has been published in the New York Times on august 19, 2011 by a group of journalists, describing debt crisis in America and consumer price inflation and also drifting of treasury bonds. Today America is in the grip of debt of $14.4 trillion mark! To bail out from financial and economic crisis, there have been substantial increase ON the global debt. A Frontline report has said that according toMckinsey Global Institute, the total amount of debt incurred by governments across the world rose by by staggering $25 trillion to $41.1 trillion over the decade ending 2010.

A Frontline has said when we compare the economic crisis of 1929 and 2007, we find one thing common the outrageous level of inequality (both in terms of income and house-hold-to debt ratio)—in both cases middle shrunk and poor despaired.

The recent explosive situation in Britain is perhaps resulting of socially and economically excluded outburst of the citizens of that country! UK government empathy towards poverty and unemployment led the people, mainly youths to rise in riots and vandalism. Likewise voices of people are rising far and wide in Arab world, Middle East for right to assert against the monopolised and atrocious governments in the regions, resulting into inequality, poverty, unemployment, corruption etc. In particular case in India-people of middle classes along with rich and capitalists are fighting to end not only corruption menace but also rising poverty and wide gap between 20 percent rich and 80 percent poor, mainly of rural areas, and non-development trend in rural areas!

AMBITIOUS NITISH KUMAR, CM OF BIHAR: MY REMINISCENCES

Thursday, 1 September 2011

NITISH KUMAR

Nitish Kumar, a suave and soft spoken since the initial days of student's movement in Bihar in middle of 1970s under the leadership of Lok Nayak Jayprakash Narayan, was silent operator in playing the games of politics. After the emergency was lifted and election of Lok Sabha was ordered in 1977, Nitish Kumar was ignored by JP and his coterie, thanks to the manoeuvrings of the then Jansangh and RSS, which became part of the then Janata Party led by Chandra Shekhar. Almost all important JP movement activists were awarded with Janata Party nominations to contest Lok sabha elections in 1977—but this man Nitish Kumar did not find berth in the nomination of Janata Party from Barh parliamentary constituency. A sad and pained, Nitish Kumar kept silence but creating a little bit murmur in Janata Party political circles.

Many people, sympathetic to Nitish including myself were very much resentful—but the harm is done! The then Jan sangh constituent of the Janata Party, nominated former mayor of Calcutta Ram Lakhan Prasad to contest from Barh because of his RSS background. The Janata Party won the Lok Sabha election with massive votes and majority not only in Bihar but in entire country. Nitish Kumar was left high and dry by hardcore Jansangh and RSS people and he developed deep-rooted hatred towards Jansangh constituent of Janta Party and RSS! At the time of split in Janata Party and fall of first non-congress government led by Morarjee Desai, on dual membership—of party and RSS—Nitish used to speak harshly against them with volume of hatred towards Jan sangh and RSS in public and private conversations.

But time is great healing factor and after many political developments, Nitish became star personality of now Bharatiya Janata party, a coalition partner of his Janta Dal (U) and remained union minister with important portfolios in Atal Behari Vajpayee government and subsequently in coalition with BJP humiliated Laloo Prasad Yadav in the assembly elections—and this is second time that he became chief minister of Bihar, heading Janata Dal (U)-BJP coalition government in Bihar! Nitish was also a close confidant of former prime minister Vishwanath Pratap Singh and became minister in his government after the ousting of Rajiv gandhi in the Lok sabha elections on Bofor scandal issue. During those days, there were many stories on Nitish, rumoured in Delhi about his personal character—it will be better for me not to write all those things at this time.

Gradually, with passing of time and political circumstances, Nitish also changed his political colours and adjusted with his principles, sauve and soft characters. Nitish was so closed to Laloo Prasad Yadav that both Nitish and Laloo were called "Ranga-Billa" in Bihar politics. But again time changed and being antagonised with Laloo, Nitish split the party and separated from Laloo and formed Samata Party under the leadership of his political Guru of that time George Fernandes. But due to lack of mass base appeal like Laloo, Nitish started changing track of his political workmanship. He started garnering his own caste—Kurmi—and after holding many caste-based rallies during those days, Nitish became a champion of his own caste men and in the process became "Kurmi chieftain" like former chief minister, Satyendra Narayan Sinha as "Rajput chieftain". Since than Nitish became too much aggressive against Laloo after mobilising his own caste men—but this politics of Nitish did not click and in the assembly elections of that time Nitish could not muster enough seats and remained high and dry. Than in the process Nitish had taken help of many Laloo's own men in politics including Sharad Yadav and got him joined the new party JD(U) and broad based the organisation and to defeat Laloo, Nitish joined hands with BJP, which was once poison for him when he was ditched after emergency in getting party nomination from Barh Lok sabha seat and subsequently he used to consider BJP, an arch enemy of backward class in implementing Mandal commission reservation to OBC during Vishwanath Pratap government at the centre and a bundle of communal forces in demolition of Babari masjid.

Nitish's allergy with media is not new! During Samata party days, Nitish became instrumental in writings to various newspapers and news magazines about unnecessary and uncalled for praise to chief minister Laloo Prasad Yadav. That time, the Samata party got a cupon published in the denomnomination of Rs 50, Rs 100, Rss 200 Rs 500 etc to collect "chanda" in the name of party fund "and removing Laloo from power and becoming chief minister of Bihar". The chanda campaign was mainly taken up by his own caste men. Many kurmi leaders used to collect chanda by selling coupons forcibly—in the process, a group of Nitish caste men encountered a passerby, who happened to be journalist, and forced him to buy coupon—reluctantly that journalist purchased the coupon and got rid of Nitish hoodlums. But the matter did not end there—the whole fact was published in national English daily prominently with scanned coupon. Lot of furore had taken place and Nitish approached the proprietor of that national English daily through a letter, written by the then general secretary of Samata party Jaya Jaitley, abusing, cursing the journalists and asking the management to dismiss him. A delegation of Samata party, comprising frequent party changer Shivanand tiwari, Lallan singh, now MP of JD(U), and many others met local management and resident editor of the said national english daily. There was time when press freedom and factual journalism was respected by everyone, particularly proprietor of the newspaper. Everything was looked into and complaint of Nitish against the journalist was ignored and that journalist was promoted subsequently and retired from that newspaper, may be still living and watching vindictiveness of Nitish Kumar, who is replca ting all his characters vigorously during his chief ministership1 Nitish has become past master in imposing "undeclared censorship" in the last six years— proprietors, journalists are given tasks by Nitish government not publish adverse reports in their newspapers and in lieu Nitish government has opened floods of advertisements to newspapers and other mode of media, putting heavy burden on state exchequer. Nitish looks journalists with contempt and very much helpful to amenable journalists!

Because of his political obstinacy and lack of political farsightedness and his role in not getting reservation to OBC during the chief minister ship of Karpoori Thakur, Nitish remained in political oblivion for many years. Nitish finally, perhaps, became legislator in 1980 from an assembly constituency in Nalanda district. By look Nitish appears a gentleman par excellence but his real face lies else where. He is shrewed politician, having many merits and demerits, political trade secrets, his hidden agenda of authoritarian style of functioning, ignoring his close party colleagues and dumping them like anything etc unlike a true politician!

Before I forget an important event, this writer had very close liaison with Nitish during his initial and ripe political days. Nitish and myself used to meet very frequently to exchange our views on many political events—he and myself were very respectful to each other. We shared many political and other developments in Bihar and other parts of the country at national—level—it will not be proper to reveal all those things at this moment. But sadly and strangely, although I am a journalists, myself became the targets of Nitish's ire many times including public meetings in which he used to even call my names. But there were days when I was said to be useful for him. A time had come, Nitish was landed in serious trouble while contesting re-election on Laloo's party nomination from Barh lok sabha seat—T N Sheshan, who was chief election commissioner, found malpractices in the elections and ordered re poll in nearly 80 booths—this would have ultimately changed the impact of result. Nitish and many of his well wishers called me up and asked me a factual report over the issue so that re poll in many booths, which have been included unnecessarily should be reduced. At about 8 in the morning I had gone to meet Nitish in his Punaichak official quarter, allotted to him by Laloo. There were virtual tears in his eyes and he narrated verbatim everything to me that complaints are exaggerated. I had written a story, based on Nitish version, official and chief electoral officer sources. Result—re poll in booths were reduced to about 28 booths from over 80. Nitish won the election with flying colours and we used to meet regularly either in social calls or in political circles. But his face used to indicate hatred towards journalists1 I must cite one recent example—I was and am in trouble because of block officials high-handedness over a piece of land of mine—i had gone to Janata Darwar of Nitish and after eight hours strenuous efforts I could meet to submit my application to Nitish—he failed to even recognise me what to expect a kind words about my complaints to him in the durwar (I have written a story on Nitish Janta darwar or feudal darwar, published in many news websites including Bihar times.com, newspapers and news magazines).

Everybody was happy with the installation of Nitish as chief minister six years back and myself was also in the same category that at least one sincere politician has become chief minister to get rid of misrule of Laloo and his company Ltd. for 15 years. Nitish also started on right tracks—improvement on many fronts were visible, particularly law and order front. people started living in peace—one commoner of remote

Purnia district village told me four years back, "what Nitish or Laloo give us—we are living in the same condition—but in Nitish regime—we lead our life peacefully and at least sleep peacefully in the night", he added. I feel this is not an ordinary commentary by a commoner—Nitish efforts started percolating at ground level, but his much-publicised measures on land reforms, health, education, poverty alleviation programmes etc are trapped in bureaucratic cobweb. Less said is better about corruption in Nitish government—it is flourishing right from panchayat-block level to secretariat headquarters level. Transfers and postings on money changing have taken drivers' seat during Nitish regime like Jagannath Mishra and Laloo regimes. Perhaps Nitish has become tiered! And his coalition compulsion compelled him to go slow. Not only that Nitish is like previous occasions gradually sidelining his trusted colleagues in the party and the government, many of his hardcore supporters and socialist brand politicians have deserted him because of his highhandedness and authoritarian style. Only sychophants in the party and government are ruling in his regime. Nitish, no doubt, was sincerely striving to develop Bihar, but he has become cold in his second term. Let us hope for the best from Nitish, comparatively a better politician to run the affairs of Bihar in comparison to other politicians of Bihar currently!

INDIAN DEMOCRACY AND ITS PREDICAMENT!

Monday, 29 August 2011

Indian democracy, although even today, considered not so old! But it has survived many predicaments and is kicking up, like a torch-bearer in the globe. Eminent scholar K N Panikkar, in a recent Essay, in a fortnightly has said, "Crisis of Indian democracy is because of the failure of the state to create a public sphere capable of generating critical engagements with social issues." I strongly feel that Indian democracy is surviving only because of principles of patriotism among country's pluralistic society and culture. Panikkar has further commented that the vibrancy of a functioning of democracy, therefore, would depend upon the social acceptance of the idea of equality, which as principle the Indian Republic has written into the Constitution. Lamentably, in practice equality has gone underground and has become a far cry in the fields political, economic and cultural in equality in India. No doubt, our Constitution has enunciated and created many measures and sufficient guarantee and safe guards to ensure democratic rights—but in actual functioning of democracy Indian people are deprived of equal rights in practice. The Constitution has provisions, like "there must be secured to all people-justice, social, economic and political; equality of status, of opportunity and before the law." But in practice Indian democratic system has failed currently in securing justice to all and democratic rights are not accessible equally to everybody.

To begin with, I must point out the deficiencies in the Indian democracy—our representative system in democracy is full with maladies. Notwithstanding the successive elections of Lok sabha and state assemblies under voting system have proved that Indian democracy is kicking up, in actual practice it has failed miserably. Under our democratic system, majority definitions have strange connotations. Strangely and sadly in our system majority is determined, who gets the largest chunk of votes—whether the percentage of vote is low or not all have exercised their franchise or the votes have been divided among multiplicity of candidates—but who ever gets highest number of votes in Lok Sabha and state assemblies elections are declared winners despite the facts that the figure of total votes, cast, are less than 50 percent of the total electorate—This amply proves that whoever candidate gets largest chunk of votes is declared winner but in actual practice—the candidate become the representative of less than 50 percent majority and thus it clearly indicates that instead of majority vote, he or she has won the elections is considered minority votes winner! In this way, Indian democracy is not giving in political sense, a rule of majority. For example, in many states and Parliament, minority governments are elected by securing less than 50 percent of total votes and they are ruling over majority of people in the country—what a traumatic experience of Indian democracy?

Moreover, in Indian democratic system, poor and downtrodden have no chance to be elected to state assemblies and Parliament except through reservation of seats as defined in the Constitution—of course there are many exception but in general practice such things are happening in the Indian democracy. Mainly, the political class in India is dominated by the affluent, educated and socially advance and powerful sections of society. Present system of representation has become exclusive platform of millionaires and multi-millionaires. To contest election has become so expensive that hardly poor could get a chance to be elected to state assemblies and Parliament. Thus majority of people of the country have no stake in having the governance under our democratic system. Such system is giving agonising moments to the deprived lots and serious resentment prevails throughout the country, especially in rural areas. Rural people being fed up of exploitation, deprivation, inequality etc, are indulging in violence in the form of Naxal movements and in many instances they are indulging in insurgency, posing a big question mark over the present democratic system.

Apart from that, cultural equality and plurality has become a far cry in the country Entire Indian society has been badly entrapped in caste and religion cobweb. They are badly divided. The Anthropological Survey of India has estimated the existence of more than 4000 communities with different culture and system in our country—Because of that facts Mahatama Gandhi, has shared the ideas of Pundit Jawahar Lal Nehru, who initially promoted the ideas of secularism during pre-independence days and later on it has become part of the Constitution—but different ideas of fundamentalists like Vinayak Damodar Savarkar and Mohammad Ali Jinna, during pre-independence days, sowed the seeds of discontent and ultimate the great Bharat was divided into two nations—India and Pakistan and seeds of communal ism are flourishing in both the countries in the form of hatred between Hindu and Muslims in India and Pakistan besides looking downtrodden and poor with hatred and Hindu-Muslim riots, particularly in Gujarat where thousand of Muslims had been massacred under Narendra Modi regime in Gujarat particularly in India! Under the present system society have been divided on religion lines. Pannikar has said, "Indian society has become religionisation of politics and politicisation of religion. In the present situation in the Indian politics religion has become a powerful mobilising force, being invoked by both communal and secular parties in India to retain power in different states and centre.

On economic front about inequality is less said is better. There has been wide gap between rich and poor—Poor are getting poorer and rich getting richer day by day under the present system. Neo-liberal economic policy has impacted more and more inequality in the Indian society. So called economic measures under new economic policy and development appear to be an eye—wash except generating much black money through corrupt practices by political class and capitalists. Practically, these policies are ruining not only the economic equality but cultural, religious and plurality of the nation. Over 80 percent of population, majority of them in rural areas, are living on Rs 20 per day while 20 percent rich, capitalists, corporates, multinationals, political classes of all hues have concentrated country's wealth in their hands. Successive governments in states and union have even failed so far to identify poor and landless in the country. Its own panels have different percentage of poor in the country (please read my other blog to get exact figures of poor given by different government panels of government). Jungles, tribal, land of poor tribal and middle class people are being indiscriminately being acquired for setting up industrial units by multi-nationals, corporates, capitalists, influential sections of political class and government itself in most of the states without paying proper compensation and rehabilitation for uprooting them from their houses and lands. Livelihood of poor is being deprived besides destroying ecological balances in the country under present system.

Last but not least, in my opinion, democratic institutions under the Constitution are being eroded by vested interests. Under the Constitution, there are specific provisions for reservation to SC, ST, Other Backward Classes, educationally and socially backward classes etc. These provisions have been implemented to some extend—but questions are being raised over such provisions by upper caste and moneyed people in the country!

Moreover, the social groups, Naxalites and others, fighting for rights to poor, tribal etc under the Constitution, are being termed anti-nationals. State power and private armies of landlords are creating violence to suppress the voice of poor and downtrodden. To change the system, violence is not the answers but the development of poor and down-trodden. Different wings under the Constitution like Judiciary, executive, legislature are under the grip of rampant corruption. Rahul Gandhi has rightly said that there are two India in existence in this country—one for minority rich and other for majority poor and downtroddenns. Even the just directives of judiciary under the laws and the Constitution are being violated by the government!

The Indian media, once considered peoples' voice, has gone to dogs. Most of the print and electronic media have been "Mudrochised" and instead of carrying stories of peoples miseries are keeping mum, thanks to "undeclared censorship by union and state governments and proprietors of newspapers". Rupert Murdoch is considered these days a devil piece in media world, who utilised his print, electronic etc media to serve his enlightened self-interest to glorify himself as world's most powerful man.

Thus, the present democratic set-up under parliamentary democracy enshrined under the Constitution is under tremendous pressures of vested interests in the country—let us hope for the best solution?

POLITICIANS' CREDIBLITY IN QUESTION!

Wednesday, 17 August 2011

Amazingly for the last several years, especially in the last two years, the entire systems of the union and state governments are paralysed. Instead of initiating welfare measures both the state and union governments are more engaged in salvaging the situation going bad to worse. Entire system is in the grip of corruption right from Kanya Kumar to Himalayas in the country. Politicians of all hues in "name of democratic system" have created worse situation, drawing a big question mark over their "credibility"! There is serious erosion in the morality of political class and politics seems to have taken shape of "business" in India! Corruption added and abated by political class in connivance with pliable bureaucracy has embedded deep in every spheres of life. 'Misdemeanour and manoeuvres among all class of politicians" came to light in indulging in corruption and encouraging corrupt practices. Result: Chain of reactions in the form of agitations by people, specially "white collared middle class" led by Anna Hazare for strict law of Lok Pal to end the corruption menace. Initially the movement against corruption was highlighted and launched by Yoga Guru Swami Ram Dev for the last two and half years was hijacked by Anna Hazare and because of lack of competence in RamDev, the movement under the leadership of Anna Hazare has taken a definite shape and it appears that something will definitely come out this time keeping in view the strong support of the movement to Anna in the country.

It all started with unearthing of scams like "two G spectrum" and loot of crores of rupees in the allotment of speturm licences by the successive union telecommunication ministers including latest one Raja, who is facing charges in scandal of allotment of "two-G spectrum" and is languishing in jail. Thereafter, corruption stories came to light in Karnataka, being ruled by BJP (for the first time in south India). B S

Yeddyurappa, the then chief minister of Karnataka, now he has resigned, was indicted by the former Lokayukta of Karnataka, Justice N. Santosh Hegde for "illegal iron ore mining", to the tune of crores of rupees by Yedduyurappa in connivance with officials of the state government. Hegde recommended launching of criminal cases against Yedyurappa and others for his "misdeeds" in siphoning crores of rupees of state exchequer. Final blow of action against Yeddu came after the final report of Hegde and he reluctantly resigned from the chief minister post and criminal cases have been instituted against him.

Subsequently, the issues of corrupt practices spread like virus fever throughout the country and chief ministers of almost all states are in the grip of charges of corruption. To begin with subsequent event—I want to begin with corrupt practices coming to fore in Bihar!The NDA government, comprising of BJP and JD(U), led by Nitish Kumrar, in its earlier five years tenure, was usually called "probity in governance", started crumbling under the weight of corrupt practices in later stage. Now there are several instances of misappropriation of funds and favouritism against the Nitish government has come to surface, puncturing the claim of "good governance of Nitish Kumar". Huge misappropriation of fund was unearthed in the reports of Comptroller and Auditor General of ndia (CAG). The report of the CAG has revealed that the state government officials have failed to submit proper accounts for funds withdrawn from state exchequer, totalling over crores of rupees, meant for developmental activities. Cases of favouritism in Bihar Industrial areas development authority (BIADA)'s land allotment have come to the notice recently. Interestingly, BIAD lands have been allotted to close relatives and close men of ministers of Nitish government and IAS official close to Nitish Kumar including P K Shahi, Praveen Amanullah JD(U) MP, Jagdish Sharma, BJP MLC Awadhesh Narayan Singh and IAS officials, close to Nitish Kumar including S Siddhartha, secretary to CM Nitish Kumar, and another IAS official Anand Kishore, IG-Prison, came to surface recently. These close relatives and close friends of officials have been allotted 10, 000 square feet to ten acres of land to them in different parts of the state to set up food processing units, cement factories, educational institutions and hospitals etc. Legally, the Biada claims that allotment have been made on "first come—first serve basis" but the procedures in hsate raise question mark over the sincerity of BIADA and Nitish government. Notwithstanding Nitish Kumar has said that BIADA land allotment is being made mountain out of mole, at the same time" Mr Clean Nitish" has also informed that other other democratic institutions are free to look into the entire matter and no body will be spared if found guilty in the wake of demands of general public as well as opposition to enquire into the matter by the CBI. THE CAG observation with regards to development fund expenditure has revealed that the officials have failed to submit detailed contentment bills for money withdrawn by state officials against abstract contingency bills involves a cumulative amount of over Rs 67,000 crore. Even the single bench of Patna High court had ordered CBI enquiry into the matter of CAG, brought to the notice by PIL by one advocate Dinu Kumar—the order of the court has been stayed by double bench and final verdict is yet to come when the judges of Patna high court are badly divided pro and against Nitish Kumar!

Issue of corruption is not different in Uttar Pradesh led by Mayawati. UP IAS Officers association has made startling disclosure and politicall observer Indu Bhusjhan Singh have disclosed that a CAG report has disclosed as many as 68 departments of state government in connection with rampant corruption and misuse of government funds. In a single case, the CAG has revealed, National rural health mission fund, totalling over Rs 8,600 crore spent on the NRHM scam in the last five years have been in majority cases have been misappropriated. These are the just a tip in the iceberg about gbobbling up of public funds by Mayawati government officials in collusion with political class. Land have been acquired for development and sold to builders to construct shopping malls and apartments by Mayawati government! Similar are the cases in Gujarat, Maharashtra, Andhra Pradesh, Madhya Pradesh, Tamil Nadiu etc in looting public funds and lands by political class in connivance with government officials. Not only that black money to the tune of hundreds of lakhs of rupees is stashed in foreign banks and foreign countries of rich and elite classes as well as capitalists and politicians. No effective measures are being taken to retrieve that money! 1n Orrisa and Chhatishgarh alone, the flood of foreign capitals have taken alarming proportion and poor and tribal are being deprived of their land and houses in forest areas in the name of setting up big industries and power plants. Change of money in hundreds of crore rupees among political class are not being ruled out!.

In Chhatshigarh, Orrisa, Bihar etc the respective state governments are up in arms against Naxalites. Instead of taking effective measures for initiating development activities, these government on its own and on provocation of union government are spreading violence against violence in the form of recruiting special police officials and starting and launching tirade against poor and tribal. Naxallites are not against democracy but they are for change in system of police and rich people terror against poor and tribal. Result: Naxal activities are increasing leaps and bound in many states and they are spreading their network in urban areas also, giving dangerous signals.

Amid all these hullah-bullah, the union government has broughtt weak Lokpal Bill, ignoring the suggestions of Anna Hazare and company. Prashant Patnaik has written an article in the Frontline, Madras based fofortnightly and has said that the steep rise in corruption is due to the change in property regime brought about by freeing of markets and privatisation drive. The struggle against corruption is important but insufficient since it looks at corruption in isolation from primitive accumulation. A powerful popular resistance alone can provide a bulwark for democracy, the Frontline article says.

Initially, the union government, which now stresses that Parliament alone is entitled to enact legislation on Lok Pal bill, had failed to identify opposition while holding discussions and deliberations with Anna Hazare and company over the form of bill despite vehement suggestions by many politicians and legal pundits. The government ignored the opposition political class and later it also ignored Anna Hazare and company suggestions for an effective Lok Pal bill. And of its own placed a Lok Pal bill, of which Frontline has described in its column, "Crusade and Farce", written by V Kenktesan, and has said, "The government's bill not only has provisions designed to shield the corrupt, but its statement objects does not even explain why allegation against only certain public functionaries will be probed—hence prospect for smooth passage of the Lokpal Bill looks dim, mainly because of divergence of opinion."

Any way, Now the Anna's agitation for an effective Lokpal Bill and subsequent public protests has put the union government and Prime Minister Manmohan Singh in dock. Support of public to Anna against public crusade against corruption is gaining momentum. Entire Manmohan singh government machinery is paralysed and general people, particularly urban middle class, have become outraged to press the union government to toe Anna's line on the bill. In the process, the constitutional right of Anna to hold agitation and hunger strike and union government's action to put restriction on Anna and put him behind bar have also outraged the people—and they are protesting the action of union government throughout the country although majority of people living in rural areas are silent Let us hope for the best to end the corruption virus in the country.

DREAMS AFTER INDIA GOT INDEPENDENCE!

Monday, 15 August 2011

Tears in the eyes of millions of people of India are yet to be wiped! Today is 15th August, independence day of the country from the British Raj yoke. I exactly remember vividly I was five and half years old when independence was achieved and in the mid-night celebration, Pundit Jawahar Lal Nehru, the them prime minister of independent India, had spoken many things and had said that unless tears are wiped from every citizens, independence would have no meaning!

Old vivid reminiscences in my mind still haunt me, my father late Satya Narayan Singh, after remaining in jail for three years continuously had been released by British Raj on the eve of independence—this was my father's last spell in Biritish Jails as he had been in jails for over a dozen times in different cases instituted by the Raj since 1928 and lived over 18 years in jails, of course with occasional release on bail bonds during trial of cases. I was happy that day! My other uncles late Bindeshwar Prasad Vidyalankar, ex-MLA, late Thakur Prasad Singh, a mukhtar by profession, Brahmdeo Singh alias Buchcha Babu, a sharp shooter and fond of classical music, Babuwan Babu, a Sanskrit scholar, and late Panchanand singh alias Panchu Babu, basically a farmer, all had been released from jails about three months back from the date of 15th August 1947, the day of independence. All were happy lots because the efforts of my entire family since the days of my great grand father late Babu Mani Singh-Roy and my grand father late Mohit Singh Roy, plunging into national movement on the inspiration of "Bal, Lal Pal" and later on Subhash Chandra Bose. I remember eyes of my father and uncles were twinkling for the services of poor after independence to carry their family legacy!

Anniversary after anniversary passed since 15the August 1947 in the country-we celebrated azadi day—but dreams of Balgangadhar Tilak,

Surendra Nath Pal, Lal of Punjab (I forgot his full name), Subhash Bose, Mahatma Gandhi, Pundit Jawahar Lal Nehru, Sardar Ballav Bhai Patel Dr Bhimrao Ambedkar, Zakir Hussain and many other leaders remained on papers and are virtually closed in the achieves of the government records rooms. Nothing tangible has happened to eliminate poverty since independence—over 80 percent population of the country still remains on Rs 23 per day. Hunger, Starvation, malnutrition, sad state of education and health, exploitation of poor, backwards, dalits, tribal are continuing! Political leaders of instead of adopting socialistic pattern of society and stress on agriculture and cottage industries in rural areas where majority of people live, have messed up the situation by adopting new liberal economicl policy, resulting into rich growing more and more rich and poor becoming more and more poor. In this way India has become two country—one for poor and one for rich. Entire economy is being controlled by politicians of all hue and cry, rich, capitalists, industrialists, corporates and multinationals, constituting about 20 percent of the population. People of rural areas and major pocket of urban parts live in abject poverty!

After independence thieves, thugs, criminals, dacoitits, robbers etc in white colour have their hey days to exploits poor people, majority in the country. Misdemeanour and maneuvering by politicians in successive union and state governments have entrapped all the welfare measures in the cobweb in collusion n with officials and rich people. Welfare measures are seldom stressed in the country!

Politicians and religious leaders are more interested in dividing society on caste and creed line throughout the nation for their vote banks. In the process, they have become corrupts inconveniences with rich, industrialists, capitalists, corporates and new class, emerging in society— neo rich people etc Natural resources are being plundered, exploitation of tribals and poor at the height, forest and fertile lands in different parts of the country are being grabbed by government and industrialists in the name of setting up industrial units—but in reality they are increasing their assets by grabbing lands and constructing buildings, factories, developing townships etc. Bureaucrats in collusion with politicians are indulging in rampant corrupt practices!

More over some tangible measures have been initiated for upliftment of poor, hardly even 18 paise of one rupee is spent on welfare measures— entire amount are gobbled up by officials and politicians, namely, MLAs, MLCs, MPs, ministers, chief ministers in almost all parts of the country.

Politicians are behaving shamelessly—mass are keeping mum because they are in search of an alternative measures to change the system. State terror is at its zenith. Left-wing ultras like Naxalites and Maoists have become only hope! They in cooperation with poor are fighting to change the system-even that is being curbed. But they are last hope!

Now let us hope for the best—revolution come but with delay and in the process wipes out evils in society.

DISPARITY: POVERTY-VIS-A-VIS RICH IN WORLD

Monday, 8 August 2011

POVERTY IN CONTEXT OF INDIA!

For the last few days, some reminiscences are haunting my mind! But today When I saw a small piece of news—"Rihanna stylist", London date-line small story on page three in The Fine Column of Telegraph, Patna edition, it reminisces many thing about plight of poor and their miserable life in the globe, particularly in India.

With such down the memory—lane, I exactly remember famous one sentence of the famous writer, Scar Wilde—"We all live in the gutter, but some of us gaze at the stars." Sadly over 80 percent population in almost all countries of the world live in poverty without food, shelter, health care etc. In India itself 80 percent people lead their life on hardly Rs 20 to Rs 25 per day.

On the other hand the particular small news in the Telegraph datelined London has stated that one Rihanna spends $14000 a week on her hair stylist to get the perfect look. In the same story, the 23-year-old star's stylist Ursula Stephen, charges $2000 a day to help ensure she looks her best, reported the Daily Mail and said "Rehanna likes to pioneer new styles but it is costing her a fortune." This small piece has shaken my conscience and compelled me to look beyond and see the plight of poor and luxury and lavish expenditure of rich. It is narration of Britishers, known for imperialist designs throughout the globe in the last over 800 years.

Analysts say the entire Europe is passing through economic down trend—but I strongly feel there is no economic crisis effect in European countries, Particularly England. Similari are many stories of wasteful expenditures In United States of America and the country is under heavy debt and more and more economic crisis is gripping that country.

Such economic crisis in Europe and US is not telling upon the health of rich people there, who lead luxurious and extravagant life at the cost of poor in these regions! Countries of these two continents are virtually controlling economic power in the world in the last several years. But now they are in the grip of serious economic crisis and US alone is paying $250 billion dollar by way of interest payment per year! Now the European countries and US are looking for financial support from the world countries to bail out from its economic morass. Particularly wasteful expenditure of US on war in Afghanistan, Pakistan, Iraq and Middle east countries and also other Muslim countries, mainly in the name of counter terrorism but in actual terms for usurping oil resources and its supremacy in the world for spreading its imperialism has put America in deep sea, as per reports of US impartial print media and also of Britain One old saying justifies the action of US, "himself a beggar and beggar at the door." Here one should also remember Tulsi Das's Ram Charit Manas in which he has said, "Jo jash karihi so tass phal chakha (one what ever deeds or misdeeds do or does—he or they taste the same taste)." It also justifies the saying of Scar Wilde and suggests that US living in gutter and gazing up at sky for its deeds and misdeeds.

In changed situation, Asia's Japan, which was recovering from the worst-ever war in 1930s and early 1940s and destruction of that country from dangerous hydrogen bombs, started a big jump and by late 1960s and early 1970 started overtaking the Europe and America by adopting new economy of cheap and best and use and throw manufacturing durable and cheapest consumer goods and also knowing kon-how of advanced technology. Now Asia's China and India are heading for economic boom. But there are vast differencves between rising economy of China and India. While China is adopting economy and advance technology for the benefits of all including poor, India, on the other hand, is adopting western styple economy of liberalisation and capitalism. Moreover, these policies of India have resulted in more and more poverty. Rich are becoming richer and poor becoming poorer. Rural areas of India continue to be neglected! Poverty has become a bane in India in this 20th century. Surprisingly India government is making only tall claims of GDP and the so called economic development of country—but on the other hand at least the government has failed to identify poor and rich in the country. Twenty percent rich people are said to be ruling the country including politicians, corporates, multi-nationals, feudal and landlords where as 80 percent people are said to be without any basic facilities including food, shelter, health, education etc and are ggroaning under poverty. Moreover, successive governments of India have no knowledge of prevailing poverty in India. Surprisingly India is yet to identify the number of poor living in the country. The India's government's own different panels, set up at different times, are not unanimous on the figures of poor in India. While its Planning commission says that 28.3 percent population of India are poor, its another Saxena panel has put the figure over 57 percent, another panel—Arjun Dasgupts panel says 77 percent people of India are poor and another Tendulkar panel has put the figure 37.2 percent. Now anybody can imagine the plight of our union government in even determining people, afflicted with poverty.

With such reasons, it is rightly said that India is two countries—one for poor, who in my opinion constitute over 80 percent, another of rich people who constitute 20 percent. Intrinsically, successive union governments, particularly of Manmohan Singh of UPA two in India proves beyond doubt that Manmohan Singh, the present prime minister is harbouring the interest of capitalist, in this socialist pattern of society and government as enunciated by Pundit Jawahar Lal Nehru. Monamohan "living in the gutter gazing up at the stars"!

"MURDOCHISATION" OF INDIAN MEDIA!

Thursday, 4 August 2011

Rupert Murdoch vis-a-vis world media. Before more and more about Rupert Murdoch, We Indian must think in right perspective—Are Indian print and electronic media except a few are following the path of Murdoch to destroy the credibility, independence and freedom of press in media of India? Some print and electronic media in India, particularly Bennet, Coleman&company Ltd (BCCL), publishers of the Times of India, Economic Times, Maharashtra Times and owner pof electronic channels are "Murdochisation" their print and electronic media. I will explain all these things in this very blog itself. Rupert Murdoch is media "moghul" in the world or "power broker" through his empire! Murdoch is known for his chain of newspapers, news magazines, electronic news channels, entertainments channels, spread over throughout the globe. His empire is$82 billion media and entertainment channels. Interestingly Murdoch had a small Australian centre-right newspapers Thereafter he expanded his media empire in Australia his home country and in the process he launched the centre-right paper—The AUSTRALIAN in 1962. He had inherited a small newspaper from his father Keith Murdoch. Successfully, Murdoch started his media ventures beyond Australia and had bought newspapers in United Kingdom in 1960s and United States in 1980s. From there Murdoch started the role of devil of the pieces. He got notoriety following his media publicity to crush trade unionism in Britain. Murdoch succeeded in dismissing 6000 employees following a strike in 1986 in Great Britain. In this misdeeds Murdoch has full support of the then Prime Minister of Britain Margaret Thatcher, who is known for trade union bashing. His long journey of dubious reached him to the height in media world and today at the age of 80 years, Murdoch is the chairman and Chief Executive Officer of his News Corporation,(founded in 1979) having revenue (year to May 31, 2011)

US$ 32.55 billion and gross profit is $11.88bn, employees—51000 and personal net worth $7.6bn,. Murdoch owns 127 newspapers throughout the world besides electronic channels like Star news, Fox News, and other entertainment channels, according to information from various news websites and newspapers, news magazines throughout the world including Indian newspapers and news magazines. Rupert, in his credit, has many misdeeds as tales to tell! Murdoch is considered friends of almost all the top leaders of various political parties and governments throughout the world, particularly Europe and America. He is thoroughly conservative, pro-capitalist and anti-liberal, anti-trade unions, and finally a retrograde personality in media world. His role in different big wars in Middle East and South—East Asia as well as anti-Muslim attitude have destroyed the credibility of media in the world. Murdoch always started campaign against Iraq, Iran, Pakistan, Afghanistan and other progressive countries like Vietnam, China, France, Germany and sided with colonial European countries like England, Israel, and US etc. All these things reflected in his print and electronic media in the last several years. His print and electronic media virtually started campaign against progressive countries. It was his print media and electronic media, which had started a campaign against progressive US President Barack Obama's birth certificate and his father's Islamic faith. It is Murdoch responsible for creating hysteria that behind every terror acts; there is invariably a Muslim hand! Many columnists of The New York Times, The Economist, and Indian news magazine—The Frontline have exposed the evil designs of Rupert. A new York Times columnist Rank rich has described the Murdoch media empire as "Islamophobia command centre" a comprehensive report of the Frontline says and adds that the Economist wrote, that it was for the first time since the powerful "East India Company" was brought to heel in the 19th century that political power over an influential private enterprises in Britain (has) been so brutally enforced" powerful. It further predicted Rupert empire fall!

More over this small story of Rupert is not enough to explain his conduct in the media world, which has become shame both for print and electronic media in the globe. His recent involvement in publishing and broadcasting in his channels and news papers, news magazines the private lives of people is highly immoral. And his involvement and also his journalist staff as well as his management have put Murdoch in serious troubles—but shamelessly he is defending himself and his publications and at the same time closing down his one of the important

Newspaper—"News of the World", responsible for phone hacking scandal. Murdoch and his son had been interrogated intensively for the crime by the committee of the British Parliament. They both faltered!

Sadly Murdoch's invasion in the shape of spreading its network in India has started giving ominous signal for print and electronic media in the country besides threat to culture, civilization, unity and integrity, and secular credentials of India. Besides spreading its tentacles in 1991 after looking its market prospects Rupert-controlled Star(Satellite Television Asia region) group in the of wake economic liberalisation policy and subsequently allowing world media to enter India after vehement opposition, now the Rupert owned Star India Group is one of the biggest media conglomerates in the country (in terms of turn over). It claims largest number of viewers around 170 million every week for its 32 channels in eight languages including Star plus, Star one, star Gold, Channel V, Star Jalsa, Star Parah, Star World, Star Movie. Star utsav, and joint venture channels such as Asia net, Sky News, FX, Fox crime, Star Vijay, Star News, ESPN and star Sports among others A front line report says and adds thatDaya Kishan Thusssu, professor of international communication at the university of Westminster has said," Mudrochisation" of Indian media as a process "which involves the shift of media power from public to private-owned, transitional, multimedia corporations controlling both delivery system and the content of global information networks." For the first time in India, BCCL, publishers of Times of India, Economic Times, Maharashtra Times are market leaders in their categories, has broken" Lakhsman rekha" in 2003 that existed between marketing and editorial departments. BCCL, surprisingly, started paid contents""service called media net", which sent journalists to cover product launches or celebrated related events for a fee. It violated blatantly journalistic ethics but regretfully BCCL management claims that is acceptable given that such "advertorials". Interestingly it also introduced "paid news" syndrome, which involves paying newspapers and broadcasters for positive coverage. It is big menace for Indian journalism. Press Council of India is sitting over the matter and nothing tangible has come out. BCCL has also introduced "private treaties:" scheme, which allows giving space to corporates in exchange of quality shares. All these action of BCCL is "Murdochisation of Indian Media by BCCL". The Editor-in-Chief of The Hindu N Ram has rightly said," This is disturbing trend. Investigative journalism has been given a bad name by the invasive spy camera." Similar concern were voiced over "Murdochisation" of

Indian media and recent trend on freedom of press and expression as well as "undeclared censorship" by owners of media houses for serving their enlightened self interest and also virus of "paid news" by eminent journalists including P Sainath, India Today group editor Aroon Purie. According to Thussu and others, the channels in Star group led the the way in developing content that is sensationalists and emphasis urban, westernised, consumerists concern with a particular emphasis on sex and celebrity culture as well as three Cs (crime, cricket, cinema). All these developments in the wake of Murdoch, going berserk must be controlled by the people of India and the union government. Is this not ominous sign for India media?

TREASURE OF SREE PADMANABHASWAMY: A HONESTY PAR EXCELLENCE!

Tuesday, 26 July 2011

YAD YADACHARIT SHRESHTHSTYWDEVETARO JAN; SYATPRMANAMN KURUTE LOKSTDNUAIWARTATE. *SRIMAD BHAGWAT GITA (CHAPTER THREE TEXT 21) (Whatever action a great man performs, common men follow. And whatever standards he sets by exemplary acts, all the world pursues)

This text of Gita aptly describes the discovery of treasures in Shree Padmanabhaswamy temple (important Vishnu shrines) in Kerala. It is not surprising but a reality how these hidden wealth in hundreds crores of rupees were safe even after a lot of moral degeneration among people in India—(Where money and wealth minting have become order of the day among people of all sections). We must congratulate and praise the successive rulers of Trabancore Cochin and temple management committee as well as people of Kerala for keeping such huge wealth for hundreds of years in safe custody. One must not dispute over the actual ownership of such huge wealth! But think and feel about the presence of Almighty in this critical hour where we Indians have gone decadent for enlightened self-interest! In this connection I must praise the present Kerala government, which has declared that huge wealth belongs to temple and the government would and is providing all securities to keep the huge wealth in proper condition in the temple complex itself. Padmanabhaswamy temple of Almighty Vishnu, the supreme God, is a symbol of Indian culture and has great religious, archaeological and historical importance, according to the CM of Kerala Oomen Chandy. Interestingly, when we compare the temples of different gods and Goddesses in different parts of the country especially in north, east and central India, we seldom finds such huge treasures notwithstanding lakhs of devouts visit then regularly and make huge offerings! In many cases, temple property is gobbled up grabbed and siphoned off by priests and management trustees of these temples. Mismanagement galore is there in almost all the temples. Loard Venketesh temple in Andhara and Shirdi Baba temple in Maharashtra are well managed. Such is not the case in even Vaishno Devi temple in Kashmir wheres crores of devout pray every year! There are many miserable tales of temple management in central, east and north India where the so called service of Almighty has no meanings for priests and management committees of famous temples and shrines of religious importance. You will fuind there that priests are more active in fleecing devouts instead of accumulating the wealth offerings to the respective God and Goddesses. Some bitter experiences, you will, find in Baidyanath Dham temple, in Deoghar under Jharkhand state. Huge offerings are made but something tangible is yet to make to renovate temple and show on records the huge wealth donated by devouts. Even Ram Krishna Asharam managed temple of Goddess Dakshnishwar Kali has similar tales. In all these places devout are discouragee devout to offer donations or offerings in sealed cover kept in the respective temple premises. These eyewitness account some time hurt and disappoint men like me how we have been morally degenerated. Even the governments under the respective religious deities have failed to curb such menace and temples of God and Godesses remain fund crunched although crores of people visit yearly and made offerings to the temple deities! The story of Padmanabhaswamy is different where honesty and pure love for Almighty exists. The entire huge Sree Padamanabhaswamy temple has beautiful scenic surroundings and huge complex, located in the main hub of city— the capital of Kerala. the temple has huge granite walls. Temple is hub of activities for devouts right from morning to evening. Records of temples showed huge offerings by devouts and successive rulers of Travancore in the last hundreds of years. It has also huge track of lands, farm lands etc right from AD117. Gold, silver, vessels, pooja utensils are many many and much and much! It has huge statue of Almighty Vishnu of solid shape in Gold. According to a Madras based fortnightly—Frontline; there are records of kings of Tranvancore had borrowed funds from temple during crisis. But of course the kings repaid the loans promptly.

There are many mysteries when the underground vaults were constructed inside the temple. Vaults have not been unlocked for more than century. The first renovation of the temple was done in by Bhasshkara Ravi Varma, a Chera king of in AD1050! There are many such examples of renovation and percolating of huge wealth in the temples in hundreds of years. So far it is said that under the directives of the Supreme Court five vaults have been opened and after inventory sealed. Ant it is said that wealth in the shape of gold, diamonds, other valuable stones, gold coins and other invaluable precious metals, worth over Rs 100 crores have been discovered—one vault, said to be oldest and having many more huge wealth is yet to be opened. Interestingly, the present successor of erstwhile Travancore rulers have not claimed the wealth but has said that it all belongs to Almighty Vishnu. Systematically, the Vishnu shrine in Kerala is being managed. There are records that compound wall of the temple was perhaps built in AD 1425. There is urgent need in the temple to decipher temple's achieves for more light on Padmanabhaswamy temple so that it could throw light on antique value of all treasures found in the temple vaults.

Apart from that the temple management committee must be backed up with full research teams to study more and more about temple treasures in such huge amount not heard and seen India. There may be one thing many temples, especially in north, east and central India have been looted and plundered by successive invaders in over thousands of years. At the same time invaders might not have reached the southern parts of the country because of presence of strong rulers and peoples' resistance and they could not succeed in robbing and plundering these deities in south India. Pages of history three enough light on this aspects! It also point out that Dravidian, and aboriginals were real inhabitants of Hindustan or Bharatvarsh instead of so called Aryan in north, central, eastern India.

Last but not the least Padmanabhaswamy temple of Lord Vishnu and its thousands of crores of huge wealth must be declared as a legacy of our society. Nobody even government must not succumb to the pressure of people for using it for public purposes. I agree with the contention of eminent historian K N Panikkar. He had rightly said that all that the kings of Travancore received belonged to the deity, to Sree Padamnabha because the kings used to consider themselves das (servant) of the deity. All these huge wealth must be kept in the museum—these are public property as these precious things must had been purchased by Travancore kings for deity from the revenue collected by citizens of the kingdom! Pannikar has given a very good suggestion—as it happened in many other countries in the globe, the entire huge wealth must be preserved as legacy of our society. These must be lodged in a museum as the treasures of many empires are of the world are kept like that. Technically and legally the huge wealth of temple unearthed and over 100 years old, the treasure will go to the government and through government to the Archaeological Survey of India. There must be a trust of experts in museology, preservation, valuation and so on such museum of such huge wealth of Padmanbhaswamy deity should be kept in a newly created museum, mainly for preserving our culture and glorious history.

My respectful sharnagat to Loard Vishnu deity in the form of Padmanabhaswamy.

MAN PROPOSES GOD DISPOSES! WND IS BEYOND CONTROL?

Friday, 22 July 2011

"Kshit, jaal, pawak, gagaan, samiraa;
Panch rachit yaah adham sharira,"
(This body is built of five elements—earth, water, fire, sky, wind)
***Shree Ramcharit Manas—Tulsi Das.

I am not so great scholar that I will tell you the philosophy of life! Just I am mentioning the crux of truth in life. More over, about plunder of natural resources by mafia or mafia's throughout the globe. Loot of water, mainly in entire Europe and land loot in the entire universe, particularly in India in the wake of neo-liberal economic policy in the last 20 years have inspired me to say somethings on plundering of natural resources by people, especially mafia throughout the world in connivance with respective governments of the land. In this free for all exercises, important elements—like wind and natural calamities, specially earthquake and bursting of jawalamukhi in mountain terrain continue to beyond the control of men-kind, you may call it scientists, discovering many unbelievable things in the world., are yet to have any control over these disastrous things In this loot and plunder of natural resources, mafia are working hard inconvenience with the government of the land, in the entire globe. One must have read a lot of looting water resources in recent years, especially in Europe and America. It is not uncommon in other countries of the world, particularly India. And land loot for corporates, capitalists, and industrialists, multinationals are also common. for setting up industries, ignoring agriculture in India, there are virtually land grabbing spree, ignoring the agriculture interest, forest cover, and uprooting of homes and lively hood of tribal and poor etc by power-that-be! Looters, plunderers, grabbers are working over time in connivance with government to make India a so called economic developed country in the world where 80 percent population are hungry and wealth is accumulated in the hands of only 20 percent of rich people. Earth is meant land available to people for farming, housing etc are the main targets of grabbers and looters including government!

But the power-that-be and grabbers have not succeeded to deprive the people of air or wind, which is available in abundance and everywhere. This air or wind is so important that men or any living thing on the earth cannot live without it for even a fraction of a second.

But one thing is very much clear that grabbers, plunderers, looters etc do not lag behind in polluting the air specially. More over, they have full control over water and it is polluted weather the water of drinking or sea or rivers and under earth.

Sky has also been conquered by scientists—major portion of sky is jammed with different satellites, working as communication channels and other purposes. Sky stations have come up—recently American scientists have covered and returned after successful mission of Atlantika. Scientists have also voiced fear that many satellites, stationed in the sky may fall and may cause disasters on the earth!

Strangely, fire is controlled—but it has such devastating effects that men-kind remain helpless when it engulfs the villages, towns, jungles, sea, rivers and many other areas. Under ground fires had engulfed Jharia coal belt areas In Jharkhand state of India for the last one hundred years—but scientists and miners did not succeed in controlling the underground fire in coal seams and it has spread to hundred miles in and around Jharia—Jharia township is under danger—Many areas are being evacuated! There are no takers of fire by grabbers and looters like land, water and other natural resources! Apart from this, there is no control over earthquake or jawalamukhi or cloudburst—such thing can happen anywhere on the earth—earth will shake and many residents will die and become shelter less—such has recently happened in Japan! Earthquake happenings are continuous chain of events throughout the globe and it happens very often anywhere on the earth. Even the sea is not untouched with earthquake. Similar are the true stories of jwalamukhi burst in mountainous region in different parts of the world. Likewise flood waters also some time bring devastation after devastation—and people become helpless to such natural furry Nobody has control over such happenings!

More over people and scientist have every reason to explore the things but must not be at the cost of destroying natural resources and ecological balances and making them hell for the living people and also other living creatures like animals, insects, birds, flora and fauna of the nature! It is true that they could not deprive people of air or wind but the demonic activities of men-kind can definitely pollute that air, disastrous for every living creature on the earth.

Hey men, Almighty has given you all enough—be satisfied do not hanker for more and more—it will invite you only sorrow and pain!

GREAT LOOT OF FARM LAND AND FOREST LAND IN INDIA!

Tuesday, 19 July 2011

Sufferings of farmers, poor, tribal, forest under neo-liberal policy:

The OXFORD Dictionary has aptly described the meaning of loot—"goods taken from enemy, spoil, booty, illicit gains made by officials money; plunder, rob, steal-home, houses, goods and left unprotected after violent events". This is exactly happening in India, specially, Maharashtra, Gujarat, Chhatishgarh, Orrisa, Bihar, Haryana, Punjab, Madhya Pradesh, Uttar Pradesh etc under neo-liberal economic policy of the union government to grab and loot lands, forest, houses from farmers and tribal in the country to hand over the "looted lands and forest areas and cover" to corporates, industrialists, capitalists, multinationals etc for setting up a chain of industries in the respective areas, obviously without any agriculture cover. The Oxford has rightly meant the word "loot" goods taken from enemies. Landowners and poor tribal have become "enemies" of the state governments and union government in their own country. Another meaning of "loot" is "left unprotected" after violence of loot! All these meaning aptly describe that land looters, grabbers, acquisitioners without any consent of concerned people and adequate compensations have field day in the entire country. Both the state governments and union governments have become villain of the pieces in their nefarious design to uproot the farmers, farm labour, tribal and other poor section of society of their houses, jungles, crop lands etc And we Indians, numbering over 80 percent of population, are tolerating all these atrocities of vested interests in connivance with both union and state governments.

Ugly faces of land grabbing and looting by governments and neo-rich individuals have begun in the last 25 to 30 years. Even today in big cities, minority is being forced to sell their houses and lands, located in prime locations. In the last twenty years, at least majority of Bengali population, and to some extend Muslims as well as majority of helpless people and their dependents have left Patna by selling or leaving their lands and houses in prime locations in Patna. Being afraid, they left and or sold their lands in comparatively less price. Now anyone can see palatial houses, multi-stories apartments, offices of multinationals, corporates on these lands in Patna, Bhagalpur, Muzaffarpur, Chapra, Siwan, Gaya etc in Bihar at least. in recent past without any legal validity Nitish government has unauthorised settled big and costly plots of lands of industrial estates to set up multi-flexes, cinemas, small and big units, apartments etc on throwaway prices. Currently, lands of Bihar industrial areas development authorities, located in different towns and cities of the state have been illegally sold without any tenders to vested interests, having close to BJP and JD-U ministers and senior bureaucrats.

Recently Mayawati government had acquired huge portion of agriculture lands in Agra and Noida areas for express highways and surprisingly sold all those lands to private parties for setting up malls and apartments, violating the very purpose of acquisition of land Aagitations are going on Bhatta-Parsoul and many other places in Uttra Pradesh and the court has also directed Mayawati government to return the lands to farmers as these lands have not been used for public purposes.

All these are under unauthorised possessions of mafias and neo-rich, close to corridors of power in successive governments in Bihar and Uttar Pradesh. In Jharkhand, most of the Bengali population and poor tribal, outnumbered by Biharis during joint Bihar are also leaving for safer places from important town areas! The recent loot of mining and other precious things in Jharkhand since the creation of Jharkhand have made the situation worse in the state. Now there is spree of setting industrial units by Mittal, Tata, and Jindal etc by land grabbing of tribal population in jungle areas. Such tales are not only in Bihar, Jharkhand and Uttar Pradesh—it is almost the same in metropolis and towns of all states in the country that minorities of every section are leaving the places for safe areas!

Real enacting of land grabbing dramas are being enacted in Orissa, Chhatishgarh, Madhya Pradesh, Jharkhand, West Bengal and also some western states like Maharashtra and Gujarat and south's mineral rich Karnataka and Andhra Pradesh. Land grabbing and loots are in big speed of course with the connivance with both states and centre. Huge areas of agriculture and forest and mountain, marine land have been acquired in Maharashtra for setting up industries in the last 50 years and now nuclear power plants, violatitave of guarantee to human lives and environment in the areas. In Gujarat, there are spree of land gabbing by government to set up corporates and multinational companies! In Karnataka, and Andhra Pradesh a different "tamasha" is being enacted to loot lands for mining purposes by vested interests, uprooting tribal and jungles, violating environment laws.

Sadly, a progressive chief minister like Navin Patnaik has created strange situations by giving huge lands in forest areas to South Korean steel giant—Posco. Forest Act and tribal laws have been kept aside and tribal have become homeless and farm less. Strong protests are there but connivance of government will ultimately prevail! Orissa government has "looted "land, forest and mining and marine lands for big industrial units like Vedant, Tata etc. Over 1000 acres of land for 12-million steel plant of Posco are being acquired under stiff resistance from farmers and local people. Over 50000 acres of land is required by Orissa government to spread the industrial network and operation is on to grab and loot land. a Madras based fortnightly the Frontline report says, "acquisition of vast tracks of lands for industrial projects has created a real estate boon in Orissa. The poor are losers as corporates houses and real estate developers vie with one another to grab land. such hype has already cost the farmers and poor and tribal population., the report says and added "worse, people's movements, are branded as pro-Maoists and innocent people and activists questioning the land acquisition move are jailed and charged with having links with the extremists."

In chhatishgarh and Madhya Pradesh, land "loot and grabbing" is in jet set-speed. Chhatishgarh government has alone "grabbed or looted" thousands of acres of lands for setting up industries, mainly power plants by corporates, multinationals, neo-rich Indians industrialist like a newspapers chain of publication—Dainink Bhashkar. A BBC report has said that present spree of land acquisition in Chhatishgarh is considered biggest in the country, which have uprooted tribal and forest in huge areas. A Centre for Science and Environment report also says that Chhatishgarh government's push is on to install 77 percent of India's thermal power capacity, 51 percent of the country's present cement need capacity and 31 million tonnes of sponge iron capacity. But the result of the fast track industrialisation will be at the cost of forest, agricultural lands and tribal population. Interestingly, at present an estimated 1.64 lakh ha of forest land has been diverted to mining in Chhatishgarh! Moreover, apart from Raman Singh, chief minister of Chhatishgarh, his ministers and their wards and relatives are playing coercive measures against land holders, particularly tribal in forest areas to hand over their lands or face consequences. A recent report says that son of minister, employed in Videocon is working overtime to coerce poor in handing over lands on small price or face the consequences. Lands are being garbed by corporates and other industrial units and being registered in the name of third parties to ultimately transfer to corporates concerned besides Chhatishgarh government's illegal pressure to acquire the lands from them.

The Frontline has also written cover stories extensively how the lands garbing are going on in India without any legal sanctions!in Chhatishgarh best quality iron ore in the forest are being exported to Japan at mere Rs 400per tonnes from the garbbed lands. In Haryana, although best land deal acquisition has been formulated but there are simmering resentment to acquire agriculture land. Strangely Haryana government is acquiring fertile lands and handing them over to builder's huge number of people is being displaced in Haryana!

On and average, same is the stories of seven sisters' states in the eastern parts of the country. Huge lands are being acquired in similar fashion in sensitive Arunacha Pradesh to create huge hydro power potential. Installation of projects will require acquisition of vast track of land belonging to different tribes, thousands will have to be displaced in addition to thousands already been displaced, the Frontline report added. Nagaland, Assam, Meghalaya, Tripura etc also passing through such agonising moments as major industrial players have thrown their lots to set units in eastern states by "grabbing lands in connivance with respective governments in the region".

Such craze of land "loot and grabbing" throughout the country in connivance with the government has created piquant situaion in the entire country Sparingly, in these days of industrial era in the wake of economic liberalisation in the country—industrialists, corporates, multinationals, neo-rich want to first create real estate in the form of lands on cheap price for future shake and if industries run or not ultimately, they will be owners of huge estate, worth crores of rupees in developed areas like Rajas, maharajas, zamindars during British raj— and they may divert the lands for other purpose in the future. No body is cared of food scarcity and to boost agriculture production. If such situation continues India will must be one of most starved nation in the world in near future. Loot and grabbing of lands continuing***********.

HUMILITY VIS-A-VIS RAT RACE

Thursday, 14 July 2011

Some time I go into deep thoughts and remember Almighty. My thinking touches wide-range of problematics topics. And very often I fell myself disappointed. The old memory lane and day-to-day happenings, exactly, compels me think about the sufferings of people like me in the entire globe. Just stranges thoughts come up in my mind! And think myself what should be the course correction. Suddenly, I remember the versions of Yuddhishthir and Yakhs when the former had gone to rescue his other Pandava brothers, who could not reply Yaksh's set of questions and wanted to take water forcibly from the lake to mitigate their thirst—and subsequently all of them died. Lastly Yuddhishthir had come and found his brother's dead—Yaksh asked him the same set of questions from Yuddhishthir. Yuddhisthir replied all questions satisfactorily and in course of reply of the last question, he said that there are differences of opinions among sages, saints, and also in scriptures like Vedas, Puranas etc about what is good and bad "acharan", mentioned in the last question—then one must follow path of the elderly scholars and pundits and also great personalities (whatever they say and do). Yaksh became happy with the scholarly replies of his questions by Yuddhisthir and his dead brothers were given life and they all took water from the lake to satisfy their thirst!

I belong to a nationalist family. And I always believed in hard work (karm). I did that during my active journalism service career of over 36 years and my hard work used to be appreciated. But when the time of dividends or benefits came, I remained isolated. What ever I got in my career were by dint of hard labour. Even after that it did not shake my faith in Bhagwad Geeta, which says karm is supreme! And I am leading my retired life by reading, writing and praying to Almighty of all faiths. I have great respect, regards in Swami Ramkrishna Paramhans philosophy

551

of religions and spiritualism like "bhakti". Ramkrishna Paramhans had practiced all religions and had said that all religions go to same end and men get salvation without any discrimination of caste, creates, faith in all religions. But I am not succeeding in full concentrations. Stray thoughts come in my mind and "maan", which it is said moves in speed more than anythings. I feel this is great lapses in me. However, gradually or some time I succeed in concentration and find Almighty helping me in dire need and consequences. I try to remember Almighty always and keep in my mind to pray the almighty always and every time. I advise my near and dear to have faith in Almighty—it will look after you. Of course death and life is not even in the hands of Almighty! The Almighty becomes faiths in death and life—but some time when I see "anhoni honi ho Gaya:"—than I feel the Almighty has control over everything.

I seriously think only two great saints—Swami Ramkrishna Paramhansh and Shirdi ke Saidewa, born in two different regions—easts and west respectively in 19th century have shown the path of salvation. And both died of dreaded cancer while serving the men kind and enlightening the people of all religions presence of Almighty everywhere, everybody etc. Perhaps they died early and of serious ailments because they had taken sorrow and pains of people to cure them and have more life spans!

Both religious giants of 19th century impressed me enough and my faith in Almighty and all religions was deep rooted. More over I remember the old reminiscences of my life and I become thankful to Almighty that IT has great blessings on me and I am carrying. Such thoughts also reverates my mind when I look back and find that people of the world are more and more in distress and sufferings!

POVERTY AND STARVATION DEATHS

Sunday, 10 July 2011

Once a sage asked his disciple, which is worst and distressful thing in man's life, without any pause the disciple replied starvation (death without food or grain) is the most distressful thing in the world!

This is evident from mentioning in almost all mythological and religious books in the entire globe like Geeta, Ramayana, Vedas, Upanishads, scriptures, Koran, Bible etc. In every religion one find such remarks this is what happening in the world. Many are dying without food alone daily and nobody is there to take care of starvation deaths. There are many areas on the globe, which are yet to be discovered and their people live like primitive age people and many of them die without food and shelter. And we people of the world are claiming of most scientific and human advancement in this 20th century—what a cruel joke with men-kind!

Food mean prepared of grains. Grains are fer tiled and cropped in lands. Cropping of grains are gradually goindg down throughout the world. People of even advanced and developed countries least bothered about farming of land and do not grow grains from lands—vast tracks of fertile lands are vacant but nobody is there for cropping in almost all countries. Lands are concentrated in few hands. Over 80 percent people on the earth, which are landless in the globe! Only because of these factors, now even food grains are being monopolised. Gradually, food or grain productions are on declining trend. Whatever grains are available throughout the world are sold on high prices. Result: Grains are not available in abundance and starvation death is increasing on the globe, especially among poor, who constitute over 80 percent in the world besides inaccessible places where men-kind live.

As per a recent survey of The United Nations' Food and agriculture Organisation (UN FAO)and Organisations for Economic Cooperation and development, OECD), published in a Madras based magazine—Frontline, the food price will soar up over 30 percent in next ten years. Currently the food price has risen by 40 percent over the past year. It would have a devastating impact on the poor of the globe. Such will be the ominous sign for the world countries, and ultimately lead to political unrest, famine and starvation. People are being forced to eat less or cannot provide food to carry their life, resulting into many more starvation deaths!Cost of cereals is likely to increase by 20 percent and price of meat, particularly chickens may soar up 30 percent very soon. Global food price hit by a record high in February, promoting demonstrations across the world. The last extreme food price rise in 2008 led to riots in 20 countries across three continents.

World food price is bound to increase in coming years and already a record high as droughts and flood threaten to seriously damage current year's harvest. Global harvest is in critical condition and warned that price would continue to rise. The slowdown in production comes amid new forecasts that the global population will climb to 9.2 billion by 2050, compared with previous estimate of 6.9 billion, the report of FAO and OECD adds and further says that agriculture production would have to increase by 70 percent to match the expected rise!

This is what happening in the world on food front and availability of food grains to starving people! Once China and India were called most starved countries of the world. Starvation deaths were beyond imagination in these two countries. In China, the situation has eased to great extend. China has adopted novel way of farming by removing its previous law of state farming. Now China government is giving bulk of farm lands to individuals for agriculture purpose on lease by taking certain quantity of grains in state coffers. Apart from that, China has also succeeded in controlling its population growth. But in India, situation is very grim. Lands continue to accumulate in the hands of certain people. Over 90 percent populations of India are landless. Land reforms measures have been initiate in half-hearted manners. Vast tracks of farm lands are unutilised. In India pace of farming is very very slow. Even government is not taking effective measures on agriculture fronts! Strangely subsidy on agriculture is gradually being withdrawn whereas subsidy on industries are increasing by leaps and bounds under neo-liberal economic policy, resulting into concession of lakhs of crores rupees to industrialists, corporates, capitalists etc. Farmers are keeping their fingers crossed and in many instances farmers' suicides are increasing throughout the country because of their being in heavy debts.

Result: agriculture production is going down year to year in India Shortage of grains have become evident. India has even today to import food grains like wheat, pulse etc from foreign countries. Such in differences of the government is giving alarming situation in the country because of shortage of food grains. Innovations in agriculture sector have become matter of the past in last 15 years. Slogans of Lal Bahadur Shastri" Jai Jawan-Jai kisan" has become bygone slogans. On and average three of 100 deaths are taking place in India daily of starvation and matter is suppressed by the government. In the entire globe such death are 15 of one hundred daily in different developed and under-developed countries in the world, as estimated by authentic international body survey, taking into ground realities in the different countries. Sadly, nobody in the corridor of power, especially in Delhi is bothered and to think to increase agriculture production in the country, especially India being an agricultural based country in the world. Worst are the condition of farm labours, who are suffering without any work in the agriculture field as owners of the lands have put their lands in barren condition.

Strangely most of the advanced and developed countries of the world do not grow to create artificial but they keep their lands ready for farming. Europe, America, Latin America, Africa, Australia and many other continents and countries, food are grown in abundance. But in many cases, they dump their produce in sea to put pressure on food price rise and export the remaining quantity on high prices to scarce country of the world. In some cases, in America, Americans put ready their lands for agriculture purpose always but do not grow—. When the prices of food grains increase worldwide they grow in abundance and export their produce at high prices.

Ominous sign for starvation deaths throughout the world!

NAXALITES

Thursday, 30 June 2011

FIGHTING FOR GOOD CAUSE!
K K Singh

For the last few months I am passing through agonising moments about the activities of Maosis or Naxalites and governments' and enlightened self-interest people condemning their activities! I am surprised and at the same time shocked over action being launched against the Naxal activities by union and various state governments. Why this? Are they not fighting for causes of poor and tribal, being exploited by state power, capitalists, industrialists, neo-rich classes, multi-nationals etc? Are they not the Indian citizens? Have they no right to fight injustice? Cannot they raise their voices for right to life of people, guaranteed under the Indian Constitution and also raise their voices against suppression of freedom of expression? Yes, they have all avenues to raise their voices against exploitation of poor, tribalsand deprived lots. Than why this state terror and so called Salwa Jud um, private army of Chhatishgarh government to suppress and kill the Maoists or Naxalites! One must remember that Naxal operation is major component of left forces and activities to highlight exploitation in the Indian Society—this movement came out in early 1960s from a West Bengal village under the heroic leadership of late Charu Mazumdar and Kanu snyal. A trade union right to agitate still continues in statue book! This movement flourished and many even after becoming martyrs joined this pious movement to change the system and many living comrades are fighting for injustices! And the system to some extend, changed also. At the same time exploitation also reached at its zenith. An edit page article "A Need To Be Fighting FIT" by a retired police chief Prakash Singh in The Times of India on June 30, obviously to provoke union and state governments, affected by naxal activities, to take effective measures to curb naxal menace, rather stirred my conscience and I thought better to speak now about the so called problems of Naxalism.

Prakash Singh has spoken many things, reminding the union home minister Chhidamabaran for lack-lustre approach to "eliminate" Maoists. In the process, Singh reminded the decision of the government to start operation against Naxalites by the plan of "clear, hold and develop" in the worst affected areas of Chhatishgarh, Jharkhand, Bihar, Orissa, west Bengal and Maharashtra to eliminate the "naxal menace" in two to three years! The operation "clear, hold and develop" to eliminate Naxalism appears to have many follies. In my opinion, there is urgent need of development in the affected regions by soothing the injured feelings of poor and tribal, which are now being saved and rescued by Maoisists from further exploitations. Development should come first. The government must come forward through heavy dose of development schemes in affected areas with sympathetic approach. The chalked out strategy of union government and affected state governments are bound to rebound and Maoists programme will take deeper root and spread to different other parts of the country as well as urban centres very soon, a member of Maoist politburo arrested recently in Bihar told intelligence officials in course of interrogation. Naxalites are fighting to save and rescue poor people and tribal in forest areas. Almost all forest areas in the country are being mortgaged by respective governments in the hands of capitalists, industrialists, multinationals, corporates etc to set up industries by uprooting home and lands and Forest covers in the region. Are these measures proper to uprootot poor tribal? If not then why not Naxalites not help the affected people from exploitation. Sadly, union government has become silent to these naked dramas of fascits— type action of different state governments! Naxalites must not keep silent and save the poor from state power clutches also to save their homes, lands, forest cover in tribal areas and also for the sake of conductive environments in the country. Moreover, it appears surprisingly that only tribal belts are suitable for setting up industrial units and not the plan areas. Forest rights of tribal are also being deprived and they are also not paid proper and adequate compensation for taking over their lands.

Capitalists' out; look and measures in the last ten to 15 years have made the situation more complicated and in the name of industrial units and markets, poor are being deprived of their due share. In plan areas, lands are still concentrated in the hands of few people and the neo-rich people in the society. Except west Bengal, nothing tangible has been done for land reforms and land for landless. Almost all the state governments and union government is keeping mum over such serious issue of land reform. Not only that over hundred year Act of land acquisition are in operation and government' especially centre is silent not to amend the act or fresh land acquisition act for land acquisition for public purposes.

Land grabbing, water grabbing, forest resources grabbing mafias have become active throughout the country and major encouragements on their activities have government support and the government has itself become land grabbers of poor in the name bringing moon by setting up industries in the tribal and plan areas of the country. But there are many right thinking politicians including Congress leader Digvijay Singh, West Bengal chief minister, Mamta Bannerjee, Bihar chief minister, Nitish Kumar (now Nitish has changed his track—initially he was for development and sympathetic approach to tackle Naxlites activities) and even left oriented mode of Congress leader Rahul Gandhi appear to have a different approach to tackle naxalism not through state terror. They are also of the opinion of heavy dose of development and due rights to poor, farmers, industrial and other workers and their trade union rights. Also sympathetic treatment to poor and tribal and to bring them in national main stream by providing those education and health factlities—and naxal ism or Maoism will gradually go down. Naxalites or Maoisits are not fighting to overthrow the government or Constitution but they want overhauling in system, which has become decadent and exploitative.

Interestingly, the union government has announced a Rs 3,300 crore integrated action plan for 60 naxalite-hit districts across nine states to ensure overall development of these areas, setting up schools, health facilities, roads and access to safe drinking water etc, Prakash singh has said in the write-up. But strangely, Praksh Singh is unnecessarily blaming the political leadership of different states either of non-serious or indifferent to the Maoist problem or making hey while sun shines. Strangely and sadly Prakash Singh has praised the Chhatishgarh BJP chief minister Raman singh for taking up Maoist head-on, obviously for eliminating Maoists or killing them or nabbing them under well planned so called salwa judum and state terror!Raman singh has taken tyranny at its zenith to kill or eliminate Maoists.

Now the tactics of Raman Singh is being replicated by his Bihar counter-part Nitish Kumar, who has also support of BJP, Over a dozen important veteran naxalites and members of central politiburo of Maioists party, have been arrested from different parts of Bihar in recent past under "well planned conspiracy hatched between Raman Singh and Nitish Kumar", a top naxalite source said. Not only is that Nitish government torturing Naxalites and their supporters and sympathisers in different parts of the state. An important Politburo member, who has been arrested by Bihar police recently, has confirmed that Maoists will spread their activities in urban areas and its consequences will be worst in Bihar, intelligence sources said.

Main reasons of not carrying development in naxal-affected areas in different parts of the country, especially in Bihar are half-hearted development measures in the affected areas. Apart from that, corruption in implementing development programme in affected areas, mainly in tribal belts and rural areas is also proving stumbling bloc in implementing development schemes in affected areas. Power-that-be or ruling politician elites, bureaucracy and power brokers are hand in glove to thwart the implementation of development measures and bulks of money are gobbled up by them! Prakash singh has also mentioned such menace in his writings and said that fruits of development are not reaching the intended beneficiaries. In Bihar such nefarious practice is much much more and least said is better.

MY SYMPATHY WITH MAOIST AND NAXALITE COMRADES FOR CHANGING THE SYSTEM. K K SINGH, Journalist, After retirement from TImes of India as chief reporter is based in Patna and writing, writing, more and more, reading, reading more and more and praying, praying almighty more and more.

NITISH KUMAR VIS-A-VIS BIHAR!

Tuesday, 28 June 2011

Many things are happening in Bihar in the last over fifteen days. People are at a loss and sad. Chief Minister Nitish Kumar is keeping mum. His government machinery and ministers are engaged in different games! After return from his China's goodwill visit, Nitish perhaps is dreaming only China and smiling! Reasons best known to him. But some time Nitish speaks gospel truth! People like me think what has gone wrong with Nitish! Strangely for every bad things, Nitish and his ministers as well as ministerial colleagues as well as BJP, JD(U) party men blame centre and previous governments for all the prevailing maladies. Forget past and build Bihar slogans do not appreciate present Nitish government!

Nitish was away in China and his health minister Ashwani Kumar Choubey away in Gujarat to take a lesson or two from Gujarat Chief Minister Narendra modi for elimination of Muslims from Bihar when killer disease is rampaging Muzaffarpur 's Tirhut region and police firing in Araria village where six persons were killed including a pregnant woman and a child.

So far over 60 children have died of killer disease in Tirhut region in the last twelve days. Although doctors initially diagnosed the disease encephalitis, Later it proved wrong. Pune lab of virology also disclosed that disease is not encephalitis! And dying spree is going on. Children from poor start are the victims and the disease has spread in entire region. Many poor have not tunrned up to Muzaffarpur hospitals because they cannot afford treatment and in the process many boys and girls died crying. Almost all hospitals including private and SKMedical college hospital, Muzaffarpur are crowded and flooded with patients. Doctors have raised their hands. In many cases it was detected that parents of children, who died of disease while in treatment in government hospitals, were not given bodies—and cruelty and inhuman treatment crossed all limits in Nitish Kumar government! Moreover, now the Pune virology lab wants of brain swab to detect the disease after test in the lab—but the state government has becme motion less. Nothing tangible is done! Only death reports are pouring in apart further spread of Kala-azar in the region in which over half a dozen have died, Nitish government is yet to make arrangements to airlift experts from other parts of the country for proper treatment of the children!

Apart from that, state has also witnessed one of the worst police firings on innocent Muslim villagers in one of the villages in eastern parts of Araria district. Police firing killed six persons including a pregnant woman and a child of Muslim community. Villagers were protesting the sealing of approach road to the village for opening a starch factory by the son of the BJP legislator. Matter was not a big deal—it would have been thrashed out amicably. But police opened unprovoked and unjustified firing. Government machinery and ministers of Nitish government reportedly put pressure on Araria district administration to clear the villager's of or starting work on starch factory. Deputy Chief Minister Sushil Kumar Modi had blessings to open starch factory by the son of the BJP legislator! Strangely, instead of giving compensation to police firing victims like such compensations to police firing victims in recent past in different parts of the state, Nitish Kumar ordered for judicial probe and announced that compensation, if any, will be given after the report of the commission. It appears discrimination because victims belonged to minority community. Hindu outfits and Nitish's alliance partner BJP reportedly put pressure on Nitish for not announcing compensation to victims!

Sadly, the matter was put under carpet for days together. Newspapers, news magazines, especially urdu dailies as well as electronic media did not take care to highlight such brutal and cruel incident for days together—this is how the media are under undeclared censorship for the last six years during Nitish government! Even a popular Urdu daily, having largest circulation and one of top beneficiaries of advertisements revenue of Bihar government kept the matter censored for days together to highlight the incident with Muslims in araria village. In this way media are supposedly in the pocket of Nitish government! Significantly, even media from outside state did not take up the matter when international media like BBC had reported the incident with full coverage.

Matter started only hotting up when a few activists from Delhi and eminent film producer Mahesh Bhatta visited the village and hear sad tale of villagers and saw the actual condition in the village. When Bhatta called the firing unprovoked and unjustified, he was abused and lambasted by BJP leaders and Hindu outfits Thereafter, chairman of the National minority commission Wazahat Habibullah air dashed from Delhi and visited the village for on the spot study. Wazahat also termed the police action and firing unprovoked, killing innocent Muslims. He also held discussions with state government officials. Strangely, Wazahat, who wanted to meet Nitish, to have first hand information about Araria incident was not given incident. Cries of people are subsiding in cacophony of Nitish's announcements galore!

MUCH HYPED NITISH CHINA VISIT!

Saturday, 11 June 2011

MUCH HYPED NITISH CHINA VISIT!

Much media-hyped chief minister of Bihar Nitish Kumar's China visit, beginning tomorrow is being welcomed by the People of the state except the toiling mass of rural areas, who are far away from any source of communication and are indifferent what is happening in the country!

Nitish is going to China with a strong continent of delegation for week-long visit of China, mainly for encouraging Buddhist tourists from that country and also to know-how technology for agriculture development in that country. Bihar is completely based on agriculture because of so many constraints like acute electricity scarcity to set up new industries. Only long and repeated announcements of Nitish will not suffice the need of the people of the state, lagging for development and considered one of low-rate states in the country in respect of development. Of course with the advent of Nitish Kumar as the chief minister of the state over six years back in coalition with Hindu party—Bharatiya Janata Party (BJP), law and order, which was at the lowest ebb, has been considerably improved. People are gradually feeling secured to some extend!

But as regards the developmental activities and also creating infrastructures, the work, which was being paced fastly in the first five years of his rule, has gradually slowed down. But his other schemes like cycles to students, kanya vivah yojana, fifty percent of reservation to backward, dalit, women in panchayat and local bodies elections are to be praised—In the second tenure of Nitish Kumar, I find only announcements to bring moon in Bihar by making a lot of announcements not only by Nitish but his ministerial colleagues also. In ground reality, nothing tangible is being done to convert these announcements in reality! Of all transport sectors and road communication have also improved to little bit. But rural roads, connecting even the block headquarters throughout the Bihar are completely in mess. Dream of new industries and bringing corporates or capitalists to invest and set-up industries are yet to see the light of the day. Electricity is biggest problem in Bihar. Recent announcements of Nitish Kumar to set-up power plants even nuclear power plants for ample of electricity will take at least ten to twelve years by than Bihar will have to give stress on agriculture and agro-based industries.

On education and health front, Nitish government has failed to bring desired development! Initially, on both these sectors, improvement was witnessed and much fan-fare was created—but later his measures slowed down. Illiterate teachers on fake marsheets were appointed at primary, middle and secondary level! Any body could expect the imparting of education in rural as well as urban areas in these schools! Sadly, the higher education is the worst causalities. Functioning of all the universities is paralysed for the last three years mainly because of tug of war between governor-cum-chancellor of universities and the Nitish government! Students are migrating to other states for higher education and even for middle and higher education; Nitish's much hyped impatrting of technical education by opening institutes also remained on paper only and only a few lower level polytechnics were set up without any infrastructures.

Interestingly, Nitish kumar's Agriculture advisor Mangla Roy, has also informed at a recent seminar on development organised by a national Hindi daily that farm sector is the only hope right now to bring some development. For this he has suggested agro-based industries and fish, goat, chicken rearing and also preparing for cold chain to export vegetables and seasonal fruits, which are grown in abundance in Bihar, to other states. Thus, this process will continue for 10 to 12 years till new power plants are erected and start power generation—only than prospects of big industries could be achieved in Bihar!

Situation is not so bright in Bihar on developmental aspects. His visit to china can bring a new hope for Bihar! Nitish and his delegation should find prospects of immediate generation of electricity besides knowing know-how on agriculture in China. One should keep in mind one thing that energy from nuclear energy will gradually turn into thing of past because of mishap in nuclear power plants in Japan and before that in many other countries and also mainly nuclear—induced serious ailments like cancer and other deadly diseases and last but not the least escalation in cost in erecting nuclear power plants. Most of European countries have already decided to say good bye to nuclear power plants. China has abandoned the plan of electricity from nuclear power plants and Germany did also the same thing. America, the main propagator nuclear energy, is also giving serious thoughts over the issue because of escalated cost as well as danger from nuclear power plants. ON the other hand surprisingly America is encouraging countries like India to set up nuclear power plants to market its plants and machinery of nuclear system in crores of dollars!

Surprisingly, till now only 13 percent of total electricity produced in the globe comes from nuclear power plants. World nuclear power plants capacity has stagnated as per an article in the FriontLine. Nuclear power output has declined by two percent over the past four years. Nuclear capital cost has surged high. In India it has been estimated that nuclear power plant cost for generating electricity has gone up five thousand dollar a kilowatt, compared with over one thousand dollar per kilowatt for coal based power and under one thousand five hundred dollar per kilowatt for producing power from wind. Renewable energy is growing rapidly throughout the globe. China is rapidly converting its plants to generate electricity from non-conventional sources like renewable energy, wind energy, hydro carbon energy etc. China, which has frozen its all nuclear power projects, already has 4.5 times more installed wind power than nuclear capacity and thus will bound to generate more electricity from wind power than nuclear power schemes. Non-conventional source of energy is gaining popularity throughout the globe.

Moreover, Nitish Kumar and his delegation must know the technical know-how of producing wind energy and also from renewable energy from China and adopt the same to Bihar. Technicality for generating electricity from wind and renewable energy is not so difficult and costly. Apart from agriculture based know-how and attracting tourism in Buddhist circuits in Chinsa, Nitish should approach China leadership for providing technology for generating electricity also.

M.F HUSSAN IS NO MORE

Friday, 10 June 2011

TRIBUTES TO M. F. HUSSAIN.

He had said, "I never wanted to become clever, esoteric abstract. I wanted to make simple statements. I wanted my canvases to have a story. I wanted my art to talk to people,"

My rich tributes to Hussain, painter, political philosopher and passionate admirer of beuteous Bollywood actresses tstartlingly to life and I pray to Almighty—may his soul rest in peace. This apart what an Indian like me can do on the demise of a great personality! WE, I mean us, Indian society, are part to be blamed to not give a share of last laugh at his birth place to a great man on the earth and Hussain died in London as Qatari citizen and cremated there! We all are part of this decadent society in India! A great man born in a village in Maharashtra, later shifted to Bombay as initially painting cinemas hoardings and billboards and later rose to height in painting field throughout the world, equating himself as famous painter Piccasso-fame. Thereafter many developments had taken place in his life and by making Bombay as his "karmkshetra", Hussain touched the sky of fame And in the last phase of his life, Hussain had been caught between devil and deep sea.

Painting or righting or speaking etc is freedom of expression—these are the things not to be seen or looked with naked eyes but with heart and mind. But we Indians have strange habits of not allying hearts and minds on anything happening on the earth! For making painting of Hindu God and Godesses and making films to raise voice against unIslamic culture, written in Quoran, Hussain has to pay heavy prices. Lot of criminal cases was lodged against him when he was on tour to foreign countries a few years back. His house was vandalised in Bombay by Hindu outfits' activists and both Muslims and Hindu have gone after his bloods. For some time, he remained in different countries of the globe for shelter but when matter worsened, Hussain moved to Qatar where he was offerred Qatari citizenship and he accepted it gladly and started remaining there. But love for motherland India never died from his heart—many of us met him in foreign countries and exchanged the reminiscenes with Hussain.

Shame to us and Indians as a whole, who could do nothing to get back Hussain to his motherland, And he crazed for Bombay faluda before his death as narrated by eminent writer and social activist Shobha Dey, who met a few hours ago with Hussan in London. Mainly the successive union governments and politicians of all hues are to be blamed for such maltreatment to Hussain. But we Indian remained silent! Does this not prove that we all Indians are to be blamed? I consider this is slur on secular democratic country like India!

Strange are the ways in India. Currently, we are crying for rampant corruption, money stashed in abroad banks and countries of neo-rich Indians etc but Hussan's honour, dignity, his bringing back to his motherland never became an issue—and we remained silent like cowards—we could not enegise us to protest against illtreatment to Hussain! This is our India where we can assemble in thousands for non-issues like demolition of mandir, masjid and many other issues but when the matter of crux come like food to poor in majority of India's rural areasr and other basic amenities, we keep silence—this does not prove that we are "murda ka desh hai."

I strongly blame every Indians for treatment with Hussain and he was compelled to accept the offer of Qartar government for citizenship and subsequently died in London and cremated there.

Last but not the least, if such trend continues and people start glorifying Babas, Sadhi, self-styled Mahatma Gandhi type men and politicians, who are no better than thieves except a few, generation to come will ask us how this happened and history will be with such sad aspects, happening in India.

OMINOUS SIGN FOR INDIA!

Thursday, 9 June 2011

OMINOUS SIGN FOR INDIA!

Strange developments are taking place in India in the recent months. Huge corruptions in corridor of power right from almost all state governments to union governments have come to light. Involvement of politicians, officials, power brokers, a few journalists in telecom scam and other scams in the country are practically breaking the back-bone of the democratic and secular fabrics of the country. Subsequently the controversy over a strong Lok Pal bill and obstinacy of civil society members led by Anna hazare is plaguing the checkmating of corruption menace in the country.

Thereafter, the hue and cry over unearthing of huge black money in foreign banks and countries of neo-rich Indians and agitation of spiritual Guru and Yoga teacher, Swami Ramdev is also posing a big question mark over the way the union government should act!

Apart from that, scams after scams in Karnataka BJP government and, corruption in implementation of NAREGA in entire country, especially in Bihar because of misuse of funds and non-utilisation of the same fund have also raised many eyebrows throughout the country.

Ongoing trend in journalism to support the dictum of power-that-be for imposing undecalred censorship on newspapers and electronic media, and also news magazines to curb the freedom of expression is also giving a cautious note that are our media are going down to the drains or giving long rope to government to go scot free although some media are playing important role in exposing the people and governments for its misdeeds.

Judiciary is also not untouchable to the recent declining trends in the country. Strangely Judges are also divided lots. Strange rulings some time wonder people—those also strange observations while hearing the cases—Judges should put on records the observation as per laws even to embarrass the government or anybody so in accoradance with law and legal procedure—they should not act like commentators, sitting in the judge's commentary boxes!

Because of partisan attitude of the union and state governments towards the plight of poor, tribals etc in the country—Naxalites are rightly spreading their network in almost all states to fight state terror and feudal landloards

Recent happenings in neighbouring Pakistan, Afghanistan etc in the wake of killing of Osama Bin Laden in US raids and increase in terrorists' activities in Pakistan and Afhganistan appears to be disturbing trend in South-East Asia. The imperialist America, which economy is gradually slipping to downward trend, is creating unnecessary problems in the region! Fast changing political game of politics in gulf countries and also in the Middle East is giving agonising moments in the entire globe, particularly India, China and their neighbouring countries. Question of a new Constitution of Nepal, hanging fire for the last two to three years and India's indifferences for playing possitive role towards its Himalayan neighbour—Nepal is bound to be rebound in harming the interest of India in future to come!

Firstly, to tackle corruption, Manmohan Singh government and almost all state governments have practically failed and new and effective law to curb the menace appears to be a distant dream. One should rightly agree with civil society that all power ful persons in power including in prime minister, lower to high officials, legislators, high court and Supreme Court judges etc must come under the perview of new Lokpal Bill! The union government is posing hurdles in framing the consensus bill to be passed by the Parliament. But the opposition leaders and MPs must be taken into confidence and their views must be solicited on the bill as ultimately they are peoples' representatives and they have to pass the bill in the Parliament! Calm and cool discussions should be intiated to p repare the draft of Lokpal bill. Let us hope for the best as the enacted bill will prove a mile stone in tackeling corruption.

Secondly, I must discuss the current agitation of Swami Ramdev, who rightly wants to bring back black money stashed in foergign banks and countries. But the way Swami Ramdev is acting it appears thast he has become an extra-constitutional authorities! Everybody should condemn the night-long action of the Delhi police in Ramlila ground to disallow Ramdev and his supporters to carry indefinite fast to press for unearthing black money (In the process many have been injured and Swami Ramdev's unseemly character to flee the venue in woman's dress do not behove well for a Swami stature of Baba Ramdev). Surprisingly many politicians and people have desribed the event by equating Jallianwala bagh massacres and J P agitation suppression! Such comparision is highly objectionable to glorify Ramdev in the name historical facts, which people remember with reverance!

Now the latest call of Ramdev to raise militant organisation for self-defence shows his true character how he is serious about the unearthing of black-money. Forgetting his spiritual sermons and non-violence preachings of Mahatama Gandhi, Swami has moved a step forward to create anarchy in the country! To press his points before government, Swami wants to terrorise the government and civil society to accept his view points without any valid reasons. His action and call will definitely aggravate the terror activities by terrorists in the country. Not only that if he is realy sincere in his adventure, Ramdev should join Naxak movements and mobilise Naxalites to stop terror and state power atrocity on poor, dalits, tribals, backward and majority section of forward classes in the country. Ramdev should concentrate his fights with Naxalites against corporates, multinationals, capitalists, American impreliasm, and state's dubious role in acquiring lands of people for starting industries in forest as well as fertile landloards in almost all parts of the country. The way Ramdev is moving will bind to rebound! For unearthing black money, the union government should also initiate immediate action as per international treaties so that crores of Indian money stashed abroad should be brought back!

Need of the hour is freedom of press! Media must play a watch-dog. The Judiciary should move cautiously in this critical hour and look the Constitution and Laws in delivering and recording hearings and judgements. No doubt that executiuve and legislative organs of the government have failed in many aspects and judiciary has to take up their roles for the welfare of people! Many fungers have be raised in past avbout corruption in judiciary and at least three for chief justices of the Supreme Court are in docks and many judges of high courts are facing impeachments because of corruption.

If the presnt trend continues and a choosen few so called politicians, civil society members, and bureacracy, judiciary as well as sadhus and sants continue to indulge in such nefarious games, the real people of India, who constitutes 80 percent of rural areas and dependent on aghriculture, will rise to the occassion and teach them a lesson—our secular democratic system will prevail.